STUDIES IN
EARLY
CHRISTIANITY

A Collection of Scholarly Essays

edited by
Everett Ferguson
ABILENE CHRISTIAN UNIVERSITY

with
David M. Scholer
NORTH PARK COLLEGE AND THEOLOGICAL SEMINARY

and
Paul Corby Finney
CENTER OF THEOLOGICAL INQUIRY

A Garland Series

CONTENTS OF SERIES

VOLUME VI

Early Christianity and Judaism

edited with introductions by
Everett Ferguson

Garland Publishing, Inc.
New York & London
1993

Introductions copyright © 1993 Everett Ferguson

Library of Congress Cataloging-in-Publication Data

Early Christianity and Judaism / edited by Everett Ferguson.
      p.   cm. — (Studies in early Christianity ; v. 6)
    Includes bibliographical references.
    ISBN 0–8153–1066–8 (alk. paper)
    1. Jewish Christians—History—Early church, ca. 30–600.
2. Judaism—Relations—Christianity.   3. Christianity and other
religions—Judaism.   4. Christianity—Early church, ca. 30–600.
I. Ferguson, Everett, 1933-   . II. Series.
BR195.J8E37   1993
261.2'6'09015—dc20   92–41463
                            CIP

Printed on acid-free, 250-year-life paper
Manufactured in the United States of America

Contents

Series Introduction

Christianity has been the formative influence on Western civilization and has maintained a significant presence as well in the Near East and, through its missions, in Africa and Asia. No one can understand Western civilization and the world today, much less religious history, without an understanding of the early history of Christianity.

The first six hundred years after the birth of Jesus were the formative period of Christian history. The theology, liturgy, and organization of the church assumed their definitive shape during this period. Since biblical studies form a separate, distinctive discipline, this series confines itself to sources outside the biblical canon, except as these sources were concerned with the interpretation and use of the biblical books. During the period covered in this series the distinctive characteristics of the Roman Catholic and Eastern Orthodox Churches emerged.

The study of early Christian literature, traditionally known as Patristics (for the church fathers), has experienced a resurgence in the late twentieth century. Evidences of this are the flourishing of a new professional society, the North American Patristics Society, a little over twenty years old; the growing number of teachers and course offerings at major universities and seminaries; the number of graduate students studying and choosing to write their dissertations in this area; the volume of books published in the field; and attendance at the quadrennial International Conferences on Patristic Studies at Oxford as well as at many smaller specialized conferences. This collection of articles reflects this recent growing interest and is intended to encourage further study. The papers at the International Conferences on Patristic Studies from the first conference in 1951 to the present have been published in the series *Studia Patristica,* and interested readers are referred to these volumes for more extensive treatment of the topics considered in this series of reprints and many other matters as well.

The volumes in this series are arranged topically to cover biography, literature, doctrines, practices, institutions, worship, missions, and daily life. Archaeology and art as well as writings are drawn on in order to give reality to the Christian movement in its early centuries. Ample

attention is also given to the relation of Christianity to pagan thought
and life, to the Roman state, to Judaism, and to doctrines and practices
that came to be judged as heretical or schismatic. Introductions to each
volume will attempt to tie the articles together so that an integrated
understanding of the history will result.

The aim of the collection is to give balanced and comprehensive
coverage. Early on I had to give up the idealism and admit the arrogance
of attempting to select the "best" article on each topic. Criteria applied in
the selection included the following: original and excellent research and
writing, subject matter of use to teachers and students, groundbreaking
importance for the history of research, foundational information for
introducing issues and options. Preference was given to articles in
English where available. Occasional French and German titles are
included as a reminder of the international nature of scholarship.

The *Encyclopedia of Early Christianity* (New York: Garland, 1990)
provides a comprehensive survey of the field written in a manner
accessible to the average reader, yet containing information useful to the
specialist. This series of reprints of Studies in Early Christianity is
designed to supplement the encyclopedia and to be used with it.

The articles were chosen with the needs of teachers and students of
early church history in mind with the hope that teachers will send
students to these volumes to acquaint them with issues and scholarship
in early Christian history. The volumes will fill the need of many
libraries that do not have all the journals in the field or do not have
complete holdings of those to which they subscribe. The series will
provide an overview of the issues in the study of early Christianity and
the resources for that study.

Understanding the development of early Christianity and its impact
on Western history and thought provides indispensable insight into the
modern world and the present situation of Christianity. It also provides
perspective on comparable developments in other periods of history and
insight into human nature in its religious dimension. Christians of all
denominations may continue to learn from the preaching, writing,
thinking, and working of the early church.

Introduction

At the beginning all Christians were Jewish Christians (or should we say Christian Jews?). The first Bible of the church was the Jewish scriptures—see the articles in Volume III. Jewish influence on early Christianity, therefore, is undoubted. Defining the exact extent of that influence is not so easy; even the concept "Jewish Christianity" is subject to various definitions.

As Christians in their numbers became predominantly Gentile, Jewish Christianity (Christian Judaism?) came to be regarded as heretical and by isolation moved into extremes further away from the mainstream of the church. Judaism itself, however, remained attractive to potential Gentile converts and to Christians themselves for a much longer period than has often been thought. Throughout antiquity Christians remained in contact and competition with Jews who did not believe in Jesus. The extent to which those contacts were personal and informed is often difficult to determine. Some of the more extreme anti-Judaic statements to be found in early Christian literature arise from a polemical context; some of the statements, on the other hand, belong to the theological context of Christian self-definition and do not at all reflect personal prejudice. Garland Publishing, Inc. has published a twenty-volume series edited by Jacob Neusner on "The Origins of Judaism," which includes a volume on *Judaism and Christianity in the First Century*. The present volume extends the story of those relationships into the fourth and fifth centuries.

Doctrinal problems in the early church are often schematized as those that come from Gentile sources—Gnosticism—and those that come from Jewish sources—Ebionites and certain other Jewish Christian sects. That now seems highly misleading, as new knowledge about Gnosticism emphasizes its connections with Judaism—see Volume V.[1]

Three strands can be discerned among Christian Jews who maintained their Jewish identity while believing in Jesus. All are known only sketchily. (1) There were those who continued the practice of the Law of Moses and maintained that Gentile converts too should observe it. These are usually designated Ebionites, and they may be a continuation of the

Jewish believers who opposed Paul in the book of Acts.[2] Their hero was
James the Just. According to the reports, they regarded Jesus as the true
prophet, a new Moses, the Messiah by his vituous life. They rejected the
sacrificial system and practiced washings for the forgiveness of sins.
(2) Others who lived by the Law accepted Gentiles without their submitting
to the Law. They are sometimes called Nazoraeans, but it is not clear that
this was a designation of a distinct group. (3) Others were subject to
Gnostic tendencies. The followers of the prophet Elkesai may be put in
this category. When the term "Jewish Christianity" is used, most often
the Ebionites are meant.

Jean Daniélou's studies have inspired (or provoked) much modern
discussion of Jewish Christianity.[3] He used the term more broadly than
is common to refer to the Jewish heritage and Jewish concepts in the
early church. Since Jewish Christianity had generally referred either to
the earliest Christianity of those racially Jews or to the later "heretical"
expressions of Jewish Christianity, much confusion resulted. The articles
at the beginning of this collection—by Robert Kraft, Marcel Simon,
Georg Strecker, Robert Murray, and A. F. J. Klijn—are part of the
renewed effort to understand and define the Jewish component in early
Christianity. The article by Strecker, taken from the English translation
of Walter Bauer's *Rechtgläubigkeit und Ketzerei im ältesten Christentum*,
had as its further context Bauer's thesis that the "heresies" preceded the
achievement of standardized orthodoxy (Volume IV).

The next two articles—by J. Munck and H. J. Schoeps—discuss the
phenomenon of "Jewish Christianity," especially as it moved away
from, or was left behind by, the majority Gentile church.[4] Schoeps has
contended for the contemporary ecumenical significance of Jewish
Christianity, particularly the Ebionite idea of parallel covenants at Sinai
and Golgotha existing side by side for Jews and Gentiles respectively.
His article gives a summary of his conclusions on the practices and
beliefs of the Ebionites.[5] A major source for Jewish Christianity is the
documents incorporated into the Pseudo-Clementines (see the article by
F. S. Jones in Volume II).

Then follows a set of articles on some aspects of possible Jewish
influence on early Christianity. Jewish theological thought is used
creatively by Moxnes in explaining a difficult concept in the *Shepherd*
of Hermas, a passage that has been an embarrassment to orthodox
theology. "The Two Ways" seems to be a Christian borrowing of the
method and content used by Jews in moral instruction (see further the
introduction and first article in Volume II). Jewish influence on early
Christianity is often seen as extensive on early Christian worship, a
position much promoted by F. Gavin.[6] In particular, the synagogue

service seems to offer the point of departure for the development of the early Christian liturgy. Rankin raises caution about too eager or too extensive an assumption of direct derivation of the Christian liturgy from the Synagogue service. The development of early Christian art is another area where Jewish influence is often postulated. The actual physical evidence for the priority of Jewish art, however, is lacking, and it seems that Jewish and Christian art developed almost concurrently around the beginning of the third century, perhaps under common Hellenistic influences.[7] One of W. H. C. Frend's articles in Volume VII, "Early Christianity and Society: A Jewish Legacy in the Pre-Constantinian Era," identifies another Jewish influence on early Christianity in the early church's attitude toward society.

The last set of articles collects studies dealing with relations between Christians and Jews. A modern Jew (Krauss) and an Orthodox Christian (Constantelos) give their perspectives on references to Jews in early Christian literature. A less than happy association between Jews and Christians was the part played by Jews in the persecution of Christians (Frend). This may not have been as extensive as some passages would suggest.[8] Two articles deal with authors involved in the debate between Christianity and Judaism—*Barnabas* and Origen. The latter, as a scholar, was one of the few Christians who sought to learn from the Jews in order to improve his exegesis of the scriptures and put the Christian argument on a firm basis.[9] Studies of early Christian relations with the Jews usually focus on the western diaspora of the Jews. Many Jews, however, lived in Syria and the lands to the east, and Christianity as it spread east stayed closer to its Semitic roots. Drijvers discusses an important center for the development of Syriac-speaking Christianity, Edessa, and Neusner discusses an important figure for Syriac Christianity who was in close contact with Jews, Aphrahat.[10]

Notes

1. Stressed by B. Pearson, *Gnosticism, Judaism, and Egyptian Christianity* (Minneapolis: Fortress, 1990).

2. G. Lüdemann, *Paulus, der Heidenapostel*, 2 vols. (Göttingen: Ruprecht, 1980, 1983).

3. *The Theology of Jewish Christianity* (Philadelphia: Westminster, 1964).

4. Note R. E. Taylor, "Attitudes of the Fathers towards Practices of Jewish Christians," *Studia Patristica* 4 (1961) : 504–11.

5. *Theologie und Geschichte des Judenchristentums* (Tübingen: Mohr, 1949); *Jewish Christianity* (Philadelphia: Fortress, 1969).

6. F. Gavin, *The Jewish Antecedents of the Christian Sacraments* (New York: KTAV, 1969 repr.); C. W. Dugmore, *The Influence of the Synagogue upon the Divine Office* (Oxford: Oxford UP, 1964).

7. P. Corby Finney, "Orpheus-David: A Connection in Iconography Between Greco-Roman Judaism and Early Christianity?" *Journal of Jewish Art* 5 (1978):6–15.

8. David M. Scholer, "Tertullian on Jewish Persecution of Christians," *Studia Patristica* 17.2 (1982):821–828.

9. N. DeLange, *Origen and the Jews: Studies in Jewish-Christian Relations in Third-Century Palestine* (Cambridge: Cambridge UP, 1976).

10. See his book, *Aphrahat and Judaism: The Christian-Jewish Argument in Fourth-Century Iran* (Leiden: Brill, 1971).

IN SEARCH OF "JEWISH CHRISTIANITY" AND ITS "THEOLOGY"

Problems of definition and methodology

by R.A. KRAFT

University of Pennsylvania

Cardinal Daniélou's volume on *The Theology of Jewish Christianity*[1] has played an extremely important role in the formation and development of my own interests and work as a student of Christian origins. While still a neophyte doctoral student at Harvard, I was given the assignment of preparing a detailed report on that book as a means not only of learning more about Christian origins and about current approaches to that subject, but also as my first real introduction to French literature. A direct result of that assignment was my first publication — a brief review of Daniélou's book[2]. Indeed, it was largely because of what Daniélou wrote about « Jewish Christian exegesis » that I decided to examine the use of Jewish sources in the *Epistle of Barnabas* as the sub-

1. *Théologie du Judéo-Christianisme* (Paris : Desclée, 1958); English edition and translation (including some revision by author) by J.A.Baker (Chicago : Regnery / London : Darton-Longman-Todd, 1964). For the series title, see below, n. 4. Page numbers will be cited by giving first the page of the original French (if the material is present in the French) marked by an asterisk (*), followed by the equivalent page number of the English translation (= *ET*). The English wording used herein is not necessarily taken from the *ET*, but may be the author's own translation. I would like to thank Mr. Harold Remus for his many valuable suggestions regarding the final form of this essay.
2. *Journal of Biblical Literature* 79 (1960), 91-94. Approximately 50 reviews or notices of the volume are listed in the bibliographies to *Biblica*. It would be a valuable project to synthesize the comments of the reviewers, but that has not been attempted here.

6

1

ject of my doctoral dissertation [3]. Thus I have a profound respect for the wealth of information contained in Daniélou's investigation, and for the stimulating manner in which he synthesizes and presents the material. It is a book that I regularly recommend to my graduate students as basic reading for their work in Christian origins.

Nevertheless, I continue to have serious reservations about the central focus of Daniélou's book as I understand it—his « theology » of « Jewish Christianity ». On the one hand, I find myself questioning the very concrete manner in which he speaks of « *the* theology » of Jewish Christianity. Is it historically accurate to suggest that anything so neat and seemingly homogeneous ever existed among early Christians ? I have no doubts that there was at work in certain Jewish circles during the hellenistic period a somewhat intangible *Zeitgeist* that clearly included many factors and ideas treated by Daniélou under the heading « Jewish Christian theology » — a spirit of the times into which Christianity was born and in which many early Christians continued to exist for a long period. But to me, there is a vast difference between often heterogeneous (sometimes even competing !) yet typical factors at work in a particular cultural milieu at a particular time, and a concrete homogeneous « theology » of the sort that Daniélou seems to be proposing.

On the other hand, I sometimes find myself uncomfortable about the *methods* employed by Daniélou in seeking to identify and isolate elements that he feels were part of this « Jewish Christian theology ». Does his search for a « theology of Jewish Christianity » arise inductively from clues provided by the ancient sources themselves ? Are there adequate criteria for determining which sources can be expected most closely to reflect this « theology » ? Are the various sources analyzed in a consistent manner in the attempt to draw relevant information from them ? Admittedly, historical investigation must by its very nature frequently involve circularity of argument, but what « controls » exist by which to regulate the argument as adequately as possible ? It is to such issues as these that I

---

3. *The Epistle of Barnabas : its Quotations and their Sources* (Harvard University, 1961) ; a précis appeared in *Harvard Theological Review* 54 (1961), 300. The dissertation is available in microfilm from the Harvard University Library.

wish to turn my attention in this critical appreciation of, and attempt to contribute to, the ongoing work of Cardinal Daniélou.

The Context of Discussion : Definitions and Presuppositions

At the outset, it should be recognized that Daniélou's treatment of « Jewish Christian theology » is the first part of a larger project in which he intends to deal with the « history of Christian doctrine(s) before Nicea »[4]. Volume two appeared in 1961 under the title « Gospel Message and Hellenistic Culture in the 2nd and 3rd Centuries », focusing on the « Greek milieu » (especially Justin, Irenaeus, Clement, Hippolytus, Origen, and Methodius[5]). A third volume on Latin theology in the same period has been promised[6]. This helps to explain the opening words of the English version of volume one :

Three worlds went to the making of the Christian Church, three cultures, three visions and expressions of truth—the Jewish[7], the Hellenistic and the Latin : and each of them produced its own distinctive Theology [p. 1 ET].

But exactly what Daniélou's reasons are for this seemingly arbitrary division of the (theological) world into three parts on the basis of cultural-ideological-linguistic criteria is not explained. Whether the evidence contained in the various witnesses from each « world » would support such a division requires close, systematic scrutiny and cannot be pursued here. But a feeling of artificiality and arbitrariness is left at the outset by this procedural presupposition in Daniélou's treatment of pre-Nicene theology.

In the same vein, Daniélou states that volume one will deal with the earliest stage of Christian theology, up to the mid-second century (pre-Justin, so it seems). But the reasons for this chronological division are not sufficiently clarified. Doubtless it has something to do with the way in which

4. Bibliothèque de Théologie : Histoire des doctrines chrétiennes avant Nicée.
5. *Message Evangélique et Culture Hellénistique aux IIe et IIIe siècles* (1961). An English translation has been promised for the near future.
6. See the opening paragraph of volume 2.
7. Probably it would be more accurate to read here « Jewish-Semitic » ; see below.

« conventional courses of instruction on the history of Christian doctrine » have tended to begin with second century Christianity and examine its relationships to Greek philosophical thought (cf. Harnack)[8]. Daniélou wishes to examine what preceded that sort of « Greek » development and to deal with the earliest stage of Christian theology. Thus he states, without any argumentation beyond a reference to the work of L. Goppelt[9], that « Christianity which had spread throughout the entire Mediterranean basin, remained Jewish in structure until the mid-second century » (19*=9 ET). Again, when discussing criteria for identifying « Jewish Christian » writings, he states that « the Jewish Christian period extends from the origin of Christianity to around the mid-second century » (21*=11 ET). Why so ? Daniélou admits that « Jewish Christian theology » survived to some degree in later Syrian Christianity, and also indicates the presence of « Jewish Christian » ideas in « heterodox » persons and movements that continued to exist beyond the second century (e.g. Ebionism and certain « gnostic » groups ; see below). He claims not to be interested in heterodox « Jewish Christian » groups per se, but only as they shed light on « orthodox » Jewish Christian ideas. This delimitation of content, with its focus on « orthodox » Jewish Christianity, also may provide a concealed clue as to the chronological assumptions behind Daniélou's presentation. Apparently « orthodox » Jewish Christianity must be in some sort of direct continuity with the « orthodox » Christian theology (theologies ? Hellenistic and Latin !) of the second and third centuries, and thus is treated within the chronological limitations noted above. But if one concentrates on the conceptual similarities between various early Christian writings and movements, without attempting to impose on them (later) theological judgments regarding « orthodoxy » or « heterodoxy, » the approximate limit of mid-second century would seem to be

---

8. See p. 1* = 2 ET : « Harnack, for example, regarded theology as born from the union of the gospel message and Greek philosophy ; and in his History of Dogma, a Jewish Christian theology finds no place simply because he never suspected its existence. »

9. Christentum und Judentum im ersten und zweiten Jahrhundert : ein Aufriss der Urgeschichte der Kirche (Gütersloh : Bertelsmann, 1954) ; English translation of the first part in Jesus, Paul and Judaism (1964). Daniélou's reference to Goppelt's work is general and rather vague.

quite arbitrary. On the other hand, it also needs to be asked whether significant alternatives to Daniélou's « Jewish Christian theology » might not have existed already in first century Christianity — whether all Christianity was, in fact, « Jewish in structure until the mid-second century » (19*=9 ET). Daniélou seems to admit that the « biblical theology » of the New Testament writings « has points of contact and affinities with extra-canonical theology... of both Hellenistic and Jewish Christian type » (p. 1 ET; cf. 433*); does this not suggest the possible existence of a theological orientation which was « hellenistic » and non-Jewish-Christian (by Daniélou's definition; see below) in « orthodox » circles prior to the middle of the second century ? But more of this problem of diversity below.

Another difficulty relating to the context in which Daniélou's discussion is presented and the presuppositions behind his presentation has to do with the meaning of the term « theology » as it is used in the phrase « the theology of Jewish Christianity » or in the above-mentioned idea that each of the « three worlds » of early Christianity « produced its own distinctive Theology. » By « theology », Daniélou claims to indicate « an attempt to construct an overall view based on the foundation provided by the divine events of the incarnation and resurrection of the Word » (433*=1 ET). By definition, this would be « orthodox » theology as over against approaches to Christianity in which incarnation and resurrection are not focal. At one point Daniélou seems to be making a contrast between the sort of « theology » for which he is searching and the particular theological positions of individual representatives of early Christianity :

Our concern is not to describe and analyze theologians, but *a Theology.* None of the great writers of the early Church belongs wholly to one tradition, to one alone of the three worlds mentioned earlier... It may not be out of order to warn the reader that a complete portrait of any particular Christian theologian of the first two, or even three, centuries will not be found either in this volume or in the second, each taken by itself. ...The principal subject remains *the world of belief* and not its outstanding exponents. In so far as the conceptions of individuals are represented here, it is rather those of the *nameless thousands of believers* who did not move between the worlds, but worshipped God through the eyes, and served him through the ordinances of their Jewish forefathers » [pp. 3-4 *ET*, italics mine].

5

Even Paul, who for Daniélou qualifies as « Jewish Christian »
(19*=9 *ET*), apparently does not represent a purely « Jewish
Christian » theological position but also stands between the
Semitic-Jewish and the hellenistic-Greek thought worlds (see
433* = 1 *ET*).

In one sense, then, Daniélou's « theology of Jewish Christianity » (as also his « hellenistic Christian theology ») seems to
be an idealistic abstraction—a purified and systematized distil-
lation of various ideas drawn from a variety of sources, without
special regard for the question of whether any *actual* person
or group of persons ever consciously adhered to such a « theology ». This « Jewish Christian theology » would be related to
actual early Christians as the Platonic world of ideas is thought
to be related to the empirical world. Yet, Daniélou also suggests that there were « nameless thousands of believers » who
actually adhered to such a « Jewish Christian theology » —
believers whose ideas are reflected in the variety of sources
from which Daniélou has collected the data by which he recon-
structs « the theology of Jewish Christianity ». Unfortunately,
the elusiveness of this group makes it difficult to measure their
precise relationship to Daniélou's « Jewish Christian theology ».

I must admit that such an approach in which concrete historical evidence seems subservient to principles accepted on
other grounds, makes me very uncomfortable[10]. For myself,
I prefer to investigate history and the ideas of people in history inductively, avoiding *a priori* judgments whenever possible. I do not find it objectionable to speak of the ideas and
theological orientation of particular individuals (e.g. the « theology » of Paul), while recognizing that not every such individual consciously attempted to achieve some sort of consistent
overview that could be called a theological « system ». Indeed,
I am willing to admit that certain theological ideas can even
be *implicit* in what a person says or believes, without the person being fully conscious of his « theology » at every point.
And certainly a given group or community can be said to
have a selfconscious theological position (e.g. Marcionite theo-

---

10. I am similarly uncomfortable with terms such as « biblical theology » or « New Testament theology » or even « theology of the Apostolic
Fathers, » all of which relegate the ideas of individual authors to a syn-
thetic abstraction based on an *a priori* judgment or assumption regarding the « unity » of the particular collection of writings.

logy) even though not every member of the group necessarily possessed a theological awareness of the details of the group position. But in each instance an identifiable historical entity (person or group) had existed and can be examined by means of critical historical methodology. It seems to me legitimate to ask whether any historically identifiable and selfconscious entity (person or group) ever existed behind Daniélou's « Jewish Christian theology » ? Is there any way of breaking through the circularity of argument whereby the reconstructed « theology » provides the primary evidence for the existence of « Jewish Christianity » as an entity, while the supposed existence of Jewish Christianity as an entity is the rationale for reconstructing Jewish Christian theology ? It is true that in Daniélou's presentation, his (orthodox) Jewish Christianity gains a semblance of concreteness by being contrasted with identifiable brands of « heterodox » Jewish Christianity (e.g. Ebionites, Elkesaites, certain « gnostic » groups), but this does not solve the problem in a convincing manner ; rather, it simply serves to further change the focus of the discussion from the meaning of « theology » for Daniélou to the meaning of « Jewish Christianity » itself.

Defining « Jewish Christianity »

For Daniélou, « Jewish Christianity » does *not* refer to a particular selfconscious group but is an umbrella term used to designate a type of Christian outlook—the expression of Christianity in thought forms borrowed from « *Spätjudentum* » (see 19* = 9f *ET*). It includes two other groupings sometimes referred to as « Jewish Christian » in modern discussions : (1) « Ebionite » and related « heterodox » groups for which Jesus is prophet or messiah, but not son of God (although Daniélou does not wish to focus on this sort of Jewish Christianity as such) ; and (2) the « orthodox » Christianity represented by the earliest community at Jerusalem, led by James and his successors (sometimes later called « Nazarenes »), for whom Jesus' messiahship implied divinity. It also includes every other early Christian or group for whom characteristically Jewish thought forms were basic, regardless of whether such Christians had any direct connection (including genealogical) with any Jewish community or with the Jewish world at large[11]. It should be noted that Daniélou simply presents this definition of « Jewish Christianity » as the way in which he chooses to use the term[12]; no attempt is made to derive the idea of such « Jewish Christianity » inductively by means of careful analysis of ancient references to particular individuals (e.g. James, Paul, Cerinthus) or groups (e.g. « Hebrews » vs. « Hellenists », « circumcision party », « Ebionites ») described in ancient sources as being closely associated with Judaism in one way or another. Indeed, the definition seems to presuppose the results of Daniélou's investigation, that a body of characteristically Jewish thought underlies most of the earliest Christian sources.

For Daniélou, « *Spätjudentum* » means the various sorts of Judaism in existence at the beginning of the common era, although for reasons not sufficiently explicated, he chooses to exclude Philo's Judaism from his investigation of Jewish Christianity and thus to concentrate on the Jewish-*Semitic* thought world[13]. He sees in the development of heterodox Jewish Christian groups a continuation of the varieties of « heterodox » Judaism: Ebionism derives from an Essenic Jewish heterodoxy which emphasized the break with the « official » Jewish cult (cf. 76*, 82* = 64, 69 *ET*); Cerinthus represents a development of zealot messianism (82* = 69 *ET*); Carpocrates reflects heterodox Jewish gnosis (98* = 85 *ET*); etc. But even « orthodox » Jewish Christianity, with its more acceptable christology, existed in a variety of forms related to the varieties in *Spätjudentum* (19* = 10 *ET*).

Daniélou claims that despite the « diverse streams » within Jewish Christianity, « there was a common mentality »: « a first form of Christian theology, Semitic-Jewish in expression » (20* = 10 *ET*), an « overall view » (433* = 1 *ET*), a « common basis » (1* = 3 *ET*), a « doctrinal system...Semitic in struc-

---

11. Apparently the reference to « their Jewish forefathers » on p. 4 *ET* either is not intended to be genealogical, or the « nameless thousands » pictured in that context (see above) are to be considered as only part of the total « Jewish Christian » group.

12. Here, Daniélou makes another passing reference to Goppelt's work noted above, n. 9.

13. See p. 20* = 10 n. 18 *ET*: « The influence of Philo is not included here, since it belongs to a type of Judaism expressed in the forms of Greek philosophy, and will therefore be of more direct concern in the study of hellenistic Christianity » (see e.g. volume 2, pp. 297-302).

ture and expression » (4 *ET*). But it must be asked, was there any conscious awareness of this « common » bond on the part of these « Jewish Christians » ? Presumably both Paul and his « superapostle » opponents at Corinth (see 2 Cor 11) would qualify as « Jewish Christian. » They would both probably even be considered christologically « orthodox » by Daniélou's standards ! But that cannot change the fact that they seem to have had radically different outlooks on the basic point (to Paul, at least) of what constituted the heart of the « gospel ». Should not the descriptive categories for our study of men and movements in history derive from the historical situations themselves—from the selfconsciousness of the participants ? How can Daniélou's abstraction « Jewish Christianity » help me to understand what was happening among early Christians ? Does it not, in fact, tend to blind me to the problems of which the historical participants were conscious in their own times, by viewing them from later perspectives quite foreign to them (e.g. Semitic-Jewish, hellenistic, Latin) ?

Probing the Sources : the Problem of Methodology

In all fairness, it must be acknowledged that Daniélou does not claim to be pursuing his subject by means of inductive historical description. Rather, he is attempting to establish a thesis which is stated at the beginning of the volume : that there was in earliest Christianity a common mentality (« Jewish Christianity ») characterized by the use of techniques and ideas derived from *Spätjudentum*. In an attempt to identify early Christian materials that derive directly from this supposed Jewish Christian outlook, Daniélou proposes three criteria : (1) a date prior to the last half of the 2nd century ; (2) use of literary genres popular in *Spätjudentum* ; and (3) presence of ideas characteristic of *Spätjudentum*, especially the use of apocalyptic imagery. But Daniélou does not think it necessary that each particular writing under consideration must meet all three requirements in order to qualify as « Jewish Christian » (21* = 11 *ET*). The arbitrary nature of the chronological criterion has already been mentioned above. The matter of literary genre is not discussed with any precision by Daniélou, but seems to be of most significance for his first category of allegedly Jewish Christian writings, namely pseudepigraphical

9

works like *Ascension of Isaiah, 2 Enoch* (Slavonic), and *Testaments of the Twelve Patriarchs*. The statement that apocalyptic is « the dominant Jewish thought form of the period » ($2* = 4 ET$; see also $21* = 11 ET$) requires further comment since it is of such central importance to Daniélou's thesis.

Daniélou offers no evidence in support of his claim about the dominance of apocalyptic in *Spätjudentum*. Certainly not every witness preserved from *Spätjudentum* was apocalyptically oriented, and certainly other interests such as ethical and philosophical wisdom, cult and calendar, history and legend were also characteristic of some Jewish sources and representatives. Even Daniélou's quick dismissal of Philo (and presumably any other such « hellenistic » Jewish witnesses) as relevant evidence for « Jewish Christianity » does not leave *Spätjudentum* without non-apocalyptic currents of thought. But if streams of Judaism existed in which apocalyptic was not particularly central, is it not possible that a similarly non-apocalyptic outlook was included among the earliest (« orthodox ») Christian theological positions ? Must there be but a *single* theological position in earliest Christianity ? Even if Philo is dismissed as « hellenistic, » does that not leave open the possibility that an early Christian « hellenistic theology » (to use Daniélou's terms) might also have existed from the earliest period ? Perhaps detailed, inductive investigation would reveal that in the earliest decades of Christian existence there were several *competing* (or at least selfconsciously different and distinguishable) theologies of « hellenistic » as well as of « Jewish » coloring, even within early Christianity of a christologically « orthodox » sort (by Daniélou's definition).

The need for adequate controls becomes most evident when Daniélou applies his criteria to the extant non-canonical literature from early Christianity. His thesis is that in earliest Christianity there is a common mentality with pronouncedly apocalyptic features. One criterion for identifying extant sources is the apocalyptic imagery. It is no surprise that the sources support the thesis ! It is to be expected that the sources will show a common mentality of some sort, since they are identified primarily with respect to the kind of thought world they represent. It is not difficult to find *something* in common between *any* series of writings from approximately the same period of history. The problem is whether the method

10

of investigation is adequate to identify what are the most significant and characteristic features of the materials, from the viewpoint of what their ancient authors and editors intended to convey. More careful and consistent attention to the methodological problems is desirable at the outset of such an investigation.

Nevertheless, Daniélou's approach has proved fruitful in a variety of ways. Some very significant patterns of thought are seen to be common to several of the allegedly Jewish Christian sources —e.g. angelology pervades documents such as *Ascension of Isaiah, 2 Enoch, Testaments of the Twelve Patriarchs, Shepherd of Hermas, Apocalypse of Peter, Epistle of the Apostles*; the « theology of the cross » is important in *Ignatius, Gospel of Peter, Odes of Solomon, Epistle of the Apostles*, and perhaps elsewhere ; ecclesiological interest is obvious in *Ascension of Isaiah, Ignatius, Shepherd of Hermas, 2 Clement*, and *Odes of Solomon*. Unfortunately, no single « doctrine » or pattern of doctrines is common to all of the sources examined, nor is there a really close unity between the particular ways in which each document expresses a particular doctrine—e.g. there is not *one* angelology common to all the angel-oriented sources, but several angelologies ; similarly there are *several* ideas concerning millennium, redemption, incarnation, the cross, etc. The « common mentality, » then, applies not to details of doctrine, but primarily to general areas of thought represented in various ways in the various sources. Unity is achieved by a process of theological abstraction ; it is not obvious in the study of the particular documents and traditions themselves.

Summary and Conclusions

It is the farthest thing from my intention to leave the impression that Daniélou's study entitled « The Theology of Jewish Christianity » has not made any significant or positive contribution to the study of early Christian history and thought. He has gathered together a wealth of evidence from various early Christian sources to suggest that Jewish ideas and interests were of great influence among early Christians. Even if the framework of his presentation appears to be overly dependent on what seem to be unexamined presuppositions, and even though his method of approach may lack sufficient controls at points (all of which is simply another way of saying that I would not have approached the subject in the same manner !), the result of his labors is an impressive description of the apocalyptic Jewish atmosphere breathed by many early Christians. Whether it is helpful to call this sort of atmosphere or *Zeitgeist* a « theology » in the rather specific manner employed by Daniélou must be left to the individual reader to decide. But whatever one wishes to call it, the material in Cardinal Daniélou's « Theology of Jewish Christianity » recaptures an aspect of early Christian thought that the student of Christian origins cannot afford to neglect. For the reasons outlined in this essay, it is probable that the rigid historical inductivist could not have produced such a bold and convenient synthesis of materials. In that instance we would all be poorer. Despite the above-mentioned difficulties, I am convinced that our understanding of early Christianity has been advanced in an important manner by Daniélou's « Theology of Jewish Christianity » with its excellent overview of the Jewish apocalyptic thought world(s) of earliest Christianity.

PROBLÈMES
DU
JUDÉO-CHRISTIANISME

par MARCEL SIMON
(Strasbourg)

Le présent exposé n'a d'autre ambition que de proposer un
rapide inventaire de quelques-uns au moins des problèmes, diffi-
ciles et complexes, que le judéo-christianisme pose à l'historien
et de fournir ainsi une base de discussion à ce Colloque.
Et tout d'abord, comment définir le judéo-christianisme ?
La tâche peut paraître simple à première vue. Un judéo-chrétien
est un homme qui se sent, qui veut être et qui est en fait, dans
les différentes manifestations de sa vie religieuse, à la fois juif
et chrétien. C'est ainsi que l'entendent communément les auteurs
ecclésiastiques de l'Antiquité (1). A y regarder de plus près
cependant, on s'aperçoit que le phénomène est singulièrement
plus difficile à cerner et à saisir. Il n'est pas très facile, en particulier, de préciser le dosage des deux éléments requis pour qu'il
y ait vraiment judéo-christianisme. Du côté chrétien, les choses
sont relativement simples : dans cette synthèse, le christianisme
implique, au minimum, la conviction que Jésus est l'un des
prophètes d'Israël. Il en va tout autrement lorsqu'il s'agit de
définir la dose de judaïsme nécessaire pour qu'un chrétien puisse
être étiqueté judéo-chrétien. Il apparaît en particulier que la
définition que chacun donnera du judéo-christianisme dépendra
dans une large mesure de sa propre position en regard du judaïsme
ou simplement de l'Ancien Testament. Pour Marcion, qui rejette
la Bible juive comme inspirée par un dieu subalterne, le Démiurge,
l'Église orthodoxe est tout entière judéo-chrétienne, du simple

---

(1) Les principaux textes patristiques sur les judéo-chrétiens sont rassem-
blés et analysés dans mon *Verus Israel, Etude sur les relations entre Chrétiens
et Juifs dans l'Empire romain*, 2ᵉ éd., Paris, 1964, pp. 277 ss.

13

fait qu'elle accepte ces écrits comme révélés et se place ainsi dans la ligne de la Synagogue. C'est là à coup sûr une vue extrémiste. Elle illustre du moins ce qu'il peut y avoir de flottant et aussi de subjectif dans cette notion à première vue très bien délimitée de judéo-christianisme. Si l'on se tourne vers les historiens modernes, on se trouve confirmé dans cette même impression, car l'on enregistre parmi eux des divergences significatives.

Elles tiennent pour une part à une lacune de notre vocabulaire, qui nous oblige, en français tout au moins, à désigner par le même terme des chrétiens d'origine juive, de naissance israélite — et si on l'entend ainsi saint Paul lui-même peut être considéré comme judéo-chrétien — et des chrétiens qui judaïsent, et il a bien pu s'en trouver parmi eux, dans l'Église ancienne, qui étaient Gentils de naissance. L'allemand dispose en l'occurrence de deux mots là où le français n'en possède qu'un. Et de ce fait certains historiens ont réservé pour les chrétiens de naissance juive le terme de *Judenchristentum* et peuvent parler, avec Walter Bauer, d'un *Judenchristentum ohne gesetzliche Bindung*, tandis qu'ils appellent *Judaismus* le christianisme judaïsant, même lorsqu'il se manifeste dans certains secteurs de l'Église des Gentils (1).

Faute de pouvoir faire cette distinction en français, qu'il soit bien entendu au départ que lorsque nous parlons de judéochristianisme nous englobons sous cette étiquette les deux catégories que je viens de mentionner : Juifs convertis mais restés attachés à l'observance, et Chrétiens de ·la Gentilité gagnés à l'observance. C'est une simplification arbitraire que de réduire, comme le fait par exemple l'article Judéo-Christianisme du *Dictionnaire de théologie catholique*, l'appellation de judéo-chrétiens aux seuls « chrétiens d'origine juive qui associent les observances de la religion mosaïque aux croyances et aux pratiques chrétiennes » (2). C'est en particulier résoudre d'emblée par la négative, avant même de l'avoir posé, le problème d'un éventuel christianisme judaïsant, d'un judéo-christianisme, dans les rangs de l'Église d'entre les Gentils. Un tel phénomène a-t-il existé et, dans l'affirmative, quelle en est l'origine ? Est-il imputable à une mission organisée par des Juifs chrétiens en dehors d'Is-

---

(1) W. BAUER, *Rechtgläubigkeit und Ketzerei im ältesten Christentum*, 2ᵉ éd., revue par G. STRECKER, Tübingen, 1964, p. 91. Sur la relation entre *Judenchristentum* et *Judaismus*, cf. par exemple, parmi les ouvrages récents, L. GOPPELT, *Christentum und Judentum im ersten und zweiten Jahrhundert*, Gütersloh, 1954, *passim*.

(2) *Dict. de théol. cathol.*, article « Judéo-chrétien », VIII, 2, 1681.

raël ? Ou à des influences du judaïsme non chrétien, de la Synagogue ? Ou simplement à une évolution interne, particulière à certains secteurs de l'Église ancienne ? Ce sont des questions qui nous retiendront tout à l'heure. Notons simplement, pour l'instant, que le terme français de judéo-christianisme recouvre à la fois *Judenchristentum* et *Judaismus*.

Mais cette constatation ne nous mène pas encore très loin. Bien des difficultés subsistent, dont témoignent clairement les deux monographies qui, jusqu'à il y a une vingtaine d'années, présentaient la vue en quelque sorte classique du judéo-christianisme : Hort, *Judaistic Christianity*, 1894, et Hoennicke, *Das Judenchristentum*, 1908. L'un et l'autre de ces auteurs évoquent d'abord, pour les rejeter aussitôt, diverses définitions possibles du judéo-christianisme, qui se recoupent au moins en partie de l'un à l'autre. Celle qu'ils retiennent en fin de compte est la même chez l'un et chez l'autre. « Le seul christianisme », écrit Hort, « qui puisse vraiment être qualifié de judéo-chrétien *(Judaistic)* est celui qui attribue une valeur permanente à la Loi juive, même plus ou moins modifiée ». Et il ajoute que ce christianisme judaïque pourrait tout aussi bien être désigné comme judaïsme chrétien *(Christian Judaism)* ; sa position n'est pas fondamentalement différente de celle de l'Islam, sauf que c'est Jésus et non pas Mahomet qui est pour lui le dernier des prophètes.

Quant à Hoennicke, il définit comme judéo-chrétienne la conception selon laquelle « le salut ne peut être acquis que par l'intermédiaire du judaïsme ». Mais alors que pour Hort une telle définition est finalement exclusive de toute autre, Hoennicke au contraire pense pouvoir la retenir concurremment avec une seconde : on peut aussi, estime-t-il, parler de judéo-christianisme chaque fois que dans le développement du christianisme on enregistre une influence d'éléments juifs ou vétéro-testamentaires venant altérer l'essence du message évangélique. En rapport avec ces deux définitions, correspondant à deux aspects du judéo-christianisme, l'ouvrage de Hoennicke se divise en deux parties bien distinctes : la première constitue une histoire du judéo-christianisme tel que l'entend Hort et que Hoennicke désigne précisément sous ce terme de *Judaismus* que je notais à l'instant ; la seconde dresse le bilan de ce que l'Église ancienne, sous la forme du *Frühkatholizismus*, a emprunté au judaïsme et à l'Ancien Testament dans son esprit, sa conception des « œuvres », son moralisme, ses institutions rituelles et son organisation sacerdotale.

Les deux auteurs sont en outre d'accord pour admettre que le judéo-christianisme, défini par son attachement à la Loi juive, dont l'observance est tenue pour nécessaire au salut, offre quelque lien avec les premiers disciples, avec l'époque apostolique, mais qu'il s'est rapidement restreint à un secteur assez peu important de l'Église, pour disparaître progressivement de la scène. Ils sont d'accord enfin pour considérer que notre documentation sur le judéo-christianisme est maigre et fragmentaire et que nous ne disposons d'aucune source importante qui puisse être avec certitude attribuée à la fraction judéo-chrétienne de l'Église ancienne.

Cette position était assez communément acceptée parmi les spécialistes lorsque H. J. Schoeps publia, en 1949, sa *Theologie und Geschichte des Judenchristentums*. A la différence de ses devanciers, Schoeps estime que nous n'en sommes pas réduits, pour nous faire une idée du judéo-christianisme, aux données maigres et peu sûres fournies par les auteurs ecclésiastiques de l'Antiquité, hérésiologues ou autres. Nous disposons d'une source fort précieuse, les *Pseudo-Clémentines*, dont le substrat primitif, tel qu'on peut le reconstituer sous les remaniements qu'il a subis, offre un caractère indubitablement judéo-chrétien. Ces écrits nous permettent donc de reconstruire de façon satisfaisante l'image du judéo-christianisme authentique. Celui-ci est caractérisé non seulement, comme le pensaient Hort et Hoennicke, par son attachement à l'observance juive, mais aussi par des traits fort originaux en matière de doctrine. Je n'ai pas le loisir de les analyser ici. Ils sont du reste bien connus, et je me contenterai de renvoyer à ce propos aux travaux de Schoeps lui-même, de Cullmann (1) et plus récemment de Strecker (2), pour n'en citer que quelques-uns. Je me bornerai à noter trois points qui, dans la démonstration de Schoeps me paraissent particulièrement importants.

1) Le type de judéo-christianisme qui s'exprime dans les *Pseudo-Clémentines* n'est pas, à ses yeux, un entre plusieurs : il est *le* judéo-christianisme. Je ne suis pas sûr que l'auteur maintienne intégralement ce point de vue aujourd'hui ;

2) Il tire son origine d'une tradition pré-chrétienne de judaïsme marginal, ésotérique et sectaire, dont il représente le point d'aboutissement final ;

---

(1) O. CULLMANN, *Le problème littéraire et historique du roman pseudo-clémentin*, Paris, 1930.
(2) G. STRECKER, *Das Judenchristentum in den Pseudoklementinen*, Berlin, 1958.

3) Le christianisme sous sa forme première, celui de la communauté jérusalémite, représente le chaînon intermédiaire entre les étapes pré-chrétiennes de ce mouvement et l'ébionisme des *Pseudo-Clémentines*. En d'autres termes, les caractères très particuliers que celui-ci présente en matière de doctrine et de rite sont déjà présents dans la première chrétienté, et en particulier chez Jacques, frère du Seigneur, qui est pour les *Pseudo-Clémentines* le grand ancêtre. Schoeps prend à cet égard très délibérément le contre-pied de ce qu'avait pensé Hort, pour lequel rien ne permettait de rattacher ce qu'il appelle l'ébionisme essénien des *Pseudo-Clémentines* à la communauté apostolique.

Une dizaine d'années plus tard, en 1958, le R. P. Daniélou publiait à son tour sa *Théologie du Judéo-Christianisme*. Le titre est évidemment inspiré de celui de Schoeps. De fait, l'auteur nous avertit que son propos est de faire « pour le judéo-christianisme orthodoxe ce que Schoeps a fait pour le judéo-christianisme hétérodoxe ». Ce qui implique qu'il n'accepte pas les vues de Schoeps touchant une filiation directe entre la communauté jérusalémite, orthodoxe par définition, et le type pseudo-clémentin de judéo-christianisme, pas plus qu'il n'accepte de voir dans celui-ci la forme unique de judéo-christianisme, le judéo-christianisme par excellence. En fait, il distingue trois acceptions possibles du terme judéo-chrétien.

1) Le mot peut désigner en premier lieu « ceux des Juifs qui reconnaissent en Jésus un prophète ou un Messie, mais non le Fils de Dieu » (1). Les Ébionites des *Pseudo-Clémentines*, entre autres, appartiennent à cette catégorie, où voisinent « des groupes de stricte observance juive et des judéo-chrétiens syncrétistes, chez qui il semble bien qu'est apparu d'abord le dualisme gnostique » (2) : gros problème, dont le R. P. Daniélou doit nous présenter lui-même quelques aspects au cours de ce colloque.

2) On peut entendre sous ce terme également « la communauté chrétienne de Jérusalem, dominée par Jacques, et les tendances qui sont les siennes ». Ce milieu, à la différence du précédent, « est parfaitement orthodoxe, mais il reste attaché à certaines formes de vie juives, sans les imposer d'ailleurs aux prosélytes venus du paganisme ». Ces judéo-chrétiens ont peu à peu disparu, après 70 ; « on les désigne parfois du nom de Nazaréens. Ils ont composé en araméen l'Évangile selon les Hébreux. Ils restent fidèles à une théologie archaïque, qui s'en tient au

---

(1) *Théologie du judéo-christianisme*, p. 17.
(2) *Op. cit.*, p. 18.

monothéisme et au messianisme de Jésus. Mais à la différence des Ébionites, ce messianisme implique la divinité du Christ » (1).

3) Enfin, et c'est ici l'apport original de l'auteur, « on peut appeler judéo-christianisme une forme de pensée chrétienne qui n'implique pas de lien avec la communauté juive, mais qui s'exprime dans des cadres empruntés au judaïsme » (2). Ainsi défini, le judéo-christianisme englobe naturellement les deux catégories précédentes de judéo-chrétiens, Juifs devenus chrétiens. Mais il s'étend bien au-delà de leurs limites. Il comprend non seulement des Juifs qui, comme Paul, ont rompu avec l'observance, mais aussi les recrues venues du paganisme. En fait, il a été un moment coextensif à l'Église. « Il y a une première théologie chrétienne d'expression juive, sémitique » et l'on peut ainsi parler, dans l'histoire du christianisme antique, d'une « période judéo-chrétienne », qui va « des origines du christianisme au milieu du second siècle environ » (3).

Comme le judaïsme de l'époque est très loin d'être une religion monolithique, comme il s'exprime dans des tendances très diverses et se ramifie en un grand nombre de sectes, on doit se demander à laquelle d'entre elles le judéo-christianisme ainsi défini emprunte ses catégories de pensée. Le R. P. Daniélou estime que les courants majeurs, Pharisiens, Esséniens, Zélotes, ont tous, à des degrés divers, imprimé leur marque au christianisme naissant. Mais en définitive, c'est surtout de l'apocalyptique que viennent les influences déterminantes : « On peut dire que toute la littérature judéo-chrétienne est apocalyptique, si l'apocalyptique constitue sa méthode théologique ». Et l'auteur précise que « cette apocalyptique était une gnose. Elle était constituée par des enseignements sur les réalités cachées du monde céleste et sur les arcanes dernières de l'avenir » (4).

Nous voici donc en présence de trois définitions différentes du judéo-christianisme — sans compter celles que l'un ou l'autre de nos auteurs a évoquées sans les retenir : par l'observance, par un système de doctrine, par des catégories de pensée. Mon propos n'est pas de chercher si on peut les accorder entre elles, ou si au contraire elles sont exclusives l'une de l'autre. Je me contenterai pour l'instant de noter que ces différences de point de vue d'un chercheur à l'autre ne font qu'illustrer la complexité du phénomène, mise en pleine lumière par les plus récents des travaux mentionnés.

(1) *Ibid.*
(2) *Op. cit.*, p. 19.
(3) *Op. cit.*, p. 20-21.
(4) *Op. cit.*, p. 35.

Le critère de l'observance me paraît incontestablement le plus sûr. Si le judéo-christianisme représente une synthèse, plus ou moins heureuse et logique, ou, si l'on préfère, une syncrèse de christianisme et de judaïsme, et comme le judaïsme, dans quelque rameau ou secte qu'on l'envisage, attribue une importance primordiale à la pratique de la Loi, comme il est, dans le pharisaïsme ou ailleurs, essentiellement une orthopraxie, il est légitime de chercher aussi du côté de la pratique ce qui peut caractériser le judéo-christianisme à toutes les étapes de son développement et sous tous ses aspects. C'est contre l'observance rituelle juive — tout au moins dans la mesure où elle prétend s'imposer même aux convertis du paganisme — que prend position saint Paul. C'est parce qu'ils cèdent à la tentation de l'observance que certains fidèles sont dénoncés dans l'Église ancienne, et par saint Jean Chrysostome à Antioche jusqu'à l'extrême fin du ive siècle, comme οἱ ἰουδαΐζοντες. Il y a là un élément ferme, qui doit à coup sûr être retenu pour une définition du judéo-christianisme au sens précis et classique : celui qu'ont adopté les auteurs ecclésiastiques de l'Antiquité et aussi les deux premiers des auteurs modernes dont je rappelais tout à l'heure les travaux et les conclusions.

Mais ceci une fois acquis, une question se pose immanquablement : comment délimiter l'observance à partir de laquelle on pourra définir le judéo-christianisme ? Ou, pour parler plus familièrement, quelle est la dose d'observance requise pour qu'un fidèle de l'Église ancienne puisse être qualifié de judéo-chrétien ?

Il me semble que nous disposons à cet égard d'une pierre de touche assez sûre, qui est le « décret apostolique » consigné au chapitre 15 des Actes des Apôtres. On sait qu'il codifie un ensemble, réduit, de prescriptions qui sont toutes de caractère rituel et dont les affinités avec les commandements dits noachiques, tels que les connaît la tradition rabbinique, sont communément reconnues. On sait également que ces prescriptions, qui représentent le minimum qu'on peut imposer même aux Gentils, mais aussi un maximum au-delà duquel on n'a pas le droit de les entraîner, ont gardé force de loi assez longtemps dans de nombreux secteurs de l'Église ancienne : témoins, entre autres, la lettre de l'Église de Lyon relatant la persécution de 177 et, pour l'Afrique, Tertullien (1). Elles fixent donc la

(1) EUSÈBE, *Hist. ecclés.*, 5, 1, 26 ; TERTULLIEN, *Apologétique*, 9, 13-14 ; cf. MINUCIUS FELIX, *Octavius*, 30, 6.

position officielle de l'Église sur la question de l'observance juive. Considérées du point de vue de la Synagogue, elles équivalent à faire des chrétiens quelque chose comme des demi-prosélytes. Nous sommes donc fondés, semble-t-il, à voir là la ligne de démarcation entre le chrétien normal et le judéo-chrétien. Sera judéo-chrétien celui qui ira au-delà de cet ἐπάναγκες, qui se pliera à d'autres prescriptions de la Loi rituelle juive. Critère empirique à coup sûr. Je le tiens personnellement pour valable, tout au moins pour les tout premiers siècles. Car l'observance du décret est peu à peu tombée en désuétude, plus ou moins vite selon les régions ; et il est venu un moment où le simple fait de continuer à s'y plier a constitué aux yeux de l'autorité ecclésiastique une présomption de judéo-christianisme : la chose apparaît très clairement chez saint Augustin par exemple, qui raille ceux de ses fidèles qui se croient tenus d'observer encore ces prescriptions surannées (1).

Il n'y a pas, à mon sens, de judéo-christianisme au sens précis sans observance, et une observance non pas simplement apparentée dans son esprit — comme peut l'être celle du *Frühkatholizismus* — mais identique dans sa teneur même et dans sa lettre à l'observance juive et synagogale. Cette fidélité à la Loi rituelle s'accompagne assez normalement de particularités doctrinales. Elles sont très nettes dans ce rameau original de judéo-christianisme que nous révèlent les *Pseudo-Clémentines*. On les retrouve sous des formes moins tranchées — christologies de type adoptianiste par exemple — dans d'autres variétés du phénomène. Mais même lorsqu'il y a identité de vues — et si nous en croyons nos sources ecclésiastiques elle a parfois existé — entre l'orthodoxie et les judéo-chrétiens, le critère de l'observance à lui seul suffit à définir ces derniers. Le témoignage de Justin Martyr entre autres, à une date où ils ne sont pas encore relégués, en dehors de la Grande Église, au rang d'une secte, est à cet égard particulièrement clair (2).

Mais à côté de ce judéo-christianisme classique, les recherches récentes ont fait apparaître d'autres formes du christianisme antique qui peuvent elles aussi, en un sens plus large, être qualifiées de judéo-chrétiennes. Nous sommes ici en terrain beaucoup plus délicat. Car si l'on veut définir un judéo-christianisme à partir de notions théologiques ou de catégories de pensée, il faut ne pas perdre de vue que le judaïsme lui-même sous ses

(1) Cf. M. Simon, *Verus Israel*, p. 390.
(2) *Dialogue avec Tryphon*, 47.

différentes formes, et en dépit de son intransigeance doctrinale, a subi l'emprise des cultures voisines, de la pensée iranienne et hellénistique en particulier. Dans ces conditions, le critère des expressions, thèmes ou formes de pensée, apparaîtra d'un maniement difficile, dans la mesure où les termes de référence eux-mêmes, empruntés au judaïsme de l'époque, trahissent parfois des influences qui ne sont pas exclusivement juives. C'est là, à mon sens, l'objection fondamentale que l'on peut faire à la définition intéressante et neuve que le R. P. Daniélou nous propose du judéo-christianisme. Il l'a d'ailleurs prévue, sur un point au moins, puisqu'il laisse en dehors de son champ d'investigation et renonce à utiliser comme terme de référence l'œuvre de Philon et plus généralement le judaïsme alexandrin, trop profondément marqué par l'hellénisme pour qu'il puisse servir à définir, par opposition au christianisme hellénistique, un judéo-christianisme. On ne peut que lui donner sur ce point entièrement raison. Mais on peut penser aussi que la précaution était insuffisante et que parmi le vaste ensemble de thèmes et de représentations qu'il reconnaît comme judéo-chrétiens, il en est qu'il est difficile de qualifier ainsi. J'hésiterais beaucoup, pour ma part, à parler de judéo-christianisme à propos de l'Épître de Barnabé par exemple, simplement parce qu'on y retrouve certains thèmes ou formes de pensée considérés comme judéo-chrétiens, alors que son auteur est essentiellement préoccupé de détourner ses lecteurs de l'observance synagogale et que, poussant à ses conséquences extrêmes l'exégèse allégorique, il va jusqu'à dénier aux commandements de la Loi, même avant le Christ, toute autre valeur que de pur symbole.

Plus généralement, il me paraît que certains éléments tenus par le R. P. Daniélou pour judéo-chrétiens pourraient avec autant de raison être étiquetés gnostiques, sauf que cette appellation est de maniement aussi délicat que celle de judéo-chrétien. Et c'est sans doute le problème le plus redoutable qui se pose dans ce secteur de la recherche que celui des relations entre judéo-christianisme et gnosticisme, les deux termes étant aussi malaisés à serrer l'un que l'autre, dès qu'on recourt, pour définir le premier, à autre chose que l'observance.

Peut-être du moins peut-on essayer de poser un ou deux principes susceptibles d'orienter les débats et la recherche. Il me semble que l'on est fondé à parler de judéo-christianisme, en un sens plus large que celui que j'ai précédemment rappelé, à propos de telle position doctrinale, tel aspect de la pensée théologique, telle particularité de la pratique liturgique ou dis-

ciplinaire qui d'une part se distinguent nettement du christianisme de type hellénistique et d'autre part offrent des affinités
précises, qu'il sera légitime d'interpréter comme l'indice d'une
filiation probable, avec l'une ou l'autre des écoles de pensée ou
sectes juives du début de notre ère. L'exemple le plus net est
fourni, ici encore, par l'ébionisme des *Pseudo-Clémentines*, dont
les singularités sont sans parallèle du côté de la Grande Église
de la Gentilité, mais prolongent en revanche en milieu chrétien
celles d'un certain judaïsme marginal et ésotérique, essénisme en
particulier.

La même constatation vaut pour divers secteurs, même
orthodoxes, de l'Église ancienne, en particulier dans les provinces orientales, et plus spécialement pour le christianisme
d'expression sémitique, araméenne ou syriaque, dont nous saisissons de plus en plus clairement l'importance, à côté du christianisme de langue grecque ou latine et d'esprit hellénistique.
C'est à coup sûr de ce côté-là que les vues du R. P. Daniélou
trouvent leur champ d'application le plus incontestable. J'hésiterais pour ma part à le suivre lorsqu'il parle d'une période
judéo-chrétienne pour l'ensemble de la chrétienté antique. On
ne le peut, me semble-t-il, qu'au prix d'une schématisation
excessive, qui ne tient pas compte des nuances multiples d'une
réalité infiniment complexe. En revanche, je suis tout disposé
à admettre avec lui qu'il a existé un secteur judéo-chrétien
— judéo-christianisme étant entendu au sens large que je viens
de proposer — beaucoup plus considérable et plus important
qu'on ne le soupçonnait communément, et qui, localisé pour
l'essentiel en Orient, de part et d'autre des frontières de l'Empire, a poussé des prolongements non négligeables aussi du
côté de l'Occident gréco-latin. Le chapitre consacré à la question
sous le titre « Éphèse, Édesse, Rome » dans la *Nouvelle Histoire
de l'Église* que le R. P. Daniélou vient d'écrire en collaboration
avec M. Marrou me paraît à cet égard avoir utilement nuancé
les positions un peu trop tranchées, à mon sens, de *Théologie
du Judéo-Christianisme* (1).

Mais une fois admis ou établi le fait même de ce judéo-christianisme, d'autres questions se posent, et d'abord celle de son
origine. Sur ce point précis, l'accord paraît relativement facile
à réaliser. Je ne pense pas qu'on puisse, en français, restreindre
le terme de judéo-christianisme aux seuls fidèles d'origine juive.

(1) J. DANIÉLOU et H. MARROU, *Nouvelle Histoire de l'Église* : I, *Des origines
à Grégoire le Grand*, Paris, 1963, pp. 70-86.

Même si on l'entend au sens précis et traditionnel — défini par l'observance — et à plus forte raison si on lui donne une acception plus large, rien n'interdit de penser — et tout, au contraire, y invite — qu'il a compté dans ses rangs des fidèles nés en dehors d'Israël, dans la Gentilité. Du moins le point de départ chronologique, la forme initiale du judéo-christianisme doivent-ils être cherchés du côté du judaïsme palestinien. Il est communément admis que ce point de départ est fourni par la première chrétienté jérusalémite, groupée autour des Douze. Celle-ci, en effet, recrutée parmi les Juifs, semble, pour autant que nous soyons renseignés sur elle, être restée fidèle aux formes de vie religieuse et cultuelle de la religion ancestrale. Plus précisément, l'influence de Jacques, frère du Seigneur, paraît avoir été considérable dans la formation et le développement de ce christianisme judaïque à ses débuts. Même si l'on accepte l'historicité du rôle médiateur et conciliateur que lui prêtent les Actes des Apôtres dans la genèse du décret sur les observances, il paraît assuré que pour sa part, et pour ceux qui gravitaient autour de lui, il ne s'est pas contenté de ce minimum codifié par le décret.

Mais le problème se pose de savoir laquelle, parmi les formes ultérieurement attestées de judéo-christianisme, peut se réclamer en droite ligne de la communauté apostolique. Plus précisément, le christianisme initial se situait-il déjà en dehors des cadres du judaïsme officiel et offrait-il déjà à quelque degré ces caractères aberrants par rapport aux normes jérusalémites, qu'elles soient sadducéennes ou pharisiennes, qui apparaissent avec une telle clarté dans l'ébionisme des *Pseudo-Clémentines* par exemple ? La question a été abondamment débattue au cours des années récentes (1). Elle est particulièrement difficile à résoudre, parce que nos sources sont à cet égard d'un laconisme fort décevant. Nous ne savons que très peu de chose sur la pensée religieuse du groupe apostolique et plus précisément sur sa position en regard des institutions rituelles du judaïsme. Si nous en croyons les Actes, les premiers chrétiens ajoutaient la foi au Christ à la pratique de la religion ancestrale, sans rien retrancher de cette dernière. Leur assiduité au Temple édifiait tout le peuple et il fallut les propos révolutionnaires proférés à l'endroit du sanctuaire par Étienne pour déclencher, mais uniquement sur le

_____

(1) Cf. entre autres, en plus de Schoeps, *Judenchristentum*, E. Lohmeyer, *Kultus und Evangelium*, Göttingen, 1942 et déjà F. C. Burkitt, *Christian Beginnings*, Londres, 1924, qui prêtent à la première communauté chrétienne une attitude hostile au culte traditionnel.

groupe des Hellénistes, la première persécution que les chrétiens aient eu à subir de la part des autorités juives (1).

Sans doute la possibilité existe, au moins théorique, de dissocier Temple et culte sacrificiel. Certains auteurs ont effectivement pensé que les premiers disciples s'étaient abstenus du second sans pour autant condamner le premier. J'hésiterais pour ma part à me rallier à cette vue des choses. Le parallèle des Esséniens ne me paraît pas entièrement probant, d'autant qu'il y a sur ce point une contradiction entre Philon, d'après lequel ils ne sacrifiaient pas du tout, et Josèphe, selon lequel ils se contentaient d'envoyer des offrandes — non sanglantes — au Temple, mais accomplissaient leurs sacrifices entre eux. On a beaucoup discuté sur ces textes, et je n'ai pas l'intention de rouvrir la discussion (2). Je noterai simplement que si l'attitude des Esséniens vis-à-vis du culte sacrificiel n'est pas entièrement claire, elle l'est en revanche vis-à-vis du Temple. Que ce soit par principe ou seulement, comme il apparaît plus vraisemblable, parce qu'il était à leurs yeux souillé par un sacerdoce indigne, ils ne le tenaient pas en très haute estime ; et les gens de Qumran tout au moins, isolés au fond de leur désert, semblent s'être abstenus de le fréquenter. Les premiers chrétiens au contraire vivent à Jérusalem même, et sont assidus au Temple. Il me paraît difficile qu'ils aient pu le faire tout en répudiant ce qui était la raison d'être même du sanctuaire unique, savoir le culte sacrificiel. Sans doute, aucun texte ne dit explicitement qu'ils sacrifiaient. Mais peut-être ne faut-il pas attacher trop de poids, en l'occurrence, à l'argument *e silentio*.

Reste la fameuse notice d'Hégésippe sur Jacques, frère du Seigneur, présenté comme un nazir, dont l'ascétisme se manifeste en particulier par l'abstention de toute nourriture carnée (3). Ceci peut, à coup sûr, et même doit impliquer qu'il s'abstenait aussi des sacrifices. De fait, Hégésippe nous dit qu'il passait ses journées dans le Temple à prier, intercédant en permanence pour le peuple. Il est très possible que le naziréat de Jacques lui ait en effet interdit de participer aux sacrifices. Mais il n'est pas sûr que ceci ait impliqué une condamnation du culte sacrificiel en soi, et pratiqué par les autres. Il l'est encore moins que

(1) Sur la position d'Étienne, cf. M. SIMON, *St. Stephen and the Hellenists in the primitive Church*, Londres, 1958.
(2) PHILON, *Quod omnis probus*, 75 ; JOSÈPHE, *Ant. Jud.*, 18, 1, 5 ; cf. A. DUPONT-SOMMER, *Les écrits esséniens découverts près de la mer Morte*, Paris, 1959, p. 47.
(3) EUSÈBE, *Hist. ecclés.*, 2, 23, 5.

l'ensemble de la communauté chrétienne primitive n'ait été composée que de nazirs végétariens. Le texte même du décret apostolique, n'interdisant que les idolothytes, les viandes étouffées ou crevées et le sang, implique que d'autres viandes, rituellement immolées, étaient consommées dans la première chrétienté. Le cas de Jacques, si nous faisons confiance à Hégésippe, n'est qu'un cas individuel : celui d'un moine vivant dans le siècle. Les arguments avancés en faveur du caractère d'emblée hétérodoxe, jugé selon les normes juives, du christianisme initial ne me paraissent pas décisifs. Il ne me paraît pas établi, en d'autres termes, qu'il procède en droite ligne d'un groupe qui déjà se situait en marge du judaïsme officiel.

Je croirais plus volontiers que c'est une confluence ultérieure entre certains éléments de la première communauté chrétienne et des groupements sectaires juifs qui a donné naissance au judéo-christianisme de type pseudo-clémentin et à telle autre forme de judéo-christianisme aberrante et proprement hérétique à la fois par rapport aux normes synagogales dans ses aspects juifs, et aux normes ecclésiastiques dans ses aspects chrétiens. C'est à ce propos que se pose la question, très controversée, elle aussi, de la migration de la communauté chrétienne de Jérusalem à Pella au début de la première guerre de Judée. Je n'ignore pas les difficultés que soulève le passage d'Eusèbe qui la relate (1). Elles ont été clairement mises en lumière en particulier par S. G. F. Brandon (2). Les arguments invoqués par lui pour nier l'historicité de l'épisode sont inégalement probants. Celui qu'il tire du caractère entièrement grec et païen de la ville de Pella, qui rendrait improbable que la communauté jérusalémite y ait cherché refuge, ne me convainc absolument pas. Car si les premiers chrétiens se trouvaient en difficulté avec les Juifs, il était fort naturel au contraire qu'ils se retirassent en pays non juif pour se mettre à l'abri. C'est une réaction du même ordre qui semble avoir inspiré à la communauté essénienne l'idée de s'exiler momentanément à Damas (3). Les circonstances dans lesquelles Eusèbe nous dit que la migration eut lieu peuvent bien être suspectes, voire largement inventées. Mais ceci ne suffit pas à infirmer la réalité du fait lui-même. Et au demeurant oet exode a pu n'affecter que quelques individus, plutôt que la communauté en corps constitué. L'existence, à Pella et dans les environs, de

---

(1) *Hist. ecclés.*, 3, 5, 2-3.
(2) *The Fall of Jerusalem and the Christian Church*, Londres, 1951, pp. 168 ss. ; même point de vue chez G. STRECKER, *op. cit.*, pp. 229 ss.
(3) Cf. A. DUPONT-SOMMER, *op. cit.*, pp. 134-135.

groupes judéo-chrétiens à une date ultérieure paraît solidement attestée. Dans ces conditions, il est possible à coup sûr que nous soyons en présence d'une légende née sur place et destinée, en rattachant ces groupes à la communauté jérusalémite, à leur conférer des quartiers de noblesse apostolique. Mais il n'est pas exclu non plus que quelques membres au moins de cette communauté jérusalémite aient effectivement émigré vers les régions transjordaniennes soit au cours de la guerre, soit avant l'ouverture des hostilités, au lendemain de la mort de Jacques, pour échapper à des violences possibles de la part des Juifs. Je serais assez disposé, quant à moi, à voir dans une fusion entre des conventicules sectaires juifs déjà installés au-delà du Jourdain et des éléments chrétiens venus de Jérusalem l'origine de groupements judéo-chrétiens hétérodoxes comme celui dont sont issues les *Pseudo-Clémentines*. La secte préchrétienne des *Nasaraioi* décrite par Épiphane et localisée par lui en Transjordanie paraît bien avoir joué un rôle dans la constitution, par intégration d'éléments chrétiens, du judéo-christianisme sectaire (1).

Je laisse de côté la redoutable question de savoir si c'est dans ces secteurs du judaïsme ou du judéo-christianisme sectaires qu'il faut chercher les racines majeures du gnosticisme : elle sera traitée ultérieurement au cours de ce colloque. Je voudrais simplement noter que ce sont ces milieux marginaux qui paraissent avoir surtout assuré la survivance de formes judéo-chrétiennes de vie religieuse. Rituellement et le plus souvent aussi doctrinalement aberrant par rapport aux normes ecclésiastiques, le judéo-christianisme, dans la mesure où il ne l'était pas déjà au départ par rapport aux formes normales de l'orthopraxie juive, a été peu à peu relégué au rang d'un phénomène sectaire, aux ramifications diverses et aux formes variées. Entendu au sens strict et classique — chrétiens, d'origine juive pour la plupart, restés attachés à l'observance — il ne semble avoir eu ni beaucoup d'importance ni une large diffusion dans l'Église ancienne. Il en va tout autrement si on l'envisage dans toute la diversité de ses aspects, rituels, théologiques ou disciplinaires, associés selon une multitude de combinaisons dont nous ne pouvons souvent que deviner la complexité. Vu sous cet angle, il est fort loin de se limiter à la seule Palestine ou à sa périphérie immédiate (2).

---

(1) ÉPIPHANE, *Panarion*, 18.
(2) Cf. sur ce point les judicieuses remarques de G. STRECKER, dans son *Addendum* à la seconde édition de W. BAUER, *Rechtgläubigkeit*, p. 247.

Le problème se pose alors des causes de sa diffusion. Il me paraît incontestable qu'il y a eu une mission judéo-chrétienne, dont l'initiative remonte en dernière analyse jusqu'aux Douze, ou à certains d'entre eux. Peut-être devons-nous nous prémunir contre une illusion d'optique, due au fait que les Actes des Apôtres sont presque exclusivement concentrés sur les voyages missionnaires de Paul, avec le seul prélude constitué par la dispersion des Hellénistes. Et peut-être aussi, sans prendre pour argent comptant tout ce que la tradition ecclésiastique croit savoir sur la façon dont les Apôtres se sont réparti le monde à évangéliser, peut-on tout de même y retrouver un noyau historique. Mais sans doute faut-il aussi faire entrer en ligne de compte, pour expliquer cette diffusion du judéo-christianisme au sens large, c'est-à-dire d'un christianisme qui porte plus nettement que le christianisme hellénistique la marque du judaïsme, d'autres causes encore. Les éléments juifs de ce christianisme ne sont pas nécessairement congénitaux, si je puis dire. Il peut s'agir parfois de caractères acquis, consécutifs à des influences latérales venues du judaïsme lui-même, de la Synagogue non chrétienne. Nous savons qu'en Orient la coexistence de communautés juives importantes avec les communautés chrétiennes a entraîné des contacts étroits, se traduisant par des influences, réciproques peut-être dans certains cas, mais certainement de la Synagogue sur l'Église. Les tendances judaïsantes plus ou moins poussées qui se manifestent jusqu'à une date souvent assez tardive dans l'histoire du christianisme oriental représentent une forme atténuée, élargie et généralement instable de judéo-christianisme. Elles naissent de relations de voisinage. Encore faut-il se demander si elles représentent un phénomène spontané, ou si au contraire elles ont été entretenues par une activité prosélytique de la part de certains milieux juifs, ce que je crois pour ma part (1). Nous aurons l'occasion de revenir sur ce problème à propos de la communication que doit nous faire M. Munck. Je ne conteste pas que ces tendances judaïsantes soient en partie spontanées, ni non plus que la seule lecture de l'Ancien Testament, reconnu par l'Église comme Écriture révélée ait pu çà et là contribuer à les faire naître. Nous avons tout près de nous, avec la curieuse histoire des

---

(1) Sur les divers aspects des contacts entre judaïsme et christianisme dans le monde antique, cf. M. SIMON, *Verus Israel, passim*. L'existence d'un judaïsme missionnaire et de tout prosélytisme juif a été niée — à mon sens sans argument décisif — par J. MUNCK, *Paulus und die Heilsgeschichte*, Copenhague, 1954, pp. 259-265.

paysans italiens de San Nicandro, venus au judaïsme simplement pour avoir lu la Bible et sans même savoir qu'il existait
encore des juifs, un exemple illustrant ce mécanisme de judaï-
sation spontanée, et de prosélytes sans prosélytisme (1). Le
fait est néanmoins assez exceptionnel. En ce qui concerne l'Église
ancienne et les formes diverses que le judéo-christianisme y a
revêtues, ni la lecture de l'Ancien Testament, ni la contagion
des pratiques synagogales, ni même la propagande juive ne me
paraissent représenter le facteur déterminant. Ils ont pu et
je pense, quant à moi, qu'ils ont dû jouer, mais à titre secondaire.

La diffusion et la persistance du judéo-christianisme sous ses
formes diverses me paraissent en définitive s'expliquer surtout
d'un côté par l'absorption dans le christianisme de groupements
sectaires juifs, de l'autre par une impulsion qui remonte en
dernière analyse jusqu'à l'époque apostolique. Ces deux facteurs
conjugués, se combinant à des degrés divers, me paraissent rendre
compte d'un phénomène dont nous saisissons de mieux en
mieux l'extrême complexité et qui mérite à coup sûr de retenir
de plus en plus l'attention des chercheurs.

DISCUSSION DE LA COMMUNICATION
DE M. SIMON

M. KRETSCHMAR fait remarquer que le problème de l'observance
de la Loi s'est posé non seulement au christianisme naissant, mais aussi
au judaïsme après 70 et, de façon plus aiguë encore, après l'interdiction
de la circoncision par Hadrien. Il n'y a pas à cet égard de différence
fondamentale entre la situation de l'Église primitive et celle de la Synagogue. Et dans la synthèse que prétend être le judéo-christianisme
l'élément juif ne représente pas une constante.

M. SIMON estime qu'il y a tout de même entre les deux groupes une
différence capitale. Le problème de l'observance s'est posé au judaïsme
sous la pression des circonstances extérieures : que peut-on encore
observer, une fois le Temple disparu et la circoncision momentanément
interdite ? Pour l'Église, il résulte d'une sorte de logique interne :
qu'est-il encore légitime d'observer ? D'autre part, la ruine du Temple
a eu pour effet d'étendre même aux Juifs de Palestine les conditions
qui étaient déjà celles de la Diaspora, et l'adaptation paraît s'être faite
assez facilement, selon la formule pharisienne de vie religieuse.

M. QUISPEL estime que le décret apostolique n'a gardé vraiment
force de loi que dans les milieux judéo-chrétiens. Ainsi que l'a montré
Molland, les milieux des *Pseudo-Clémentines*, parce que le décret n'im-

(1) Sur cet intéressant épisode d'histoire religieuse contemporaine, cf. ELENA
CASSIN, *San Nicandro, histoire d'une conversion*, Paris, 1957.

pose pas la circoncision aux convertis de la Gentilité, s'abstiennent eux aussi de la rendre obligatoire. Le texte occidental des Actes spiritualise les prescriptions du décret, preuve qu'il n'était pas observé dans les milieux pagano-chrétiens. Il y aurait donc lieu de définir le judéo-christianisme non par la seule observance, mais à partir d'une mission palestinienne, en tenant compte aussi d'influences ultérieures venues de la Synagogue.

M. SIMON reconnaît comme M. Quispel l'intérêt de la démonstration de M. Molland touchant les *Pseudo-Clémentines*. Mais les Ébionites n'en établissent pas moins une hiérarchie entre les fidèles circoncis, qui représentent une élite, et les autres. Et par ailleurs, en appliquant le mot *porneia* du décret au fait de ne pas se plier aux ablutions rituelles après les relations sexuelles, alors qu'il paraît désigner, dans le décret même, des mariages à des degrés de parenté prohibés par la Loi mosaïque, les *Pseudo-Clémentines* en durcissent l'interprétation dans un sens plus strictement judaïsant. Et les textes de Tertullien et de la lettre de l'Église de Lyon cités par M. Simon dans son exposé montrent que certains secteurs au moins de l'Église des Gentils se considèrent comme liés par le décret.

M. CLAVIER pense que le terme de judaïsants pourrait être retenu pour désigner les chrétiens de la Gentilité qui réintroduisent l'observance, celui de judéo-chrétiens étant alors réservé pour les fidèles d'origine juive restés attachés à l'observance. Mais comme le fait observer le P. Daniélou, il manque à côté du participe un substantif correspondant à *Judaismus*. M. Clavier souligne en outre qu'il y avait dans les vues de F. C. Baur touchant l'opposition entre les Jérusalémites et Paul un élément de vérité.

Revenant sur la difficulté qu'il y a à définir le judéo-christianisme à partir de représentations, le P. DANIÉLOU reconnaît que le judaïsme à l'état pur, c'est-à-dire totalement exempt d'influences non juives, n'existe pas. Mais c'est à travers le fond judéo-biblique que ces influences se sont exercées et ont été élaborées, si bien que nous disposons d'un système de référence qui est véritablement juif.

M. BLACK rappelle que le judaïsme lui-même présente à cet égard une grande variété de nuances, et des oppositions sur le problème même de la Loi. On peut distinguer en gros deux courants majeurs : le judaïsme normatif de type pharisaïque, et un courant qui paraît représenter, en face des Pharisiens, la vieille tradition sacerdotale. C'est de ce dernier que paraissent dériver pour la plupart les premières sectes judéo-chrétiennes.

Appendix 1

On the Problem of Jewish Christianity

by Georg Strecker

In the preceding investigation, Walter Bauer posed for himself the task of examining critically the widely held view that "for the period of Christian origins, ecclesiastical doctrine . . . already represents what is primary, while heresies, on the other hand, somehow are a deviation from the genuine" (above, xxiv). He concluded that this understanding of history which has dominated ecclesiastical historiography since Eusebius is not correct, but that for broad areas the heresies were "primary." It is surprising that he did not buttress this conclusion *in extenso* with reference to the problem of Jewish Christianity. This is especially remarkable because here the generalization drawn by the ecclesiastically approved view of history would be most clearly open to refutation—Jewish Christianity, according to the witness of the New Testament, stands at the beginning of the development of church history, so that it is not the gentile Christian "ecclesiastical doctrine" that represents what is primary, but rather a Jewish Christian theology.[1] This fact was forgotten quite early in the ecclesiastical heresiological tradition. The Jewish Christians usually were classified as "Ebionites" in the ecclesiastical catalogues of sects or else, in a highly one-sided presentation, they were deprecated as an insignificant minority by comparison with the "great

1. Cf. already above, 236; also H. Koch's review of Bauer (see below, p. 287) with reference to the "most ancient Jewish Christianity in Palestine": "Here also the dogmatically determined historiography of the heresiarchs accused the 'Ebionites' of apostasy or of relapse into Judaism while in reality they were merely the 'conservatives' who did not go along with the Pauline-hellenistic developments" (345).

church." Thus implicitly the idea of apostasy from the ecclesiastical doctrine also was applied [246] to them.[2] The more recent treatments have for the most part followed the older pattern of ecclesiastical historiography without contradiction.[3] From the fact that there is only a sparse tradition of Jewish Christian witnesses they incorrectly conclude that Jewish Christianity was actually insignificant, without taking into consideration that our knowledge is determined by the ecclesiastical tradition and that even the various titles of Jewish Christian literature[4] seem to demand some critical reservations with respect

2. Cf. among others Jerome *Epistle* 112.13: "As long as the Nazoreans want to be both Jews and Christians, they are neither Jews nor Christians." See also below, 272 ff.
3. Cf. for example A. von Harnack, *History of Dogma*, 1 (ET by N. Buchanan from German 1894[3] ed.; London: Williams and Norgate, 1894; repr. New York: Dover, 1961): 290 f.; [= 4th German ed. of 1909, p. 313; but in this appendix on Jewish Christianity, Harnack does not point specifically to the year 70 as a watershed; see also p. 330 = ET 308 f.] cf. also H. Lietzman, *History*, 1: 183: after the destruction of Jerusalem "Jewish Christianity lacked not only a racial, but also a religious basis for its former claims, and thus was forgotten in the mainstream church. It sank into oblivion in the lonely deserts of east Jordan"; also O. Cullmann, "Ebioniten," RGG[3], 2 (1958): 297 f., speaks of a "process of retardation into a heretical sect"; M. Simon, *Verus Israel: Étude sur les relations entre Chrétiens et Juifs dans l'Empire Romain (135-145)* (Paris: Boccard, 1948; supplemented reprint 1964), p. 313, claims that "Jewish Christianity outside of Palestine, in view of its initial Israelite recruitment, represents only a rather sporadic phenomenon without much extent. In Palestine itself, the Ebionites are a minority in relation to the mainstream church, in uninterrupted regression and condemned by their position itself to disappear sooner or later." It is inexplicable that L. E. Elliott-Binns quotes this with approval (*Galilean Christianity*, Studies in Biblical Theology 16 [Chatham: SCM, 1956], p. 77 n. 4), even though he correctly recognizes the disparity between actual Jewish Christianity and the uniform characterization of it in the heresiological tradition (78; cf. also 50). The year 70 is usually regarded as the time of transition into the "sectarian situation" —e.g. A. von Harnack, *Mission*[2], 1: 63; H.-J. Schoeps, *Theologie und Geschichte des Judenchristentums* (Tübingen: Mohr, 1949), p. 7; J. Munck, "Jewish Christianity in post-Apostolic Times," NTS 6 (1959-60): 103-116. The influence of the destruction of the Jerusalem temple on Judaism and on Jewish Christianity is quite often overestimated. Such influence was small wherever Jewish Christianity, like diaspora Judaism, had come to be largely independent of the temple cult. Naturally, Jewish Christianity like "official" Judaism, was capable of adapting itself to the new situation. It has been demonstrated elsewhere that the tradition of the flight of the primitive Jerusalem community to Pella during the Jewish war is a legend without historical value and therefore may not be used in this connection; see G. Strecker, *Das Judenchristentum in den Pseudoklementinen*, TU 70 (1958), pp. 229 ff. The defense by Elliott-Binns of the historicity of that event (*Galilean Christianity*, pp. 65-71; in opposition to S. G. F. Brandon) cannot remove the fundamental doubts about the quality of the tradition. His thesis about a unification of the Jerusalem and Galilean communities in Pella (pp. 68 f.) is pure speculation.
4. Cf. G. Strecker, "Ebioniten," RAC 4 (1959), pp. 492 ff.

242

to the judgment of the mainstream church. Therefore no further justification is required for [247] the attempt to apply Bauer's conception of history to Jewish Christianity as well.

Jewish Christianity is, to be sure, a complex thing. It is found both in a Palestinian as well as a hellenistic environment and it was subjected to various influences. Hellenistic Jewish Christianity does not represent a closed unity, but the transition from Jewish Christianity to gentile Christianity is fluid, as is shown on the one hand by the adoption of gentile Christian forms by Jewish Christians and on the other by the Judaizing of Christians from the gentile sphere. The latter process is not only to be assumed for the earliest period— as a result of the direct effects of the Jewish synagogue upon the development of gentile Christianity—but is also attested for the later period.[5] And to what extent can a boundary be drawn with precision between Palestinian and hellenistic Jewish Christianity? Further, there is the problem of genetic definition: if the Christians of Jewish descent are designated "Jewish Christians," it must be asked what criteria there are for so doing. Relationships at the level of the history of tradition should also be explored—as, for example, between the later Jewish Christians and the primitive Jerusalem community or the Jewish Christianity of the New Testament. And is it possible to regard the Jewish Christianity of the New Testament as a unity? The testimony of the Pauline letters as well as the statements (admittedly questionable in particular instances) of the other New Testament writings suggest the opposite already in the early period.[6] A multi-

5. Cf. John Chrysostom *Adversus Judaeos* (PG 48, 844 and 849 f.); Simon, *Verus Israel*, 379 f. The large-scale work of J. Daniélou, *Theology of Jewish Christianity* (ET by J. A. Baker from the 1958 French; Chicago: Regnery, 1964) has a misleading title. That sort of Jewish Christianity, the theology of which it attempts to present, never existed as an entity that can be identified in terms of the history of religions. Actually, this book is an undoubtedly worthwhile presentation of Semitic (Jewish) forms of life and thought within Christian theology. But even in this respect the book is incomplete and has not taken into consideration hellenistic analogies nor the problem of the history of tradition. For a critical evaluation, see the valuable review by A. Orbe, "Une théologie du judéo-christianisme," *Recherches de science religieuse* 47 (1959): 544-549; in addition, Munck, "Jewish Christianity," 108 ff.
6. In taking up the thesis proposed by W. Lütgert, W. Schmithals has indeed argued that besides Pauline Christianity, there existed a comprehensive counter-church of Jewish Christian gnosticism; see the bibliography given below, p. 307 [the shorter studies on Galatians, Philippians, and Romans have now appeared in revised form in *Paulus und die Gnostiker*, Theologische Forschung 35 (Hamburg: Evangelisher Verlag, 1965), along with an article on "Die historische

243

tude of problems that go far beyond the [248] restricted range of an "appendix" arise. Thus some limitations must be set. We shall deal with the legalistic Jewish Christianity situated in Greek-speaking Syria, and will examine from the perspective of this investigation (1) the indirect witness of the *Didascalia* and then (2) the Jewish Christian *Kērygmata Petrou* ("Proclamations" or "Sermons of Peter"; abbreviated KP) source of the pseudo-Clementines, and compare our results with (3) the so-called ecclesiastical position, which in this instance means with the statements about Ebionitism made by the ecclesiastical heresiologists.

1. *The Didascalia.* The author who, around the first half of the third century, wrote the *Didascalia* in Syria [7] claims that he is setting forth the "catholic doctrine" (title; 24 [204.8 f. = 6.12.1], etc.) and

Situation der Thessalonicherbriefe"]—on 1 Thessalonians, see also p. 64 n. 123 of the article on Galatians. [248] On the problem of Philippians, cf. also the investigation by H. Koester listed below, p. 308, which modifies the conclusions of Schmithals somewhat.
7. On this matter, see the following: P. Galtier, "La date de la Didascalie des Apôtres," *Revue d'Histoire Ecclésiastique* 42 (1947): 315-351; B. Altaner, *Patrology* (ET by H. C. Graef from the German 1958[5] ed.; London: Nelson, 1960), p. 56 (see German 1960[6] ed. with A. Stuiber, p. 48); J. Quasten, *Patrology 2: The Ante-Nicene Literature after Irenaeus* (Utrecht: Spectrum, 1953), 147; G. Bardie, "Didascalie des Apôtres," *Dictionnaire de Spiritualité,* 3 (Paris, 1955): 863-865; Harnack, *Geschichte,* 2 (*Chronologie*).2: 488 ff. (his suggestion of post-Novatian interpolations is not convincing). [In what follows, references to *Didascalia* are given according to its normal (broad) chapter divisions, with page and line from Connolly's ET (see below) and the equivalent passage from the *Apostolic Constitutions* (by book, section, and paragraph, following Funk's ed., listed below) appended in that order—e.g. *Didasc.* 8 (80.21 = 2.27.7) means chapter 8 of *Didascalia*, material found on p. 80 line 21 of Connolly's ET, which parallels *Apostolic Constitutions* 2.27.7. The standard German translation by (H. Achelis and) J. Flemming, which is referred to by page and line in the original form of this appendix, has also been consulted at every point.] For the text of the *Didascalia*, reference has been made to the following editions and studies: P. Bötticher (P. de Lagarde), *Didascalia apostolorum syriace* (Leipzig, 1854); M. D. Gibson, *The Didascalia Apostolorum in Syriac,* Horae Semiticae 1 (London, 1903); H. Achelis and J. Flemming, *Die syrische Didaskalia,* TU 10.2 (1904), with variant Syriac readings on pp. 225-235 [Achelis is responsible for the commentary on pp. 257-387; Flemming for the text, German translation, notes, and pp. 243-247]; F. X. Funk, *Didascalia et Constitutiones Apostolorum* (in two volumes, Paderborn, 1905; reprint 1960), a reconstruction of the text in Latin according to the Latin and Syriac evidence, and a comparison with the *Apostolic Constitutions;* R. H. Connolly, *Didascalia Apostolorum: the Syriac version translated and accompanied by the Verona Latin fragments* (Oxford: Clarendon, 1929), an ET of the Syriac text and comparison with the Latin fragments. Cf. also E. Tidner, *Didascaliae Apostolorum Canonum Ecclesiasticorum Traditionis Apostolicae versiones Latinae,* TU 75 (1963). [For an ET of the Ethiopic version, see J. M. Harden, *The Ethiopic Didascalia* (London: SPCK, 1920).]

244

that he represents the "catholic church, holy and perfect" (9 [86.1 = 2.26.1]; cf. 8 [80.21 = 2.25.7], etc.). The consciousness of catholicity appears to permeate the church of his time—in any event it presents itself as such when the recommended practice of fasting is defended by reference to the custom "of all the faithful throughout the world" (21 [180.19 f. = 5.12.5]), and becomes concrete in the dispute with the heretics, "who have erred by thinking that there are other churches" (23 [199.1 f. = 6.5.5]) and "who with evil words blaspheme the catholic church which is the receptacle of the holy spirit" (25 [212.30 = 6.14(18).7]). In opposition to them, it is necessary to preserve the catholicity of the church by making a clear break with them (25 [210.24 ff. = 6.14(18).1-2]) and to deal with the believers who have fallen away to their side either by [249] excluding them from the church's fellowship or by converting them from their error (25 [210.20 ff. = 6.14(18).1; and 214.14 ff. = 6.14(18).10]). The author supports the "catholic doctrine" which he represents through the apostolic claim made by his work in its title and in the fiction of apostolic authorship that it maintains throughout. Thereby he gains a legitimation that could not be achieved on the basis of his own authority, and at the same time his work acquires a universality corresponding to the presupposed missionary activity of the apostles (25 [214.24 ff. = 6.14(18).11]). On the surface, it seems that the catholic ideal has been widely realized. In opposition to the dangers of heresy, a firmly established episcopal office guarantees the purity of the church.[8] The reference to the "holy scriptures" is a polemical thrust at the heresies—it is a familiar indication of a "catholic" self-understanding.[9] Even the triadic structure of the credo fits into this framework.[10]

Thus in the *Didascalia* the claim of catholicity and the claim of orthodoxy go hand in hand. But are we dealing with anything more than a claim? It is true that when the author speaks about traveling

8. Cf. the instructions for the office of bishop in chapter 4 (28 ff. = 2.1-6). It is significant that the admonition which is characteristic for the *Didascalia*, to use church discipline with moderation, is justified by reference to the dangers that threaten the outsiders from the side of the heresies (7 [64.28 ff. = 2.21.2]).
9. *Didasc.* 20 (172.12 = 5.7.14), 24 (204.12 = 6.12.2), 25 (212.39 = 6.14[18].7), 26 (242.13 f. and 244.7 ff. = 6.21[27].1 and 2); cf. Bauer, above, 195 ff.
10. *Didasc.* 19 (167.3 ff. = 5.6.10), 24 (204.10 ff. = 6.12.1), 26 (258.13 ff. = 6.23[30].8—cf. the codices!)—in pointed confrontation with the heretics; cf. especially the passage listed from 24, where the short form of the credo is attached to an implicit warning against the heresies.

245

Christians he makes a distinction between adherents of the church
and heretics (12 [120.28 ff. = 2.58.1]), but the question remains completely open as to how extensive is the ecclesiastical background
referred to here. Considering the forms in which the "catholic doctrine" of the *Didascalia* appears, it is striking that it diverges significantly from the character of "orthodoxy" with which we are familiar.
To be sure a monarchial episcopate is presupposed, but the concept
of succession that was for the most part simply taken for granted in
the mainstream church of the third century is not mentioned. This
is all the more surprising since the apostolic fiction maintained by
the book plainly requires such a basis for the episcopal office.[11] [250]
The use of the New Testament scriptures also is striking. The stereotyped reference to the "holy scriptures" is expanded as an exhortation to read "the holy scriptures and the gospel of God"
(2 [20.4 f. = 1.7.17]), or "the law, the book of the kings and the

---

11. Cf. Achelis(-Flemming), *Didaskalia*, p. 270. The more or less contemporary
"basic writing" that underlies the ps.-Clementines (see below, 258), on the
other hand, reports the installation of Clement or of Zachaeus by the apostle
Peter on the basis of a supposed order for the episcopal consecration—ps.-Clemen-
tine *Epistle of Clement to James* (ET in ANF 8: 218-222), *Hom.* 3.60 ff., *Rec.*
3.65 f. (cf. Strecker, *Judenchristentum*, pp. 97 ff.). On this problem, see also W.
[250] Ullmann, "The Significance of the Epistula Clementis in the Pseudo-Clementines," *Journal of Theological Studies* 11 (1960): 295-317; this is an expansion
of the presentation, "Some Remarks on the Significance of the Epistula Clementis in the Pseudo-Clementines," *Studia Patristica* 4, TU 79 (1961): 330-337.
According to Ullmann the *Epistle of Clement to James*, which is in the form
of a testament of Peter to Clement, endeavors to establish the legal basis for the
transmission of Peter's authority to the papacy ("Remarks," 334 and elsewhere).
Ullmann correctly recognizes that the *Epistle of Clement to James* presupposes
the concept of apostolic succession, but he is wrong in his contention that the
reference to the Roman community determines the character of the letter. From
the viewpoint of literary analysis, the *Epistle* derives from the author of the
"basic writing" behind the ps.-Clementines. Correspondingly, its content relates
directly to the ps.-Clementine story. As an introduction to the work, this epistle
was fashioned in connection with the other introductory writing, the *Epistle of
Peter to James* (below, 260 n. 57), and attempts to prepare for the significance
of the speeches of Peter that are referred to in what follows, and at the same
time to indicate that the journeys of Peter and Clement ended in Rome. Herein
lies the purpose of the *Epistle of Clement to James*, not in the establishing of a
foundation for the Roman claim, of which no indications are found elsewhere
in the Clementine romance. How little the Roman claim lies in the background
is disclosed through a comparison with the episcopal installation of Zachaeus in
Caesarea; Zachaeus is also the successor of Peter (*Hom.* 3.60.1, *ant' emou!*), and
is even legitimated through being an eyewitness (*Hom.* 3.63.1).

246

36

prophets, and the gospel" (2 [14.12 ff. = 1.5.2]), or even "law, prophets, and gospel" (4 [34.21 ff. = 2.5.3]). The designation "gospel" apparently means the gospel literature, which is the most important part of the New Testament canon for the author.[12] The gospel of Matthew is preferred.[13] But acquaintance with the gospel of Mark is not to be ruled out, and knowledge of Luke [251] and of John is highly probable.[14] Thus caution is in order with respect to the con-

12. Achelis(-Flemming), *Didaskalia*, p. 333. In *Didascalia* 8 (81.29 f. = 2.25.1) the introductory formula ["in David and in all the prophets and in the gospel also, our savior prays for our sins . . ."] alludes to an episode from the story of Jesus (cf. Luke 23.34 [and the similar "gospel" material about how "our savior made intercession for sinners before his father," found in *Didasc.* 6 (52.14 ff. = 2.16.1); cf. also 24 (212.10 f. = 6.14[18].4)]), just as elsewhere the "gospel" introduces only synoptic material, and not quotations from the canonical epistles (the "apostolos"). [But see n. 14 below on possible "gospel" material from John.] 13. Cf. Achelis(-Flemming), *Didaskalia*, pp. 318 ff. [and Connolly, *Didascalia*, lxx ff.]. Matthew is the only gospel cited by name (21 [182.11 = 5.14.11]—"but in the gospel of Matthew it is written thus. . ."). This introductory formula can hardly be the result of an interpolation as was suggested by Connolly (*ad loc.* and p. lxxi); rather, it is confirmed by the content of the quotation. Reference is made to Matt. 28.1 f., which is part of the material peculiar to Matthew, and the quotation from Matt. 12.40 that follows has been shown to belong to the Matthean redactional material (see G. Strecker, *Der Weg der Gerechtigkeit: Untersuchungen zur Theologie des Matthäus*, FRLANT 82 [1962]: 103 f.). 14. Achelis(-Flemming), *Didaskalia*, pp. 319 ff. [and Connolly, lxx f.]. According to Harnack, *Geschichte*, 2 (*Chronologie*).2: 492 f., the gospel of John was "not used as an evangelical platform," but the testimonies adduced by Achelis (pp. 241 and 320) should not be belittled. With a high degree of probability John 6.38 f. (in 11 [118.3 ff. = 2.55.2]), 7.24 (in 11 [114.23 f. = 2.51.1]), and 12.25 (in combination with Matt 10.39, in 19 [166.16 f. = 5.6.7]) are cited. Therefore one also will have to favorably evaluate allusions to John 13.4 f. and 14 f. in *Didasc.* 16 (150.10 ff. and 16 = 3.13.4 f. ["in the gospel"]). To be sure, the Syriac manuscript Harrisianus does not contain a translation of this passage. However, this omission includes the larger context and is insignificant in view of the numerous omissions in this manuscript. Finally, the possibility also must be left open that the pericope concerning the adulteress in *Didasc.* 8 (76.16 ff. = 2.24.3) was accessible to the author because it was included in his copy of the Fourth Gospel (cf. certain manuscripts of John 7.53 ff.)—contrary to Achelis(-Flemming), 319, and Connolly, lxxi f. Even though Papias and the *Gospel of the Hebrews* transmitted a similar narrative, according to the report of Eusebius (EH 3.39.17), there is still no proof that the *Didascalia* is dependent on them. The fact that the notice of Eusebius and the *Didascalia* agree in avoiding the word "adulteress" is not a sufficient argument. Against this hypothesis it can be argued (1) that no other connections can be established between the *Didascalia* on the one hand and Papias and/or the *Gospel of the Hebrews* on the other—for the latter, such connections are not to be expected since the *Gospel of the Hebrews* is native to Egypt and not to Syria; and (2) that the content of the pericope as it was known to Papias and to the *Gospel of the Hebrews* cannot be determined any longer, but verbal agreements exist in part between *Didascalia* and John 7.53 ff.

247

jecture that the author made use of a harmony of the gospels [15]—
in view of the freedom of the manner of quotation and the citation
of mixed texts from Old and New Testament writings, the use of such
a harmony can hardly be established. This holds true with one exception. It is almost universally recognized that the author either
directly or indirectly used the so-called *Gospel of Peter*, [16] a compilation based on the canonical gospels. The surprising agreements
in the account of Jesus' passion can hardly be explained otherwise,
particularly the statement that it was Herod, not the procurator
Pilate, who had Jesus crucified (21 [190.4 = 5.19.5]), but also in a
more general way the exoneration of Pilate that immediately precedes this passage, the dating of the resurrection of Jesus in the
night [252] preceding Sunday (21 [190.10 f. = 5.19.6]), and the emphasis upon fasting during holy week.[17] The casual manner in which this
gospel is used (formulas of citation do not occur [18]) is all the more
significant since we are dealing with the gospel of "Syrian-Antiochian
heretics" (see above, 66) and Serapion of Antioch already devoted
an official refutation to the book.[19] As the *Didascalia* shows, Serapion's judgment was not able to prevail very quickly throughout the
area of the Syrian church. The outlook of its author with respect
to what may be considered "catholic doctrine" is rather different from
that of the occupant of the bishop's throne in Antioch.[20]

---

15. Harnack, *Geschichte*, 2 (*Chronologie*).2: 494.

16. Cf. [Connolly, *Didascalia*, lxxv ff.;] C. Maurer in Hennecke-Schneemelcher,
1: 179 ff.; L. Vaganay, *L'évangile de Pierre*[2] (Paris: Gabalda, 1930), pp. 167-169;
Harnack, *Bruchstücke des Evangeliums und der Apokalypse des Petrus*, TU 9.2
(1893[2]). Harnack also attempts, without much success, to trace John 7.53 ff. back
to the *Gospel of Peter;* cf. on the contrary Vaganay, pp. 186 f.

17. Compare *Didasc.* 21 (190.6 ff. = 5.19.6), "thus it is fitting for you to fast on
Friday and Saturday and also to take your vigil and watch on Saturday," and
Gospel of Peter 5.27, "on account of all these things we fasted and sat there and
cried night and day until Sabbath." See also below, 250 n. 26.

18. With the possible exception of 21 (183.4 ff. = 5.14.14-15), where the relationship to the *Gospel of Peter* is not entirely clear ["and he said to us, teaching us,
'Are you fasting. . . ?'" These words are spoken in the presence of Levi after the
resurrection—cf. *Gospel of Peter* 14.60 and n. 25 below].

19. EH 6.12 (see above, 115); Zahn, *Geschichte*, 1.1:177-179, and 2: 743 ff.;
Harnack, *Geschichte*, 1.1: 11.

20. Eusebius, on the other hand, later included the *Gospel of Peter* among the
heretical writings; EH 3.3.2 and 3.25.6 ff.

We will bypass the question of *Didascalia*'s relation to the rest of the canon [21] and also the problem of its use of so-called agrapha, in which it does not go beyond the bounds of what is common in patristic literature of the third [253] century.[22] But in connection with what has been said, we must refer to the relation of the author of the *Didascalia* to Judaism.[23] Of course, one should not overestimate

21. The number of canonical New Testament writings presupposed by *Didascalia* is not as extensive as Achelis had affirmed (*Didaskalia*, pp. 321 ff.). In addition to the four gospels, the *Gospel of Peter*, and the book of Acts, there is clear acquaintance with some Pauline epistles, especially the Pastorals (Achelis, pp. 322 f.; [cf. Connolly, lxxii]). But in regard to the remaining canonical works, judgment must be reserved. The idea that the author knew Hebrews is not supported by any real evidence. Nor is it demonstrable that his Pauline corpus comprised fourteen letters, as Achelis supposed (323; [cf. Connolly, lxxii]). Knowledge of the catholic Epistles is also questionable. The parallel between *Didascalia* 12 (122.29 ff. = 2.58.4) and James 2.2 f. does not prove that James is being cited because, as Achelis himself acknowledged (322), it is precisely the colorful statements of the version in James that are absent from *Didascalia*. It is self-evident that use of 1 John cannot be inferred from the fact that the Johannine gospel is quoted. Only for a knowledge of 1 Peter is there some basis: *Didascalia* 1 (2.6 = 1. introduction) seems to refer to 1 Pet. 1.2, *Didasc.* 4 (32.26 = 2.3.3) to 1 Pet. 4.8, and *Didasc.* 9 (86.1 f. = 2.26.1) to 1 Pet. 2.9 (Achelis, 322; [Connolly, lxxii]). There is no denying the existence of these parallels. Moreover, the material in *Didasc.* 4 is presented as a direct quotation. But surprisingly, the quotation is said to be spoken by the "Lord," so that one must ask whether this logion was actually transmitted to the author of the *Didascalia* as part of 1 Peter, or whether it may not have been independent of that document. This supposed evidence also is compromised by the discovery that the passage ultimately derives from an Old Testament text (Prov. 10.12) even though the wording in *Didasc.* 4 is closer to the text of 1 Peter [253] than to that of the Old Testament. The same applies to the material in *Didasc.* 9, where the text that supposedly is cited (1 Pet. 2.9) actually is an indirect quotation of Exod. 19.6 and 23.22 (LXX). As was true in the case of *Didasc.* 4, the wording of *Didasc.* 9 is closer to the New Testament text than to the Old Testament. But this is hardly decisive. The text in question appears in a series of ecclesiological predications which were well known and probably orally transmitted. The same is true of *Didasc.* 1, where the wording of 1 Pet. 1.2 is not reproduced exactly either. The conclusion that the author of *Didascalia* knew 1 Peter is not compelling, to say the least. Finally, with reference to the Apocalypse [cf. Connolly, lxxiii], even Achelis recognized that the few allusions do not go beyond the stock of commonly used liturgical formulae in the ancient church (323 f.). There is thus no reason for assuming that the author of the *Didascalia* knew and used the Apocalypse.

22. Cf. Achelis(-Flemming), *Didaskalia*, pp. 336 ff.; [Connolly, lxxiii; and above, n. 12].

23. Details in Achelis(-Flemming), *Didaskalia*, p. 361; C. Schmidt, *Studien zu den Pseudo-Klementinen*, TU 46.1 (1929): 252; L. Goppelt, *Christentum und Judentum im ersten und zweiten Jahrhundert* (Gutersloh: Bertelsmann, 1954), pp. 205-207. [Cf. also Connolly, lxxxviii f.]

249

the evidence that will be cited here. The fact that the author speaks of the Jews as "brothers" in chapter 21 (184.31 = 5.14.23, and 187.8 = 5.17.1) is based on the Old Testament [24] and perhaps goes back to a literary source that could also have contained the idea of intercessory fasting for the brethren from the Jewish people.[25] Behind it lies an understanding of the history of salvation that concentrates primarily upon the past and less upon the current situation (cf. 21 [184.17 ff. = 5.14.22], 23 [198.10 ff. = 6.5.4 ff.]). Nevertheless, this assessment of Judaism also has a root in the author's present experience, as is indicated by the fact that the *Didascalia* betrays a detailed acquaintance with Jewish customs and teachings. The following examples will suffice: the unusual etymological derivation of the Jewish name from the Hebrew root *YDH* in chapter 13 (126.22 = 2.60.3—"'Jew' means 'confession'"); the precise presentation of Jewish [254] sabbath customs;[26] the distinction between the passover and the feast of the unleavened bread,[27] the dating of the

24. The former passage continues: "For even if they hate you, we must call them brothers, for thus it is written for us in Isaiah, 'Call those who hate and despise you "brothers," because the name of the Lord is praised'" (Isa. 66.5).
25. In terms of its content, *Didasc.* 21 (180.29 f. = 5.13.1, "when you fast, pray and intercede for those who are perishing, as we also did when our savior suffered") has parallels in the *Gospel of Peter* 5.27 (see above, 248 n. 17). The later citation in *Didasc.* 21 (183.5 ff. = 5.14.15) seems to be a resumption of the same tradition, which Achelis already claimed was part of the *Gospel of Peter* (327)—"but he [the Lord] said to us, teaching us, 'would that you not fast these days for my sake; or do I have need that you should afflict your soul? [cf. Isa. 58.4-5]. But for the sake of your brothers you did it, and you will do it on these days on which you fast, on the fourth [day] of the week [= Wednesday] and on Friday, for all time" [see also above, n. 18]. The possibility that a source lies behind this material becomes more probable in view of the way it differs from its present context; it refers to fasting on Wednesday and Friday, [254] but immediately thereafter *Didasc.* 21 (183.18 ff. = 5.14.17) speaks of fasting during the holy week, from Monday "till the night after the sabbath." With respect to the designation of the Jews as "brothers" it follows that it was originally contained in the source which was either closely related to or identical with the *Gospel of Peter* (above, and n. 18), and was placed into the larger context by the author of the *Didascalia*. Accordingly, it is on the basis of this source used in chap. 21 (180.29 f. = 5.13.1, and 183.5 ff. = 5.14.15) that the intercession was made to relate to the Jewish people even in the subsequent treatment (184.22 = 5.14.22, 185.3 ff. = 5.14.24, 185.10 f. = 5.15.1), without being limited to them, as is clear from the earlier reference to gentile unbelievers (180.10-181.1 = 5.12.4-5.13.1).
26. *Didasc.* 21 (191.4 ff. = 5.20.1 ff.). However, the injunction for Sabbath observance "you shall not lift your foot to do any work, nor shall you speak a word with your mouth" (191.16 ff. = 5.20.5) is not derived from a Jewish tractate (Achelis) but from Isa. 58.13; see Connolly, lxxxviii [following Funk, *ad loc.*].
27. *Didasc.* 21 (192.18 = 5.20.10); cf. Achelis(-Flemming), *Didaskalia*, p. 361; Josephus *Antiq.* 3.(10.5.)248 f.

250

40

lament over the destruction of Jerusalem on the ninth of Ab.[28] These are statements which one may not explain simply by assuming that the author had been of Jewish origin. Such a hypothesis cannot be based upon observations that in reality do nothing more than to identify various items of information.[29] Hence it is more probably the case that there was an active relationship between Christians and Jews in the author's world. Even though with regard to particulars the question of the extent to which such a contact contributed significantly to the development of the outlook of the author and the practice of his community must remain open,[30] it is quite clear that the Syrian environment of the *Didascalia* supports an intensive influence of Jewish thought and conceptual material.

The "catholic doctrine" of the *Didascalia* unfolds itself in the controversy [255] with the "heresies." This problem is treated in chapter 23, "On Heresies and Schisms" (194 ff. = 6.1.1 ff.). Already at the beginning of the *Didascalia* the problem of heresy is mentioned,[31] and it is called to mind repeatedly in what follows.[32] The heresies form a constant danger to the church (23 [199.21 ff. = 6.5.8]). Hence the warning at the start of chapter 23, "guard yourselves against all hateful, reprehensible, and abominable heresies and flee them as you

28. *Didasc.* 21 (191.23 = 5.20.6). It is true that a clear distinction between Jewish and Jewish Christian influence cannot always be made. Thus some of the texts that have been cited may have derived from Jewish Christian influence (see below). Nevertheless, the distinction itself should not be abandoned—it is suggested by the author of *Didascalia* when on the one hand he can speak of the "Jews" (13 [126.22 = 2.60.3] or of "the people" (21 [189.19, 190.26 f., 191.7 ff. = 5.19.2 and 9, 5.20.2 ff.], etc.), and on the other of the "dear brothers" who came "from the people [and] became believers" (26 [233.7 f. = 6.18 (23).11]).
29. Contrary to Achelis(-Flemming), *Didaskalia*, pp. 384 f., and Quasten, *Patrology*, 2: 147. Even though the author knows of a replacement of Israel by the church in the development of salvation history (21 and 23; see above, 249 f.), he does not reveal any special sympathy for the fate of the Jewish people—in contrast to Rom. 9-11, for example.
30. Goppelt, *Christentum und Judentum*, p. 206, states that the instructions to the bishop, the "juridical functions," and the community's "simple ideal for living" are examples of the "high estimation" for the "Jewish tradition." But with respect to the orders of office and community the author is primarily dependent on Christian traditions as is indicated, for example, by his extensive use of the pastoral Epistles.
31. *Didasc.* 5 (38.1 = 2.6.17). The sinners have "fallen into the pernicious corruption of the heresies concerning which the decisive word is (still) to be spoken."
32. *Didasc.* 7 (64.28 ff. = 2.21.3), 12 (120.32 = 2.58.1), 13 (128.16 = 2.62.3), 23 (194 ff. = 6.1.1 ff.), 25 (210.20 ff. = 6.14[18].1).

251

41

would a blazing fire" (197.22 ff. = 6.5.1), and the instruction in chapter 25 to have no fellowship with the heretics (210.24 ff. = 6.14[18].1). Nor are references to the frightful ultimate fate of the heretics lacking in these contexts (194.13 ff. = 6.1.2, 197.25 ff. = 6.5.2, 212.29 ff. = 6.14[18].7 ff.).

Apparently the author presupposes the existence of a number of heresies. This is not merely part of the fictitious character of this work, with its apostolic claim addressed to the church's past, present, and future, but is also based on actual experiences (cf. chaps. 7 and 12, above n. 32). What actual picture emerges? Following a general warning about heresies in chapter 23 (199.21-31 = 6.5.8 f.), the author presents the "beginning of heresies," namely, the appearance of Simon Magus from his confrontation with the apostles in Jerusalem (!) to the macabre contest of the miracle workers (Simon Magus and Peter) in Rome (200.1-202.6 = 6.7-9). Of course, this does not permit us to draw an inference as to the present situation of the author. The presentation is rather reminiscent of the accounts of the apocryphal acts of the apostles.[33] But even the summary presentation of the heresies that follows in *Didasc.* 23 is not immune to criticism. In a very schematic manner "all heresies" are accused of rejecting "the law and the prophets," blaspheming "God almighty," and denying the resurrection (202.8-11 = 6.10.1). In addition there are the false teachings of particular groups—"many of them taught that a man should not marry, and said that if one did not marry, that would constitute sanctification" (202.12-14 = 6.10.2; cf. 204.14 ff. = 6.12.1); "others of them taught that a man should eat no meat . . ." (202.15 f. = 6.10.3). These assertions, like the preceding portrayal of the heresy of Simon [256] Magus, do not seem to presuppose the existence of an actual situation of controversy, but remain remarkably schematic and lack concreteness. Similarly, they are taken up again only in brief summary statements, without the addition of more specific information.[34] Apparently the author follows an established

33. Cf. Lipsius, *Apokryphen Apostelgeschichten,* 2: 59 ff., 321, 328 (but here the text of the Didascalia is regarded as an abbreviation of the report found in *Apostolic Constitutions* 6.9). Hegesippus already associated Cleobios with Simon Magus (Eusebius EH 4.22.5; cf. Hilgenfeld, *Ketzergeschichte,* p. 32; F. X. Funk, *Die Apostolischen Konstitutionen* (Rottenburg, 1891), p. 74, [and also his *Didascalia* 1: 317 f.].
34. Cf. *Didasc.* 24 (202.23-204.4 = 6.11.1-2, 204.9 ff. = 6.12.1), 26 (240.22 ff. = 6.20[24].1).

pattern of presentation that does not reveal any connection with his own situation. This leads to a further observation—the false teachings to which *Didascalia* refers can be identified with the gnostic theological ideas opposed by the "great church." [35] But in the actual body of the *Didascalia* gnostic influences can be confirmed neither in a positive nor in a negative (antithetical) manner. The heresiological statements summarize material formulated and transmitted in the church tradition. It is a different matter with the last part of the heresiological characterization that is given in *Didasc.* 23—"others said that one should abstain only from the flesh of swine, and should eat what the law declares to be clean, and ought to be circumcised according to the law" (202.17-20 = 6.10.4). In contrast to the gnostic rejection of the Old Testament, the ceremonial law of the Old Testament is here expressly acknowledged as binding. In a subsequent section the author will apply to the above-mentioned "heresy" a notion peculiar to him concerning the "second legislation" (24 [204.1-4 = 6.11.2]; see below, 256). This makes it likely that the former passage contains a reflection of a concrete situation. While the question may remain open whether this notice originally was attached to the older traditional formulation—the above-mentioned repetition of the basic wording in chapter 24 would support this—or whether it was composed by the author, it is certain that the author connects the relevant doctrinal position to the present. Thus we are here provided with the clue by means of which we can reconstruct the "heresy" opposed by the author of the *Didascalia*.

It has already become clear that the heretical group under discussion is not to be characterized as a vegetarian Jewish Christianity [257] that rejected marriage, the eating of meat, and the Old Testament, such as is attested by Epiphanius.[36] Instead, the fundamental

35. It suffices to refer to the summary treatments of Hilgenfeld, especially with regard to the teaching of the Syrian gnostic Cerdo (*Ketzergeschichte*, pp. 316 ff. and especially 332 f.). According to Harnack, the characterization found in *Didascalia* conforms to "the Marcionites" (*Marcion*[2], p. 341*). However, it is difficult to make a distinction between gnostic and Marcionite outlooks here, as is often true with such isolated assertions. Against Harnack it can be argued that Marcion does not seem to have rejected explicitly the idea of an eschatological resurrection; and further, that in our passage the *Didascalia* ascribes the prohibition of marriage and of eating meat not to one single group but to different heretical groups.

36. Cf. Achelis(-Flemming), *Didaskalia*, pp. 355 f.; Schoeps, *Theologie*, pp. 179 n. 3, and 191.

253

acknowledgment of the Old Testament law is assured. Of course, the author can also clothe his polemic in the kind of Old Testament terminology that does not allow us to recognize its actual setting. The assertion that in the true law "no distinctions with regard to food, no burning of incense, no sacrifices and burnt offerings" were mentioned (26 [218.21 ff. = 6.16.2]). can be regarded only as literary decoration at a time subsequent to the destruction of Jerusalem.[37] But in other respects the dependence on the Old Testament still can refer to current situations. The ritual baths after sexual contamination (26 [242.6 ff. = 6.21(27).1 ff.]; cf. 24 [204.25 ff. = 6.12.2]) reflect Lev. 15.16 ff. without being derived in a literary sense from that passage. The explicit nature of the controversy and also the direct or indirect address to the heretics indicate a current situation. The observance of the sabbath is also counted among the characteristic features of the heretics, as the context attests (26 [233.7 ff. = 6.18(23).11]); probably this is true also of circumcision, to which not only the last part of the statement quoted above (on 253) refers but also the emphatically positive description of ecclesiastical life (24 [204.21 = 6.12.2], "spiritual circumcision of the heart"; 26 [218.25 = 6.16(20).2], "uncircumcision"). Finally, it is possible that the observance of the Old Testament food laws is to be included here, although it is mentioned only in the summary passages in chapters 23-24 (202.17 ff. = 6.10.4, 204.1 ff. = 6.11.2; see above, 253).

According to Connolly and W. C. van Unnik,[38] the heretics of the *Didascalia* were "Judaizing Christians" who had adopted some aspects of Jewish observance but not the totality of Jewish regulations. Therefore they did not actually live in association with Judaism and are not to be designated as Jewish Christians.[39] But while it cannot be denied that Syriac Christianity exhibits strong Judaizing tendencies, one should not connect the people addressed in the *Didascalia* with such trends. Since they are interested in Jewish observances,

37. Cf. also *Didasc.* 9 (98.15 ff. = 2.35.1), and perhaps 26 (216.3 f. = 6.15.1, and 252.3 f. = 6.22[28].1)?
38. Van Unnik, "De beteeknis van de mozaische vet voor de kerk van Christus volgens de syrische Didascalie," *Nederlandsch Archief voor Kerkgeschiedenes* 31 (1939): 65-100. [Connolly, lxxxiii, does not explicitly argue for such an interpretation, despite Strecker's claim, but seems to leave the question open.]
39. Van Unnik, "Beteeknis," pp. 95 ff. Cf. similarly J. Thomas, *Mouvement baptiste*, pp. 406 f.; Simon, *Verus Israel*, pp. 362 ff.

they are explicitly [258] designated "heretics," [40] a verdict which would be extraordinary with respect to Judaizing Christians, whose basic mistake did not so much involve questions of faith as questions of ecclesiastical discipline. The same can be said with reference to their practice of circumcision, which provides tight bonds to Judaism and goes far beyond mere "Judaizing." [41] Therefore, the deduction is more likely that we are dealing here with Jewish Christians. It is not accidental that the author, at the beginning of his instruction about the "second legislation" (or "repetition of the law") in chapter 26, spoke to those who "from among the people have turned to faith in God our savior Jesus Christ" (216.1 ff. = 6.15[19].1), just as in chapter 21 he also interpreted the quotation from Isaiah 9.1 f. by referring it to the church made up of Jews and gentiles (186.4 ff. = 5.16.2 ff.).

In spite of the apparent close connection between the Jewish Christian "heretics" and the community of the author, it is not to be assumed that they actually belong to the community of the *Didascalia*.[42] It is striking that where the order of the congregation and its spiritual life is especially treated, a Jewish Christian peril is not mentioned. Controversies concerning the authority of the bishop and the other office holders would hardly be absent in the event of a struggle within the community. The question of how "catholic doctrine" is to defend itself against heresy is not concerned with the problem of the inner life of the community, but the community is presupposed as a self-contained entity that seeks to defend itself against sin and apostasy (cf. *Didasc.* 5 ff. [37 ff. = 2.7 ff.]). The Jewish Christian "heretics" stand outside the community of the *Disascalia*.

With this result we have reached a point of departure for the question concerning the relationship between heresy and catholicism in the world of the *Didascalia*. Apparently a complete separation was not involved; rather the previously mentioned contacts permit

40. *Didasc.* 23 (202.17 ff. = 6.10.4), 24 (203.23 ff. = 6.11.1 f.); in 26, compare also 242.6 = 6.21(27).1 with 240.22 ff. = 6.20(24).1.
41. The objection that no christological heresy is mentioned (van Unnik, "Beteeknis," p. 96) does not carry much weight, because first of all it is doubtful whether the author of the *Didascalia*, in view of his very practical purpose, would even be aware of such a deviation; second, it is not impossible that the Jewish Christians who are addressed were in agreement with the community of the *Didascalia* in christological matters.
42. Contrary to Schmidt, *Studien*, pp. 253, 260.

the assumption of a lively relationship in which the leading role of "catholic doctrine" was not considered to be incontestable. The powerful language with which the faithful are warned against "heresy" [259] in chapter 23 (194.7 ff. 6.1.1, 197.22 ff. = 6.5.1, 1.99.1 ff. = 6.5.5, etc.) is eloquent proof of this. The statements made by the author about the form and content of the Jewish Christian "heresy" make it seem questionable that it formed an actual sect.[43] It is instructive to note that it is in his confrontation with his Jewish Christian opponents that the author develops the theory, so central for the *Didascalia*, of the "second legeslation" (or "repetition of the law") —i.e. the contrasting of the Old Testament decalogue [= the "real" law] with the ceremonial rules [the *deuterōsis* or "second legislation"] which had been added after the generation in the wilderness worshipped the golden calf (26 [216.1 ff. = 6.15(19).1 ff.]). Although it cannot be established as probable that the author himself constructed this theory in dependence upon a Jewish Christian theological concept,[44] since a corresponding interpretation of the Old Testament had long been used even in ecclesiastical circles in the controversy with Judaism,[45] its pointed application to the Jewish Christian situation (cf. 26 [216.1-5 = 6.15(19).1]) shows that the Jewish Christian "heretics" had a special importance in the world of the *Didascalia*. We can even go a step further; the fact that the author addresses the Jewish Christian "heretics" with the term "dear brothers"

---

43. Cf. *Didasc.* 26 (240.1 = 6.19[24].3)—they live "in the dispersion among the gentiles." Of course, this also applies to Judaism after the year 135. But the context refers to Jewish Christianity.
44. Contrary to Schmidt, *Studien*, pp. 262 ff., and Schoeps, *Theologie*, p. 180. The theory of false pericopes, which is found in the "KP" document of the ps.-Clementines (see above, 244, and below, 257 f.), cannot be considered as a predecessor since it shows no dependence on Exod. 32; nor does it contrast two stages of written law, but rather, contrasts the falsification of the law with the oral revelation of "the true prophet" (see Strecker, *Judenchristentum*, pp. 162 ff.). The criticism of the Old Testament in the *Didascalia* comes somewhat closer to the Jewish Christian "AJ II" source of the ps.–Clementines [= *Rec.* 1.33–44.2 and 53.4b-71, according to Strecker, *Judenchristentum*, pp. 221–254, and in Hennecke-Schneemelcher, 2: 106], which like the *Didascalia* sees the starting point of the outdated legislation in the veneration of the golden calf by the generation in the desert (*Rec.* 1.36), and holds that sacrifice is replaced by baptism (1.39). However, the author of the *Didascalia* thinks, among other things, of the elimination of the ritual baths through Christian baptism (cf. 26 [224.17 f. = 6.17(22).1, and 248.10 ff. = 6.21(27).7]), while for the "AJ II" source the Jewish ritual laws of purification do not belong to the "second legislation." [For an extended discussion of the concept of *deuterōsis* or "second legislation" in the *Didascalia*, see Connolly, lvii–lxix.]
45. As is pointed out correctly by van Unnik, "Beteeknis," pp. 86-95.

(216.3 = 6.15[19].1, 233.7 = 6.18[23].11) can now no longer be understood as a self-evident *captatio benevolentiae* [attempt to gain good will] resulting from pastoral concern, but can also include the acknowledgement that the Jewish Christian "heresy" actually predominates. The reckoning of the dates for fasting as observed in the author's community is expressly [260] traced back to the reckoning by "believing Hebrews" (21 [187.12 f. = 5.17.2]). Since the designation "believers" in a similar context means only Christians and not Jews, this statement can only be referred to Jewish Christians.[46] The influence of the Jewish Christian "heresy" on the "catholic" ecclesiastical orientation of the *Didascalia* is evident there. The author presupposes Jewish Christian influences. Furthermore, he considers the possibility that the "heretics" might accept those who have been excluded from the church (7 [64.28 ff. = 2.21.2]) or that they themselves might even take part in the worship in his community.[47] As a result, the notion that the "heretical" Jewish Christians were the ones who separated themselves from the church seems much less probable than that the church of the *Didascalia* itself was faced with the task of separating itself from the "heretics."[48] The opposite view is no longer as self-evident as the heresiological outlook would like to imagine, and it is not difficult to conclude that in this part of Syria Jewish Christianity occupied a dominant "orthodox" position superior to "catholicism."

2. *The "Kērygmata Petrou" Source.* We would not be able to draw this conclusion with confidence if we were not in the position of being able to appeal to a direct witness for Jewish Christianity in Greek-

---

46. It could be argued that the preceding sentence, "begin [your fasting] when your brothers who are of the people keep the passover" (187.7 f. = 5.17.1), already should be considered as a reference to the Jewish Christian opponents. This accords with the reading in Epiphanius (*Her.* 70.10.2— *hoi adelphoi humōn hoi ek peritomēs*), which, however, is regarded as doubtful by Connolly (note, *ad loc.*), following Funk (*Didascalia* 2: 7). That the author of the *Didascalia* recognized the connection between the Jewish Christian practice of fasting and the Jewish practice is revealed also by the instructions, "thus you must fast when that people is celebrating the passover" (21 [192.16 f. = 5.20.10]). Therefore a serious objection against the available textual tradition cannot be raised. [The point being argued by Funk and Connolly is that Epiphanius has paraphrased the original Syriac, which they accept as a satisfactory text.]

47. *Didasc.* 12 (120.31 f. = 2.58.1). The fact that these statements are formulated in the plural ("heresies") does not, in view of the tremendous influence of the Jewish Christians, exclude the possibility that they are primarily under consideration.

48. Cf. also Achelis(-Flemming), *Didaskalia*, p. 357.

257

speaking Syria. The *Kērygmata Petrou* source (= KP, "Proclamations of Peter") contained in the "basic writing" that underlies the pseudo-Clementines contains a Jewish Christian theology that is approximately contemporaneous with the author of the *Didascalia* or perhaps a few decades earlier. This document, which was literary in character but can be reconstructed only in part, is especially valuable for our inquiry since we cannot assume that it was literarily dependent on the *Didascalia* or vice versa, in spite of their geographical proximity.[49] KP is a [261] pseudo-Petrine treatise. It contains material about (1) the "true prophet," how he passed through the world, and his relationship to the hostile female prophecy; also about (2) the exposition of the law by the "true prophet" with material about the "false pericopes"; connected with this are (3) anti-Pauline statements, which attempt to show Paul as an opponent of Peter and as one who was not approved by James, the representative of the true doctrine and bishop of Jerusalem; finally (4) material about baptism is given in which the strongly legalistic character of the work becomes evident.[50]

An important piece of evidence for establishing geographical locus and orientation in terms of the history of theology is the testimony a writing gives with respect to the New Testament canon. The *KP* source is acquainted with the four canonical gospels, the Acts of the Apostles, Galatians and 1 Corinthians.[51] It is significant that neither the catholic epistles nor the Apocalypse are known. Thus there is a basic distinction between the attitude of the *Kerygmata* and the situation that obtained in the West and in wide areas of the East at that time, in which the catholic epistles were in use and the validity of the Apocalypse was only partially contested.[52] However, even at a later period these writings were slow to find acceptance in northern

49. Cf. above, 256 n. 44; Strecker, *Judenchristentum*, p. 215 n. 2.
50. For a treatment of various details as well as a reconstruction of the "basic writing" and the KP source, cf. Strecker, *Judenchristentum*, *passim*. A summary presentation with selected texts in translation is found in Strecker, "The Kerygmata Petrou," in Hennecke-Schneemelcher 2, 102-127 [in the same volume, see also J. Irmscher's introduction to the ps-Clementines on 532-535].
51. Strecker, *Judenchristentum*, p. 218.
52. Cf., among others, J. Leipoldt, *Die Entstehung des neutestamentlichen Kanons*, 1 (Leipzig, 1907): 58 f.

258

and eastern Syria.[53] Even the *Didascalia* does not yet show acquaintance with the catholic epistles and the Apocalypse, as was noted above (249 n. 21). This establishes a relation between the KP document and the *Didascalia*, and confirms the view that both are to be placed in a Syrian locale.

It is noteworthy that, in contrast to the assumption of the ecclesiastical heresiologists,[54] the Jewish Christian *Kerygmata* show no knowledge of a Jewish Christian gospel.[55] Therein the *Kerygmata* [262] stand even closer to the "catholic" tradition than does the *Didascalia* which, as we have seen (248 f.), shows a positive relationship to the apocryphal *Gospel of Peter* in spite of Serapion's negative verdict. This and the fact that the *Kerygmata* quote as a matter of course the four gospels that later became canonized is a fundamental argument for the view that the Jewish Christianity represented by the *Kerygmata* had not cut itself off from the "great church," but lived in a situation in which it could candidly accept the development toward the New Testament canon.

This can be corroborated through another line of approach. When we take into consideration the fact that the Pauline letters and the book of Acts are not quoted with approval in the KP document,[56]

53. Zahn, *Geschichte*, 1: 373 ff.; Leipoldt, *Entstehung*, pp. 74, 222; Bauer, *Der Apostolos der Syrer*, pp. 76 f.
54. Cf. Irenaeus AH 1.26.2 (= 1.22), on the Ebionite use of "Matthew"; below, 277 f.
55. G. Quispel ("L'évangile selon Thomas et les Clémentines," *Vigiliae Christianae*, 12 [1958]: 181-196) attempted to prove that a Jewish Christian gospel is cited respectively in the so-called *Gospel of Thomas* and in the ps.-Clementines. [262] However, this attempt is not convincing. It presupposes that the ps.-Clementine quotations from scripture disclose the use of an apocryphal Jewish Christian gospel (cf. the contrary view in Strecker, *Judenchristentum*, pp. 117 ff.), and takes into consideration neither the literary stratification of the ps.-Clementine romance nor the demonstrably free manner of handling scriptural evidence on the part of the ps.-Clementine editor. Contrary to Quispel, cf. also A. F. J. Klijn, "A Survey of the Researches into the Western Text of the Gospel and Acts (1949–1959), Part 2," *Novum Testamentum*, 3 (1959): 176 f.: E. Haenchen, "Literatur zum Thomasevangelium," *Theologische Rundschau*, 27 (1961): 165, 168.
56. It is true that in *Hom*. 3.53.3 we find the influence of a reading which is also attested in Acts 3.22 f. But the parallel passage in *Rec*. 1.36.2 differs. Thus it is not impossible that the (alleged) influence of Acts is to be attributed to a later stratum of tradition in the development of the ps.-Clementine romance. On the problem of anti-Paulinism, see below, 263 f.

259

49

it would appear that only the Old Testament and the four gospels are quoted as holy scripture. This is without precedent in Greek-speaking Syria around the year 200, but has a striking parallel in the canon of the Edessene Christians, who besides the Old Testament, used only the four gospels, and these in the harmonized form found in Tatian's *Diatessaron* (see above, 30 ff.). Of course the *Kerygmata* are not to be assigned to Edessene Christianity; they were not originally written in Syriac and betray no acquaintance with the *Diatessaron*. But this parallel probably can enable us to fix more precisely their geographical position and their place in the spectrum of the history of theology—it makes it clear that the Jewish Christianity of the KP was located on the dividing line between Greek and Edessene Syria. This type of Jewish Christianity is a witness for the history of the development of the New Testament canon in this region. It is [263] subject to the fluctuation which is characteristic of the formation of the New Testament canon in the developing mainstream church.

This fundamental openness toward a line of development taken by the "great church" is especially significant since the milieu in which the Jewish Christianity of the *Kerygmata* emerged also presupposes influences that are non-ecclesiastical—namely, Jewish and pagan. That Judaism is an important factor in the environment of the author can already be learned from the prefixed "Epistle of Peter to James" (= EP) which serves as an introduction to KP [57] and explicitly presents the followers of Moses (EP 1.2) as an example to the disciples of Jesus (EP 2.1). It becomes obvious that behind EP there is not only an appeal to history (Moses handing over his teaching office to the seventy, Num. 11.25), and not only a literary fiction (the reference to a Jewish Christian body of seventy brethren should probably be considered such, based on Luke 10.1!), but there are actual references to contemporary Judaism. Thus it is expressly stated that Judaism could serve as an example "to this very day" (EP 1.3), and the document goes beyond biblical allusions in mentioning particular details of a Jewish mode of instruction such as the Jewish confessional formula (EP 1.3 and 5) and especially the idea of the

57. [This *Epistula Petri* (= EP) and another short document called the *Contestatio* or "Testimony Regarding the Recipients of the Epistle" were prefixed to KP already in the "basic writing" behind the ps.-Clementines, according to Strecker. See his treatment in Hennecke-Schneemelcher, 2: 102-115, which includes an ET (by G. Ogg) of these two introductory writings; see also above, 184 n. 78.]

260

50

"contradictions of the scriptures," which are brought into harmony by means of a Jewish "guiding principle" or rule (EP 1.4 f.). This derives from a Judaism which is not really "official" but rather "heretical," from which other statements of the KP documents also come, such as the explanation of the theory of false pericopes in particular.[58] It is also characteristic of KP that its Jewish Christian self-understanding affirms the continuity between ancient Israel and Judaism— not only because the followers of Moses serve as an example in EP, but also because the figure of the true prophet Jesus is important in this connection. He is to guarantee the continuity between the old and the new Israel (*Hom.* 8.5-7), and thus on the basis of this coordination of contents which finds no essential conflict between the law of Moses and the proclamation of the "true prophet," the teaching of Moses and the message of Jesus are identified.[59] It is only logical that [264] with such a common foundation, contact with Judaism would also be maintained. The absence of an anti-Jewish polemic, which was so freely practiced in the "great church" of the same period,[60] also suggests that the Jewish Christianity of the *Kerygmata* existed in close relationship to Judaism. This corresponds to the situation regularly encountered with Jewish Christianity, which normally grew from the soil of Palestinian or hellenistic Judaism.

The Jewish Christianity of the *Kerygmata* was also in close contact with paganism. Even though the fictitious nature of the introductory

---

58. Cf. Strecker, *Judenchristentum*, pp. 166 ff.
59. Cf. EP 2.5, *Hom.* 9.19.3, etc.; Strecker, *Judenchristentum*, pp. 151 f., 163 ff. The nature of the Judaism confronted by the *Kerygmata* cannot be dealt with in detail here. That it does not refer to the Essenic Judaism of the Qumran sect has been shown elsewhere: see Strecker, *Judenchristentum*, pp. 215 ff. [cf. J. A. Fitzmyer, "The Qumran Scrolls, the Ebionites, and their Literature," *Theological Studies*, 16 (1955): 335-372 (reprinted in K. Standahl, *The Scrolls and the New Testament* [New York: Harper, 1957], pp. 208-231)]; contrary to Schoeps, *Theologie*, pp. 252 ff., 316, and also *Urgemeinde-Judenchristentum-Gnosis* (1956), pp. 68 ff.; K. Schubert, "Die [264] jüdischen und jüdenchristlichen Sekten im Lichte des Handschriftenfundes von 'En Fešcha," *Zeitschrift für katholische Theologie,* 74 (1952): 1 ff.; O. Cullmann, "Die neuentdeckten Qumrantexte und das Judenchristentum der Pseudoklementinen," *Neutestamentliche Studien für R. Bultmann,* ZNW Beiheft 21 (1954): 35 ff.; K. Rudolph, *Die Mandäer* 1, *Prolegomena: Das Mandäerproblem,* FRLANT 74 (1960): 226 f. and *passim.* The Qumran texts are, however, an important witness for the diversity of Judaism in the period of the New Testament and earlier.
60. Cf. e.g. Justin, *Dialogue;* Tertullian *Adversus Judaeos.* In contrast to Matt. 23.25 f., the critique of Pharisaic attitudes is not applied to the totality of the Pharisees in the *Kerygmata* (*Hom.* 11.29.1).

epistle should not be underestimated, on the basis of Peter's plea "not to pass on to any one of the gentiles the books of the *Kerygmata*, not even to a member of our own tribe before he has passed probation" (EP 1.2, 3.1), we may conjecture that the author's situation brought him into confrontation with gentiles. Perhaps this is true also of the statement that "some of the gentiles" have rejected Peter's "lawful" proclamation (EP 2.3). It becomes especially clear from the baptismal instruction of the *Kerygmata* (*Hom.* 11.21-33 and parallel material) included in the discourses of Peter at Tripolis (*Hom.* 8-11 = *Rec.* 4-6). Just as the external framework, which was part of the "basic document," presupposes a gentile audience (*Hom.* 11.1.1 f.), the content of the baptismal instruction does likewise. It alludes to the polytheistic cult of idols (*Hom.* 11.21.4, 11.31.1, etc.), which is also characterized by "lust" (*epithymia*—*Hom.* 11.26.1; cf. 11.11.5, 11.15.1 and 4 ff., etc.). It contains the demand for the adoption of ritual cleansings, which it presupposes are not being observed by the hearers.[61] Accordingly, it is the gentile populace (not the Jewish) that is the main objective of the Jewish Christian missionary activity. [265]

The fact that the Jewish Christianity of the *Kerygmata* carried on its discussion with both Jewish and gentile parties, coupled with the realization that the KP document reflects tendencies at work in the development of the canon of the ecclesiastical mainstream, should not encourage us to draw far-reaching inferences concerning an actual or even simply a geographical classification of KP within the sphere of the ecclesiastical mainstream. And even though a basic openness toward the tendencies at work in the development of the New Testament canon of the ecclesiastical mainstream is evident, the form and the content of the Jewish Christian theology of the *Kerygmata* are not determined by a confrontation with the "great church." Although the teaching on baptism in the KP document provides an insight into the practices of the Jewish Christian mission to gentiles, it is characteristic that this missionary activity does not reveal opposition on the part of a mainstream mission. The Jewish Christian theological tenets of the *Kerygmata* do not imply a polemical atti-

---

61. *Hom.* 11.28. But *Hom.* 11.30.2 states, on the contrary, that the hearers observed "things that pertain to purity" (*ta tēs hagneias merē*) during the time of idolatry. *Hagneia* apparently must be understood in a wider sense. It does not designate ritual practices but signifies an ethical attitude (cf. *Hom.* 11.31 ff.).

262

tude toward the "great church." Apparently a serious controversy with the representatives of the "great church" has not (yet) taken place. It was not necessary because the real partner in the discussion was not the "great church" and because, as has been said, the formation of this type of Jewish Christianity took place primarily in a Jewish and pagan setting.

It should, of course, be asked whether the anti-Paulinism of the KP document contains a polemic against the "great church." [62] One could get that impression from the *Epistula Petri*. Here Peter says that already in his lifetime some of the gentiles have rejected his "lawful preaching" since they "have preferred the lawless and senseless teaching of the hostile man" (EP 2.3 f.). This material seems to reflect a later development, subsequent to Peter's death. This becomes even clearer in Peter's prediction: "But if they falsely assert such a thing while I am still alive, how much more will those who come later venture to do so after my death" (EP 2.7). One must conclude that the author is aware of Pauline teachings in his immediate environment or its wider setting. But this conclusion is as far as one can go in this respect, for the anti-Paulinism of the *Kerygmata* does not reveal an actual controversy taking place between the ecclesiastical mainstream and Jewish Christianity. The author remains [266] bound to his sources, the Pauline letters and the picture of Paul in Acts. His knowledge derives essentially from literary sources. This is also indicated by particular references that have the appearance of citations.[63] The anti-Pauline statements of the *Kerygmata* thus can confirm that the Jewish Christianity of KP did have access to the writings of the mainstream church, but they do not lead us back to an actual controversy. From a formal point of view, their purpose is to give

---

62. In my opinion it is an assured result of scholarship that the *Kerygmata* originally polemicized against Paul alone, and not in some sort of combined fashion against Simon-Paul or Marcion-Paul (cf. Strecker, *Judenchristentum*, pp. 187 ff., 154 n. 1). The suggestion has recently been made by W. Schmithals [266] that from the very beginning the polemic was directed against Simon-Paul (*Das kirchliche Apostelamt*, FRLANT 79 [1961], p. 153 n. 305; p. 198 n. 481). But this does not take into consideration the problems involved in reconstructing the Jewish Christian element in the ps.-Clementines. One must begin with an analysis of the introductory writings, the *Epistula Petri* and the *Contestatio* (see above, 260 n. 57). They show no demonstrable confusion of the "hostile man" (*ekthros anthrōpos*, EP 2.3) with Simon Magus, but the identification with Paul is evident in the allusions to Gal. 2.11 ff. (EP 2.4).

63. Cf. the examples listed in Strecker, *Judenchristentum*, p. 218.

263

color to the apostolic fiction of Peter's doctrinal discourses as expressed especially in the reference to the controversy between Peter and Paul in Antioch.[64] With reference to content, their purpose is the explication of the Jewish Christian self-understanding. The pseudo-Petrine doctrinal discourses as a whole are not directed primarily against Pauline thought, but their anti-Paulinism should be interpreted as a specific expression of the Jewish Christian legalistic system.[65]

From this perspective the picture of the Jewish Christianity of the *Kerygmata* comes into focus. If the references to the Pauline letters and to Acts are set aside as a literary matter, then the relationship to the "great church" can be defined with more precision. There appears to exist no direct interconnection nor any genetic dependence, but the structural elements of the theology of the *Kerygmata* must be attributed to an earlier independent Jewish Christian tradition. This follows from the fact that the citation of gospel texts is made in a rather unpretentious manner with such introductory formulas as: "For thus the prophet has sworn to us saying" (*Hom.* 11.26.2), "for he said thus" (EP 2.5), "and when he said" (*Hom.* 3.50.2), etc. Apparently the readers made regular use of the gospel writings being cited. [267] Insofar as the author is explaining the theology of the *Kerygmata* by means of the citations,[66] he is not resorting directly to the tradition of the "great church"; rather, the Jewish Christianity of the *Kerygmata* presupposes a tradition which may have developed in the region bordering Osröenian Syria, and which paralleled in part that stream of tradition represented on the other side by the "great church."

How much the theology of this Jewish Christianity must be considered to be fundamentally autonomous is further indicated by its

---

64. EP 2.4; *Hom.* 17.19; Gal. 2.11 ff.

65. The warning against false "prophets, apostles, and teachers" as well as the admonition to accept only messengers who have been approved by the "bishop" James (*Hom.* 11.35.3-6 and par.) could be construed as indicating the presence of a current polemic. But this warning also is related to the basically literary anti-Paulinism (the sequence of offices is paralleled in 1 Cor. 12.28). Furthermore, the motif of James is related to the apostolic fiction and cannot be transferred to the period [267] of the author. Even here, the contemporization indicates nothing more than the presence of a legalistic self-understanding.

66. The quotations from the gospels underline the validity of the law (EP 2.5), the doctrine of the falsified pericopes in the scriptures (*Hom.* 3.50.1), the anti-Paulinism (*Hom.* 11.18.1), and the teaching on baptism with its related injunctions to purity (*Hom.* 11.26.2, 11.29.2).

teaching on baptism. On the one hand this appears against the background of gnostic dualism. The original materialism of this dualism is taken over by the *Kerygmata*, with some modifications, but it is still assumed that the "first birth" (*prōtē genēsis*), the natural origin of man, is identical with enslavement to lust (*epithymia*, Hom. 11.26 and par.). This recalls the deprecation of the cosmos in gnostic systems.[67] But at the same time a judaistic interpretation is also apparent—the task of the Spirit at baptism is not related to a sacramental event but rather to the evaluation of the good deeds of the baptized. The Spirit "offers the good works of the baptized as gifts to God" (*Hom.* 11.26.3 and par.). Not the act of baptism but man's ethically related "fear" (*phobos*) brings about the rebirth—i.e. the exchange of man's natural destiny for "being born to God" (*Hom.* 11.26.1, 11.27.2 and par.). Therefore in the last analysis the rationale for the act of baptism consists solely in the divine command (*Hom.* 11.26.1 and par.). This peculiar doctrine of baptism also leads to the baptismal exhortation (*Hom.* 11.27.3 ff. and par.), which is clearly distinguished from the unique baptismal instruction that precedes by its directions concerning ritual baths of purification (*Hom.* 11.28.2, 11.30.1). This distinction is also indicated by the specific terminology used: while the *baptisma* or the passive voice *baptisthēnai* are regularly used for the act of baptism, the lustrations are designated by *kathareuein* or *loutrō plunein;*[68] [268] and while baptism as an act of initiation is connected with "rebirth" (*Hom.* 11.24.2, 11.26.1 ff; *Contestatio* 1.2) with the phrase "living water" appearing in this context (*hydōr zōn; Hom.* 11.26.2 and 4; *Contestatio* 1.2), this designation is not applied to the lustrations which can be repeated. It is apparent that directions of this sort have no parallels in mainstream gentile Christian practices, but express the genuine

67. Cf. Strecker, *Judenchristentum*, pp. 158, 199 f.
68. *Hom.* 11.28.1 ff.; also *Hom.* 11.30.1 f., 11.33.4 (*baptizesthai* or *baptistheisē*). K. Rudolph also called attention to this terminological distinction, but at the same time he emphasized the unity of baptism and lustrations because the significance [268] of the water as "a vehicle of divine power" is present in both (*Die Mandäer* 1, 241; cf. 235). Since KP does not really seem to attest a magical-sacramental character for the baptismal act, it would be more accurate to speak of a moralistic understanding as the common basis for baptism and lustrations. This also distinguishes the Jewish Christianity of the *Kerygmata* from the views of baptism and lustrations held by the Elchasaites and Mandaeans. Moreover, the *Book of Elchasai* also distinguishes between baptism and lustrations (cf. Strecker, "Elkesai," RAC 4 [1959]: 1181), and thus reveals its originally Christian nature; cf. also below, 269. [For ET of the fragments of the "Book of Elchasai," see Hennecke-Schneemelcher, 2: 745-750, by J. Irmscher and R. McL. Wilson.]

265

Jewish Christian character of the material.[69] The KP source also bases its injunctions for the ritual baths on the Old Testament Jewish law (cf. Lev. 15.24, 18.19) or on the instructions of the "true prophet" who summons men to surpass the pharisaic way of life (*Hom.* 11.28.1, 11.29.1 ff.; cf. Matt. 23.25 f.).

The consequences of the peculiar Jewish Christian legalistic outlook are not fully developed in the *Kerygmata*. Baptism serves as the sole rite of initiation, not circumcision.[70] But *Contestatio* 1.1 advises that the books of Peter's proclamations be transmitted only to a "circumcised and believing" candidate for the teaching office. This, however, does not imply that circumcision had the function of a rite of initiation, since the immediate context does not deal with the introduction into the community, nor with baptism, but only with the transmission of the books. Furthermore, the earlier statement in EP 3.1, which has the same purpose, [269] does not mention any requirement of circumcision. Although the supposed evidence in *Contestatio* 1.1 also may permit the conclusion that the author knew of circumcised persons who were members of the Christian community, it seems that this passage should be understood primarily as a literary intensification of the rule found in EP 3.1, and that inferences of a more far-reaching sort cannot be drawn. Since statements corresponding to this cannot be demonstrated elsewhere in KP, it is probably correct to suppose that in the Jewish Christianity represented by the *Kerygmata* baptism has taken the place of circumcision. However, this does not imply that the Jewish Christian practice of baptism has been borrowed from the ecclesiastical mainstream, although the parallelism with ecclesiastical baptism extends beyond the mere act—if baptism

---

69. For Jewish ritual baths, cf. Babylonian Talmud *Berakot* 21b (3.4); Josephus *Against Apion* 2. 203; W. Brandt, *Die jüdischen Baptismen*, ZAW Beiheft 18 (1910): 44 f., 52, 55; A. Oepke, "louō," TDNT 4: 300 f. = TWbNT 4: 303 f.
70. This was correctly emphasized by E. Molland, "La circoncision, le baptême et l'autorité du décret apostolique (Actes XV 28 sq.) dan les milieux judéochrétiens des pseudo-Clémentines," *Studia Theologica*, 9 (1955): 1-39 [repr. in Molland, *Opuscala Patristica* (Oslo, 1970)], against Schoeps (*Theologie*, pp. 115, 138). Molland's position with respect to source analysis, however, is untenable; it follows O. Cullman (*Le problème littéraire et historique du roman pseudoclémentin* [Paris, 1930]) in positing a "Journeys of Peter" source (*Periodoi Petrou*) between the "basic writing" and KP, but fails to recognize that the demonstrable multiplicity of special sources behind the "basic writing" makes it necessary to stratify the tradition further at this point.

266

is performed, according to the mysterious circumlocution, "in the thrice-blessed name," it is hardly possible that any formula other than the ecclesiastical triadic formula is meant.[71] But according to what has been said it is evident that the witnesses for the baptismal practice do not stand in contradiction to the independent character of the *Kerygmata*, but they enable us to recognize the stream of tradition that is common to the *Kerygmata* and to the "great church," just as was true of the use of the "canonical" gospel writings (above, 258-260).

Can we conclude from all this that the Jewish Christianity of the KP document was not a sectarian conventicle—that it cannot be considered as a sectarian minority that stood over against an orthodox majority? [72] K. Rudolph has disputed these results and affirmed a close relationship to the so-called baptizing sects on the grounds that in his view the "living water" in the *Kerygmata* stands in opposition to the fire, baptism by water is in contrast to sacrifices, and ritual baths play an important role.[73] However, his argumentation does not really take into account the problem of the literary criticism of the ps.-Clementines, but he endeavors to take his point of departure from the "contents of the entire complex insofar as they are instructive for our purposes." [74] On the contrary, it is necessary to stress that this

71. *Epi tē trismakaria eponomasia, Hom.* 11.26.3. In *Hom.* 11.26.2, according to the extant text, Matt. 28.19 is expressly quoted along with John 3.5. This citation of Matthew belongs to a later stage of the tradition. The parallel passage in *Rec.* 6.9 shows that the triadic formula of Matt. 28.19 is not yet found in the "basic writing." But even in the earlier form of the quotation (in *Hom.* 11.26.2) the influence of Matthew's gospel seems to be present in the phrase "you will never enter the kingdom of the heavens" (*ou mē eiselthēte . . . tōn ouranōn*), which reflects Matt. 5.20 [cf. John 3.3 and 5, and the variants].
72. Cf. Strecker, *Judenchristentum*, p. 215.
73. Rudolph, *Die Mandäer*, 1: 240.
74. Rudolph, *Die Mandäer*, 1: 240 n. 1. E. S. Drower also is content to state: "My own interest in the *Homilies* is, of course, confined to similarities found in them [270] to the secret teaching of the Nazoraeans" (*The Secret Adam: A Study of Nasorean Gnosis* [Oxford: Clarendon, 1960], pp. 45 n. 1, 88 ff.). Similarly P. Beskow (*Rex Gloriae: The Kingship of Christ in the Early Church* [Stockholm: Almqvist and Wiksell, 1962]) does not wish to contribute to the "confusion" concerning the question of the sources of the ps.-Clementines by introducing a "new basis for source division" (256). One would hardly have expected such a major undertaking in an investigation dealing with the kingship of Christ. But it is not unreasonable to require that even this type of investigation should at least take a position worthy of the name on the problem of the ps.-Clementine sources. In its present form Breskow's work itself contributes to the "goodly measure of confusion" on this subject insofar as this author, in spite of his failure to take

[270] sort of approach does not do justice to the complicated stratification of traditions reflected in the ps.-Clementines, and overlooks the fact that the specific meaning of the supposed Jewish Christian "contents" varies with each changing situation in the history of tradition—thus the "contents" can be identified only by means of literary-critical classification. But even apart from the methodological problem, Rudolph's thesis is open to serious objections. Although the antithesis between baptism and sacrifice appears not only in the "AJ II" source of the ps.-Clementines (in Rec. 1.39 and 55; see above, 256 n. 44), but is also found in Rec. 1.48.5, the latter is part of a context (Rec. 1.44.3-53.4a) in which the author of the "basic writing" gathered together heterogeneous materials. Thus one would obviously suppose that the passage in Recognitions 1.48.5 had been influenced not by the KP source but by the context (Rec. 1.39 belongs to "AJ II"). This assumption is confirmed by the fact that the KP document does not contain such an antithesis between baptism and sacrifice elsewhere. The rejection of temple sacrifices found in the Kerygmata is not relevant to the present problem.[75] And finally it is doubtful on principle that the antithesis between sacrifice and baptism constitutes a sufficient criterion for connecting the KP document with the "baptizing sects," since this sort of direct relationship cannot be affirmed for the "AJ II" source, in spite of the admitted antithesis, and since the antithesis between baptism and sacrifice is not clearly evidenced in the literature of the actual baptizing sects.[76] [271]

---

a position on the source critical problem, thinks he is in a position to make the straightforward claim, as startling as it is unfounded, that "It is sufficient for our purposes to point out that in one section of PsC there is a deposit of Greek speculation, which has nothing whatever to do with more or less hypothetical 'Ebionite' concepts" (256).

75. In reply to Rudolph, Die Mandäer, 1: 240 n. 4.

76. It should be noted that the "AJ II" source speaks of a contrast between a single act of baptism over against sacrifice and not of an antithesis between various ritual baths and the sacrificial cult (cf. also Rec. 1.55 and 69 f.). This indicates a Christian [271] background. Wherever ritual baths were practiced alongside baptism within the Christian sphere, a careful distinction is made (cf. above, 265 f.). The antithesis of ritual baths and sacrificial cult presupposes another environment, namely, a Jewish world of ideas; it is not even generally found among the baptizing sects, and what evidence exists is ambiguous (for the Essenes cf. Josephus Antiq. 18.[1.5.]19; for the Book of Elchasai [above, 265 n. 68], Epiphanius Her. 19.3.6 f.—but is this from the Elchasaites?). This sort of contrast is not present in the Jewish Christian literature of the ps.-Clementines.

268

58

An allusion to the practice of the baptizing sects could perhaps be seen in the notion of the "daily baths of Peter," if it were possible to trace this idea back to the KP document.[77] But this cannot be demonstrated. First of all, the pseudo-Clementines do not speak of "daily" baths of Peter. The "basic writing" only mentions occasional baths (Hom. 8.2.5, 10.26.2 and par.). The editor of the Homilies-recension has elaborated on this motif in secondary fashion, but still has not understood it in the sense of "daily" baths (cf. Hom. 10.1.2, 11.1.1, 14.3.1; etc.). It is only in Epiphanius that such a reference occurs (Her. 30.2.4, 30.15.3, 30.16.1, 30.21.1), which is a typical example of the liberties he takes with his sources. Secondly, it is clear that the notion of "Peter's baths" cannot be traced back to the KP source, but is a legitimate part of the narrative framework of the Clement romance. Thus it would seem plausible that the idea was inserted by the author of the "basic writing" since he is responsible for the narrative of the romance. This is consistent with the archaizing manner of presentation used by the author of the "basic writing," who also employs Judaizing features elsewhere.[78]

Of course, it cannot be denied that the KP document refers to injunctions for ritual baths. But it has already been shown that in the Kerygmata the ritual baths are distinguished from baptism proper and that they reflect not a gnostic but a genuinely Jewish background.[79] These baths [272] do not go beyond the Jewish sphere of thought and therefore cannot be used as an argument to show that the Kerygmata belongs in the same category as the so-called baptizing sects. The Book of Elchasai (above, 265 n. 68) serves as a counter-example. Its injunctions for ritual baths depend not so much on Jewish as on Christian presuppositions, and its demand for a

77. So. K. Rudolph, Die Mandäer, 1: 240, n. 5.
78. Strecker, Judenchristentum, pp. 213, 257 f.
79. Above, 267 f. Rudolph has demonstrated that Jewish commandments for ritual baths are also known in Mandaeanism (Die Mandäer, 2, Der Kult [1961]: 109 ff.). Beyond that, he sought to establish that the Mandaean baptism could, in the final analysis, be traced back to Jewish ritual baths (402). This hypothesis is rather daring, since unambiguous examples of the repetition of the Mandaean baptismal bath are not given (if we ignore the modern reports, which can hardly be utilized as evidence for the more ancient period). This criticism should not detract from the significance of Rudolph's work. Without doubt, his detailed presentation of recent literature and the results of his discussions on particular problems of basic importance make this investigation one of the most valuable contributions to the present state of Mandaean studies.

269

baptismal bath for "grievous sinners" (Hippolytus *Ref.* 9.15.1 f.) and for baths at time of sickness (*Ref.* 9.15.4 ff. and par.) can with more justification be considered elements of a baptizing sect.[80]

Finally, the notion of "living water" does not provide grounds for a real argument. The expression does occur in gnostic literature,[81] but nothing can be made of this fact because one should in principle make a differentiation between baptizing the gnostic circles, and only in particular instances can an identity be established.[82] Moreover, the notion is not limited to gnosticism, but is met also in the ecclesiastical milieu,[83] quite apart from the fact that in the KP source this expression appears exclusively [273] in connection with the water of baptism and is not used in relation to ritual baths (see above, 265 f.).

In conclusion it can be said that Rudolph's attempt to postulate a sectarian situation for the Jewish Christianity of the KP by connecting it with the so-called baptizing sects is not convincing. We can now affirm with greater assurance that the Jewish Christianity of the *Kerygmata* should be understood in the context of Bauer's hypothesis.[84] The relations to the "great church" are primarily on a liter-

80. Strecker, "Elchesai," cols. 1171 ff. E. Peterson ("Die Behandlung der Tollwut bei den Elchasaiten nach Hippolyt," *Frühkirche, Judentum und Gnosis* [New York: Herder, 1959], pp. 221-235; a revised form of "Le traitement de la rage par les Elkésaïtes d'après Hippolyte," *Recherche de science religieuse*, 34 [1947]: 232-238) has attempted to prove that the lustrations of the Elchasaites were not intended to avert sicknesses, but that sicknesses named in the *Book of Elchasai* symbolize sin. "Madness" (*Ref.* 9.15.4) is to be understood as "concupiscence" (227 ff.). But Peterson's proposal leaves unanswered the question of why the *Book of Elchasai* can in other places refer to sexual sins without circumlocution (Hippolytus *Ref.* 9.15.1 and 3) if in fact it spoke symbolically in this passage. Furthermore, Peterson did not take into consideration the fact that in the Elchasaite traditions cited by Epiphanius, lustrations against sicknesses also are mentioned (Epiphanius *Her.* 30.17.4). Finally, Hippolytus quotes another fragment in which Elchasai's injunctions to ritual baths are explicitly directed to sick people (*Ref.* 9.16.1). In the original form of his essay, Peterson attributed this last passage to an interpolator (237), which must be taken as an admission of the weakness of his approach. The fact that this interpretation is not repeated in his revised version is no improvement, since he does not provide an alternative solution.
81. Strecker, *Judenchristentum,* p. 202.
82. Contrary to Rudolph, *Die Mandäer,* 1: 245; 2: 379.
83. *Didache* 7; perhaps also *Barnabas* 11.11, etc.; T. Klauser, "Taufet in lebendigem Wasser! Zum religions-und kulturgeschichtlichen Verständnis von Didache 7, 1-3." *Pisciculi* (Festschrift for F. J. Dölger, Münster, 1939), pp. 157-164.
84. Only the historical problem is posed here. A dogmatically conditioned definition of the concept of "heresy" would not advance the historical analysis. This must also be said of H. Köster's article "Häretiker im Urchristentum" (RGG³, 3 [1959]: 17-21; see below, 307 n. 21), which takes its point of departure from the "faith of the community in the revelation of God that took place once and for

270

ary level and there is no indication of an active confrontation. Rather this Jewish Christianity has its own theology, independent of main-stream Christianity, which precludes the possibility that it is "sectarian" in nature. The widespread notion that Jewish Christianity separated itself from the "great church" and subsequently led a cloistered existence as a sect (cf. above, 242 n. 3) must be revised. It is much more probable that in the world from which the *Kerygmata* derives, Jewish Christianity was the sole representative of Christianity and the problem of its relationship to the "great church" had not yet arisen. This conclusion is indirectly supported by Bauer's recognition that other parts of Syria also served as the original homeland for non-ecclesiastical gnostic [274] groups, and the situation did not indicate the prior presence of ecclesiastical orthodoxy (above, pp. 1 ff.). It is also supported by the witness of the *Didascalia* which, as has been demonstrated above, reflects confrontations between a "catholic" community and a Jewish Christianity that apparently enjoyed unrestricted prominence in Syria up to that time. This verdict stands even if the Jewish Christians addressed in the *Didascalia* are not to be identified with the community of the author of KP. The evidence of the *Didascalia* confirms from the ecclesiastical viewpoint the situation of Syrian Jewish Christianity as it is presented in the *Kerygmata*. In this part of Syria around the end of the second and beginning of the third century Jewish Christianity is independent of the "great church," and has an appearance that does not conform to the usual heresiological characterization.

---

all," and considers as "heretical" (1) an overemphasis on the time-bound historical character of the revelation or, (2) the absolutizing of the transcendent content of the revelation (18). However, Köster's presentation of the "heretics" is not based on this theological point of departure but proceeds phenomenologically on the basis of statements by New Testament writers concerning the Christian groups which are opposed to them (18 ff.). This discrepancy can be interpreted as constituting an indirect admission that sufficient criteria for the historical application of the theological concept cannot be developed, but rather that the historical phenomenon of "heresy" resists theological classification. This also is evidence for the correctness of Bauer's thesis. If the theological definition of heresy were consistently applied to the whole New Testament and were not used simply to describe anti-ecclesiastical groups, this would not only lead to difficulties, but the problem would also be raised as to what extent the theology of the New Testament writers or of the traditions used by them should be exempt from the concept of "heresy" in that sense. Against such a schematic application of a theological understanding we could also point to the usage of *hairesis* in the New Testament, which does not yet suggest the later heresiological-dogmatical meaning.

271

3. *The Ecclesiastical Attitude and "Ebionism."* In the heresiological classifications Jewish Christianity has a well established position under the rubric "Ebionites." In the older secondary literature the Hebrew equivalent of this name [*'ebionim* = "poor"] was traced back to a messianic self-designation of the primitive community.[85] However, while this explanation seems quite plausible at first sight, it cannot be verified. In the Pauline letters those references to the "poor" (*ptōchoi*) which relate to the situation of the Jerusalem community and have been interpreted in the above sense do not demonstrably require anything but a literal interpretation. They are not messianological in nature.[86] Even if it is admitted that [275] at an early period a broad stream of piety based on a Jewish ideal of poverty found acceptance in Christianity,[87] there is no reason to assume that the earliest community as a whole followed that ideal. The reports in Acts about a general community of goods in the Jerusalem community are largely legendary or else Lukan generalizations of non-typical isolated epi-

---

85. E.g. Holl, *Gesammelte Aufsätze*, 2: 60; Lietzmann, *An die Römer*[4], 122 ff.
86. Rom. 15.26, Gal. 2.10. E. Bammel's attempt to the contrary is not convincing. His argument that the expression *ptōchoi* in Rom. 15.26 could not have the literal meaning "poor" because "then it is inconceivable that the collection would be continued after the need for it had disappeared" (TDNT 6, 909 = TWbNT 6, 909.5 f.) is not decisive because it has not been proven that the reason for the collection was a specific emergency in Jerusalem—Acts 11.27-30 cannot be used in support of this thesis (Strecker, "Die sogenannte Zweite Jerusalemreise des Paulus," ZNW 53 [1962]: 67-77). It is not impossible, on the contrary, that the collection resulted from a general concern for the socially deprived, and that the Jerusalem authorities would have added legal overtones to its accomplishment. When in Rom. 15.26 *tōn hagiōn* appears as partitive genitive describing *tous ptōchous* ("the poor from among the saints"), this certainly does not convey a "general meaning" which "would not definitely exclude non-Christian Jerusalem" (Bammel, TDNT 6, 909 = TWbNT 6, 908.33 f.; G. Klein also disagrees, "Die Verleugnung des Petrus," ZTK 58 [1961]: 320, n. 5; this essay has been reprinted in *Reconstruktion und Interpretation: Gesammelte Aufsätze zum Neuen Testament* [München: Kaiser, 1969]), but employs the eschatological designation of the community that is frequent in Paul ("saints"—Rom. 1.7, 1 Cor. 1.2, 2 Cor. 1.1, etc.). Thus *ptōchoi* refers to only one group within the community and a literal interpretation of "poor" is the most logical. This can also be demonstrated for Gal. 2.10 (A. Oepke, *Der Brief des Paulus an die Galater*[2], Theologische Handkommentar zum Neuen Testament 9 [Berlin: Evangelische Verlagsanstalt, 1960], p. 54), and is confirmed by 2 Cor. 9.12 (*ta hysterēmata* [!] *tōn hagiōn*).
87. Cf. e.g. Luke 6.20 f., 12.13 ff., 16.19 ff.; James 1.9 ff., 2.5 ff., 5.1 ff., etc.; M. Dibelius, *Der Brief des Jakobus*, Meyer Kommentar 15 (Göttingen: Vandenhoeck, 1956; expanded by H. Greeven, 1957[9], 1964[11], etc.), p. 37 ff.

sodes.[88] The title *Ebiōnaioi* appears first in Irenaeus (AH 1.26.2 [= 1.22]), and even if it was already used as a fixed designation for the sect prior to Irenaeus, as is probable (see below, 278), it does not date back to earliest Christian times with that meaning since it does not occur at all in Justin's statements about Jewish Christianity (*Dial.* 47). Therefore it is not probable that it was originally used as a general Jewish Christian self-designation; instead, we assume that the name was originally applied to a specific Jewish Christian group which felt especially obligated to uphold the Jewish ideal of poverty. Later the title was transformed by the heresiologists into a general designation for "sectarian" Jewish Christianity. Such a schematic procedure corresponds to the usual heresiological pattern, as will become clear. Thus critical discretion with regard to the data of the church fathers is mandatory as we proceed to investigate their accounts in detail.

After the first part of his *Dialogue with Trypho the Jew,* which deals with the transitory value of Jewish ceremonial law (9-42), Justin speaks of the divine majesty of Jesus in a second section (43-118). At the intersection of these two major sections there is an excursus criticizing those Christians who combine the observance of the Jewish law with faith in Christ (47). Trypho's question, whether a member of the Jewish people can be saved if he believes in Jesus as the Christ but also observes the Mosaic commandments [276] is answered as follows: (1) Jewish Christians can be saved if they hold fast to the Jewish law without demanding such observance from others nor regarding it to be necessary for salvation (47.1)—this is Justin's view, even though there are gentile Christians who reject any social contact with Jewish Christians (47.2). (2) Jewish Christians who force their gentile brothers to keep Jewish observances or who withhold fellowship from them are not acknowledged as true Christians by Justin (47.3). (3) For those who have been misled by Jewish Christians to accept Jewish observances, salvation is possible if they hold fast to the confession of Christ (47:4a). (4) Christians who have turned

88. Acts 2.44 f., 4.36 f., 5.1 ff.; E. Haenchen, *Die Apostelgeschichte*[4], Meyer Kommentar 3 (1961), *ad loc.* Epiphanius later traced the name of the Ebionites back to the community of goods in the earliest community of Acts 4-5 (*Her.* 30.17.2) [See also J. A. Fitzmyer, "Jewish Christianity in Acts in the Light of the Qumran Scrolls," in *Studies in Luke-Acts,* ed. L. E. Keck and J. L. Martyn (1961) p. 244.]

273

to Judaism and forsaken faith in Christ and who are not converted prior to their death will not be saved (47.4b). (5) The descendants of Abraham who live in accordance with the Jewish law and who are not converted to Christ, but in their synagogues curse the be-, lievers in Christ will not be saved (47.5). In spite of its logical arrangement this list cannot be attributed to mere abstraction. It presupposes actual knowledge about the "Jewish" attitude. This is demonstrated not only by the concluding reference to the Jewish "eighteen benedictions" (*Shemoneh Esreh*) [89] but also by the fact that in other passages, Justin also is well-informed about Judaism,[90] not the least of which are the statements that according to Jewish Christian theology Christ had been a "man from among men" (48.4) and "had been elected" to be Messiah-Christ (48.3, 49.1).

From Justin's data the following can be discovered about the form and the self-understanding of the Jewish Christianity known to him. The general mark of identification relates to Jewish observances, namely the observance of circumcision and sabbath (47.2), of months and purification (cf. 46.2). Of course, sacrifice is no longer part of Jewish cultic practice, as is stated elsewhere (46.2). Justin's witness about the large variety of beliefs and practices within Jewish Christian theology is significant. The indefinite formulation "for there are also some" (*kai gar eisi tines*, 48.4) already indicates that an adoptionistic christology was not a general feature of all Jewish Christian circles. In fact, the presence of a preexistence [277] Christology in Jewish Christian literature can be demonstrated.[91] On the other hand, an adoptionistic christological confession is considered possible also among gentile Christians (48.4). Above, all there were different approaches to the gentile mission—legalistic Jewish Christianity wavers between a basically tolerant attitude that grants gentile Christians freedom from the law (47.1 f.), and another attitude that expects gentile Christians to maintain Jewish observances also (47.3).

---

89. On this subject, see H. Strack-P. Billerbeck, *Kommentar zum Neuen Testament aus Talmud und Midrasch,* 1 (München: Beck, 1926): 406 ff.; 4 (1928): 208 f.; K. G. Kuhn, *Achtzehngebet und Vaterunser und der Reim* (1950).
90. E.g. on Jewish teachings concerning the Messiah in *Dial.* 8; A. von Harnack, *Judentum und Judenchristentum in Justins Dialog mit Trypho. . . ,* TU 39.1 (1913), *passim.*
91. Jerome *Commentary on Genesis* 1.1; ps.-Clementine *Rec.* 1.43 f.; Strecker, "Ebioniten," col. 497.

274

The heresiological situation reflected in this account is somewhat clearer. In the gentile Christian church the appraisal of legalistic Jewish Christianity apparently has not yet advanced beyond the stage of expressing a personal point of view. This is indicated by the introductory words "as it seems to me" (*hōs men emoi dokei*, 47.1-2) and also by the extremely personal tone of Justin's statements in general,[92] and his references to other possible points of view (47.2, 48.4). There is nothing to indicate the existence of a developed heresiological stance, or even an official ecclesiastical differentiation. Nor is there evidence that Jewish Christians were classified with other "heretical" groups. A basic tolerance is possible in which the norm of behavior can depend on the attitude of the Jewish Christians, with the principle that the person excluded from the church's fellowship is the one who excludes himself (47.2 f.). It is therefore quite consistent that the concept *hairesis* is not applied to Jewish Christians. Here Justin's assessment of Jewish Christianity differs greatly from his presentation of other religious groups. The parties of Judaism are designated "heresies" (62.3, 80.4). Above all, gnostics and Marcionites are numbered among the *haireseis* (*Dial.* 35.3, 51.2, 80.3 f.; *Apol.* 26.8). If Justin's *Syntagma* described "all heresies"[93] it would not have included heretics of Jewish Christian provenance, but probably dealt primarily with gnostic-Marcionite teachings.[94]

The author Hegesippus is quoted by Eusebius as an outstanding representative of the correct doctrine (EH 4.21 f.) whose travels, by his own admission, were aimed at confirming that "the law, [278] the prophets, and the Lord" possess authority "in every transmission of doctrine[95] and in every city" (EH 4.22.3). To the extent that the preserved fragments permit us to recognize the outline of his own conception, Hegesippus shows parallels to Justin's heresiological thought in a surprising way. The danger that threatens the church originates primarily from gnostics (EH 4.22.5; see above, 189). The

---

92. "I am of the opinion" (*apophainomai*, 47.2,4,5), "I am not in agreement" (*egō ou sunainos eimi*, 47.2), "I do not accept" (*ouk apodechomai*, 47.3), "I suspect" (*hypolambanō*, 47.4).
93. Apology 26.8, *syntagma kata pasōn tōn gegenēmenōn haireseōn syntetagmenon.*
94. *Apol.* 26 names the heretics Simon (Magus), Menander, and Marcion.
95. This is the meaning of *diadochē;* for a discussion and bibliography cf. Altaner, *Patrology*, 149 f. (see the German 6th ed. with A. Stuiber, p. 118), and above 196 n. 2.

275

concept *hairesis* is applied to Jewish groups,[96] but a corresponding characterization of Jewish Christianity is lacking. The name "Ebionite" apparently is unknown to him, and the problem of the relationship between Jewish Christianity and orthodoxy is never raised. The absence of that sort of question is not necessarily due to the Jewish Christian tradition in which Hegesippus undoubtedly stands, which even permits him to view the Jerusalem community as the authentic prototype of orthodoxy (EH 3.32, 4.22.4). For our purposes, his witness is all the more valuable since it cannot be demonstrated that he was dependent on Justin.[97] Thus, with Justin, Hegesippus is an important informant concerning the openness of the heresiological situation in the second half of the second century.

Justin's literary influence is noticeable in the writings of Ireneaeus, in which Justin's work against Marcion is cited (AH 4.6.2 [= 4.11.2]) and Justin's literary heritage has also been utilized in general.[98] It is therefore all the more surprising that Irenaeus' reports concerning the Ebionites do not refer back to the position taken by Justin to which we have already referred. Irenaeus describes the *"Ebionaei"* in AH 1.26.2 (= 1.22), subsequent to the heresiological characterization of Cerinthus (26.1 [= 21]) and prior to the treatment of the Nicolaitans (26.3 [= 23]), Cerdo (27.1 [= 24]), and Marcion (27.2 ff. [= 25.1-2]). They are said to acknowledge the creator God, possess a christology similar to Cerinthus and Carpocrates,[99] and [279] use only "the gospel according to Matthew." The apostle Paul is rejected

---

96. EH 2.23.8 f., *tines oun tōn hepta haireseōn tōn en tō laō. . . ;* cf. 4.22.5. The names of the seven Jewish heresies are found in EH 4.22.7; cf. also 3.23.3 and 6 (also 3.19 and 3.32.2).
97. Cf. Hilgenfeld, *Ketzergeschichte*, pp. 30 ff., contrary to A. von Harnack, *Zur Quellenkritik der Geschichte des Gnostizismus* (1873), pp. 36 ff.
98. Cf. AH 5.26.2 (= 5.26.3)—is this material taken from Justin's *Syntagma?* See Bardenhewer, *Geschichte²,* 1: 407. [On the general problem of Justin's lost *Syntagma,* see P. Prigent, *Justin et l'Ancien Testament* (Paris: Gabalda, 1964).]
99. The *"non"* must be deleted; it disturbs the meaning of the text which apparently intended first to emphasize the contrast between Ebionites and Cerinthus-Carpocrates, and then the agreement with them. The deletion is confirmed by Hippolytus *Ref.* 7.34 (*ta de peri ton christon homoios tō Kērinthō kai Karpokratei mytheuousin*) and also through Irenaeus' description of Ebionite christology in AH 3.21.1 (= 3.23) and 5.1.3. [279] The reading could have originated through assimilation to the preceding *"dominum"* (cf. Harvey's note, *ad loc.*).

276

by them as an apostate from the law. They have their own peculiar interpretation of the "prophecies" (*prophetica*), practice circumcision, and also observe the Jewish law in general.

No doubt, this description is influenced by the immediate context— e.g. in the emphasis on God's creatorhood. But it is also clear that the statements which in part are rather general in tone presuppose a concrete tradition not only in the reference to the similar christological ideas of Cerinthus and Carpocrates but also in the other reports, even though at first glance they may seem to be rather unintelligible. The statements receive partial explanation through the other passages: In AH 3.21.1 (= 3.23) Irenaeus mentions that the Jewish translators Theodotion and Aquila do not read *parthenos* ("virgin") [100] in Isa. 7.14 but *neanis* ("young woman") and that the "Ebionites," who regard Jesus as a natural son of Joseph, follow them (cf. also 3.21.9 [= 3.29]). Here a "natural christology" is clearly reported as the christological position of the Ebionites (cf. 5.1.3). This confirms the reference back to Cerinthus and Carpocrates (1.26.2 [= 1.22]) for whom the notion of a natural birth of Jesus is also asserted (1.25.1 [= 1.20] and 1.26.1 [= 1.21.1]). Perhaps this christology can shed new light upon the obscure remark about the "peculiar interpretation of the prophets" among the Ebionites (1.26.2 [=1.22]). Is Irenaeus thinking of the interpretation of Isaiah 7.14 along the lines of an Ebionite christology? For support one could refer to Symmachus' translation, which like that of Theodotion and Aquila reads *neanis*— if indeed Symmachus had been a Jewish Christian.[101]

AH 3.11.7 (= 3.11.10) contains a brief notice about the gospel of Matthew which was the sole gospel used by the Ebionites and, as

---

100. This is the reading of the "Septuagint"; cf. the detailed discussion of this passage in Justin *Dial.* 43 f., 66 ff. (esp. 84).

101. Cf. Origen's *Hexapla;* Hilgenfeld, *Ketzergeschichte,* p. 440. According to Eusebius EH 6.17, Symmachus was a Jewish Christian; this is supported by Harnack, *Geschichte,* 1.1: 209-212; 2.1: 165 f.; *History of Dogma,* 1: 305, n. 1 (= 5th German ed., 1: 327 n. 1); Schoeps, *Theologie, passim.* But according to Epiphanius, Symmachus had been a Samaritan who defected to Judaism (*On Weights and Measures* 16). [For a survey of the subject, see H. B. Swete, *An Introduction to the Old Testament in Greek* (Cambridge: University Press, 1902², supplemented ed. by R. Ottley, 1914, repr. KTAV 1968), pp. 49-53; also S. Jellicoe, *The Septuagint and Modern Study* (Oxford: Clarendon, 1968), pp. 94-99.]

277

Irenaeus remarks, contradicts their specific christology. Obviously, Irenaeus is thinking of the canonical gospel with its doctrine of the virgin birth in the infancy narrative (Matt. 1.18 ff.) which cannot be brought into harmony with an adoptionist christology. But it must be asked whether such a contradiction ought to be postulated for Jewish Christianity? [280] It can only be claimed if the Ebionites mentioned by Irenaeus actually used the canonical Matthew. But it is more probable that behind the phrase "gospel according to Matthew" is hidden another gospel writing similar to the canonical gospel or perhaps even dependent on it, but not identical with it. This is true of the so-called *Gospel of the Ebionites* which, according to Epiphanius, was a mutilated Matthaean gospel.[102] The infancy narratives are lacking in the latter, so that the assumption of a contradiction is resolved if we suppose that Irenaeus' notice reflects some confusion.

That Irenaeus could have confused the *Gospel of the Ebionites* with the canonical Matthew is conceivable since he does not have independent knowledge of the Ebionites. The fact that his report contains only a few concrete details that are frequently repeated[103] points in the same direction. Basically, his reports can be reduced to the information which is explicitly or implicitly contained in 1.26.2 (= 1.22). This would suggest that Irenaeus had used a fixed source corresponding most nearly to that passage, from which the remaining references are also taken. In favor of this assumption is the fact that the name "Ebionites" is first attested in Irenaeus, where it seems to be taken for granted as the designation for legalistic Jewish Christianity. Irenaeus probably found this name in the suggested source.

102. Epiphanius *Her.* 29.9.4, 30.13.2, 30.14.2; cf. P. Vielhauer on "Jewish-Christian Gospels" in Hennecke-Schneemelcher, 1: 117 ff.
103. AH 5.1.3 deserves notice as a further reference to the Ebionite christological confession. Here the comment is offered that instead of a "mixture of the heavenly wine" (*commixtio vini caelestis*) the Ebionites accept "only worldly water" (*solam aquam saecularem* [?]—on the textual problem cf. the editions of Stieren or Harvey, *ad loc.*). Epiphanius later speaks of a Jewish Christian meal with unleavened bread and water (*Her.* 30.16.1). However, one must question whether our passage ought to be interpreted in the light of Epiphanius' information or whether commonly held Christian notions about a meal with water have, in secondary fashion, here been transferred to Jewish Christianity (cf. G. Gentz, "Aquarii," RAC 1 (1950): 574 f.). There is danger of over-interpreting this section since its thrust is to be understood christologically and not sacramentally. AH 4.33.4 (= 4.52.1) also deserves notice with its general pronouncement of judgment against the Ebionites. The anti-Pauline passage in AH 3.15.1 to which Hilgenfeld refers (*Ketzergeschichte*, p. 421, n. 711) is not relevant to this discussion, as is indicated by its immediate and its wider context.

This is not the place to inquire into the more comprehensive question as to the source materials from which Irenaeus' report about the Ebionites is derived. No detailed argumentation is necessary to show that this source cannot be identified with the *Syntagma* of Justin. [281] The name Ebionites as well as the content of Irenaeus' report and its heresiological presuppositions are completely alien to Justin. This difference in outlook marks a development in the patristic evaluation of Jewish Christianity. The complex nature of Jewish Christianity, which was self-evident to Justin, is now no longer seen. Jewish Christianity now is classified as a self-contained unit alongside of other groups. The designation *Ebiōnaioi*, which probably originated in a concrete situation and was not a general label, has become the name of a sect. The term loses its original theological significance and is degraded to a heresiological technical term. A tendency toward schematization, which becomes characteristic of subsequent heresiology, comes into operation.

In *Ref.* 7.34, Hippolytus is largely dependent on Irenaeus' report.[104] His claim that the Ebionites acknowledge God as creator together with the explicit comparison of the Ebionites with the heretics Cerinthus and Carpocrates and the summary statement about "Jewish customs" are reminiscent of Irenaeus, AH 1.26.2 (= 1.22). Even his subsequent observations only appear to go beyond what is found in Irenaeus. Hippolytus' reflections on the elevation of Jesus to the position of Messiah-Christ add nothing really new but merely transfer to the Ebionites what Irenaeus said about Cerinthus or Carpocrates.[105] For the remainder, Hippolytus has introduced into his

104. It is assumed that Hippolytus wrote this work; see also Harnack, *Geschichte*, 2 (*Chronologie*). 2: 211, n. 2. The frequently noted attempts of P. Nautin (*Hippolyte et Josipe* [Paris, 1947] and *Hippolyte, Contre les hérésies. Étude et édition critique* [Paris, 1949]) to attribute Hippolytus' literary activity to an almost unknown Josippus or to an equally little known Hippolytus lead to even greater difficulties than those involved in the objections Batiffol once raised against the commonly accepted literary-historical judgment concerning Hippolytus (*Anciennes littératures chrétiennes: La littérature grecque* [Paris, 1897], pp. 156 f.). Contrary to Nautin cf., among others, M. Richard in *Mélanges de science religieuse*, 5-10 (1948–1953) and *Recherches de science religieuse*, 43 (1953): 379 ff.; H. Elfers, "Neue Untersuchungen über die Kirchenordnung Hippolytus von Rom," *Abhandlungen über Theologie und Kirche*, Festschrift for K. Adam, ed. M. Reding (Düsseldorf, 1952), pp. 181-198. [For further bibliography on the discussion, see Altaner, *Patrology*, p. 185, and Quasten, *Patrology*, 2: 169.]
105. The distinction between "Jesus" and "Christ" as well as the idea of his adoption are found in Irenaeus' treatment of Cerinthus (AH 1.26.1 [= 1.21]; cf. the reference in 1.26.2 [= 1.22]; a relationship to Jewish Christianity is already attested in Justin *Dial.* 48.3-49.1). On the other hand, the anthropological sig-

279

discussion terminology and concepts from the Pauline doctrine of justification. Of course, this does not represent an independent tradition, but it expresses the intention to theologize and conceptualize [282] which characterizes the whole of Hippolytus' "Philosophumena" (cf. *Ref.* preface.11). The *Epitome* of the work repeats the same material in abbreviated form—the sketch of Ebionite tenets derived from Irenaeus and Hippolytus' own Paulinizing judgment (*Ref.* 10.22). Finally, it is also significant that for Hippolytus the sequence of heresies immediately preceding his section on Ebionites corresponds to Irenaeus' schema. Thus the genesis of this material in terms of its literary history is not problematic.

On the other hand it is remarkable that in the next chapter, *Refutation* 7.35, "Ebion" is mentioned as the supposed hero from whom the Ebionites derived their name. This is the first appearance of that name in the heresiological literature and it cannot be traced back to Irenaeus. Where did this name originate, for which there is obviously no historical basis? [106] Reference could be made to Lipsius' witnesses for the *Syntagma* of Hippolytus,[107] which likewise mention "Ebion": Pseudo-Tertullian *Against Heresies* 48 (11); Epiphanius *Heresy* 30.1 f; and Filaster *Heresy* 37 (9). But since E. Schwartz's brilliant explanations [108] this attestation has become questionable: Filaster probably used Epiphanius; Pseudo-Tertullian is still "an unknown quantity which first must be solved" (p. 38); and the treatment in Epiphanius is demonstrably confused while the sources he employed still have not been identified.[109] In order to answer our

---

nificance of the adoption [i.e. anyone who lives as Jesus did can become "Christ"] derives from the report about Carpocrates (AH 1.25.1 [= 1.20.1]; Hippolytus *Ref.* 7.32.3).

106. Hilgenfeld, *Ketzergeschichte*, pp. 436 ff., shows unusual confidence in the reports of the church fathers when he accepts as genuine a monothelitic tract which, according to the witness of Anastasius (seventh century), was attributed to Ebion.

107. [R. A. Lipsius, *Zur Quellenkritik des Epiphanios* (Vienna, 1865).]

108. Schwartz, "Zwei Predigten Hippolyts," *Sitzungsberichte der Bayrischen Akademie der Wissenschaften*, 3 (München, 1936): 36 ff.

109. On the indiscriminate use of the ps.-Clementines by Epiphanius, cf. Strecker, *Judenchristentum*, pp. 265 f., and "Elkesai," 1175 f. Indeed, on the basis of the reports on the Nazoraeans M. Black asserts that Epiphanius' treatment is trustworthy (*The Scrolls and Christian Origins: Studies in the Jewish Background of the New Testament* [New York: Scribner's, 1961], pp. 67 ff.). But his argument only shows in exemplary fashion that Epiphanius' literary efforts are capable of producing such an impression.

question, therefore, it would be better not to make use of Lipsius' threefold attestation. Nevertheless, it should be discussed whether this designation could derive from the *Syntagma*. Tertullian, who also refers to "Ebion," [110] encourages this possibility. It is therefore impossible to regard Hippolytus' *Refutation* as the place of origin for this name since Tertullian belongs to an earlier period. Since Tertullian also made use of local Roman tradition [283] elsewhere [111] the possibility cannot be excluded that he was here under the direct or indirect influence of the *Syntagma* which was composed much earlier than the writing of the *Refutation* and perhaps immediately after the appearance of Noëtus in Rome. [112] This possibility is supported by the fact that in the immediate context, also without any parallel in Irenaeus, Hippolytus deals with the Byzantian Theodotus who appeared in Rome and was excommunicated by Bishop Victor. [113] Theodotus is mentioned also in chapter 3 of Hippolytus' homily against Noëtus. [114] Both the excommunication of Theodotus and the composition of the writing against Noëtus suit the time of origin of the *Syntagma*. Thus it is reasonable to conclude that *Refutation* 7.35 as a whole is based on the *Syntagma*. Perhaps we may go one step further and assume that it was Hippolytus himself who, on the basis of false etymology, conjectured that the founder of the sect had been a person named "Ebion." The context even seems to indicate how this misunderstanding could have arisen. While Hippolytus deals with "Ebionites" in *Refutation* 7.34, depending on Irenaeus, the name "Ebion" occurs in 7.35, in the chapter that goes back to the *Syntagma*,

110. *On the Flesh of Christ* 14, 18, 24; *On the Veiling of Virgins* 6.1; *Prescription Against Heretics* 33.5 and 10 f.
111. Cf. e.g. Harnack, *Marcion*2, p. 17°.
112. According to Photius (*Library*, codex 121) Hippolytus' *Syntagma* covered thirty-two heresies beginning with the Dositheans and ending with the adherents of Noëtus. Its time of composition should be fixed considerably before the *Refutation* since according to the preface to book one of the *Refutation*, the earlier draft was written "some time ago" (*palai*). The grounds for Harnack's dating of the *Syntagma* (*Geschichte* 2 [*Chronologie*]. 2: 223: during the first decade of the third century) are convincing only insofar as the work could not have appeared after 210. Since Photius applied the word *biblidarion* to the *Syntagma*, it follows that it was small in size and (contrary to the widely held assumption) could not have contained Hippolytus' *Homily against the Heresy of Noëtus*, as has been demonstrated conclusively by Schwartz ("Zwei Predigten," 37).
113. *Ref.* 7.9 and 35, 10.23; Eusebius EH 5.28.6; Hilgenfeld, *Ketzergeschichte*, p. 611.
114. [Ed. by Schwartz, "Zwei Predigten"; cf. also Migne PG 10.817. ET by S. Salmond in ANF 5: 223-231.]

281

and is juxtaposed with the names of "Cerinthus" and "Theodotus." Therefore, it would seem that the name originated in the *Syntagma* by means of a somewhat automatic assimilation to other founders of sects—apart from the other argument based on the fact that Hippolytus provides the earliest attestation of this name.

The foundation for the later heresiological treatment of Ebionitism has been provided by Irenaeus and Hippolytus. Henceforth, the doctrine and the practice of Jewish Christians will be reported in a stereotyped manner. Observance of Jewish customs, rejection of Paul, a "natural christology," and derivation from a certain "Ebion" as founder of the sect—all of this is subsumed under the concept *hairesis tōn Ebiōnaiōn*, "Ebionite heresy." By being identified as "Ebionism," Jewish Christianity [284] becomes an established heresiological entity which is treated in the one place provided in the catalogue of sects. The heresiologists who are supposed to have used Hippolytus' *Syntagma* (above, 280) can confirm this. The individual details that they have to offer are nothing but assimilations to the extant heresiological material, and cannot claim to be derived from firsthand knowledge (cf. Pseudo-Tertullian and Filaster). This also applies to Epiphanius. The comparison with other heresies mentioned by name (*Her.* 30.1) is just as much a secondary literary embellishment as the seemingly significant reference to "the earliest" Ebionite position (*ta prōta*), which introduced a line of development in Ebionite christological outlook stretching from a "natural" (30.2) to an Elchasaitic Christology (30.3 and 17), but is really a literary device whereby the diverse sources and disorganized bits of information are held together. This indicates, to be sure, that in distinction from other heresiologists, Epiphanius had access to sources hitherto unknown in the West, but it also shows that he did not really understand the significance of these bits of information, but rather grouped them according to a general heresiological point of view in which matters of detail are not differentiated.[115]

Origen's evidence also agrees at first with the heresiological reporting. Jewish observances (*Homily* 3.5 on Genesis), rejection of Paul (e.g. *Against Celsus* 5.65 and *Homily* 17.2 on Jeremiah), and

---

115. On the heresiological outlook of Epiphanius, cf. P. Fraenkel, "Histoire sainte et hérésie chez Épiphane de Salamine," *Revue de théologie et de philosophie*, 12 (1962): 175-191. Unfortunately Fraenkel does not follow Bauer's approach.

282

natural christology (*Homily* 17 on Luke) also are typical characteristics of the Ebionites according to Origen. He can also designate
them as "heretics" (*Against Celsus* 5.65). However, it is remarkable
that Origen does not reflect the heresiological pattern in other respects
—e.g. the common stereotyped comparison with Cerinthus and Carpocrates is not made. It is also characteristic of Origen to interpret
the name of the Ebionites ironically as indicating "the poverty of
their spirit." [116] What is especially important is the new information
he provides. Origen knows of Jewish Christians who teach that Jesus
was born in a natural way [285] but he is also aware of others who
acknowledge the virgin birth (*Against Celsus* 5.61; *Commentary on
Matthew*, 17.12). He is informed about their literal interpretation of
the Bible (*Commentary on Matthew*, 11.12), and also about their
celebration of the passover (*Commentary on Matthew*, series 79). His
reports apparently are based at least in part on his own substantiated
observation. He is aware that the Jewish Christian rejection of Paul
continues "to this day" (*Homily* 19 on Jeremiah). And there is other
evidence to confirm that the christology of Jewish Christians cannot
be limited to the notion of Jesus' natural birth, but also has room for
declarations concerning his preexistence.[117]

The idea that Origen's knowledge of Jewish Christianity was based
on personal observation explains his exceptional attitude of openness.
Origen admits that Jewish Christian theology was more complex than
would be possible according to the heresiological pattern. Even Eusebius, who elsewhere follows Origen's presentation for the most part,
by no means remains within the limits of the heresiological pattern,
but is also aware (perhaps on the basis of personal observation) of
Jewish Christians who live in Kokaba,[118] and he knows "Ebionites"
who celebrate the Lord's day as well as the sabbath.[119] The reporting
of Origen and Eusebius differs from the usual heresiological approach
not only by virtue of its factual knowledge; chronological and geo-
graphic differences are also reflected. Whereas Origen and Eusebius

116. *On First Principles* 4.3.8; *Against Celsus* 2.1, and *passim*. This interpretation
probably originated with Origen himself. It agrees with his knowledge of Hebrew
and is not found prior to him but appears rather frequently afterward. Cf. Strecker,
Judenchristentum, p. 123.
117. Strecker, "Ebioniten," col. 496 f.
118. *Onomasticon* (ed. Klostermann, GCS, 11.1 [1904], 172); [cf. Hilgenfeld,
Ketzergeschichte, pp. 426 n. 715, 428 n. 734 (cf. n. 731)].
119. EH 3.27.5; cf. *Apostolic Constitutions* 7.23.

283

attest that in the eastern church the complexity of Jewish Christianity is still acknowledged (even if only with regard to particular details) in the third and fourth century, the western church had already forced Jewish Christianity into a fixed heresiological pattern by the end of the second and beginning of the third century. This pattern was the result of a gradual development since the relatively open position of Justin, (and of Hegesippus), was replaced around the end of the second century by the typically heresiological approach. It is clear from the witness of Origen and Eusebius that even after standardization took place in the West, the East remained open with respect to the actual situation. It was not until much later that the final transfer of the heresiological pattern in the East seems to have become possible. Epiphanius can be named as the first witness to this development. [286] Theodoret and the later fathers, who wrote in complete dependence on their predecessors, mark the ultimate victory of the heresiological outlook.[120]

Walter Bauer had established that the early opponents of heresy, from Clement to Dionysius of Corinth, stood in close relation to Rome (see above, 106 ff.). It can now be added that this is also true with respect to the heresiological approach itself. The Roman character of Justin's literary endeavors is well known, in spite of his Samaritan origin and his sojourn in Asia Minor. Even though it may be supposed that his source material comes partly from the East, it was given its ultimate shape in Rome. Bauer showed in detail the connections between Hegesippus and Rome (above, 103, 107). This Roman orientation is especially true of Irenaeus, the first ecclesiastical author of whose systematic heresiological activity we have knowledge. His account of the heresies grew out of the ecclesiastical situation at Lyons— out of his struggle with Valentinian gnosticism. His journey to see Eleutherus of Rome (Eusebius EH 5.4) and his entry into the passover controversy through his letter to Bishop Victor (EH 5.24.10 ff.) are sufficient evidence for recognizing the strong ties by which he and his community felt themselves bound to the Roman ecclesiastical position. And that Hippolytus represents Roman tradition does not need to be argued, in spite of his actual alienation from the official

---

120. In several respects, Jerome occupies a unique position. He has connections with both East and West. As is well known, his information is no more reliable than that of Epiphanius. We cannot deal with it in more detail here.

284

incumbent of the Roman episcopal chair and his corresponding enum-
eration among the schismatics. Without any doubt, systematically
practiced heresiology begins in Rome. The later penetration into the
East of the heresiological attitude toward Jewish Christianity indicates that a Roman principle gained "ecumenical" validity. In this
respect, Bauer's claims receive substantial confirmation.

The variations in configuration and success of the heresiological
point of view corroborate the results gained from the direct and indirect evidence for Jewish Christianity in Syria—namely, that the
situation with regard to Jewish Christianity is complex, both in terms
of its own theological frame of thought and also in its relationship
to the "great church." This complexity contradicts the heresiological
pattern. And to the extent that later Jewish Christianity can be un-
covered, even greater variety is encountered there.[121] The simplistic,
[287] dogmatically determined classification of Jewish Christianity as a
heresy which confronts the "great church" as a homogeneous unit
does not do justice to the complex situation existing within legalistic
Jewish Christianity. Walter Bauer's opinion that "the Judaists soon
became a heresy, rejected with conviction by the gentile Christians,"
and that the Jewish Christians were "repulsed" by gentile Christianity
(above, 236 f.) needs to be corrected. Not only is there "significant
diversity" within the gentile Christian situation, but the same holds
true for Jewish Christianity. The fact that Jewish Christianity was a
polymorphic entity and that a heresiological principle emanating from
Rome could succeed against it only gradually provides not only a
correcting supplement, but above all an additional substantiation of
Bauer's historical perspective.

121. There are few witnesses, the Jewish Christian gospels cannot [287] be dated
with sufficient certainty, and the reports of Jerome and Epiphanius are unreliable
even when they deal with the contemporary situation rather than with past events.
On the activity of Jewish Christian groups on into Islamic times, cf. A. Schlatter,
"Die Entwicklung des jüdischen Christentums zum Islam," Evangelisches Mis-
sionsmagazin, 62 (1918): 251-264; Harnack, Lehrbuch der Dogmengeschichte⁴,
2 (Tübingen: Mohr, 1909; repr. Darmstadt, 1964): 534 ff. [this appendix on
Islam is not included in the ET, History of Dogma, 4 (1898)]; Schoeps, Theologie, pp. 334-342; Strecker, "Elkesai," col. 1177.

285

11

"Disaffected Judaism" and Early Christianity: Some Predisposing Factors

Robert Murray, S.J.
Heythrop College, University of London

It is proposed to try to clarify our understanding of early Judaism and Christianity, in the centuries of their formation and growing apart, by using the polarities "insider/outsider" and "self/other" with reference to consciousness, judgment and action. Once Christianity is a distinct entity, it becomes possible to apply these polarized categories clearly and fruitfully. But how are we to analyse the milieu in which Christianity arose? We have come to recognize how mistaken it was to read the characteristics of rabbinic Judaism back into the period before the rise of the School of Jamnia. But every student soon learns how hard it remains to reconstruct—even hypothetically—the movements in Judaism between the two destructions of Jerusalem in 586 B.C.E. and 70 C.E.

How are we to apply our polarities to the Jewish world which was the matrix of Christianity? The gospels picture Jesus as appealing now to "outsiders," now (less often, perhaps) to "insiders." What mutual attitudes were already determining people's reactions to Jesus? Who viewed whom as what in contemporary Judaism, and what effect may these views and feelings have had on the new movement?

What follows is a personal attempt to sketch a picture of some factors which, we may reasonably suspect, affected the self-understanding of Christianity. To some extent, this paper continues a line of thought first explored in public two years ago, in an article entitled "Jews, Hebrews and Christians: some needed distinctions."[1] That piece, admittedly speculative and provisional, arose from longstanding dissatisfaction with the way most writers who consider religious movements in the last centuries B.C.E. and the first centuries C.E. seem content with undifferentiated senses of "Jewish/Judaism" and "Jewish Christian[-ity]." Both the origin of the term *Ioudaios* and its eventually accepted denotation make it uneasily applicable to move-

---

[1] *Novum Testamentum* 24 (1982), 194-208.

ments (however disparate) which rejected the Jerusalem temple and its "establishment" of priesthood and schools. Despite the light thrown on this crucial period by many scholars, dissatisfaction with the terminology and classification for kinds of "Judaism" and "Christianity" continues, as my previous article began by documenting and trying to analyse.[2] My tentative advocacy of "dissident Hebrews" (suggested by Josephus, AJ XI, 8, 6) has won no public acclaim; no doubt "Hebrew" has already caused quite enough trouble in early Christian sources. There is no doubt that we must stay with "Jewish" and "Judaism"; that family was and remains so elastic and inclusive that even its most non-conformist branches should not be excluded from the name. But we constantly need qualifying and differentiating adjectives—above all when talking about movements of the kinds just referred to. To some extent, these involve traditional northern sentiment vis-à-vis Judaea. Of late, H.L. Ginsberg has expressed his sense of need for a term distinct from "Israelite" or "Jewish," namely "Israelian,"[3] to refer to Israel in the restricted sense of the old northern kingdom, and to characteristics of its religious understanding which continued to be influential when the heritage of the greater Israel was claimed by Judah. Ginsberg sees that his insight entails further discussion about the meaning and origin of "Judaism," and about how other more open concepts of the heritage were repressed in Nehemiah's time (op. cit., 3-18).

It seems likely, as several scholars have supposed, that anger on the part of those disqualified, further intensified by other motives such as repugnance to the new calendar of the restored cult, lies not only at the root of various movements hostile to the Judaean "establishment," but also behind much of the literature which that establishment could not possibly canonize. How that literature may best be designated remains disputable. In this paper I look not so much at questions of genre as of *Tendenz*, especially that which I call "disaffected." The literature has at its head that great monument of vision and theological reflection, 1 Enoch; it is this, rather than the pious Jewish book of Daniel, which is the archetypal apocalypse, systematically working out a vision inspired by ancient religious traditions[4] in

---

[2] See, for example, R. E. Brown, "Not Jewish Christianity and Gentile Christianity but types of Jewish/Gentile Christianity" CBQ 45 (1983), 74-79, though he does not attempt to locate the sources of confusion as or where I do.

[3] *The Israelian Heritage of Judaism* (New York: Jewish Theological Seminary of America, 1982), 1-2.

[4] This is increasingly recognized for 1 Enoch. See James C. VanderKam, *Enoch and the Growth of the Apocalyptic Tradition*, CBQ Monograph Series 16, (Washington, D.C.: 1984); John J. Collins, *The Apocalyptic Imagination* (New York: Crossroad, 1984), chs.

order to make unbearable evils explicable, and hope for the future conceivable.

In my article of 1982 I argued that "Jewish Christianity" could never be understood unless "Jewish" is differentiated so as to allow for at least the following two kinds of background: the first is "Jewish" in the proper sense, that is, accepting the Jerusalem establishment's terms of reference; the second inherits old quarrels with Jerusalem— either that going back to early opposition to the new calendar and temple, or the later quarrel which led to the secession to Qumran.[5] I briefly sketched the lines on which the various New Testament books might be classified in this regard, and hinted at how this differentiation might fruitfully be extended into the developing history of the early Church. I asked finally "Is it possible that the charge against the Jews that they crucified Jesus (very explicit in Melito and early Syriac writers) was formulated by angry Galileans before ever it was by non-Israelite Gentiles?"

This is the starting-point for the present paper. Unfortunately circumstances have not permitted me to undertake the detailed research which I proposed as desirable in the previous article, nor to correlate my hunches with all the relevant work of other scholars. This sequel is again speculative and provisional. Nonetheless, it suggests lines along which to follow up my suggestion.

Given that the early Church's quarrel with "Judaism" was focused on the interpretation of Jesus, we might naturally suppose it was essentially, even entirely, about the refusal to accept him as a prophet and God-sent Messiah, and the charge that the Jewish leaders had

---

1 and 2. While agreeing with those who emphasize the ancient Mesopotamian sources, however, it will be clear that my inclination to see the power of myth still working from the old royal cult puts me in the tradition of Frank Moore Cross. I have been especially stimulated by Jonathan Z. Smith's article "Wisdom and Apocalyptic" (1975), reprinted in Paul D. Hanson (ed.), *Visionaries and their Apocalypses* (Philadelphia: Fortress, 1983) as ch. 6, and also by Margaret Barker's "Some Reflections upon the Enoch Myth", JSOT 15 (1980), 7-29.

[5] In saying "at least two kinds," my aim is only to avoid complexity at this point. My 1982 article was open to the criticism made by W.L.Horbury in JSNT 19 (1983), 48, that I exaggerate the incidence of dissident movements, and also assimilate known ones to each other too much. This is far from my intention, which is to clarify, not to blur the picture. Nevertheless, if various movements arise in opposition to the same institution, they may show certain similarities, may influence each other and may gravitate towards each other. Compare, for example, the history of religious dissent from the Anglican Church in England since the sixteenth century. (This suggests the further thought that an undifferentiated use of "Jewish" in the period under study could be compared to using the term "Anglican" to cover not only members of the established Church but also all Protestants in England!)

delivered him to death by the agency of the Romans. But the New Testament and early Christian witness is more complicated. Stephen, arraigned before the Sanhedrin, expounds a lengthy charge sheet against the Jews and against the very idea of a temple before he ever mentions Jesus. Several books of the New Testament and the sub-apostolic period show that Enoch is regarded as equivalent to Scripture, and links with the "disaffected" literature can be multiplied.

But let us return to the central figure of Jesus. The very categories available for interpreting his teaching and nature were multiple and reflected the oppositions which we must consider. There was not one single Messianism, on the Davidic model. Judaism and the opposition movements had different models for conceiving of the saviour expected from God. One model, that of Melchizedek, appears, on the available evidence, to have flourished especially in the circles revealed by the Qumran discoveries. Jesus' conquest of rebellious spirits, both in the synoptics, in Paul, Peter and in Revelation, again suggests the thought-world of Enoch. There is indeed a case to be considered that already existing hostility to Jerusalem Judaism, and ideas developed in terms other than those of its schools, conditioned the new quarrel about the rejection of Jesus.

I propose to sketch such a case by outlining a number of ideas, beliefs, or practical positions and activities, which may link at least parts of the early Church with movements already hostile to Jerusalem Judaism. There is time only for a sketch; part of the case has been well established by others, while part is frankly speculative and may not appeal to many. If it impresses anyone, that will be by virtue of accumulated hints pointing one way, rather than force of certain facts. I do not presume to reconstruct "trajectories"—to use a fashionable but not quite apt metaphor. (Trajectories arise from aimed firing and are determined by ballistic laws.) Rather I may seem like an amateur water-diviner, exploring with forked hazel twig or bent copper rods to trace lost underground channels. Some channels may be verified, some may be possible, others will remain uncertain. Another imaginative model might be the discovery by aerial photography of ancient settlements and earthworks which cannot be seen from the ground. Both this and "dowsing" involve inevitable imprecision, but yet can direct us towards accurate and fruitful investigation later, and eventually help to produce a new map.

Up to now, attempts to sketch the sectarian map have inevitably been dominated by Josephus' four "philosophies." Of course, his account must never be neglected, but it leaves us with acute problems. Only three of his groups are mentioned in the New Testament; the Essenes are never named. While I do not oppose the majority view that the Qumran people were Josephus' Essenes, the books in their library imply things Josephus never tells us. They treasured Enoch and Judilees, both dedicated to an older calendar than that in use in the second temple. The former appeals to astronomy and uses an angelic myth of the origin of evil to attack the "sinners" who were now in control, the latter claims that the old calendar had been revealed to the patriarchs. Here we have evidence of a quarrel with the Jerusalem establishment both distinct from the Samaritan quarrel and earlier than that which brought about the secession to Qumran. But the Qumran people also used a calendar akin to that of Jubilees, even though the *Mōreh ha-ṣedeq* and his followers seem to have come out from the Zadokite temple priesthood who followed the postexilic calendar, while the sect's approach to *halakhah* has seemed near enough to that of the Pharisees to make scholars such as Louis Ginzberg and C. Rabin relate the Damascus document to that movement.[6] The precise location of the Qumran sect (or Essenes) on the map of Palestinian movements still presents baffling problems as regards both its antecedents, its own quarrel with Jerusalem, and what it became or contributed to. It is not new to trace its influence both to some features of early Christianity and to Qara'ism. What is perhaps newer, in relation to the map which I see forming, is the realization that there were more streams leading from the thought-world of Enoch (whatever the name of the group whose dissatisfaction it expressed) to the early Church than has been generally recognized up to now.[7] Even if those streams do not always express actual hostility in every case, the fact that a quarrel lies behind Enoch, and that Christianity has a new quarrel, justifies our examining early Christianity more carefully in the light of "disaffected"Judaism.

1 Enoch uses a myth of angelic rebellion and the consequent disturbance of divine order (both cosmic and in human society) to attack the "sinners," who are not named but are clearly those who have changed the calendar. David Suter takes the function of the myth "as a *paradigm* (rather than an etiology) of the origin of evil . . . . In the

---

[6] L. Ginzberg, *Eine unbekannte jüdische Sekte* (New York: 1922), E.T. *An Unknown Jewish Sect* (New York: 1970); C. Rabin, *Qumran Studies* (Oxford, 1957).

[7] Despite R.H. Charles' judgement that "the influence of 1 Enoch on the New Testament has been greater than that of all the other apocryphal and pseudepigraphical books put together" (*The Book of Enoch* [Oxford, 1912], p. xcv). See W.J.Dalton, *Christ's Proclamation to the Spirits* (Rome: 1965), ch. VI; G.W.E.Nickelsburg, "Riches, the Rich and God's Judgment in 1 Enoch 92-105 and the Gospel According to Luke," NTS 25 (1979), 324-344; "Enoch, Levi and Peter: Recipients of Revelation in Upper Galilee," JBL 100 (1981), 575-600, and his contribution to the present volume; also M. Barker, "Some Reflections. . ." (note 4 above).

Damascus Document, Jude and 2 Peter, the paradigmatic function of
the myth is expanded into a *typology* of the origin of evil in the form
of lists of great sinners in each generation—lists headed by the fallen
angels".[8] The myth works analogically and "possesses a number of
possibilities for meaning that may not be exhausted by any one
version" (ibid.). I believe that the "Parables," though the latest part of
the book, still exemplify this function. They are called as they are
precisely as heavenly visions which can give insight about both the
cosmos and society. Thus in 43: 3-4 Enoch asks about the circulation
of the stars "according to the number of the angels, and [how] they
keep faith with each other," and he is told "The Lord of Spirits hath
showed thee their parable (Charles renders 'parabolic meaning'):
these are the names of the holy who dwell on the earth . . . ." This
scheme of heavenly realities as paradigms to interpret earthly events
is, surely, the key to interpreting the Book of Revelation. Indeed, it
makes me less attracted by appeals to Philonic Platonism as the
thought-world of Hebrews, or of the Odes of Solomon where they say:
"The likeness of that which is below is that which is above" (Od. 34:
4). This whole area of visionary expression is well discussed by
Christopher Rowland, who proposes to define the scope of apocalyptic literature using the formula in M. Hagigah 2.1: "What is above,
what is beneath, what was beforetime and what will be hereafter."[9]

So far I have discussed only the *function* of the Enochic angel
myth and how this kind of thinking continues in early Christianity. To
turn to the content and message, I am attracted (more than the
majority of scholars in this field) by Margaret Barker's thesis that the
story of the angelic rebellion developed from an *older* tradition
concerning rebellious members of the heavenly host, the traces of
which are in Isaiah 14: 12 ff., 24: 21-22, and in Psalms 82 and 58.[10]
Genesis 6 contains a truncated fragment of the myth in a form which
presupposes a fuller form, one containing elements preserved in 1

---

[8] "Fallen Angel, Fallen Priest: The Problem of Family Purity in 1 Enoch," HUCA 50
(1979), 115-35, 116-117.

[9] *The Open Heaven* (London: SPCK, 1982), ch. 2; see also John J. Collins, *The
Apocalyptic Imagination* (n. 4 above), 9-16. On the contrast between cosmic order and
human disorder in 1 Enoch 2-5 and early Christian literature (e.g. 1 Clement and
Aphrahat, Dem XIV), see R. Murray, "Hellenistic-Jewish Rhetoric in Aphrahat," Or.
Chr. An. 221 (1983), 79-85. But this is a widely-based *topos*, present already in Isaiah 1:
1-2 and Jeremiah 5: 22-25, independently developed by Stoic writers, and found in
Jewish as well as Christian literature.

[10] M. Barker, "Some Reflections. . ." (n. 4 above). Her reconstruction of the context,
development and eventual transmutation of the ancient myth is the subject of a whole
book, the publication of which is expected.

Enoch.[11] Genesis 3, reworking and largely demythologizing another rebellion myth, known from Ezekiel 28, is a deliberate *substitute*, pre-emptively given priority, in order to play down any responsibility for evil other than plain human disobedience. (However, it is left unexplained how the serpent, a creature of God, has already become capable of supernatural malice before the story begins!) Mrs Barker believes the original locus of the rebellion myth was in the old royal cult, a major function of which was to maintain control of all hostile forces, both natural and supernatural. The king, as the earthly representative of the "Holy One of Israel," directed the constantly necessary campaign against the other, disorderly, "Holy Ones," and the this-worldly forces under their influence.[12] This hypothesis of the myth's antiquity in its "pre-angelic" form fits with the strong probability that the pentecontad solar calendar, which the authors of Enoch, Jubilees and the Damascus Document insist was divinely revealed, was simply the old Palestinian agrarian calendar as developed in a solar year structure in the first temple. The variants in what we may call the "old calendarist" literature arise from diverging memories of what it was like before the breach of continuity and the introduction of the lunar-solar calendar which Jerusalem's new masters brought back from Babylon.[13]

I am further impressed by Mrs Barker's argument that the revelation of dangerous and corrupting "wisdom" is an integral part of the myth from the beginning, rather than a distinct theme eventually combined with that of rebellion and fall through lust. This is contrary

---

[11] J.T. Milik, *The Books of Enoch: Aramaic Fragments of Qumran Cave 4* (Oxford: Clarendon Press, 1976), 30-32, maintains simply that the Enoch story is older than and implied by the Genesis story. In this bald form his view has not won acceptance. A view as expressed above remains possible and corresponds to the view that the account of Enoch in Gen 5 presupposes a fuller tradition (cf. VanderKam, *Enoch*. . . [n. 4 above], ch. II).

[12] Cf. J.Z. Smith, "Wisdom and Apocalyptic" (n. 4 above), especially 109, in the reprint. Cf. my interpretation of Isaiah 33: R. Murray, "Prophecy and the Cult," in R.J. Coggins, A. Phillips and M.A. Knibb, eds., *Israel's Prophetic Heritage* (Cambridge: University Press, 1982), 200-216, especially 205-16.

[13] Cf. J. Morgenstern, "The Calendar of the Book of Jubilees: its Origin and its Character" VT 5 (1955), 34-76, summing up his long series of calendar studies in HUCA, 1924-1947. For the recent debate see J. VanderKam, "The Origin, Character and Early History of the 364-Day Calendar," CBQ 41 (1979), 209-217 and "The 364-Day Calendar in the Enochic Literature", in K.H. Richards ed., *SBL 1983 Seminar Papers* (Chico, CA: Scholars Press, 1983), 157-65; P.R. Davies, "Calendrical Change and Qumran Origins: An Assessment of VanderKam's Theory," CBQ 45 (1983), 80-89. It is not necessary here to take sides in this difficult discussion. I wonder if it is possible that the *Mōreh ha-ṣedeq* at some point was converted to "old calendarism", and that this was a major reason why he seceded?

to the current "orthodoxy," which places the revelation story later in
the redaction history. Since it is clear that the Enoch tradition grows
and develops, the story may be *redactionally* subsequent, but I still
want to hold that its substance belongs to the old myth.[14] (Its absence
leaves Gen 6:4 with no explanation of how mankind became wicked.)

This rather lengthy discussion of the Enochic angel myth's antiquity may seem remote from my main theme. But it is important if it is
true. If 1 Enoch began from one writer's vision, not much before 200
B.C.E., and its influence passed to the Qumran people, it could be a
limited phenomenon which eventually touched early Christianity
here and there. And such a minimal view used to be common. But if
the roots of Enoch are in memories of the ancient cult, preserved by
the "people of the land" who had experienced not exile and intensive
spiritual development but abandonment, desolation and then ideological oppression by those who returned (breaking up marriages, dis-
qualifying levites and robbing people of the security of their ancestral
calendar), then it is likely that disaffection was both widespread and
deep, ready for catalysts to organize it into new movements—rather as
in northern Europe and Britain there were many disaffected circles all
ready to become Protestants when the Reformation finally broke. I
believe that in the New Testament, if we do not restrict ourselves to
explicit citations of Enoch or implicit allusions, but look for a vision of
the cosmos and the whole moral situation of mankind corresponding
to that reflected in 1 Enoch, much important evidence points towards
that very world-view, rather than towards that of rabbinic Judaism's
forefathers.

Altogether, angels and evil spirits play a much more substantial
part in the New Testament than is typical, as far as I know, of the
approximately contemporary Jewish literature. Mark's presentation of
Jesus as demonstrating a new, divine authority, different not only in
its basis, but qualitatively different from that of the scribes (Mk 1:22),
is substantiated by Jesus' command of all spirits, both the angels who
minister to him in the desert (Mk 1:13) and the demons whose power
is shown in disease. These last he casts out with absolute authority
(Mk 1:27). The spirits acknowledge Jesus by titles belonging both to
the king and to his heavenly patron in the ancient royal cult: "Holy

---

[14] J.J. Collins, in his valuable article "The Apocalyptic Technique: Setting and
Function in the Book of Watchers," CBQ 44 (1982), 91-111, takes Mrs. Barker to hold a
less nuancé position than is actually the case. My own position here is analogous to
what I would maintain regarding numerous gospel pericopes, where I accept literary-
critical arguments for recognizing redactional activity, yet still in many cases judge it
more likely that the essentials go back to words and acts of Jesus.

one of God" (Mk 1:24), "Son of God" (Mk 3:11), "Son of the Most High God" (Mk 5:7—El Elyon!).[15] We enlightened moderns have not taken the spirits seriously enough. That insoluble problem for the redaction critics, the Marcan Messianic secret, may find its solution also here. Jesus "would not allow the demons to speak, because they knew him" (Mk 1:34). Part of Jesus' strategy was to keep the advantage of surprise over the hostile spirits till his victory was complete—as Ignatius recognized (Eph 19).[16]

At the time of Jesus' appearance, though the rebel spirits have been cast down by God and imprisoned (Isai 24: 22; most fully, 1 Enoch 10, 18, 21 etc.; Jude 6; 2 Peter 2: 4), they have power over vulnerable victims whom they "bind" by disease (Lk 13: 16). But Jesus is the stronger one who comes, releases the victims, and binds their oppressors (Mk 3: 27). The power of binding and loosing, which he gives to his disciples, was the power of exorcism (Mk 3: 15) before it was translated by Jewish Christians into anything like rabbinic authority (Mt 16: 19; 18: 18). The latter, according to the picture in the gospels, is not so much evil as superseded. If Jesus attacks the scribes and pharisees as blind leaders of the blind, he is seen to be speaking for a public which expects something else of God than a blessing on the institutions which maintain and develop a safe *halakhah* to live by. But if that public breathed an air constantly contested by angels and demons, and was acquainted with the Qumran covenanters' conviction of being involved in a cosmic war between the sons of light, allied with the angels, and the sons of darkness, the lot of Belial, then much in the New Testament clicks into place. Indeed, there is a cosmic war in progress, but the meaning of Jesus' life, death and resurrection is that through him, victory for God has already been definitively won. He has triumphed over the demonic powers controlling the world (Col 2: 15) and announced his victory, immediately after the paradox of his death, to the imprisoned disobedient spirits (1 Peter 3: 19). The Enochic myth provides the seer John with the means of interpreting both the challenge realized immediately in the birth of

---

[15] These occur also, of course, on the lips of a good angel in the Lukan Annunciation narrative (Lk 1:32-35)!

[16] Cf. J.M. Hull, *Hellenistic Magic and the Synoptic Tradition* (London: SCM, 1974), especially p. 69. Significant also for my argument for ancient roots is Josephus' belief that exorcism went back to Solomon, a feature not preserved in canonical Scripture (AJ VIII,45; Hull, p. 34). I disagree with Hull's view, however, that the "magical" element in Mark and Luke represents the infiltration of alien, Hellenistic ideas. If Matthew has the least "magical" ideas, that is because it is the most "Jewish" gospel (in the restricted sense of that term); Mark and Luke reflect circles open to other religious concepts.

the Messiah (Rev 12: 7-9) and the future final stages of the cosmic drama (Rev 20).

Meanwhile, till the rebellious spirits are finally bound and destroyed, all who have recognized Jesus as God's son, sent from heaven to rally the sons of light (1 Thess. 5: 5; Col 1: 12-13) are engaged in a battle which consists in a day-to-day ascetical struggle, but which is their part in the cosmic war (1 Thess. 5: 8-9, Eph 6: 10-17). The kind of imagery which expresses this vision links the Qumran Community Rule (1QS 3-4) and the War Scroll, through the New Testament passages just alluded to and the "Two Ways" catechesis in Barnabas (18-20) and the Didache (1-6), to the early Syriac ascetical literature. This forms one of our most clearly traceable underground streams— even if decisive proof is still lacking that these ideas, together with the consecrated celibacy of ascetics stripped for action, go back behind Christianity to the Qumran Covenanters.[17]

Likewise, besides the symbolism of participation in spiritual warfare, the claim to live and worship in fellowship with the angels of God may well be another stream joining early Christianity to the world of Enoch and the Qumran people. For the latter, this claim is expressed e.g. in 1QS 17:7-8, 1QSa 2:8-9 and 1QM 12. In early Christianity the ascetical life soon came to be regarded as a *vita angelica* on earth.[18] But already, in the New Testament, Christians see themselves as united with the heavenly worshipping community (Heb 12: 22-24 and, implicitly, in all the visions of heavenly cult in the book of Revelation).[19] The same book sees churches as having presiding angels (chs. 2-3). The Sanctus, the angelic hymn which proves its antiquity by its similarity in all early eucharistic anaphoras, has its most probable immediate antecedents in the Qumran "Angelic Liturgy" and the Parables of Enoch;[20] its remoter roots are, of course, in Isaiah's vision in the first temple.

In all this, the pre-Christian antecedents seem to point mainly towards "disaffected" groups, behind which we may recognize attach-

---

[17] Cf. R. Murray, "The Exhortation to Candidates for Ascetical Vows at Baptism in the Ancient Syriac Church," NTS 21 (1974-5), 59-80.

[18] Cf. P. Nagel, *Die Motivierung der Askese in der alten Kirche und der Ursprung des Mönchtums*, TU 95 (1966), 34-48.

[19] Cf. E. Peterson, *Das Buch von den Engeln*, E.T. *The Angels and the Liturgy*, (London; Darton, Longman and Todd, 1964), ch.1. More speculatively, G. Dautzenberg in his *Urchristliche Prophetie* (Stuttgart: Kohlhammer, 1975) finds the possible antecedents of early Christian glossolalia (236), which Paul apparently understood as the language of the angels, in the Testament of Job, assigned by both Philonenko and Dautzenberg to the Therapeutae (ibid., 108-118).

[20] Cf. B.D. Spinks, "The Jewish Sources for the Sanctus", HeyJ 21 (1980), 168-79.

ment to features remembered from the old temple cult. Such an appeal to the past of Israel will have taken various forms: not only the way of transformation by canonization on the part of the Jerusalem scribes, but also ways that expressed claims to inheritance on the part of disaffected groups. What are we to say of Merkavah mysticism, whose roots have been thought to lie not far from those who composed the "Angelic Liturgy"? Are we entitled to imagine that a kind of spirituality which was born in sectarian circles later flourished (however suspect) in contact with rabbinic Judaism, as well as influencing Christianity? If we could reach any safe conclusions about the Therapeutae, who may (if certain works are justifiably ascribed to them) have claimed to live in fellowship with angels,[21] this would make it more possible to chart our hidden streams. Philo does not present the Therapeutae as sectarian or as anything other than admirable to him as a good Jew.

When we consider Messianism, the expectation of an anointed agent through whom it was hoped that God would again act to deliver Israel and institute his kingdom on earth, and when likewise we consider the ways in which the early Christians saw Jesus as fulfilling such expectations, then (as I observed above) we must recognize several models of Messianism. One approach is to consider what functions in the Lord's service were understood to require anointing. Obviously, these were kingship, priesthood and prophethood. Evidently, the royal messianism in the Davidic tradition (and therefore beloved of Jerusalem Judaism, inspiring texts such as the Psalms of Solomon 17-18) is claimed for Jesus, for example in the infancy narratives, Romans 1:3 and carries over into Ignatius (Rom 7) and the Didache (9). A priestly messiah appears to be expected at Qumran (1QS 9:11), though this remains obscure; the expectation is clearer in the Testament of Levi (18),[22] which of course reflects at least redaction by Christians. Along this line, we may remember some Syrian Christians' concern to give Jesus a title to priesthood through the hands of John the Baptist[23]; this claim is hardly compatible with the way in which Hebrews ascribes priesthood to Jesus. With the idea of a priestly messiah we are, if not among sects, at least moving farther (if

---

[21] Not explicit in Philo, De Vita Contemplativa (our main source); but cf. Testament of Job (n. 19 above), in J.H. Charlesworth ed., *The Old Testament Pseudepigrapha* I (Garden City, N.Y.: Doubleday, 1984), translation, introduction and commentary, 829-68; cf. also the Apocalypse of Zosimus or History of the Rechabites, ibid., vol. II.
[22] For a recent summary of the position on the data from Qumran and on Test. Levi, see J.J. Collins, *The Apocalyptic Imagination* (n. 4 above), 111-112,122-126.
[23] Cf. R. Murray, *Symbols of Church and Kingdom: A Study in Early Syriac Tradition* (Cambridge: University Press, 1975), 178-80.

I am not mistaken) from the preferred concepts of Jerusalem Judaism. Finally, an eschatological prophet was expected in the light of Deut 18:15 ff., as is referred to, apparently, in 1QS 9:11, and in the questions to John the Baptist (Jn 1:21). This kind of figure appears to occupy the Messianic role for the Samaritans, even though they rejected the prophets canonized by the Jerusalem tradition. Among the reactions to Jesus was to acclaim him as a prophet (Lk 7: 16), but this does not necessarily point to messianic expectations. However, in John 6, the cry that Jesus is "*the* prophet who is to come into the world" leads immediately to an attempt to make him king, a proceeding which Jesus decisively forestalls (Jn 6: 14-15). Would any of this have happened in a world of religion safely controlled by the Jerusalem scribes and rabbis?

Another approach to Messianism is to ask what kind of person, possessed of what nature, was expected as messiah. All the models of messiah-ship summarized in the previous paragraph remain within the human sphere. But there is a range of data which reveals the expectation that a divine figure will exercise messianic functions. Modern New Testament scholarship has conspired to play down the existence of any 'Jewish' background for the early Christian conviction of the preexistence of the Messiah, Holy One and Son of the Most High God, whose incarnation the angel announces to Mary (Lk 1:32-35). But the tide is turning from "hellenistic" theories, as Martin Hengel's *The Son of God* illustrates.[24] Further, the Qumran Melchizedek fragments reveal a figure who functions in the heavenly order, who judges on terms drawn from Ps 82, and for whom is the "day of favor" (which in Isa 61:2 is the Lord's). That passage in Isaiah is spoken by one anointed by YHWH, and in Lk 4:18-19, Jesus claims to be the one signified. The figure named Melchizedek in the fragments is to vanquish Belial, the leader of the forces of evil (Melchireshà in 4Q 'Amram^b).[25]

Not only these texts are fragmentary; so must be my argument. Still it seems to come together to establish the theme of a figure active in the heavenly sphere whose functions are closely associated with God himself. This figure bears the name used in Hebrews as the basis for a different kind of argument, one concerning the kind of priesthood which can appropriately serve as a model for speaking of Jesus' death as salvific. I see no link, beyond the name, between the Melchizedek

---

[24] *Der Sohn Gottes* (Tübingen, 1975); English Trans. London: SCM, 1976.
[25] See Paul J. Kobelski, *Mechizedek and Melchireša*, CBQ Monograph Series 10 (1981); for a summary of the position, J.J. Collins, *The Apocalyptic Imagination* (n. 4 above), 132.

figure in Hebrews and the Qumran figure, who seems to be identified with Michael. It is different, however, when we turn back to the source of the name. The biblical Melchizedek was a priest-king (therefore presumably with a double title to be anointed) in Salem (understood to be Jerusalem), so the Davidic king could be addressed as "a priest for ever according to the order of Melchizedek" (Ps 110). If the same name was believed to be borne by a heavenly figure, surely this suggested some kind of identity, representative or symbolic, between the king and a heavenly patron bearing the same name as the supposed founder of his line of royal priesthood.

Once again we are led back, by yet another path, from ideas apparently used by early Christianity, to aspects of the royal cult in the first temple. These the redactors of the canonical Tanach did not wish to emphasize, though they let traces remain, especially in the royal covenant tradition as we see it in Ps 89, with its close parallelism between the sovereignty of YHWH and that of the king, or in that remarkable phrase in 1 Chron 29:23, "Solomon sat on the throne of YHWH as king instead of David". Do we need to look further for the model for the Elect One sitting on God's throne in Parables of Enoch 51:3? Is there, even, a simpler or more plausible background for the "Son of Man" in Dan 7? Whether, or how much, Jesus may have meant people to understand his self-designation as "Son of Man" on these lines is an unanswerable question. It is not clear even that the early Church understood it in such a way (unless perhaps Stephen did in his dying vision, Acts 7: 56). But I propose it as a hypothesis worth considering, that the memory of the old "royal theology" which linked the king especially to YHWH as *his* patron, flowed into the early Christian belief in the glorification of Jesus as the Christ. If this could be true, once again it looks as if the streams had flowed through terrain not perfectly controlled by those who had taken over the hierarchical functions in Jerusalem.

Before turning to subjects nearer to actual quarrels with the latter, however, I would like to conclude this section with a suggestion about the background of the christological "hymn" in Philippians 2. The favoured sources seem to be Adam and the Isaian Servant, or the Isaian Servant mediated through Wisdom of Solomon 2-5, as is argued by Dieter Georgi.[26] But none of these options seem to me to fit well

---

[26] "Der vorpaulinische Hymnus Phil 2,6-11," in E. Dinkler (ed.), *Zeit und Geschichte* (Tübingen: Mohr, 1964), 263-93; on Wisdom 2-5 in relation to the Isaian Servant, see G.W.E. Nickelsburg, *Resurrection, Immortality and Eternal Life in Intertestamental Judaism*, Harvard Theological Studies 26 (Cambridge, MA: Harvard University Press, 1972), ch. 2, especially 62-66.

enough as regards either sharing the divine nature or an actual attempt to usurp equality with God. The story in Genesis 3 never says that Adam and Eve actually formed the desire to become like gods. Surely the most appropriate place to look is the use in Isaiah 14:12-15 of the myth of a star-god who tried to usurp the throne of El, but was cast down and imprisoned; variants of the myth doubtless underlie Ezekiel 28 and Isai 24:21-22, and I suppose the Enochic rebellion story to be also related to it. The "hymn" in Philippians (the inverted commas reflect an abiding lack of conviction about this fashionable identification of the genre) pictures Jesus as actually having the right, but renouncing the claim, to equality. His self-abasement, rewarded by exaltation, exactly reverses the pattern of the old myth with an elegance which makes me, at least, feel no need to look further elsewhere. On this view, the other suggestions may still find a place in the creative mixture; Adam has a certain aura of royal wisdom, and the Isaian Servant (which I see as a figure like T.S. Eliot's "familiar compound ghost" in *Little Gidding*) must have, among its components, a lot to do with sacral kingship.

Again, we are fed back to the sort of background for apocalypticism variously proposed by Jonathan Z. Smith and Margaret Barker.[27] And we are looking for the roots of at least some early christology in a direction to which Martin Hengel points (without pursuing it). The same, perhaps, might be true of E.P. Sanders's conclusion that "Paul presents an *essentially different type of religiousness from any found in Palestinian Jewish literature*,"[28] but I believe the essential next step depends on making distinctions in "Jewish" and also between kinds of "apocalyptic" literature, and on searching among heirs of ancient Israel who may have had mixed or negative feelings about being called Jewish. In my previous article I suggested that the Damascus Christians among whom Paul was converted had a dissenting background, and that "his conversion to Jesus. . . also meant making peace with dissenters. This could help to explain his subsequent intense concern with reconciliation."[29]

I have postponed till now the identifiable points at issue between the "disaffected" and Jerusalem, for various reasons. I do not in the least intend to undermine the essential and obvious truth that the new Christian movement had a new quarrel with all elements in the Jerusalem establishment and with anyone else who ought, in Chris-

---

[27] See Smith, "Wisdom and Apocalyptic" and Barker, "Some Reflections. . .", in note 4 above.

[28] *Paul and Palestinian Judaism* (London: SCM, 1977), 543.

[29] Murray, "Jews, Hebrews and Christians" (n. 1 above), 204.

tian eyes, to have been able to recognize Jesus as God's chosen messenger and messiah. What leads the student of Christian origins back to 1 Enoch and the Qumran people is not the survival of their quarrels, as such, but rather of elements of their world-view and "spirituality".

As we have observed, the angelic rebellion myth in 1 Enoch is used to picture disorder on earth as in heaven. Through the abuse of calendrical "wisdom," "sinners" have thrown the seasons into confusion by changing the calendar (1 Enoch 80). As the Enoch tradition develops, further charges become clear. The temple has been polluted by "blinded shepherds" (ibid. 89), and the sinners who are in power exploit the poor (94-104). The same attachment to the old calendar and the same accusations against temple and oppression reappear in the Damascus Document (esp. 2-5). The last two themes are familiar, in various forms, in the preaching of Jesus and his followers, but the devotion to the old calendar cannot be traced into Christianity. Annie Jaubert made an imaginative and exciting attempt to do this, but it has not won credence.[30] There remains the puzzling statement in the third-century *Didascalia* (21) that Jesus and the disciples ate the passover on the third day of the week.[31] This could be explained on Mlle Jaubert's theory, but the theory itself creates too many other problems.

If, however, Enochic and Essene "Old Calendarism" did not pass into Christianity (which too clearly aimed, at first, to relativize the value of almost all religious observances), may we perhaps see a shadow of it in the Colossians' attachment to calendrical concerns as well as to the influence of supernatural powers (Col 2:8-23)? Further, if "Old Calendarism" as such did not survive, Christianity remained vulnerable to outbreaks of this kind of conservatism—witness the Quartodeciman dispute in the second century, the dispute between the Celtic Church and Rome about the reckoning of Easter, Russian Old Calendarism, and other conservative movements such as the "Old Believers," and Catholic reactionary movements such as that which has rejected liturgical change since Vatican II. The last two examples also show how easily the apocalyptic language of Antichrist comes to the lips of those whose sense of an eternally changeless liturgy is threatened.

The Temple is a more fruitful subject for examination. Few would disagree that here, from the prophetic criticism of presumptuous

---

[30] *La Date de la Cène* (Paris: 1957), English Trans. *The Date of the Last Supper* (Staten Island, N.Y.: Alba House, 1965).

[31] *Didascalia Apostolorum*, R.H. Connolly ed (Oxford: Clarendon Press, 1929), 181.

reliance on the temple cult through the Enochic and Essene criticisms
to those voiced in early Christianity, we have more of a visible stream
than an underground channel. Here a few summary remarks must
suffice. Of course there are different attitudes to the Temple in the
New Testament. Jesus appears to have respected it and chosen to
teach in its courts, but he also relativized its value and foretold its
destruction without any sense of final disaster. Among New Testament writers, Luke, especially in Acts, shows a positive attitude to the
Temple. This attitude makes his insertion of Stephen's speech all the
more striking. Stephen's violent attack (Acts 7), which finally denies
the value of a temple as such, has often been analysed as reflecting
disaffected, perhaps Samaritan sentiment. Similar hostility can probably be discerned in the Book of Revelation (esp. ch. 11). The Letter
to the Hebrews, which I am inclined to see as addressed to readers of
"dissident" background, seems curiously unaware of the Temple.[32]
The writer's meditation concentrates on the desert tabernacle in a
timeless present. This might imply alienation from the actual Temple,
but it would be hard, if not impossible, to prove such a case. After all,
Josephus discusses the temple cult in the present tense after it has
ceased (C. Apionem II, 193-8). Likewise, the activity of the priests is
mentioned in the present tense by 1 Clement (40), and the sacrifices
by various Christian critics (e.g. Barnabas 2, Ad Diognetum 3) who
seem unaware that their mockery no longer has an existing target.

However, apart from attitudes to the Jerusalem Temple itself,
there is a particular phenomenon which may even be regarded as a
distinct stream. This is the taste for designing "blueprints" for the
ideal temple and/or temple city, with the characteristic of more
emphasis on squareness than was realized in the second Temple or in
that of Herod. This activity begins, to our knowledge, with Ezekiel's
visionary plan, which is insistent on squareness (Ez 40-43), 1 Enoch
90:28 looks forward to a new temple brought by God, but does not
describe its plan. The most developed "blueprint" for an ideal temple
is, of course, the Temple Scroll found at Qumran and possibly referred
to in CD 5:2ff.[33] (I cannot discuss here the problems of relationship
between these documents and the Qumran community.) As a Mosaic
pseudepigraph, the Temple Scroll stands with Jubilees in claiming
the authority of Torah. Its reckoning of feasts seems to be by some
form of the older calendar, and it proposes a plan of an ideal temple
city and temple arranged in concentric squares, on lines nearer to

---

[32] Murray, "Jews, Hebrews and Christians" (n. 1 above), 205.
[33] Cf. B. Z. Wacholder, The Dawn of Qumran (Cincinnati: Hebrew Union College
Press, 1983), 112-29.

Ezekiel than to the second Temple. To be sure, much of the scroll consists of detailed *halakhah,* and to that extent, like much in the Qumran documents, is in a different value system from most early Christian teaching. (However, the marriage code for the king in 11Q Temple 57, 15-18, apparently referred to in CD 5:2, can suggest a halachic background for Jesus' teaching on divorce, as J. Fitzmyer has argued.)[34] But to return to the square plan, it is striking that in Revelation 21 the holy city is a perfect cube, with twelve gates commemorating the twelve tribes, as in 11Q Temple 40-41. Yet it contains *no temple,* God and the Lamb being its only temple (Rev 21:22). There could hardly be a more vivid symbolization of early Christianity's claim to need no temple as such (except for metaphors transferring the theme to Christ, the apostles and Christians), nor of the claim that, whatever authority had resided in the Temple, Jesus transcends and supersedes it. Is there, in a way, a "stream" from the authority-claim made by Jubilees and the Temple Scroll to the new movement which acknowledged Jesus as the living and final source of Torah?

The last strand which I wish to mention is that of anger on behalf of the oppressed poor, which comes out so strongly in the Epistle of Enoch and again in New Testament writers, especially Luke. But here it is enough to refer to the work of George Nickelsburg.[35] Of course, anyone can be angry with oppressors, and if this proposed link stood alone it would hardly secure a whole chain. The same might be said of Nickelsburg's suggestion of a significant link, consisting in the location of revelation scenes in Upper Galilee on the slopes of Hermon (where the angels had conspired to rebel, 1 Enoch 6:6!), which could connect Enoch (ibid. 13:7-9), Levi (Test, Levi 6:6) and Jesus' words to Peter (Mt 16:17-19).[36] But Nickelsburg's arguments do not stand alone as imaginative speculations. They relate to a broader picture which is becoming clearer, and they are confirmed by the convergence of similar interpretations of other phenomena.

I am very conscious of the incompleteness of this sketch. If it takes two to make a quarrel, traditions of hostility need to be traced from both ends of the relationship, and I have consistently neglected any approach from what I have called the "establishment" side. I must leave that to others, especially those trained by Jacob Neusner. If

---

[34] "The Matthean Divorce Texts and some New Testament Evidence", TS 37 (1976), 197-226.
[35] *Resurrection. . .* (n. 26 above), ch. 4; "Riches, the Rich and God's Judgment. . ." (n. 7 above).
[36] G. W. E. Nickelsburg, "Enoch, Peter and Levi. . ." (n. 7 above).

there is any merit in the approach adopted in this paper, I hope it will be tested from the side of the Judaism which was the object of the disaffection discussed here—the Judaism which was rallied and reorganized by the rabbis of Jamnia to become the dominant surviving form. I have sketched a case for an alternative and partially distinct development from the religion of ancient Israel—an alternative which had its own attitudes to the works canonized by the Jews as *Tanach*, and which also treasured other expressions of a heritage believed to be older, and to have a higher authority than the reconstruction in force in Jerusalem. I have proposed the hypothesis that significant features of early Christianity reflect this alternative and disaffected background, and can be ascribed partly to its influence.

E.P. Sanders quotes approvingly "Schweitzer's argument that a theme cannot be central which does not explain anything else".[37] I suggest that the hypothesis explored in this paper can explain far more about early Christianity than scholars have been able to see, as long as they were tied to a set of fixed assumptions about Judaism, apocalypticism, Hellenism and several other problematical categories. It has been assumed that the early Christians created new theological insights by interaction with the hellenistic world. But who *knows* that that is the dominant influence, rather than older religious ideas and traditions which had come down in Israel and, in related forms, in the whole near East? Why should this material not have been at hand in already formed complexes, ready to facilitate that extraordinary burst of theologizing about Jesus which Martin Hengel insists was so early, and not merely the product of the interaction between the Christian message and the hellenistic world?[38]

To appreciate this hypothesis, we must rethink assumptions about the relationship of early Christianity to "Jewish" sources, and about that of the un-canonized literature to canonical *Tanach*. I Enoch and the works related to it have been interpreted mainly with regard to Mesopotamian sources and the canonical *Tanach*. But, by looking beside and behind the latter within Israelite tradition, it may be possible to discover an alternative tradition which did not win. There are abundant points of contact between that alternative tradition and the canonical Scriptures, but they are points of contact, not necessarily indications of simple dependence. Many features of the alternative tradition favored the new Christian movement as the Jerusalem establishment could not, and those whose dreams were formed by the

---

[37] *Paul and Palestinian Judaism* (n. 28 above), 441.
[38] *The Son of God* (n. 24 above), especially p. 2, but this is the thesis of the whole book.

alternative tradition could have reasons to recognize Jesus different from those which a Jerusalem priest or rabbi might formulate.

And so back to our key categories in this conference. I suggest that Christianity inherited older ways of being "outsiders" in the Jewish family, ant that early Christian ideas of "self" and "other" had a complex prehistory. I suggest that an ironically and tragically fateful scenario for the future of the Israelite family was scripted when the exiled élite returned from Babylon under the Persians, and imposed their revision of religion on brethren stubbornly attached to other and older ways of thinking about the powers of heaven and earth.

New Testament Stud. 20, pp. 419–431

A. F. J. KLIJN

THE STUDY OF
JEWISH CHRISTIANITY

In 1830 F. C. Baur tried to demonstrate that the early Church was split up into Jewish Christians and Gentile Christians, but more than a hundred years later H. Köster wrote: '...a label such as, for example, "Jewish-Christians" is misleading insofar as everyone in the first generation of Christianity was a Jewish-Christian anyway...'.[1] In spite of this observation it still seemed possible to organize a 'colloque' on Jewish Christianity[2] and to publish a book with many contributions to this subject.[3] But it cannot be denied that the word 'Jewish Christian' poses a problem which we shall study in the present essay. First we shall give a brief survey of the study of Jewish Christianity from F. C. Baur to the present time in order to show the development of the word 'Jewish Christian', and with the results of this survey we shall then try to show what can be regarded as belonging to the field of Jewish Christianity at the present moment.

Modern study of Jewish Christianity began with F. C. Baur in 1830. He started from I Cor. i. 11–12 where it is said that some Christians called themselves after Paul and others after Apollos, Cephas or Christ. He suggested that we are actually dealing with only two groups of Christians, some who considered themselves to be followers of Paul and others who were followers of Peter. The Petrine group was supposed to be identical with the group called after Christ 'weil sie die unmittelbare Verbindung mit Christus als Hauptmerkmal des ächten apostolischen Ansehens aufstellte...'.[4] Paul's opponents can also be detected in his other letters: 'Dieselben judaisirenden Gegner, gegen welche sich der Apostel in den beiden Briefen an die korinthische Gemeinde so nachdrücklich erklärte, begegnen uns auch in anderen Briefen desselben Apostels in mehreren Stellen...'[5] The same group he found in post-apostolic times in the writings of Irenaeus, Eusebius and Epiphanius, in so far as they wrote about Jewish-Christian heresies.[6] Baur

---

[1] H. Köster, 'ΓΝѠΜΑΙ ΔΙΑΦΟΡΟΙ: the origin and nature of diversification in the history of early Christianity', *H. Th. Rev.* LVIII (1965), 279–318, esp. p. 380.

[2] *Aspects du Judéo-Christianisme*, colloque de Strasbourg, 23–25 avril 1964 (Paris, 1965).

[3] *Judéo-Christianisme*. Recherches historiques et théologiques offertes en hommage au Cardinal Jean Daniélou (Paris, 1972).

[4] F. C. Baur, 'Die Christuspartei in der korinthischen Gemeinde, der Gegensatz des petrinischen und paulinischen Christenthums in der ältesten Kirche, der Apostel Paulus in Rom', *Tübinger Zeitschr. für Theol.* (1831), 3. H. pp. 61–206, p. 84, cf. pp. 97/8.

[5] Baur, *art. cit.* p. 107, about Philippians, p. 107, and about Galatians, pp. 108–14.

[6] Baur, *art. cit.* pp. 114–15, cf. Irenaeus, *adv. haer.* I. 26, Eusebius, *hist. eccl.* III. 27 and Epiphanius, *pan.* XXX.

also tried to prove that the Church in Rome was founded by Peter's followers who lived originally in Jerusalem,[1] in connection with which he wrote:

Ja, wie aus dem Briefe an die Römer selbst deutlich zu ersehen ist, hatten schon damals in pharisäischen Sinne judaisirende Irrlehre derselben Art, wie diejenigen waren, die die Gemeinde in Galatien, Korinth und an andern Orten von der ihnen durch den Apostel Paulus gegebenen Richtung abzulenken suchten, auch in Rom nicht ohne Erfolg denselben Versuch gemacht.[2]

According to Baur a very important witness for this Petrine Christianity was the Pseudo-Clementine writings. Baur emphasized the struggle between Simon Magus (a name denoting the apostle Paul) and Peter described in these writings. He considered of special significance the passage *Homil.* XVII 13 in which it is said by Peter that real apostleship cannot be based upon revelation but must go back to a personal acquaintance with Jesus.[3]

This means that Baur pointed to two different groups in the early Church, of which the Jewish Christians are the oldest party. They were found in the Church of Jerusalem, at the beginning in the Church of Rome and finally in Jewish-Christian sects like the Ebionites. Paul's opponents in Galatia, Philippi and especially Corinth were representatives of the same group. They showed their adherence to Peter and proclaimed that Paul could not be called a legitimate apostle.

At the end of the nineteenth century Baur had lost all his followers. As the last one we may consider Hilgenfeld, of whom Schoeps wrote:

Als der letzte Säule der Schule, Adolf Hilgenfeld, in 1906 die Augen schloß, war durch Ritschl, Lechler, Harnack u.a. der Tübinger Standpunkt bereits so gründlich abgetan, daß die während der letzten fünfundzwanzig Jahre in der 'Zeitschrift für wissenschaftliche Theologie' veröffentlichen Arbeiten Hilgenfelds u.a. kaum mehr Beachtung gefunden haben.[4]

But even Hilgenfeld differed from Baur. He was fully aware of the differences within the group which Baur called Jewish Christian.[5] He accepted roughly two main groups. Taking as his basis the information given by ecclesiastical writers about Jewish-Christian sects he came to the conclusion that the Nazoraeans were descendants of the non-Pharisaic group of Jewish Christians in the early Church of Jerusalem, although their members were faithful followers of the Jewish Law. This group came into contact with the doctrine of Elchasai at a later date.[6] Apart from this group he noticed the extreme group of the Ebionites, as they are called by ecclesiastical writers,[7] who 'den Paulus ausschließenden Christenthum als Weltreligion durchführen wollte'.[8]

Hilgenfeld regarded himself as a follower of Baur. As his real opponents he

[1] Baur, *art. cit.* pp. 163-4.   [2] *Ibid.* 165-6.
[3] *Ibid.* 116-17, cf. Gal. ii. 12.
[4] H. J. Schoeps, *Theologie und Geschichte des Judenchristentums* (Tübingen, 1949).
[5] A. Hilgenfeld, *Judentum und Judenchristentum* (Leipzig, 1886, reprint Hildensheim, 1566), pp. 116-17.   [6] *Ibid.* p. 117.
[7] *Ibid.* pp. 117-20.   [8] *Ibid.* p. 118.

mentioned those who tried to prove that the 'Urapostel' lived in peace with
Paul; who said that these 'Urapostel' must be distinguished from the anti-
Pauline group in the original Church of Jerusalem and that this last group
disappeared within a short time.[1]

It is obvious how difficult it is to speak of Jewish Christians in general if we
have to accept different groups within the early Church of Jerusalem. It
becomes, however, still more problematic as soon as we become aware of the
fact that Christians of Jewish as well as those of Gentile descent can be called
Jewish Christians since their Christian ideas were taken from Judaism. These
problems had to be dealt with at the beginning of this century. We choose
three scholars who went into this problem, viz. Hort who wrote a monograph
about Jewish Christianity, and Harnack and Seeberg who had to write about
the subject in connection with their 'Dogmengeschichten'.[2]

These three scholars tried to show that the word 'Jewish-Christian' is open
to misunderstanding since Christianity as a whole originated within a Jewish
community and its early development took place under the influence of
Jewish ideas.[3] But they still insisted that a special kind of Christianity be
called 'Jewish-Christian'. According to Hort it can be applied to Christians
'ascribing universal validity to national ordinances'.[4] Harnack wrote:

Dieser Ausdruck ist ausschließlich für solche Christen zu verwenden, welche im ganzen
Umfange oder in irgend welchem Masse, sei es auch in einem Minimum, die nationalen und
politischen Formen des Judenthums und die Beobachtung des mosaischen Gesetzes ohne
Umdeutung als für das Christenthum, mindestens für das Christenthum geborener Juden,
wesentlich festhielten oder diese Formen zwar verwarfen, aber doch eine Prärogative des
jüdischen Volkes auch im Christenthum annahmen.[5]

And Seeberg regarded it as Christianity 'sofern sie prinzipiell das Christentum
mit dem angestammten Judentum, seinen Satzungen, Bräuchen und Ten-
denzen verband'.[6]

Harnack said that the original Church of Jerusalem was Jewish Christian
and that in Palestine it was a majority group.[7] He referred to Justin Martyr
in order to show that Jewish Christianity displayed a variety of forms.[8]
According to Harnack we may accept that we find a similar variety as in

[1] *Ibid.* p. 10.
[2] F. J. A. Hort, *Judaistic Christianity* (Cambridge and London, 1894); A. Harnack, *Lehrbuch der
Dogmengeschichte* (Tübingen, 1909⁴), pp. 310–34; and R. Seeberg, *Lehrbuch der Dogmengeschichte*,
(Leipzig, 1922³, reprint Darmstadt, 1965), pp. 249–67.
[3] Hort *op. cit.* pp. 1–5, Harnack, *op. cit.* pp. 310–11, and Seeberg, *op. cit.* pp. 249–55.
[4] Hort, *op. cit.* p. 5.
[5] Harnack, *op. cit.* pp. 311–12.
[6] Seeberg, *op. cit.* p. 250.
[7] Harnack, *op. cit.* p. 313.
[8] Justin Martyr, *Dial. c. Tryphone* 47, speaks about the following possibilities: Christians living
according to the Jewish Law will not be saved unless they ask other Christians to do the same or when
they do not wish to live in communion with other Christians; some Christians disagreeing with
Justin say that Christians living according to the Law cannot be saved; Justin himself applies this to
Christians who did not live according to the Law first but later changed their way of living and also
to Jews who are not Christians.

Judaism itself. Apart from a legalistic attitude one may accept the influence of Oriental religions and Greek philosophy. Harnack pointed to two main branches. From the ecclesiastical writers we know about Nazoraeans and Ebionites, which are only two names for the same group. From Paul's letters we know of Gnostic Jewish Christianity. To that group the Ebionites, according to Epiphanius, belonged, the Elchasaites[1] and also Symmachus.[2]

These Jewish Christians, who lived mainly in Palestine and the Syrian area, did not influence the development of the Church and its doctrine, according to Harnack.[3]

If we compare Harnack with Baur, we see that both apply the name 'Jewish Christian' to the same group of Christians. Harnack, however, accepted more than one Jewish-Christian community and denied any influence on the Gentile Christian Church.

Seeberg and Hort emphasized the agreement in opinion between the apostles in Jerusalem and the rest of the Church. Both pointed to Hegesippus who, being a Palestinian Christian, did not notice any deviation from his ideas in Gentile Christian Churches.[4] Because of this supposed agreement Hort and Seeberg had to accept a wide gap between the Church in Jerusalem and later Jewish-Christian groups in the Syrian area. They assumed that the year A.D. 135 was very important because from that time on Jews were not allowed to live in Jerusalem any longer. Hort wrote that after 135 Jewish Christians came to live in isolation and antagonism to the Gentile Christian Church in Jerusalem.[5] Seeberg favoured the same opinion, stating that Jewish Christianity lived 'in einem Wettbewerb mit der Autorität der neuen Kirche in Jerusalem'.[6] Hort even went so far as to deny any reflection of the original Jerusalem Church.[7] Seeberg gave a more detailed picture of the development. He supposed that in the Jerusalem Church there existed a Pharisaic group of Christians which can be compared with the extreme Jewish Christians mentioned by Justin Martyr. This again is the same group as that mentioned by Irenaeus and Origen under the name Ebionites. Their main characteristic was their anti-Pauline attitude. This group joined

---

[1] Epiphanius based his description of the Ebionites mainly on the *Periodoi Petrou*, one of the sources of the Pseudo-Clementines. Deviations from Irenaeus and Hippolytus were supposed to be due to the influence of Elchasai on the Ebionite doctrine, cf. *pan.* XXX. 3. 2 and 17. 5–6.

[2] Harnack noticed the agreement between remarks about the Elchasaite doctrine of a returning Christ (cf. Hippolytus, *ref.* IX. 14. 2 and X. 29. 1–3 and Epiphanius, *pan.* LIII. 1. 8) and Marius Victorinus, *in ep. ad Gal.* 1. 15: *dicunt* (sc. Symmachians) *enim eum ipsum Adam esse, et esse animam generalem. et alia huiusmodi blasphema.*

[3] Harnack, *Dogmengeschichte*, p. 317.

[4] Hort, *Judaistic Christianity*, pp. 164–9, and Seeberg, *Dogmengeschichte*, pp. 253–4. Seeberg refers to Eusebius, *hist. eccl.* IV. 22. 1–4, where Hegesippus is quoted as saying that the Church in Corinth lived according to the true doctrine up to Bishop Primus, and calls the primitive Church 'virgin' since she was not polluted by heretical doctrines, cf. also III. 32. 7.

[5] Hort, *op. cit.* p. 200.

[6] Seeberg, *op. cit.* p. 255.

[7] Hort, *op. cit.* p. 176, contrary to J. B. Lightfoot, *Saint Paul's Epistle to the Galatians* (London, 1884[8]), p. 317.

Christians with gnostic ideas. In this way there came into being 'ein gnostisch-pharisäistisches Judenchristentum'. This group already existed in the time of Paul, who dealt with them in his letter to the Colossians. The same group is to be found in the Pastoral Epistles and is responsible for the Pseudo-Clementines. They can be identified with the Ebionites mentioned by Epiphanius.[1] Contrary to Harnack, Seeberg accepted a group of Nazoraeans with more orthodox principles than the Ebionites.[2]

This means that Seeberg supposed that an anti-Pauline group belonging to the Jerusalem Church came into contact with gnosticizing communities at an early date and can be found again in Jewish-Christian heresies after 135. Moreover, Seeberg stated that the Jewish Christians did not influence the development of the orthodox Church and its doctrines.[3]

If we examine these ideas we notice that the study of Jewish Christianity does not deal with a particular group of Christians with special ideas but with the development of a particular regional branch of that Church. Scholars tried to trace the origin, development and influence of the Church of Jerusalem in the light of and in connection with Christian life in Palestine and Syria. This life is reflected in writings such as the Pseudo-Clementines, the Jewish-Christian Gospels and groups like the Ebionites and Nazoraeans. Scholars accepted some relation between the Church of Jerusalem or part of it and later Christianity in Palestine and Syria, but the development was not supposed to be uninterrupted. That interruption took place in the year 135, after which gnostic ideas became more and more influential. The isolated position of these Christians does not make them interesting for our study of the Church as a whole. This remained the opinion up to the middle of this century, as we learn from Lietzmann's *History of the Early Church*[4] and from W. Bauer's study on heresy and orthodoxy in the early Church, which almost totally neglected the Jewish-Christian influence on early Christian life and doctrine.[5]

A new impetus to Jewish-Christian studies was given by H.-J. Schoeps who called his work 'die späte Rehabilitierung eines geläuterten Tübinger

---

[1] Seeberg, *op. cit.* p. 259.

[2] Seeberg agrees with Th. Zahn, *Geschichte des neutestamentlichen Kanons*, II (Erlangen–Leipzig, 1890), pp. 668–73. The Nazoraeans are mentioned for the first time by Epiphanius, *pan.* XXIX, and later by Jerome and Augustine.

[3] Seeberg, *op. cit.* pp. 250 and 266.

[4] H. Lietzmann, *Geschichte der alten Kirche*, I (Berlin–Leipzig, 1937²), pp. 184–99, supposed a rather great difference between Jerusalem and later Jewish Christianity and wrote, p. 184: 'die geschichtliche Entwickelung ging über die Männer von Jerusalem hinweg'. After Pella Jewish Christianity was influenced by Jewish sects. More in agreement with Harnack seems E. Meyer, *Ursprung und Anfänge des Christentums*, III (Stuttgart–Berlin, 1923, reprint Darmstadt, 1962), pp. 583–602, who appears to accept a close relationship between the original Jerusalem Church – already isolated from the rest of the Church during Paul's lifetime – and the Ebionites and Nazoraeans.

[5] See W. Bauer, 'Rechtgläubigkeit und Ketzerei im ältesten Christentum', in: *Beiträge z. hist. Theol.* 10 (Tübingen, 1933), herausgegeben von G. Strecker (1964), p. 245. H. J. Schonfield, *The History of Jewish Christianity from the first to the twentieth Century* (London, 1936), did not contribute to the study of this subject.

Standpunktes'.[1] This caused some misunderstanding, because of which he had to write a second book about the subject, but it is doubtful whether he really can be called a follower of Baur.[2]

Schoeps wanted to write about the flourishing period of Ebionite Christianity in the second and third century.[3] As a major witness for this period he accepted the Pseudo-Clementines, which he called representatives of 'die intransigente Partei des Justinischen Berichtes'.[4] This party was in turn identified with the Pharisaic Christians mentioned in Acts xv. 5[5] and with Paul's opponents mentioned in his letters to the Galatians and Corinthians.[6] In order to give a clear picture of Ebionite life and practices he drew attention to the translation of the Old Testament of Symmachus, the Didascalia, quotations of Jewish-Christian Gospels found among ecclesiastical writers and remarks on Jewish-Christian sects in the same sources. The historicity of the flight of Jerusalem Christians to Pella and the relation between these Christians and the Ebionites is demonstrated not only by Eusebius' information but especially by passages in Symmachus and the Pseudo-Clementines.[7]

We notice some agreement and disagreement between Schoeps and his predecessors. He agrees with the generally accepted view that the Jerusalem Church was split up into different parties, of which the Pharisaic one was extreme Jewish Christian. Already Seeberg supposed a relation between this party and the origin of the Pseudo-Clementines. Like Harnack, Seeberg and Lietzmann, Schoeps also wrote about the Ebionites: '...einen aktiven Einfluß auf die kirchliche Entwicklung haben sie (sc. the Ebionites) damals (sc. in the third century) schon nicht mehr ausgeübt'.[8] He differed from other scholars by denying that Paul's opponents and the Pseudo-Clementines should be called gnostic. Only the Elchasaites are representatives of a 'Gnostisches Ebionitismus', according to Schoeps.[9]

However, after the many studies devoted to the sources of the Clementines in this and the previous century[10] it was impossible to return to a point of view that excludes any gnostic influence on these writings. For this reason Schoeps did not influence the studies appearing after 1950. Goppelt reflected the well-established facts, assuming that no Jewish Christianity existed in the

---

[1] H. J. Schoeps, *Theologie und Geschichte des Judenchristentums* (Tübingen, 1949), p. 5.
[2] H. J. Schoeps, *Urgemeinde Judenchristentum Gnosis* (Tübingen, 1956), in which also a list of reviews can be found.
[3] Schoeps, *Theologie*, p. 295.
[4] Schoeps, *Theologie*, p. 8.
[5] Schoeps, *Theologie*, p. 261, and *Urgemeinde...*, p. 23.
[6] See Gal. ii. 12; II Cor. xi. 5 and xii. 11, see also Acts xxi. 18 ff., Schoeps, *Urgemeinde...*, pp. 7–8.
[7] Schoeps refers to *Rec.* 1. 37 (Syriac translation), 1. 39 (Latin translation) and Symmachus. *Ecclesiastes* 12. 5.
[8] Schoeps, *Theologie*, p. 295.
[9] Schoeps, *Theologie*, pp. 325–34.
[10] See survey of these studies in G. Strecker, *Das Judenchristentum der Pseudoklementinen*, in: *Texte u. Unters.* 70. Bd (Berlin, 1958), pp. 1–34.

diaspora after the year A.D. 70[1] and that the Church of Jerusalem as a whole disappeared into 'judaistisches Sektierertum'.[2] Apart from 'die nomistisch-judaistische Grundströmung'[3] represented by the well-known Jewish-Christian sects he spoke of 'synkretistische Sonderbildungen'[4] which included groups like the Elchasaites and a work such as the *Kerygmata Petrou*, one of the sources of the Pseudo-Clementines.

The accepted ideas are represented in the well-known encyclopaedias. Kümmel stated that those members of the Church can be called Jewish Christian 'deren Glieder ausschließlich oder im wesentlichen aus geborenen Juden bestehen und die sich bewußt auf dem Boden des Judentums halten',[5] but he limited his survey to a description of the Palestine Church for which he considered the inquiries into the Pseudo-Clementines as of no importance.[6] Strecker wrote that 'Ebionitismus' is 'eine complexe Größe' whereupon he devoted parts of his article to Paul's opponents, Jewish-Christian sects and Gospels, the Pseudo-Clementines and Elchasai without going into the possibility of a historical and doctrinal relationship existing between them.[7]

About ten years after Schoeps' study Daniélou published a theology of Jewish Christianity.[8] In general his ideas about this phenomenon are not new. He maintains that the name can be applied to three forms of Christianity. In the first place we know of a group which denied that Christ is God. This group was studied, according to Daniélou, by Schoeps. To this group also belonged Paul's opponents, but this Jewish Christianity 'à côté de ces groupes de stricte observance juive, présente des judéo-chrétiens syncrétistes...'.[9]

In the second place the name can be given to the Christians of the original Church of Jerusalem. According to Daniélou this community was 'parfaitement orthodoxe'. The group disappeared after a short time.[10]

In the third place Jewish Christianity is 'une forme de pensée chrétienne qui n'implique pas de lien avec la communauté juive, mais qui s'exprime dans des cadres empruntés au judaisme'.[11] Daniélou was only interested in this last group.

It is not new to define Jewish Christianity as second-century Christianity in general. Already Hort, Harnack and Seeberg wrote about the Jewish origin of the Christian Church and the development of Jewish ideas in the different Christian communities. Daniélou went into many of these Jewish

---

[1] L. Goppelt, *Christentum und Judentum im ersten und zweiten Jahrhundert*, in: *Beitr. z. Förd. christl. Theol.* 2. R., 55. B. (Gütersloh, 1954), p. 97.
[2] *Ibid.* p. 167.
[3] *Ibid.* p. 167-8.
[4] *Ibid.* pp. 168-76.
[5] W. G. Kümmel, s.v. 'Judenchristentum', in: *Rel. in Gesch. u. Gegenw.* iii³, c. 967-76, c. 967. See also his 'Urchristentum', in: *Theol. Rundschau* xxii (1954), 138-211, esp. pp. 147-51. Kümmel, Judenchristentum..., c. 968.
[7] G. Strecker, s.v. 'Ebionitismus', in: *Reallex. f. Ant. u. Christentum* iv, c. 487-500.
[8] J. Daniélou, *Théologie du Judéo-Christianisme* (Desclée, 1957).
[9] *Ibid.* p. 18.
[10] *Ibid.*   [11] *Ibid.* p. 19.

influences but he failed to demonstrate that the different examples can be combined into a 'Théologie du Judéo-Christianisme'. Neither are his ideas about the other groups of Jewish Christians clear in any way. He failed to consider possible groups in the original Church of Jerusalem and in a chapter about heterodox Jewish Christianity he spoke of groups and writings such as the Elchasaites and the Pseudo-Clementines and and also of Carpocrates, the well-known gnostic leader.[1]

Nevertheless we may say that Daniélou took a step which had to be taken sooner or later. It is impossible to isolate the Jerusalem Church, Palestinian or Syriac Christianity from the rest of the Church in the Graeco-Roman world. We are dealing with one Christian movement in which the Jewish ideas and practices and the Jews themselves played their part in Jerusalem and Rome, Ephesus and Alexandria. For this reason it is impossible to define the term 'Jewish-Christian' because it proved to be a name that can readily be replaced by 'Christian'.[2]

This, however, does not mean that studies on Jewish Christianity did not deal with particular subjects. From Baur to the present time scholars were struck by the immense Jewish influence on the Church *apart from the many ideas already adopted in the New Testament and taken over by ecclesiastical writers of a later date.* It was this wealth of ideas which Baur deemed present in one group of Christians only, but which Daniélou finally showed to be present all over the Christian world during the first centuries. The object of the study of Jewish Christianity is to detect the presence, the origin, the development and the disappearance of this Jewish influence. This influence consisted of Jewish practices like circumcision; a Jewish way of life, like distinguishing between pure and impure food; or Jewish haggadic material, like speculations about Adam.

In Greek and Latin writings known to us the quantity of this material is scant, because in the Greek and Latin world Jewish influence was not only comparatively small but also eliminated within a short time. There are, however, still a number of subjects which from the very beginning of Jewish Christian studies attracted the attention of scholars.

In the Pauline epistles we find Christians opposing Paul's preaching who

---

[1] *Ibid.* pp. 67–98. Daniélou's study was frequently reviewed, but see especially R. A. Kraft, 'In Search of "Jewish Christianity" and its "Theology"', in: *Judéo-Christianisme...*, pp. 81–92.

[2] A number of ideas about definitions: J. Munck, 'Jewish-Christianity in Post-Apostolic Times', *N.T.S.* VI (1959/60), 103–16, p. 103: 'The words "Jewish-Christian" and "Jewish Christianity" are used in several different senses within the field of New Testament research. Some scholars – no doubt oneself included on occasion – use them with varying significance in the same article or book, so that the reader is either led astray, or discovers that the words do not have the same meaning every time they occur'; M. Simon, 'Problèmes du Judéo-Christianisme', in: *Aspects...*. pp. 1–17: M. Simon and A. Benoit, *Le Judaïsme et le Christianisme Antique* (Paris, 1968), p. 258: 'On a maintes fois souligné la difficulté qu'il y a à définir le judéo-christianisme', and R. N. Longenecker, *The Christology of the Early Jewish Christianity*, in: *Stud. in Bibl. Theol.*, sec. Ser. XVII (London, 1970), 1: 'The expression Jewish Christianity is employed in a variety of ways today.'

are of Jewish descent,[1] favour Jewish practices,[2] or, in some way, interlard their preaching with Jewish haggadic material.[3] These groups can also be found in the letters of Ignatius.[4] The origin, development, influence and interrelationship of these groups are still matters of dispute,[5] but they show that the Church was accompanied from its beginning by Christians much more openly in favour of their Jewish background than people in the Apostolic Church and later orthodoxy were able to accept.

Of particular interest is the origin of two local Churches, viz. the one in Rome and the other in Alexandria. According to very old traditions Rome was founded by Christians of Jewish descent.[6] Conflicts between them and Christians of a Gentile background are known from Paul's letter to this Church. Strong emphasis on the text of the Old Testament in Clement's letter to Corinth[7] and particular ideas about Christ and the Holy Spirit in the *Pastor Hermae* are witnesses of Jewish influence.[8] Interesting too is a sermon called Pseudo-Cyprian, *adversus Iudaeos*, in which the Jewish members of the Roman Church are admonished to stop boasting of their Jewish descent.[9] Apart from these signs of Jewish influence we may draw attention to Latin writings like V Esra and the *Passio Perpetuae* in which Daniélou discovered many examples of the influence of Jewish apocalyptic ideas.[10]

It is not impossible to imagine that Irenaeus' chapter about the Ebionites was inspired by particular groups in the Western Church which did not wish to adjust themselves to a development in which there was no room for some ancient, originally Jewish, ideas.[11]

The origin of the Alexandrian Church is also unknown, though we may gather from Acts that Christians had been living in this city at a very early

---

[1] II Cor. xi. 22, cf. Phil. iii. 5 and Tit. i. 10.

[2] Gal. ii. 3-4. vi. 12 and Col. ii. 16. [3] Tit. i. 14.

[4] Ignatius, *Magn.* VII. 1; IX. 1; X. 2, *Philad.* VI and VIII. 2.

[5] The idea that the pseudo-apostles (II Cor. xi. 13) came from Jerusalem, cf. E. Käsemann, 'Die Legitimität des Apostels. Eine Untersuchung zu II Korinther 10–13', *Zeitschr. f. d. neutestamentl. Wissensch.* XLI (1942), 33–71, was not accepted, cf. R. Bultmann, 'Exegetische Probleme des zweiten Korintherbriefes', *Symb. Bibl. Upsalienses* IX (1947), 21, but see G. Strecker, 'Christentum und Judentum in den ersten beiden Jahrhunderten', *Evang. Theol.* XVI (1956), 458–77, p. 464. General information about the opponents in H. Köster, 'Häretiker im Urchristentum', in: *Rel. in Gesch. u. Gegenw.* III³, c. 17–21. See literature for Corinthians in D. Georgi, *Die Gegner des Paulus im 2. Korintherbrief*, in: *Wissensch. Monogr. z.A.u.N.T.* 11. Bd (Neukirchen, 1964); for Galatians in R. Jewett, 'The Agitators and the Galatian Congregation', *N.T.S.* XVII (1970/71), 198–212; for Philippians in A. F. J. Klijn, 'Paul's Opponents in Philippians III', *Nov. Test.* VII (1964/5), 278–84 and for Colossians in J. Lähnemann, 'Der Kolosserbrief', *Stud. z.N.T.* III (1971), 63–81.

[6] Ambrosiaster, *Comm. in ep. ad Rom.*, in: Migne, *Patr. Lat.* XVII, c. 46A.

[7] See D. A. Hagner, 'The Use of the Old and New Testament in Clement of Rome', in: *Suppl. to Nov. Test.* XXXIV (Leiden, 1973).

[8] S. Giet, 'Un courant judéo-chrétien à Rome au milieu de IIe siècle, in: *Aspects...*, pp. 95–112.

[9] D. van Damme, 'Pseudo-Cyrian, Adversus Iudaeos. Gegen die Judenchristen. Die älteste lateinische Predigt', in: *Paradosis* XII (Freiburg, 1969).

[10] J. Daniélou, 'La littérature Latine avant Tertullien', *Revue des Études Lat.* XLVIII, *1970* (Paris, 1971), pp. 357–75, and J. Daniélou, 'Le Ve Esdras et le Judéo-Christianisme Latin au second siècle', in: *Ex Orbe Religionum I, Studia G. Widengren Oblata*, in: *Stud. in the Hist. of Rel.* (Supplem. to *Numen*) XXI (Leiden, 1972), pp. 162–71. The Jewish apocalypses more than influenced Christianity since they were adopted by the Christian Church. [11] Irenaeus, *adv. haer.* I. 26. 2.

date.[1] The presence of two Gospels which were not accepted by the Church attests the existence of two groups in this city.[2] The Gospel of the Egyptians represents the gnostic Christians and the Gospel of the Hebrews Christians of Jewish descent. It is important to realize that the Gospel of the Hebrews and the Gospel of the Egyptians, mentioned by Clement of Alexandria and Origen, were not connected with a particular sect by these writers.[3] They were initially used by a Church which as a whole followed ideas different from those developed later. When they were introduced into the Alexandrian Church we can imagine that many Alexandrian Christians organized themselves in small groups of which one is called 'Ebionite' by Origen.[4]

We may accept that many haggadic ideas in the Gnostic writings found in Nag Hammadi were already known at this time.[5] They disappeared in the official Church but were taken up by those who grouped themselves in gnostic circles where Jewish ideas started to lead their own life.

In Asia Minor the influence of Jewish ideas was substantial from the very beginning, as can be seen from the letters to Galatia, Colossians and the Pastoral Epistles. The influence of Judaism can also be derived from the custom of celebrating Easter on the fourteenth of the month Nisan[6] and the doctrine of millenarianism.[7]

These are only a few remarks to show that a vast field of Jewish-Christian ideas is now known. The majority of Christians of Jewish descent were, however, living in the area of Palestine and Syria. The Church had its origin in a Jewish community in Jerusalem. From all Jewish Christian studies we know that it is difficult to obtain a clear picture of this Church. In Acts we read that there existed different parties in this Church,[8] but it is

---

[1] Cf. Acts xviii. 24–5.

[2] This can also be derived from the text of the New Testament used in Egypt, see A. F. J. Klijn, 'A Survey of the Researches into the Western Text of the Gospels and Acts, Part II (1949–69)', in: *Suppl. to Nov. Test.* XXI (Leiden, 1969), 32–50 and 66–70.

[3] The Gospel of the Hebrews is mentioned by Clement, *strom.* II. 9. 45 and v. 14. 96, and by Origen, *in Joh.* II. 12, cf. *hom. in Jer.* xv. 4 and *in Matth.* xv. 14.

[4] The Ebionites are not mentioned by Clement, but cf. Origen, *de princ.* IV. 3. 8, *hom. in Luc.* XVII. *hom. in Gen.* III. 5, *hom. in Jer.* XIX. 12, *in Matth.* XI. 12 and XVI. 12, *in Matth. comm. ser.* 79, *in Luc.*, XIV 18 ff., *in epist. ad Rom.* III. 11, *in epist. ad Tit.*, and *c. Cels.* II. 1, v. 61 and v. 66.

[5] M. Krause, 'Aussagen über das Alte Testament in z.T. bisher unveröffentlichen gnostischen Texten aus Nag Hammadi', in: *Ex Orbe...*, pp. 448–56, and B. A. Pearson, 'Jewish Haggadic Traditions in the Testimony of Truth From Nag Hammadi (CG IX, 3)', in: *Ex Orbe...*, pp. 457–70, with literature.

[6] See B. Lohse, *Das Passafest der Quartadezimaner*, in: *Beitr. z. Förd. christl. Theol.* LIV (1953).

[7] See J. Daniélou, 'La Typologie millénariste de la Semaine dans le Christianisme primitif', *Vig. Christ.* II (1948), 1–16 and H. Bietenhard, 'The Millennial Hope in the Early Church', *Scot. J. Theol.* VI (1953), 12–30.

[8] See B. Reicke, *Glaube und Leben in der Urgemeinde, Abhandl. z. Theol. des A.u.N.T.* XXXII (Zürich, 1957), and B. Reicke, 'Die Verfassung der Urgemeinde im Lichte jüdischer Dokumente', *Theol. Zeitschr.* X (1954), 95–112. See also J. Munck, *Paulus und die Heilsgeschichte*, (København, 1954), who emphasized the unanimity between Paul and the 'twelve'. In this connection it would be important to know who are meant by ἅγιοι, cf. Rom. xv. 25–6 and 31; I Cor. xvi. 1; II Cor. viii. 4, ix. 1 and 12, who receive support from Gentile Christian Churches, cf. K. F. Nickle, *The Collection*, in: *Stud. in Bibl. Theol.* XLVIII (London, 1966), and D. Georgi, 'Die Geschichte der Kollekte des Paulus für Jerusalem', in: *Theol. Forsch.* XXXVIII (Hamburg, 1965).

questionable whether we are allowed to trace the development of these parties with the help of information furnished by writings such as the Pseudo-Clementines[1] and groups like the Nazoraeans.[2] Many studies going into the sources of the synoptic Gospels pretend to discover traces of ideas favoured in Jerusalem, in Palestine or by Aramaic-speaking Christians,[3] but the information is often too scant to obtain a complete picture of a Church which was obviously far from uniform. The same can be said of archaeological discoveries.[4]

It is still a matter of dispute what the relationship between the Jerusalem Church and the rest of the Jewish population in that city was.[5] This, of course, has something to do with the flight to Pella mentioned by Eusebius. If the Christians really went to Pella, we may accept that they did not join the Jews in their struggle against Rome.[6] But even if these Christians escaped, it is still not clear whether they adhered to the ideas known to them while still in Jerusalem. Epiphanius wrote that in the region of Pella the Jerusalem Christians split up into two different sects, viz. the Nazoraeans and the Ebionites.[7] As we have seen, it is still an almost generally accepted view

---

[1] See Strecker, Christentum..., p. 466, but especially G. Strecker, *Das Judenchristentum der Pseudoklementinen*, in: *Texte u. Unters.* 70 (Berlin, 1958), p. 214 (about the *Kerygmata Petrou*): 'Der Gnostizismus und Hellenismus der Kerygmen schließen eine unmittelbare Beziehung zu der Urgemeinde aus'. Cf. also W. Schmithals, *Paul and James*, in: *Stud. in Bibl. Theol.* XLVI (London, 1963), 105: '...it is impossible to gain from their (Jewish Christian sects') traditions authentic material for the attitude of the primitive Jewish Christian church' and especially J. Munck, 'Jewish Christianity in Post-apostolic times', *N.T.S.* VI (1959/60), 103–16.

[2] See A. F. J. Klijn, 'Jerome's quotations from a Nazoraean interpretation of Isaiah', in: *Judéo-Christianisme...*, pp. 241–53.

[3] See E. Käsemann, 'Die Anfänge Christlicher Theologie', in: *Exegetische Versuche und Besinnungen*, II (Göttingen, 1965²), 82–104 (first published 1960), S. Schulz, *Q. Die Spruchquelle der Evangelisten*, (Zürich, 1972), and H. W. Kuhn, *Ältere Sammlungen im Markusevangelium* (Göttingen, 1973), esp. p. 232.

[4] See P. E. Testa, 'Il Simbolismo dei Giudeo-Cristiani', in: *Pubblicazioni dello Studium Biblicum Franciscanum N.* 14 (Gerusalemme, 1962), B. Bagatti, *L'Église de la Circoncision* (Jérusalem, 1965), L. Randellini, *La Chiesa dei Guideo-Cristiani* (Brescia, 1967) and E. Testa, *L'Huile de la Foi* (Jérusalem, 1967). See also the information taken from rabbinic sources by A. Schlatter, *Synagoge und Kirche bis zum Barkochba-Aufstand. Vier Studien zur Geschichte des Rabbinats und der jüdischen Christenheit in den ersten zwei Jahrhunderten* (Stuttgart, 1966, written in 1897, 1898, 1899 and 1915). The conclusions about Jewish Christianity drawn from a tenth-century Arabic writing by S. Pines, 'The Jewish Christians of the early centuries of Christianity according to a new source', *Proc. Israel Acad. Sci. and Hum.* II, no. 13 (1966), were not very favourably received, cf. E. Bammel, 'Excerpts from a New Gospel', *Nov. Test.* X (1968), 1–9 and S. Stern, 'Abd al-Jabbar's account of how Christ's religion was falsified by the adoption of Roman customs', *J. Th. Stud.*, n.s. XIX (1968/9), 128–85.

[5] The opinion of S. G. F. Brandon, *The Fall of Jerusalem and the Christian Church* (London, 1968²), that the Jerusalem Church fought with the other Jews side by side against the Romans and was totally annihilated except for some fugitives who went to Alexandria, did not receive wide acceptance, but cf. M. Goguel, *La Naissance du Christianisme* (Paris, 1946), p. 154: 'L'exode des Chrétiens ne prouve pas qu'ils se soient détachés des espérances nationales juives et désintéressés du sort de la ville de Jérusalem.'

[6] For this reason Brandon denied the historicity of this flight, see *op. cit.* pp. 168–73 and 263–4, and S. G. F. Brandon, *Jesus and the Zealots* (Manchester, 1967), p. 209. Of the same opinion are Strecker, *Judenchristentum...*, pp. 228–31, and J. Munck, 'Jewish Christianity'..., pp. 103–4. It is accepted by Schoeps, *Theologie*, pp. 47 and 269, and especially recently by M. Simon, 'La Migration à Pella. Légende ou Réalité?', in: *Judéo-Christianisme...*, pp. 37–54.

[7] See Epiphanius, *pan.* XXIX. 7. 8 (Nazoraeans) and XXX. 2. 7 (Ebionites).

that Christians from the Palestine area fell a victim to gnostic and baptist sects. This picture has to be modified. Epiphanius and Jerome wrote about the Nazoraeans in Beroea who lived according to the Jewish Law but accepted the virgin birth and the existence of a Gentile Church.[1] It is not impossible that these Aramaic-speaking Christians were descended from the main body of Jerusalem Christians.[2] Epiphanius' description of the Ebionites is a mixture of information given by Irenaeus and Hippolytus, on the one hand, and by an 'Ebionite' Gospel and the *Periodoi Petrou* on the other.[3] Actually he is a witness for the existence of some writings from which the Pseudo-Clementines originated and an apocryphal Gospel of unknown origin. The contents of these writings show that in the Syriac area Christians adhered to specific ideas, very often taken over from their Jewish environment. We should not refer to these as heretical groups, but consider them part of a vulgar Christianity which shows a great variety of different ideas, some more and some less in agreement with the general development in the Graeco-Roman world. It is interesting to see how a writing like the Didascalia tried to remove some Jewish practices from the Church.[4]

It is necessary to draw attention to the Elchasaites and the origin of the Edessene Church. The Elchasaites have always been regarded as a Jewish Christian sect although stamped by Gnostic ideas. They became very important since it became known recently that Mani grew up within an Elchasaite community.[5] The Edessene Church became important since the time it was maintained that the Gospel of Thomas originated in this Church, which displays a form that is supposed to be very ancient by some scholars.[6]

It is obvious that some of these general statements need correction. To call the Elchasaites 'Jewish Christian' is questionable. We are dealing with a Jewish apocalyptic sect which originated in Parthia but was influenced at a later date by Christian ideas of a kind that can be compared with those found in the Pseudo-Clementines.[7] Christianity in Edessa is interesting but it

---

[1] Epiphanius, *pan.* XXIX. 7. 7 and Jerome, *epist.* 112. 13 and *in Is.* 9. 1.

[2] See Klijn, Jerome's Quotations...

[3] A. F. J. Klijn and G. J. Reinink, *Patristic evidence for Jewish-Christian sects*, in: *Suppl. to Nov. Test.* XXXVI (Leiden, 1973), 28–38.

[4] Strecker, *Judenchristemtum...*, p. 214, supposed that the *Kerygmata Petrou* did not originate within a sect but that the contents 'der Fluktuation der werdenden Großkirche unterworfen waren', and we read on p. 215 n. 2: 'Ein Beispiel für das Ineinandergreifen von Katholizismus und Judenchristentum stellt die Didaskalia dar; sie setzt sich mit einer Gruppe von Judenchristen in der eigenen Gemeinde auseinander.' Later he obviously changed his mind, since in his appendix to a reprint of Bauer's *Rechtgläubigkeit...*, pp. 248–60, he wrote that the Didascalia were directed to a Jewish-Christian heresy outside the official Church. This seems to be incorrect.

[5] See A. Henrichs–L. Koenen, 'Ein griechischer Mani-Codex', in: *Zeitschr. für Papyrologie und Epigraphik*, Band 5, Heft 2 (Bonn, 1970).

[6] See Köster, 'ΓΝΩΜΑΙ...', pp. 300–1, and J. M. Robinson, 'Logoi Sophon – Zur Gattung der Spruchquelle Q', in: H. Köster and J. M. Robinson, *Entwicklungslinien durch die Welt des frühen Christentums* (Tübingen, 1971), pp. 67–106.

[7] See A. F. J. Klijn and G. J. Reinink, 'Elchasai and Mani', to be published in *Vigiliae Christianae*. The idea of Christ returning throughout the ages which was introduced into Elchasaitism at a secondary stage, cf. Hippolytus, *ref.* IX. 14. 1; x. 29. 2 and Epiphanius, *pan.* LIII. is to be found

is wrong to think that this Church was founded by Palestinian or even Jerusalem Christians.[1] One of the main characteristics of this area with so many Jewish inhabitants was that the different communities adhered to their original ideas, at best adapting them to ideas taken over from the outside world. It would be well to remember that Christianity was preached as the fulfilment of already existing Jewish convictions. It is this phenomenon which makes Jewish Christianity into such a varied whole of ideas.

From what has been said above it follows that the study of Jewish Christianity is still worth while. It deals with such Jewish elements in the primitive Church as are not available in the New Testament and were either neglected or adapted by a developing orthodoxy.[2] Of course it is impossible to compile 'a' or 'the' theology of Jewish Christianity. The many Jewish-Christian ideas which may collectively be called 'Jewish Christianity' cannot be combined into one clear-cut or well-defined theology. We are dealing with isolated phenomena and can, therefore, only speak of the Jewish Christianity of a particular writing or of a particular group of Christians. In these cases we mean that in a writing or among a group we can detect ideas having a Jewish background and which were not accepted by the established Church.

in *Rec.* II. 22. 4. Special oaths are mentioned in Hippolytus, *ref.* IX. 15. 2 and 5 and Epiphanius, *pan.* XIX. 1. 6 and 6. 4, cf. *Hom., Diamart.* 2. 1 and 4. 1.

[1] See J. C. L. Gibson, 'From Qumran to Edessa or the Aramaic-speaking Church before and after 70 A.D.', *Annual of the Leeds Univ. Oriental Soc.* V (1963–5), 24–39; G. Quispel, 'The discussion of Judaic Christianity', *Vig. Christ.* XXII (1968), 81–93; L. W. Barnard, 'The origin and emergence of the Church in Edessa during the first two centuries A.D.', *Vig. Christ.* XXII (1968), 151–75, but see also H. J. W. Drijvers, 'Edessa und das jüdische Christentum', *Vig. Christ.* XXIV (1970), 4–33.

[2] For a fine example of adaptation see G. Kretschmar, *Studien zur frühchristlicheen Trinitätstheologie*, in: *Beitr. z. Hist. Theol.* XXI (Tübingen, 1956).

New Test. Stud. **6.** *pp.* 103-16.

J. MUNCK

JEWISH CHRISTIANITY IN POST-APOSTOLIC TIMES[1]

The words 'Jewish-Christian' and 'Jewish Christianity' are used in several different senses within the field of New Testament research. Some scholars—no doubt oneself included on occasion—use them with varying significance in the same article or book, so that the reader is either led astray, or discovers that the words do not have the same meaning every time they occur. The aim of the following is to draw attention to this fact, of which perhaps not everyone is aware, and to attempt to reach a clearer usage of the term Jewish Christianity; and I shall therefore now try to formulate and answer certain questions that may throw light on the conditions described by the terms in question, and on the use of these terms.

I

The first question to be considered is whether we can learn anything about primitive Jewish Christianity, that is, about the church of Jerusalem and the other Palestinian churches in the period before A.D. 70, from sources other than the New Testament writings. We therefore put the following simple question: What information can we gather as to primitive Jewish Christianity with the help of what is commonly known as Jewish Christianity in the post-apostolic period? And in order to answer this question in the limited time at our disposal, we will consider three separate questions: (1) Did primitive Jewish Christianity survive the destruction of Jerusalem in A.D. 70? (2) Do the Pseudo-Clementine writings contain a reliable account of primitive Jewish Christianity? (3) Can we get back to primitive Jewish Christianity by way of the so-called Jewish-Christian gospels?

The first question is: Did primitive Jewish Christianity survive the destruction of Jerusalem in A.D. 70? In his History of the Church (*H.E.* III, 5, 3) Eusebius says that the members of the church in Jerusalem, by means of a prophecy made to those most esteemed among them in a revelation, were commanded to leave the city and settle in a town in Peraea called Pella. And when these holy ones had left Jerusalem and the whole land of Judaea, the Jews were visited by the wrath of the Lord. This emigration of descendants of the adherents of primitive Jewish Christianity is generally regarded as a historical fact,[2] although it seems obvious that we here have an edifying

---

[1] Presidential Address to S.N.T.S. delivered at Norwich, 8 September 1959.

[2] H. J. Lawlor, *Eusebiana* (Oxford, 1912), pp. 28–34, assumes Eusebius' and Epiphanius' source for this to have been Hegesippus. This assumption is attacked in the criticism of Lawlor's conception of Hegesippus' work put forward by me in an article on Papias to be published in *H.T.R.*

111

story designed to show that the Jews were not visited by the wrath of God until the Jewish Christians had escaped.[1]

If this story is accepted as historically correct, it explains the existence of so-called Jewish Christians in this area at a later period, but this very fact may have contributed to the creation of the story. Acceptance of it disregards the fact that flight does not necessarily mean that the fugitives settle elsewhere: many ancient emigrations lasted only a short time, and ended with a return:[2] for example, the flight of the infant Jesus and his parents, of the members of the church of Jerusalem after the persecution connected with Stephen, and of the apostle Peter after the death of Herod Agrippa. It must at all events be stressed that no one maintains that primitive Jewish Christianity continued to exist in Pella; on the contrary, something quite different—a heretical form of Jewish Christianity—arose among the emigrants. Schoeps terms this a paradox in world history.[3] It would be more reasonable to say that the story of the flight of the Jewish Christians is not historical.[4] With the destruction of Jerusalem in A.D. 70 the primitive church of Jerusalem, with its authority and significance for the whole Church, vanished for ever. The Jewish Christianity to be found later in Palestine and Syria, including Pella, is of a new type, having no connexion with primitive Jewish Christianity.

We now come to our second question: Do the Pseudo-Clementine writings give a reliable account of primitive Jewish Christianity? On the face of it this novel, or rather ψευδὴς ἱστορία about the earliest history of Christianity before Paul, with Peter as the chief character, here regarded as a missionary to the heathen, is quite untrustworthy. Like Jewish writings of the type of Aristeas and III Macc., it is neither historically reliable, nor intended to be so; it is merely intended to look plausible. It also resembles them in that the doctrines it states are so general that they are difficult to date.[5] We have here a parallel to the high priest Eleazar's remarks on the Jewish laws as to food (Aristeas §§ 130–69), and the Jewish translators' statements as to the ideal king (Aristeas §§ 187–292), which are not made *ad hoc*, but presuppose a tradition; so that the important but difficult question is why the writer has chosen to put forward those particular traditional views at that moment of time, and for those readers; in the case of the Pseudo-Clementine writings we must ask why the author, the editors, and the translator have chosen to set down such traditions as the remarks on the True Prophet and on the true

[1] Cf. another theme, that only when the righteous man (in this case James, the brother of the Lord) is dead, will Jerusalem perish (Eusebius *H.E.* ii, 23, 19–20). Cf. 'Discours d'adieu etc.', *Mélanges Maurice Goguel* (Neuchâtel-Paris, 1950), p. 160, note 3.
[2] See F. H. Cramer, 'Expulsion of Astrologers from Ancient Rome', *Classica et Mediaevalia*, xii (1951), pp. 9–50.
[3] H. J. Schoeps, *Theologie und Geschichte des Judenchristentums* (Tübingen, 1949), p. 270.
[4] Cf. G. Strecker, *Das Judenchristentum in den Pseudoklementinen* (T.U. vol. 70, 1958), pp. 229–31. S. G. F. Brandon, *The Fall of Jerusalem and the Christian Church* (London, 1951), pp. 168–73, 263–4.
[5] See Moses Hadas's important articles on and editions of Aristeas and III Macc. (Harper and Brothers, 1951 and 1953). See now also G. Zuntz, 'Aristeas Studies' I and II, *J. Sem. Stud.* iv, 1 (1959), 21–36; iv, 2 (1959), 109–26.

and false pericopes at that particular time and in that particular connexion. Obviously it was not the author's aim to codify the opinions of past ages for the benefit of modern scholars. It therefore seems unfortunate to begin by distinguishing sources, before the 'Sitz im Leben' of the work is clearly understood. The latest reconsiderations of the sources of Aristeas indicate to my mind the need for caution in dealing with the sources of the Pseudo-Clementine writings.

But to return to our question. There is not time here for a satisfactory discussion of source classification in the Pseudo-Clementine writings; our aim must be to investigate whether the sources—held by many to be ancient—behind the writings take us back to primitive Jewish Christianity. Some of the dogmas stressed by Schoeps[1] in the original work (G) have been the subject of research which may help us. In an article, 'La circoncision, le baptême et l'autorité du décret apostolique (Actes xv. 28 sq.) dans les milieux judéo-chrétiens des Pseudo-Clémentines',[2] Molland has shown that in the Jewish-Christian circles from which the Pseudo-Clementine writings issued there was no question of circumcision, but only of baptism. The doctrine of the True Prophet has been discussed by Cerfaux in his article 'Le Vrai Prophète des Clémentines',[3] where he assumes that it was originally an apologetic application of Deuteronomy's prophecy of the coming Prophet, round which have collected other fragments of heretical origin.

These articles do not merely show that the doctrines they discuss are not primitive Jewish-Christian; they also make it plain that the way ahead in research into the Pseudo-Clementine writings and Jewish Christianity lies, not in the somewhat undifferentiated classification of sources, but in applying the same historical-critical method and strict accuracy to these adjacent fields as to the New Testament writings, in order to understand the individual texts and to grasp them as a whole. I wish that my New Testament colleagues would begin to write commentaries on the patristic writings, which are of importance to New Testament studies, so that one might get to the bottom of these texts and their problems. The constructions would then be fewer, but built on a better foundation.

But some will perhaps be cautious of so audacious an idea. Some years ago, I was being shown the Greek agora in Athens, where a whole district of the city has had to make way for the excavation of this site, with its buildings from the time of Athens' greatness; our knowledgeable and witty guide told us that there had also been some talk of digging under the railway to Piraeus,

[1] See the above-mentioned book by Schoeps, and also *Aus frühchristlicher Zeit* (Tübingen, 1950), and *Urgemeinde, Judenchristentum, Gnosis* (Tübingen, 1956), and several articles. Schoeps has modified his original opinions on some points, but methodically there is no change.

[2] *Studia Theologica*, IX (1955), 1–39, see pp. 8–25. Molland's critical examination has to some extent been anticipated by earlier investigations; these are attacked by Schoeps in *Theologie*, etc., who takes his stand on what is generally accepted as being Jewish-Christian!

[3] *Recherches de Science religieuse*, XVIII (1928), 143–63, reprinted in *Recueil Lucien Cerfaux* (Gembloux, 1954), I, 301–19.

and continuing on the other side of it, in order to complete this great excavation. He was not sure that it would be a good idea. Up to now, he said, we have always been able to assume that the buildings we could not find lay in the area that had not yet been excavated. But if we start digging there as well, then where are we going to put them?

Our third question is: Can we get back to primitive Jewish Christianity by way of the so-called Jewish-Christian gospels? In the case of the Pseudo-Clementine writings, we have to try to make our way back to the second century—if we can—by means of a complicated classification of sources, about which no two scholars are in complete agreement. But here matters are different.

The Jewish-Christian gospels are believed to belong to the second century, but only fragments of them have survived, and the traditions concerning them are of very mixed value. The latest discussion of the three gospels—the Gospel of the Nazaraeans, the Gospel of the Ebionites, and the Gospel according to the Hebrews—is that by Vielhauer in the third edition of Hennecke's *Neutestamentliche Apokryphen*, which has just been published.[1] A study of the surviving fragments of these Jewish-Christian gospels will show that they contain occasional syncretistic or heretical features, but not the special dogmas which one would expect to find in Jewish-Christian circles. Vielhauer's work deserves praise. There is, however, one point to which I must add a few critical remarks. As proof of the Jewish-Christian character of the Gospel according to the Hebrews, Vielhauer cites the importance attached in it to James, the brother of the Lord, since according to the New Testament (Gal. ii and Acts xv; xxi. 18ff.) and Hegesippus (Eusebius *H.E.* II, 23, 4–18) James represented a strict form of Jewish Christianity, and was the leader of the primitive church of Jerusalem. But this assumption by Vielhauer is not supported either by Gal. ii, or by Acts xv and xxi. 18ff., where James takes a different view from the Judaistic opponents; and the text of Hegesippus in Eusebius is corrupt.[2] In the revelation to James of the Risen Christ, preserved in Jerome (*De vir. ill.* 2), Vielhauer finds James described as the first witness, and thus as the most important evidence for the Resurrection; this reading, however, is not based on the text, but on an application to it of Holl's interpretation of I Cor. xv. 1 ff.[3]

[1] Edgar Hennecke, *Neutestamentliche Apokryphen*, etc., 3rd ed., edited by W. Schneemelcher (Tübingen, 1959), I, 75–108.

[2] Cf. *Paulus und die Heilsgeschichte* (Aarhus-Copenhagen, 1954), pp. 105–11; 226–37.

[3] Karl Holl, 'Der Kirchenbegriff des Paulus in seinem Verhältnis zu dem der Urgemeinde'. *Ges. Aufsätze zur Kirchengeschichte* (Tübingen, 1928), II, 44–67, especially pp. 45–54; cf. *Paulus und die Heilsgeschichte*, pp. 282 ff.—The strongest description of the place of James in the Salvation story is to be found in the newly discovered Gospel of Thomas. Vielhauer stresses this passage, Logion 12. as a remarkable parallel. Parallel is hardly the right term, as the passage is far stronger than the text in the Gospel according to the Hebrews. It is more like the statements made about James in the corrupt Hegesippus quotation in Eusebius *H.E.* II, 23, 5 ff. See *Paulus und die Heilsgeschichte*. p. 108, note 76, and p. 109, note 83. For parallels to the statement about James in the Gospel of Thomas, see Ginzberg, *The Legends of the Jews* (Philadelphia, 1947), V, 67-8, especially the passages

These considerations make it clear that the fragments of the so-called Jewish-Christian gospels do not contain Jewish-Christian features linking them with primitive Jewish Christianity. Even though the occasion of the quotations as a rule has little or no connexion with this, it is important to establish this negative point because it illustrates the nature of our material, and stresses the difficulty of drawing certain often-drawn conclusions from such un-positive matter.

II

The question we have asked, whether we can learn anything about primitive Jewish Christianity from sources other than the New Testament writings, must be answered in the negative. Primitive Jewish Christianity ceased to exist at the destruction of Jerusalem, and neither the Pseudo-Clementine writings nor the so-called Jewish-Christian gospels take us back to it. In what has hitherto been said, we have cautiously accepted a conception of primitive Jewish Christianity in which circumcision and observance of the Mosaic Law are taken to be the distinguishing marks; but this is of course not the only possible interpretation of primitive Jewish Christianity, and in my opinion not the right one. In the first case we have a religion that does not take its rise in Jesus, but—as is typical of Hegel's philosophy—becomes Christianity only by a μετάβασις εἰς ἄλλο γένος. But if Christianity had a character of its own from the beginning, we get a historically probable blend of Jewish and Christian elements, in which the decisive factor is Jesus Christ, and which is therefore from the start a new religion, Christianity.

Hitherto, the obscurity surrounding Jewish Christianity has helped to support the theory that Christianity was a Jewish sect from the beginning. According to Eusebius, primitive Jewish Christianity continued in the East Jordan region. And the Pseudo-Clementine writings and the so-called Jewish-Christian gospels bore witness that Jewish-Christian communities of this kind had survived, and had expressed their special doctrines in these writings. If we have been right in arguing that the later so-called Jewish Christianity was not a continuation of primitive Jewish Christianity, and that the literary productions of so-called Jewish-Christian circles likewise have no connexion with primitive Jewish Christianity, we must next ask whence, in that case, the later Jewish Christianity had its origin.

There is a conception of late Judaism and early Christianity that attaches great importance to gnosticism. It will not be discussed here, for several reasons, the most important being that we are investigating the meaning of a concept—'Jewish Christianity'—with many different senses, and it will not help us to introduce another, equally complicated concept into the investiga-

showing that the world was created for the sake of Abraham, Moses, David, or the Messiah. Cf. also Hermas *Vis.* II, 4, 1, on the Church: διὰ ταύτην ὁ κόσμος κατηρτίσθη with Dibelius' note in Lietzmann's *Handbuch*, Ergänzungsband, p. 452.

tion. The doctrine of our schooldays still holds good, that one cannot solve an equation with two unknown quantities.

Apart from the already rejected view that it derives from primitive Jewish Christianity, the possibilities seem to be either that the later so-called Jewish Christianity derives from the Jewish religious community, as Marcel Simon has attempted to prove in his valuable book *Verus Israel*,[1] or that it resulted from an internal development of the Church. These two possibilities are not mutually exclusive, but it is important that it should be clear whether it is a question of the result of Jewish missionary activity, or whether the adoption of Jewish customs originated in an internal church development.

The latter possibility has become more probable since the recent publication of Daniélou's *Théologie du Judéo-Christianisme*,[2] in which the term 'Jewish Christianity' is used to describe the earliest phase of the history of the Church. Daniélou points out that the word can be used in three different ways: it can be used first of what we have here called primitive Jewish Christianity—though Daniélou is rather of the Tübingen school—secondly, of a group half-way between the Jews and the Christians, such as the Ebionites, and lastly, of a Christian way of thinking which does not spring from a connexion with the Jewish religious community, but which expresses itself in borrowed Jewish forms. In this wider sense even the apostle Paul is a Jewish Christian. Jewish Christianity of this kind is to be found not only among Jews who have become Christians, but also among Gentile Christians, for in all missionary work there is a long interval of time between the first establishing of the gospel in a new nation, and the expression of the gospel in the terms of that nation's civilization.[3]

Daniélou's work is valuable, and deserves detailed discussion. But I must add that I disagree with him in many particulars, and as regards method. As obvious improvements, I may mention that we avoid the Gentile Christianity which has hitherto been an important, but undoubtedly wrong factor in the earliest history of the Church.[4] We learn that we must go back to Judaism in order to get a better understanding of the earliest theological and ecclesiastical development. And it is refreshing to see both heretical Jewish Christianity and gnosticism treated as elements in the history of the Church—not merely as a basis on which 'Christianity' was formed and

[1] *Verus Israel* (Paris, 1948, Bibl. des Écoles Françaises d'Athènes et de Rome, Fasc. 166). Simon first bases his opinion on a missionary Judaism which to my mind never existed (cf. *Paulus und die Heilsgeschichte*, pp. 259–65), and secondly, underestimates the importance of the internal Church debate as to the Old Testament and the Law. This debate I regard as the necessary preliminary to a new interest in the Jewish attitude to the Law, and with it the adoption of Jewish customs and doctrines, or conversion to the Jewish religious community. The only exception to this is the conversion to Judaism during the persecutions which Simon also discusses.

[2] *Histoire des doctrines chrétiennes avant Nicée*, vol. 1 (Tournai, 1958).

[3] Daniélou points out that it is Goppelt, in his book *Christentum und Judentum* (Gütersloh, 1954) who has demonstrated the significance of this Jewish Christianity.

[4] As for instance in Bultmann's *Theologie des Neuen Testaments* (Tübingen, 1948–53), pp. 64–182.

produced, but also as spheres that were themselves influenced and determined by the life and movement of the great Church.

Daniélou's use of the term 'Jewish Christianity' for the earliest Church is easily understandable as a provocative challenge to the earlier view of the question, which may be briefly described as Harnack's opinion. But we can hardly continue to use it, because the word is already charged with associations which it would be difficult to avoid in the new usage. The fundamental truth that the earliest Church was determined by its origin in Judaism must be related to the fact that the large majority of its members were Gentiles. The Jewish-Christian missionaries of the first generation set a Jewish-Christian stamp on the Gentile Church.

We must therefore consider the attitude taken by the Gentile Church towards the Old Testament Jewish features of the ecclesiastical inheritance from the Jewish-Christian apostles. From the beginning the Old Testament is the Bible. It is the source of the arguments used by Jesus in his discussions with the Jews, and it is used by the first disciples in dealing with the Jews and the Gentiles, as we see in Acts. We find the same thing in the epistles of Paul. The Christians have the same Bible as the Jews, but the latter do not understand it properly, as is shown particularly by the religion of the Law, and its justification by works. From the start the Old Testament was a Christian book, the revelation of God. There may thus be Jewish traditions in the Christian interpretation of this Christian book, just as there may be in the Christian life of the apostolic churches. This is something that is taken for granted, accepted without conscious awareness, and therefore not discussed, until the Church of the Gentiles begins to develop a Gentile-Christian theology and practice.

But it must here be emphasized that this struggle to create a Gentile-Christian theology and piety gave great support to Old Testament Jewish features which had not been stressed to this extent, or in this way, by the apostles. As early as Paul's epistle to the Galatians we see these Gentile Christians showing more zeal for the Law than did the Jewish Christians, not to mention Paul; they were willing to be circumcised and to undertake to keep the whole Mosaic Law in order to belong to Christ. In Acts the Gentile-Christian Luke lays great stress on the connexion between the Church and Judaism. We see how Christianity takes its rise in Judaism, and how it is forced to break away because of the unbelief of the Jews. This separation is not the work of man: it is God who step by step directs and determines the decisions made by the Christian leaders. Thus nothing takes place that is not due to the guidance of the Holy Ghost, or to a revelation showing what is to be done. Faltering and reluctant, the disciples and apostles are compelled to go to the Gentiles, or to seek new mission fields.[1]

[1] Although the talk of rejudaization is right enough in theory, we must be cautious in applying it to the gospels. Matthew in particular has features which are generally taken to be rejudaization, but which can more probably be attributed to Jesus' conflict with the Jews about the relation between the Mosaic law and the will of God.

In the time of the Apostolic Fathers, which to Daniélou is the Jewish-Christian era of the Church, we find in several points the same emphasis on Old Testament Jewish features, not, be it noted, as being Jewish, but on the contrary as being truly Christian. Just as the Galatians were more zealous for the Law than was their Jewish-Christian apostle, so we find in this later generation of Gentile Christians a similar zeal to fulfil the New Law and live according to a nomistic Christianity. True, neither circumcision nor Pharisaic obedience to the Law is required, but so much importance is attached to good works in the Jewish sense that the distance from the apostles and their age is strikingly clear.[1]

As in the case of the Galatians,[2] one of the reasons for this may be that the Church's Bible is the *Greek* Old Testament, the Septuagint, with its greater stress on the Law, and it was only gradually that New Testament writings were added to this first Christian canon. Even after the two Covenants were united in the canon of the Church there was tension between them, which has revealed itself time and again in the history of the Church. The attitude of Jesus and the apostles to the Law could be forgotten, and this was not, as has been assumed in the case of the earliest Church, due to the influence of Judaism. It seems to be possible in any age for Old Testament features, interpreted without reference to Jesus' and the apostles' fight against justification by works of the Law, to be regarded as true Christianity. Perhaps Tertullian's assertion: *anima naturaliter Christiana* should be changed to the more probable: *anima naturaliter Judaica.*

As an example of later Gentile-Christian use of the Old Testament, may I remind you of Macaulay's description of the Earl of Crawford, in his *History of England.*[3] I do not know whether the description is accurate, and perhaps I should also mention that this section of his *History of England* is about Scotland, but at all events Macaulay says of Crawford: 'He had a text from the Pentateuch or the Prophets ready for every occasion. He filled the despatches with allusions to Ishmael and Hagar, Hannah and Eli, Elijah, Nehemiah, and Zerubbabel, and adorned his oratory with quotations from Ezra and Haggai. It is a circumstance strikingly characteristic of the man, and the school in which he had been trained, that, in all the mass of the writing which has come down to us, there is not a single word indicating that he had ever in his life heard of the New Testament.'

For the Gentile Church in the second century the Old Testament had a special significance which later ages have had no need to remember. This significance is connected with the fact that, in the past, age was synonymous with authority. When a Jewish apologist was trying to maintain his people

---

[1] See T. F. Torrance, *The Doctrine of Grace in the Apostolic Fathers* (Edinburgh, 1948), and his remarks on the difficulty experienced by the first Gentile Christians in understanding the New Testament message, pp. 135–41.

[2] Cf. *Paulus und die Heilsgeschichte*, pp. 122–6.

[3] Longmans, Green, and Co. (1866), vol. III, ch. XIII, p. 24.

in the religion of their fathers he pointed out that Moses was far older than all the Greek sages. This proof of age was taken over by the Christians from the Jews: Christianity is older than all other religions and revelations. It was established at the creation of the world: in the beginning, i.e. in Christ, God created the heaven and the earth. It is difficult now at this point of time to visualize how effective the Christian teaching would have been without the Old Testament.

It is true that it is also in the time of the Apostolic Fathers that the apostles and their tradition gain importance. It was apostles such as Paul, and not the twelve earliest disciples, that had brought the gospel to the Gentiles; but in the post-apostolic period the Gentile churches took over the Jewish-Christian gospels—presumably one by one—containing the Palestinian tradition of the twelve earliest disciples who followed Jesus. And these disciples, who had been sent out into Israel, and only a few of whom had worked outside Palestine, were now regarded by the Gentile churches as apostles to the Gentiles, as those who in Jerusalem divided the world among them and set forth to preach to all the nations of the earth. We find the Gentile-Christian bishop Papias of Hierapolis, whose very name betrays his origin among the heathen of North Phrygia, collecting traditions from Palestine, and about the Palestinian disciples of Jesus, for use in his interpretations of the words of the Lord.

While the earliest Church had no doubt that the apostles were in agreement with the Old Testament, we find a new feature in the post-apostolic period, in that the apostles and James, the brother of the Lord, are given a connexion with the priesthood in the Temple at Jerusalem. Jesus himself, with his disciples, had wandered in those parts of it to which only priests were admitted (*Oxyrhynchos Papyri*, vol. v, 1907, no. 840), and only James might enter the Temple (according to Hegesippus, in Eusebius *H.E.* ii, 23, 5), while John 'who leant back on the Lord's breast, was a priest, wearing the sacerdotal plate' (according to Polycrates' letter in Eusebius *H.E.* iii, 31, 3). Thus the new Covenant is linked with the old, the Old Testament service in the temple with the Christian leaders of the earliest age, from whom the Christian bishops and presbyters trace their descent.

And not only does the Church claim its own ancestry in the Old Testament and Judaism; it maintains that the same applies to the heretics: they also are related to the Jewish sects. As far back as Irenaeus, perhaps even as far as Justin, in his lost treatise against the heretics, the Church Fathers traced the ancestry of the heretics by deriving one heresy from another; in the same way, the heresies of the day were from an early date linked with the Jewish parties or heresies. This learned hypothesis of the Fathers has recently been revived in connexion with the Qumran finds.

III

The significance of these finds extends also to the research into the late Jewish writings hitherto known as Apocrypha and Pseudepigrapha. For one thing, a theory has arisen connecting some of these writings with the Qumran sect, and seeing them as expressions of the doctrines and life of that community.[1] For another, the possibility has been put forward by Daniélou and others, that a number of writings hitherto held to be Jewish may now be regarded as Jewish-Christian. Formerly it was assumed that these late Jewish writings had been adapted by Christians, so that their present form was due partly to the original Jewish authors, partly to the later Christian editors. The new hypothesis is that they were written by Jewish-Christian authors, so that the Jewish and Christian elements are no longer regarded as two separate stages in the creation of the writings, but as characteristics present from the beginning. Whether scholars have tried to consign late Jewish writings to the Qumran sect, or to attribute them to Jewish-Christian authors, the result has been valuable observations; but as yet it cannot be said that scholarship as a whole has accepted these new views.

It would of course be of the greatest importance for Jewish Christianity if the number of Jewish-Christian texts, hitherto so small, could be increased. And it may seem hazardous to say anything about this research while it is still in progress. But since this tendency touches on our subject—a working definition of the term 'Jewish Christianity'—the question must be mentioned, and doubt expressed as to whether the material so badly needed in this field is to be gained here. This must be said, despite the fact that with our present scanty material the subject of Jewish Christianity will continue to be a mystery—unless, of course, we improve our methods, and concentrate on what it is possible for us to learn, rather than on what we would like to learn.

Since the time at our disposal is limited, I will substantiate this doubt as to the Jewish-Christian origin of the apocryphal writings by taking a single example, namely Daniélou's book. On p. 21 of that work the following criteria are given for determining whether writings are Jewish-Christian: (1) The chronology: does it belong to the period between the beginning of Christianity and approximately the middle of the second century? (2) The literary style: does it contain the late Jewish literary forms now known to us from Qumran? (3) The dogmatic criterion ('le critère doctrinal'): do we find the characteristic Jewish-Christian categories, especially the apocalyptic?

[1] As a single example, and as regards a single work, I may mention the recently concluded research by Marc Philonenko, 'Les Interpolations chrétiennes des Testaments des Douze Patriarches et les Manuscrits de Qoumrân', I–II, Rev. d'Hist. et de Philos. Relig. (1958), pp. 309–43 and (1959). pp. 14–38. A warning against the above-mentioned tendency is given by Bent Noack, 'Qumran and the Book of Jubilees', Svensk exeg. årsbok XXII–XXIII (1957–8), 191–207.

The danger in extending the conception of 'Jewish Christianity' with the aid of such criteria[1] lies in the fact that it may easily end in making everything Jewish-Christian. There is nothing else left. In other words, we have a parallel to the research into gnosticism, where insufficiently defined limits allow everything to be included as gnostic. Even the opponents of the movement, such as Paul and Plotinus, are declared to be gnostics.

Daniélou has with great erudition succeeded in describing a whole period as Jewish-Christian by demonstrating its origin in the undisputed Jewish Christianity of the earliest Church, its extensive inheritance of Jewish or Jewish-Christian features, and the many interconnexions that seem to confirm the truth of the conception. But the disparity between the various writings, and the demonstrable connexions between the time of the apostles and this period, and again between the latter and the succeeding Fathers, show that what we have is a picture of a period and a setting with certain features in common, but not a distinct movement that can be given so definite a name as 'Jewish Christianity'. And if this is so, then this phase of Church history must be called by another name.

It is difficult to lay down clear rules, that will be generally acceptable, for distinguishing between what is commonly known as Jewish and Hellenistic, Jewish and Jewish-Christian, Jewish-Christian and Gentile-Christian. An instance is the discussion as to whether something is Hellenistic or Jewish.[2] Moreover, it is confusing that Hellenistic features, taken over by Judaism in certain spheres, should have been described as Jewish. If we then continue to assume Jewish influence in every case where these Jewish-Hellenistic features occur, without considering that they may have been taken over directly from Hellenism, as in the Jewish writings, we shall get a regrettable expansion of Judaism and Jewish-influenced writings.

Nor is it easy to distinguish between Jewish and Jewish-Christian.[3] Here also the application of these terms ought not to depend only on the particular points, but on the context into which these points are inserted. A loan from Judaism may have a certain importance in the writings of the Fathers, and still be repeated in medieval commentaries, but there is little point in stressing its origin when it is a question of understanding it in its new context within the Church and its history.

As regards the difference between Jewish Christianity and Gentile Christianity, Daniélou's book has accentuated an already very difficult problem. Here as elsewhere, details of Jewish origin cannot be used to prove

---

[1] Compare Daniélou's interpretation of Hippolytus' account of the doctrines of the Naassenes (p. 95) with the far more cautious treatment of the Apocryphon of John in R. McL. Wilson, *The Gnostic Problem* (London, 1958), p. 154.

[2] See, for instance, the discussion of II Cor. v. 1 ff. in W. D. Davies, *Paul and Rabbinic Judaism* (London, 1955), pp. 312 ff.

[3] See Dibelius (*H.N.T.* 11, 3rd ed., Tübingen, 1937), and Lohmeyer (*Meyer*, 9, 8th ed., Göttingen, 1930), on Phil. iii. 2 ff. In opposition to most exegetists of the older school they both stress the fact that Paul's opponents here are Jews, not Judaists.

that something or other, or someone or other, is 'Jewish-Christian'.[1] The interpretation of the details, here as elsewhere, must be based upon the whole. The many different standpoints in the post-apostolic Church can with more or less accuracy be described as Jewish-Christian, for example, the views of the authors of the Epistle to the Hebrews and the Epistle of Barnabas, Ignatius and his opponents in his Epistle to the Philadelphians viii. 2, Papias and Marcion.

IV

Let us now turn to those definitions which we set out to achieve. Our first thesis concerns primitive Jewish Christianity, namely the meagre results of the mission of the twelve earliest disciples in Palestine, with Jerusalem as the starting-point, and it is as follows: (1) *After primitive Jewish Christianity perished with the destruction of Jerusalem in A.D. 70, all later Jewish Christianity has its origin in the Gentile-Christian Church of the post-apostolic period.*

We shall not discuss here whether primitive Jewish Christianity was mainly or partly Judaistic, but merely observe that in Galatians we find Gentile Christians who had recently become Judaists.

The next thesis concerns that part of Church history which Daniélou has termed 'Jewish Christianity'. What he is right in stressing is the powerful Jewish element that has stamped this Gentile Church. But this is not the most decisive factor for that important but all too neglected period of Church history. It is therefore unreasonable to name it after its Jewish inheritance, however justified Daniélou may be in stressing this in the face of the lack of understanding of this aspect in former days. We will therefore give it another name, and include this in our second thesis: (2) *The post-apostolic Gentile Church was Jewish-Christian in the sense that its founders were Jewish-Christian apostles such as Paul, and it therefore possessed a tradition that contained Jewish elements, which were taken over and adapted by the Church.*

It would be a mistake consistently to attribute Jewish features in the post-apostolic Gentile Church to the heritage from primitive Jewish Christianity, as will appear in the third and last thesis. Every instance must be treated separately.

The third thesis is as follows: *Heretical Jewish Christianity, which originated in the post-apostolic Gentile Church, may possibly also, in addition to this internal ecclesiastical development, be based on a relationship with the Jewish religious community.*

---

[1] It can, for instance, be pointed out that according to Harnack, *Marcion*, 2nd ed. (T.U. vol. 45, 1924), p. 22, Marcion is familiar with the Jewish interpretations of the Old Testament. It is doubtful whether, like Harnack, one can conclude from this that Marcion was at one time closely connected with Judaism, and that his attitude to the Old Testament and Judaism is to be taken as resentment. The latter is at all events superfluous, since the Old Testament-Jewish features of the Church were at that time overstressed to such a degree that they provided enough to react against. R. M. Grant has recently argued convincingly that Marcion's distinction between the righteous God and the just creator goes back to theological distinctions in Judaism (*Vig. Christ.* XI, 1957, pp. 145 f.).

A possible connexion of this kind between Christianity and Judaism is not due to Judaism, which has never been a missionary religion. Christianity, on the other hand, concentrated its missionary activity on Israel from the beginning, and although this circumstance changes considerably after the death of the apostles, there are still possibilities for contact between the two religions. A possible contact of this kind deserves consideration beside the decisive factor—the internal Church debate on the Law and the Gospel—that determines whether possible contact between the two religions is to have any influence on the Church.

A different circumstance is the adoption of Jewish learning which sporadically occurs, and which is known to us in particular in connexion with Origen and Jerome. Conversely, part of the Jewish heritage through Jewish Christianity was reduced at an early stage to the adoption of Jewish learning.

V

Our present undertaking may perhaps seem both over-confident and superficial. At a time dominated by specialized research we have ventured to discuss the general terms of our subject. We have done so in the conviction that these questions ought to be discussed, and that the discussion ought to be public; for if not, all the many special papers being written are based on a solution of the great fundamental questions which is at the most mentioned in a footnote, and more generally simply assumed, and never discussed.

As a young man, feeling my way towards the study of the New Testament, I wrote a book about Clement of Alexandria. There were many surprises in the change from patristics to the New Testament. In patristics—a map with many blank spaces—there was always a feeling of gratitude for the work already done by others, and pleasure when they had reached entirely different interpretations of the texts. In the New Testament there seemed to be less elbow-room. Everything appeared to have been settled already, in our grandfathers' generation, or earlier still. Jülicher had solved all the problems in the Parables, in the synoptic gospels the Two Sources theory prevailed, and Paul was dominated by the Tübingen school. Having criticized the traditions of the primitive Church concerning the New Testament writings and primitive Christianity, the professors had themselves come to represent tradition and authority, and there was no room for young scholars, for it was not permissible to doubt what all believed. Brilliant impartiality had ended in stolid conservatism.

Today, the atmosphere in biblical studies is more placid than it has ever been since Old Testament criticism was launched in the nineteenth century. Our difficulties today come, not from the Church behind us, but rather from the strong traditionalism that governs our studies—a traditionalism mainly liberal, let me hasten to add. Let us give the younger generation opportunity

123

and encouragement to question the important, but perhaps not always true or permanently valid views put forward by the generations before us. Let us go further, and urge them to question what we ourselves tell them.

With a subject like the New Testament, consisting of a certain number of facts, and a larger number of theories, and assumed rather than substantiated suppositions, it is necessary to go through it from time to time, in order not to forget what is fact and what is theory. In carrying out such a revision, the definition of such concepts as 'Jewish Christianity' must also be reconsidered, since clear-cut concepts are an essential basis of impartial critical research.

EBIONITE CHRISTIANITY

[In the *J.T.S.* of April 1951, pp. 96–99, Professor T. W. Manson reviewed two books by Professor H. J. Schoeps, dealing with Jewish Christianity. The latter was so good as to send to the Editor recently a summary of the results of his studies in this subject, and by Dr. Manson's advice this summary, apart from a few omissions, is here offered to the reader. Dr. Manson believes that there is fruitful work to be done in this field of inquiry, which has been much neglected in the past; and he hopes that this summary may stimulate interest in the subject. The translation is by the Editor.]

DEFINITE authorities, the pseudo-Clementine Romance (consisting of Homilies and Recognitions), Symmachus' translation of the Bible, remains of apocryphal gospels, patristic and rabbinic information, disclose to us the theology of Jewish-Christian communities of the middle and later part of the second century. Jewish Christianity obviously took many forms and varied in different districts. But the sources just mentioned are attached, almost without exception, to groups in Coele-Syria or Transjordan, composed of the descendants of the first Christians who left Jerusalem and probably also of others who moved from Palestine shortly before A.D. 70 and round A.D. 135. In this way information and traditions have been preserved, which go back to the middle of the first century and reveal the opposition of their fathers at Jerusalem to St. Paul and the growing Gentile Christian church. This opposition, mirrored in the oldest strata of the pseudo-Clementine Romance, had practical importance for these groups, because their fathers' arguments could also be applied for their own defence against Marcion and the Christian 'gnosis'. It is proposed in the following pages to sketch briefly their tenets in respect of their Christology, their opposition to St. Paul, and their attitude to the Jewish law, so far as the positive and negative evidence permits.

1. *The Ebionite Picture of Jesus Christ*

In Jesus the Ebionites saw the teacher and the pattern of perfect 'Chassiduth'. On account of the merit of his life, they held, he was called by God to be the Christ, that is, the messianic Prophet. 'Had another similarly fulfilled the precepts of the law, he would similarly have become the Christ, for in virtue of like deeds others also can become a Christ', says Hippolytus (Philos. vii. 34, 1 f.) with regard to their belief. The Ebionites saw in Jesus the *saddiq*, who in a unique degree perfectly fulfilled the law. In their view, however, he fulfilled it as a human being, not as Son of God, but as Son of man, who was consecrated to be Messiah and equipped by God with power, not through true pre-existence or at the moment of birth, but only on the day of his baptism through the act, announced in the words of Ps. 2⁷, of adoption through baptism, i.e. through the Holy Spirit present in the baptismal water.

Among the Ebionites this 'adoptionist Christology' was combined with the apocalyptic expectation of the Son of man which prevailed in the primitive community, the expectation that 'Rabbi Jeshu ha-Nozri', transfigured into the angelic form of the Son of man on the clouds of heaven, would soon return at the hour of salvation for the last judgement upon the living and the dead. The disappointment of this expectation, the fact of the delay of the 'parousia', is to blame for the result that the fading of the strong eschatological interest in the fourth and fifth centuries led to the end of the Ebionite movement. The delay of the 'parousia', it is true, promoted the development of the Catholic church; but in face of this hard fact the growth of the primitive Jerusalem community could not continue, since the latter held fast to a primitive stage of Christology, that is to say, the expectation of the 'parousia' of the Son of man.

Apart from this expectation, however, the Ebionite picture of Jesus was also characterized by a quite different feature, the belief that he was the messianic prophet, the true prophet promised by Moses. Such a prophet had been widely expected in Judaism at the beginning of the Christian era, and the messianic doctrine, that the true prophet had come in Jesus, is a feature of the primitive community. This doctrine links the primitive community with the Jewish Christianity of Epiphanius and the pseudo-Clementines, and also distinguishes it markedly and definitely from those Jews whose messianic hopes were entirely directed to the remoter future.

The Ebionite belief, that Jesus was 'the true prophet', that is to say, the messianic prophet promised by Moses, whom God would raise up 'like unto me' (Deut. 18¹⁵), led among them to a complete parallelism of the two personalities. Both were sent by God to make covenants with mankind. As Moses was steward of the Jews (Luke 12⁴²), so was Jesus steward for the Gentiles (Hom. 2, 52). But since the teaching of both is the same, God accepts every man who believes one of them (Hom. 8, 6).

Thus for the Ebionites conversion to Christ and conversion to the holy God and to the Jewish law (Hom. 4, 22) are one and the same.

2. The Ebionite Opposition to St. Paul

On the basis of this position the Ebionites were bound, as a matter of principle, to adopt a position of hostility to the teaching of the apostle Paul and to the man himself. No direct evidence of teaching against the Pauline theology has been preserved in the sources which have survived to us, but instead we find an all the more violent polemic against his apostleship, its purpose being to discredit him as a deceiver (2 Cor. 6[8]), as an enemy (Gal. 4[16]), indeed as the Evil One himself (2 Thess. 2[1]), who has given heresy a footing in the church of Christ. His teachings they disparage as 'the false gospel'. The Ebionites who figure in Ps.-Clement in this matter merely renew once more the accusations of their fathers, the Judaizers in the Pauline missionary churches, and thus make their fathers' standpoint for the first time quite clear. In particular we can perceive from the passage Hom. 17, 13–20, that the Ebionites and their forerunners condemned St. Paul's appeal to a vision of the risen Lord as a demonic illusion. His apostleship, based on 'visions and revelations,' they held to be illegitimate, since apostleship was only legitimized by personal intercourse with the earthly Jesus.

It is clear that from the outset the circle of the twelve (together with James) and the Jerusalem Christians regarded the status of an eyewitness of the Elect One, that is, physical companionship with him, as essential for the rank of an apostle and the office of teaching, and conceded to St. Paul at most the function of 'a worker together with us', as the Clementine Peter (Hom. 17, 20) expresses it. We may compare Rec. 2, 55: 'he who does not learn the law from teachers, but regards himself as a teacher and rejects the instruction of the disciples of Jesus, must necessarily fall into absurdities with regard to God'. Indeed Peter in this connexion expresses the further opinion that Saul-Paul had indeed a vision which came from Jesus, but that it was of the kind which Jesus in anger would allow to an enemy (Hom. 17, 14). Hence St. Paul's thought is said to be the opposite of the teaching of Jesus (17, 18).

These polemics, which we only possess in truncated form, probably derive from ancient ebionitic Acts of the Apostles giving a very malicious presentation of the anti-christian activity of St. Paul previous to the martyrdom of St. Stephen, of his conversion, and of the events in Antioch. On this view, as 'the enemy' in his Jewish period contended for a Mosaism whose moral and spiritual truth had been sacrificed to ritual requirements, so he later became opposed to the whole Mosaic law. Having by his interference already frustrated the efforts of the primitive

community and of James for the conversion of the Jews to the Mosaic
law reformed by the prophet Jesus, after his conversion he still remained
the persecutor of the *true* law.

3. *The Ebionite Understanding of the Law*

The Ebionites of the second and third century were, like their fathers,
the 'certain of the sect of the Pharisees who believed' (Acts 15⁵), plain
and professed 'enthusiasts for the law' (Acts 21²⁰). They call their teaching 'the proclamation of the law', but carried the Mosaic law to new
extremes of strictness by their insistence, as a matter of principle, on
vegetarianism (which was to overcome the imperfections of the Jewish
'schechitha'), by the command of poverty and community of goods, as
well as by a vigorous system of purifications, extending from ritual
washings to a singular water-mysticism culminating in the act of
baptism. But, while on one side they increased the severity of the law,
they also took a decisive and historically very important line in carrying
through a systematic revision of the Mosaic law; that is to say, they cut
out the sanguinary cult of animal sacrifice, after that, the institution of
the kingship in Israel, then the erroneous—that is to say, the unfulfilled
—prophecies of scripture, as well as, lastly, the divine utterances of an
anthropomorphic character, as being 'erroneous sections', which had
been subsequently inserted into the Mosaic torah. Jesus was for them
the reformer of the Jewish law, whose teaching was the criticism of the
torah as a means of spreading the knowledge what in the law is truth,
and what is error, wrongly introduced.

In Ebionite belief, therefore, the reformation of the law by Jesus was
connected above all with the sacrificial cult, and in connexion with such
an estimate of Jesus' opposition to the sanguinary sacrificial cult of
atonement we see a further reason why the Ebionites were bound to
reject the Pauline teaching. For St. Paul's soteriological estimate of the
death of Jesus as an atoning sacrifice is—ebionitically speaking—the
greatest paradox which can be conceived, a blasphemy so great that it
alone at once proves him to be a type of the false prophet. Not by the
all-encompassing sacrifice of the Son of God, as the church, following
St. Paul, teaches, did Christianity become free from the Jewish sacrificial
worship, but Jesus by the waters of baptism extinguished the fire of
sacrifice—such is Ebionite belief. In any case, in the Ebionite theology
Jesus' specific task was the abolition of sacrifice; and thereby he proved
himself the 'true prophet', precisely because, alongside complete allegiance to and affirmation of the Mosaic law in all other respects, he
brought to an end the sacrificial torah.

All the Ebionite deductions from and additions to the law, commanded by Jesus, the alleviations as well as the increased burdens, have, however, as their sole purpose the expression of the will of God as the authority behind the scriptures, in order to set up once more the broken unity between the law and the will of God. In the last resort they assessed the law by reference to Jesus; in his life and in his teaching they saw the correct fulfilment of the Mosaic law. That which in it was of God he confirmed; that which was not of God he abolished. For them Ebionite theology simply meant the establishment of this in detail. In opposition to the Pauline teaching their purpose in this connexion was, as the content of the true worship of God, to revere him only, not to live a defiled life, to do good, not to commit injustice (Hom. 7, 8). Through 'righteousness by means of works' (*justitia in operibus*, Rec. 2, 36) the 'higher righteousness' required by Jesus, the true Prophet, would be attained.

4. *The Ebionites' Place in History*

Especially surprising is the hostility of the Ebionites to the Jewish sacrificial cultus, a hostility which was also directed against the cult-places of the Jerusalem temple, on the ground that the temple was a debased form of the old tabernacle of God's choice. Since in Jewish religious history, from the nomadic Rechabites through the Maccabean era to the Essenes of the period before and after Christ, movements continually occurred which were opposed to the sacrificial cultus of the Jerusalem priesthood, it is possible to place the Ebionites in a clearly definable context in the history of ideas, especially as their inner connexion with the Essenes seems close. Obviously in their line of descent are especially also those groups that are represented by the writings, which have become known, since my books were completed, through the discovery of the scrolls from 'Ain Feshkha. A comparison of their views, together with several characteristic agreements in detail, at least yields a very similar Christology (*more ṣedeq*: 'the true prophet'), the same glorification of the poor and probably also (Sektenkanon ix. 3) a common attitude of reserve towards the sanguinary sacrificial cultus. As I was able to show elsewhere,[1] the Zadokite group of 'Ain Feshkha, the church of Damascus, Essenes, and Ebionites probably had a doctrinal connexion. This was rendered possible by the exodus of the primitive community to Transjordan, where from of old time Jewish minority groups opposed to civilization and the cultus had settled.

That the Ebionites of patristic literature and the Clementine Romance are in fact the physical descendants of the original Jerusalem community, also follows—apart from the testimony of Eusebius and Epiphanius—

[1] H. J. Schoeps, 'Handelt es sich wirklich um ebionitische Dokumente?' *Zeitschrift für Religions- und Geistesgeschichte*, 1951, Heft 4.

from two explanatory statements of the Ebionite source of the pseudo-Clementine Romance (Rec. 1, 37 *syr.*; Rec. 1, 39), which hitherto have been for the most part overlooked: 'The wisdom of God transported them, for their deliverance, to a safe place in the country, and this before the outbreak of the war, which was to result in the destruction of the unbelieving Jews.'

The descendants of the primitive Jerusalem community were able to maintain themselves in their new homes, remote from the highways of the world, hardly more than 350 years. In accordance with the usual fate of sectaries, they seem latterly to have broken apart or at least to have branched out in many diverging lines. So far as they did not find their way back to the Catholic church, they were finally submerged in the motley mixture of religions in the Near East, after their watchwords and their programme for the reform of the Jewish law had met with no approval on any side, and the strength of their eschatological expectation had been gradually broken by the fact of the delay in the 'parousia', since this was not compensated, as it was in the great church, by any special sacramental mysticism. So far, however, as their religious teaching and doctrinal formulations are concerned, these, more or less modified and recast, again came to the light of day—along several lines of connexion—in the third, and up to the present time last revealed, religion in world-history, Islam.   H. J. SCHOEPS

Studia Theologia 28 (1974) pp. 49–56

God and His Angel in the Shepherd of Hermas

HALVOR MOXNES

The first study of the background to angel-Christology in the Early Church was undertaken by W. Lueken in 1898.[1] In the 1940's two works by M. Werner and C. Barbel dealing with this subject appeared almost simultaneously.[2]

Werner argued that angel-Christology was the oldest possible Christology, developing from the Son of Man figure in Enoch, in fact, *the* Christology of the Early Church, until it was rejected by the growing orthodoxy. Werner met with heavy opposition, especially from W. Michaelis,[3] who showed that at least as far as NT is concerned, Werner's thesis does not hold true. Barbel dealt with patristic evidence; he understood angel-Christology as 'malak Yahweh' appearances in OT being interpreted as appearances of Christ. After that, there have been no full studies of the problem, but useful contributions have been made in works by J. Daniélou[4] and G. Kretschmar.[5]

The question of angel-Christology has been widely discussed in works about the Shepherd of Hermas, as the first document where the term 'angel' seems to be used for Christ. Most of the discussion, however, has concentrated upon the angel figure in the parables, Sim. VIII and IX. These parables have long, detailed and somewhat inconsistent explanations.[6] This has led to different answers to the question of the identity of this angel.

---

[1] Michael. Gött. 1898. For the history of the study of angel-Christology, see the review by C. Barbel in the 2nd ed. of his book, *Christos Angelos*, 1964, pp. 235–52.

[2] M. Werner, Die Entstehung des christlichen Dogmas, Bern 1941. C. Barbel, *Christos Angelos*, Bonn 1941.

[3] *Zur Engelchristologie im Urchristentum*, Basel 1942.

[4] *Théologie du judéo-christianisme*, Tournai 1958.

[5] *Studien zur frühchristlichen Trinitätstheologie*, Tübingen 1956.

[6] Both ὁ ἀνὴρ ὁ ἔνδοξος and other pictures in Sim. IX are explained to be the Son of God. Most puzzling is the explanation in Sim. VIII, where the angel is said to be the archangel Michael and not the Son of God.

M. Dibelius in his commentary[7] holds the angel to be Christ. He shows how angelology, pneumatology, and Christology are connected. The inconsistencies, especially in the interpretation of Sim. VIII, Dibelius attributes to the fact that the underlying Jewish material has not been fully Christianized.[8] J. Lebreton[9] also declares the angel to be Christ, with the same function as the Son of God elsewhere in the book.

Among recent works, S. Giet[10] rejects the possibility of seeing the angel as Christ, partly in "Auseinandersetzung" with Daniélou.[11] Giet finds that the angel is not equal to, but subordinate to God, and he will not see ὁ ἀνηρ ὁ ἔνδοξος in Sim. IX together with the angel. The identification of the angel as Michael in Sim. VIII is the decisive proof.[12] With some modifications, this is also the view held by L. Pernveden.[13] G. F. Snyder likewise rejects the idea of angel-Christology, but speaks of Christological functions carried out by various angels, seeing ὁ σεμνότατος ἄγγελος in Vis. V and ὁ ἔνδοξος ἄγγελος in Sim. V:4.4 as two different angel-figures.[14]

This seems to ascribe too much inconsistency to Hermas. Even if the titles vary, this angel has several functions that are not ascribed to other angels. He does not seem to be a part of the dualistic pattern [15] and there is a consistency in his functions throughout the book. I therefore still think that there is one supreme angel-figure in Hermas and that to the question "Who is meant by this angel?", the most plausible answer is "the Son of God, Christ". But the texts where the angel occurs should not be interpreted as dogmatic statements about Christ. Dogmatic questions (e. g. about subordination) should not be automatically raised; they might very well be beyond the scope of Hermas.

I would like to draw attention to some texts outside the parables where the angel is mentioned in discourses between the shepherd and Hermas, viz. Vis. V, Mand. V:1.7, Sim. V:4.4 and VII.[16] These texts have been used for comparison between the functions of the angel and the Son of God, but not studied carefully in their own context.

---

[7] Der Hirt des Hermas, *HNT*, Erg. b. IV, Tübingen 1923, esp. pp. 572–76.

[8] p. 576.

[9] *Historie du dogme de la trinité*, t. II, Paris 1928, pp. 651–59.

[10] *Hermas et les pasteurs*, Paris 1963, pp. 227 f.

[11] op. cit. esp. pp. 169–75.

[12] pp. 228 f.

[13] *The concept of the church in the Shepherd of Hermas*, Lund 1966, esp. pp. 58–64.

[14] *The Shepherd of Hermas. The Apostolic fathers*, vol. 6, Camden 1968, pp. 60 f, 105.

[15] As are the two angels in Mand. VI:2.

[16] Sim. IX:1.1ff and X (in Latin) may also be included, but as they do not add any substantially new material, they will not be treated separately.

There is reason to believe that we will here find Hermas' own view stated more clearly than in the parables, where he is working with material from the tradition.[17] Even if the angel figure as such is not explained in these passages, they are a good starting point to see what Hermas thinks of the *function* of the angel,[18] especially in relation to God's own work. This will place the angel within the central message of the book, repentance and Christian life, and not isolate him as a dogmatic theme. I will therefore argue that in further discussion of angel-Christology in Hermas, these texts should be paid sufficient attention.

Vis. V is the introduction to the Mandates and shows many similarities to the OT theophany pattern. The shepherd appears for the first time and says: Ἀπεστάλην ὑπὸ τοῦ σεμνοτάτου ἀγγέλου, ἵνα μετὰ σοῦ οἰκήσω τὰς λοιπὰς ἡμέρας τῆς ζωῆς σου. He will show Hermas what is helpful to him with respect to what the Lord's will is. The shepherd is identified as the angel of repentance and Hermas' guardian angel.[19]

The one who sends the shepherd has a specific purpose in doing so; he has plans for Hermas and the Christians (indicated by the ἵνα-clause). This is also the case in other passages where ἀποστέλλειν is used.[20] But whose will is it that is carried out in this way? Only in Vis. V:2 is the angel the subject of ἀποστέλλειν; in the other instances it is ὁ κύριος, the Lord himself.[21] In Mand. XII:6.1 we find the passive form of the verb, ἀπεστάλην, without any subject explicitly given. From the context, however, it is quite obvious that it must be God.

---

[17] See M. Dibelius, p. 572, on his methodology in interpreting the Christology of the parables.

[18] The different titles used of the angel: ὁ σεμνότατος, ὁ ἔνδοξος ἄγγελος, ὁ ἄγγελος κυρίου, are of little help for the identification of the angel. The adjectives may be used of angels, but are not primarily religious terms, see W. Foerster, *TWNT* VII, pp. 190–95 and G. Kittel, ibid. II, pp. 257 f. ὁ ἄγγελος κυρίου may be the only exception, but the inconsistency in Hermas' use of the titles tells us not to overstress the evidence from this title, see n. 55. The use of the superlative σεμνότατος, however, might indicate that this is a superior angel.

[19] The identification of the shepherd has also been much discussed, see e.g. M. Dibelius, pp. 494–96 and E. Peterson, *Kritische Analyse der fünften Vision des Hermas, in Frühkirche, Judentum und Gnosis*, Freib. 1959, pp. 276 ff. S. Giet, pp. 181–84 will make him a Christ figure, except for in Sim. IX, p. 168. This seems to overinterpret the messenger-language used of him. G. F. Snyder speaks of "Christological function", pp. 60 f.

[20] The purpose is here indicated by an infinitive, Sim. VIII:6.3 and Mand. XII:6.1.

[21] J.-P. Audet, *Affinités littéraires et doctrinales du Manuel de Discipline*, RB 60. 1953, pp. 45 ff, holds that ὁ κύριος in Hermas is always used of God and not of his Son. That is hardly correct, see e.g. S. Giet, pp. 164 ff, but in the texts we are discussing, ὁ κύριος clearly refers to God.

This use of ἀποστέλλειν goes well together with the biblical usage. It is the word LXX uses for שלח, expressing a goal-directed action with a specific purpose. The passive without a subject will be understood in a religious context as denoting an act by God.[22] As a translation of the pu'al of שלח it is comparatively rare in the OT itself; it is used of an angel in Dan. 10:11. But one can see how the passive use has developed within the LXX by comparing the Theodotion and LXX versions of Dan. 4:13,23.[23] Intertestamental and NT writings also give evidence of this use of ἀποστέλλειν.[24]

Other passages dealing with the shepherd's coming to Hermas, using other verbs, show the same pattern. ὁ κύριος is subject in Sim. VIII:11.1, also in Mand. IV:2.1, where the purpose of the shepherd's coming is to give Hermas understanding. A similar function occurs in Sim. IX:1.3, where he is sent by the angel! This wider context then confirms our first result: there is no difference between the language used of the angel and of the Lord.

The ἵνα-clause in our sentence: ἵνα μετὰ σοῦ οἰκήσω τὰς λοιπὰς ἡμέρας τῆς ζωῆς σου and also Mand. XII:6.1: μεθ' ὑμῶν εἶναι, support this. A similar promise is often used in OT to express divine protection. It can be revealed by God himself,[25] or by his angel.[26] Promises in this form are also found in NT.[27] The sentence here, then, stands in a long tradition as a divine promise.

The evidence is clear. ἀποστέλλειν, used of angels being sent is elsewhere in Hermas only used with ὁ κύριος as subject; and the biblical material has shown that the use with ὁ κύριος is the original one, which gives meaning to the term when used of the angel. Only God sends angels; in Judaism this is clearly a divine prerogative.[28] Here, then, ὁ σεμνότατος ἄγγελος has the same function as God, or we should rather say that 'God-language' is used of this angel. So far he is not found to have any specific profile of his own. ὁ κύριος and this angel seem to be interchangeable. We will see whether this is also the case in other texts.

---

[22] K. H. Rengstorf, *TWNT* I, p. 402, n. 34.

[23] Theodotion follows TM: ιρ και ἅγιος ἀπ' οὐρανοῦ κατέβη, whereas LXX has ἄγγελος ἀπεστάλη ... ἐκ τοῦ οὐρανοῦ, in 4:23 extended to ἀπεστάλη παρὰ τοῦ κυρίου.

[24] Tob. 3:17, 4. Esdras 4:1, 5:31 etc. (Latin), Luke 1:19,26, Hebr. 1:14.

[25] Gen. 15:1.

[26] Judg. 6:12,16 and Gen. 16:7 ff, showing how the distinctions between the Lord and his angel are gliding.

[27] e.g. Acts 18:10, cf. Matt. 28:20. See also J. Jeremias, *Jesu Verheissung für die Völker*, Stuttg. 1956, p. 33.

[28] See O. Betz, *Der Paraklet*, Leiden 1963, pp. 170 ff.

Mand. V:1.7 is an exhortation to avoid ill temper. Typical of our text are several expressions giving reasons why Hermas and the Christians are able to fulfil this commandment. First the promise of the presence of the shepherd is mentioned, and secondly: ἐδικαιώθησαν γὰρ πάντες ὑπὸ τοῦ σεμνοτάτου ἀγγέλου. ἐδικαιώθησαν is not to be taken in a Pauline sense, as a unique Christological statement, but should be seen within the wider context of Hermas' concept of righteousness.

The commandments in the Mandates can sometimes be summed up as: "do δικαιοσύνη and you will live to God".[29] But this righteousness, acted out in men's lives, comes from God;[30] those who have faith in him cannot be led away from it.[31] It is a gift of God to the Christians, creating that community where men should live according to righteousness.[32] God's giving of justification is not a finished act. It also has a future; in Sim. V:7.1 δικαιωθῇ refers to his judgement and expresses the reward to the Christians. His activity in forgiving, healing, sins must also be seen as an act of his righteousness.

From this context, ἐδικαιώθησαν ... ὑπὸ τοῦ σεμνοτάτου ἀγγέλου, referring to an act in the past, has the same implications for the Christians as when God is acting: it makes it possible to live according to the commandments of God. Again, no specific acts on his part are referred to; he has no functions of his own, but shares in those of God.[33]

Sim. V:4.4 is a part of a dialogue between Hermas and the shepherd; Hermas is rebuked because he asks for an explanation of the parable in V:2. He should have asked the Lord, because σὺ δὲ ἐνδεδυναμωμένος ὑπὸ τοῦ ἁγίου ἀγγέλου καὶ εἰληφὼς παρ' αὐτοῦ τοιαύτην ἔντευξιν and the Lord is very merciful, πολυεύσπλαγχνός, and gives unceasingly to all who ask him.

The mercy of God stands in the very centre of Hermas' message. If he urges Christians to repent, it is because God's mercy makes repentance

---

[29] Mand. I:2, V:2.1, VI:2.10.

[30] Vis. III: 1.6.

[31] Mand. V:2.1.

[32] Vis. III:9.1.

[33] Is it possible to see Sim. IX:17.4 f as a Christological interpretation of ἐδικαιώθησαν ... ὑπο τοῦ σεμνοτάτου ἀγγέλου? Sim. IX is most likely later than the rest of Similitudines (M. Dibelius, p. 421, G. F. Snyder, pp. 4 ff, but S. Giet, pp. 289 ff) and takes up and develops the themes from Vis. III and Sim. VII. Sim. IX:17.4 f tells that to be called by the name of the Son of God means to receive a seal. Thereby man becomes a member of το γένος τῶν δικαίων and he is supposed to keep his righteousness. IX:16.3 f identifies the seal with water; it is likely that traditions about Jewish water-rites have been combined with Christian baptism, see E. Peterson, p. 329 and S. Giet, pp. 171 f.

possible.[34] It is also this merciful Lord who strengthens those who repent; his mercy and his power to strengthen go together.[35] The verb δυναμοῦν can be used in imperative: strengthen yourself![36] Most often, however, this strengthening is due to God's help, either directly or through mediaries.[37]

Our passage, 'strengthened by the glorious angel,' should be seen as fulfilling the conditions for receiving the mercy of the Lord: to be God's servant and have the Lord in one's heart (V:4.3). In this connection we should pay attention to two instances where δυναμοῦν marks the transition from 'then' to 'now', Sim. IX:1.2 and Vis. III:12.3, where the strengthening has a clear connection with repentance.[38]

Hermas has also received prayer, ἔντευξις, from the angel. Ἔντευξις is seen as some sort of power; only the prayers of the man who serves God with a whole mind have power.[39] This is clearly shown in Sim. II:5 f., where it is also explicitly stated that man has got this prayer as a gift from God: ἥν ἔλαβεν παρὰ τοῦ κυρίου, the same expression that in our text is used of the angel: εἰληφὼς παρ' αὐτοῦ τοιαύτην ἔντευξιν.

The strengthening that makes man a true servant of God and the powerful prayer, these are truly God's own gifts. And the function of the angel in this respect is to such a degree identical with God's own that the process in Sim. V:4.3 f. can be described without him.[40]

Sim. VII shows the same tendency as the other texts and gives few new elements. We notice that the activities within the passage are divided between the angel and the Lord, not completely consistently, it seems.[41] That the angel and God are interchangeable in this text, can be tested by comparing it to Vis. I:3, which shows many striking similarities.[42]

[34] Mand. IX:1 f. For the eschatological background to πολυεύσπλαγχνός, see H. Köster, *TWNT* VII, pp. 558 f.
[35] Vis. III:12.3, I:3.2. Cf. the use of the formula ὁ τὰ πάντα κτίσας καὶ δυναμώσας in a similar context, Sim. VII:4.
[36] Mand. V:2.8.
[37] Mand. XII:6.4, Sim. VI:1.2.
[38] Once more we will look to Sim. IX for illumination of our passage. Here (IX:13.7) the strengthening by receiving the power of the holy spirits and the inclusion among the servants of God is attributed to the receiving of the name of the Son of God, as we found in IX:17.
[39] Esp. Mand. XI:2 ff, also V:1.6.
[40] See Sim. VI:3.6.
[41] Hermas' family has sinned against the angel, but it is God who can give forgiveness. The angel has handed Hermas over to be punished, but it is God who has decided to show him the reason for it.
[42] Sin against the angel (Sim. VII)/ God (Vis. 1) provokes the anger of the angel/ God. But the result, afflictions for Hermas, is the same; the aim is repentance. And in both instances hope comes from the mercy of God.

We shall look more closely at the element of men's sin evoking the anger of the angel. παραπιχραίνειν, in the passive, is a hapax legomenon in Hermas and the Apostolic fathers; in NT it is only used in Hebrews.[43] For the implications of this word, we will have to go back to OT.

The LXX uses παραπιχραίνειν as a translation of two different Hebrew words: כעס, to make angry, and מרה, to be rebellious. As a translation of כעס it is always used with God as its object, synonymous to παροργίζειν.[44] Other instances seem similar, even if actually rendering the Hebrew מרה, with God as its object,[45] or, more interesting in our context, his word or his spirit.[46]

The use of παραπιχραίνειν of the angel is then clearly derived from the use about God. Vis. I:3.1 uses ὀργίζεται ὁ Θεός in a parallel passage to παρεπιχράνθη ὁ ... ἄγγελος and the viewpoint that sin is an offence against God in his majesty is underlined by Vis. I:1.6.

CONCLUSIONS

1. The result of our study of the function of the angel in these texts is that it is difficult to distinguish between God and his angel. The angel is sharing in God's own work; he seems to have no activity apart from that. We seem to be nearer to the OT understanding of the 'malak Yahweh' more than to any specific angelic figure in later development of angelology. This angel cannot be identified with any of the other angels in the Shepherd. There is *one* angel of ultimate importance. This angel is a part of the framework of the book; he appears in Vis. V, Sim. IX:1 and X, texts that are important for the redaction and the structure of the Shepherd.

2. We have not come much nearer to an explanation of the immediate background to this angel. In recent years many attempts have been made to show the connections between Hermas and Qumran,[47] but it has not been possible to establish any positive evidence of influence from Qumran

---

[43] Hebr. 3:16 and 3:8 in citing Ps. 94:8 (this and the following OT citations are from LXX).

[44] See Jer. 51:3, 39:29,32. W. Michaelis, *TWNT* VI, pp. 125 ff.

[45] Ps. 5:11.

[46] Ps. 104:28, 105:33.

[47] The article by J.-P. Audet, n. 21, created the basis for further discussion, see H. Braun, *Qumran und das Neue Testament*, Tübingen 1966, esp. pp. 184 ff. Audet is followed in his positive view upon the influence from Qumran on Hermas by J. Daniélou et al., but has also met with heavy criticism, esp. from Braun, p. 189. There seems to be a consensus, however, that the dualism in anthropology and pneumatology shows great similarities.

messianology upon Hermas.[48] The picture of the archangel Michael in
Qumran corresponds by and large to that in Judaism in general. This is
clearly the underlying tradition of the parable in Sim. VIII, and it bears
many similarities to the function of the angel in the texts we have discussed.[49] But these texts have certain elements to which there are no parallels, e.g. the sending of the shepherd, sin against the angel, the use of
παραπικραίνειν. The evidence from these texts then speaks against a restless
identification between this angel and Michael.[50] He cannot be the only explanation.

3. The picture of the angel in the texts outside the parables is open to a
more specific Christological interpretation. As we have tried to show, it
may be closer to the interpretation of the parables.[51] This might show how
Christology has influenced angelology.

This can be demonstrated upon the motive of the angel sending the shepherd. S. Giet has shown the influence from the Gospel of John upon Hermas, especially Sim. IX.[52] Is John to send or to be sent is an important
Christological term.[53] That Jesus is sent by God proves his legitimacy. But
what is quite new compared to the tradition is that Jesus himself is here
described as one who sends, who shares this right with God.[54] We find
the same closeness to God and the same interchangeability in functions that
we observed regarding the angel and God in Hermas. Maybe this influence
can account for what seems to be a revival of the OT picture of 'malak
Yahweh', which was discontinued during the intertestamental period until
it reappeared in interpretations of OT texts.[55]

---

[48] The suggestion from W. H. Brownlee that the angel in 1QM XVII:6 f is a Messianic figure, Messianic motifs of Qumran and the NT, NTS 3, 1956–57, p. 204, do
not seem to be a possible interpretation, see, e.g., A. S. van der Woude, *Die messia-
nische Vorstellungen der Gemeinde von Qumran,* Assen 1957, pp. 140 ff. But for later
Arabic sources referring Arius' doctrine of Christ as an angel to influence from the Essenes, see R. de Vaux, *A propos des manuscrits de la Mer Morte,* RB 57, 1950, pp. 422 ff.

[49] The acts of God and Michael seem to be interwoven, 1QS III:24 f. Michael is
the highest among angels, 1QM XVII:6 ff, and he is the lord of 'all the sons of justice',
1QM XIII:10.

[50] As W. Lueken, p. 155, also S. Giet, p. 228.

[51] See n. 33, 38.

[52] S. Giet, pp. 157 ff.

[53] The verb used is πέμπειν.

[54] Of the sending of the paraclete, John 16:7, 15:26, 14:26. See O. Betz, *Der Paraklet,* pp. 170 ff.

[55] J. Lebreton, pp. 655 f, points to Philo and Clemens of Alexandria interpreting
ὁ ἄγγελος κυρίου in OT theophanies as Logos and Christ respectively. Lebreton will
explain the angel in Hermas from this interpretation. But he only states formal similarities, the title and the angel appearing in visions, and does not study his functions.

UN CHAPITRE
D'ÉTHIQUE JUDÉO-CHRÉTIENNE :
LES DEUX VOIES

par W. Rordorf

Université de Neuchâtel

Il est bien connu que la *Didaché*, découverte par P. Bryennios et publiée par lui en 1883, s'ouvre par cette phrase : « Il y a deux voies, une de la vie et une de la mort. » L'enseignement des deux voies, qui est un enseignement éthique, couvre l'essentiel des chapitres 1-5 de l'écrit[1]. Très tôt, on a pris l'habitude de le désigner comme *manual of the Two Ways*[2], comme *die beiden Wege*[3] ou *zwei Wege*[4], ou plus simplement comme le *duae viae*[5]. L'enseignement des deux voies, conservé sous différentes formes dans plusieurs écrits chrétiens des premiers siècles[6], n'a cessé de susciter la curiosité des savants. Les recherches faites depuis bientôt un siècle se sont concentrées, entre autres, sur deux problèmes : 1. la question de la provenance du *duae viae* ; 2. la question du *Sitz im Leben* du *duae viae* ; à quoi j'aimerais ajouter un troisième problème, celui

---

1. Pour le moment, nous laisserons de côté la question de savoir si, oui ou non, le chap. 6 forme la fin du *duae viae*, et si le chap. 16 appartenait primitivement aussi au *duae viae* (cf. *infra*, notes 32 et 36, et p. 125).

2. Ainsi C. Taylor, *The Teaching of the Twelve Apostles with illustrations from the Talmud*, 1886.

3. Ainsi A. Harnack, *Die Apostellehre und die jüdischen beiden Wege*, 1886 (2e éd. 1896).

4. Ainsi R. Knopf, *Die Lehre der zwölf Apostel*, 1920.

5. La *Doctrina apostolorum*, connue en partie en 1884 déjà, commence en effet par les mots : *Viae duae sunt in saeculo, uitae et mortis...*

6. A part *Did.* 1-5, il faut signaler notamment *Barn.* 18-20, *Doctrina apost.*, *Canons eccl.* 4-13 et *Epitome des can. eccl., Const. apost.* VII, 1-18, *Vie de Chenoute* (arabe), et quelques textes pseudo-athanasiens. Cf. S. Giet, *L'énigme de la Didachè*, 1970, p. 19-26.

du *Nachleben* du *duae viae* dans le christianisme, qui, me semble-t-il, a été quelque peu négligé. Dans ce qui suit, je me permettrai de reprendre chacun de ces problèmes, l'un après l'autre ; je m'efforcerai de faire le point des recherches passées et de tirer les conclusions qui s'imposent pour la recherche actuelle.

1. La question de la provenance du duae viae[7]

La ressemblance entre *Didaché* 1-5 et *Epître de Barnabé* 18-20 a frappé déjà les premiers éditeurs de la *Didaché*. D'abord, on ne songeait qu'à deux solutions possibles du problème : ou bien la *Didaché* suit, dans la section du *duae viae*, l'*Epître de Barnabé* (ainsi Bryennios, Harnack), ou bien c'est le contraire, et *Barnabé* dépend ici de la *Didaché* (ainsi Zahn, Funk). C'est C. Taylor[8] qui avança l'hypothèse d'une source commune qu'il croyait juive ; Harnack s'est rallié à son point de vue[9].

Dès que le texte complet de la *Doctrina apostolorum* fut connu et édité[10], on eut un nouveau problème à résoudre : était-ce une traduction latine de la *Didaché* ou un texte indépendant qui serait même plus proche de la source commune supposée de *Didaché* et de *Barnabé* ? La deuxième réponse semblait plus plausible[11]. Mais elle n'aidait pas à déterminer si la source commune était de provenance chrétienne ou juive.

---

7. On trouve des résumés de l'histoire de la recherche dans J.-P. AUDET, *La Didachè. Instructions des apôtres*, 1958, p. 2-21 ; P. PRIGENT-R.A. KRAFT, *Epître de Barnabé*, SC 172, 1971, 12-20. Cf. aussi A. TURCK, *Evangélisation et catéchèse aux deux premiers siècles*, 1962.

8. Dans l'ouvrage cité à la note 2 ; avant lui, semble-t-il, J. WORDSWORTH, « Christian Life, Ritual and Discipline at the Close of the First Century », *The Guardian*, London, 19 mars 1884, Supp., cité par J.-P. AUDET, *op. cit.*, p. 12, n. 3.

9. Dans l'ouvrage cité à la note 3 ; cf. *Die Apostellehre*, dans *Realencycl. für prot. Theol. und Kirche*, 3e éd. I (1896), p. 723 ss. ; *Didache*, dans *The New Schaff-Herzog Encycl. of Rel. Knowl.* III (1909), p. 423.

10. Par J. SCHLECHT, *Doctrina XII apostolorum*, 1900 ; cf. L. WOHLEB, *Die lateinische Uebersetzung der Didache kritisch und sprachlich untersucht*, 1913.

11. Cf. E. HENNECKE, « Die Grundschrift der Didache und ihre Rezensionen », *ZNW* 2 (1901), p. 58-72 ; E.J. GOODSPEED, « The Didache, Barnabas and the Doctrina », *Angl. Theol. Rev.* 27 (1945), p. 228-247 ; B. ALTANER, « Zum Problem der lateinischen Doctrina apostolorum », *Vig. Chr.* 6 (1952), p. 1-47.

Un fervent défenseur de l'origine juive du *duae viae* fut A. Seeberg. Dans plusieurs publications [12], il essaya de prouver l'existence d'un catéchisme chrétien primitif contenant les deux voies, des prescriptions alimentaires (cf. *Did.* 6 !), des instructions sur le baptême, la prière, l'eucharistie (cf. *Did.* 7-10 !) et un enseignement doctrinal, à l'instar du catéchisme qu'utilisaient les Juifs pour initier leurs prosélytes, et qui s'inspirait en partie du « Code de Sainteté » (Lév. 17 ss.) [13]. A cause de leur hardiesse, les thèses de Seeberg ne trouvèrent pas l'écho qu'elles auraient mérité [14] ; toujours est-il que P. Carrington [15] et, à sa suite, E.G. Selwyn [16] s'en inspirèrent visiblement dans leurs travaux beaucoup plus connus sur le catéchisme chrétien primitif ; mais ces deux auteurs n'incluaient pas le *duae viae* dans leurs recherches (en tout cas pas directement).

Après Seeberg, la question de la provenance — juive ou chrétienne — du *duae viae* ne fut plus au premier plan. Ce désintérêt est dû à J.A. Robinson qui, dès 1912 [17], reprit la thèse des premiers éditeurs de la *Didaché*, à savoir que le *duae viae* de la *Didaché* dépendrait de celui de l'*Epître de Barnabé* puisque ce dernier est une partie intégrante de *toute* l'Epître qui forme une unité littéraire. Robinson fut suivi par la majorité des savants [18]. Du même coup, le problème de la provenance du *duae viae* pouvait sembler tranché : il serait tout simplement

12. *Der Katechismus der Urchristenheit*, 1903 ; *Das Evangelium Christi*, 1905 ; *Die beiden Wege und das Aposteldekret*, 1906 ; *Die Didache des Judentums und der Urchristenheit*, 1908.

13. G. KLEIN, *Der älteste christliche Katechismus und die jüdische Propaganda-Literatur*, 1909, allait encore beaucoup plus loin : d'après lui, tout l'enseignement moral chrétien reposerait pratiquement sur Gen. 6,12 et Ps 34 (33) !

14. Cf. F. HAHN, dans son introduction à l'ouvrage *Der Katechismus der Urchristenheit* réimprimé, 1966 ; cf. aussi A. TURCK, *op. cit.* (note 7), p. 20 ss.

15. *The Primitive Christian Catechism*, 1940.

16. *The First Epistle of St. Peter*, 2ᵉ éd. 1947, Essay II, p. 363-466.

17. « The Problem of the Didache », *JTS* 13 (1912), p. 339-356 ; cf. *Barnabas, Hermas and the Didache*, 1920 ; « The Epistle of Barnabas and the Didache », *JTS* 35 (1934), p. 113-146 ; 225-248.

18. Ne mentionnons que J. MUILENBURG, *The Literary Relations of the Epistle of Barnabas and the Teaching of the Twelve Apostles*, 1929 ; R.H. CONNOLLY, « The Didache in Relation to the Epistle of Barnabas », *JTS* 33 (1932), p. 237-253 ; « The Didache and Montanism », *Down. Rev.* 55 (1937), p. 477-489 ; F.E. VOKES, *The Riddle of the Didache. Fact or Fiction, Heresy or Catholicism ?*, 1938 (M. Vokes me disait récemment qu'il ne maintient plus sa thèse de l'origine montaniste de la *Didaché*).

la création de l'auteur de l'*Epître de Barnabé*. Rares furent les voix critiques qui osèrent dire que le problème d'une éventuelle source commune à *Barnabé* et à la *Didaché* restait entier [19].

Les découvertes de Qumran obligèrent les savants à reprendre le problème resté en suspens. En effet, le *Manuel de discipline* (III,13-IV,26) contient une instruction sur les deux esprits, qui ressemble en maints points au *duae viae* que nous trouvons dans l'*Epître de Barnabé* et dans la *Didaché* ; il semble même que la forme du *duae viae* représentée par la *Doctrina apostolorum* s'en rapproche davantage, ce qui confirmerait, après coup, l'avis exprimé jadis par Hennecke, Goodspeed, Altaner [20]. Le Père Audet a le mérite de s'être penché le premier sur ce problème et d'avoir démontré, dans le détail, que le *duae viae* chrétien devait dépendre, d'une manière ou d'une autre, de son modèle qumranien [21]. Sa démonstration a trouvé un large écho positif [22]. Le Cardinal Daniélou, dans plusieurs publications [23], a exposé les mêmes vues. S. Wibbing [24] a étayé cette thèse en prouvant que les listes chrétiennes de vertus et de vices dépendent de la même section du *Manuel de discipline* de Qumran. A son tour, E. Kamlah [25] a décelé l'arrière-fond *religionsgeschichtlich* de cette forme de parénèse dans les écrits du Bas-judaïsme et du christianisme primitif.

---

19. J.-P. AUDET, *op cit.* (note 7), p. 20 s., cite les noms suivants : J.V. Bartlet, B. Capelle, A.J. McLean, C.H. Turner, B.H. Streeter, J.M. Creed, Th. Klauser.

20. Cf. note 11.

21. Cf. son article « Affinités littéraires et doctrinales du *Manuel de discipline* », *RB* 59, 1952, p. 219-238 ; et son grand commentaire de la *Didaché*, 1958, p. 121-163.

22. Cf. les éditions les plus récentes de la *Didaché* et de l'*Epître de Barnabé*, par R.A. KRAFT, *The Apostolic Fathers* III, 1965, et P. PRIGENT-R.A. KRAFT, *Sources chrétiennes* 172, 1971. Cf. aussi J. LIEBAERT, *Les enseignements moraux des Pères apostoliques*, 1970, p. 99 s.

23. Cf. par ex. « Une source de la spiritualité chrétienne dans les manuscrits de la Mer Morte : la doctrine des deux esprits », *Dieu vivant* 25 (1953), p. 127 ss. ; *Les manuscrits de la Mer Morte et les Origines du christianisme*, 1957, p. 39 ss. ; *Théologie du Judéo-christianisme*, 1958, p. 38 ss., 370 ss. ; et encore assez récemment *La catéchèse aux premiers siècles*, 1968, p. 127 ss.

24. *Die Tugend- und Lasterkataloge im Neuen Testament*, BZNW 25, 1959.

25. *Die Form der katalogischen Paränese im Neuen Testament*, WUNT 7, 1964. Cf. déjà A. WLOSOK, *Laktanz und die philosophische Gnosis*, 1960, p. 107 ss.

La lumière semble donc faite sur la provenance du *duae
viae* : il serait issu d'une tradition essénienne dualiste et aurait
fait son chemin dans le christianisme [26]. Pourtant, il y a des
questions qui se posent et que la recherche future devra prendre en considération si elle veut arriver à des résultats solidement établis. Voici ces questions :

1. Il ne faut pas perdre de vue que la comparaison entre
le *Manuel de discipline* qumranien et les différentes formes
du *duae viae* chrétien porte uniquement sur le *cadre dualiste*
(qui est absent dans 1a *Didaché* !) et sur le genre littéraire
général de l'instruction qui met côte à côte une liste de vertus
et une liste de vices ; mais dans le détail du contenu et du
vocabulaire, les ressemblances font défaut. D'autre part, à en
croire le Père Audet, le *duae viae* de la *Didaché* serait adressé
« aux Gentils » [27] et se situerait par conséquent dans une orientation non pas particulariste (qumranienne), mais universaliste.
On est donc obligé d'admettre, avec le Père Audet [28], que « le
duae viae a connu, sans doute dans 1a première période de
son histoire (pré-chrétienne ?), une phase recensionnelle assez
active ».

2. Somme toute, la parenté entre le *Manuel de discipline* et
le *duae viae*, éblouissante parce que découverte récemment,
ne semble pas être beaucoup plus étroite que celle qu'on avait
établie, avant la « nouvelle vague » qumranienne, entre l'instruction catéchétique des prosélytes juifs et le *duae viae* que
l'on croyait être un enseignement catéchétique chrétien [29]. Bien

26. H. BRAUN, *Qumran und das Neue Testament* II, 1966, p. 184 ss.,
286 ss., résume la discussion d'une manière très nuancée et compétente.
Pour E. ROBILLARD (« L'Epître de Barnabé : trois époques, trois théologies,
trois rédacteurs », *RB* 78, 1971, p. 184-209), ce serait Barnabé, le compagnon
de Paul, qui aurait repris le *duae viae* juif, à des fins missionnaires !
27. En effet, J.-P. AUDET, *op. cit.* (note 7), p. 91 ss., fait confiance au
titre long de l'écrit qui aurait eu, en milieu juif, la teneur suivante :
Διδαχὴ χυρίου (= Dieu !) τοῖς ἔθν᾽σιν.
28. *Op. cit.* (note 7), p. 158. De même PRIGENT, dans *SC* 172, 1971, p. 20.
Cf. les remarques critiques de F.E. VOKES, « The Didache — Still debated »,
Church Quarterly 3, 1970, p. 58 s., 62.
29. Cf. en particulier A. BENOÎT, *Le baptême chrétien au second siècle*,
1953, p. 5-33, mais aussi D. DAUBE, *The New Testament and Rabbinic
Judaism*, 1956, p. 106 ss. La règle d'or et les devoirs domestiques incor-
porés au *duae viae* se situent aussi plutôt dans ce contexte : cf. A. DIHLE,
Die goldene Regel, 1962, et D. SCHROEDER, *Die Haustafeln des Neuen Tes-*

que nous soyons mal renseignés sur le baptême des prosélytes juifs à l'époque du christianisme primitif, les parallèles qu'il présente avec le baptême chrétien sont indéniables [30]. La recherche future ne devra pas négliger cette donnée du problème.

3. Il y a autre chose : c'est l'arrière-fond vétéro-testamentaire du *duae viae*. Je ne pense pas ici aux allusions au thème des deux voies qu'on trouve dans l'Ancien Testament, mais je pense au genre très précis du *Bundesformular* que K. Baltzer [31] a décelé dans certains textes bibliques, et qu'il retrouve, sous des formes nouvelles, précisément dans le *Manuel de discipline* qumranien et le *duae viae* chrétien. Il vaudra la peine de prendre au sérieux, à l'avenir, aussi cette vision des choses [32].

Etant donné la complexité du problème de la provenance du *duae viae*, il faudra surtout éviter les solutions simplistes, unilatérales ; il ne semble pas, en effet, que le *duae viae* (dans *toutes* ces formes) vienne de Qumran, ni qu'il dérive uniquement de l'instruction donnée aux prosélytes juifs, ni encore qu'il soit une expression tardive de la morale de l'alliance ancrée dans le *Bundesformular*. A titre d'hypothèse, je verrais l'évolution plutôt de la manière suivante : la tradition éthique vétéro-testamentaire rattachée au *Bundesformular* a subi, dans certaines couches du Bas-judaïsme (pas dans toutes) une modification nettement dualiste sous le coup de l'influence parse (dans ce domaine, je suivrais volontiers Kamlah). Le christianisme a hérité de ces deux courants dualiste et non-dualiste. Dans le Nouveau Testament, nous retrouvons ces deux tradi-

taments (thèse, Hambourg), 1959. A. ADAM, dans *ZKG* 68, 1957, p. 30 ss., est très précis : il voit dans le *duae viae* le manuel catéchétique des prosélytes juifs de l'Adiabène.

30. M. DUJARIER, *Le parrainage des adultes aux trois premiers siècles de l'Eglise*, 1962, tout en traitant de l'arrière-fond qumranien possible (p. 103 ss.), n'a pas laissé de côté ce problème (p. 73 ss.). Cf. aussi J. JEREMIAS, *Die Kindertaufe in den ersten vier Jahrhunderten*, 1958, p. 28 ss.

31. *Das Bundesformular*, WMANT 4, 2e éd. 1964. Cf. le bon résumé en français de J. L'HOUR, *La morale de l'alliance*, dans *Cahiers de la RB* 5, 1966. Voir aussi : J. BECKER, *Untersuchungen zur Entstehungsgeschichte der Testamente der zwölf Patriarchen*, 1970.

32. E. KAMLAH, *op. cit.* (note 25), p. 163, n. 1, se fait la critique beaucoup trop facile ! Notons cependant que les deux auteurs tombent d'accord pour dire que le chap. 16 de la *Didaché* appartenait au *duae viae* primitif. Cf. H. KÖSTER, *Synoptische Ueberlieferung bei den apostolischen Vätern*, 1957, p. 160, 173, 189 s., et R.A. KRAFT, *op. cit.* (note 22), p. 12 ss.

tions [33]. Ne serait-il pas possible que les différentes formes du *duae viae* chrétien reflètent également les *deux* traditions ? Dans cette optique, la *Doctrina apostolorum* et l'*Epître de Barnabé* s'inscriraient dans la lignée *dualiste* de l'instruction morale telle qu'elle se trouve dans le *Manuel de discipline*, tandis que la *Didaché* et les documents dérivés représenteraient la lignée non-dualiste de l'instruction morale telle qu'elle s'est formée au cours de l'histoire d'Israël et qu'elle a passé dans l'enseignement sapientiel et synagogal du judaïsme (et éventuellement dans la catéchèse donnée aux prosélytes) [34]. L'étude de la question du *Sitz im Leben* nous apportera peut-être d'autres lumières à ce sujet. [35].

2. La question du Sitz im Leben du duae viae

En *Didaché* 7,1, nous lisons ceci : « Au sujet du baptême, baptisez ainsi : après avoir enseigné tout ce qui précède (ταῦτα πάντα προειπόντες), baptisez au nom du Père et du Fils et du Saint Esprit. » Les mots ταῦτα πάντα προειπόντες doivent se rapporter aux chapitres 1-5(6) [36] de la *Didaché*, qui contien-

---

33. En gros (c'est bien *cum grano salis* que je le dis !), les évangiles synoptiques représentent la tradition non-dualiste, tandis que les littératures johannique et paulinienne reflètent la tradition dualiste.

34. Cf. J.P. AUDET, *op. cit.*, p. 255 s. R.A. KRAFT, *op. cit.* (note 22), p. 136, met l'accent sur le critère de l'intensité eschatologique pour distinguer les traditions ; il s'approche par là de mon point de vue. A mon sens, cependant, le critère de la présence ou de l'absence du cadre dualiste va encore plus au centre du problème.

35. Il est assez vain de vouloir dire ce qui formait le *contenu* exact du *duae viae* pré-chrétien. Bien entendu, la « section évangélique » (*Did.* 1,3-2,1) ne s'y lisait pas. Le Père Giet, *op. cit.* (note 6), p. 153 ss., aimerait préciser davantage : le *duae viae* juif n'aurait contenu ni le *double* commandement de l'amour, ni l' « instruction du sage » (*Did.* 3, 1-6), ni même (éventuellement) la voie de la mort. Ce n'est pas ici le lieu de discuter ces thèses. En ce qui concerne le double commandement de l'amour, cf. la critique implicite que fait C. BURCHARD, dans *Der Ruf Jesu und die Antwort der Gemeinde, Festschrift für Joachim Jeremias*, 1970, p. 39-62.

36. *Did.* 6,1, semble être la fin du *duae viae*. Cependant, le précepte concernant les aliments (6,3) plonge ses racines dans une tradition également très ancienne ; cf. le décret apostolique qui est reflété, sous une forme archaïque et dans un contexte catéchétique, dans les *Pseudo-Clémentines* ; cf. à ce sujet les travaux de E. MOLLAND, dans *Opuscula Patristica*, 1970, p. 25-60 ; A.F.J. KLIJN, dans *NT* 10, 1968, p. 305-312 ; M. SIMON, dans *BJRL* 52, 1969-70, p. 437-460 ; et Y. TISSOT, dans *RB* 77, 1970,

nent justement le *duae viae*. En conséquence, les premiers éditeurs de la *Didaché*, Bryennios et Harnack, estimaient que le *duae viae* formait sans doute une partie de l'enseignement *catéchétique* préparatoire au baptême, dans les milieux d'où l'écrit est issu [37]. Par la suite, cette interprétation fut unanimement reçue par le monde savant. C'est J.-P. Audet qui, le premier à ma connaissance, l'a mise en question [38]. Il part de l'observation du fait que les mots ταῦτα πάντα προειπόντες ne se trouvent que dans le manuscrit de Constantinople (de 1056) et dans la version géorgienne, mais pas dans le remaniement de la *Didaché* au VIIe livre des *Constitutions apostoliques*, de la fin du IVe siècle. Il ne voit qu'une explication possible de ce fait : le compilateur des *Constitutions apostoliques* n'a pas trouvé les mots en question dans le texte de la *Didaché* qu'il a utilisé. En outre, il reconnaît dans les mots ταῦτα πάντα προειπόντες une insertion dans le texte, stylistiquement maladroite, de seconde main, qu'il n'hésite pas à supprimer dans son édition du texte grec [39]. La leçon particulière du manuscrit de Constantinople serait une glose de copiste qui refléterait l'usage de l'Eglise d'Egypte de se servir du *duae viae* pour l'instruction des catéchumènes [40].

La thèse du Père Audet est assez fragile. En ce qui concerne la question du style de *Didaché* 7,1, P. Nautin [41] l'a déjà montré. On peut aussi faire remarquer que le style de l' « addition » ne semble pas étranger aux habitudes d'expression du rédacteur de la *Didaché*, puisqu'il se sert, en 11,1, d'une formule presque identique : ταῦτα πάντα τὰ προειρημένα. Mais ce

p. 321-346. On peut même se poser la question de savoir si *Did.* 6, 2-3 ne montre pas que le *duae viae* s'adressait primitivement à des craignant-Dieu (cf. les préceptes noachiques de la tradition rabbinique : BILLERBECK III, 36 ss.); c'est la thèse de M. Simon (cf. déjà J.-P. AUDET, *op. cit.*, p. 354, et A. STUIBER, dans *Texte und Untersuchungen* 79, 1961, p. 323-329). Or, dans le christianisme, l'ensemble de 6,2-3 se rattachera plutôt à une tradition ascétique : cf. *infra*, p. 125 s.

37. A. HARNACK, *Die Lehre der zwölf Apostel*, 1884, p. 22, laissait ouverte la question de savoir s'il s'agissait d'un discours baptismal précédant immédiatement le baptême ou d'un véritable enseignement catéchétique.

38. *Op. cit.* (note 7), p. 58 ss.; cf. p. 358 s.

39. *Ibid.*, p. 232.

40. Cf. ATHANASE, *Lettre festale* 39, mais aussi *Can. eccl.* 12.

41. Dans *RHR* 155, 1959, p. 206 s. Cf. aussi B. BOTTE, dans *BTAM* 8, 1958, p. 168.

qui est plus grave, le Père Audet ne se pose même pas la question de savoir si le compilateur des *Constitutions apostoliques* aurait pu avoir intérêt à changer le texte de la *Didaché* du fait que, *de son temps et dans son Eglise, le duae viae* n'était plus utilisé pour l'instruction des catéchumènes [42]. On a l'impression que c'est la bonne réponse quand on lit l'exposé du contenu de la catéchèse baptismale en *Const. apost.* VII, 39 ss.

Si la critique de *Didaché* 7,1 par le P. Audet semble donc injustifiée [43], la question du *Sitz im Leben* du *duae viae* n'est pas pour autant résolue. En effet, il demeure que le *duae viae* ne fut pas exclusivement employé dans la catéchèse préparant au baptême. Une preuve en est l'*Epître de Barnabé* : selon toute vraisemblance, elle s'adresse à des chrétiens déjà baptisés [44] ; à la fin, elle leur rappelle l'enseignement des deux voies [45]. Dans la *Didaché*, le *duae viae* a donc sa place dans l'enseignement prébaptismal ; dans l'*Epître de Barnabé*, au contraire, elle a sa place dans l'enseignement postbaptismal. Pouvons-nous en dire davantage sur l'enseignement éthique *pré*baptismal et son *Sitz im Leben* ?

Posons d'abord une question, préliminaire, mais importante : A qui le *duae viae* s'adresse-t-il ? A des judéo-chrétiens ? Ou à des pagano-chrétiens ? Est-ce que les titres de la *Didaché* peuvent nous donner le renseignement désiré ? En effet, le manuscrit de Constantinople porte deux titres : « *Didaché* des douze Apôtres » et « *Didaché* du Seigneur aux gentils par les douze Apôtres ». Il ne s'agit pas de trancher ici le problème de la relation de ces deux titres entre eux et par rapport à l'écrit, problème qui est très compliqué [46]. Il est hors de doute, cependant, que le titre long (qui semble inspiré par Matth. 28,19 s.)

---

42. Un indice linguistique qui va dans ce sens : pourquoi s'exprime-t-il, juste ici, de la manière suivante : ἤδη μὲν καὶ πρότερον διεταξάμεθα ? Cette formule semble s'inspirer de ταῦτα πάντα προειπόντες de *Did.* 7,1.

43. Le Cardinal Daniélou, dans ses publications à ce sujet (cf. note 23), a toujours fait confiance au texte de *Did.* 7,1.

44. Cf. G. SCHILLE, « Zur urchristlichen Tauflehre. Stilistische Beobachtungen am Barnabasbrief », ZNW 49, 1958, p. 31-52.

45. Cf. les allusions au *duae viae* dans *I* et *II Clément*, dans le *Pasteur* d'HERMAS, donc dans des écrits qui s'adressent tous à des chrétiens baptisés.

46. J.-P. AUDET, *op. cit.*, p. 91 ss., le complique encore ; cf. P. NAUTIN, dans *RHR* 155, 1959, p. 210 ss.

entend présenter la *Didaché* comme un enseignement donné
aux convertis venus du paganisme [47]. Un passage du *duae viae*
lui-même confirme cette interprétation : en *Did.* 2,2, il est dit :
« Tu ne tueras point, tu ne commettras pas d'adultère [48]. Tu
ne t'adonneras ni à la pédérastie, ni à la fornication, ni au
vol, ni à la magie, ni à la sorcellerie. Tu ne supprimeras pas
l'enfant par avortement et tu ne tueras point l'enfant déjà né. »
Les préceptes visant la pédérastie, la magie, l'avortement et
l'exposition des enfants, qui s'ajoutent aux commandements
du décalogue, se comprennent mieux s'ils sont adressés à d'an-
ciens païens [49]. Le *duae viae* semble donc avoir été destiné à
des craignant-Dieu ou à des prosélytes, en milieu juif, et à des
pagano-chrétiens, en milieu chrétien.

Cette constatation peut nous aider à comprendre pourquoi
la *Didaché* parle du *duae viae* comme partie de l'enseignement
catéchétique préparant au baptême. Souvent, en effet, on a eu
l'impression que ce témoignage de la *Didaché* était absolument
insolite dans la littérature chrétienne primitive. Le Nouveau
Testament (à part *Hébr.* 6, 1 ss.) ne semble rien nous dire sur
une catéchèse prébaptismale ; le gros de l'enseignement moral
du Nouveau Testament semble rattaché à la parénèse postbaptismale [50] ; les récits de baptêmes contenus dans le *Livre
des Actes* nous suggèrent que l'on a baptisé sans perdre beaucoup de temps avec une catéchèse préliminaire. Cependant,
n'oublions pas que les premiers baptêmes étaient des baptêmes
de juifs ou de craignant-Dieu convertis au christianisme. Ceux-ci
n'avaient plus besoin d'être initiés à la morale de l'alliance,
ils la connaissaient et la pratiquaient avant même de devenir
chrétiens. Par conséquent, leur foi au Christ Jésus suffisait
pour qu'ils soient admis au baptême. Tout autre fut la situation, dès que les premiers convertis du paganisme demandèrent
le baptême : il fallait les instruire, préalablement à leur bap-

---

47. Ainsi déjà Harnack, *op. cit.* (note 37), p. 27 ss., contre Bryennios.
48. La *Doctrina apostolorum* met en tête le péché d'adultère, suivant
en cela l'ordre du décalogue dans les Septante (cf. aussi PHILON, *De
decalogo*, § 121 ; CLÉMENT D'ALEXANDRIE, *Protr.* 108 ; *Paed.* II, 89, 1 ; III,
89, 1). Il se pourrait que cet ordre soit primitif (cf. S. GIET, *op. cit.* [note
6], p. 103). Ce serait encore un indice pour situer l'origine du *duae viae*
dans un milieu de « diaspora » juive et chrétienne.
49. Cf. J.-P. AUDET, *op. cit.* (note 7), p. 286 ss. Voir aussi *Did.* 3,4.
50. Cf. par exemple F. HAHN, *op. cit.* (note 14), p. XXVIII ; c'est une des
critiques qu'il fait aux études de A. Seeberg.

tème, dans les rudiments de l'éthique correspondant à la foi en un seul Dieu. Saint Irénée, apparemment en connaissance de cause, s'exprime ainsi :

> Voilà pourquoi encore Paul, qui fut l'apôtre des gentils, déclare : *Plus qu'eux tous, j'ai peiné* (*1 Cor.* 15,10). Pour ceux-là (sc. les apôtres des juifs), en effet, l'enseignement était aisé... Car, lors même que ceux de la circoncision ne mettaient pas en pratique les paroles de Dieu, parce qu'ils les méprisaient, ils n'en avaient pas moins été instruits par avance à ne commettre ni adultère, ni fornication, ni vol, ni fraude, et ils savaient que tout ce qui porte préjudice au prochain est mal et objet d'exécration pour Dieu : aussi se laissaient-ils persuader sans peine de s'abstenir de ces choses, eux qui avaient déjà appris tout cela. Mais aux gentils, il fallait enseigner même cela, à savoir que de telles actions sont mauvaises, préjudiciables, inutiles et qu'elles sont dommageables à ceux qui les commettent. Pour ce motif, celui qui reçut l'apostolat à destination des gentils peina plus que ceux qui prêchèrent le Fils de Dieu parmi les circoncis [51].

Non seulement nous devons postuler que telle était bien la situation de la mission parmi les païens, au premier siècle déjà, mais nous avons des indices qui confirment cette vue. En plus de ce que M. Dujarier [52] a signalé, à propos du Nouveau Testament, on peut citer deux textes du début du IIe siècle qui, selon toute vraisemblance, supposent un enseignement éthique prébaptismal. Il s'agit de la lettre de Pline le Jeune, d'une part, et d'un passage du Livre d'Elkesaï, d'autre part. Dans sa lettre bien connue à Trajan (X,96,7), Pline dit, en parlant des chrétiens qu'il a interrogés :

> Ils affirmaient que toute leur faute, ou leur erreur, s'était bornée à avoir l'habitude de se réunir à jour fixe avant le lever du soleil, de chanter entre eux alternativement un hymne au Christ comme à un dieu, de s'engager par serment non à perpétrer quelque crime, mais à ne commettre ni vol, ni brigandage, ni adultère, à ne pas manquer à la parole donnée, à ne pas nier un dépôt réclamé en justice.

D'après l'interprétation de ce passage qu'a donnée H. Lietzmann [53], et qui reste toujours la plus plausible, l'« engagement » (sacramentum) dont parle le texte, serait l'enga-

---

51. *Adv. haer.*, IV, 24 1-2 ; trad. de A. ROUSSEAU, SC 100**, 1965, p. 699 ss. Y a-t-il, dans ce texte, des allusions au *duae viae* ?

52. *Op. cit.* (note 30), p. 117 ss. Cf. J. DANIÉLOU, *La catéchèse aux premiers siècles*, 1968, p. 37 ss.

53. « Die liturgischen Angaben des Pliniusbriefs », dans *Geschichtliche Studien für A. Hauck zum 70. Geburtstag*, 1916, p. 34 ss.

gement baptismal. A ce moment-là, nous devons supposer qu'une instruction éthique précédait le baptême. La même conclusion s'impose quant au passage du Livre d'Elkesaï que cite Hippolyte [54] en ces termes :

> (Que celui qui se plonge dans l'eau dise :) Voici que je prends à témoin le ciel, l'eau, les esprits saints, les anges de la prière, l'huile, le sel et la terre. J'atteste ces sept témoins que désormais je ne pécherai plus, je ne commettrai plus ni adultères, ni vols, ni injustices, ni actes inspirés par la cupidité ou la haine, ni parjures, bref que je ne me complairai plus dans aucune action mauvaise.

Bien qu'il soit ici question d'un deuxième baptême, comme acte de pénitence, qui se fait par auto-immersion, il est hors de doute qu'il se rattache étroitement aux rites du premier baptême.

Nous pouvons ajouter à cela le témoignage des *Kérygmes de Pierre* pseudo-clémentins, un peu plus tardif, il est vrai [55]. Ces prédications de Pierre sont particulièrement intéressantes pour notre propos parce qu'elles reflètent indubitablement un enseignement éthique prébaptismal qui s'avère très proche du *duae viae*. Ne citons que la VII<e> *Homélie* [56]: Pierre prêche d'abord à Tyr. Comme ailleurs [57], il souligne l'importance de suivre les préceptes du décret apostolique et donne ensuite une explication de la règle d'or qui reprend une partie des dix commandements (cf. *Did.* 1,2 ; 2,2-3). Après cette catéchèse (le texte grec emploie déjà le verbe κατηγεῖν !) qui dure plusieurs jours, les auditeurs se font baptiser en masse. Pierre passe ensuite à Sidon où il reprend son enseignement catéchétique qui mène à un grand nombre de baptêmes, en ces termes :

> Je ne refuse pas de vous indiquer la manière dont vous pourrez être sauvés, ayant appris moi-même, de la bouche du Prophète de la Vérité, les règles posées d'avance par Dieu... Connaissant donc ces actions, les bonnes et les mauvaises, je vous les signale comme étant deux voies, et je vous indique quelle est celle qui conduit à la perdition et quelle

---

54. *Ref. omn. haer*, IX, 15,5-6. Cf. à propos de ce passage E. Peterson, *Frühkirche, Judentum und Gnosis*, 1959, p. 221-235. G. Kretschmar, *Studien zur frühchristlichen Trinitätstheologie*, 1956, p. 212, a raison de renvoyer aussi au baptême des prosélytes juifs. Cf. d'ailleurs la *Contestatio* pseudo-clémentine (1,1).

55. Cf. G. Strecker, « Die Kerygmata Petrou », dans *Neutestamentliche Apokryphen* (ed. Hennecke-Schneemelcher), 3<e> éd., 1964, p. 63 ss.

56. On pourrait aussi citer la XI<e> et la XVIII<e> *Homélie*.

57. Cf. les travaux mentionnés en note 36.

est celle qui mène au salut sous la direction de Dieu. La voie que suivent les hommes marchant à leur perte est large et parfaitement unie : elle mène sans fatigue à la perdition. La voie des hommes qui travaillent à se sauver est étroite et raboteuse, mais à la fin elle fait aboutir au salut ceux qui l'ont péniblement suivie [58]. A ces deux routes président l'incrédulité et la foi.

Je crois qu'il faut aussi mentionner, dans ce contexte, le rite baptismal de l'*abrenuntiatio*. Bien qu'il soit attesté *expressis verbis* seulement à la fin du IIe siècle [59], ses racines doivent remonter plus haut dans le temps. En effet, il est impensable qu'on ait créé, à la fin du IIe siècle, un rite de renonciation à Satan, à ses anges et à ses œuvres, rite qui exprime un dualisme eschatologique très marqué. Ce rite doit être relié à une conception dualiste juive et judéo-chrétienne à laquelle étaient rattachées à leur tour, nous l'avons vu, certaines formes du *duae viae*. Or le rite de la renonciation à Satan implique l'existence d'une catéchèse éthique préalable [60].

C'est dire qu'il y a eu, sans doute, une tradition ininterrompue d'enseignement éthique prébaptismal dans l'Eglise chrétienne des deux premiers siècles, tradition qui plonge ses racines dans le judaïsme, qui a son *Sitz im Leben* dans le contexte de l'initiation des convertis païens, et qui mène jusqu'à l'institution du catéchuménat chrétien à la fin du IIe siècle. Le *duae viae* a eu sa place dans cette tradition [61].

Pour terminer ce chapitre, j'aimerais encore exprimer un vœu. L'intérêt que l'on porte aux traditions « catéchétiques » dans l'Eglise naissante a augmenté sensiblement, ces dernières années. On s'interroge sur la structure catéchétique du Sermon sur la montagne [62], voire des Evangiles synoptiques tout

---

58. L'influence de *Matth.* 7,13 s. est ici sensible.

59. Cf. H. KIRSTEN, *Die Taufabsage*, 1960 ; G. KRETSCHMAR, dans *Leiturgia* 5, 1970, p. 72 et 96 ss.

60. TERTULLIEN, *De cor.* 3,2, nous dit d'ailleurs que la première renonciation se faisait quelque temps avant le baptême déjà. Il faut ajouter à cela le témoignage de JUSTIN, *Apol.*, I, 64 (cf. aussi *II Clém.* 17,1).

61. Il est plus difficile de dire si l'on peut comparer le catéchuménat chrétien et le « catéchuménat » qumranien (affirmativement, J. DANIÉLOU, dans *RHPHR* 35, 1955, p. 105 ss.) ; le contexte est en tout cas assez différent.

62. Cf. E. MASSAUX, *Influence de l'Evangile de Saint Matthieu sur la littérature chrétienne avant Saint Irénée*, 1950 ; G. BORNKAMM, *Ueberlieferung und Auslegung im Matthäusevangelium*, WMANT 1, 4e éd. 1965, p. 15 (cf. *idem*, dans *Mélanges Dodd*, 1956, p. 225) ; J. JEREMIAS, *Die*

entiers [63] ; de même, on réétudie, après Carrington et Selwyn, les éléments catéchétiques dans la parénèse épistolaire du Nouveau Testament [64]. Mais on oublie généralement de préciser si l'on parle d'une catéchèse pré- ou postbaptismale. Il serait sage, me semble-t-il, de distinguer mieux ces deux choses, et de réserver le terme de catéchèse à l'enseignement dont on est sûr qu'il se donnait *avant* le baptême. L'application d'une certaine rigueur de méthode, dans ce domaine, clarifierait la situation, et nous apporterait du même coup, j'en suis convaincu, de nouvelles lumières quant à l'enseignement éthique préalable au baptême [65].

3. Le Nachleben du duae viae dans le christianisme

Dans les premières décennies qui suivirent la découverte de la *Didaché*, on a relevé pratiquement tous les passages dans la littérature chrétienne des trois premiers siècles qui citent le *duae viae* ou qui semblent y faire allusion [66]. Deux textes sont venus s'ajouter, en 1907 et 1914. Il s'agit de la *Démonstration de la prédication apostolique* de saint Irénée [67], et du Sermon

Bergpredigt (*Calwer Hefte* 27), 2e éd. 1960, p. 17 ss. ; C.H. Dodd, « The primitive Catechism and the Sayings of Jesus », dans *New Testament Essays. Studies in Memory of T.W. Manson*, 1959, p. 106-118 ; W.D. Davies, *The Setting of the Sermon on the Mount*, 1964, p. 370 ss. ; O. Hanssen, dans *Der Ruf Jesu und die Antwort der Gemeinde. Festschrift für Joachim Jeremias*, 1970, p. 94-111.

63. Cf. G. Schille, dans *NTS* 4, 1957-1958, p. 1-24 ; 101-114.

64. C.H. Dodd, *Gospel and Law*, 6e éd. 1965 ; W. Schrage, *Die konkreten Einzelgebote in der paulinischen Paränese*, 1961 ; K. Wegenast, *Das Verständnis der Tradition bei Paulus und in den Deuteropaulinen* (*WMANT* 8), 1962 ; cf. aussi G. Schille, dans *ZNW* 46, 1955, p. 81 ss. ; 48, 1957, p. 270-280 ; 51, 1960, p. 112-131 ; F.L. Cross, *I. Peter. A Paschal Liturgy*, 1954 ; M.E. Boismard, dans *RB* 63, 1956, p. 182-208 ; 64, 1957, p. 161-183.

65. Le rapport étroit entre le *duac viae* de la *Didaché* et le Sermon sur la Montagne est indéniable (cf. les travaux mentionnés à la note 62). Auraient-ils le même *Sitz im Leben* ? Cf. aussi J. Daniélou, *La catéchèse aux premiers siècles*, 1968, p. 134 s.

66. A. Harnack, dans son édition de la *Didaché* (note 37), présentait déjà un riche dossier de parallèles, mais c'est surtout A. Seeberg qui, dans ses différentes publications (cf. note 12), a rassemblé une vaste documentation à ce sujet ; cf. aussi G. Resch, *Das Aposteldecret*, 1905, p. 92 ss.

67. Publiée par Mgr Ter-Mekerttschian, dans *Texte und Untersuchungen* 31, 1, 1907.

De centesima, de sexagesima, de tricesima[68]. A. Turck[69] a le mérite d'avoir fait le rapprochement entre le premier texte et le *duae viae*. En ce qui concerne le Sermon, J. Daniélou[70] a vu qu'il cite *Did.* 6,2 ; nous y reviendrons.

Ce n'est pas mon ambition de reprendre cette liste des citations et allusions ; on ne peut d'ailleurs jamais dire avec certitude si les allusions qu'on croit avoir trouvées, se réfèrent vraiment au *duae viae*. J'aimerais plutôt étudier quelques textes des IVe, V^e et VIe siècles qui me semblent influencés par le *duae viae* et dont on n'a peut-être pas assez tenu compte. Ces textes nous montreront en même temps que le *Sitz im Leben* du *duae viae* a changé, au cours de son histoire.

Un premier texte à citer est l'*Epitome des Institutions divines* de Lactance. Dans les chapitres 53-62, où Lactance reprend le VIe livre des Institutions *De vero culto*, l'influence du *duae viae* est indéniable[71]. En effet, nous n'y trouvons pas seulement des allusions à l'un ou l'autre passage du *duae viae*, mais — qui plus est — nous y trouvons toute la trame du *duae viae* tel qu'il nous est conservé dans la *Didaché* et la *Doctrina apostolorum*. En tête est placé le thème des deux voies de la vie et de la mort. La voie de la vie est explicitée de la manière suivante : premièrement, on doit aimer Dieu qui nous a faits, deuxièmement, on doit aimer le prochain. L'amour du prochain est explicité, à son tour, par la règle d'or (cf. *Did./Doctr.* 1,1-2). Il faut d'abord combattre les vices, ensuite planter les vertus[72]. Pour combattre les vices, il faut commencer par arracher leurs racines dans le cœur : les passions (*ira, avaritia, libido*) ; ensuite, on sera capable d'accomplir le décalogue et les autres préceptes chrétiens (cf. *Did./Doct.* 2-4)[73]. Enfin, on

---

68. Publié par R. Reitzenstein, « Eine frühchristliche Schrift von den dreierlei Früchten des christlichen Lebens », *ZNW* 15, 1914, p. 60-90.

69. *Op. cit.* (note 7), p. 128 ss.

70. Dans son compte rendu du livre de J. Liébaert, *Les enseignements moraux des Pères apostoliques*, dans *RSR* 59, 1971, p. 68. Cf. maintenant son article dans *Vig. Chr.* 25, 1971, p. 71-81.

71. Malgré l'affirmation contraire de B. Altaner, *art. cit.* (note 11), p. 162. Cf. M. Gerhardt, *Das Leben und die Schriften des Lactantius* (thèse, Erlangen), 1924, p. 121-128.

72. Ou, comme le dit Lactance en une formule : *primum est enim non nocere, proximum, prodesse*. Encore Ambroise, *De officiis* I, suit ce schéma, et en cela, il dépasse précisément Cicéron.

73. Il est vrai que *Did./Doct.* font juste l'inverse de Lactance : elles rappellent d'abord les péchés condamnés par le décalogue pour montrer ensuite quelles passions poussent l'homme à commettre ces péchés.

pourra passer à la vertu chrétienne qu'est la charité (cf. *Did.* 1,3-2,1). Bien entendu, Lactance développe l'enseignement primitif du *duae viae* à la lumière de la philosophie chrétienne qui était la sienne ; mais il est d'autant plus intéressant de constater qu'un ancien manuel d'éthique judéo-chrétienne a pu lui servir de base pour le faire, parce que cet enseignement s'avérait assez substantiel pour ne pas être abandonné, et en même temps assez souple pour pouvoir être transformé en fonction des besoins d'une nouvelle époque. Cet essai de Lactance, innovateur et en même temps profondément attaché à la tradition, pourrait peut-être nous inspirer aujourd'hui où il s'agit également de reformuler l'éthique chrétienne dans un langage nouveau [74].

Un deuxième texte que j'aimerais citer est le sermon qui se trouve à la fin des *Canons d'Hippolyte* [75]. Le canon 38, le dernier du recueil, porte comme titre : « De la nuit où est ressuscité notre Seigneur : que personne ne dorme en cette nuit-là et qu'on se baigne (auparavant). De celui qui pèche après le baptême, et explication de cela ; de l'interdiction de ce qu'il ne faut pas (faire), et de la pratique de ce qu'il faut (faire). » Dans la table des titres, au début du recueil, on lit ensuite : « Et si quelqu'un veut imiter les anges. » Bien vite, l'auteur passe au discours direct ; cette partie du canon 38 semble donc être un sermon prononcé pendant la vigile pascale. Le prédicateur — le moment était bien choisi pour le faire — rappelle la liturgie du baptême pour exhorter ses auditeurs [76]. S'ils ont rejeté Satan, il faut qu'ils persévèrent, comme de bons soldats, dans leur promesse, et ne retournent pas aux mauvaises actions, autrement le Seigneur ne les reconnaîtra pas comme siens au moment du jugement : qu'ils « marchent dans les préceptes du Christ ». Puis vient une longue liste « de ce qu'il ne faut pas faire », liste qui, par le genre littéraire ainsi que par le contenu, ressemble de très près au *duae viae* ; elle est suivie, à la fin, d'une liste des choses

---

74. Cf., d'une manière générale, les belles remarques de J. DANIÉLOU, *La catéchèse aux premiers siècles*, 1968, p. 170 ss.

75. Cf. la récente édition de R.-G. COQUIN, dans *Patrologia Orientalis* 31. 2, 1966, p. 413 ss. Pour l'éditeur, les *Canons d'Hippolyte* ont été rédigés en Egypte, en 340 environ.

76. On peut supposer qu'il y avait aussi, parmi eux, de nouveaux baptisés.

« qu'il faut faire » qui, elle, rappelle la « section évangélique »
du *duae viae*. La liste des choses « qu'il ne faut pas faire »
se termine de cette façon : « Si le chrétien persévère en tout
cela, c'est-à-dire imite le Christ, il sera à sa droite, sera envoyé
avec les anges et sera honoré par lui ; parce qu'il a pris la
couronne du bien, a accompli la charge et gardé la foi, il
recevra la couronne de vie qui a été annoncée à ceux qui l'ai-
ment », — passage qui rappelle la fin de la *Doctrina apostolorum*. Or, le texte continue ainsi : « Si le chrétien veut être
dans un rang angélique, qu'il s'éloigne des femmes une fois
pour toutes et dispose dans son cœur de ne pas les regarder
ni de manger avec elles. En hâte qu'il distribue tous ses biens
aux faibles, qu'il ait la règle des anges dans l'humilité du
cœur et du corps. » Le prédicateur s'adresse ici à une autre
classe de chrétiens, qui va au-delà de ce que fait le commun
des fidèles ; ces chrétiens d'élite vivent dans le célibat et sont
volontairement pauvres, prêts à la souffrance et « prêts à la
mort à toute heure, à cause du Christ, pour la foi », comme
dit le texte. Ils ont à subir les trois tentations du Christ, « qui
sont la gourmandise, l'orgueil et la cupidité ». Il est intéressant
de noter que cette partie du sermon a des parallèles étroits
dans certains textes monastiques rattachés au même milieu [77].
Il faut ajouter à ces textes le *Syntagama doctrinae* et la *Foi
des 318 Pères* pseudo-athanasiens qui, comme il est bien connu,
incorporent des résumés du *duae viae*. Là aussi, nous trouvons
ces deux classes de chrétiens : en principe, le *duae viae*
s'adresse à tous les chrétiens, mais il reçoit un supplément
réservé aux μονάζοντες qui va dans la même ligne que le sermon conservé dans les *Canons d'Hippolyte*. Si on lit ces textes,
on est tenté de dire que le chapitre 6 de la *Didaché* auquel
ces textes se réfèrent, reflète la même tradition ascétique ; il
semblerait que la forme du *duae viae* attestée par le manuscrit de Constantinople a été marquée par cette tradition [78].

77. Il s'agit du *Traité sur la virginité* pseudo-athanasien (qui a d'ailleurs
utilisé les prières de *Did.* 9-10), de deux traités d'Evagre le Pontique et
d'un texte de Jean Cassien, signalés par R.-G. COQUIN, *op. cit.* (note 74),
p. 311 ss.
78. La parenté de ce manuscrit avec le *Liber graduum* a été remarquée
par A. ADAM, *art. cit.* (note 29), p. 25 s., par E. PETERSON, *op. cit.* (note 54),
p. 150 s., et par G. KRETSCHMAR, dans *ZThK* 61, 1964, p. 40 s. (Ce dernier
rattache la tradition en question aux ascètes itinérants syriens ; elle

Si nous nous tournons vers l'Occident, nous trouvons une confirmation de ce que nous venons de voir. Dans son explication de la parabole du Semeur (*Matth.* 13,1 ss., par.), l'auteur du sermon *De centesima, de sexagesima, de tricesima*[79] distingue trois classes de chrétiens : les martyrs qui produisent « cent », les ascètes qui produisent « soixante », et les continents qui produisent « trente » fruits. Pour appuyer son point de vue, il glisse, dans la partie sur les martyrs, la citation d'une *scriptura* qui dit ceci : *si potes quidem, fili, omnia praecepta domini facere, eris consummatus ; sin autem, uel duo praecepta, amare dominum ex totis praecordiis et similem tibi quasi < te ipsum >.* Le début est une citation presque textuelle de *Didaché* 6,2a[80] ; la fin est un commentaire précieux de la phrase plutôt obscure de *Did.* 6,2b : « sinon, ce qui t'est possible, fais-le » : nous apprenons maintenant que « ce qui est possible » est le double commandement de l'amour, c'est-à-dire le contenu même du *duae viae* qui en est l'explication. L'auteur du sermon s'empresse d'ajouter que l'accomplissement du double commandement de l'amour n'est pas encore la perfection, mais qu'il y a, sur le chemin (*uia*) qui mène à la perfection, plusieurs degrés (*gradus*) à franchir. Nous sommes dans la même optique que nous avons trouvée dans le sermon à la fin des *Canons d'Hippolyte* : le *duae viae* est bon pour la masse des fidèles, mais le chrétien « parfait » va plus loin dans son effort d'ascèse et dans sa disposition au martyre.

Au VIᵉ siècle, la situation a encore une fois évolué : le *duae viae* n'est plus un enseignement qui s'adresse à tous les fidèles et qui reçoit, dans les cercles des ascètes, un supplément caractéristique, mais il est devenu une partie de la règle monastique elle-même, tant en Egypte qu'en Occident. Pour l'Egypte, nous avons le témoignage bien connu de la *Vie de Chenoute* arabe[81] ;

---

remonterait au christianisme primitif et se refléterait dans l'Evangile de Matthieu et dans l'Apocalypse de Jean.) Dans les autres textes qui reproduisent le *duae viae* (cf. note 6), l'équivalent de *Did.* 6, 2-3 manque ; les *Const. apost.* VII, 19-21, laissent tomber *Did.* 6,2.

79. Pour R. REITZENSTEIN, *art. cit.* (note 68), le sermon serait écrit en Afrique du Nord, à la fin du IIᵉ siècle déjà (cf. aussi J. DANIÉLOU, *art. cit.* [note 70]) ; d'après D. DE BRUYNE, dans *ZNW* 15, 1914, p. 281, il serait du IIIᵉ siècle.

80. Seul changement : ὅλον τὸν ζυγόν est devenu *omnia praecepta*.

81. Cf. L.E. ISELIN, dans *Texte und Untersuchungen* 13, 1, 1895, p. 10 s. Le texte arabe est du VIIᵉ siècle seulement, mais il est la traduction d'un texte copte qui remonte au VIᵉ siècle, sinon au Vᵉ siècle. L'enseignement

pour l'Occident, nous avons la *Regula Benedicti* [82]. A mes yeux, il est indéniable que saint Benoît, dans le prologue et le quatrième chapitre de sa *Règle*, s'est inspiré d'une forme du *duae viae*. Dans le prologue, le maître s'adresse au fils et lui enseigne, dans la ligne du Psaume 34(33), la « voie de la vie » qui nous dit de faire le bien et d'éviter le mal ; cette voie du salut est dure et étroite, surtout au début, mais elle mène celui qui persévère à la vie éternelle. Le 4e chapitre donne la liste des choses à faire et à éviter ; elle commence par le double commandement de l'amour et cite aussi la règle d'or (cf. *Did./Doct.* 1,2), puis elle fait suivre des préceptes qui se rattachent à la deuxième table du décalogue (cf. *Did./Doctr.* 2). Le reste du chapitre a aussi beaucoup de parallèles de détail avec *Did./Doctr.* 3-4 et avec *Did.* 1,3-2,1. Bien entendu, des préceptes de caractère typiquement monastique se trouvent maintenant mêlés à l'enseignement primitif du *duae viae*, mais la trame de celui-ci est encore visible.

Une fois que le *duae viae* a fait son chemin dans la tradition monastique, il a cessé d'exister en dehors d'elle [83]. Il se peut que les Vaudois aient fait une tentative pour utiliser le *duae viae* dans leur prédication qui appelait essentiellement à la conversion ; mais ce n'est pas sûr [84].

Aujourd'hui où nous savons l'importance que le *duae viae* a eu pour l'Eglise ancienne, on doit se poser la question de savoir s'il ne faudrait pas lui refaire une place dans notre enseignement catéchétique. Je ne saurais mieux exprimer la valeur du *duae viae* qu'en me servant des propres paroles du

des deux voies semble d'ailleurs avoir joué un rôle dans la tradition cénobitique antérieure déjà : cf. la première catéchèse de Pachome, éditée et traduite par L.-Th. LEFORT, dans *CSCO* 159, 2e éd. 1965, p. 1 ss. et 160, 2e éd. 1964, p. 1 ss. Par contre, les Règles de saint Basile ne semblent pas s'inspirer du *duae viae* malgré leur emploi du double commandement de l'amour.

82. Cf. la récente édition de R. HANSLIK, dans *CSEL* 75, 1960. D'après B. STEIDLE, *Die Regel St. Benedikts*, 1952, p. 24 ss., Benoît se serait éventuellement inspiré de la règle des moines de Lérins.

83. Outre le manuscrit de Constantinople qui a conservé le texte même de la *Didaché*, ce sont seulement quelques écrits médiévaux qui gardent le vague souvenir de cet « apocryphe » ; cf. J. SCHLECHT, *Doctrina XII Apostolorum*, 1901, p. 62 ss., et J.-P. AUDET, *op. cit.*, p. 87 ss.

84. Cf. à ce sujet H. BÖHMER, dans *Realencycl. für prot. Theol. und Kirche*, 3e éd., 20, 1908, p. 827.

Cardinal Daniélou [85] : « Le thème des deux voies est beaucoup plus qu'un schéma pédagogique ou une méthode de présentation. On aurait pu le croire, à voir la description de la voie de la vie se présenter comme un traité des vertus et celle de la mort comme un traité des vices. Il s'agit en fait de beaucoup plus que cela. Mettre le candidat au baptême devant les deux voies qui s'ouvrent à lui, c'est le placer devant une option décisive : la renonciation à Satan ou l'adhésion à Jésus-Christ. Toute la tradition biblique en témoigne. La voie de la vie est celle de celui qui a choisi Dieu. C'est ce qui donne à l'ensemble de la catéchèse morale présentée selon le schéma des deux voies ce caractère de conflit, de lutte, spécifique du temps de préparation au baptême, et d'ailleurs de toute la vie chrétienne. Mais il s'agit alors de tout autre chose que d'une « bonne éducation ». Cette « morale » est bien plutôt l'exposé d'une réalité surnaturelle qui manifeste que l'âme doit être arrachée au pouvoir des forces du mal. Elle indique le chemin concret de la foi vécue. Le thème des deux voies est donc un « lieu » catéchétique essentiel. »

85. *Op. cit.* (note 74), p. 130 s.

RABBINIC PARALLELS IN EARLY CHURCH ORDERS

By F. GAVIN, The General Theological Seminary, New York

A S long ago as 1910 Schwartz in hise ssay Über die pseudo-apostolischen Kirchenordnungen (in *Schriften der wissenschaftlichen Gesellschaft in Strassburg*), advanced some contentions regarding the so-called "Egyptian Church Order" which were independently confirmed by Dom Connolly, *The So-called Egyptian Church Order and Derived Documents* (in *Texts and Studies*, Cambridge, VIII:4) six years later. We have every assurance that in this document we possess the text of the *Apostolic Tradition* of Hippolytus, written in the early decades of the 3rd century. The circumstances of its writing and the *tendenz* of the writer give us good grounds for maintaining that the *A. T.* represents the usage of the Roman Church of the later 2nd century. So important a discovery has made necessary a radically new departure in the study of the early Christian liturgy, of which recent development we possess Lietzmann's fine monograph, *Messe und Herrenmahl* (Bonn, 1926) and Völker's *Mysterium und Agape* (Gotha, 1927). Yungklaus has written on Die Gemeinde Hippolyts (*T. u. U.*, 46, 2, Leipzig, 1928), and other significant studies will undoubtedly appear in the near future. With two 2nd century Church Orders—the *Didache* and the *A. T.* of Hippolytus—we have Christian texts roughly contemporaneous with the Tannaitic tradition of Rabbinic Judaism, as redacted in the Mishna, Tosefta, and the baraitot.

We are then in a position to examine afresh the question of the relationship maintaining between the two faiths, on the basis of material which is of the same date. Despite the parting of the ways between Judaism and Christianity, the two religions continued to influence each other in many ways. This interaction was not from one side alone: when Judaism waived its claim to the LXX and practically abandoned it to the Church; when it surrendered the ancient recitation of the Ten Com-

55

mandments in the Synagogue service "because of the Minim"
(cf. Ber. 12a; P. 1.8 (3c); Elbogen, *Der jüdische Gottesdienst in
seiner geschichtlichen Entwicklung*,[2] Frankfurt a.M., 1924, p. 242);
when the method of ordination by *semika* was changed to that
by nomination; when Jewish apologetic was concerned to defend
its claim to be the true "Israel of God" against Christian polemic
(cf. Bonwetsch, Der Schriftbeweis für die Kirche als das wahre
Israel, in *Theologische Studien Theodor Zahn* . . . *dargebracht*,
Leipzig, 1908, pp. 1–22; Marmorstein, *Religionsgeschichtliche
Studien* I, Pressburg, 1910, pp. 1–26, where as *e. g.*, pp. 14, 7
n. 2, relevant references are given), we have definite tokens
of the reaction upon Judaism of Christianity. We are now to
examine some instances of influence of Judaism upon the Church
as shown in Early Church Orders.

Our first instance will deal with certain parallels between the
rites and rubrics of Jewish proselyte and Christian baptism. For
the former we have two descriptions, in a baraitha in Yeb. 47,
and in the small tractate Gerim I.1–5; for the latter, the accounts
in *Didache* VII and in Hippolytus' *A. T.* (The latter is most
conveniently accessible in Connolly, *op. cit.*, pp. 180–185, a
conflated text based upon Hauler, *Didascaliae apostolorum frag-
menta veronensia latina* . . . , Leipzig, 1900, pp. 110–112, and
supplemented by Horner, *The Statutes of the Apostles, or Canones
Ecclesiastici*, London, 1904, translation, pp. 148–153.) *Did.* VII
begins: "Having first rehearsed all these things," referring to
the catechumenal instructions represented by I–VI, which is
a revision in a Christian direction of a Jewish manual for the
instruction of proselytes (Cf. Knopf's edition, Tübingen, 1920,
p. 2 *et ad loc.*) It continues: "Baptize in living water. If, however, thou hast not living water, baptize in other water. If thou
canst not in cold, then in warm." The same specification of
"living" or running water appears in Justin Martyr, I Apol. 61.
It was the normal procedure in Judaism, in accordance with
Lev. 14.5, 50; Num. 19.17, and underlies the controversy between
Bet Hillel and Bet Shammai in Sab. 15a (the date of which is
discussed by Lerner in *MWJ* 1885, p. 113; cf. also Katzenelson,
in *MGWJ* 1900 (44.10) pp. 416–447, and Ber. 22a; Ḥag. 11a;
Yoma 31a; Sifra Mes. 6.3 (Weiss ed. Vienna, 1862, 77b), 'Emor

4.7 (96b), etc.). The Christian rubric has in view the existence of bath-houses where, in the event described, baptisms could be administered. There is a Rabbinic provision in the case of an aged and weak High Priest that warm be mixed with the cold water of his *tebilah* to take off the chill (cf. Yoma III.5; P. Ber. III.4 (6c); Ber. 22a), where allowance is made for other than living water.

We shall now turn to the evidence offered by the *Apostolic Tradition*. The Latin of the Hippolytan rite is at this point defective, but we possess the Ethiopic and Coptic: "At the time of the cock-crow they shall first pray over the water, and it shall be either such as flows into the tank (Coptic κολυμβήθρα), or is caused to flow down upon it" (so Coptic and Arabic). Of the Canons of Hippolytus No. XIX (ed. Riedel, *Die Kirchenrechtsquellen des Patriarchats Alexandrien*, Leipzig, 1900) reads: "At cock-crow let them cause them to go to the water of a *clean running stream,*" which probably represents an original "running water." The *Testamentum D. N. J. C.* (ed. Rahmani, 1899, II.8) stipulates that "the water be pure and flowing." The convergence of the whole *corpus* of allied Hippolytan readings postulates some provision requiring "living" water, and the Coptic κολυμβήθρα is strikingly like the *bet ha-tebilah* of Gerim 1.3. The Ethiopic adds: "this shall maintain unless there be a scarcity of water, in which case they shall carry water . . . having drawn it from a well" (Horner, op. cit., p. 152).

There follows a very significant rubric in the non-Latin versions of the *A. T.*: "All the women shall loose their hair, and they shall be forbidden to wear their ornaments and their gold; and none shall go down having anything alien with them into the water" (Horner, *op. cit.*, pp. 21 (152–153) Ethiopic; 100–101 (253) Arabic; 316 Sahidic). In Haneberg, *Canones S. Hippolyti* (1870) Canon XIX.7 reads: Solvant crinium nodos, ne cum illis descendat in aquam regenerationis quidquam peregrinum de spiritibus peregrinis (pp. 39, 75). He points out (ibid. p. 112) that this reason is not given by the Coptic and Syriac. The related passage in the latter version (ed. Rahmani, p. 126) has: "The Bishop is to see to it that no man wears a ring nor a woman a golden ornament, since it is not fitting to have anything alien with them in the water." Rogers (in *JTS* XIII, p. 414) does not seem to have found the clue to this rubric, which is simply the provision, familiar to the Rabbis, that nothing shall intervene to prevent the water touching every part of the body. The baraitha in B. K. 82a, quoting Lev. 14.9 ("wash his flesh in water") interprets the injunction to mean "in such a way that no separating element (*ḥoṣeṣ*) intervene between the water and the body." Further provisions against anything that may serve as a "separating element" are to be found in Sabb. VI.1: "a woman may not take her *tebilah* until she have loosed the band about her head;" Miḳ. IX.1: "These things act as a 'separation,'—woolen and linen fillets with which women are wont to plait their hair. But R. Judah said that such do not act as a separation, as the water can reach the person through them." Cf. also Niddah 66.

But it is in the rite as a whole and in the administration of the act of Baptism that the most striking likeness to Jewish procedure appears. It may suffice to mention two facts regarding the *A. T.* rite: (1) there is no baptismal "formula" in the later sense of the word; (2) there is no "administrator" or officiant in the proper meaning of the term, for the rite is practically self-administered. (1) In the place of the use of a proper "formula" of Baptism, the Latin (Hauler, op. cit., pp. 110–111; cf. Horner, p. 153) gives us the *traditio* and *redditio symboli*, which are strikingly like the summary of obligations and duties, and the formal address of congratulation in Jewish proselyte baptism given in Yeb. 47 and Gerim I.1–4. (2) Easton has drawn attention to the Old Latin readings in the N. T. which imply self-baptism (*AJT*, XXIV, Oct. 1920, pp. 513–518): in Lk. 3.12; 11.38; 12.50, and the use of the middle of βαπτίζειν in Acts 22.16 and I Cor. 10.2. The Syriac, like the Hebrew, term,— '*amad* and *tabal*—is middle, while the Greek verb, βαπτίζειν, is transitive. This ancient viewpoint is still fundamental to the rite of Hippolytus, for in the administration of Baptism the priest's part is confined to having his hand on the head of the baptizand.

We must pass from this brief consideration of Baptism to other usages represented in the Church Orders, chiefly those concerned with the *Agape* or Agape-Eucharist. Some of these affiances I have discussed elsewhere (*Jewish Antecedents of the Christian Sacraments*, London, S. P. C. K., 1928, and Macmillan, N. Y.). The ancestral type of the Christian Agape or Agape-Eucharist is most certainly the *kiddush* as it was observed by a *ḥaburah*. The evidence of the N. T.,—where there is linguistic assimilation to the current Rabbinic language, as well as a controlling *tendenz* dictated by current Christian liturgical procedure,—is especially interesting in the narratives of the miraculous feedings. Strack-Billerbeck have furnished, for example, to Mark 5.39ff. and 8.6ff., conclusive parallels from Rabbinic sources. A comparison of the accounts of the Institution of the Eucharist in St. Luke (cf. also his characteristic "breaking of the bread" in 24.30, 35, and Acts 2.42, 46; 20.7, 11; 27.35, etc.) with the Matthaean-Markan and the Pauline traditions suggest the early confusion between what later came to be sharply distinguished as the Agape and the Eucharist respectively. Discussion of this very important subject had not materially advanced since Keating's essay, *The Agape and the Eucharist in the Early Church* (1901), despite Leclercq's learned monograph on the evidence of the Didache (*Monumenta Historiae Liturgiae Ecclesiae Antiquae*). until the publication of Lietzmann's work, followed by Völker's *Mysterium und Agape*.

When we turn to Did. IX-X and XIV to see what is the yield of that primitive document, our attention should first be directed to the preceding section (VIII.1) where the direction is given: "Let not your fasts be with the hypocrites, for they fast on Mondays and Thursdays, but do you fast on Wednesdays and Fridays." There is more here than the simple prohibition to fast on the same days as did the devout Jews (cf. Meg. Taan. XII; Taan. 12a; Elbogen, *Geschichte*,² pp. 76–77). The exigencies of anti-Jewish controversy still dictate the terms and condition the course of Christian liturgical procedure and customs. Sections IX and X contain each two blessings and one petition, each several one terminating in its proper doxology. (There is a dislocated fragment in X.4, which if transposed to introduce X.3 will make the three sections correspond.) The form of all six prayers is Jewish, and abundant evidence has been collected

which demonstrate the dependence, from Kohler in *J. E.*,
Knopf, the latest commentator on the Didache, to Dr. Finkelstein in The Birkat ha-Mazon in *JQR* (XIX.3, Jan. 1929,
pp. 211ff.). The summary result is: *Did.* IX.2 (the blessing over
the cup) has the Jewish blessing in mind (cf. Ber. VI.1), for the
Christian allusion to Ps. 79(80).9ff. in the words "the holy vine
of David thy child" uses as its point of departure the Rabbinic
words "fruit of the vine." The blessing of the bread (Cf. Ber
ibid.) and the Rabbinic thanksgiving after the meal may in
conflation have furnished the antecedents for Did. IX.3, heightened and developed into their Christian form. The petition in
Did. IX.4 has as its immediate background the 10th petition
of the Tefillah or 'Amidah (cf. Meg. 17b) and the Musaf for
the Day of Atonement. The same structure underlies section X
of the Didache, and Finkelstein has found in it a close relationship to the *Birkat ha-Mazon.* In his article (loc. cit., pp. 215–216)
he puts into parallel columns the substance of Did. X with the
three thanksgivings of the *Birkat ha-M.* He also suggests (ibid.
p. 234), that even the eschatological close (Did. X.6) is not
without Rabbinic affiliations. The order of the three paragraphs
in the Did. is not that of the *Berakah*, but it may be asked
whether the Christian usage here represented may not have
preserved a still more ancient Jewish tradition, since the sequence
is more in line with the words of the Torah in Deut. 8.10. Finkelstein urges that the core of these three prayers is probably
Maccabean, in which case the significance of the Didache evidence is heightened. The whole procedure given in the Christian
source is guided by the same instinct represented by the statements of R. Akiba: "It is forbidden to taste of aught before a
blessing has been pronounced upon it" (Ber. 35a), and of Tos.
Ber. VII.24 (Zuckermandel, p. 17): The devout Jew is to "eat
his bread, pronouncing a blessing before and after."

Elbogen (in *Festschrift zu Israel Lewy's 70tem Geburtstag*,
Breslau, 1911, pp. 173–187) has discussed the origin of the
Synagogue *kiddush* as from the domestic custom of a household
or *ḥaburah*. The transference of this home-observance to the
Synagogue, especially prevailing in Babylonia, is marked by the
reminiscence of its original association in the words: אין קידוש

אלא במקום סעודה (Pes. 101a). Tos. Ber. V.3 presupposes a kind of community-centre near the synagogue where transients could be entertained: "Travellers who are at table with the father of a family, at the coming of the Sabbath go as soon as dusk comes, into the Synagogue. Then they return and the cup is mixed and the Blessing of the Day pronounced over it." There is confusion in the Tannaitic sources, and no little controversy,—over the exact sequence, order, and number of the various blessings,—and it is difficult to establish a definite chronological succession of the several stages. The Rabbinic evidence is chiefly to be found in: Ber. VI–VIII; Tos. III.7; IV.8; V–VI; the relevant sections of Babli (cf. 35a, 43a, etc.), P. 10d, and in Pes. 101–102.

A similar confusion confronts us when we try to disentangle the evidence presented by the various recensions—chiefly the Verona Latin fragments and the Ethiopic—of the Hippolytan Agape and its relationship to the Eucharist. These two versions (the former in Hauler, pp. 113–114; the latter in Horner's translation, pp. 157–158) describe two kinds of congregational supper. The Latin gives us the picture of the supper held in a private house, with its master acting as host, but with an ecclesiastic present to preside. The food is either to be "consumed on the premises" (to borrow a popular phrase well known in England), or to be taken away as *apoforetum*. They are enjoined to observe due decorum. Each is to be prompt in receiving from the presiding ecclesiastic,—a bishop is the normal person, though a presbyter or deacon will do,—a bit of blessed bread called εὐλογία (= *benedictio*), which is carefully distinguished from that of the Eucharist. Laymen cannot "bless" the food. Exorcized, not blessed, bread is to be given to the catechumens, who are not to recline with the believers.

The Ethiopic contemplates a somewhat different situation. There is first a section (Statute 36) "Concerning Widows and Virgins and at what time the bishop should fast." The text offers some interesting features: while we lack the Latin, we possess the Sahidic (in Funk's edition, II p. 112), and Lietzmann has transferred into a note (op. cit., pp. 183–184, transcription from Vindob. Hist. 7) the original Greek of the passage in question, by which the inaccurate rendition of the Ethiopic may be corrected. There is one phrase of particular interest: "The Bishop cannot fast" (as do the widows, virgins, and the lesser clergy, at will) "save only when all the folk fast. If perchance anyone wish to offer, he may not say him nay. For in all cases he who breaks (the bread) must partake" (ἐκλάσας δὲ πάντως γεύεται). The whole substance of this is Rabbinic. Klein (*ZNTW* IX, p. 135) adduces the following from R. H. 29b: "A Tannaitic tradition reports: One may not break bread and say grace for his guests except he eat with them, save when he do so for his children and those of his own household in order to train them in proper religious observance" ת״ר לא יפרוס אדם פרוסה לאורחים אלא אם כן אוכל עמהם אבל פורס הוא לבניו ובני ביתו כדי לחנכן במצות וגו'. In Ber. 47a "R. Judah ben R. Samuel ben Shelat said in the name of Rab: Those who recline at table are not permitted to eat anything until he who breaks bread partakes thereof." אמר רבי יהודה בריה דרב שמואל בר שילט משמיה דרב אין המסובין רשאין לאכול כלום עד שיטעום הבוצע. Lietzmann (op. cit., p. 210, note 2) quotes: המברך צריך שיטעום from Ber. 52a: "He who says the Grace must taste of the food,"—which is practically reproduced by the Greek.

It may be well at this point to return to the Latin, and for the sake of clearness, to quote from it:

> Catecuminis vero panis exorcizatus detur et calicem singuli offerant. Catecuminis in cena dominica non concumbat. Per omnem vero oblationem memor sit qui offert ejus, qui illum vocavit; propterea enim depraecatus est, ut ingrediatur sub tecto ejus. Edentes vero et bibentes cum honestate id agite et non ad ebrietatem et non ut aliquis inrideat, aut tristetur qui vocat vos in vestra inquietudine, sed ut oret, ut dignus efficiatur, ut ingrediantur sancti ad eum. (Hauler, op. cit., pp. 113–114.)

Certain observations may here be made on the above: (1) the catechumens, who are not to receive the "blessed" but only the "exorcized" bread, are yet to offer each his own cup. (2) The guest is to be mindful of his host,—by implication, is expected to pray for him. He is not to put him to shame by his unseemly conduct, but to conduct himself so that his host will be honored by his presence. There are several points of affiliation with Jewish customs which illuminate this religious hospitality. The

order of procedure at a dinner-party, as given in Tos. Ber. IV.8 (Zuckermandel, p. 9), is as follows: the guests are seated on *subsellia* or *cathedrae* until all assemble. Wine is brought, over which each recites his own blessing. They then recline, and a second cup is brought, which is blessed for all by one only (Cf. P. ibid., 10d, and Ber. 43a). In Ber. VI.6 the distinction is clearly drawn: "When one sits he says his own blessing, but when he reclines, one says it for all. If wine be brought during a meal, each says his own blessing over it; if after the meal, one recites it for all." The "cup of blessing" in the Christian Agape seems to belong only to the solemn Supper of the Congregation, on which see below. But the private "offering" of a cup by each several person seems to have been the rule not only for the catechumen, but (if the Sahidic text of Canon 48 be trustworthy ("It is fitting for all, before they drink, to take a cup and give thanks (εὐχαριστεῖν) over it") for the believer as well. In Ber. 46a R. Yoḥanan in the name of R. Simeon ben Yoḥai directs that the host break the bread and say Grace, while the guest is to say the thanksgiving; the former, that he may dispense hospitality generously, and the latter, that he may invoke a blessing upon his host. What is he to say? "May it be Thy will that the host be not put to shame in this world, nor confounded in the world to come." א"ר יוחנן משום בן יוחי בעל הבית
בוצע ואורח מברך בעל הבית בוצע כדי שיבצע בעין יפה ואורח מברך כדי
שיברך בעל הבית מאי מברך יהי רצון שלא יבוש בעל הבית בעולם הזה ולא
יכלם לעולם הבא.

In the "bringing in of lamps at the supper of the congregation," which is represented only by the Ethiopic (cf. Horner, op. cit., pp. 159–161), we have a most interesting and curious mosaic of originally Rabbinic materials. The text has no exact parallel in the other versions, unless the other type of supper spoken of above, represent it. Dom Connolly urges however (op. cit., pp. 112–116) that some service of this character must have been in the original *A. T.* since the Canons of Hippolytus (Cf. Achelis' edition, in *T. u. U.* VI (1891) c. 32 §§164–168) and the *Testamentum* (ed. Cooper and Maclean, Edinburgh, 1902, p. 129) contain related sections, as does *A. C.* VIII.37ff. For the church represented by the *Canons* the service has become a

Sunday night supper for the poor, the expenses being defrayed
by an individual host, and the occasion being accompanied by
the Lighting of the Lamp (cf. Lietzmann's description and discussion, *op. cit.*, pp. 198–201). In the *Testamentum* it has become
only a solemn lighting of the light by the Deacon, possibly the
immediate prototype of the lighting of the Paschal Light in the
Latin rite of mediaeval and modern times. This ancient observance has left as a permanent memorial this first Christian
hymn outside the N. T.,—the Φῶς ἱλαρόν, so old that it was
archaic by the time of St. Basil.

The text of the rite from the Ethiopic (Horner, *op. cit.* pp.
27–29; translation pp. 160–161) follows:

"*Concerning the bringing in of lamps at the supper of the congregation.*
When the evening has come, the bishop being there, the deacon shall
bring in a lamp, and standing in the midst of the faithful, being about
to give thanks, the bishop shall first give the salutation, saying: 'The
Lord (be) with you.' And the people shall also say: 'With thy spirit.'
'Let us give thanks unto the Lord.' And they shall say: 'Right and just,
both greatness and exaltation with glory are due to him.' And he shall
not say: 'Lift up your hearts,' because that shall be said at the Oblation.
And he prays thus, saying: 'We give thee thanks, God, through thy son
Jesus Christ our Lord, because thou hast enlightened us by the reveal-
ing of the incorruptible light; we having therefore finished the lenght of
a day and having come to the beginning of the night, and having been
satiated with the light of the day, which thou hast created for our satisfaction, and now since we have not been deficient of the light of the
evening by thy grace, we sanctify thee and we glorify thee through thy
Son Jesus Christ our Lord, through whom to thee (be) glory and might
and honour with the Holy Spirit now' etc. And they shall say: 'Amen.'
And having risen up therefore after supper, the children having prayed,
they shall say the psalms, and the virgins: and afterwards the deacon,
holding the mingled cup of the Presphora, shall say the psalm from that
which is written Haleluya, (and) after that the presbyter has commanded:
'And likewise from those psalms.' And afterwards the bishop having
offered the cup, as is proper for the cup, he shall say the psalm Haleluya;
and all of them as he recites the psalms shall say Haleluya, which is to
say: 'We praise him who is God (most high): glorified and praised is
he who founded all the world with one word.' And likewise, the psalm
having been completed, he shall give thanks over the cup, and shall
give of the fragments to all of the faithful. And as they are eating their
supper, those who are the believers shall take a little bread from the
hand of the bishop before they partake of their own bread, for it is Eulogia
and not Eucharist as the Body of our Lord."

Allowing for a generous degree of development in the document represented by the Ethiopic recension, we may see in it evidence of a Christian conflation of a number of Rabbinic practices. Indications of the ancestry and prototypes of the usages here redacted can be gathered from sundry Jewish customs, of which the observations following suggest a selected group. (1) Elbogen in his Eingang und Ausgang des Sabbats nach talmudischen Quellen (in Lewy's *Festschrift*, Breslau, pp. 179–181) has studied the development of the *kiddush*, from the originally domestic fellowship-meal, in the course of which the Sabbath was greeted; when dusk came was said the Grace (ברכת המזון), and the sanctification of the day (cf. Tos. Ber. V.4). Later—possibly after the Bar Kochba War—came the introduction of the visit to the Synagogue. With the same events occur the institution of a Friday evening service there, which was earlier in Babylonia than in Palestine (cf. Pes. 100b: בני אדם שקדשו בבית הכנסת). Thus the *kiddush* came to be transferred to the Synagogue, and we have a two-fold tradition. (Cf. Elbogen, *Der jüdische Gottesdienst in seiner geschichtlichen Entwicklung*,[2] 1924, p. 111.)

(2) Of the three chief duties of the housewife one was the kindling of the Sabbath-light, as we learn from authentic Tannaitic tradition (cf. Sabb. II.6). This was a major obligation (cf. Ber. R. 17.14 end), and appears together with the other two in the summary instruction of the female convert in Gerim I.4 (cf. also P. Sabb. I.4 (5b) for the importance of this observance).

(3) Ber. VI.3 prescribes the blessing to be recited over "any (food) whose growth is not from the earth" as ending in the words: שהכל ניהיה בדברו. As Babli understands it, a baraitha construes the provision to include meat, milk, eggs, cheese, etc. (Ber. 40b). Since bread and wine (as well as some other foodstuffs) have their own proper blessing, this would seem to be a "common" form to be used where no special blessing was provided. There is a similar formula in Tos. B. M. VI.15 (ed. Zuckermandel, p. 385) which reads: מי שאמר והיה העולם (ברוך הוא), and this appears in the congratulatory address to the newly baptized convert in Gerim 1.5: במי נדבקת אשריך במי שאמר והיה העולם וגו'. It is also to be found in many other places in the

Tannaitic sources: Mekilta—בא 5d, בשלח 13d, 15c, יתרו 8 (26b), 11 (28a), משפטים 10 (31c), 12 (32c), 18 (34b, c); Ber. R. 81d; Sotah 10b; Sanh. 19a; Sabb. 139a; Meg. 13b etc. (cf. Zunz, *Gottesdienstliche Vorträge*,² 1892, p. 389 and n. *e*; Elbogen, *Jüd. Gottesd.*,² p. 525).

(4) Ber. VII.3 gives us the word used by the leader in the common Grace to be recited by certain groups: נברך), which corresponds exactly to the Greek: εὐχαριστήσωμεν.

(5) The recitation of the Hallel-psalms (113–118) was associated with the celebration of Passover, and was taken over from the Temple to the Synagogue for that Feast, then later associated also with the New-Moon (cf. Elbogen, *Jüd. Gottesd.* pp. 125, 249).

(6) The Passover prayer of R. Gamaliel in Pes. X.5 reads in part: "We are in duty bound to thank, praise, adore, glorify, extol, honour, bless, exalt, and reverence Him, who wrought these miracles for our ancestors, and for us, for he brought us from bondage to freedom, changed our sorrow into joy . . . *led us from darkness into a great light*" and ends: "Let us therefore say in His presence: Halleluyah!" The latter word was in early Tanniatic times used as a congregational response (cf. P. Sabb. XVI.1 (15c); Sukkah 38b), and then the custom came gradually to be discarded.

While we are not yet clear as to the details of the evolution of the rite represented by the Ethiopic recension of this portion of the *A. T.* (for it may well have been a local Egyptian use, grafted on to the translated Hippolytan text as a substitute for the type of congregational supper represented by the Verona Latin fragments discussed above), there is little doubt as to the spirit and controlling factors involved in it. It must have been very primitive, and certainly lay very near the soil from which Christianity sprang. It is noteworthy that an originally private and quasi-domestic observance should have become a Church service, parallel to the course of the evolution of the *kiddush*. The internal development as well is analogous. Just why the deacon should have come to be the person who should kindle the lamp, is not clear. With the developing tradition and the transmutations due to translation, the original blessing (modeled on the "common" form of the Rabbis) could easily have become: "We praise him who is God . . . who founded all the world with one word." Can we account for the choice of this particular formula, by the suggestion that the proper formula for the blessing of the cup had been specially allocated to the Eucharistic cup? Since "Let us give thanks" derives from Hebrew usage; since the very term εὐλογία, in the Latin *benedictio*, is entirely unidiomatic; since the awkward use of the Greek εὐχαριστεῖν throughout bespeaks a sense that it was regarded as transitive; since the very choice of the psalms, and the use of the response *Hallelujah* belongs to current and earlier Jewish usage, we shall be justified in seeing in this archaic Christian service (leaving the Eucharist out of our present view) as well as in the rite, rubrics, and ideas of Christian baptism evident dependence upon Jewish ideas, archetypes, and antecedents.

THE EXTENT OF THE INFLUENCE OF THE SYNAGOGUE SERVICE UPON CHRISTIAN WORSHIP

Mark Lidzbarski in the story of his youth (Auf rauhem Wege, p.112) relates a tale his grandfather told of a man who, seeing a beggar wearing a coat that was all over patches, asked the wearer if he knew what patch was the original cloth. The beggar answered that of the original coat nothing now remained. So, said the grandfather, is the present state of the various religions ; patch holds to patch but it cannot be said with any certainty that any patch represents the original fabric. It would seem that the sceptical caution of Lidzbarski's grandparent is being justified so far as an answer may be given to the question : What did the Synagogue service contribute to the worship of the Church ? *Beyond the outer form* of worship, is there anything in the content of the Christian service that derives from the Synagogue, apart from the Old Testament and its ideas which constitute a gift of Judaism as a whole to Christianity ?

In regard to the question of the contribution of the Synagogue to Christian worship, two works of Christian scholars, namely, Oesterley's "The Jewish Background of the Christian Liturgy " written in 1925 and " The Influence of the Synagogue upon the Divine Office " (1944) by Dugmore, allow us, by contrast, to see the progress and tendency of investigation. The latter work considerably diminishes the number of contacts which Oesterley, twenty years previously, perceived as existing between Jewish and Christian prayers. This change of outlook is due to Dugmore's appreciation of the Cairo Genizah fragments published by Schechter and of the work of Finkelstein[1] on the Jewish Synagogue service which enables him to trace the growth and development of that service and to give approximate dates to certain of its liturgical elements, especially to the benedictions that compose the *'Amidah* prayer in their old Palestinian form (cf. Dugmore, p. 114 f). These dates together with the fact that after the middle of the second century—more precisely, through the Bar Kokhba war c. 135—the separation of Jew from Jewish Christian was complete and the influence of the Synagogue upon the Church brought to an end, provide a chronological criterion in regard to the question of the Jewish liturgical contribution. Moreover, since none of the early Christian Service-books, e.g. the Sacramentary of Sarapion, is older than the fourth century, the inquiry must be limited to those prayers which are preserved in Christian literature prior to the middle of the second century or which otherwise seem to be entitled to be regarded as prior to that date.

The application of chronological evidence which, as we have stated, diminishes the possible borrowings from the Synagogue so far as the content of Christian prayers is concerned, may be best exemplified by two instances of Dugmore's criticism of Oesterley's conclusions. Oesterley (p. 130) suggests that a certain prayer from the Service-book of Sarapion ("Grant us knowledge and faith and piety and sanctification . . . Grant that we seek Thee and love Thee. Grant that we may search Thy divine words and study them . . .") is based upon the Jewish *'Ahabhah* prayer. But, says Dugmore (p. 77), the *'Ahabhah* prayer which Oesterley so compares "was probably not known before

---

[1] FINKELSTEIN, *La Kedouscha et les Bénédictions du Schema, REJ*, xciii (1932) ; *The Development of the Amidah, JQR*, N.S. Vol. xvi.

the end of the second century A.D." Thus the *'Ahabhah* prayer would appear to be ruled out of the comparison. The most that Dugmore will concede to Oesterley is that it is possible that the Sarapion prayer " may reflect an early Christian prayer modelled on the Palestinian version of the IVth Benediction of the *'Amidah.*" This concession, it will be seen, does not amount to much when the stages of influence and the point of contact have to be removed backwards to earlier forms of prayer in both religions. When now we compare the Palestinian version of the IVth Benediction (date c. A.D. 10-40) (" O favour us, Our Father, with knowledge from Thyself and understanding and discernment from Thy *Torah.*. Blessed art Thou, O Lord, which vouchsafest knowledge "), it might well seem that if people are going to thank or pray to God for knowledge and enlightenment at all, what similarity there is in the Jewish and Christian prayers is explicable without the hypothesis of contact at an earlier stage of development of the one or the other. Again, to give the second example, it is held by Oesterley (p. 127) that the IIIrd Benediction of the *'Amidah* has influenced the words of the early Christian prayer which appears in the First Epistle of Clement to the Corinthians (A.D. 96) which (ch. lix. 3) runs : " (Grant us) to hope in Thy Name, the first source of all creation ; open the eyes of our heart to know Thee, that Thou alone art the Highest among the highest, and remainest Holy among the holy ones." The point of comparison between the two passages is the holiness of God, the phrase " Holy among the holy ones " being parallel to the words of the IIIrd Benediction in its modern version as given by Singer : " and holy is Thy Name ; and holy ones praise Thee every day." But any conclusion we might base upon this comparison is, Dugmore points out, nugatory, for in the old Palestinian version of this Benediction, which was not composed till 10-40 A.D., the phrase " and holy ones praise Thee every day " is absent. In the time of the composition of I Clement it is unlikely that any expansion of the old Palestinian tradition had arisen.

Though the thesis of Dugmore is that " such early Christian prayers as have survived do not suggest any wholesale borrowing from the liturgy of the Synagogue " (p. 113), yet he himself concedes more than his own criteria allow to those who trace borrowings in the early Christian prayers from the Synagogue. Dugmore (p. 107) himself holds for example that the First Epistle of Clement, ch. lix-lxi., which represents the Roman form of prayer at the end of the first century, has incorporated the Ist and IInd Benedictions of the *'Amidah.* There is nothing against this from the standpoint of time, for Benediction I in its earliest form would appear to bé pre-Maccabean and the oldest version of Benediction II to belong to the first century before the Christian era (cf. Dugmore p. 114 f). But what the impartial reader of the prayer in Clement will find is that there is nothing in it to suggest any dependence upon Benediction I ; and that while in lix. 3 there is resemblance to Benediction II in the Palestinian version, what resemblance there is is due to the fact that I Clem. lix. has drawn freely from *The Song of Hannah* (I Sam. 2), which has also in phraseology and thought inspired the second Benediction. The prayer in I Clem. lix. 3, like the *Magnificat* (Luke i., 46-55), is based upon Hannah's song, that is, upon the *scriptures* not on the liturgy, upon the theme of the sovereign God as disposer of the destinies of men. Again, in regard to a well-known prayer of the *Didache* (of uncertain date: according to Dix, 190 A.D.) which Oesterley (p. 131) says " reads like a Christian adaptation " of the Xth Benediction, some analysis may prove illuminating. Dugmore indeed warns against Oesterley's conclusion but he omits to examine it. Now, the Didache-prayer runs thus : "As this broken bread was scattered upon the mountains, but was brought together and became one, so let Thy Church be gathered together from the ends of the earth unto Thy Kingdom." The thing that strikes us first as we compare this with the Benediction is that there is absolutely nothing in the latter relating to that which is the chief picture of the Christian prayer, viz. that of corn or bread scattered upon mountains. Nor in the Christian prayer is there anything about sounding or blowing horns or lifting up banners as in the Jewish. There is, however, similarity in the "let Thy Church be gathered together from the ends of the earth " of the Didache to the words of the Benediction in its *modern* version : " and gather us as one from the four corners of the earth." But this similarity, minimal as it is, is diminished almost to vanishing point when we reflect that the form of the Xth Benediction (A.D. 40-70), with which the author of the Didache would be acquainted, if he had known of it at all, would have been : " Blow the great horn of our freedom and lift a banner to gather our exiles. Blessed art Thou, O Lord, who gathered the dispersed of Thy people Israel." Thus the notion of *gathering the dispersed* remains alone as common element in both prayers while the words "ends (corners) of the earth " disappear from the comparison altogether. One could hardly be so bold as to claim on the basis of what is left any real contact between the prayers in question.

What we have written so far, though it might be further elaborated, suggests that, arising from the new evidence which the Genizah fragments offer, certain conclusions now fall to be drawn and certain issues require to be weighed in connection with the inquiry into the influence of Judaism, so far as the Synagogue service is concerned, upon the new religion which sprang from her. We may claim to have shown that it is time that the question of this influence be formulated in a new way, namely, that it should take this form : What is the reason for the scantiness of the contribution of the Synagogue to Christian worship so far as the latter has found expression in the ancient *prayers* of the Church ? It is our task now to seek to answer this question.

II

It would seem, *a priori*, to be highly improbable that the Synagogue service of the period before and the century and a half after the Christian era should have made no contribution to Christian prayer. Phrases of praise, thanksgiving, invocation, adoration heard in the Synagogue must have lived on in the affection and hearts and upon the tongues of those Jewish men and women who now formed the first Christian congregations. How is this to be reconciled with the scantiness of the traces of borrowing on the part of the known prayers of the ancient Church ? Some of the factors relevant to or explanatory of this scantiness may be set forth as follows :—

(*a*) The Synagogue service has given the pattern (praise—prayer—reading of scripture—homily or sermon) of that part of the Christian service which is called pro-anaphoral, *i.e.* the part prior to the eucharistic prayer which consecrates the oblation of bread and wine in the sacrament. This pattern form is common to both religions as a "means of grace " or of approach to God. In Lidzbarski's story of the beggar's coat of patches, we may assume that although none of the patches could be certified as belonging to the original coat, nevertheless the *form* of the original coat was well preserved. A new religion or a new sect must invariably justify itself by claiming to possess a new content of thought and teaching, while it may not be able, or desire, to dispense with the old form. Besides the pattern which the Church in its pro-anaphoral portion of its service took from the Synagogue, Christianity has made extensive borrowings from Judaism in regard to form. The Passover meal (or perhaps

175

the weekly *Kiddush* ceremony), Baptism, Laying on of hands, and even some minor features of Jewish ritual such as occur in the Mishnah tractate *Yoma*, have made their mark on Christianity as modes of religious expression and vehicles of its thought and practice or as the basis of a new religious form or ritual. But without considering such loans or the Old Testament, which acts as a perpetual stream of Hebrew influence upon the Church, and confining our attention to the Synagogue service alone, we find that the contribution of the latter to the Church service was a particular pattern of worship, the pro-anaphoral form.

(*b*) The Sabbath and the Sunday. The first Christians, as the New Testament (Acts i. 46) informs us, were, after the death of Jesus, to be found "daily with one accord in the temple." It is also to be supposed that they continued to attend the Synagogue service on the Sabbath and other days. And very early their own Sunday gathering or service must have attained a position with them similar to the Sabbath Synagogue service. Now, it is very unlikely that the fixed prayers of the Sabbath Synagogue service were repeated the very next day at the Christian gathering for worship in some other place without any variation or that they were merely altered to be made suitable to the new circumstances. It is true, of course, that these Jewish Christians could not acquire an entirely new religious vocabulary of prayer. *Extempore* prayers were characteristic of the early Christian gatherings and without doubt must have fallen into the old channels of expression and must often have contained more than merely echoes of the familiar and fixed Jewish prayers. But *extempore* prayers once said, like water that has been spilt, cannot be collected again. Moreover, even those *extempore* Sunday prayers must have had, in the new situation, as their main characteristic, thoughts and teachings which were relevant to the new faith and to the new day of worship; and whenever—after a period of considerable length—other fixed prayers ranged themselves alongside the one hitherto only fixed prayer, the " Lord's Prayer," it is unlikely that they were modelled on the Synagogue service of the day before. It is probable that they became *fixed* because they were particularly expressive of the new faith. Prayer that is felt to be effective must revolve round what is taught, believed, and preached. Judged by this standard the Jewish Synagogue prayers are conspicuously relevant and it may be assumed that the Jewish Christian prayers had also this relevancy in respect of what was believed and taught by them. The Sunday had a particular doctrinal reference, namely the belief that on this day Jesus had risen from the dead ; and St. Paul's description of the content of his preaching, viz. "Jesus Christ and him crucified" (I Cor. ii. 1), can with certainty be regarded as applicable to the preaching throughout the Church everywhere. Prayer before becoming fixed and even when fixed is apt to retain an incalculable element and wherever men pray they inevitably use similar terms, but the fixed prayers of a religious community will, on the whole, be a reflection of the message the community teaches and believes. This is the reason why borrowings on the part of the Church service from the Synagogue service are scant and the proof of them difficult.

There were a number of topics, themes and doctrines common to Jesus and to the Jewish Christians (of whom the Church was composed) and we cannot suppose that the latter, of the same race and culture, devised a linguistic technique for praying concerning the same things in different ways from their brethren. It would be as unnatural to suppose so as it would be to speak of *borrowing* when we recognise an obvious likeness in language in prayers of both communities concerning, for example, the coming of God's Kingdom and the doing of His will everywhere among men. The Old Testament was the only sacred scripture of the Church for a long time and here was a source rich in liturgical expressions that are the heritage of both Jew and Christian, and in the subject-matter of prayer. In general it is not necessary to seek to derive from elsewhere what the Old Testament itself can account for. No doubt the congregational response *Amen* did, as is widely stated, pass over from the Synagogue to the Church although that word is also the congregational response in the Old Testament. It would have been in the circumstances absurd, had the thought ever occurred, to seek to invent another word to express congregational response. Likewise the dependence of the first three petitions of the Lord's Prayer and the old pre-Christian *Half-kaddish* which Jesus must have known well seems fairly clear, even if, in respect of these petitions, both prayers express in their own way thoughts of which neither had a monopoly. The Lord's Prayer thus bears upon it the influence of the Synagogue even before such a thing as a Christian Church or a Church service existed. It did not arise, as the other prayers of the Church did, out of the Sunday service. And that the Jewish Christian Church felt no strong necessity or desire to proceed along the lines of the Synagogue service is evident further from what we must now consider.

(c) Conflict : the cultivation of dissimilarities. The early occurrence of tension between Jews and Jewish Christians had the effect of emphasising differences rather than resemblances in the content of their worship. One account of this tension concerns the Decalogue, which had a place in the Christian service, where it may have come from the Temple or the Synagogue or because of its scriptural and doctrinal importance alone. We cannot simply decide without more ado, as Dugmore does (p. 105, 110), that the Decalogue owed its presence in the Church service because it was recited in the Synagogue service. But, in any case, we see from the Talmud (J. Ber 1.8; B. Ber 12a) that, apparently some time after the middle of the first century, the Synagogue saw itself compelled to effect a change in its service on account of particular views which the Jewish Christians held about the Decalogue. This change must have been made after a long time and much thought. We are told that the Synagogue dropped the recital of The Decalogue " because of the idle talk (Goldschmidt—*Rederei*) of the Minim." Rashi's comment on this (cf. Goldschmidt's note on Ber 12a) explains that the idle talkers asserted that only the Ten Commandments represented the truly Divine Law. In other words, the recital of the Decalogue in the Christian service had, and must have had from the beginning, an anti-Synagogual tendency stressing the validity of the Decalogue in contrast to the Ceremonial Law. Its presence in the Christian service was not a sign of following in the path of the Synagogue service but of just the opposite, and the action of the Synagogue was the reply. The comment of Rashi confirms the interpretation that has been given of Pliny's letter (112 A.D.) to Trajan describing the character of the Christian gatherings, namely that Pliny refers to the place the Decalogue took in their worship. The Jewish Christian sectaries were doctrinaire Biblicists, interpreting the Old Testament in the light of the new Evangel, and the Decalogue was the scriptural focus of their polemic in regard to the Law.

We have only to consider such facts concerning the earliest Christian worship as may be gathered from the New Testament, to see how little disposed the Church was to proceed along the lines of the Synagogue service. In Corinth (I Cor. xi. 4f) women pray and prophesy at the Church service. The Apostle Paul does not object to this procedure but only forbids their appearing unveiled. The Church here, it is true, is not entirely Jewish Christian, indeed essentially non-Jewish, but nevertheless under the tutelage of the Jew Paul. Then here in Corinth and elsewhere we learn of the rite of " the holy kiss " (Rom. xvi. 16 ; I Cor. xvi. 20, etc.). A society which in its Sunday gatherings had established this custom of the kiss of brotherhood—in the early days administered promiscuously—cannot have been conscious of any need of keeping in line with the Synagogue service. Other usages, though not so intimately connected with the service of worship, reflect the same picture of independence. Some have sought for the prototype of the Christian *agape* or love-feast in the banquets of the Essenes. But it is difficult to give this feast of the Church any convincing location in Judaism. The same problem presents itself in regard to a peculiar rite, namely baptism *for the dead* (i.e., in behalf of the dead, I C. xv. 29). The Christian Church was very eclectic and independent from the start and we may understand why it has been asked : Did the Church owe anything to the pagan cult-associations of the age ?

(*d*) In the "Apostolic Constitutions" (4th century), there are what appear to be large fragments of Jewish prayers which have been worked over for Christian use in Church services. These prayers are those to which Bossuet first drew attention and which Dr. Goodenough (By Light, Light, The Mystic Gospel of Hellenistic Judaism, 1935, p. 306f) shows do not derive from normative Judaism but are of a mystic type. The fragments are an indication that the breach occasioned in the second century between Jews and Christians was now becoming to some extent narrower. They are samples of liturgical effort on the part of Christians in or about the time of the appearance of the first extant service-manuals. But of much importance is the source from which the borrowing is made. Goodenough regards this mystical non-normative Judaism as having drawn from the pagan mystery religions before the Christian era and as having been the well from which Christianity drew. If this be so, then the Church service must not be examined solely in comparison with the normative Synagogue service.

O. S. Rankin.

Early Synagogue and Jewish Catacomb Art
and its Relation to Christian Art

by Joseph Gutmann, Detroit, Michigan

Contents

I. The Dura Synagogue Paintings

1. Description of the Dura Synagogue and its Panels

No archaeological discovery in recent decades has so revolutionized our thinking as the excavation of the Dura-Europos synagogue in 1932. Clark Hopkins clearly states the case:

"if . . . a biblical scholar or a student of ancient art . . . were told that the building was a synagogue and the paintings were scenes from the Old Testament, he simply would not have believed it. It could not be; there was absolutely no precedent, nor could there be any. The stern injunction in the

Ten Commandments against the making of graven images would be sufficient to prove him right."[1] (Pl. I, fig. 1.)

Since the amazing Dura paintings could hardly be anticipated, or accounted for, by classical Jewish or Christian historical scholarship, they have raised serious questions about the prevailing historiography devoted to that period. Above all, the Dura paintings have forced scholars to undertake a critical re-evaluation of so-called 'normative rabbinic Judaism' and its rigid iconoclasm which historians presumed as established fact.

The Dura synagogue paintings have also demanded a re-examination of the conventional scholarly assumption that a negative attitude toward images characterizes every period of Jewish history.

Dura has re-opened an older debate in art history — whether indeed the origins of Christian art may be rooted in an antecedent — now lost — Jewish art.

The Dura synagogue is the first major Jewish artistic monument ever to be found; its paintings are the earliest known significant continuous cycle of biblical images. Figural biblical decoration of similar complexity and extent does not appear in Christian art until two hundred years later, in the fifth century. The synagogue, excavated by an expedition of Yale University and the Académie des Inscriptions et Belles Lettres, was located in Dura-Europos, a city which stood between Damascus and Bagdad on the right bank of the Euphrates river (the reconstructed synagogue is now in the National Museum in Damascus, Syria). Dura-Europos in the third century was a provincial Syrian frontier town, occupied by a Roman garrison stationed there to defend it against the Sasanians. The preservation of the synagogue can be attributed to Roman military skill. To protect the city's walls against Sasanian siege operations, which actually occurred in 256 A.D., a number of buildings close to the city wall were covered with an earthen embankment. Since the synagogue stood close to the western city wall, it was within the area of these fortifications, and hence was preserved. The excavated synagogue was dated by inscription 244/45. It had been rebuilt and enlarged in order to replace an earlier, late second-century A.D. synagogue, originally a private house.

The synagogue complex consisted of a house of assembly (the synagogue proper), a pillared forecourt, and a precinct surrounded by chambers facing the street through which it was approached. Some of the quarters in this precinct may have served as a hostel for transients and as residences for synagogue officials. The house of assembly was a *Breithausbau*, familiar from Syro-Palestinian domestic architecture, and had two entrances on the east wall. The measurements of the synagogue were 13.65 m. in length, 7.68 m. in width and 7 m. in height. The inside walls were completely covered with five horizontal bands of decoration running around the four sides. The lowest band above the two-tiered benches was a decorative dado with panels depicting animals, masks of the New Comedy type, and simulated marble incrustation. The three middle bands portray some 58 biblical episodes in about 28 preserved panels (roughly 60% of the original

[1] C. HOPKINS, The Discovery of Dura-Europos, 131.

decoration). The decorative band next to the ceiling has been almost completely destroyed. The central, middle band, measuring 1.50 m., is the largest and is bound, on the west wall, to the horizontal band above it by simulated painted columns. All the horizontal bands converge on and are interrupted on the west wall by the Torah niche, above which are two panels flanked by two vertical wing panels on each side. The Torah niche is oriented towards Jerusalem. Next to it was placed a special seat for Samuel, the elder of the synagogue. Greek, Aramaic and Middle Iranian inscriptions[2] were found on the walls. A flat ceiling with large decorative or inscribed tiles originally covered the house of assembly.

The Jewish population of Dura, consisting perhaps of some 65 members, was probably made up of merchants and traders stemming from Syro-Palestine and nearby Mesopotamia. Dura was not an intellectual center; no gymnasium or theatre was found there. The Jews most likely catered to and supplied the Roman garrison stationed there to ward off an expected Sasanian attack. Many scholars agree that the program of the synagogue paintings is unlikely to have been invented at Dura. Perhaps it imitated a similar program which one of the Jewish merchants saw in a synagogue in a major Jewish center, Antioch, Palmyra or Tiberias.

To date the Dura synagogue paintings have elicited more than ten major studies by leading scholars, all concentrating on the iconography – the meaning of individual scenes or of the entire cycle of paintings. SUKENIK and SCHNEID wrote an evaluation in Hebrew; EHRENSTEIN and KÜMMEL composed a commentary in German; AUBERT, DU MESNIL and GRABAR presented their findings in French; ROSTOVTZEFF, SONNE, LEVEEN, WISCHNITZER wrote in English. These studies all antedating 1956, were sagaciously and critically examined in the magnificent final report on the synagogue by CARL KRAELING. Since KRAELING published his book, GOODENOUGH's three-volume work on the Dura synagogue paintings has appeared. Recently PERKINS and HOPKINS wrote on the Dura synagogue, but their books address iconographic problems only peripherally.

Little agreement exists among scholars as to the sequence of the synagogue paintings – whether they are to be read clockwise or counter-clockwise, radiating towards or away from the Torah niche, from the lower to the upper register or vice versa. Nor does agreement exist as to the identification of individual panels. Following KRAELING's numbering, we list the divergence of opinions among scholars as to the identification of each scene (fig. 2, p. 1316).

The West Wall (pl. II, fig. 3; pl. III, fig. 4; pl. IV, fig. 5):

Above the Torah niche is depicted the Sacrifice of Isaac (Genesis 22) – the person in the tent has been construed as one of Abraham's servants (KRAELING, PERKINS), Isaac freed from his bonds (GRABAR, HOPKINS), Abraham (DU MESNIL),

---

[2] R. BRUNNER, The Iranian Epigraphic Remains from Dura-Europos, Journal of the American Oriental Society, 92 (1972), 496, suggests that these inscriptions may have been written by Jewish scribes in the service of the Persian army. The Iranian inscriptions contain the names of the visitors, dates of viewing and invocations of peace.

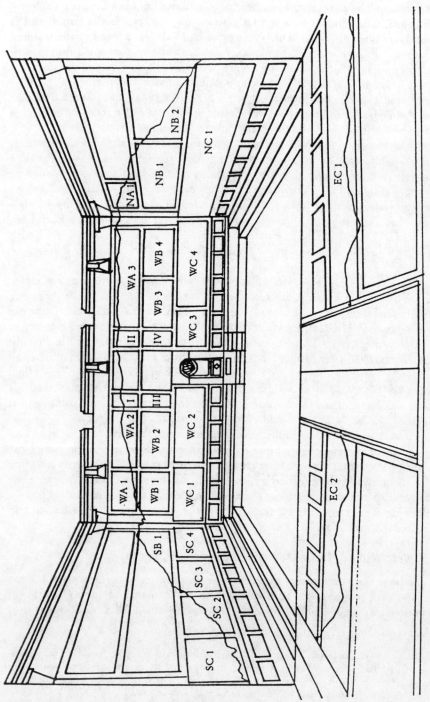

Fig. 2. Diagram of all paintings of the Dura synagogue paintings, according to CARL KRAELING

Sarah (GOODENOUGH), the Jebusite Ornan (WISCHNITZER), Ishmael (SCHUBERT). The building surrounded by cultic objects has been interpreted by most scholars as the Temple of Jerusalem.

Lower Central Panel: Scholars are generally agreed that this represents Jacob blessing his sons and the sons of Joseph (Genesis 48–49), and David, the pious king.

Upper Central Panel: Many scholars agree with KRAELING that David, the messianic king over Israel, is depicted here. Other interpretations are: Joseph and his brethren in Egypt (WISCHNITZER), Pharaoh confronted by Moses and Aaron (LEVEEN), Moses' Blessing (SONNE), Apotheosis of Moses with Aaron and Hur (DU MESNIL), The Glorification of Israel (GOODENOUGH).

Wing Panel I: It is generally agreed that the panel depicts Moses receiving the law (Exodus 24). Some scholars feel that Joshua and the angel are represented (SONNE, SUKENIK).

Wing Panel II: There is general agreement that Moses is depicted standing before the Burning Bush (Exodus 3).

Wing Panel III: Many scholars identify this figure as Abraham (KRAELING, WISCHNITZER, HOPKINS, PERKINS). Other interpretations are: Joshua (SUKENIK, LEVEEN), Jacob (SONNE), Moses (GOODENOUGH, AVI-YONAH), Enoch (HEMPEL), Elijah (MASER).

Wing Panel IV: Ezra (KRAELING, DU MESNIL, PERKINS), Samuel or Nathan (WISCHNITZER), Josiah (GRABAR), Samuel the Elder (SONNE), Moses (GOODENOUGH, LEVEEN, SUKENIK, AVI-YONAH).

WC 1: It is generally agreed that the panel represents Elijah restoring the widow's son (I Kings 17).

WC 2: There is general agreement that depicted are Esther and the triumph of Mordecai (Esther 6–9).

WC 3: General agreement that Samuel anointing David is depicted (I Samuel 16).

WC 4: General agreement that Pharaoh and the infancy of Moses are shown (Exodus 1–2). The scene on the right is interpreted as Jochebed depositing Moses in the ark (KRAELING), Pharaoh's daughter laying the child at Pharaoh's feet (HOPKINS), a Hebrew woman in childbirth (SONNE).

WB 1: Well of Be'er (KRAELING), Waters of Marah (SUKENIK), Wells of Elim (SONNE), Moses giving the Law (WISCHNITZER), Feast of Tabernacles (DU MESNIL), Miriam's Well (NORDSTRÖM, GUTMANN).

WB 2: General agreement that the panel depicts the Consecration of the Tabernacle and its priests (Exodus 40 and Numbers 7), Open Mystic Temple of the priests (GOODENOUGH).

WB 3: General agreement that the Temple of Solomon is shown. Other interpretations: Restored Temple of Josiah (GRABAR, LEVEEN), Beth Shemesh (WISCHNITZER, DU MESNIL), Closed Mystic Temple (GOODENOUGH), Heavenly Temple (GOLDSTEIN, HOPKINS).

WB 4: General agreement: the Ark in the Land of the Philistines and its Return (I Samuel 5–6); The Ark versus Paganism (GOODENOUGH).

WA 1: Saul among the prophets (WISCHNITZER), Jacob's Burial (SONNE), Joseph greeting his brethren in Egypt (DU MESNIL), Anointing of Solomon(?) (KRAELING).

WA 2: Many scholars agree that Solomon and the Queen of Sheba are depicted (I Kings 10). Other interpretations: Judgment of Solomon (WISCHNITZER, DU MESNIL, GRABAR) Pharaoh's Council with the midwives (SONNE).

WA 3: General agreement that the Exodus from Egypt and the Crossing of the Red Sea are shown (Exodus 12–14).

The North Wall (pl. V, fig. 6):

NC 1: General agreement that what is depicted is Ezekiel's Vision and the Resurrection of the Dry Bones (Ezekiel 37). The last scene of the panel has been variously interpreted: Joab's Punishment (WISCHNITZER, DU MESNIL, GRABAR), Ezekiel's Execution (SUKENIK, LEVEEN, GOODENOUGH, AVI-YONAH), Jehoiakim's Death (KRAELING), Beheading the Prince of Edom (SONNE), Mattathias killing the apostate Jew (STERN, HOPKINS).

NB 1: General agreement that the Battle of Eben-Ezer and the Capture of the Ark are illustrated (I Samuel 4).

NB 2: Most scholars follow KRAELING and identify this scene as Hannah and Samuel at Shiloh; Samuel and Eli at Shiloh (WISCHNITZER, GRABAR) (I Samuel 1–3).

NA 1: General agreement that Jacob's Dream is shown (Genesis 28).

The East Wall:

EC 1: David sparing Saul in the Wilderness of Ziph (KRAELING), Wars of Gog and Magog (SONNE), David's War with the Philistines (SUKENIK), Victory of Judas Maccabaeus over Gorgias (HOPKINS).

EC 2: Belshazzar's Feast and the Fall of Babylon (?) (KRAELING), Cleansing of the Jerusalem Temple (HOPKINS), Wars of Gog and Magog (SONNE), Elijah fed by Ravens (WISCHNITZER), Abraham frightening the birds away from the sacrifice (?) (LEVEEN, SUKENIK), Drunkenness of Noah (?) (DU MESNIL).

The South Wall (pl. VI, fig. 7):

SC 1: Elijah proclaims a Drought and leaves for Cherith (?) (KRAELING) (I Kings 16–17).

SC 2: General agreement that Elijah and the Widow of Zarapeth are represented (I Kings 17).

SC 3: General agreement that the Sacrifice of the Baal Prophets on Mount Carmel is depicted (I Kings 18).

SC 4: General agreement that Elijah's Sacrifice on Mount Carmel is shown (I Kings 18).

SB 1: Dedication of Solomon's Temple (KRAELING), Aaron's Death (SONNE), Joseph's Bones carried to Canaan (WISCHNITZER), Setting up the Tabernacle (HOPKINS), Procession of the Ark (DU MESNIL, GRABAR), Joshua crossing the Jordan with the Ark (GUTMANN).

Although the individual scenes deal with such well-known biblical personages as Abraham, Isaac, Jacob, Moses, Aaron, Samuel, Elijah, Ezekiel, David, Solomon, Mordecai, Esther and Ahasuerus, many scholars have noted that details in many scenes can only be understood by recourse to the vast *aggadah* in targumic and midrashic literature contemporary with the synagogue paintings. Thus we find in the panels such legendary amplifications as:

WC 2: Ahasuerus sits on Solomon's Throne (pl. III, fig. 4).
WC 3: Samuel anoints David in the presence of six brothers (pl. IV, fig. 5).
WC 4: The nude princess rescues the child Moses from the Nile (pl. IV, fig. 5).
WB 1: Miriam's Well nourishes the children of Israel in the Wilderness (pl. III, fig. 4).
WA 3: The Israelites departing from Egypt are armed and cross the Red Sea, which has divided into twelve paths (pl. IV, fig. 5).
SC 3: Hiel hides in the altar of the Baal prophets and is bitten by a snake (pl. V, fig. 6).
Over the Torah niche: God Himself (and not an angel) intercedes in the Sacrifice of Isaac; the ram stands next to a tree (and is not entangled in the thicket) (pl. II, fig. 3).

While many of the identifications of KRAELING's magisterial work are accepted by scholars, recent research has added new information on some of the panels treated by KRAELING and has suggested other identifications.

SB 1: I would suggest identifying this scene as the Crossing of the Jordan with the Ark under Joshua — a scene playing a prominent role in later church art (pl. V, fig. 6). According to Jewish legends, the crossing of the river Jordan was an occasion of many wonders, to which all the peoples of the earth were witness.[3]
NC 1: The last scene in the Vision of Ezekiel panel should, I believe, be identified as Mattathias killing the apostate Jew (pl. VI, fig. 7).[4] This episode and the following one in EC 1, which HOPKINS identifies as Judas Maccabaeus' Victory over Gorgias, are drawn from the Books of Maccabees. If these identifications prove correct, they raise interesting questions as to what third-century Jews knew about these books, which were not canonized as part of the Hebrew Bible, but were included by the Church

---

[3] J. GUTMANN, The Dura-Europos Synagogue, 141, and L. GINZBERG, The Legends of the Jews (Philadelphia, 1946–1947), IV, 5f., VI, 172.
[4] H. STERN, Quelques problèmes d'iconographie paléochrétienne et juive, Cahiers archéologiques, 12 (1962), 104–113.

Fathers in the Vulgate.[5] The significance of the split Mount of Olives in the Ezekiel panel's depiction of the Resurrection of Dry Bones was not adequately underscored by KRAELING (page 191). According to Jewish tradition, all the righteous dead will roll underground and will emerge at the Mount of Olives on the day of resurrection.[6]

SC 4: The legend of Ḥiel hiding in the altar of the Baal prophets was also known to the Church Father Ephraem Syrus (pl. V, fig. 6).[7]

WC 3: KRAELING noted, on page 168, that Josephus adopts the I Chronicles 2:13—15 reading of six brothers instead of the seven brothers of David recorded in I Samuel 16:10 (pl. IV, fig. 5). Many of the aristocratic Byzantine Psalter depictions of the Anointing of David, dating from the tenth century on, also prefer showing only six brothers of David. The contradiction between the Chronicles and the Samuel accounts is resolved in a ninth-century Christian source. Written by Pseudo-Jerome, the pertinent section reads:

> "The question has been raised why this man [Jesse] is said to have eight sons when in Paralipomenon [I Chronicles 2:13—15] there are said to be no more than seven. This is the explanation: He [Jesse] numbered among his sons the prophet Nathan, the son of his son Shimea whom he had reared and cared for in the place of his son. For his eight sons are said to have been led into the presence of Samuel and the eighth [David] was with the flocks. Among these sons it is clear that Nathan had been brought before Samuel, the one who is called Jonathan. In the last part of Samuel [II Samuel 21:21 and I Chronicles 20:7] it is said concerning this man, Jonathan, the son of Shimea, David's brother [that when Goliath, the giant of Gath taunted Israel] he slew him. And the fact should be noted that everywhere he is called a prophet. Nathan is written, not Jonathan."[8]

This story may be based on a lost midrash. One of the seven brothers of David was not really a brother, but was merely treated as such; thus reducing the traditional number of brothers to six.

WB 1: This scene should be identified as Miriam's Well (pl. III, fig. 4). According to midrashic and targumic accounts, also found in 1 Corinthians 7:21 and in the writings of the Hellenistic Jewish tragedian Ezekiel, a

[5] C. HOPKINS, Discovery of Dura-Europos, 171 ff. Cf. S. ZEITLIN, The First Book of Maccabees (New York, 1950), 61 ff.

[6] H. RIESENFELD, The Resurrection in Ezekiel . . ., in: GUTMANN, No Graven Images, 144—145 and J. GUTMANN, The Messianic Temple . . ., in: GUTMANN, Temple of Solomon, 132, 143—145. Cf. also G. STEMBERGER, Zur Auferstehungslehre in der rabbinischen Literatur, Kairos, 3/4 (1973), 259—60; E. GARTE, The Theme of Resurrection in the Dura-Europos Synagogue Paintings, Jewish Quarterly Review, 64 (1973), 1—15 brings no new information.

[7] L. GINZBERG, Die Haggada bei den Kirchenvätern (Amsterdam, 1899), 80—82.

[8] A. SALTMAN, ed., Pseudo-Jerome, Quaestiones on the Book of Samuel (Leiden, 1975), 91; J. GUTMANN, Jewish Elements in the Paris Psalter, Marsyas, 6 (1950—1953), 48. GINZBERG, op. cit., VI, 264, n. 88.

rock-well followed the Israelites in their Wilderness wanderings and set itself up before the Tabernacle at each new encampment; twelve streams of water gushed from the rock-well, one to each of the twelve tribes. KRAELING and recent articles on the subject recognize that, except for Moses and his staff, most of the elements in the panel are accounted for in the targumic-midrashic narratives. In my opinion, the only narratives which allude to both Moses and his rod and the twelve springs gushing from the rock-well are found in the Koran and Byzantine literature.[9] Sura 7:160 reads: "We inspired Moses, when his people asked for water, saying: Smite the rock with your staff! And there gushed forth therefrom twelve springs, so that each tribe knew their drinking place." The Koran and Byzantine writings may here preserve a version of the legend illustrated at Dura, but lost to us in surviving rabbinic writings.

WC 4: The nude princess in the water (KRAELING, page 176ff.) has been reconsidered in several articles, which reveal that the motif of the nude princess is also found in later Christian and Jewish illustrated manuscripts (pl. IV, fig. 5).[10]

WA 3: KRAELING (page 83ff.) observed that the Israelites were armed and that they crossed the Red Sea via twelve paths (pl. IV, fig. 5). Recent studies indicate that these two motifs are also found in Christian art and literature as well as in medieval Jewish art.[11]

Above the Torah niche: KRAELING noted that, in the depiction of the Sacrifice of Isaac (pl. II, fig. 3) a hand (symbolic of God) is substituted for the biblical angel, and that the ram is standing next to a tree rather than being entangled in the thicket (KRAELING, page 57f.). As a reward for Abraham's and Isaac's obedience to God's will, God, according to rabbinic tradition, will guarantee the forgiveness of Israel's sins.[12] In deviating

---

[9] C. O. NORDSTRÖM, The Water Miracles of Moses in Jewish Legend and Byzantine Art, in: GUTMANN, No Graven Images, 297–308; J. MILGROM, Moses Sweetens the 'Bitter Waters' of the 'Portable Well', an Interpretation at the Dura-Europos Synagogue, Journal of Jewish Art, 5 (1978), 45–47. Cf. also R. STICHEL, Außerkanonische Elemente in byzantinischen Illustrationen des Alten Testaments, Römische Quartalschrift, 69 (1974), 175 n. 66.

[10] J. GUTMANN, The Haggadic Motif in Jewish Iconography, Eretz-Israel, 6 (1960), 17–18, n. 5, and ID., Medieval Jewish Image: Controversies, Contributions, Conceptions, in: Aspects of Jewish Culture in the Middle Ages, ed. P. E. SZARMACH (Albany, 1979), 123 and 132, n. 8. Cf also K. and U. SCHUBERT, Die Errettung des Mose aus den Wassern des Nil in der Kunst des spätantiken Judentums und das Weiterwirken dieses Motivs in der frühchristlichen und jüdisch-mittelalterlichen Kunst, in: Studien zum Pentateuch: Walter Kornfeld zum 60. Geburtstag, ed. G. BRAULIK (Wien, 1977), 59–68.

[11] NORDSTRÖM, The Water Miracles of Moses . . ., 286–297. J. GUTMANN, Hebrew Manuscript Painting (New York, 1978), 65 and Vulgate to Exodus 13:18.

[12] For a full treatment of this subject, cf. J. GUTMANN, The Sacrifice of Isaac: Variations on a Theme in Early Jewish and Christian Art, Festschrift für Josef Fink (in press). R. WISCHNITZER, Number Symbolism in Dura-Synagogue Paintings, Joshua Finkel Festschrift, ed. by S. B. HOENIG and L. D. STITSKIN (New York, 1974), 159–171, claims that the numbers 12 and 7 in various Dura scenes were placed there for dramatic effect. All

from the biblical text, the rabbis wanted to stress their belief that, instead of relying on divine messengers, God intervenes directly in human affairs. The pentateuchal narrative about the ram entangled in the thicket by its horns, as if by accident, is replaced with a depiction of the ram standing next to a tree, as if awaiting the divine acting out of the miracle.

2. Scholarly Theories on the Judaism of Dura and the Meaning of the Entire Cycle

Scholars have attempted not only to discover the meaning of individual scenes, but the purpose and meaning of the entire cycle. Basically, scholars have taken one of three positions:

1. that no unifying idea lies behind the painting cycle.
2. that one governing idea or theological theme underlies the paintings.
3. that several diverse messages are expressed.

1. ROSTOVTZEFF, SUKENIK and LEVEEN see no governing idea behind the cycle of paintings. They feel that the individual panels merely related to special liturgical readings of the Sabbath and the festivals and enabled the worshippers to visualize some of the episodes as they were being read and interpreted in the synagogue.

2. Scholars like GRABAR, SONNE, WISCHNITZER and GOODENOUGH find a unified theological theme reflected in the painting cycle. GRABAR finds that the scenes are a tribute to the sovereignty of God — analogous to programs found in Roman Imperial art. This is expressed in the central group of paintings through the enthroned Anointed and his symbol. The second band reflects it through focus on the power of the ark, God's sacred palladium which brings to naught the plans of hostile rulers. In the first band, God assures his people a glorious future. The covenantal promise guaranteed by certain past events and persons is depicted in band three.

SONNE finds the claim of Rabbi Simon reflected in the Dura paintings: There are three crowns: "the crown of Torah, the crown of Priesthood, and the crown of Kingdom" (Pirkei Avot 4:17). Hence, for him, the third band spells out the Crown of Torah with Moses as the dominant figure. The second band bespeaks the Crown of Priesthood with Aaron as the main figure, and the first band the Crown of Kingdom in which are portrayed various kingdoms to be overthrown in preparation for the messianic kingdom.

WISCHNITZER sees a messianic theme pervading the whole body of paintings. Band three shows the witnesses of the coming salvation; the second band, the trials and tribulations that will usher in the messianic era; the first band, the salvation cycle presenting the heroes of the messianic drama. Another unit is

---

of the Dura scenes discussed are simply aggadic elaborations. If any symbolism adheres to these numbers, it must be sought in the aggadic texts themselves and not in the Dura paintings.

formed by the triptych with the ancestors surrounded by the prophets of salvation. Depicted in the aedicula of the niche is the Messianic Temple, holding the entire program together.

GOODENOUGH sees reflected in the paintings the Philonic doctrine of the soul's mystic ascent to true being and the hope of victory over death.

3. DU MESNIL DU BUISSON and KRAELING see no unified idea, but a cycle containing many diverse religious themes. DU MESNIL classifies the paintings by subject matter and sees the third band as historical, the second as liturgical, dealing with the covenant relationship between God and Israel which expresses itself in cultic performance, and the first band as moralistic, showing how God protects his own while punishing the wicked and rewarding the good. KRAELING suggests that the paintings reflect many diverse religious ideas. He concludes that such themes as the historical covenant relationship, reward and punishment, salvation and the messianic expectation were dictated by practical considerations – to inculcate historical, moral or liturgical lessons or combinations of them.

Thus each scholar finds a different meaning in the cycle of paintings depending on the conceptual framework he brings to his interpretations. In reading these widely divergent reconstructions, we are not always certain that the same synagogue is being discussed. KRAELING has rightly rejected most of the proffered interpretations which would impose a scholarly straitjacket on the painting cycle. He feels that the scholars make interesting combinations, assume similar mentalities in those who commissioned the paintings and "create a situation in which almost everything can mean something else and in which almost anything can mean almost everything" (page 355). KRAELING also notes that many interpreters have a tendency to stress details of a painting which are then related to a midrash, and employ details of a midrash which are then applied to the paintings. KRAELING's own conclusions, however, as Moses Hadas pointed out, leave the reader with "a sense of bafflement . . . surely something more is involved than a discontinuous series of crude representations of Bible stories . . .?"[13]

Although differing widely in their interpretation of the paintings, most scholars who have written on the subject – GOLDSTEIN and GOODENOUGH excepted – are generally agreed that any explanation of the paintings must be rooted in "normative rabbinic Judaism," the definition of Judaism coined by GEORGE FOOT MOORE in his classic work on rabbinic Judaism, 'Judaism in the First Centuries of the Christian Era'. GOLDSTEIN in a review-article concluded that the Dura paintings do not reflect a "normative legalistic rabbinic Judaism," but rather a rabbinic Judaism which had adopted what he terms an "eschatological-material mysticism."[14] GOODENOUGH and his disciples maintain that the paintings can only be understood in terms of a mystic Hellenistic Judaism. GOODENOUGH concluded that "normative rabbinic Judaism" had been at most something of a minor sect – the religion of the intellectual minority responsible for the compilation of the Babylonian and Jerusalem Talmuds.

---

[13] M. HADAS, Review of KRAELING's Synagogue, Commentary, 24 (1957), 81.
[14] J. A. GOLDSTEIN, Review of GOODENOUGH's Jewish Symbols, Journal of Near Eastern Studies, 28 (1969), 212–218.

According to GOODENOUGH, the rabbis with their aniconic and anti-mystical attitudes would have been utterly repelled by the Dura artistic representations. Hence, he argued, rabbinic literature is an unreliable guide for unravelling what he called the 'interpretation' of symbols: the articulate, objective explanation or meaning of symbols, an explanation or meaning which usually changes in each culture, or the 'value' of symbols: the emotional, subjective response to a 'live' symbol, which remains essentially the same in differing cultures. When, therefore, Judaism took over 'live' symbols from the Greco-Roman world, the 'interpretation' of the symbols changed, while their 'value' remained the same. The masses, divorced from rabbinic jurisdiction and influence, worshipped in synagogues decorated with 'live' pagan symbols; they subscribed to a popular 'mystical' Judaism whose chief literary remains are discoverable in the writings of the Hellenistic Jewish philosopher Philo. In Volume X (page 206), GOODENOUGH states his case as follows:

> "For the Judaism that seems expressed here is a Judaism which finds its meaning in mystic victory, a victory reached by two paths, the cosmic and the abstractly ontological . . . the artist [of Dura], like Philo, presumed that the Old Testament text is to be understood not only through its Greek translation, but through its re-evaluation in terms of Greek philosophy and religion."

MORTON SMITH and MICHAEL AVI-YONAH in their perceptive articles place GOODENOUGH's work in proper perspective.[15] Both authors refute some of GOODENOUGH's basic contentions, his rigid categories of a 'mystic' and 'normative rabbinic' Judaism for instance, and his ironclad Jungian concepts of the 'value' and 'interpretation' of symbols.

3. A New Interpretation of the Dura Synagogue Cycle

Recent scholarship has quite conclusively shown that we can no longer speak of one undifferentiated rabbinic Judaism pervasive in all areas of Palestine, Babylonia and the Diaspora, but that we must speak of distinct regional variations in rabbinic Judaism. Thus the Judaism in Palestine, Babylonia and the Diaspora included many variations on the basic theme of rabbinic Judaism.[16]

As only 60 % of the paintings are intact, we may never be able to recover the meaning of the entire cycle. I believe, however, that what remains gives us a picture of the rabbinic Judaism which probably prevailed in Roman Dura in the third century and that the program yields sufficient information to spell out some major ideas and concerns of Durene Jewry. Durene Jewry — perhaps also Jews in

---

[15] M. SMITH, Goodenough's *Jewish Symbols* in Retrospect, in: GUTMANN, The Synagogue, 194–209 and M. AVI-YONAH, Goodenough's Evaluation of the Dura Synagogue: A Critique, in: GUTMANN, Dura-Europos Synagogue, 117–135.

[16] Cf. J. GUTMANN, ed., Ancient Synagogues: The State of Research (Chico, 1981).

nearby Syro-Palestine and Northern Mesopotamia — may have resorted to religious propaganda just as their neighbors did. The purpose of the programs visible in a proximate Christian building and in cult buildings dedicated to Zeus Theos, Palmyrene gods, and Mithras was to gain converts. No doubt the Jews of Dura, by giving visual expression to their religion, aimed at a similar purpose.

A radical new Judaism had come into existence by the first century A.D., a Judaism out of which Christianity grew and was nourished. This new Judaism had substituted prayers within synagogues for sacrifices in the Temple. It elevated the scholar-rabbi and did away with priestly intermediaries. It offered eternal life through personal salvation of the soul and ultimate bodily resurrection, and no longer concentrated on promising fertility of the land. It developed a new system of authority based on a revealed two-fold Law — the Written and the Oral — in preference to the Pentateuch, the authoritative text of the priestly, Temple-centered Judaism. Within the new Oral Law, we find no connected historical narrative or biography, as is the case in the Bible. In fact, the 'Old Testament' or biblical text was no longer viewed as a literal document, but as a divine source for solving contemporary problems. In the Oral Law, scriptural proof was now adduced to illumine a non-biblical concept, be it in the form of a moral teaching or a law. Combining verses and stories drawn from different biblical books, preferring an aggadic elaboration to a biblical text — this was now simply a means to make the point of an identical lesson and to prove the essential unity and timelessness of God's entire revelation.[17] By the mid-third century, the patriarch and the Palestinian scholar class, which had religious jurisdiction over Jews in the Roman empire, were compelled by an ever growing Christian population to focus increasingly on scriptural exegesis and eisegesis in order to answer and expose Christian claims. Both religious factions struggled for control of Scripture with rabbinic concepts and tools in order to win converts and to hold onto their coreligionists. In Palestine, we find the emergence, largely under Christian pressure, of the homiletical midrash and the targumim, Aramaic paraphrases of the Bible. The concentration on preaching by elaborating on and interpreting Scriptures was a primary concern for Palestinian scholars. Babylonian scholars lived in the midst of religions, such as the Zoroastrian, which did not recognize the Bible as a sacred book, and in a land where Christianity made no major inroads; they were not challenged to the same extent as their Palestinian colleagues to develop scriptural interpretation.[18]

If the Dura synagogue paintings reflect this type of Palestinian Judaism, are the 'Old Testament' stories here, too, used simply as prooftexts for the purpose of legitimating a non-biblical concept, liturgical ceremony, or teaching? Already in late Roman art, we find Greek mythological stories employed without regard to their original narrative sequence. As in Dura, they probably served as prooftexts to spell out and underwrite a new liturgical-theological context or program on the

---

[17] Cf. E. RIVKIN, The Shaping of Jewish History (New York, 1971), 42ff. and IDEM, A Hidden Revolution (Nashville, 1978).

[18] Cf. J. NEUSNER, A History of the Jews in Babylonia, II (Leiden, 1966), 72ff.

contemporary mystery religions.[19] In the Dura synagogue, the apparently discontinuous series of pictures represent one of the oldest examples of an art genre whose images are organized around a set of liturgical and ceremonial ideas dependent on or bound to sacred texts and a congregation, a community praying and performing religious rites within that space. The sacred texts which supply most of the visual materials at Dura are not biblical narratives, but contemporary Palestinian targumim and midrashic works. How is this manifest?

In the second band of the Dura paintings, the largest of the three figurative bands, the substitution of the biblical ark for the Torah ark-chest (the container of God's entire revelation to Israel) is done purposely. Furthermore, the biblical scenes, torn out of their narrative biblical context, serve as proofs of new theological ideas. All the panels in the second band reveal the long history of the ark — how it sustained Israel in the desert, performed miracles in the land of the Philistines and finally came to rest in the synagogal Torah shrine where it continued to assure the faithful the salvation of the soul and the bodily resurrection they craved. Although following no narrative sequential order, the scenes are bound together, not by the Bible, but the words of a hymn probably sung during the actual liturgical procession when the ark, kept outside the synagogue, was brought in for synagogal worship. Hence the congregation recounted through song in the procession what is depicted in the second band of the wall. This second band assures the continued efficacy of Torah (symbolized by the Torah ark) for all believers in rabbinic Judaism and hence guaranteed them salvation and resurrection;[20] the first band spells the message out more clearly, more emphatically, the message that salvation and resurrection will come only with the future messianic age. Personal salvation is perhaps suggested by such scenes as Moses saved by the princess and Elijah triumphing over the Baal prophets through God's personal and direct intervention. The promise of personal resurrection may be what was conveyed by the Ezekiel panel and Elijah restoring the widow's son. The scene of Mattathias killing the apostate Jew and Ahasuerus on Solomon's throne may have had messianic implications.

It must be remembered that the favorable climate which existed for Jews under Roman rule during the short reign of Alexander Severus early in the third century had dissipated by the time of the Dura paintings.[21] Oppression and heavy taxation were the rule under the crumbling Roman empire in the third century. The Parthians had persecuted the Jews in Babylonia during the early part of the third century, but their Sasanian successors a generation later had a most favorable attitude towards Jews.

Ahasuerus on Solomon's throne may be Shapur I in disguise, the claimed rightful heir to Cyrus and Darius of the ancient Achaemenian empire — kings glorified in Jewish tradition since they encouraged Jews to return to Judea and

---

[19] Cf. M. L. THOMPSON, The Monumental and Literary Evidence for Programmatic Painting in Antiquity, Marsyas, 9 (1960–1961), 36ff.

[20] Cf. J. GUTMANN, Programmatic Painting in the Dura Synagogue, in: GUTMANN, The Dura-Europos Synagogue, 137–154.

[21] M. AVI-YONAH, The Jews of Palestine (New York, 1976), 115ff.

1. Dura Synagogue: Southwest corner, reconstruction in the National Museum, Damascus

PLATE II

GUTMAN

3. Dura Synagogue: Central area with Torah shrine, West wall

4. Dura Synagogue: West wall, south half

PLATE IV   GUTMANN

6. Dura Synagogue: South wall

PLATE VI   GUTMANN

7. Dura Synagogue, North wall

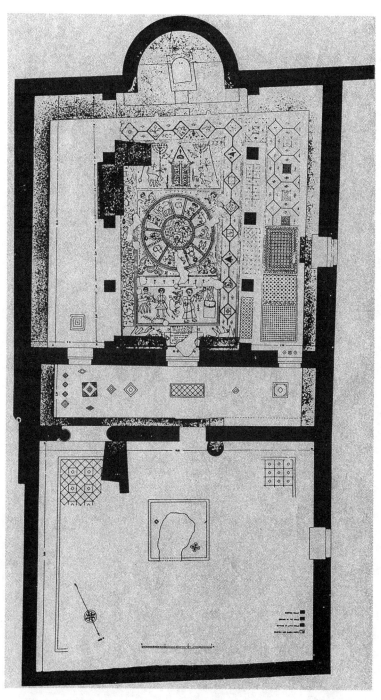

8. Beth-Alpha Synagogue: Diagram of main floor. Beth-Alpha, Israel

PLATE VIII

GUTMANN

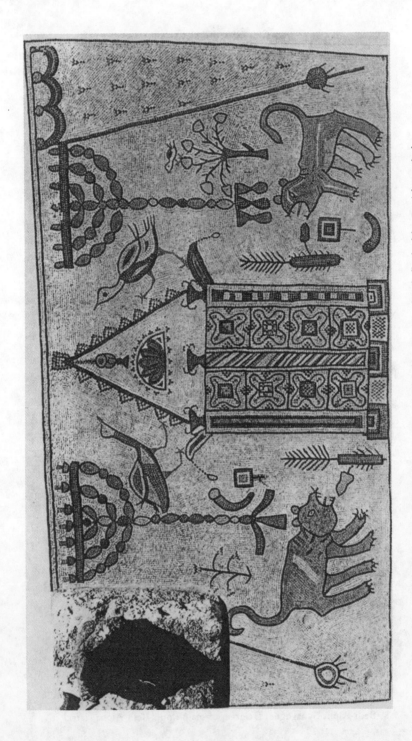

9. Beth-Alpha Synagogue: Upper mosaic panel showing Torah ark flanked by Jewish symbols

helped rebuild the Second Temple. Jews may have seen in Shapur the Sasanian, God's appointed redeemer who would conquer Edom (Rome), the destroyer of the Jerusalem Temple, and would help usher in the messianic age with the restoration of the Davidic kingdom in Jerusalem and the Temple gloriously rebuilt.[22] The depiction of Mattathias killing the apostate Jew may have had a similarly disguised messianic symbolism. Mattathias, zealous fighter for God's law, rose up against Greco-Roman civilization, and it was from his loins the Hasmoneans sprang. Only in this scene is Roman military gear worn by the soldiers who are standing by to watch Mattathias kill the apostate Jew — again a possible allusion to the hoped for collapse of the Roman empire. The cycle in the first band begins next to the Torah niche with the anointing of the youthful David, the promised messianic king, and ends over the Torah niche in the uppermost panel with David enthroned as the messianic king over all Israel,[23] the ultimate fulfillment and promise of rabbinic Judaism. The message of salvation, resurrection and messianic expectation may be pervasive in all of the first band panels — lack of textual sources describing such a program make interpretation difficult and we can only sketch some of the ideas in broad outline rather than specific detail.[24]

It must also be pointed out that the artists of Dura painted no narrative biblical scenes such as we are accustomed to seeing in some later Christian manuscripts and church cycles; they merely rendered moral, ethical, and spiritual lessons ultimately derived from the Bible — the same lessons the congregation heard and became familiar with through the liturgy and rabbinic sermons, later recorded in the Targumim, Midrashim and Prayerbook. Hence, I fully agree with HENRI STERN when he writes:

> "To my mind, the explanation of the scheme must be sought among current opinions of the members of the Jewish community who commissioned the frescoes, and not in complicated philosophical and mystical speculations far removed from the subjects represented."[25]

The Durenes were not Hellenistic philosophers à la the cultivated Alexandrian Philo nor were they akin to the naive fundamentalists common in our own day; they were probably unsophisticated merchants who simply gave visual expression to a Judaism familiar to them, but strange to us. The midrashic interpretations in the paintings were not a matter of special erudition; the congregation was more familiar with them through sermons and Aramaic paraphrases than with the literal sense of the Bible.[26] The entire program is held together by the central

---

[22] Cf. A. H. CUTLER, Third-Century Palestinian Rabbinic Attitudes towards the Prospect of the Fall of Rome, Jewish Social Studies, 31 (1969), 275–285; AVI-YONAH, Jews of Palestine, 127ff.

[23] KRAELING, op. cit. 220.

[24] The writer hopes to document in greater depth in a future study the conclusions given here.

[25] H. STERN, The Orpheus in the Synagogue of Dura-Europos: A Correction, Journal of the Warburg and Courtauld Institutes, 22 (1959), 373.

[26] Cf. M. KLEIN, Palestinian Targum and Synagogue Mosaics, Immanuel, 11 (1980), 34, who writes: "The Palestinian Targumim are particularly expansive in theological matters such as

panel over the Torah niche which functions like the keystone of an arch. With its ultimate promise of personal salvation and resurrection in a messianically restored land of Israel, the panel gives visual expression to the pious wish the builders and donors of the Dura synagogue recorded on one of the ceiling tiles: "their reward, all whatever . . . that the world which is to come . . . assured to them."[27]

The four figures flanking the central scenes are also likely to have specific meanings. The two top figures, identified as Moses, may represent the revelation and giving of Torah – the Written and the Oral Law. The two bottom figures, possibly biblical, are difficult to interpret, but perhaps embody the two basic components of synagogal worship, recitation of prayer[28] and reading of Scripture (Torah). They may have been placed next to the two sanctuaries – the Tabernacle and the Temple – to underscore what rabbinic statements make amply clear, that prayers are a fitting substitute for sacrifices and that reading Scripture (Torah) in the synagogue is equal to performing cultic Temple rites.[29]

Next to the Torah niche is a special seat, called in contemporary sources the 'cathedra of Moses',[30] on which Samuel, the priest and elder of the synagogue, probably sat. This chair may represent the chain of rabbinic tradition. According to tradition (pl. II, fig. 3), Moses received

"The [Written and Oral] Law from Sinai [top figures] . . . transmitted it to the Prophets [two bottom figures(?)], and the Prophets transmitted it to the men of the Great Synagogue [of whom Samuel the Elder was a disciple][31]" (Pirkei Avot 1:1).

Samuel, seated in the 'cathedra of Moses', was probably endowed with authority, ultimately inherited from Moses through the chain of tradition, to interpret and adjudicate the Law.

II. The Second Commandment and Synagogue Images

The Dura synagogue paintings have aroused great surprise since they fly in the face of the supposed and assumed strict observance of the so-called Second Commandment. Much confusion has stemmed from the assertion of scholars that the Second Commandment is to be viewed as an unchanging phenomenon, a

God's providence and direct intervention in the world, sin and the day of Judgment, reward and retribution, . . . the Messiah and the End of Days."

[27] KRAELING, op. cit., 263–264.
[28] Cf. KRAELING, ibid., 166f. on the gesture of adoration and submission.
[29] GUTMANN, Programmatic Painting, op. cit., 149–150.
[30] Cf. I. RENOV, The Seat of Moses, in: GUTMANN, The Synagogue, 233–238.
[31] KRAELING, op. cit., 333.

monolithic concept never transcending its own particular historical context. Such pietistic, literal interpretations frequently gloss over the fact that, within the Bible and the Talmud, different and diverse attitudes are expressed toward images. Exodus 20:4—5 may clearly pronounce: "You shall not make for yourself a sculptured image or any likeness," but Exodus 35:31—34 elevates the artist to heights unparalleled in extant ancient Near Eastern texts: "He [God] has endowed him [Bezalel] with a divine spirit of skill, ability and knowledge in every kind of craft."[32]

It would be more to the point to speak of Second Commandments in the plural, not only in the Bible but in subsequent interpretations of the commandment. When the Hebrew Bible underwent a process of canonization and the predominantly negative attitude expressed in some biblical books was held binding on subsequent Jewish societies, the Second Commandment had to be dealt with and interpreted to suit new societal contexts — contexts very much at variance with those of the biblical period for which the commandment had originally been intended. New interpretations of the Second Commandment had to be promulgated. Thus multiple Second Commandments have been formulated in the course of Jewish history. These commandments, though based on the original biblical injunction, have meant something different in each new historical context and must be evaluated accordingly.

First-century Palestinian Jewry, for example, frequently cited the aniconic proscription of the biblical Second Commandment and hence violently objected to the contemplated placement of a statue of the Roman emperor Caligula in the Jerusalem Temple (Josephus, Antiquities XVII, 8:2 and Wars II, 10:1). Third- and fourth-century Palestinian Jewry evinced a different attitude. The Palestinian Talmud records: "In the days of Rabbi Yoḥanan they began painting figures on walls, and he did not protest against this practice," and "In the days of Rabbi Abin (Abun) they began to have figural mosaics, and he did not protest against it."[33] Rabbi Yoḥanan, one of the most prominent rabbis of third-century Palestine, lived in Sepphoris and Tiberias in the very period when the Dura synagogue murals were painted, and Rabbi Abin also lived in Tiberias when fine figural mosaics like the recently unearthed fourth-century synagogue mosaic in Ḥammath-Tiberias was commissioned.

Why the difference in attitude toward images? First-century Jewry, resenting the ever mounting oppression of Rome, refused to place an imperial image in the Temple on the ground that it would be idolatrous to worship the detested emperor. No doubt the refusal also had political implications, for first-century Palestinian Jewry wanted to reject a symbol of the hated Roman power.

---

[32] Cf. J. GUTMANN, The 'Second Commandment' and the Image in Judaism, in: GUTMANN, No Graven Images, XIII—XXX, 3—16 and ID., Deuteronomy: Religious Reformation or Iconoclastic Revolution? in: GUTMANN, Image and Word, 5—25.

[33] Cf. KLEIN, op. cit., 33—45; G. J. BLIDSTEIN, Prostration and Mosaics in Talmudic Law, Bulletin of the Institute of Jewish Studies, 2 (1974), 19—39, and J. M. BAUMGARTEN, Art in the Synagogue: Some Talmudic Views, in: GUTMANN, The Synagogue, 79—89.

By contrast, during the time of the Dura synagogue paintings, the Patriarch Judah II and his loyal supporter, Rabbi Yoḥanan, the head of the Palestinian academy at Tiberias assumed a different attitude toward Rome and art. Judah II was reported on intimate terms with the Roman emperor Alexander Severus. He not only dressed like a Roman dignitary and wore his hair in the Roman fashion, but he and Yoḥanan diligently studied and encouraged the use of Greek. Like an emperor, the patriarch was surrounded by a bodyguard of Goths who could ward off any attack, verbal or physical.[34] Is it any wonder, therefore, that we find synagogue paintings and later synagogue mosaics imitating standard Roman practice?

It should be noted that attitudes toward Rome were not static in Jewish Palestinian life; they fluctuated considerably, depending on the position taken by Roman emperors toward Jews.

Similarly, we read that no objection was voiced in the third century when the statue of a king was installed in the important synagogue of Nehardea, Babylonia, where the father of Mar Samuel, Samuel and Rav prayed.[35] It might be argued, of course, that the Zoroastrian religion in Babylonia had no cult of emperor worship, so that a royal statue could be tolerated in a synagogue, while the statue of a divine Roman emperor was intolerable in Palestine on the ground of idol worship. The statue can also be viewed as having little to do with the Second Commandment, but simply as a demonstration of loyalty to the reigning monarch by third-century Babylonian Jewry. The exilarchs of third-century Babylonia were dignitaries of high rank in the Sasanian empire. They ruled like oriental despots and were surrounded by slaves and numerous attendants. The exilarch appointed Samuel as advisor and head of the academy of Nehardea. Samuel remained on intimate terms with the exilarch and with King Shapur I. It was he who declared that "the law of the land is just as binding on Jews as their own law." His allegiance to the reigning monarch was so strong that he refused to mourn when 12,000 Jews died in the Persian assault on Caesarea Mazaca, the Cappadocian capital, during Shapur's Asia Minor campaign.[36] Seen against this background, the changes in attitudes toward the Second Commandment not only become understandable, but are freed from their distorted, literal confines. As a matter of fact, had the Second Commandment as found in the Pentateuch been taken literally, it is quite obvious that Solomon with his sculpted images of cherubim and oxen would have deserved to be roundly condemned and censured. Yet no biblical writer ever accused Solomon of having violated or transgressed the Second Commandment.

---

[34] Cf. H. GRÄTZ, Geschichte der Juden, IV (Leipzig, 1908), 221 ff.; L. I. LEVINE, The Jewish Patriarch (Nasi) in Third-Century Palestine, in: Aufstieg und Niedergang der römischen Welt (= ANRW), II, 19.2, ed. W. HAASE (Berlin, 1979), 649 ff.; AVI-YONAH, Jews of Palestine, op. cit., 59 ff.

[35] Babylonian Talmud, Rosh Hashanah 24 b; Avodah Zarah 43 b speaks only of Samuel's father and Levi. Rav was head of the Sura academy.

[36] NEUSNER, op. cit., 39 ff. and 64 ff.

III. Stylistic Problems of the Dura Synagogue Paintings

Although many studies have emerged on the iconography of individual scenes and on the entire program of the Dura synagogue paintings, no thorough study has been devoted to the style of the Dura panels. The paintings are frequently called frescoes, but the paint was applied to the plaster by use of the al secco method. It is now generally accepted that one local master artist and his assistants executed the cycle of paintings: the decoration of the aedicula of the Torah niche, it has been noted, shows brush work and figure painting different from the rest of the murals. The panels were probably conceived as a unit, and were not added individually as some scholars maintain. The coherent organization, the balanced use of red-green color backgrounds leading the eye from one composition to another, give the impression that the walls were completed in their entirety. Analysis of the paintings — the largest body of ancient wall paintings outside Italy — has been made difficult by scholarly determination to fit the Dura paintings into well-defined categories, pigeon holes. Such scholars as DANIEL SCHLUMBERGER and ROSTOVTZEFF want to categorize them as belonging to Parthian art, although Parthian art is to this day ill-defined and quite scanty. RANUCCIO BIANCHI BANDINELLI and others want to see the Dura paintings as 'provincial' Roman art — a pejorative term denoting inferior art which merely copied, and in a crude and naive manner, trends emanating from the Roman capital. The few studies specifically devoted to the synagogue paintings have tried to place them either in the Roman or Parthian camp, or have tried to divide up the elements of individual compositions by giving them vague, meaningless labels like Oriental, Iranian, East or West Hellenistic, etc.

There is little doubt that Dura was a frontier town of strategic military importance. Its location on the crossroads of major cultures of the East and West exposed it to diverse cultural traditions. We can point to the purely geometric black ribbon design with triple dots separating each panel as a distinct Greco-Roman tradition; the dado treatment of theatre masks is also reminiscent of Greco-Roman practice at Antioch, and the shell motif in the Torah niche is comparable to Roman examples. Continuous narrative scenes involving stories of myths or mystery cults are basically Western, as we can see in Pompeii. In the East, the predominant form of continuous narrative conveys historical state propaganda of military victories and ritual court processions of vassal fealty and submission or the offering of sacrifices. Similarly, we can point to such non-Roman traditions as the seated king figures with ankles close together and knees spread apart so that the hem of the tunic falls gracefully across their laps and the tailored suit — a sleeved tunic or jacket over trousers — worn by many figures.

The greatest controversy rages around the strict frontality of all the figures — a convention frequently called 'Oriental,' even though the profile view is adhered to in the reliefs and paintings of the ancient Near East and frontality appears only in isolated figures both in the ancient Near East and Greco-Roman art. When used frontality appears as a result of the function of the figure within the total composition, one of many possible postures in which figures can be rendered. It is not an artistic convention pervading the entire composition. Frontality as a conscious compositional technique is at home primarily in the first-century art of Palmyra and Hatra. Thus such labels for frontality as Oriental, Parthian, East Hellenistic, etc. are misleading, as frontality first appears primarily in the immediate regions of Dura.

Furthermore, the artists at Dura had no choice of several contrasting and different artistic traditions. They knew only one style, which they applied to all monuments at Dura. Their style probably perpetuated a conservative local tradition. Undoubtedly, the artists at Dura were trained to work in an atelier with a limited number of figural and architectural models which could be applied to all commissions received. The models were in all likelihood derived from the style — the pictorial idiom — fashionable in nearby major cities of northern Meso-potamia and eastern Syria. Some panels in the Dura synagogue show naive copying of necessary elements of the narrative and leave the impression of a long established artistic tradition, a tradition expressed perhaps in a more sophisticated manner in synagogues of major trade centers like Palmyra.

For a stylistic analysis of the Dura synagogue paintings, then, it becomes important to recognize that many diverse traditions from both the East and the West co-existed in the Near Eastern trade centers and that new elements were constantly being introduced, possibly through portable crafts which passed along the trade routes. A nearby center like Palmyra had synthesized the diverse artistic traditions into a distinctive new style which can be called neither Roman nor Parthian, eastern nor western, although it may contain elements of each. This style should be analyzed on its own aesthetic terms rather than being viewed as a provincial or syncretistic product of other art styles. To what extent these static compositions with their tall stiff figures, rigid, strict frontality, staring eyes, stylized, schematized folds of the robe, luxurious colors and denial of space influenced similar later Roman art, or whether in both cases we are dealing not so much with influence as with independent conscious choice arising out of similar needs, deserves investigation.[37]

[37] Cf. M. ROSTOVTZEFF, Dura and the Problem of Parthian Art, Yale Classical Studies, 5 (1935), 155–304; H. J. W. DRIJVERS, The Religion of Palmyra, Iconography of Religions, XV 15 (Leiden, 1976), 7ff.; A. PERKINS, The Art of Dura-Europos (Oxford, 1973), 114ff.; C. HOPKINS, The Discovery of Dura-Europos (New Haven and London, 1979), 176ff.; D. TAWIL, The Purim Panel in Dura in the Light of Parthian and Sasanian Art, Journal of Near Eastern Studies, 38 (1979), 93–109; E. HILL, Roman Elements in the Settings of the Synagogue Frescoes at Dura, Marsyas, 1 (1941), 1–15; R. BRILLIANT, Painting at Dura-Europos and Roman Art, in: GUTMANN, Dura-Europos Synagogue, 23–30. For a balanced approach to the stylistic problems of the Dura synagogue, cf. B. GOLDMAN, The Dura Costumes and Parthian Art, in: GUTMANN, Dura-Europos Synagogue, 53–77 and the un-published M. A. thesis of my student, L. C. BRANTIGAN, The Artistic Sources of the Paintings in the Synagogue at Dura-Europos, Wayne State University, 1976. Cf. also the fine stylistic and iconographic comments on the "Ezekiel panel" by H. KAISER-MINN, Die Erschaffung des Menschen auf den spätantiken Monumenten des 3. und 4. Jahrhunderts (Münster, 1981), 79–82.

1. Artistic Sources of Inspiration for the Dura Paintings

Since the Dura synagogue murals are as yet an isolated phenomenon − no other synagogue has been found with so elaborate a program of biblical paintings − the question of the sources for the Dura paintings or their impact on later Christian art remains open for debate. The most common theory, held by such scholars as KURT WEITZMANN, CARL KRAELING, CARL-OTTO NORDSTRÖM, BEZALEL NARKISS, MICHAEL AVI-YONAH, is that illustrated Jewish manuscripts served as possible guides for the Dura artists. These scholars are convinced that the Dura-Europos synagogue paintings as well as later Old Testament cycles found on church walls or in later Christian manuscripts reflect an earlier Jewish illustrated Septuagint tradition. These illustrated Septuagint manuscripts were papyrus rolls and probably originated in Alexandria, Egypt.

Some scholars, like AVI-YONAH, would modify the above statement. The Septuagint translation of the Hebrew Bible, they claim, was too sacred to be illustrated figuratively. We know, however, that in Hellenistic centers like Alexandria biblical stories were transformed into epic poems, tragedies and histories in a manner reminiscent of Hellenistic works, and it is this biblical literary genre that was probably illustrated. JOSEF STRZYGOWSKI, in his path-breaking work, 'Orient oder Rom' (1901), already theorized that Hellenistic Jews may have had an art which served as a source for some of the Christian Old Testament images. However, KURT WEITZMANN and his followers attempt to re-construct from available evidence vast illuminated narrative cycles which he is convinced must have existed in classical Homeric and Euripidean manuscripts; he is led to the conclusion that Jews would probably have been inspired to imitate the Greek practice and to illustrate their own Septuagint or related manuscripts. This theory rests largely on an argumentum ex silentio, since no extensive illustrated classical or Christian manuscripts are known, which securely antedate the fifth century A. D., while the earliest surviving illustrated Jewish manuscript comes from late ninth-century Islamic Palestine.

Aside from the fact that no illustrated Jewish manuscript exists before the ninth century and such early Jewish manuscripts as the Dead Sea Scrolls are not il-lustrated, it should be pointed out that the iconography of the Dura paintings primarily reflects contemporary Palestinian and not Egyptian literature. Furthermore, if such illustrated manuscript models were at hand for the Dura synagogue artists − it would literally have required a library of illustrated biblical manuscripts since the Dura scenes range from the Book of Genesis to Maccabees − why, we might ask, does the style of the Dura synagogue paintings not reflect the Hellenistic style of the assumed Alexandrian illustrated manuscripts?[38]

---

[38] Cf. K. WEITZMANN, The Illustrated Septuagint, and: The Question of Jewish Pictorial Sources on Old Testament Illustration, in: GUTMANN, No Graven Images, 201ff. and 309ff.; KRAELING, op. cit., 398ff.; M. AVI-YONAH, Goodenough's Evaluation of the Dura Paintings, in: GUTMANN, Dura-Europos Synagogue, 127−128; B. NARKISS, The Sign of Jonah, Gesta, 18 (1979), 71; C. O. NORDSTRÖM, Das späte Judentum und die Anfänge der christlichen Kunst, Byzantina, 2 (1973), 3−7 and J. GUTMANN, The Illustrated Jewish

2. The Influence of the Dura Synagogue Paintings on Later Christian Art

Scholars have also tried to find iconographic parallels between the Dura paintings and later Jewish and Christian art. The few iconographic similarities adduced in support of a putative manuscript source for the Dura paintings are not sufficiently convincing. The details in the scenes chosen for comparison are of such a general nature — standard representations for reclining, standing or gesturing figures to meet narrative requirements — that neither the Dura paintings nor its immediate archetype need, of necessity, have been the source of inspiration. Furthermore, the style in both costume and representation in the later Christian depictions varies considerably from the Dura paintings — which again indicates that one was not copied from the other or that they both derived from a single source.

Extra-canonical Jewish elements appearing in later Christian art are also frequently cited to bolster theories positing the existence of a now lost illustrated Jewish manuscript tradition. These aggadic elaborations drawn from targumim and midrashic books are often illustrated in Christian art, especially manuscripts; however, these Jewish exegetical and homiletical additions to the biblical stories were adapted by Christian writers. It is these Christian literary works — and not lost illustrated Jewish manuscripts — which probably served as direct sources of inspiration for the Christian depictions.[39]

If illustrated manuscripts are not behind the Dura synagogue paintings, and it is admitted that the small Dura congregation did not invent this impressive cycle, what were the immediate sources of inspiration? Some scholars are coming to the conclusion that "pattern books, panels and cartoons, copied and copied again, served wall paintings in Dura as they had in Pompeii . . ."[40]

IV. Early Jewish Biblical Images and Symbols outside the Dura Synagogue

Biblical images outside of the Dura synagogue paintings are rare in early Jewish art. Although a fresco found in first-century Pompeii has been identified

---

Manuscript in Antiquity: The Present State of the Question, in: GUTMANN, No Graven Images, 232–248.

[39] Cf. the literature and excellent summation of this problem in R. STICHEL, Die Namen Noes, seines Bruders und seiner Frau, Abh. d. Akad. d. Wiss. in Göttingen, philol.-hist. Kl., III 112 (Göttingen, 1979), 103 ff.

[40] M. L. THOMPSON, Hypothetical Models of the Dura Paintings, in: GUTMANN, Dura-Europos Synagogue, 47. To the authors enumerated by THOMPSON and GUTMANN in: GUT-MANN, No Graven Images, XLI ff., the following authors also posit pattern books, sketch books, etc., as sources of artistic inspiration. Cf. V. GERVERS, An Early Christian Curtain in the Royal Ontario Museum, Studies in Textile History in Memory of Harold B. Burnham, ed. V. GERVERS (Toronto, 1977), 58; M. A. COLLEDGE, The Art of Palmyra (London, 1976), 217 and C. DAUPHIN, Byzantine Pattern Books: A Re-examination of the Problem in the Light of the 'Inhabited Scroll', Art History, 1 (1978), 400–423.

as Jewish and labeled the 'Judgment of Solomon', the identification is highly doubtful in light of the erotica in the other paintings in the room and the lack of substantive evidence.[41] The depiction of 'King David Leaping and Dancing' on a marble Roman table plate has been shown to be a modern forgery.[42]

Synagogue mosaics dating from the fourth to the sixth century, predominantly from Palestine, do reveal biblical images. From a Gaza synagogue, dated 508/509, we have a mosaic showing King David (the name is spelled out in Hebrew next to the king's head) in the guise of Orpheus — a related depiction of this motif is already found in the central panel over the Torah niche of the Dura synagogue.[43] The fifth-century synagogue of Gerasa, Jordan, depicts Noah and his sons and the animals coming out of the ark; the image of Daniel and the lions appears on a floor mosaic of the sixth-century synagogue near Jericho, and the Sacrifice of Isaac is shown in the sixth-century mosaic floor of the Beth-Alpha synagogue (pl. VII, fig. 8).[44] Mosaics depicting Noah's ark and scenes from the life of Samson have been claimed as Jewish since a fifth-century building in Mopsuestia, Turkey, was identified as a synagogue by some scholars. The issue has not been entirely resolved, but it appears likely that the building is a church.[45]

The synagogue mosaic designs show close similarities to Christian and pagan mosaics; in the case of the Beth-Alpha Sacrifice of Isaac (pl. VII, fig. 8), I was able to show that it is based on an early Christian model of the same theme.[46]

1. Jewish Catacomb Paintings

The Jewish catacombs of Rome and the catacombs of Beth She'arim, Israel have no biblical depictions, although sarcophagi with pagan personifications of the four seasons and Dionysiac putti and such myths as Leda and the Swan have been found. The Jewish catacombs of Rome probably date from the second half of the third century and the fourth century and their development appears to run parallel to Christian catacombs. The Beth She'arim catacombs date from the late second century to the fourth century. The catacombs of Rome and their gold-leaf glasses and sarcophagi, especially those of Vigna Randanini (Via Appia) and Via Nomentana (Torlonia), are — apart from some Jewish religious symbols — in-

[41] Cf. J. GUTMANN, Was there Biblical Art at Pompeii?, Antike Kunst, 15 (1972), 36—40.
[42] Cf. J. GUTMANN, Prolegomenon, The Synagogue, XXVI, n. 21.
[43] Cf. P. C. FINNEY, Orpheus-David: A Connection in Iconography between Greco-Roman Judaism and Christianity, Journal of Jewish Art, 5 (1978), 6—15, and M. BARASCH, The David Mosaic of Gaza, Assaph, 1 (1980), 1—42.
[44] No comprehensive work exists on synagogue mosaics. Cf. the essays and bibliographies on synagogue mosaics in L. I. LEVINE, ed., Ancient Synagogues Revealed (Jerusalem, 1981) and E. KITZINGER, Israeli Mosaics of the Byzantine Period (New York, 1965).
[45] Cf. STICHEL, Die Namen Noes, 15 ff., for the state of research on this problem.
[46] J. GUTMANN, The Sacrifice of Isaac, op. cit. (in press). Cf. also DAUPHIN, op. cit., 400—423.

distinguishable from both Roman and Christian catacombs in style, composition and technique, and many of the motifs used.[47]

2. The Meaning of Religious Symbols in Early Jewish Art

Jewish religious symbols found in Jewish catacombs, on gold glasses and on synagogue mosaics (pl. VIII, fig. 9), have not yet received an adequate explanation. We usually find a Torah ark, open or closed, surrounded by seven-branched lampstands, lulav and etrog, shofar and a shovel-shaped object. The Torah ark has been interpreted as a sacred portal leading to the dwelling of the Divine,[48] but it could also be interpreted as the container of Torah — symbolic of God's entire revelation to Israel. The ram's horn (*shofar*) may stand for Rosh Hashanah when God, according to rabbinic tradition, remembers the Akedah (Sacrifice of Abraham) and accounts it to Israel's credit for the forgiveness of Israel's sins.[49] The lulav and etrog probably refer to the synagogal celebration of Sukkot. The shovel-shaped object has been variously interpreted as a charity collection box, a lectern, a circumcision knife, an incense shovel and a magrepha.[50] Although the generally accepted interpretation is an incense shovel, it presents difficulties. The *maḥtah* (incense shovel) was linked in the Temple with Yom Kippur (Leviticus 16), but no such ceremony is described or known for the synagogue. Again, the meaning of the two menorot on either side of the Torah ark yields no ready answer. We are not certain whether bronze or silver menorot actually stood next to the Torah ark, singly or in pairs, although some literary and archaeological evidence makes the above a possibility.[51] If the other symbols can

---

[47] The most important work on Jewish catacombs is still the unpublished Ph. D. dissertation of H.-L. HEMPEL, Die Bedeutung des Alten Testamentes für die Programme der früh-christlichen Grabmalerei, Johannes Gutenberg University, Mainz, 1956, 84–102. Cf. also H. BRANDENBURG, Überlegungen zum Ursprung der frühchristlichen Kunst, Atti del IX congresso internazionale di archeologia cristiana, I (Rome, 1978), 331–360, 480. The Jewish gold glasses probably all date from the fourth century. Cf. I. SCHÜLER, A Note on Jewish Gold Glasses, Journal of Glass Studies, 8 (1966), 48–61 and B. NARKISS, The Jewish Realm, in: Age of Spirituality: Late Antique and Early Christian Art, Third to Seventh Century, ed. K. WEITZMANN (New York, 1979), 366–389. B. MAZAR, N. AVIGAD, Beth She'arim, I, III (Jerusalem, 1973, 1976). Cf. also H. J. LEON, The Jews of Ancient Rome (Philadelphia, 1960).

[48] B. GOLDMAN, The Sacred Portal: A Primary Symbol of Ancient Judaic Art (Detroit, 1966).

[49] Cf., for instance, Babylonian Talmud, Rosh Hashanah 16a; Bereshit Rabbah 56:10; Tanhuma Wa-Yera 46.

[50] Cf. E. L. SUKENIK, Designs of the Lectern in Ancient Synagogues, Journal of the Palestine Oriental Society, 13–14 (1933–34), 221–225; M. NARKISS, The Snuff Shovel as a Jewish Symbol, Journal of the Palestine Oriental Society, 15 (1935), 14–28; J. YASSER, The Magrepha of the Herodian Temple, Journal of the American Musicological Society, 13 (1960), 24–42.

[51] Cf. J. GUTMANN, Prolegomenon, The Synagogue, XVIII. Cf. also M. SMITH, The Image of God, Bulletin of the John Rylands Library, 40 (1958), 473–512, and J. GUTMANN, A Note on the Temple Menorah, in: ID., No Graven Images, 36–38, for other pertinent literature.

be linked with synagogal celebrations, did the seven-branched lampstand perhaps symbolize the Sabbath – the seventh day of rest?

The zodiac and the seasons, frequently together with Helios, the sun god riding his chariot, are shown in four synagogue mosaics – Beth-Alpha (pl. VII, fig. 8), Hammath-Tiberias, Na'aran and Husifa – and have been subjected to extensive research. Helios has been interpreted as God (SUKENIK, STEMBERGER, GOODENOUGH), or Elijah (WISCHNITZER); the zodiac cycle has been linked with the Sukkot holiday (WISCHNITZER), imbued with mystic Hellenistic meaning (GOODENOUGH, WILKENSON), dismissed as a decorative motif (STRAUSS), seen as a symbol of the passage of time – God's order (CHIAT), endowed with profound eschatological or messianic meaning (RENOV, SONNE, STEMBERGER), and construed as having liturgical or actual calendrical significance (STERNBERG, AVI-YONAH, HACHLILI, MAIER).[52]

No convincing explanation has been forthcoming, but some recent suggestions may have some relevance for the zodiac panels.

In 'Midrash Devarim Rabbah' we read:

"The Holy One Blessed-Be-He showed Abraham all of the zodiac (*mazalot*) surrounding his *shekhinah* (Divine Presence); . . . and said: just as the zodiac surrounds Me, with My glory in the center, so shall your descendants multiply and camp under many flags, with My *shekhinah* in the center."

This citation is one of the few rabbinic quotes that may have an association with the mosaic floors, in that Helios may represent the *shekhinah* (God's Divine Presence) in the center.[53] Another scholar feels that:

"We have simply the visual equivalent of the oral-auditory *yotzer* – whose theme should be redefined as light, by the way, not creation – and which says in words what the mosaic says in stone: *mehadesh bekhol yom tamid ma'aseh bereshit* (Who renews each day the work of creation)."[54]

---

[52] G. STEMBERGER, Die Bedeutung des Tierkreises auf Mosaikböden spätantiker Synagogen, Kairos, 17 (1975), 11–56 and J. MAIER, Die Sonne im religiösen Denken des antiken Judentum, in: ANRW, II, 19.1, ed. W. HAASE (Berlin–New York 1979), 382–385, especially 384 n. 158, give the pertinent bibliography and researches on this topic. Cf. additional bibliography: J. WILKINSON, The Beit-Alpha Synagogue Mosaic: Towards an Interpretation, Journal of Jewish Art, 5 (1978), 16–28; M. CHIAT, Synagogues and Churches in Byzantine Beth She'an, Journal of Jewish Art, 7 (1980), 13–17 and R. HACHLILI, The Zodiac in Ancient Jewish Art: Representation and Significance, Bulletin of the American School of Oriental Research, 228 (1977), 61–77.

[53] KLEIN, op. cit., 44.

[54] L. A. HOFFMAN, Censoring In and Censoring Out: A Function of Liturgical Language, in: GUTMANN, Ancient Synagogues: The State of Research (Chico, 1981), 23. Cf. also G. M. A. HANFMANN, The Continuity of Classical Art: Culture, Myth and Faith, in: Age of Spirituality: A Symposium, ed. K. WEITZMANN (New York, 1980), 82.

JOSEPH YAHALOM has recently shown that the signs of the zodiac and the literary inscriptions on synagogue mosaics reveal striking analogies with contemporary synagogal *piyyutim* (liturgical poems).[55]

Early Jewish art, still a relatively new field of study, comprises a period ranging from the third to the sixth century. Comprehensive analyses of the style of the Dura synagogue, Jewish catacomb paintings and synagogue mosaics, their relation to Christian and pagan art are a desideratum. Re-evaluation of the iconography of this early art in the light of new historical conceptual tools is also needed.

Selected Bibliography

AUBERT, M., La peinture de la synagogue de Doura, Gazette des beaux-arts, 20 (1938), 1–24.

AVIGAD, N., Beth She'arim, III. Jerusalem, 1976.

AVI-YONAH, M., Goodenough's Evaluation of the Dura Paintings: A Critique, in: GUTMANN, Dura-Europos Synagogue, 117–135.

–,   Art in Ancient Palestine, Jerusalem, 1981.

BAUMGARTEN, J. M., Art in the Synagogue: Some Talmudic Views, Judaism, 19 (1970), 196–206. Reprinted in: GUTMANN, The Synagogue, 79–89.

BARASCH, M., The David Mosaic at Gaza, Eretz-Israel, 10 (1971), 94–99.

BICKERMAN, E. J., Symbolism in the Dura Synagogue, Harvard Theological Review, 58 (1965), 127–151.

BLIDSTEIN, G. J., Prostration and Mosaics in Talmudic Law, Bulletin of the Institute of Jewish Studies, 2 (1974), 19–39.

BRANDENBURG, H., Überlegungen zum Ursprung der frühchristlichen Bildkunst, Atti del IX congresso internazionale di archeologia cristiana, I (Rome, 1978), 331–360.

BRANTIGAN, L., The Artistic Sources of the Paintings of the Synagogue at Dura-Europos, Unpublished M. A. thesis, Wayne State University, 1976.

BREASTED, J. H., Oriental Forerunners of Byzantine Painting. Chicago, 1924.

BRILLIANT, R., Painting at Dura-Europos and Roman Art, in: GUTMANN, Dura-Europos Synagogue, 23–30.

BRUNNER, R., The Iranian Epigraphic Remains from Dura-Europos, Journal of the American Oriental Society, 92 (1972), 496.

COHEN, S. J. D., Epigraphical Rabbis, The Jewish Quarterly Review, 72 (1981), 1–17.

DAUPHIN, C., Byzantine Pattern Books: A Re-examination of the Problem in the Light of the 'Inhabited Scroll', Art History, 1 (1978), 400–423.

EHRENSTEIN, T., Über die Fresken der Synagoge von Dura-Europos, eine Studie. Vienna, 1937.

EISSFELDT, O., Dura-Europos, Reallexikon für Antike und Christentum, IV (1959), 1358–1370.

FINNEY, P. C., Orpheus-David: A Connection in Iconography between Greco-Roman Judaism and Christianity, Journal of Jewish Art, 5 (1978), 6–15.

GARTE, E., The Theme of Resurrection in the Dura-Europos Synagogue Paintings, Jewish Quarterly Review, 64 (1973), 1–15.

---

[55] J. YAHALOM, Synagogue Inscriptions in Palestine – A Stylistic Classification, Immanuel, 10 (1980), 47–56.

GOLDMAN, B., The Sacred Portal. Detroit, 1966.
–, The Dura Synagogue Costumes and Parthian Art, in: GUTMANN, Dura-Europos Synagogue, 53–77.
GOLDSTEIN, J. A., Review of Goodenough's Jewish Symbols, Journal of Near Eastern Studies, 28 (1969), 212–218.
GOODENOUGH, E. R., Jewish Symbols in the Greco-Roman Period. 13 vols. New York, 1953–1968.
–, The Crown of Victory in Judaism, Art Bulletin, 28 (1946), 139–159.
–, The Evaluation of Symbols Recurrent in Time as Illustrated in Judaism, Eranos Jahrbuch, 20 (1951), 285–319.
–, The Paintings of the Dura-Europos Synagogue: Method and an Application, Israel Exploration Journal, 8 (1958), 69–79.
–, and M. AVI-YONAH, Dura-Europos, Encyclopaedia Judaica, VI (1971), 275–298.
GRABAR, A., Le thème religieux des fresques de la synagogue de Doura, Revue de l'histoire des religions, 123 (1941), 143–192 and 124 (1941), 5–35.
–, Images bibliques d'Apamée et fresques de la synagogue de Doura, Cahiers archéologiques, 5 (1951), 9–14. Reprinted in: GUTMANN, No Graven Images, 114–119.
GUTMANN, J., Die Synagoge von Dura-Europos, Reallexikon zur byzantinischen Kunst, I (1966), 1230–1240.
–, ed., The Dura-Europos Synagogue: A Re-evaluation (1932–1972). Missoula, 1973.
–, ed., No Graven Images: Studies in Art and the Hebrew Bible. New York, 1971.
–, ed., The Synagogue: Studies in Origins, Archaeology and Architecture. New York, 1975.
–, ed., The Image and the Word: Confrontations in Judaism, Christianity and Islam. Missoula, 1977.
–, ed., Ancient Synagogues: The State of Research. Chico, 1981.
–, Programmatic Painting in the Dura Synagogue, in: GUTMANN, Dura-Europos Synagogue, 137–154.
–, Was there Biblical Art at Pompeii?, Antike Kunst, 14 (1972), 36–40.
–, The Illustrated Jewish Manuscript in Antiquity: The Present State of the Question, Gesta, 5 (1966), 39–44. Reprinted in: GUTMANN, No Graven Images, 232–248.
–, The 'Second Commandment' and the Image in Judaism, in: GUTMANN, No Graven Images, XIII–XXX, 3–16 and ID., Deuteronomy: Religious Reformation or Iconoclastic Revolution?, in: GUTMANN, Image and Word, 5–25.
–, The Haggadic Motif in Jewish Iconography, Eretz-Israel, 6 (1960), 17–18.
–, Medieval Jewish Image: Controversies, Contributions, Conceptions, in: Aspects of Jewish Culture in the Middle Ages, ed. P. E. SZARMACH. Albany, 1979.
–, The Sacrifice of Isaac: Variations on a Theme in Early Jewish and Christian Art, Festschrift für Josef Fink (in press).

HACHLILI, R., The Zodiac in Ancient Jewish Art: Representation and Significance, Bulletin of the American Schools of Oriental Research, 228 (1977), 61–77.
HEMPEL, H. L., Die Bedeutung des Alten Testamentes für die Programme der frühchristlichen Grabmalerei. Unpublished Ph. D. dissertation, Johannes Gutenberg University, Mainz, 1956.
–, Jüdische Traditionen in frühmittelalterlichen Miniaturen, Beiträge zur Kunstgeschichte und Archäologie des Frühmittelalters. Akten zum VII. Internationalen Kongress für Frühmittelalterforschung, 1958, Graz – Köln, 1962, 53–65. Reprinted in: GUTMANN, No Graven Images, 347–361.
HILL, E., Roman Elements in the Settings of the Synagogue Frescoes at Dura, Marsyas, 1 (1941), 1–15.
HOPKINS, C., Introduction: The Excavations of the Dura Synagogue Paintings, in: GUTMANN, Dura-Europos Synagogue, 11–22.

—, Jewish Prototypes of Early Christian Art, Illustrated London News (29 July, 1933), 188–191.

—, The Discovery of Dura-Europos, ed. B. GOLDMAN. New Haven and London, 1979.

KITTEL, G., Die ältesten jüdischen Bilder: eine Aufgabe für die wissenschaftliche Gemeinschaftsarbeit, Forschungen zur Judenfrage, 4 (1940), 237–249.

KITZINGER, E., Israeli Mosaics of the Byzantine Period. New York, 1965.

KLEIN, M., Palestinian Targum and Synagogue Mosaics, Immanuel, 11 (1980), 33–45.

KRAELING, C. H., The Synagogue, Excavations at Dura-Europos, Final Report VIII. 1. New Haven, 1956. New York 1979².

—, The Meaning of the Ezekiel Panel in the Synagogue at Dura, Bulletin of the American Schools of Oriental Research, 78 (1940), 12–18.

KRETSCHMAR, G., Ein Beitrag zur Frage nach dem Verhältnis zwischen jüdischer und christlicher Kunst in der Antike, in: Abraham unser Vater, Festschrift für Otto Michel. Leiden, 1963, 295–310. Reprinted in: GUTMANN, No Graven Images, 156–184.

KÜMMEL, W. G., Die älteste religiöse Kunst der Juden, Judaica, 2 (1946), 1–56.

LEON, H. J., The Jews of Ancient Rome. Philadelphia, 1960.

LEVEEN, J., The Wall Paintings at Dura-Europos, in: The Hebrew Bible in Art. London, 1944. Reprint, New York, 1974.

LEVINE, L. I., Ancient Synagogues Revealed. Jerusalem, 1981.

LIFSHITZ, B., L'ancienne synagogue de Tibériade; sa mosaïque et ses inscriptions, Journal for the Study of Judaism, 4 (1973), 43–55.

MASER, P., Der Greis unter den Sternen, Kairos, 18 (1976), 162–177.

MAZAR, B., Beth She'arim, I. Jerusalem, 1973.

MESNIL DU BUISSON, COMTE R. DU, Les peintures de la synagogue de Doura-Europos 245–256 après J.-C. Rome, 1939.

—, Une peinture de la synagogue de Dura-Europos, Gazette des beaux-arts, 14 (1935), 193–203.

—, Les miracles de l'eau dans le désert d'après les peintures de la synagogue de Doura-Europos, Revue de l'histoire des religions, 111 (1935), 110–117.

—, Un temple du soleil dans la synagogue de Doura-Europos, Gazette des beaux-arts, 16 (1936), 83–94.

MEYER, R., Betrachtungen zu drei Fresken der Synagoge von Dura-Europos, Theologische Literaturzeitung, 74 (1949), 29–38.

MILGROM, J., Moses Sweetens the 'Bitter Waters' of the 'Portable Well', an Interpretation of the Dura-Europos Synagogue, Journal of Jewish Art, 5 (1978), 45–47.

NEUSNER, J., Early Rabbinic Judaism. Leiden, 1975.

NOCK, A. D., The Synagogue Murals of Dura-Europos, in: Harry A. Wolfson Jubilee Volume, II. Jerusalem, 1965, 632–633.

NORDSTRÖM, C.-O., The Water Miracles of Moses in Jewish Legend and Byzantine Art, Orientalia Suecana, 7 (1958), 78–109. Reprinted in: GUTMANN, No Graven Images, 277–308.

—, Rabbinic Features in Byzantine and Catalan Art, Cahiers archéologiques, 15 (1965), 179–205.

—, Das späte Judentum und die Anfänge der christlichen Kunst, Byzantina, 2 (1973), 3–7.

NOTH, M., Dura-Europos und seine Synagoge, Zeitschrift des deutschen Palestina-Vereins, 75 (1959), 164–181.

PERKINS, A., The Art of Dura-Europos. Oxford, 1973.

RENOV, I., A View of Herod's Temple from Nicanor's Gate in a Mural Panel of the Dura-Europos Synagogue, Israel Exploration Journal, 20 (1970), 67–74; 21 (1971), 220–221.

—, The Seat of Moses, in: GUTMANN, The Synagogue, 233–238.

ROSENTHAL, E., Some Notes on the Synagogue Paintings in Relation to Late Antique Book-painting, in: The Illumination of the Vergilius Romanus. Zürich, 1972.

ROSTOVTZEFF, M., Dura-Europos and its Art, Oxford, 1938.

—, Die Synagoge von Dura, Römische Quartalschrift, 42 (1934), 203–218.

—, Dura and the Problem of Parthian Art, Yale Classical Studies, 5 (1935), 155–304.

SCHNEID, O., The Paintings of the Synagogue at Dura-Europos. Tel-Aviv, 1946 (in Hebrew).

SCHUBERT, K., Spätantike Vorlagen der mittelalterlichen jüdischen Buchillustration, in: ID., Judentum, 32–39.

—, ed., Judentum im Mittelalter. Catalog of exhibition at Schloss Halbturn. Burgenland, 1978.

—, Das Problem der Entstehung einer jüdischen Kunst im Lichte der literarischen Quellen des Judentums, Kairos, 16 (1974), 1–13.

—, Die Bedeutung des Bildes für die Ausstattung spätantiker Synagogen, Kairos, 17 (1975), 11–23.

SCHUBERT, U., Die Kunst des spätantiken Judentums, in: ID., Judentum, 17–31.

—, Spätantikes Judentum und frühchristliche Kunst. Studia Judaica Austriaca, II. Vienna, 1974.

—, Die Errettung des Mose aus den Wassern des Nil in der Kunst des spätantiken Juden-tum und das Weiterwirken dieses Motivs in der frühchristlichen und jüdisch-mittel-alterlichen Kunst, in: Studien zum Pentateuch. Walter Kornfeld zum 60. Geburtstag, ed. G. BRAULIK. Vienna, 1977, 59–68.

SCHÜLER, I., A Note on Jewish Gold Glasses, Journal of Glass Studies, 8 (1966), 48–61.

SHANKS, H., Judaism in Stone. The Archaeology of Ancient Synagogues. New York, 1979.

SIMON, M., Remarques sur les synagogues à images de Doura et de Palestine, Recherches d'histoire judéo-chrétienne. Paris, 1962, 188–208.

SMITH, M., Goodenough's *Jewish Symbols* in Retrospect, Journal of Biblical Literature, 86 (1967), 53–68. Reprinted in: GUTMANN, The Synagogue, 194–209.

—, The Image of God, Bulletin of the John Rylands Library, 40 (1958), 473–512.

SONNE, I., The Paintings of the Dura Synagogue, Hebrew Union College Annual, 20 (1947), 255–362.

STECHOW, W., Jacob Blessing the Sons of Joseph, Gazette des beaux-arts, 23 (1943), 193–208. Reprinted in: GUTMANN, No Graven Images, 261–276.

STEMBERGER, G., Die Bedeutung des Tierkreises auf Mosaikböden spätantiker Synagogen, Kairos, 17 (1975), 11–56.

STERN, H., The Orpheus in the Synagogue of Dura-Europos, The Journal of the Warburg and Courtauld Institutes, 21 (1958), 1–6.

—, Quelques problèmes d'iconographie paléochrétienne et juive, Cahiers archéologiques, 12 (1962), 99–113.

—, Un nouvel Orphée-David dans une mosaïque du VIᵉ siècle, Comptes rendus, Académie des inscriptions et belles lettres (1970), 63–79.

STICHEL, R., Die Namen Noes, seines Bruders und seiner Frau. Abh. d. Akad. d. Wiss. in Göttingen, philol.-hist. Kl., III 112. Göttingen, 1979.

—, Außerkanonische Elemente in byzantinischen Illustrationen des Alten Testaments, Römische Quartalschrift, 69 (1974), 159–181.

STRAUSS, H., Jüdische Quellen frühchristlicher Kunst: Optische oder literarische Anregung?, Zeitschrift für die neutestamentliche Wissenschaft, 57 (1966), 114–136. Reprinted in: GUTMANN, No Graven Images, 362–384.

—, Irrwege ikonologischer Forschung, Emuna, 1 (1977), 1–26.

SUKENIK, E. L., The Synagogue of Dura-Europos and its Paintings. Jerusalem, 1947 (in Hebrew).

—, The Ezekiel Panel in the Wall Decoration of the Synagogue of Dura-Europos, Journal of the Jewish Palestine Oriental Society, 18 (1938), 57–62.

TAWIL, D., The Purim Panel in Dura in the Light of Parthian and Sasanian Art, Journal of Near Eastern Studies, 38 (1979), 93–109.

THOMPSON, M. L., Hypothetical Models of the Dura Paintings, in: GUTMANN, Dura-Europos Synagogue, 31–52.

DE VAUX, R., Un détail de la synagogue de Doura, Revue biblique, 47 (1938), 383–387.

WEITZMANN, K., The Illustrated Septuagint, and: The Question of Jewish Pictorial Sources on Old Testament Illustration, in: Studies in Classical and Byzantine Manuscript Illumination, ed. H. L. KESSLER. Chicago and London, 1971. Reprinted in: GUTMANN, No Graven Images, 201ff. and 309ff.

–, ed., Age of Spirituality: Late Antique and Early Christian Art, Third to Seventh Century. New York, 1979.

WIDENGREN, G., Quelques rapports entre Juifs et Iraniens à l'époque des Parthes. Supplement to Vetus Testamentum, 4 (1975), 197–241.

WISCHNITZER, R., The Messianic Theme in the Paintings of the Dura Synagogue. Chicago, 1948.

–, The Conception of the Resurrection in the Ezekiel Panel of the Dura Synagogue, Journal of Biblical Literature, 60 (1941), 43–55.

–, The Samuel Cycle in the Wall Decoration of the Synagogue at Dura-Europos, Proceedings of the American Academy for Jewish Research, 11 (1941), 85–103.

–, The 'Closed Temple' Panel in the Synagogue of Dura-Europos, Journal of the American Oriental Society, 91 (1971), 367–378.

–, Number Symbolism in Dura Synagogue Paintings, Joshua Fischel Festschrift, ed. S. B. HOENIG and L. D. STITSKIN. New York, 1974, 159–171.

WODTKE, G., Malereien der Synagoge in Dura und ihre Parallelen in der christlichen Kunst, Zeitschrift für die neutestamentliche Wissenschaft, 34 (1935), 51–62.

List of Illustrations

THE JEWS IN THE WORKS OF THE CHURCH FATHERS.

FOR the history and science of Judaism, and especially for a full understanding of the Agada, the study of the Church Fathers undeniably possesses considerable importance. Naturally all of them are not of the same value. Those who lived in Italy, Spain, or Gaul, and had little communication with Jews, are of minor significance for Jewish literature, compared with the Fathers of Palestine, Syria, and Egypt. I shall therefore pay the most attention to those Fathers whose writings promise the richest results, and we can herein confidently follow the lead of Jerome, who, in his reply to his opponent Rufinus's charge, that he associated too much with Jews, quoted the examples of Origen, Clement, and Eusebius, none of whom disdained to receive instruction from teachers of the Hebrew race (Lib. I., adv. Ruff., c. 13, vol. ii., p. 469, Ed. Vallarsi). If the first notable Father, Justin, and Ephraem Syrus, Jerome's younger contemporary, be added, we obtain the following list of Ecclesiastics, whose writings are of especial interest to us :— Justin Martyr, Clemens Alexandrinus, Origen, Eusebius, Ephraem Syrus, and Jerome.

In the last four decades, since the importance of Patristic literature has obtained a gradually increasing recognition in Jewish circles, students have always sought in the Fathers for Agadic elements which they might collate with Hebrew sources. The fact has, however, been lost sight of, that these Agadas have not always come direct from the Jews. Many of those found in the Church literature must be regarded as the product of independent development. The Agadic exegesis of the Scriptures was peculiar to the spirit of the times, and flourished among the Christians as exuberantly as among the Jews. The accounts in the Church Fathers of Judaism and of Jewish conditions and modes of life are, in my opinion, no less worthy of regard than the Agadic elements there preserved. I shall, therefore, direct my main attention to this class of notices, and only speak of such Agadas as were expressly and explicitly borrowed from the Jews.

For the works of Justin, Clement, Origen and Eusebius, I have used Migne's *Patrologie* (M.); for Ephraem, the Roman edition (R.) of 1732-43; for Jerome, Vallarsi's edition (V.), Verona, 1734-42. Other editions will be quoted occasionally.

I.

JUSTIN MARTYR.

Justin Martyr was born about 100 A.D., in Flavia Neapolis, formerly called Sichem, in the country of the Samaritans. He terms himself a Samaritan, which does not, however, mean that he belonged to the religious sect of the Samaritans, but that they were his countrymen.[1] He, indeed, expressly states that he was one of the uncircumcised.[2] At a later period he came to Ephesus, the scene of his dialogue with the Jew, Tryphon (Eusebius *H. E.*, iv. 18); and here he zealously propagated Christianity among the Jews.[3] The date of the Dialogue coincides with the period of the revolt under Bar Cochba (132—135). That obstinate contest is frequently mentioned in it;[4] and Tryphon is described as a fugitive who escaped from the turmoil of Palestine to peaceful Ephesus.[5]

---

[1] *Dial.* c. 120 (vi. 755, M.), ... ἀπὸ τοῦ γένους τοῦ ἐμοῦ, λέγω δὲ τῶν Σαμαρέων.

[2] *Ib.* c. 29 (vi. 537, M.), τίς οὖν ἔτι μοι περιτομῆς λόγος . . . .

[3] This follows from several passages of the *Dialogue*; v. Wetzer-Welte's *Kirchenlexicon*, vi. 2067.

[4] *E.g. Dial.* c. 108 (vi. 725, M.), cp. *Apol.* I. 31 (vi. 376, M.).

[5] At the beginning of the *Dialogue.*

These data alone should have sufficed to prove the historical character of the Dialogue. Nevertheless, scholars have apparently favoured the theory that it is only a literary framework for presenting Justin's views, and is purely imaginary. Emphasis is laid upon the fact that Tryphon makes concessions to Justin such as no faithful Jew would possibly have made.[1] The obvious explanation is that politeness induced Tryphon to adopt a conciliatory and yielding tone. Throughout the Dialogue he appears as an enlightened Jew, imbued with Hellenistic culture, who is anxious to exhibit extreme courtesy towards his adversary. He is introduced as a man of education and a philosopher. When Justin remarks, in the course of the interview, that he has no oratorical ability, the Jew replies with tact: "You must be jesting ; your conversation proves you a past master in rhetoric."[2] Tryphon's concessions are, moreover, in most cases, only hypothetical ; and Justin very often imitates him in this respect, admitting even once for instance, for the sake of argument, that Jesus was nothing more than a *Magus.*[3] Besides, details are given which are unsuitable to a fictitious dialogue, but have a meaning if we assume that the writer reports events which actually took place. On the first day, we are told, no strangers were present at the interview ; on the second day, however, Tryphon is joined by some Jews of Ephesus, who take a part in the discussion.[4] One of them begs that a remark which had pleased him might be repeated, and Justin complies with the request.[5] Another of those who had accompanied Tryphon on the second day, called Mnaseas, also joins in

---

[1] Weizsaecker, *Jahrb. für Theologie* XII. (1867), p. 63.

[2] *Dial.* c. 58 (vi. 606, M.), οὐ κατασκευὴν λόγων ἐν μόνῃ τέχνῃ ἐπιδείκνυσθαι σπεύδω . . . . Καὶ ὁ Τρύφων· εἰρωνεύεσθαι δέ μοι δοκεῖς, λέγων δύναμιν λόγων τεχνικῶν μὴ κεκτῆσθαι.

[3] *Apol.* I. c. 30 (vi. 273, M.).

[4] *Dial.* c. 118. (vi. 749, M.), διὰ τοὺς σήμερον σύν σοι ἀφιγμένους . . . .

[5] *Ib.* c. 74 (vi. 649, M.).

the debate.[1] This circumstance suggests the inference
that not only Tryphon, who from the first inspired Justin
with respect as a man of Hellenic culture, but that other
members of the Jewish community of Ephesus were also
sufficiently well educated to be able to stand their ground
against the learned Church Father. Occasionally they give
audible token of their satisfaction or disapproval,[2] even
applauding and hissing, just as in a theatre.[3] Justin
repeatedly, in the course of the disputation, bears testimony to the respect he feels for his learned opponent, and
promises, when the Dialogue appears in its written form,
to truthfully present Tryphon's views.[4] At the close of the
debate, Jew and Christian confess that they have learnt
much from one another, and part with expressions of
mutual goodwill.[5] These details can only be reminiscences
of a real event.

That Tryphon was the famous sage Tarphon (טרפון) is
more justly discredited. Justin's description of his antagonist does not tally with what we know of R. Tarphon.
The Tanaite was certainly not a philosopher of Tryphon's
type. Though Tarphon and Tryphon are not identical,
Graetz thinks the name was purposely chosen by the
Father, so that he might be able to boast that he had won
over the eminent teacher, Tarphon, to Christianity.[6] But
it is questionable whether the Hebrew טרפון really cor-

---

[1] *Ib.* c. 85 (vi. 677, M.), οὗ καὶ πάλιν ἐπιμνησθήσομαι διὰ τούτου, τοὺς μὴ
καὶ χθὲς σύνοντας ἡμῖν . . . . Καὶ Μνασέας δέ τις ὀνόματι τῶν συνελθόντων
αὐτοῖς τῇ δευτέρᾳ ἡμέρᾳ εἶπε . . . .

[2] *Ib.* c. 38 (vi. 557, M.), μὴ ταράσσεσθε δέ, ἀλλὰ μᾶλλον προθυμότεροι
γενόμενοι ἀκροαταὶ καὶ ἐξετασταὶ μένετε καταφρονοῦντες τῆς παραδόσεως τῶν
ὑμετέρων διδασκάλων.

[3] *Ib.* c. 122 (vi. 760, M.), καὶ ὥσπερ ἐν θεάτρῳ ἀνέκραγόν τινες τῶν τῇ
δευτέρᾳ ἀφιγμένων.

[4] *Ib.* c. 80 (vi. 664. M.), τῶν γεγενημένων ἡμῖν λόγων ἁπάντων . . . .
σύνταξιν ποιήσομαι ἐν οἷς καὶ τοῦτο ὁμολογοῦντά με ὃ καὶ πρὸς ὑμᾶς
ὁμολογῶ, ἐγγράψω.

[5] *Ib. ad'fin.*

[6] *Gnosticismus u. Judenth.*, p. 17.

responds to the Greek Τρύφων, in which case only could Justin have intended טרפון by his Τρύφων. Jerome, in his list of the oldest Tanaim, calls ר' טרפון Telphon.[1] He would have probably written Τρύφων had the two names been equivalent.[2] Goldfahn's theory that Tryphon was selected by Justin, because it sounded like δρύπτω, needs no refutation.[3]

Accepting the historical character of the Dialogue, we naturally cannot seek for covert allusions in the name Tryphon. It was probably in common use among the Jews of that age, and there is nothing remarkable in the fact of Justin's having happened to meet a Jew with this name. The same is the case with Mnaseas, which was also frequent from an early period. We find it in Josephus (*Cont. Apion.* i. 23). ר' שמעון בן מנסיא, of a subsequent date, is frequently mentioned in Mishna, Tosefta, Talmud and Midrash; in T. Babli (Beza 30*b*) the name is spelt מנשיא. Zunz quotes a Mnasea, grandson of a Mnasea, from the Seder-ha-doroth, fol. 68*b* (Gesammelte Schriften II., p. 23). Tryphon and Mnasea were thus ordinary names among the Jews; and nothing is less surprising than that Justin's chief opponent in the Dialogue, and another Jew of Ephesus, should have borne them.

Justin's writings constitute the first attempt which has come down to us to justify Christianity before the bar of the ancient religious powers, Heathenism and Judaism. Early Christendom still clung somewhat nervously to the old faith. Christians still practised many Jewish customs,[4] and Justin feels the need of offering an excuse for the

---

[1] In Is. viii. 11.

[2] A. Geiger, *Jüd. Zeitschrift* v. 173, proposes to read instead of Delphon (a variant of Telphon) simply *Tarphon*; this is surely inadmissible; טרפון is perhaps the same as Τερπών (Fick, *Griech. Personennamen*, p. 81), which corresponds more closely to the form Telphon.

[3] Goldfahn, *Justin Martyr und die Agada* in Graetz's *Monatsschrift* XXII. (1873), p. 49, *et seq.*

[4] Smith-Wace, *Dict. of Christian Biography*, III. 581.

Christian transference of the Sabbath-day to Sunday.[1] Judaism has no right, the Father thinks, to thrust out its daughter Christianity, for it has also produced other heresies which it does not disown. The Sadducees, Genistae, Meristae, Galilaei, Helleniani, Pharisaei and Baptistae are all Jewish sects, so that it becomes a matter of some difficulty to decide which among them represents the real Judaism.[2] To this argument Justin attaches special importance, deeming it expedient at the same time to apologise to the Jews for the harshness of his words.[3] The Jews, he urges, had sent emissaries in all directions to calumniate the new sect.[4] This charge recurs in almost every Church Father; it is also frequently asserted that the Hebrews were zealously engaged in proselytizing. Thus in Justin's time, we may conclude with a high degree of probability, Judaism still retained its power of expansion. The prophetic promise that the Word of God would reach distant nations the Hebrews saw fulfilled in the accession of proselytes to their ranks, the Christians, in the spread of their own creed.[5]

---

[1] *Dial.* c. 24 (vi. 528, M.).

[2] The names of these sects are cited by Eusebius, *H. E.* iv. 22 (xx. 381, M.), from the work of an older author, Hegesippus. There they are called ᾿Εσσαῖοι, Γαλιλαῖοι, ῾Ημεροβάπτισται, Μασβοθαῖοι, Σαμαρεῖται, Σαδδουκαῖοι, Φαρισσαῖοι. In the *Indiculum Haerescon*, which is ascribed to Jerome, the *Hemerobaptistae, qui quotidie corpora sua et domum et supellectilem lavant* figure as the tenth sect. We recognise this sect as the טובלי שחרית of *Berach*, III. 6c ; they must not be confused with the Essenes. Justin's Baptistae are very likely the same as these Hemerobaptistae. Concerning the Genistae, Meristae, Galilaei and Helleneiani the views of scholars are widely divergent, and we will leave the question open. It is remarkable, however, that the *Essaeans* are mentioned neither by Justin nor by Eusebius, and not even by Isodorus, *Orig. libr.* VIII. ; the Christians probably felt that they themselves had taken their origin from this sect, and were, therefore, unwilling to designate them as heretics.

[3] *Dial.* c. 80 (vi. 665, M.), καὶ μὴ ἀηδῶς ἀκούσητέ μου πάντα ἃ φρονῶ λέγοντος. [4] *Ib.* c. 108 (vi. 725, M.).

[5] *Ib.* c. 122 (vi. 760, M.), concerning Is. xlix. 6, ταῦτα ὑμεῖς μὲν εἰς τὸν Γηόραν καὶ τοὺς προσηλύτους εἰρῆσθαι νομίζετε.—Γηόρα is either גרים or גולה.

Jewish religious teachers are frequently mentioned by
Justin, usually under the title of Rabbi,[1] sometimes also
simply as διδάσκαλοι;[2] in a few instances, as heads of
the Synagogue, ἀρχισυνάγωγοι;[3] an insulting epithet is
invariably added. The Rabbinical teachings are termed
traditions, παραδόσεις.[4] Instruction was given at the conclusion of divine worship.[5] Disputations between learned
Christians and Jewish Rabbis were the order of the day.
Numerous specimens are found in Hebrew literature.
Justin ridicules the tactics of the Jewish controversialists,
who always hunted up their opponents' weak points, like
the fly which settles on sore places. If, at a disputation,
a multitude of well-considered and well-weighed arguments are adduced, the Jews will always discover a neglected point open to attack.[6] Such controversies might
sometimes prove disadvantageous to Judaism, where expert
Christian dialecticians overwhelmed ignorant Jews with
arguments which they were not prepared to answer, and
by which they would have to acknowledge themselves
beaten. Justin strove personally for the conversion of
the Jews; his efforts were, however, futile, owing to the
accident that he met his match in his opponents at Ephesus. Ordinary Jews, not specially skilled in controversy,
were strictly enjoined to avoid polemics with Christians.[7]
And even Tryphon, who presented so bold a front to his
opponent, regretted his breach of this rule.[8] By this we

---

[1] Dial c. 112 (vi. 736, M.), Θελόντων 'Ραββί, 'Ραββί καλεῖσθαι.
[2] Ib. c. 110 (vi. 729, M.), et passim.   [3] Ib. c. 137 (vi. 792, M.).
[4] Ib. c. 38 (vi. 557, M.), et passim.
[5] Ib. c. 137 (vi. 792, M.), διδάσκουσιν . . . . μετὰ τὴν προσευχήν.
[6] Ib. c. 115 (vi. 744, M.), "Ωσπερ γὰρ αἱ μυῖαι ἐπὶ τὰ ἕλκη προστρέχετε
καὶ ἐφίπτασθε. κἄν γαρ μυρία τις εἴπῃ καλῶς, ἓν δὲ σμικρὸν ὁτιοῦν εἴπῃ μὴ
εὐάρεστον ὑμῖν, ἢ μὴ νοούμενον ἢ μὴ πρὸς τὸ ἀκριβές, τῶν μὲν πολλῶν
καλῶν οὐ πεφρόντικατε, τοῦ δὲ μικροῦ ῥηματίου ἐπιλαμβάνεσθε, καὶ κατασκευ-
άζειν αὐτὸ ὡς ἀσέβημα καὶ ἀδίκημα σπουδάζετε.
[7] Ib. c. 112 (vi. 736, M.), ἣ καὶ ἡμῶν ἐξηγουμένων παραγγέλλουσιν ὑμῖν
μηδὲ ὅλως ἐπαίειν, μηδὲ εἰς κοινωνίαν λόγων ἐλθεῖν.
[8] Ib. c. 38 (vi. 556, M.), καὶ ὁ Τρύφων εἶπεν . . . . καλὸν ἦν πεισθέντας
ἡμᾶς τοῖς διδασκάλοις νομοθετήσασι μηδενὶ ἐξ ὑμῶν ὁμιλεῖν . . . .

may gather how the Rabbinic regulations were respected by the people at large. A Jew of Ephesus tells us that for the solution of his doubts and difficulties he often referred to the Rabbis, whom the people regarded as their appointed leaders.[1]

The differences between the Synagogue and the Church turn mostly on the exegesis of Holy Writ; a large portion of the Agada in the Midrash and Talmud is a polemic against Christianity. The text of the Scriptures also constituted an important subject of controversy; the Christians usually read into the Bible more than it contained. Moreover, instead of admitting that their copies were often incorrect, they cherished the delusion that the Jews had falsified and mutilated the text for polemical purposes. This charge already occurs in Justin, who accuses the Jews of altering παρθένος in Is. vii. 14 into νεᾶνις, in order to nullify a Christological argument.[2] He quotes many passages which, he alleges, are only to be found in the old texts, but have been omitted from the new editions.[3] But he is honest enough to reject a manifest Christological gloss interpolated in the Greek version, and gives the preference in this case to the Hebrew text.[4]

In Justin we also meet with a charge which, as far as we know, does not recur in any other Church Father. He accuses the Rabbis of encouraging immorality by sanctioning polygamy among their co-religionists, and

---

[1] *Ib.* c. 94 (vi. 701, M.).   [2] *Ib.* c. 68 (vi. 633, M.).

[3] *Ib.* c. 72 (vi. 645), on Jerem. xi. 19, καὶ ἐπειδὴ ἡ περικοπὴ ἡ ἐκ τῶν λόγων τοῦ Ἱερεμίου ἔτι ἐστὶν ἐγγεγραμμένη ἔν τισιν ἀντιγράφοις τῶν ἐν συναγωγαῖς Ἰουδαίων· πρὸ γὰρ ὀλίγου χρόνου ταῦτα ἐξέκοψαν. He cites similar passages to the same effect.

[4] This gloss is the notorious ἀπὸ τοῦ ξύλου which was said to be the reading in Ps. xcvi. (xcv.). Besides occurring in Justin, *Dial.* c. 73 (vi 645, M.), this interpolation is found only in Latin Fathers, such as Tertullian, Ambrosius, Augustinus, Leo and Gregorius Magnus, who manage to talk a great deal of nonsense concerning the "a ligno."

permitting them to lust after fair women.[1] He blames the facility with which marriages are contracted. When a Jew is abroad, the first thing he does is to take another wife.[2] This matrimonial liberty was indeed, as a matter of fact, a painful characteristic of Talmudic times.

Justin, too, is the first who imputes to the Jews the crime of mocking at and insulting Jesus. This accusation was fraught with terrible consequences for them. It is repeated by all the Fathers of the first four centuries, and though the accounts have been frequently examined, the precise character and truth of this charge have never yet been definitely established. I take the liberty, therefore, of discussing this branch of our subject in some detail.

Although the Fathers are clear as to the fact of a curse pronounced by the Jews, they differ widely as to the object of the curse. Some assert that Jesus was cursed; others that the malediction was directed against Christianity or the Christians. Starting from this point of difference, we classify the weightier statements bearing on this subject under three heads.

I. Malediction against Jesus. Justin, *Dialogue*, c. 103 (vi. 720, M.), (cp. vi. 553, M.), καὶ μάλιστα τοὺς ἐν ταῖς συναγωγαῖς, καταναθεματίσαντας καὶ καταναθεματίζοντας ἐπ' αὐτὸν τοῦτον τὸν Χριστὸν; Origen, *Hom. in Jerem.* xviii. 12 (xiii. 487, M.), Εἴσελθε εἰς τὰς τῶν Ἰουδαίων συναγωγάς, καὶ ἴδε τὸν Ἰησοῦν καθ' ἡμέραν ὑπ' αὐτῶν τῇ γλώσσῃ τῆς βλασφημίας μαστιγούμενον.

II. Against Christians and Christianity. Justin, *Dialogue*, c. 16 (vi. 512, M.), καταρώμενοι ἐν ταῖς συναγωγαῖς ὑμῶν τοὺς πιστεύοντας ἐπὶ τὸν Χριστὸν. Similarly *ib.* c.

---

[1] *Dial.* c. 134 (vi. 785, M.), τοῖς ἀσυνέτοις καὶ τυφλοῖς διδασκάλοις ὑμῶν, οἵτινες καὶ μέχρι νῦν καὶ τέσσαρας καὶ πέντε ἔχειν ὑμᾶς ἕκαστον συγχωροῦσι καὶ ἐὰν εὐμορφόν τις ἰδὼν ἐπιθυμήσῃ αὐτῆς.

[2] *Ib.* c. 141 (vi. 800, M.), καὶ ὅσας βούλεται λαμβάνειν γυναῖκας, ὁποῖον πράττουσιν οἱ ἀπὸ τοῦ γένους ὑμῶν ἄνθρωποι, κατὰ πᾶσαν γῆν, ἔνθα ἂν ἐπιδημήσωσιν ἢ προσπεμφθῶσιν, ἀγόμενοι ὀνόματι γάμου γυναῖκας.

93, (vi. 700, M.)[1]; Origen, *Hom. in Jerem.* xviii. 12 (xiii. 485, M.), καὶ μέχρι νῦν, ὑπὸ παρανόμου ἀρχιερέως λόγου προστάσσομενοι Ἐβιωναῖοι[2] τύπτουσι τὸν Ἀπόστολον Ἰησοῦ Χριστοῦ λόγοις δυσφήμοις. III. Against the Nazarenes. Epiphanius, *Haeres.*, xxix. 9, Πάνυ δὲ οὗτοι ἐχθροὶ τοῖς Ἰουδαίοις ὑπάρχουσιν. Οὐ μόνον γὰρ οἱ τῶν Ἰουδαίων παῖδες πρὸς τούτους κέκτηνται μῖσος, ἀλ ἀνιστάμενοι ἔσωθεν (*l.* ἔωθεν) καὶ μέσης ἡμέρας καὶ περὶ τὴν ἑσπέραν, τρὶς τῆς ἡμέρας, ὅτε τὰς εὐχὰς ἐπιτελοῦσιν ἐν ταῖς αὐτῶν συναγωγαῖς, ἐπαρῶνται αὐτοῖς καὶ ἀναθεματίζουσι φάσκοντες, ὅτι ἐπικαταράσαι ὁ Θεὸς τοὺς Ναζωραίους. Jerome in Isaiah ii. 18, Sub nomine Nazaraeorum anathematizant vocabulum Christianum. *Ib.* 49, 7, Christo sub nomine Nazaraeorum maledicunt. *Ib.* 52, 4, sub nomine, ut saepe dixi, Nazaraeorum ter die in Christianos congerunt maledicta, etc., etc.

This last group is in various ways most instructive. We learn from it that the curse was pronounced thrice daily; the eighteen Benedictions are obviously suggested. Epiphanius has further the important notice that it was recited ὅτε τὰς εὐχὰς ἐπιτελοῦσιν, which does not mean " at the conclusion of the prayers,"[3] but "while they read the prayers." The commination was thus a portion of the daily service, and has long since been justly identified with the ברכת המינים, "the prayer against heretics." That this blessing differed in Talmudic times from its present form is quite clear. It must then have explicitly named the Nazarenes, for Epiphanius gives us the definite formula, " May God curse the Nazarenes." The Talmud, which fully discusses this "blessing," nowhere hints that the Nazarenes

---

[1] On this v. Goldfahn, *ibid*, p. 56.

[2] The Ebionites, as is the case in many other respects, are here placed on a level with the Jews; what is predicated about them applies also to the Jews.

[3] This is Schuerer's opinion : *Geschichte des jüd. Volkes im Zeitalter Jesu Christi*, II. 387. The passage of Justin adduced there is not exactly in place.

I 2

figured in it. Indeed, although several Christian sects are named in that extensive literature, the Nazarenes do not once occur in it.[1] This by no means proves that this name was unknown to the Talmudic doctors. Probably נוצרי very often occurred in the Talmud, but has been erased by the mediæval censors. There were sufficient grounds for this. Catholic Christendom hated other Christian heresies as much as Judaism did, and therefore tolerated allusions to them in the Talmud. But it would not permit mention of the Nazarenes, for these, at an earlier period, were synonymous with the Christians. The Christians were called Nazarenes,[2] a name which they have retained in Jewish literature to this day. Our quotation from Jerome now becomes clear : *The Jews curse the Christians or Christ under the name of Nazarenes*, i.e., the malediction in the liturgy is nominally directed against the Nazarenes but really against the Christians. From the turn of the phrase, it is evident that Jerome thought he had made a discovery. "How artful the Jews are," he seems to say, "they curse the Nazarenes when they mean the Christians." This then is established, that the so-called Benediction of the Minim contained, in ancient times, the term נוצרי; and, in fact, a gloss of Rashi, which escaped the censors, and is still preserved in later authorities, makes it clear that, in his days even, the Blessing still retained the term נוצרי.[3]

The problem still remains, Which expression is it that has replaced the original נוצרי? What word has been substituted for it by the censors or out of fear of them ? J. Derenbourg assumes that the original form of the Benediction consisted of the following three parts :
ולמלשינים על תהי תקוה וכל עושי רשעה כרגע יאבדו וכל

---

[1] That בינצרפי in b. Sabb. 116a is the same as בינצרני is only a conjecture of several scholars, which, however, cannot be defended.

[2] Cp. Tertullian in *Marc.* vi. 8, unde .... nos Judaei Nazaraeos appellant. Jerome, *On Sacr.*, 143, 16 (ed. Lagarde II. p. 175) : et nos .... apud veteres Nazaraei dicebamur.

[3] V. M. Bloch, *Institutionen des Judenthums*, I. 193.

אויבינו מהרה יכרתו, and that, instead of ולמלשינים,
the word ולמינים or ולמשרתים was substituted in R
Gamaliel's days, while, at a still later date, והזדים was
added against the Romans.[1] I consider this supposition
highly improbable. We can hardly believe that the
term ולמלשינים would have been dropped, when we
reflect how much cause there was in every age for the
retention of a commination against the dangerous *Dela-
tores.* Besides, the Christians cannot, in this prayer, be
designated by the term מינים, which is manifestly the same
as μιναῖοι or Minaei; for the Christians regarded this sect
as damnable heretics, and would not have had the slightest
objection to their being cursed by the Jews. The truth
seems to be that the covert reference lies in the phrase
וכל עושי רשעה. It is with regard to these words that the
Codices of the Liturgy exhibit such numerous variations,
which proves that they were not part of the original form
of the prayer. Maimonides does not read וכל עושי רשעה,
but וכל אפיקורסים.[2] This passage, then, is the one directed
against the heretics. The modern וכל עושי רשעה, which
looks so innocent, must have been adopted as a cover for the
far more suspicious and dangerous expression נוצרים. So,
too, in another passage (*Jerusalem Berachot*, 5d, ed. Kro-
toschin) the expression רשע is used as the designation
of a sect תני כולל של מינים ושל הרשעים במכניע זדים.
Tosefta Berachot iv. 25 has, instead of רשעים, the more
forcible פושעים. *Massechet Derech Eretz Rabba* (beginning
of chap. ii.) has הצדוקים והמסורות והרשעים; *Exodus Rabba*,
c. 19, מינים ומשומדין ורשעי ישראל. In all these passages
the word רשעים can only refer to a sect. I believe that
the second phrase read originally וכל הנוצרים כרגע
יאבדו. As, however, נוצרי was primarily the title of Jesus,
the earlier Fathers were correct in asserting that the Jews
cursed Jesus, inasmuch as the expression may refer equally

---

[1] *Revue des Etudes Juives*, xiv. 30.
[2] Derenbourg, *ibid.*

to Jesus or to Christianity. As in their time Christians
and Nazarenes were still identical, they had no need to
explain the difference of designation. In Epiphanius' and
Jerome's days the Nazarenes were only a sect, and no
longer formed the whole of Catholic Christendom. These
Fathers found it, therefore, necessary to say that the Jews
in their formula of malediction cursed the Nazarenes, but
meant the Christians.

Thus the accounts of the Church Fathers on this head
are harmonised.

Returning to Justin, we note that Agadic elements are
to be found in his writings in considerable quantity; most
of them have been thoroughly discussed by Goldfahn in his
essay, "Justin Martyr and the Agada." (Graetz's *Monatsschrift* xxii., 1873, and in a separate reprint.)

II.

CLEMENT OF ALEXANDRIA.

The writings of Titus Flavius Clemens of Alexandria
offer but few materials of interest for Jewish literature.
His distinguishing excellence consisted in a sound knowledge of Hellenic literature rather than of theology.
His information about Judaism he seems to have derived
exclusively from Greek writings, particularly from
Philo and Josephus. A persecution of the Christians,
which raged in Alexandria in the years 202 and 203,
drove Clement to seek safety in flight, and he appears
to have taken up his residence for a short while in
Syria (Euseb. *H. E.*, VI. 11). Here he may have gleaned
something from the Jews at first hand. Of Hebrew he
was not altogether ignorant. Most of his explanations
of terms are indeed unfortunate, and argue little for
an intimate knowledge of the language. But that he
possessed a certain acquaintance with Hebrew is proved
by the prolix remarks found in his writings on the

characteristics which distinguish Hebrew from other languages.[1] It should also be borne in mind that his quotations sometimes differ from the Septuagint, and this variation would seem to show that he consulted the original text.[2] Only on the supposition that Clement had a command of Hebrew can we account for the fact that he criticises adversely those who, when reading Scripture, pervert its plain meaning by their tones, and place a forced construction on clear and wise laws by their transposition of points and accents.[3] That this reproach is aimed at the Jews is obvious. And it is a valuable testimony, from a comparatively early period, to the free and unrestricted manner in which the text of Holy Writ was handled for Agadic purposes.

Hostile expressions against the Jews are not found in his writings. His essay Κανὼν ἐκκλησιαστικὸς ἢ πρὸς τοὺς Ἰουδαΐζοντας (Euseb. *H. E.*, VI., 13) may have contained some ; but the work, with the exception of a few fragments, is lost. He argues that the Jews have no right to twit Christianity with its numerous sects, seeing that Judaism is also rent by factions, but that nevertheless its professors strive their hardest to win converts.[4] He betrays his contempt by the anxiety which he expresses in his exposition not to be confounded with the vulgar Jews.[5] Apart

---

[1] *Strom.* vi. 15 (viii. 353, M.), Ἔχει δ᾽ οὖν καὶ ἄλλας τινὰς ἰδιότητας ἡ Ἐβραίων διάλεκτος, καθάπερ καὶ ἑκάστη τῶν λοιπῶν . . . .

[2] A striking deviation in the translation of Leviticus xi. 13, 14 (Deut xiv. 12) is noticeable, Ἀλλ᾽ οὐδ᾽ ἰκτῖνα ἢ ὠκύπτερον μαστοφαγῇ ἢ ἀετὸν φαγεῖν φησίν . . . . *Paed.* iii. 11 (viii. 653, M.). The words ὠκύπτερον μαστοφαγῇ are wanting in the LXX.

[3] *Strom.* iii. 4, end (viii. 1144), Οὗτοι εἰσιν οἱ κατὰ τὴν ἀνάγνωσιν φωνῆς τόνῳ διαστρέφοντες τὰς Γραφὰς πρὸς τὰς ἰδίας ἡδονάς, καί τινων προσῳδιῶν καὶ στιγμῶν μεταθέσει τὰ παραγγελθέντα σωφρόνως τε καὶ συμφερόντως βιαζόμενοι πρὸς ἡδυπαθείας τὰς ἑαυτῶν.

[4] *Ib.*. viii. 15 (ix. 524, M.), πρὸς τὰ ὑπὸ Ἑλλήνων καὶ Ἰουδαίων ἐπιφερόμενα ἡμῖν ἐγκλήματα ἀπολογήσασθαι . . . . Πρὸς οὓς φαμέν· Ὅτι καὶ παρ᾽ ὑμῖν τοῖς Ἰουδαίοις . . . . πάμπολλοι γεγόνασιν αἱρέσεις· καὶ οὐ δήπου φατὲ δεῖν ὀκνεῖν . . . . ἰουδαΐζειν.

[5] *Ib.* vii. 8 (ix. 553, M.), Ἰουδαίων τῶν χυδαίων.

from these isolated instances, he is a defender of Judaism rather than an antagonist. In his Stromata an endeavour is made to prove that the Greek philosophers obtained their wisdom from Jewish teachers, and that the Jewish law stands higher than Hellenic law.

Agadic elements are more plentiful in Clement's writings than the course of his studies would naturally lead us to expect. He lays great value on the traditions of the true and hidden sense of Scripture[1] preserved by Jewish teachers, whom he knows as the μύσται, a term probably current in Alexandria.[2] As he, however, usually quotes traditions without naming the μύσται in connection with them, it is a matter of some difficulty to distinguish in his writings those elements which are of specifically Jewish origin. But as a proof that his works do contain genuine Jewish traditions I quote the following specimens. He tells us (*Strom.* I. 23, viii. 900 M.) on the authority of the μύσται, that Moses slew the Egyptian with a "mere" word, φασὶ δὲ οἱ μύσται λόγῳ μόνῳ ἀνελεῖν τὸν Αἰγύπτιον. This is identical with the well-known tradition which explains the text (Exod. ii. 14) הלהרגני אתה אומר as meaning that Moses pronounced the Ineffable Name, and thereby destroyed the Egyptian taskmaster. (See *Exodus Rabba*, and Rashi *ad locum.*)

Clement notes (*ibid.* viii., 897 M.), that the law-giver had several Hebrew names besides his Egyptian one—Moses; his parents called him at his circumcision יהויקים;[3] and after his death he received, according to the Mystae, a new name, Μελχί (מלכי ?). This is undoubtedly a genuine Jewish Agada; though I cannot, at present, trace its parallel in

---

[1] *Strom.* i. 12 (viii. 753, M.), τὰς ἀποκρύφους τῆς ἀληθοῦς γνωσίως παραδόσεις . . . .

[2] *Vide infra.*

[3] This observation is also noteworthy from a sociological point of view ; we are thereby informed that already in the second century it was customary among the Jews to give their sons names on the occasion of their circumcision (but see Luke i., 59).

Jewish sources. There is a discussion in T. B. *Sota,* 12*a*, and
Exod. R. 1, between some Tanaites on the name Moses[1]; but
there is no hint of Jehojakim, or of the name conferred
upon the leader after his death. It should also be noticed
that the phrase μετὰ τὴν ἀνάληψιν implies another Agada;
that Moses, like Enoch and Elijah, did not die, but was
translated to heaven. This legend is clearly alluded to
in Jude, verses 8, 9. It is also found in detail in *Deut.
R.*, *ad finem* Babylonian Talmud *Sota* 13*b*, לא מת משה.
Cp. also *Baba Bathra*, 17*a*, where it is said that Moses
belonged to those against whom the angel of death
was powerless, לא שלט בהם מלאך המות. Maimonides
quotes the legend at the beginning of his Introduction to
the Talmud.

After these undoubted specimens of Jewish Agadas we
feel ourselves justified in ascribing a Jewish origin to some
of Clement's obscurer legends. Clement notes, in connection with Genesis xv. 5, that Abraham, according to
the opinions of some, perceived the divine wonders of the
Creation and the beautiful order of nature. This exegesis
is opposed to the Christian interpretation, which sees in
the text a reference to Jesus, the Son of God (*Strom.* v. 1,
ix. 20 M.): "Ὕστερον δέ, ἀναβλέψας. εἰς τὸν οὐρανον, εἴτε
τὸν υἱὸν ἐν τῷ πνεύματι ἰδών, ὡς ἐξηγοῦνται τινες, εἴτε ἄγγελον
εὔδοξον, εἴτε καὶ ἄλλως ἐπιγνοὺς Θεὸν κρείττονα τῆς ποιήσεως,
καὶ πάσης τῆς αὐτῇ τάξεως.

The Midrash, commenting on the same verse (*Gen. R.*, c.
44), says that the contemplation of the star-spangled firma-
ment made the patriarch feel himself an astrologer, which
agrees with his having realised the order of nature.[2] Even
the added touch that Abraham saw an angel is not merely
invented by Clement; for the Midrash remarks (on verse
7) that Michael was the saviour of Abraham and would

---

[1] ר' מאיר אומר טוב שמו רבי יהודה אומר טוביה שמו ר' נחמיה אמר
הנון לנביאות.

[2] נביא את ואין את אסטרולוגוס.

become ultimately the saviour of his posterity. Clement
had doubtless heard this Agada, but reproduced it in the
wrong place. Clement states that Buzzi, Urias the son of
Samaia, and Habakkuk were Jeremiah's contemporaries.
προφητεύουσι δὲ καὶ Βουζὶ καὶ Οὐρίας ὁ υἱὸς Σαμαίου καὶ
Ἀμβακούμ σὺν αὐτῷ. Strom. i., 21 (viii., 849). Cp.
Strom. i. 21 (viii., 872 M.), where Σοφωνίας Βουζὶ follow
after Jeremiah. This notice is evidently based on an
Agada. And, in fact, Seder Olam R., c. xx. ad finem,
collates the following passages :—דבר ה' אל צפניה כו' דברי

ירמיהו בן חלקיהו אשר היה דבר ה' אליו וכו' וגם איש היה
מתנבא בשם ה' וכו' היה היה דבר ה' אל יחזקיאל בן בוזי
וכו' כולם נתנבאו סמוך לחורבן.

According to this quotation, Zephaniah, Jeremiah, Uriah
(Jerem. xvi. 20), and Ezekiel were contemporary prophets ;
this is in complete agreement with Clement. We are thus
also in a position to identify Clement's enigmatic Buzi—
who has given this Father's editors so much trouble—with
Ezekiel, son of Buzi. Either " Ezekiel " has dropped out,
or his father is really meant, in accordance with the
tradition that where a prophet's father is named, he too
was a prophet.

Graetz, in his Hagadische Elementen bei den Kirchenvätern
(Fränkel's Monatsschrift, III., 1854, p. 311), first drew
attention to the agreement between Clement and the
Seder Olam Rabbi. I will give one more striking instance.
Clement says, Strom. i., 21 (viii., 842 M.), that Elisha
commenced to prophesy at the age of forty, and prophesied for a period of six years. Whence is this statement, which is given with as much emphasis as if it
rested on Scriptural authority, derived? The Seder
Olam R., c. xix., says :—מכאן אתה מחשב כמה שנים פרנס
אלישע את ישראל·····יותר משושים שנה. Undoubtedly we
ought to read in the Greek, not ἕξ, but ἑξήκοντα (instead of
ξ', equal to 60, ϛ', equal to 6, was written by mistake). This
tradition, then, Clement has in common with the Seder
Olam. That Elisha commenced his prophetic career at the

age of forty we do not find in any of the Jewish sources ; it must nevertheless have been a common tradition, and the same supposition would account for many other of Clement's statements. In conclusion, we may note that this Father was acquainted with many more traditions than he gives. He, for example, alludes to an exposition of the Mystae in connection with the sacrificial ritual, but does not say anything more definite about it.

III.

ORIGEN.

Origen was born, probably, in Alexandria, about 185 or 186 A.D. It is generally assumed that his parents were Christians, but this was probably the case on one side only. His father's name, Leonides, has been preserved, but not that of his mother. This omission is not accidental, but is due to the reverence of pious Christian writers for Origen's memory, which led them to suppress his mother's name on account of her Jewish descent.[1] The fact that she knew enough of Hebrew to teach her son,[2] and that he occupied himself with the study of that language, contrary —according to Jerome—to the usage of his nation and age, are strong evidence in favour of this view.[3] His impulse to Hebrew studies he probably received from his Jewish mother.[4] In his capacity as Bishop of Cæsarea, in Palestine, Origen must have come into frequent contact with learned Jews, as indeed appears from his writings. He mentions again and again his *Magister Hebraeus*, on whose authority he gives several Agadas.[5] His depen-

---

[1] *Strom.* ii. 20 (viii. 872, M.), δι᾽ αἰτίας ἃς ἴσασιν οἱ μύσται.

[2] Jerome, *Ep.* xxxix. *ad Paulam*, c. 1, Tum vero quod in Origine quoque illo Graecia tota miratur, in paucis non- dicam mensibus, sed diebus, ita Hebraeae linguae vicerat difficultates, ut *in discendis canendisque Psalmis cum matre contenderet.*

[3] Cp. Smith-Wace, *op.. cit.*, iv. 976.

[4] Jerome, *De viris illustr.* 54, contra aetatis gentisque suae naturam.

[5] *De Princ.*, 1, 3, 4, iv. 26 ; in the Greek Fragment, ὁ Ἑβραῖος. I may

dence on Jewish masters is already emphatically noted by Jerome.[1] He often mentions the views of the Jews, by which phrase he refers not to the teaching of certain individuals, but to the method of exegesis universally prevalent among the Hebrews of his time.[2] Those of them with whom he cultivated personal intercourse were distinguished by their scientific attainments. The one Jew whom he names is no less considerable a personage than Hillel, the Patriarch's son, or Jullos, as Origen calls him.[3] His other Jewish acquaintances were either closely related to the patriarch's family or occupied a high position on account of their erudition.[4] No wonder that with such opponents Origen carefully avoids, in his polemic, offensive expressions; forming, in this respect, a noble exception to the usual practice of the Church fathers. Origen fights principles, not their representatives or exponents. Occasionally, however, a harsh sentence against his Jewish antagonists escapes him.[5] He even ventures to assert that the Jews of his time could no longer boast of men of real knowledge.[6] Consistently with this adverse judgment, Origen labours chiefly to refute the scriptural exposition of Jewish teachers, and to establish in lieu thereof his own exegesis. He not only had private interviews with Jewish

---

remark here that I give my quotations in Greek when the original writings of Origen remain, and in Latin when only the Latin translation has survived.

[1] Jerome, *Lib.* i. *adv. Ruff.*, c. 13 ; cp. the Introduction supra.

[2] *E.g.*, *Ep. ad Africanus* § 12, φασὶ δὲ οἱ Ἑβραῖοι. For other quotations see infra.

[3] My especial authority for this is Graetz's "*Hillel, the son of the Patriarchs*" (*Monatsschrift* xxx., 1881, p. 433, etc.). My revered teacher, Professor W. Bacher, in his *Hagada of the Palestinian Amoraim*, i. 92 and 107 § 2, suggests the hypothesis that Origen also had intercourse with Hoschja.

[4] Grätz, *op. cit.*

[5] *Hom.* x. *in Jerem.* § 8 (xiii. 368, M.), βλέπετε αὐτῶν τὰς καρδίας διεσθιομένας ὑπὸ τῶν δυνάμεων ἀντικειμένων.

[6] *Ib.* § 3 (xvii. 361, Gr. Text is not clear), Neque magistri neque doctores in Judaea aliqui remanserunt: et licet sint innumerabiles qui sibi sapientiam vindicent, non est jam sermo Dei in eis.

teachers, but also engaged in public disputations in the
presence of large audiences, which included among their
ranks competent controversialists. This we gather from
several expressions in his writings.[1] The principal topics
discussed at these meetings may be summarised as follows:—

1. *The Scriptural Text.*—The copies of the Bible that
circulated among the Christians were, as we have already
had occasion to remark, corrupt in several passages. At
a disputation between Jews and Christians, the former,
naturally enough, alluded to these mistakes, and mocked
their opponents for allowing such obvious blunders. This
kind of argument, the first beginnings of which we have
traced in Justin, plays an important part in Origen. The
wish to free the Church from the just reproaches of the
Jews on this score, led him to undertake that gigantic
enterprise, the fruit of which is the Hexapla.[2]

2. *The Apocrypha.*—Another point of difference was the

---

[1] *Contra Celsum* I. 45 (xi. 744, M.), Μέμνημ̕αι δέ ποτε ἐν τινι πρὸς ᾿Ιου-
δαίων λεγομένους σοφοὺς διαλέξει χρησάμενος τοιούτῳ λόγῳ, πλείονων
κρινόντων τὸ λεγόμενον. *Ib.* I. 55 (xi. 761, M.), Μέμνηναι δέ ποτε, ἐν τινι
πρὸς τους λεγομένους παρὰ ᾿Ιουδαίοις σοφοὺς ἐνζητήσει ταῖς προφητείαις
ταύταις (*Jesaja* liii.) χρησάμενος· ἐφ᾿ οἷς ἔλεγεν ὁ ᾿Ιουδαῖος . . . . *Ib.* i. 56
(xi. 764, M.), καὶ μέμνημαί γε πάνυ θλίψας τὸν ᾿Ιουδαῖον νομιζόμενον σοφὸν
ἐκ τῆς λέξεως ταύτης· ὃς πρὸς αὐτὴν ἀπορῶν, εἶπε τὰ τῷ ἑαυτοῦ ᾿Ιουδαϊσμῷ
ἀκόλουθα, etc., etc.

[2] Epiphanius, *De ponderibus et mensuris*, c. 2, ᾿Ωριγένης . . . . ἀποκα-
τέστησε τῷ ἑκάστῳ τόπῳ τὸν ἐλλείποντα λογον . . . . ἵνα μὴ παραλείψῃ
᾿Ιουδαῖος καὶ Σαμαρείταις ἐπιλαμβάνεσθαι τῶν ἐν ταῖς ἁγίαις ᾿Εκκλησίαις
θείων Γραφῶν—Ruffinus lib. v. Invect. adv. Hieronymum, c. 4, Apostatae
quidem et Judaei interpretati sunt ea, quorum lectione Judaei maxime
utuntur. Et quia frequenter si disputatio incidisset, vel immutata
esse aliquanta, vel deesse, vel abundare in nostris Scripturis mentiebantur,
voluit *Origenes* nostris ostendere, qualis apud Judaeos Scripturarum
lectio teneretur . . . . ut sciremus non quid nobis, sed quid Judaeis
adversum nos certantibus aut deesse, aut abundare videntur. Origen
recurs frequently to the Jewish method of reading, *e.g.*, *Hom.
in Num.* xvi. 4, Hebraei habere se scriptum dicunt.— *Comm. in Ep. ad
Rom.* lib. ii. § 13 (xiv. 909, M.), ipsi in Hebraeis exemplaribus habere se
dicunt . . . .

Apocrypha, to which the Church attached an exaggerated importance, notwithstanding its frequent want of taste and silliness, over which the Jews could only make merry. The history of Susanna was always derided by them for this reason.[1] The Jews had an Apocrypha of their own, which they valued; but this seems to have been distinguished from what we term Agada only in as far as it was already written down, while most other Agadas were still orally circulated.[2] Origen draws no distinction between the Jewish Apocrypha and Jewish traditions, knowing that they merged into one.[3] It is especially noteworthy that he also knew of the existence of certain mystic writings, by which he could not have meant either Apocrypha or Agada, for both these classes of literature were known to him under their proper names.[4] He must have been thinking of such works as treat of the מעשה מרכבה, or מעשה בראשית, etc., writings which, according to

---

[1] *Epistola ad Africanum de historia Susannae* § 5, Ἀσκοῦμεν δὲ μὴ ἀγνοεῖν καὶ τὰς [sc. γραφὰς] παρ' ἐκείνοις, ἵνα, πρὸς Ἰουδαίους διαλεγόμενοι, μὴ προφέρωμεν αὐτοῖς τὰ μὴ κείμενα ἐν τοῖς ἀντιγράφοις αὐτῶν, καὶ ἵνα συγχρησώμεθα τοῖς φερομένοις παρ' ἐκείνοις· εἰ καὶ ἐν τοῖς ἡμετέροις οὐ κεῖται βιβλίοις· τοιαύτης γὰρ οὔσης ἡμῶν τῆς πρὸς αὐτοὺς ἐν ταῖς ζητήσεσι παρασκευῆς, οὐ καταφρονήσουσιν, οὐδ' ὡς ἔθος αὐτοῖς, γελάσονται τοὺς ἀπὸ τῶν ἐθνῶν πιστεύοντας ὡς ἀληθῆ, καὶ παρ' αὐτοῖς ἀναγεγραμμένα ἀγνοοῦντας.—*Ib.* § 4, Ὥρα τοίνυν εἰ μὴ λανθάνει ὑμᾶς τὰ τοιαῦτα, ἀθετεῖν τὰ ἐν ταῖς Ἐκκλησίαις φερόμενα ἀντίγραφα, καὶ νομοτεθῆσαι τῇ ἀδελφότητι, ἀποθέσθαι μὲν τὰς παρ' αὐτοῖς ἐπιφερομενας ἱερὰς βίβλους, κολακεύειν δὲ Ἰουδαίους, καὶ πείθειν, ἵνα μεταδῶσιν ἡμῖν τῶν καθαρῶν, καὶ μηδὲν πλάσμα ἐχόντων.—From these concessions may be observed how weak the Church felt itself at that time. Later on the victorious Church used quite a different language.

[2] *Ib.* § 9, Σαφὲς δ' ὅτι αἱ παραδόσεις λέγουσι πεπρίσθαι Ἡσαΐαν τὸν προφήτην. καὶ ἔν τινι ἀποκρύφῳ τοῦτο φέρεται. A Hagada, therefore, which existed in an *apocryphon*, *i.e.* which was established in writing. Probably it is a reference to Ἀναβατικὸν Ἡσαΐου, which is mentioned several times.

[3] In Matt. xvii. 2 (xii. 1477, M.), εἴτε ἐκ παραδοσέων, εἴτε καὶ ἐπιβάλλον τις, εἴτε καὶ ἐξ ἀποκρύφων . . . .

[4] *In Matt. Comm. ser.* § 28 (xiii. 1636, M.), Ex libris secretioribus, qui apud Judaeos feruntur . . . .

the Talmud, were wont to be withheld from the uninitiated and especially from Christians and heretics.

3. *Christian Dogmas.*—The mysterious birth of Christ still formed a point of controversy between Jews and Christians. Justin, who knew that the Jews could not and would not accept Christ's divinity, also touches on this theme.[1] Origen reports a far harsher judgment as the belief of the Jews. He says in his commentary on John xx. 14 (xiv., 608 M.), that the Jews spoke after the following fashion: Ἡμεῖς μᾶλλον ἕνα πατέρα ἔχομεν τὸν Θεὸν ἤπερ σύ, ὁ φάσκων μὲν ἐκ παρθένου γεγεννῆσθαι, ἐκ πορνείας γὲ γεγεννημένος. Jesus' illegitimate birth was always a firmly held dogma in Judaism, which found clear expression in its ancient and modern literature, passed over to the heathens of antiquity and lives to-day in the consciousness of every simple-minded Jew, who only knows as much on this subject as he has learnt from his parents. Must not this conviction have found expression in the Talmud? Has that monumental work, which contains such valuable evidence on the events of the first Christian centuries, nothing to tell us concerning this Jewish dogma? Certainly it has. The Talmud here agrees with Origen. The founder of the dominant creed it calls ישׁו בר פנדרא, or ישׁו פנדרא.[2] What does פנדרא mean? Although much has been written about this term, its significance and etymology have not been fixed. I here suggest an explanation, quite different from those hitherto proposed. In Sifri Deut., § 320, תהפוכות (Deut. xxxii. 20) is thus interpreted, הפכפכנים הם פורנים הם, "They are a common and degraded people." פורנים is the Hebrew transcription, with the plural suffix, of the Greek πόρνοι, as Levy (*Neuhebr. Wörterb.*, iv. 18a) correctly states. The Greek term πόρνος has become naturalised in the Rabbinic

---

[1] *Dial.* c. 49 (vi. 581, M.), ὁ Τρύφων . . . . καὶ γὰρ πάντες ἡμεῖς τὸν Χριστὸν ἄνθρωπον ἐξ ἀνθρώπων προσδοκῶμεν γενήσεσθαι.

[2] Also פנכרא, which is even written פנתרא.

dialect, in which πορνεῖον and πόρνη also occur. Now, this passage in the Sifri has, as a *varia lectio*, פרדנים. Levy gives πόρδων as its equivalent, but this has nothing in common with πόρνοι. We believe that a purely phonetic phenomenon accounts for this variant. Between the liquids " r " and " n," the dental " d " has been inserted, a procedure familiar to philologists. פרדנים is thus the same as πόρνοι. The feminine form πόρνη shows a similar phonetic transformation in the word פרדנית.[1] We now arrive at the conclusion of this chain of reasoning. פנדרא and פרדנית (disregarding the feminine suffix) only differ in the relative position of the liquids "n" and " r." That these frequently change their places in the Rabbinic dialect in the case of words borrowed from the Greek is well known. It may therefore be confidently assumed that פנדרא is nothing but πόρνη, modified by phonetic influences. ישו בר פנדרא would thus mean Jesus, the son of the prostitute, or in Origen's phrase ὁ ἐκ πορνείας γεγεννημένος, or as the Pesikta Rabbathi has it ברא דזניתא. This explanation sums up the beliefs held in Jewish circles concerning Jesus.[2] This does not shut out the view that the present form of the word פנדרא, which sounds like παρθένος, may also have been influenced by the Christian dogma that Jesus was the son of a virgin. The opposition between ἐκ παρθένου and ἐκ πορνείας forms even in Origen a sort of play upon words, and Jewish popular wit was probably not slow to take advantage of the similarity of sound.

4. *Abrogation of the Mosaic Law.*—The Pauline doctrine that Jesus' advent superseded the Law of Moses encountered a lively opposition down to the third century. The contradiction between Christ's declaration that not an iota of the Law shall be given up, and his followers' disregard of the

---

[1] This disagrees with the view of Levy, iv. 102*a*.

[2] I think it unnecessary to cite the Rabbinical passages relating to Jesus, as they are accessible in the Essay of Laible, *Jesus Christus im Talmud* (Berlin, 1891).

most essential Jewish observances was too glaring not to
be noticed and severely reprehended by impartial heathens,
who told the Christians that their spiritual conception
of the Scriptures did not justify their neglect of the ceremonial laws; for there were Jews who also conceived their
law spiritually and yet scrupulously practised all of them.[1]
Origen nevertheless pours out the vials of his contempt on
Jews "after the flesh."[2] He finds it unnecessary to wash
the hands before meals; the sole requisite is spiritual
purity.[3] The fulfilment of the laws in a spiritual sense
sometimes assumes a very comical aspect!

Origen brings against the Jews a charge already met
with in Justin; viz., that the Jews falsify and mutilate
the Scriptures.[4] He is convinced that there is a want of
agreement between the old and new copies of the Jewish
Bible, and that much which exhibited a Christian tendency
in the former, has been disfigured in the latter.[5] He is
unconscious that he is here guilty of a self-contradiction;
for he often admits that the Jews possess the genuine, the
Christians the corrupt text of Holy Writ.[6] Especially instructive is Origen's testimony to the great attraction
which Judaism possessed for the heathens. There must
have been still many proselytes to Judaism in his day;

---

[1] *Contra Celsum* I. § 1 (xi. 793, [M.), μηδὲ τοῦτο κατανοήσας, ὅτι οἱ ἀπὸ
Ἰουδαίων εἰς τὸν Ἰησοῦν πιστεύοντες οὐ καταλελοίπασι τὸν πάτριον
νόμον. Origen adds to this (§ 3), The Jew of Celsus ought rather to
have said, τινὲς δὲ (ὑμῶν) καὶ διηγούμενοι ὡς ἐπαγγέλλεσθε, πνευματικῶς,
οὐδὲν ἧττον τὰ πάτρια τηρεῖτε.

[2] *Comm. in Matt.* xi. 12 (xiii. 939, M.), οἱ σωματικοὶ Ἰουδαῖοι.

[3] *Ib.* xi. 8 (xiii. 928, M.), Ὤιοντο γὰρ κοινὰς μὲν καὶ ἀκαθάρτους εἶναι,
χεῖρας τὰς τῶν μὴ νιψαμένων πρὸ τοῦ ἀρτοφαγεῖν . . . . Ἡμεῖς δὲ οὐ κατὰ τὴν
τῶν παρ᾽ ἐκείνοις πρεσβυτέρων παράδοσιν . . . . καθαίρειν πειρώμεθα . . . .

[4] *Hom. in Jerem.* xvi. 10 (viii. 451, M.), Judaei qui exemplaria non-
nulla falsarunt.—The Greek text is here damaged.

[5] *In Matt. Comm. ser.* § 28 (xiii. 1636, M.) in Scripturis *veteribus* quae
legebantur in Synagogis eorum.

[6] *Hom. in Jerem.* xvi. 10 (xiii. 450, M.), Εἶτα ἄλλη ἐστὶ προφητεία, ἣν
οὐκ οἶδ᾽ ὅπως παρὰ τοῖς Ἑβδομήκοντα οὐχ᾽ εὕρομεν δὲ ἐν ταῖς ἐκδόσεσι,
δηλονότι κειμένην ἐν τῷ Ἑβραικῷ . . . .

otherwise there is no adequate reason for the vehement indignation with which he attacks the Judaizers, forgetting himself so far as to utter curses and imprecations, altogether unworthy of him, against those who were converted to the old faith.[1] Among the Christians, too, there were several "Judaizers." Many, especially women, kept the Sabbath on the same day of the week as the Jews; washed and adorned themselves in honour of the day.[2] Origen maintains that the Sabbath in the "carnal" sense, as the Jews conceive it, cannot possibly be observed; to carry out its ordinances literally, one would have to abide in the same place for twenty-four hours, without stirring. This point was often treated in controversies. It forms, even in Jerome's writings, the subject of a lively dispute between Jews and Christians.[3] Besides the Sabbath, the Passover

---

[1] *In Matt. Comm. ser.* § 16 (xiii. 1621, M.), Arbitror ergo omnem hominem qui ex conversatione gentili Judaeorum factus est proselytus, filium gehennae fuisse et priusquam proselytus efficiatur.

[2] *Hom. in Jerem.* xii. 13 (xvii. 396, M.), Καὶ περὶ σαββάτου γυναῖκες μὴ ἀκούσωσι τοῦ προφητοῦ, οὐκ ἀκούουσι κεκρυμμένως, ἀλλὰ ἀκούουσι φανερῶς. Οὐ λούονται τὴν ἡμέραν τοῦ σαββάτου . . . .

[3] *Comm. in Ep. ad Rom.* vi. 2 (xiv. 1094, M), Quid enim tam impossibile, quam Sabbati observatio secundum litteram Legis, ut in multis saepe jam diximus? Jubetur enim non exire de domo sua, non se movere de loco suo, nihil oneris levare. Quae quia impossibilia vident Judaei, qui secundum carnem legem observant, inepta quaedam et ridicula commentantur, quibus impossibilitatem Legis sarcire videantur. Origen omits to tell us what these stupidities are. We discover them, however, through Jerome, *Ep. ad Algasiam*, c. 10 (iv. 207, ed. Martianay), Praeterea quia jussum est, ut diebus Sabbathorum sedeat unusquisque in domo sua, et non egrediatur, neque ambulet de loco, in quo *habitat, si quando eos juxta litteras experimur arctare*, ut non jaceant, non ambulent, non stent, sed tantum sedeant, sic velint praecepta servare, solent respondere et dicere : *Barachibas et Simon et Helles magistri nostri tradiderunt nobis, ut bis mille pedes ambulemus in Sabbatho*, et cetera istiusmodi. The answer of the Jew would probably in the original Hebrew run as follows : קבלה היא בידנו מפי ר' עקיבה משום ר' שמעון ר' שמעון שאמר הלל, etc. In the Talmud and Midrash we frequently note apologetic utterance against the reproach of the Christians in reference to the keeping of the Sabbath, of which a few have been collected by N. Brüll, *Grätz Jubelschrift*, p. 191, N. 1. The laws concerning circumcision were declared by

was also kept according to Jewish rites by numerous Christians who prepared unleavened bread.[1] Origen asserts, that this sympathy with Judaism was not spontaneous, but was the artificial work of missionaries, who carried on a zealous propaganda on behalf of the ancient faith, and cajoled Christians to practise its rites.[2]

Origen has a large number of Hebrew traditions or Agadas; in this respect he stands, among the Church Fathers, second only to Jerome. It should be noted that Origen knows Jewish traditions which have reference to the Gospels. He gives, in the name of the Jews, an explanation of the term κορβᾶν, קָרְבָּן, which occurs in the New Testament.[3] Iscariot, Judas the traitor's surname, also seems to have had a traditional, though erroneous, Jewish interpretation.[4] His account of the Tetragrammaton and of the word pronounced in its stead, points to a genuine Jewish tradition.[5] The Midrashim or Agadas, in the strict sense of the terms, which Origen quotes so profusely, he probably owed to his intercourse with distinguished Jewish friends.

Origen as impossible as those concerning the keeping of the Sabbath. See on that point Diestel, *History of the Old Testament*, p. 27, and Bacher, *Ag. of the Pal. Amor.*, I. 92, N. 4.

[1] *Hom. in Jerem.* xii. 13 (xiii. 396, M.). Ὅσοι ἐν ὑμῖν (ἐγγὺς γάρ ἐστι τὸ πάσχα) ἄζυμα ἄγετε. I quote the text with some emendations.

[2] *In Matt. Comm. ser.* § 16 (xiii. 1621, M.), [Judaei] diligenter circumeunt plurima loca mundi, ut advenas Judaizare suadeant.

[3] *Comm. in Matt.* xi. 9 (xiii. 929, M.), οἱ δὲ φαρισαῖοι καὶ οἱ γραμματεῖς τοιαύτην ἐναντιουμένην τῷ νόμῳ παράδοσιν ἐκδεδώκασιν, ἀσαφέστερον ἐν τῷ Εὐαγγελίῳ κειμένην, ᾗ οὐδ᾽ αὐτοὶ ἐπιβεβλήκαμεν ἄν, εἰ μὴ τῶν Ἑβραίων τις ἐπιδέδωκεν ἡμῖν τὰ κατὰ τὸν τόπον οὕτως ἔχοντα .... Κορβᾶν ἐστι ὃ ὀφείλεις μοι, τουτέστι, δῶρον. The same words, but not in the name of the Jew, are also found in *Theophylactus in Matt.* xv. 5.

[4] *In Matt. Comm. ser.* §78 (xiii. 1727, M.), Audivi quendam exponentem patriam proditoris Judae secundum interpretationem Hebraicam *exsuffocatum* vocari.

[5] *Selecta in Psalm* ii. (xii. 1104, M.), κύριον γὰρ ἐνθάδε ἀντὶ τοῦ Ἰα ἢ εἴρηκεν, καὶ ἔστιν ἡ ἀρχὴ τοῦ ψαλμοῦ παρ᾽ Ἐβραίοις "Ἀλληλουία". ἔστι δέ τι τετραγράμματον ἀνεκφώνητον παρ᾽ αὐτοῖς, ὅπερ καὶ ἐπὶ τοῦ πετάλου τοῦ χρυσοῦ τοῦ ἀρχιερέως ἀναγέγραπται, καὶ λέγεται μὲν τῇ Ἀδωναΐ προσηγορίᾳ, οὐχὶ τούτου γεγραμμένου ἐν τῷ τετραγραμμάτῳ.

K 2

His introductions to some of these Agadas show that he had a certain respect for them.[1] Most of them are also to be found in Jewish sources. Some have already been compared by Graetz in his *Hagadische Elemente bei den Kirchenvätern.* We will confine our attention to a few selected specimens, which will serve to show how useful it would be to collect and investigate the Agadas scattered through Origen's writings.

1.—" THE GARDEN OF EDEN, THE CENTRE OF THE WORLD."

Selecta in Gen. ii. 8 (xii. 100, M.), Οὐκοῦν παραδεδώκασιν Ἑβραῖοι, ὅτι ὁ τόπος ἐν ᾧ ἐφύτευσεν τὸν παράδεισον ἢ τὸν κῆπον Κύριος ὁ Θεός, Ἐδὲμ καλεῖτα· καὶ φάσιν αὐτὸν μέσον εἶναι τοῦ κόσμου, ὡς κόρην ὀφθαλμοῦ· διὸ καὶ τὸν ποταμὸν τὸν Φείσων, ἑρμηνεύεσθαι σ τ ό μ α κ ό ρ η ς, ὡς ἐκ τοῦ Ἐδὲμ ἐκπορευομένου τοῦ ποταμοῦ τοῦ πρώτου.

A remarkable Midrash of which I have failed to find an exact counterpart in Jewish writings. It may be a conclusion drawn from the old assumption that Palestine is the centre of the earth, while Eden was supposed to be in or near to Palestine. The precise situation of Paradise forms the subject of a Talmudic controversy. T. B. *Erubin,* 19a:— גן עדן א'ר ר'ש לקיש אם בארץ ישראל הוא בית שאן פיתחה פיתחא בית גרם בערביא ואם. On the other hand, Midrash Ps. xxi. 3, tells us : שערי גן עדן סמוכין להר המוריה. The interpretation of פישון as פי אישון is unknown to me in Jewish sources.

2.—POTIPHAR AND JOSEPH.

Origen says in a *catena regia*, quoted from a MS. in Montfaucon's Hexapla on Genesis xxxvii. 36 : " Phutirpharem eundem ipsum esse tradunt, qui Josephi herus et socer

---

[1] *Hom. in Isajam* I. § 5 (xiii. 225, M.), Cur non dicamus in praesenti traditionem quandam Judaeorum verisimilem quidem, nec tamen veram ..... It is a reference to the well-known tradition of the murder of the prophet Isaiah.

fuit. Narrantque Aseneth illam matrem suam apud patrem accusasse, quod insidias in Josephum struxisset, non autem ab eo insidiis appetita fuisset. Quam ille Josepho sponsam dedit"..... The same tradition is given more explicitly in Jerome, *Quest. Heb.*, in Gen. xxxvii. 36 : "Putiphar eunucho. Ubi quæritur, quomodo postea uxorem habere dicatur. Tradunt Hebræi emptum ab hoc Joseph ob nimiam pulchritudinem in turpe ministerium, et a Domino virilibus ejus arefactis, postea electum esse juxta morem Hierophantarum in pontificatum Neilopoleos, et hujus filiam esse Aseneth, quam postea Joseph uxorem acceperit."[1]

Three features are to be distinguished in these notices, (*a*) Potiphar, Gen. xxxvii. 36, is identified with Potipherah, Gen. xli. 45, and Asenath is, accordingly, Joseph's former master's daughter; (*b*) Asenath, according to this account, felt and evinced sympathy with her father's slave before his imprisonment; (*c*) Potiphar, inflamed by the sight of Joseph's beauty, contemplated the commission of an unnatural crime, but was stricken with impotence. The whole of this tradition, with the exception of the second part, which does not really belong to it, occurs in Jewish sources. We read in T. B. *Sota*, 136:—ויקנדו פוטיפר אמר רב שקנאו לעצמו [בא גבריאל וכרכו] בא גבריאל ופירעו מעיקרא כתיב פוטיפר ולבסוף פוטיפרע. The words placed within brackets are erased by Rashi, because they are tautologous. R. Nathan, of the *Aruch*, retains them, and explains, סירכו לבצים ופרעו לניד. This view is obviously preferable to Rashi's. The words כריס פרעה form the basis of the interpretation סירכו ופירעו. We thus have here the express tradition that Potiphar is identical with Potipherah, and was stricken with impotence as a punishment for his evil intentions towards Joseph.

The same legend is recorded in other portions of Rabbinic literature. *Gen. R.*, c. 86, פוטיפר שהיה פורע עצמו לע"ז

---

[1] This tradition is not found in Rahmer's *Hebrew Traditions in the Works of Hieronymus*, Breslau, 1861.

כיון שירד הפר לשם נעשה פוטנן כריס פרעה שנכרהרס מלמד
שלא לקחו אלא לתשמיש וסירסו הקב"ה בגופו. Levy, *Neuhebr.*
Wörterbuch, and Fürst, *Glossarium Græco-hebræum,* p. 163 *b.*,
give φωτεινός as the Greek original of פוטנן. Kohut's *Aruch
Completum,* VI., 315*b*, agrees with Perles' *Rabbinische Sprach-
u. Sagen-Kunde,* p. 21, that פוטנן is derived from πουτάνα=
putana. Both explanations are incorrect; for φωτεινός would
imply a eulogy of Potiphar, where none was intended by the
Midrash, and "putana" is not Latin but Romaic. I venture
to suggest that פוטנן=σπάδων, a eunuch; σπάδων is the
rendering of סריס, which the Septuagint and Vulgate give
generally as well as Gen. xxxvii. 36, in the particular passage
under discussion (see H. Rönsch, *Itala u. Vulgata,* second
edition, p. 246). The name פוטיפרע, which sounded so
strange to the Hebrew ear demanded an Agadic interpretation. It was accordingly bisected; the first half, פוטי,
was explained in three ways: (*a*) as derived from פטם,
Gen. R., c. 86, שהיה מפטם עגלים לע"ז; (*b*) from φῶς
"light," *Tanchuma* II., וישב, § 16, למה נקרא שמו פוטיפר
שהבהיק לביתו של פרעה,[1] cp. *Jelamdenu,* quoted in *Aruch,*
s. v., פט II., פוטיאל שהאיר במעשים טובים שאת אומר ביוונית
פוטיא; (*c*) from σπάδων, a "eunuch," *Gen. R.,* ib., where the
words כריס פרעה are added to confirm the derivation. פרץ,
the second component of the name, was interpreted in two
ways: (*a*) as derived from פרע, to untie or loosen, *Gen. R.,*
ib., שהיה פורע עצמו לע"ז; (*b*) from פרע, to cut out, T. B.
Sota, 13*b*, בא גבריאל ופירעו. Musafia, in *Kohut* I. 211, was
guided by a right instinct when he adds וי"מ שהוא מסרס מסרס.
He also thought of σπάδων. Our interpretation is confirmed
by a passage in *Shir R.* I. 1, בל יתיצב לפני השוכים זה
פוטיפר שהחשיך הקב"ה עיניו וסירסו. This completely excludes the idea of Potiphar's enlightenment, or, according
to Fürst, *ibid.,* his conversion. In the *Tanchuma,* Potiphar

---

[1] The passage שנכנס לביתו של פרעה ונעשה ביתו פוטינום should be
emended into כיון שנכנס יוסף לביתו נעשה [פוטיפרע] פוטנן, according
to *Gen. Rab.* and *Yalkut.*

is not represented as the enlightened but as the enlightener, *i. e.*, the steward over Pharaoh's house, an office which has no obvious connection with *spiritual* enlightenment.

3.—DIVISION OF THE RED SEA INTO TWELVE PARTS.

Hom. in Exod. v. 5 (xii. 330, M.), Audivi a majoribus traditum, quod in ista digressione maris, singulis quibusque tribubus filiorum Israel, singulæ aquarum divisiones factæ sunt, et propria unicuique tribui in mari aperta est via, idque ostendi ex eo, quod in Psalmis (cxxxv. 13) scriptum est: *Qui divisit mare rubrum in divisiones.* Per quod multæ divisiones docentur factæ, non una. Sed et per hoc quod dicitur: Ita Benjamin junior in stupore...... (Psalm. lxviii. 28) nihilominus unicuique tribui propius enumerari videtur ingressus. Hæc a majoribus observata in Scripturis divinis, religiosum credidi non tacere. Cp. Eusebius Comm. in Ps. lxxvii. 13 (xxiii. 113, M.), φασὶ γοῦν Ἑβραίων παῖδες εἰς ιβ΄ τμήματα διηρῆσθαι αὐτὴν κατ᾽ ἀριθμὸν τῶν ιβ΄ φυλῶν τοῦ λαοῦ.

Every detail of this Midrash is found with wonderful similarity in the Jewish sources.

The division of the Red Sea into twelve parts, corresponding to the number of the tribes, is recounted in the *Mechilta* (Exod. xiv. 16) נחלק לשנים עשר גזרים. In Midrash on Psalm cxxxvi. 15, in Yalkut Habakkuk, § 565, and in Yalkut Exodus, § 245, נחלק לשנים is a mistake for ב' ל' עשר. Even the verse with which this tradition is connected is the same in Origen and the Midrash. In the *Mechilta* (Exod. xiv. 15), the passage commencing מהו אומר לגוזר ים סוף לגזרים, breaks off abruptly. The expected conclusion is the deduction that the sea was divided into twelve parts. Maimonides knew this Midrash in its full form. Commentary on *Aboth* V. 4: שנבקעו לדרכים רבים כמספר השבטים והוא אמרו לגוזר וכו'. In *Aboth de R. Nathan*, c. XXXIII. (v. I.), the circumstance is added that the tribes expressly stipulated that the sea should be divided into sections, אמר להם משה קומו עברו

אמרו לא נעבור עד שנעשה לפנינו נזרים נזרים גזרים שנאמר לגוזר וכו'.

Ps. lxviii. 28, from which, Origen says, the same tradition
is derived, is connected with it in the *Mechilta*, ibid. 6, *Sota*,
36*b*, Midrash on Ps. lxviii. 14, where we read that the tribes
disputed as to which of them was to be the first to pass
through the Red Sea; the result could only have been that
they crossed simultaneously by different routes.

4.—REPENTANCE OF KORAH'S SONS.

Comm. in Ep. ad Rom. x. 7 (xiv. 1262, M.), Non puto
absurdum videri si ea quæ nobis de his etiam in veteri Tes-
tamento a patribus rationaliter tradita sunt, his scilicet,
qui ex Hebræis ad Christi fidem venerunt, in medium profe-
ramus.   Aiebant ergo tres illos filios Core, quorum nomina
invenimus in Exodo (vi. 24)...... Aser...... Elchana...... et
Abiasaph......, cum pater eorum Core pecasset una cum
Dathan et Abiram...... istos segregasse a cœtu nefario et
ab impia conspiratione sequestratos unanimiter ad Deum
precem pœnitentiæ profudisse: atque exauditos a Deo non
solum veniam pœnæ, sed et prophetiæ gratiam meruisse, et
hoc quoque eis a deo poscentibus esse præstitum, ne quid
triste aut exitiabile prophetare juberentur: et ob hoc omnes
psalmos quicunque nominibus eorum attitulati referuntur,
nihil triste adversum peccatores aut asperum continere.

Only that part of this beautiful Agada which refers to the
repentance of Korah's sons is to be found in Jewish sources.
A passage in Midrash to Ps. xlv. 4, runs as follows:—כך בני
קרח לא היו יכולין לומר שירה לפני הק'ב'ה בפיהם עד שרחש
לכם וקבלם מיד ולמה לא היו יכולין לומר שירה בפיהם לפי
שהיתה שאול פתוחה מתחתיהם ואש בלהטת סביבותיהם:
The שירה here mentioned is parallel to Origen's *preces pœnitentiæ*.   This elucidates the passage in T. B. *Sanhedrin*, 110*a*
(*Megilla*, 14*a*):—מקום נהבצר להם בניהנם וישבו עליו ואמרו
שירה.   That this Agada is ancient appears from the un-
familiar word נהבצר; cp. also Midrash on Psalms i. 5,
and xlv. 1.   In the Jewish sources we miss the fine touches
of the gift of prophecy bestowed on Korah's sons, and of

the always comforting nature of the Korachide Psalms. Perhaps others will be fortunate enough to discover these points too.

5.—ISRAEL'S STRENGTH CONSISTS IN PRAYER.

Hom. in Num., xiii. 5 (xii. 672, M.), Ut autem scias tale aliquid cogitasser egem (Balak), ex scripturae verbis intellige, quæ ego a magistro quodam, qui ex Hebræis crediderat, exposita didici. Scriptum est ergo (Num. xxii. 4) : *Et dixit Moab ad seniores Madjan : Nunc, ablinget synagoga hæc omnes, qui in circuitu nostro sunt, sicut ablingit vitulus herbam campi.* Aiebat ergo magister ille, qui ex Hebræis crediderat : Cur, inquit, tali usus est exemplo, dicens : sicut ablingit vitulus herbam campi ? Ob hoc sine dubio, quia vitulus ore obrumpit herbam de campo et lingua tanquam falce quæcunque invenerit, secat. Ita ergo et populus hic, quasi vitulus ore et labiis pugnat, et arma habet in verbis ac precibus. Haec igitur sciens rex mittit ad Balaam, ut et ipse deferat verbis verba contraria et precibus preces.

This is a well-known Midrash. *Sifri* Num. xxii. 4, § 157 ; *Num. R.* c. 20, 3; *Tanchuma* II. ; בלק, § 4 ; Rashi, *ad locum* : מה שור כחו בפיו אף הם כחם בפיהם.

6.—PHINEAS AND ELIJAH IDENTICAL.

Comm. in Joann. vi. 7 (xiv. 225, M.), Οἱ Ἑβραῖοι παραδιδόασι Φινεὲς τὸν Ἐλεαζάρου υἱὸν . . . . αὐτὸν εἶναι Ἡλίαν καὶ ἀθάνατον ἐν τοῖς Ἀριθμοῖς αὐτῷ διὰ τῆς ὀνομαζομένης εἰρήνης ἐπηγγέλθαι.

Jerome knows the same tradition, which he thinks the Jews took from an apocryphal work. Eliam esse Phineas Hebræi ex Apocryphis persuasum habent (V. 813 Vallarsi). The sentence, פנחס הוא אליהו is only found in *Yalkut Num.* 772, in the name of R. Simeon b. Lakish and ascribed to a Midrash as its original source. Its preservation in a miscellaneous collection is noteworthy. The ordinary Midrashim seem to have purposely suppressed it, because it smacked of Apocrypha. Its omission is particularly noticeable in

Tanchuma II., פנחס, § 3: את לו נתן הנני לו אמור לכן
,בריתי שלום וכן הוא אומר בריתי היתה אתו דהחיים והשלום,
which, as it stands, makes no sense. The *Yalkut*, ib., on
the basis of Malachi ii. 5, infers that the peace promised Phineas was eternal life: וחיי הזה העולם חיי לו ונתן
העולם הבא ונתן לו שכר טוב והיתה לו ולזרעו אחריו ברית
כהונת עולם. Here, too, Origen, gives the correct tradition
that Phineas' immortality is implied in the word שלום.

7.—ALLEGORICAL INTERPRETATION OF THE SERAPHIM.

De Princ. I. 3, 4 (xi. 143, M.), Ἔλεγε δὲ ὁ Ἑβραῖος τὰ ἐν
τῷ Ἡσαίᾳ δύο σεραφὶμ ἑξαπτέρυγα κεκραγότα ἕτερον πρὸς
ἕτερον .... τὸν Μονογενῆ εἶναι τοῦ θεοῦ καὶ τὸ Πνεῦμα τὸ
ἅγιον. Cp. *De Princ.* iv. 26 (xi. 400, M.), Nam et Hebræus
doctor ista tradebat: pro eo quod initium omnium vel finis
non possit ab ullo comprehendi, nisi tantummodo a Domino
Jesu Christo, et a Spirito sancto, aiebat per figuram visio-
nis Isaiam dixisse, duos seraphim solos esse, qui duabus
quidem alis operiunt faciem Dei, duabus vero pedes, et duabus
volant clamantes ad invicem sibi dicentes: Sanctus, sanctus, sanctus, etc. The same tradition was also known to
Jerome, in Ep. xli. (lxv.) *Ad Pammachium et Oceanum*,
who, however, rightly stigmatizes it as an odious and
godless exposition. Had it not been expressly so stated,
one could hardly believe that a Jew said it. The Christian
terms, at least, are to be placed to a Church Father's
account. I could not find this interpretation in the
Jewish sources, and none will regret its absence.

8.—DANIEL, CHANANIAH, MISHAEL AND AZARIAH
WERE EUNUCHS.

Comm. in Matt. xv. 5 (xiii. 1225, M.), Φασὶ δὲ Ἑβραίων
παῖδες τὸν Δανιὴλ καὶ τοὺς τρεῖς σὺν αὐτῷ Ἀνανιαν, Ἀζαρίαν
Μισαήλ, ἐν Βαβυλῶνι εὐνουχίσθαι, πληρουμένης τῆς πρὸς
τὸν Ἐζεκίαν εἰρημένης προφητείας ὑπὸ Ἡσαίου ἐν τῷ "Ἀπὸ
τοῦ σπέρματός σου λήψονται, καὶ ποιήσουσι σπαδόντας ἐν τῳ
οἴκῳ τοῦ βασίλεως Βαβυλῶνος" (Is. xxxix. 7). Φασὶ δὲ ὅτι

περὶ τούτων καὶ Ἡσαΐας ἐπροφήτευσε φάσκων " Μή λεγέτω ὁ ἀλλογενής ὁ προσκείμενος κυρίῳ. ἀφοριεῖ μὲ ἄρα κύριος ἀπὸ τοῦ λαοῦ αὐτοῦ," καὶ τὰ ἑξῆς, ἕως τοῦ "κρείττονα υἱῶν καὶ θυγατέρων" (Is. lvi. 35).

Origen gives the tradition with more fulness of detail in *Hom.* in Ezek. iv., § 8 (xiii. 703, M.). On Ezek. xiv. 15 : Audivi quondam a quodam Hebræo hunc locum exponente atque dicente, ideo hos nominatos, quia unusquisque eorum (Daniel, Job, Noe) tria tempora viderit, lætum, triste et rursum lætum...... Noe...... vidit mundum ante diluvium ......in diluvio......, rursum in resurrectione omnium peccatorum. Dicit mihi aliquis: concedo de Noe, ut tria tempora viderit : quid respondebis mihi de Daniele? Et hic ante captivitatem in patria floruit nobilitate, et deinceps in Babylonem translatus *eunuchus effectus est,* ut manifeste ex libro illius intelligi potest; vidit et reversionem in Jerusalem. Ut autem probetur quod ante captivitatem eunuchus factus sit, assumamus id quod ad Ezechiam dictum est (Is. xxix. 7)...... Job...... fuit locuples...... deinde accepit diabolus potestatem adversus eum ;...... post hæc apparet ei Dominus. *Ib.* § 5 (xiii. 700, M.). Daniel qui traditus est eunuchorum principi cum Anania, Azaria, Misaela, eunuchus fuit...... Quomodo filii Danielis docebuntur, quem eunuchum fuisse Judæi tradunt? Verum quia fertilis et sancta fuit anima illius, et propheticis divinisque sermonibus multos liberos procreavit...... Catena Regia in Prophetas ad Ezek. xiv. 5 : Υἱοὺς ἔχει ὁ Δανιὴλ κατὰ τὴν αὐτὴν πνευματικὴν γένναν, οὓς ἐγέννησεν ἡ προφητεία αὐτοῦ. υἱοὺς γὰρ σαρκικοὺς οὐκ ἔσχεν. Εὐνοῦχος γὰρ ἦν, ὥς φασι.

The same tradition we find in Jerome lib. I., adv. Jovin., c. 25 : Superfluum est de Daniele dicere, cum Hebræi usque hodie autument et illum et tres pueros fuisse eunuchos, ex illa dei sententia (II. Reg. xx. 18)......

Jerome on Daniel i. 3 : Unde et arbitrantur Hebræi Danielem et Azariam et Ananiam et Misaelem fuisse eunuchos......Epiphanius, *de Vitis Prophetarum* (xliv. 424, M. *ser gr.*): Καὶ ἦν ἀνὴρ σώφρων, ὥστε θαυμάζειν τοὺς Ἰου-

156　　　*The Jewish Quarterly Review.*

δαίους πιστεύοντας εἰς αὐτὸν εἶναι σπαδόντα. Later Church
Fathers also give the same tradition, which they have
however drawn from Origen and Jerome.

This Agada is widely disseminated in Jewish literature.
All the details correspond; the statement that Daniel and
his companions were eunuchs; the verse from which this is
deduced; the question how they could have afterwards
begotten children, etc. We read in B. *Sanhedrin*, 93*b* :—

ומבניך אשר יצאו ממך אשר הוליד יקחו והיו סריסים בהיכל
מלך בבל רב אמר סריסים ממש...... מאי טוב מבנים ומבנות
מבנים שהיו להם כבר ומרו ...... From which we see that
this tradition did not survive in the popular consciousness;
it is stated as simply an individual opinion. Of the many
views enunciated, the most noteworthy is R. Jochanan's,
ib. 93*a* : עלו [חנניה משאל ועזריה] לארץ ישראל ונשאו נשים
והולידו בנים ובנות. This, as Rashi remarks, stands in direct
opposition to the above. Cp. *Gen. R.*, c. 99; *Num. R.*, c. 13;
Esther R., c. 4; *Pirke de R. E.*, c. LII.

9.—MOSES, AUTHOR OF ELEVEN PSALMS.

Selecta in Psalmos, p. 514 (xii. 1055, M.), "Ὕστερον δὲ κινού-
μενος περί τινων λογίων Θεοῦ Ἰουλλῷ τῷ πατριάρχῃ καί τινι
τῶν χρηματιζόντων παρὰ Ἰουδαίοις σοφῶν ἀκήκοα, ὅτι δι'
ὅλης τῆς βίβλου ψαλμῶν .... οἱ παρ' Ἑβραίοις ἀνεπίγραφοι
ἢ ἐπιγραφὴν μὲν ἔχοντες, οὐχὶ δὲ το ὄνομα τοῦ γράψαντος,
ἐκείνου εἰσὶν οὗ τὸ ὄνομα φέρεται ἐν τῷ πρὸ τούτων ἐπιγραφὴν
ἔχοντι ψαλμῷ. καὶ περὶ τούτων λέγων, πρότερον μὲν ἔφασκεν,
ὅτι τρισκαίδεκα εἰσὶν ὁ του Μωυσέως εἶτα δὲ ἐξ ὧν ἀκήκοα
καὶ αὐτὸς .... τὴν ἀνέφερον ἐπ' αὐτὸν, ὅτι εἰσὶν ἔνδεκα, εἶτα
πυθόμενος, τοῦ παρ' αὐτοῖς δοκοῦντος σοφοῦ, ἐμάνθανον, ὅτι
εἶεν ἔνδεκα.

Jerome. *adv. Ruff.*, c. 13, quotes the whole of this passage.
He knows the tradition of Moses' authorship, gives it, however, not in the name of the Jews, but as a firmly established
and self-evident truth:—Qui [Moses] non solum nobis
quinque reliquit libros,...... sed undecim quoque Psalmos,
ab octogesimo nono [LXX.]...... usque ad nonagesimum

nonum. Quod autem in plerisque codicibus nonagesimus octavus habet titulum *Psalmus David,* in Hebraico non habetur, hanc habente scriptura sancta consuetudinem, ut omnes psalmi qui cujus sint titulos non habent, his deputentur, quorum in prioribus psalmis nomina continentur (Ep. cxl. ad Cyprianum, c. 2).

This Midrash also is found in Jewish sources; *Pesikta de R. Kahana,* 198*a,* ed. Buber: משה אמר מזמורים עשר אחד כנגד אחד עשר שבטים שבירך ואלו הן......אמר ר' יהושוע עד כאן שמעתי מכאן ואילך את מחשב לעצמך. R. Joshua's words imply that this was an ancient tradition. It is found also in Midrash on Psalm xc. 3, *Yalkut Ps.,* § 841, Rashi to Psalm xc. 1; cp. Midrash on Psalm xc. 4: מזמורים עשר אחד שאמר משה בטכסים של נביאים אמרן.

10.—BEASTS AS EXECUTORS OF DIVINE PUNISHMENT.

Hom. in Ezek. iv. 7 (xiii. 701, M.), and *in Ezek.* xiv. 4: Aiunt etiam Judæi, si quando lupi homines devoraverint impetum facientes in domos, et cæteræ bestiæ, ut historia refert leones quondam in humanum genus immissos, et alio tempore ursos (II. Reg. xvii. 2) istius modi devorationes ex Dei indignatione descendere.

I have not found a parallel in Jewish sources, but the root idea is patent and needs no special tradition.

S. KRAUSS.

(*To be Continued.*)

THE JEWS IN THE WORKS OF THE CHURCH FATHERS.

IV.

EUSEBIUS.

EUSEBIUS, whose best work was accomplished on Palestinian soil, in Cæsarea, must often have come into contact with Jews, and been instructed by them on several points. He is bitterer in tone against the Jews than Origen. " Jew," with him, is a term of opprobrium. He repeatedly calls his opponent Marcellus a Jew (*Eccles. Theol.* II. 2, 3). The phrase, " one of the circumcised," [1] which he employs, likewise covers a world of scorn and contempt. His work, *Demonstratio Evangelica*, was avowedly written as a direct attack on the Jews.[2] He holds that, in their exposition of Scripture, the Jews are guilty of serious errors, and efforts should be made to induce them to abandon their heresies; that is to say : Religious disputations should be encouraged with the view of persuading them to give up their faith.[3]

Eusebius regards the condition of the Jews as lamentable. What they felt most bitterly was the harsh law which denied them the solace of visiting the holy city of Jerusalem. He describes the wailing and weeping of the poor Jews when they caught even a distant glimpse of Zion's ruins.[4]

---

[1] *Dem. Ev.* i. 6 (xxii. 49, M.), τις τῶν ἐκ περιτομῆς.

[2] *Ib.* i. 1, 11, οὐ . . . κατὰ Ἰουδαίων, ἄπαγε, πολλοῦ γε καὶ δεῖ . . .

[3] *Ib.* iv. 16 (xxii. 317, M.), Διόπερ εἰκὸς τοὺς ἐκ περιτομῆς ἀποσφάλλεσθαι . . .

[4] *Comm. in Psalm* lviii. 7-12 (xxiii. 541, M.), Διὸ εἰσέτι καὶ σήμερον ἀμφὶ μὲν τοὺς ὅρους καὶ κύκλῳ παριόντες πόρρωθεν ἵστανται μηδ᾽ ἐξ ἀπόπτου

Eusebius was as much under the influence of Jewish tradition as his predecessors and several of his successors. It has nearly the same authority with him as the Scriptures, and he calls it ἄγραφος παράδοσις=" unwritten tradition."[1] Its depositaries he terms δευτερρταί,[2] and he characterises them in the following happy fashion : "There are people gifted with an uncommon strength of intellect; and whose faculties have been trained to penetrate to the very heart of Scripture. The children of the Hebrews call them δευτερωταί, because they expound Holy Writ."[3] Eusebius also distinguishes between esoteric and exoteric exegesis. The Agadas he frequently classes with the exoteric exposition.[4] Though there is no clear statement to that effect, we may confidently assume that Eusebius enjoyed direct intercourse with Jews. Cæsarea, the Father's residence, was inhabited by learned Hebrews; and we know from the Talmud that disputations between Jews and Christians were frequent in this town. It will also clearly appear from passages to be hereafter quoted, that Eusebius had a Jewish teacher. His Agadas, of which we give a few specimens, he owed to Jews.

τὸ πάλαι νενομισμένον αὐτοῖς ἱερὸν ἔδαφος θεάσασθαι καταξιούμενοι, ἔξωθεν δὲ κυκλοῦντες, πίστιν ἐπάγουσι τήν . . . Γραφῇ (Ps. liii. 7).— *Ib.* lxix. 26—29 (xxiii. 153, M.), Ἰουδαίων δὲ οὐδένα τολμῶντα ἐπιβαίνειν τῇ πόλει, μήτε γε οἰκεῖν αὐτόθι. ἀλλ' οὐδὲ οἴκησις Ἰουδαϊκὴ περιλέλειπται ἐν τῷ τόπῳ, ὡς τινα τῶν Ἑλλήνων οἰκεῖν ἐν αὐτῇ δύνασθαι.

[1] *Hist. Ev.* iv. 22 (xx. 384, M.), ἐκ Ἰουδαϊκῆς ἀγράφου παραδόσεως.

[2] *Praep. Ev.* xi. 5 (xxi. 852, M.), Δευτερωταί . . . οὕτω δὲ φίλον τοὺς ἐξηγητὰς τῶν παρ' αὐτοῖς Γραφῶν ὀνομάζειν.

[3] *Ib.* xii. 1 (xxi. 952, M.), τοῖς . . . τὴν ἕξιν προβεβηκόσι, καὶ πολιοῖς τὰ φρόνημα, ἐμβαθύνειν καὶ δοκιμάζειν τὸν νοῦν τῶν λεγομένων ἐπιτέτραπται. Τουτοὺς δὲ παισὶν Ἑβραίων Δευτερωτὰς φίλον ἦν ὀνομάζειν ὥσπερ ἑρμηνευτὰς καὶ ἐξηγητὰς ὄντας τῆς τῶν Γραφῶν διανοίας.

[4] *Dem. Ev.* vi. 18 (xxii. 461, M.), ὁ δέ γε Ἰώσηπος καὶ τὰς ἔξωθεν Ἰουδαϊκὰς δευτερώσεις ἀπηκριβωκώς . . . ἐπάκουσον. The subject here discussed is the earthquake, the legend concerning which is to be found in the *Seder Olam.*, c. xx. הוא ובישעיה הרעש לפני שנתים אומר הוא ובעמוס אומר בשנת מות המלך עזיהו כי' והוא היה ביום הרעש שנאמר וינוסו אמות הספים.

F 2

1.—ABRAHAM OBEYED THE PRECEPTS OF THE TORAH
BEFORE THE REVELATION.

Demonstratio Evang. I. 6.   Μεμαρτύρηται γοῦν τὰ προ-
στάγματα καὶ τὰς ἐντολὰς, τά τε δικαιώματα καὶ τὰ νόμιμα
τοῦ θεοῦ, πρὸ τῆς Μωσέως διαταγῆς πεφυλαγμένος.   Eusebius
infers this from Gen. xxvi. 3, 4, 5.

This is one of the best known Agadas, cp. T. B. Joma,
28b:—עקב אמר רב קיים אברהם כל התורה כלה שנאמר
אשר שמע.   Even the verse on which the statement is
based is the same in the Father and the Talmud.   Compare
Baba Meziah, 85b and 87a, where R. Meir already asserts :
אברהם אבינו אוכל חולין בטהרה היה.

2.—KING HEZEKIAH'S SIN.

Commentary on Isaiah xxxix. 1. (VI. 362 M.).   συνεξετά-
ξουσιν ἡμῖν καὶ διερευνωμένοις τὰ κατὰ τοὺς παρόντας τόπους,
ὁ τῶν Ἰουδαίων διδάσκαλος ἔλεγεν νενοσηκέναι μεν τον Ἐζεκίαν,
ἐπεὶ μὴ εἰρήκει ᾠδὴν εἰς τὸν θεὸν εὐχαριστήριον ἐπὶ τῇ πτώσει
τῶν Ἀσσυρίων, ὡς Μωϋσῆς ᾖδεν ἐπὶ τῇ ἀπωλείᾳ τῶν Αἰγυπτίων
καὶ ὡς Δεβόρρα ἐπὶ τῇ ἀπωλείᾳ τοῦ Σισάρα καὶ ὡς Ἄννα ἐπὶ
τῇ γεννήσει του Σαμουήλ.

Jerome, *ad locum*, quotes the same tradition.

This Agada, which is already noteworthy for the direct
statement prefacing it—that Eusebius learnt it from his
Jewish teacher—is one of the most widely disseminated in
Jewish literature.   The reflection that Hezekiah was guilty
of ingratitude in not chanting a hymn of praise to God
after Sennacherib's fall, also occurs in T. B. *Sanhedrin*, 94a:
למרבה המשרה ולשלום אין קץ · אמר ר' תנחום דרש בר קפרא
בציפורי מפני מה כל מ"ם שבאמצע תיבה פתוח וזה סתום
בקש הקב"ה לעשות חזקיה משיח וסנחריב גוג ומגוג · אמר
מדת הדין לפני הקב"ה ומה דוד מלך ישראל שאמר כמה שירות
ותושבחות לפניך לא עשיתו משיח חזקיה שעשית לו כל הנסים

Ib., הללו ולא אמר שירה לפניך תעשה משיח · לכך נסתרם
גנאי הוא לחזקיה וסיעתו שלא אמרו שירה.

In *Exodus R.,* c. 18, and T. B. *Pesachim,* 117a, it is related
that Hezekiah sang a hymn of praise (Hallel) before the
destruction of the Assyrian hordes, but there is no hint of
his having been censured·for omitting to sing one after the
occurrence. In *Shir R.,* on c. IV. v. 8, an excuse is put into
Hezekiah's mouth:—ראוי היה חזקיה לומר שירה על מפלת
סנחריב אמר חזקיה תורה שאני עוסק בה מכפרת על
השירה.

In *Echa R.,* c. I., the excuse takes the following form:—
חזקיה אמר אין בי כח·····לומר שירה. From all these passages it is obvious that Hezekiah's omission to compose a
special hymn of praise largely exercised the imagination of
the Agadists. In T. J. *Pesachim,* towards the end, a dictum
is found, couched in so authoritative a form that it sounds
almost like an Halacha, to the effect that a miraculous deliverance should be followed by a thanksgiving:—כשהקב"ה
עושה לכם נסים תהיו אומרין שירה. To this the cogent
objection is raised that Mordecai and Esther did not sing
a hymn after Haman's fall. *Jalkut,* on Isaiah, § 306, quotes
a passage from the lost Jelamdenu, in which the duty of
a thanksgiving is deduced from Exodus xv. 1: ויאמרו לאמר
לדורות. A contrast is also drawn between the songs
of Moses, Deborah and David, and Hezekiah's culpable
negligence—a feature also dwelt upon in Eusebius. In
all the above passages, however, we miss the detail,
found in the Father's recital of the legend, that Hezekiah's sickness was a Divine punishment for his omission
of a thanksgiving. Nevertheless, this, too, comes from
a Jewish source. The following passage is excerpted
from Jelamdenu by the Jalkut on 2 Kings, § 243:—
כשעלה סנחריב עליו והפילו האלהים לפניו הוה ליה למימר
שירה על מפלתו ולא אמר ומה היה לו והפילו האלהים במטה
כדי שיאמר שירה שנאמר מכתב לחזקיהו.

This legend illustrates the advantages that would accrue
from a systematic history of the Agada. Such a history is

however only possible after a comparison of all available
auxiliary sources, among which the Church Fathers occupy
an important place.

3.—BERODACH BALADAN AND HEZEKIAH.

Comm. in Is. xxix. 1 (vi. 361 M.) τὸν δὲ Βαβυλώνιον
ἐγνωκέναι τὴν ἀπὸ τῆς νόσου ῥῶσιν αὐτοῦ καὶ ἀπεσταλκέναι
πρὸς αὐτὸν ἄνδρας......ἐπειδὴ συνέβη τὴν ἡμέραν ἐκείνην καθ'
ἣν τὸ σημεῖον τῆς τοῦ ἡλίου ἀναδρομῆς ὡρῶν γεγενῆσθαι δι-
σπλασίων, μὴ γάρ λατεῖν τοῦ το τοὺς Βαβυλωνίους δεινοὺς ὄντας
περὶ τὴν τῶν ἄστρων δε ὡρίαν καὶ......συνεῖδον ὡς ὑπὸ κρείτ-
τονος περιήνέχθη εἰς τουπισὼ δυναμέως ...... ταῦτα μὲν ὁ
Ἑβραῖος.

The same Agada is given in Ephraem Syrus' work (*Op.
Syr.* I. 562, 563 R.) on 2 Kings xx. 10, as one of Jacob
Edessenus' *Scholia.* It is introduced in the following impressive phrases:—במלא הלין סוכלא מטשיא אית דלו לכל
נש ידיע ודאן זדקא דלגליא אנא איתוהי הא אמר אנא. Graetz
has discussed the latter passage in the *Monatsschrift,* 1854,
p. 383. The Agada inspires him, however, with but little
respect, because it is not given by Ephraem but by Jacob
Edessenus, who belongs to a later period. The passage in the
commentary on the parallel chapter in Isaiah, which is, indeed, given in Ephraem's name, Graetz suspects to have been
interpolated from Jacob Edessenus' *Scholion.* The historian
has however overlooked the fact that the earlier Father,
Eusebius, also has this Agada. By the time it reached
Edessenus, it had received several additions, *e.g.,* the recital
of the miracle of the turning back of the sun by the Nine-
vite Jews to the Babylonian king; and the statement that
his native Jewish subjects enlightened him as to Hezekiah's
importance. The Agada, in the form in which Eusebius
presents it, is found in Jewish sources. Thus T. B. *Sanhedrin,* 96a:—בעת ההיא שלח בראדך בלאדן......משום כי חלה
חזקיה ויחזיק שדר ליה? ותשב השמש עשר מעלות......א'ל מאי

האי א׳ל הזקה חלש ואיתפח אמר איכא גברא כי האי ולא בעינא
לעדורי ליה שלמא. The detail is, however, wanting that
the Babylonians, by their knowledge of astronomy, discovered that the sun-dial had turned back. We read,
instead, in a passage excerpted from the Pesikta (*Jalkut*,
2 Kings, § 244) another account of the manner in which
the Babylonians were apprised of the miracle. מרודך בן
יבלאדן היה למוד לאכול בשש שעות וישן עד תשע שעות
וכיון שחזר גלגל חמה ישן לו ועמד ומצאו שחרית בקש להרוג
את כל עבדיו אמר הנחתם אותי לישן כל היום וכל הלילה
אמרו ליה מרי יומא הוא דהדר ביה ואלוהו של חזקיה החזירו
אמר להם איכה כי האי גברא כו׳.

We must confess that the Church Father's narrative, *viz.*,
that the Babylonians discovered the miracle by their astro-
nomical calculations, is more reasonable than the Jalkut
legend. Here is another illustration of the usefulness of
foreign sources for the purpose of rectifying the Agadas,
so many of which sound strange.

4.—The Traitor Shebna.

Comm. in Is. xii. 10, 11 (VI. 249 M.). Ἔλεγε τοίνυν ὁ
Ἑβραῖος ἀρχιερέα γεγενῆσθαι τὸν Σομνάν (שבנא) τρυφητὴν
τινα καὶ τὸν βίον ἄσεμνον ἄνδρα, ὡς καὶ προδοῦναι τὸν λαόν.

Jerome comments on the passage "Supra diximus Sob-
nam fuisse pontificem qui Assyriis prodidat civitatem, sed
quia hoc traditionis est Hebraicæ et Scriptura non lo-
quitur..."

All the details of this Agada recur in Jewish sources.
Thus, *Leviticus R.*, c. 5, זה שבנא כהן גדול היה. Shebna's
treachery is discussed in T. B. *Sanhedrin* 26a. Eusebius's
brief suggestion that Shebna was sensual (τρυφητής) is
repeated in T. B. *Sanhedrin*, 26a, אמר ר׳ אלעזר שבנא בעל
הנאה היה כתיב הכא בא אל הסוכן וכתיב התם ותהי
לו סוכנת.

This somewhat obscure passage Rashi explains in the following gloss, כמשמעו וי״א משכב זכר. After what the Father tells us, we must decide that the explanation of the יש אומרים hits the correct sense of the Agada.

5.—INTERPRETATION OF ZECH. XI. 8.

The text ואכחיד את שלשת הרעים בירח אחד received, from a very early period, the following Christological interpretation: That, after Jesus' advent, the three powerful estates, Sovereignty, Priesthood and Prophecy, disappeared from Israel's midst. This explanation recurs in Eusebius, *Dem. Ev.* X. 1 (XX. 747 M.). Jerome (on Zech. xi. 8) quotes it only to reject it. His sound common sense leads him to prefer the Jewish exegesis, which applies the text to Moses, Aaron and Miriam. Strange to say, he does not give it in the Jews' name, as Graetz already noted in the *Monatssch.* 1854, p. 189. The historian has neglected to consult the older authority, Eusebius, whom Jerome follows in so many places. It is clearly evident from Eusebius, *ibid.*, that this exegesis was not specially Jewish, but was general at that period. The passage quoted by Graetz from T. B. *Taanith* 9*a*:—ואכחיד את שלשת הרעים בירח אחד וכי בירח אחד מתו והלא מרים מתה בניכן ואהרן באב ומשה באדר, completely coincides with *Seder Olam R.,* c. X., which first mentions the distinctive blessings these three pastors brought the people:—אהרן = עמוד ענן · משה = מן · מרים = באר.

V.

EPHRAEM SYRUS.

In passionate hatred of the Jews, in contempt and active hostility towards the people of the covenant, Ephraem of Syria surpasses all the Church Fathers who came before and all those who went after him. His voluminous writings are filled with rage and animosity against the Jews. He would like to destroy them with the fire of his words and to draw down upon their heads, by his prayers, the avenging lightning of an offended Deity. Whence this hatred? Whence this malignant spirit of persecution? It is difficult to find an adequate reason, especially as Ephraem hardly ever came into contact with the Jews, and therefore could never have been insulted by them. His resentment seems to have been aroused and stimulated by the marvellous power of resistance shown by the old creed. In his immediate neighbourhood, Babylon, the ancient people flourished with unexpected vigour. The serious blow which Julian the Apostate dealt Christianity, and which was indirectly of benefit to the Jews, may also have contributed to the contemporary Father's prejudice. He sought to relieve his feelings by pouring out vials of wrath on the defenceless Hebrews.

Ephraem terms the Jews טעיא גזירא, the circumcised vagabonds.[1] Judaism is a worthless vineyard that cannot bear fruit.[2] He frequently refers to their wretched condition, which he regards as a punishment sent from God.[3] Because they reviled Jesus, the Lord has banished them from their land, and and now they are condemned to wander over the whole surface of the earth.[4]

The golden hopes which the Emperor Julian's policy raised in the Jews' hearts, proved vain and illusory. As soon as Christianity triumphed, it turned with redoubled fury on its indestructible foe. After Julian's death Ephraem composed four hymns: against the Emperor Julian, the

---

[1] *Op. Syr.* II. 469. Cp. Lengerke, *De Ephraemi Syri arte Hermeneutica* (Königsberg, 1838), p. 15.

[2] See Zingerle, *Bibliothek der Kirchenväter*, II., 292.

[3] In Gen. xlix. 8 (*Op. Syr.* I., 108).

[4] In 2 *Reg.* ii. at the end (*Op. Syr.* I., 523) נרשו אנון לבד מן אתרא דלהון וזרקו להון בכל פניתא דמתעמרניתא.

Apostate; against the heresies; and against the Jews.[1] We quote from these envenomed productions the following passages: "The Jewish people broke out into maddening noise; the circumcised blew their trumpets and rejoiced that he [Julian] was a magician and worshipper of idols. They saw again the image of the beast on his [Julian's] gold pieces; they again viewed the bull of shame, and danced round it with trumpets and timbrels, for they recognised in this beast[2] their ancient golden calf. The heathen bull, imprinted on their hearts, he stamped on his coins for the delectation of the Jews, who were enamoured of him.[3] The circumcised blew their trumpets and behaved like madmen.[4] Jerusalem put to shame the accursed crucifiers who had dared to announce that they would rebuild the ruins their sins had wrought.[5] Fire broke out and destroyed the scholars who had read in Daniel that the desolation would endure for ever. Look! you (Christians) live at peace, free from the 'possessed,' free from contact with the servants of the devil."[6]

What especially exasperates Ephraem is that the Jews will not give up their hopes; notwithstanding the calamities with which they have been visited, they still cherish the firm conviction that the Future belongs to them and their religion—not to Christianity. The narrative of the two concubines who appeared before Solomon for judgment, is applied by Ephraem to the rival creeds, the Church and the Synagogue. Of the latter, he says: The Synagogue continually protests that her son is the living child and pleasing to God. She, furthermore, loudly asserts that the

---

[1] על יולינוס מלכא דאחנף ועל יולפנא טעיא ועל יהודיא in *S. Ephraemi Syri Carmina Nisibena*, Ed. Bickel (Lipsiae, 1866), and Overbeck, *S. Ephraemi Syri . . . . aliorumque Opera Selecta* (= O), Oxonii, 1865. The hymns are translated into German by Hahn in the periodical *Zeitschrift für Katholische Theologie*, II. 335 (Innsbruck, 1878).

[2] An allusion on a coin of Julian with an altar and a beast, being the sign of the restitution of Paganism.

[3] O. p. 8.   [4] O. p. 12.   [5] O. p. 18.   [6] O. p. 19.

Law of Moses is endowed with eternal life. Thus the Synagogue of the misguided perpetually contends with the Church of Jesus.[1] The hopes of the Jews find still more emphatic expression in the view that, as soon as the expected Messiah shall have arrived,[2] God's people will reign supreme.

It is interesting to learn the precise nature of these hopes which dominated the Jewish mind in the fourth century. A passage bearing on this subject may here be appropriately quoted from the Sermon against the Jews:—"Now, look! this people dreams that it will return; the people which angered God in all that it did awaits and demands a time when it will have satisfaction. As soon as this people hears of a return, they lift up their voices and shout, 'Jerusalem will be rebuilt!' Again and again they listen, for they long for the return. 'The fame of the capital will be great; its name will be glorious,' they repeatedly exclaim."

Very honourable to the Jews is the testimony which an embittered foe, like Ephraem, is forced to bear to the expansive power of Judaism, even at that time of severe oppression. We learn from Ephraem, as we have learnt from Justin and Origen, that the old faith received at this period numerous accessions from heathendom. Ephraem, of course, declares that the heathens are deluded by Jewish missionaries.[3]

Christianity still felt itself called upon to defend its

---

[1] In 1 *Reg.* iii. 16 (*Op. Syr.* I. 452) • תרתין נשׂין לעדתא ולכנושתא דמזן
כנושתא דין • • • • השׂא מן קעיא ואמרא דברא דילה חי הו לאלהא ולה
שפר • ותוב׃דנמוסא דמשׁא דמית חיّא דלעלם יהב ליה • הי הכיל כנושתא
דטצّיא עם עדתא דמשׁיחא אמינאית נציא.

[2] In 1 *Reg.* i. 5 (*Op. Syr.* I. 441):—אלא אף ביומתן מתחזה שׁועליה ואית
ליה סברא דלשׁולתניה דתאבל נסק במאיתיתה דהר משׁיחא דמסבא לה.

[3] In 2 *Reg.* xix. 1 (*Op. Syr.* I., 558): טופסא אנّין דמכבנّותהון דّשׁיעא
הנון דמנסין להימנות דהّלי אלהא ומׁשׁדלין מחתחתין להון למשׁבק לעדתה
דמשׁיחّא ודלכנושׁתא דסטנא נסטון.

position against the Jews. In the Sermon against the Jews, Ephraem exhorts them: "Come let us examine the prophets and see whether their predictions have been fulfilled." From the course of the address we learn the chief points of controversy between Jews and Christians at this period. Opening with the challenge, "Let the accursed Jews search the Scriptures and become wise," Ephraem seeks, in the first place, to deduce from Gen. xlix. 10, 11, that the Jews' hopes are futile. "If Judah wields the sceptre and has an interpreter, the prophecies are not fulfilled. But if the sceptre has departed and the voice of prophecy is silent, then should the Jews be ashamed of their obstinacy and stiffneckedness." Another point of controversy was the interpretation of Zechariah ix. 9, and of Psalm viii. 3. It is easy to understand that Ephraem indirectly attacks the Jewish exegesis on several other points. The passages have been collated by Gerson, *Die Commentarien des Ephraem Syrus im Verhältniss zur Jüdischen Exegese* (Breslau, 1868), page 8. To this brochure the reader is referred.

Intrinsically Ephraem's commentaries are incomparably more valuable than those of the Church Fathers whom we have already discussed. Ephraem proceeded to the exposition of the Scriptures with a sufficient equipment of preliminary studies. In the first place he possessed a good knowledge of Hebrew. This, however, is not the general opinion. Abraham Geiger, for example, said (*Jüdische Zeitschrift*, VII. 69), " It is quite natural that Ephraem, though ignorant of Hebrew, should have interlarded his commentaries with Midrashic elements which he learnt from his intercourse with the Jews," a statement absolutely unwarranted.

Schaf, more recently (Smith-Wace's *Dictionary of Christian Biography*, II. 142), also seeks to prove from a few instances that Ephraem was unacquainted with Hebrew. Although, in itself, it does not greatly concern Jewish literature whether any individual Father of the Church knew Hebrew or not, still this point ought to be settled in order to enable us to appraise Ephraem's efforts at their just value. It is by no means the same thing whether Jewish exegesis is criticised by a competent Hebraist or by an ignoramus. If it should turn out that Ephraem understood the Hebrew text, it is clearly unfair to charge him with rashly intruding into a domain in which he was incompetent to judge.

In his Commentaries Ephraem frequently refers to the original text. This should show whether he knew Hebrew or not. The mere reference counts for something. Neither Clement of Alexandria, nor Basil, nor Gregory of Nazianzus ever quotes the original text.

1. *Commentary on Genesis* i. 1 (*Op. Syr.* I. 116), Ephraem discusses the Hebrew word את:—

הדא ברת קלא קדימות סימא עבריתא איתיה דאיתיה סורייאת
ל. הנו דין לשמיא ולארדתא לו דין ית אלא את

This remark is unobjectionable.

2. *Gen.* i. 2. He endeavours to explain the obscure תהו ובהו, according to Severus' *Excerpts*, as follows:—

תהו ובהו · הנו דן צדיא ושהיא בצחחא דין אחרנא אמר
ארעה איתיה הות לא מתחזניתא ולא מתקנתא ולא מתחזניתא
אמר איתיה הות מטל תהומא דמיא הו דקבא הוא וחשיר ליה
מן שית פנירתא בדמות עולא הו דכריך בשלית אבנו מרבעא
דאמיה ולא מתקנתא מטל דלא גליין הוי אפיה.

Schaf sees, in this quotation, a clear proof that Ephraem did not know what תהו ובהו meant. But when we examine the passage in question carefully, we see that the expression צדיא ושהיא, "empty and desolate" is a correct rendering. The next excerpt in Severus, to the effect that the earth was invisible because of the multitude of waters that covered it, and that this invisibility constituted an imperfection, is the expansion of a just idea, but is not intended to be taken as literal exegesis. Ephraem himself, in fact, only says, I. 6:— דאיתיה הות תהו ובהו הנו דין
דשהיא הות וצדיא.

3. *Gen.* i. 21 (I. 18). Ephraem speaks of the Behemoth— Job xl. 15 (10) and Psalm l. (xlix.) 10—as none but a sound

Hebraist could. To me it is inconceivable how Schaf can quote this passage in support of his theory. It runs as follows:—

תנינא דין רוׄבא דאתבריו ואפן ללויתן נבׄא בימא מתמרין
ליה אלׄא לבהמות איוב ביבשא משרא לׄא אף דוד דעבדׄא אמר
דעל אלף טורׄין איתיה מרעיתיה הנודין מרבועיתיה כבר דין
בתר דאתבריו אתפלגו להון אתרׄותא דלויתן נאמר בימא
ובהמות ביבשא.

This rendering of Behemoth is not strange and peculiar, as Schaf supposes. The ancient translators differ as to the meaning. The Septuaginta has, in Psalms and Job, τὰ θηρία (Vulgate *jumenta*). Aquila and Theodotion, in both passages, κτήνη (Field, *Hexapla* II. 76, 173), while the *Peschito* gives in Psalms בעירא ותורא, but in Job only בהמות.

4. Schaf is guilty of a serious error in remarking that Ephraem could have had but a slight acquaintance with Hebrew, seeing that he is forced to have recourse to Syrian roots, in order to explain Hebrew words. His instance is where on Gen. xi. 29 (I. 59) the Father says:—הי דמטל שופרה אתקרית אסכה, "Sara was called Isca because of her beauty." Schaf seems to be unaware that this is an Agadic interpretation which, however, rests on the fact that in the Hebrew word a Syriac root was discerned. *Seder Olam R.* c. II., towards the end, ולמה נקרא שמה יסכה שהכל סכין ביפיה; more definitely in *Megilla*, 14a, and *Sanhedrin*, 69b, יסכה שהכל סכין ביפיה; according to another interpretation, שסכתה ברוח הקדש. (Cp. Gerson, *ib.*, p. 19, who, however, does not cite the passage from the *Seder Olam.*) In languages as closely correlated as Hebrew and Syriac, this mode of exposition is perfectly legitimate. In the *Mechilta* on Ex. xii. 4, תכסו is explained from the Syriac (לשון סורסי). Will any one assert that the author of that interpretation did not understand Hebrew? Why then should this exegesis appear strange when employed by Ephraem, especially as it is obviously homiletic and Agadic, rather than

grammatical? Compare the Syriac derivation of the names of Job's three daughters (Job xlii. 4).

5. *Gen.* xxxvi. 24 (I. 184):—חלף דאשכח מ״א עבריא אמר— אֹשכח גנבֹ״א במדברא. Ephraem's explanation here coincides with that given by Onkelos and the Samaritan version, as is already noted by J. Perles, *Meletemata Peschittoniana,* page 9.

6. In the sermon against the Jews (*Op. Syr.* III. 218), Ephraem translates the words בני ארוני (Gen. xlix. 11) " and his ass, my son." But in his commentary (I. 108, 190) the correct rendering, " the ass's colt " is twice given ; and in the Sermon, too, the same rendering occurs (III. 224). This error, therefore, proves nothing against Ephraem's knowledge of Hebrew, as Schaf himself is inclined to admit.

7. *Deut.* ix. 9 (I. 273). Ephraem says:—איכא גיר דאמר— דצלית דצמית כתיב בעבריא. He had, therefore, read the original text and understood it.

8. *Joshua* xv. 28 (I. 305):—לא כד קורֹ״ה הנו • ובזיותֹ״ה ידעו הנון דפשקו לסורתא מנא איתוהי הי ברת קלא עבריתא בזיותיה סמו. Ephraem exposes a mistake in the *Peschito* and appeals to the Hebrew text.

9. At the beginning of his commentary to the Book of Judges (I. 308), he draws a distinction between the terms שפטים and שבטים which is irreproachable.

10. *Jud.* v. 30 (I. 316) עבריא אמר • חכימֹתא דדרוכהא עני אכותה. It is indeed surprising that he should have understood שרותיה in the sense of concubines. This may, however, be an exegetical licence and not a real mistake.

11. On 1 *Sam.* xxi. 8 (I. 376), ברת קלא עבריתא ינעצר' גוניתא הי לן עם עבריא ומרניאת מתפשקא על מא דסעריז אילין דעצרין לזיתא ולענֹבא. " The word נעצר is common to Syriac and Hebrew. It specially refers to the pressing of grapes and olives." With the imperfect sources at our command we cannot tell that נעצר had not this meaning

in Hebrew. But our author has certainly a right to draw an inference from Syriac to Hebrew.

12. 2 *Kings* iii. 1 (I. 523), he explains the Hebrew term נקד.—נקדא דהרכא אמר כתבא שמאהו דמן עבריא נבה ותורגמיה דיש ל'עותא דענא הנו דמתרסא סונא דענא. No objection can be offered either to the note that here Hebrew and Syriac coincide or to the explanation suggested.

13. 2 *Kings* viii. 18 (1. 539), עבריא דין תוב סוכלא אהרנא והפכא מחוא • הנו • אמר לא מאחא תאחא. This is a studied reference to the Hebrew text.

We deem it unnecessary to give further proofs in support of our assertion, that Ephraem had a considerable knowledge of the sacred tongue.

We now turn to the question: What is Ephraem's relation to the Jewish Agada? After Lengerke, Gaertz and Gerson's thorough investigations, such a question might possibly be deemed superfluous; but such is not the case. That the Father incorporated with his commentaries a mass of Agadas and Midrashim is clear. But how did he come by them? Were his informants contemporary Jews, or Christians of the school of Edessa or Nisibis? All the other Church Fathers, to whom we have referred in this Essay, usually quote Agadas in the name of the Jews. Ephraem never does so. We frequently meet with such phrases as:—אנשין מן ספרא • אנשא מן מפשקונא • אית דאמרין • אנשין אמרו • אנשין איך משלמנותהון • אנשין אמרו מן משלמנותא דקדמיע • ברויא (Lengerke, pp. 14-20), the majority of which refer to the Jews. That he never distinctly names them shows his marked hostility. Hence it is extremely unlikely that any direct communication took place between the Jews and Ephraem. He would scarcely have so far overcome his prejudices as to associate with Jews. Of course, it is conceivable that there may have been two periods in Ephraem's life; one, when he was on intimate terms with Jews, and obtained an extensive acquaintance with their views; another, when he avoided saying anything in their name. This is however, after all, a mere hypothesis, unsupported by historical facts. The question itself we have not sufficient information to settle.

The Agadas found in Ephraem's writings are too numerous to be exhaustively treated within the limits of the present essay. I refer the reader to the works of Lengerke, Graetz and Gerson, and will only quote a few specimens which those investigators have left unnoticed.

I. Comm. in *Exod.* xiv. 24 (*Op. Syr.* I. 215): מפשטא הי כשיטא הות ליה אידיה למשה איך הי דהות מן בתרכן בקרביה דעמלק. Moses, at the passage of the Red Sea, stretched forth his hands in the same manner as he afterwards did in the battle with Amalek. This remark is quite in the Agadic vein, though I have failed to find its parallel in the Jewish authorities.

II. 1 *Kings* iii. 5 (I. 451): אפלא בזנא אחרנא גבדא עבדיא נסכו להון בנשא רחב ורות ומעכא ברת מלכא דגשור Ephraem defends the view that heathen women could only become the wives of Jews after embracing their husbands' creed. Rahab, Ruth, and Maacha, the daughter of the king of Geshur, are given as instances. The Book of Ruth is the authority for the statement in Ruth's case; the Agada in the case of Rahab. Thus T. B. *Megilla*, 14*a*: חולדה הנביאה מבני בניה של רחב הזונה היתה דאגיירה ונסבה יהושע •

T. B. *Sebachim*, 115*b*, ואהר חמשים שנה ארגיירה.

Shir R. on I. 2, רחב שמעה וארגירה.

Ib. on VI. 2, *Exod. R.*, c. 26, הלא שמעה רחב ובאה ודבקה בך.

About Maacha's conversion I could find nothing in the Agada.

III. 2 *Sam.* xi. 14 (I. 408): אנשין מן אמדין דיואב אשתודע מלתא דדויד עם ברת שבע··· וידע הוא עלת קריתה דאוריא··· איתי הכיל לעבדא מדם דארתפקד אלא לאגרדא סמה לותיה וכבר דדמה ושמה דדויד בזורה הו. "Many assert that Joab

discovered David's relations with Bathsheba, and knew why
Urijah had been summoned. He therefore executed the
orders he had received from the king, but preserved the
letter of authorisation, so as to have David's life and repu-
tation at his mercy." Ephraem spins out the legend at
great length. Joab, he tells us, wished to enact, with David,
the rôle of Abner with Ishbosheth. He was also continually under the apprehension that David would call him to
account for Abner's murder. The letter concerning Urijah
would, he thought, save him from death and give him the
upper hand. Here is undoubtedly a genuine Jewish tradition, but I have, unfortunately, been unable to trace it to
Jewish sources.

IV. 2 *Kings* iv. (I. 256):— אמרין דאנתרתא הדא אנרתא
דעובדיא הות הו דבביתא דאחאב בנכסיא תלמידיה דאליא דפצי
אנון למאא נביין··· ובכפנא תרסי אנון···דמיא מן דבא בהו שרכא
יזף כספא מן בית מלכא ודאשתבק בתר מותה חובה לאנרתה
"They say that this woman was the widow of Obadiah,
Ahab's former steward and Elijah's disciple, who had rescued
four hundred prophets from Jezebel's hands and maintained
them during the famine. During the distress he had borrowed money of the royal household, and at his death the
debt was still unpaid." The parallel of this beautiful Agada
is found complete in every detail, in the Jewish sources.
That the woman was Obadiah's wife is stated in the *Targum
Jonathan* on the passage עבדך עובדיה בעלי מית. The
steward's indebtedness is referred to in *Exod. R.*, c. 31:—
כספו לא נתן בנשך זה עובדיה שהיה עשיר אפוטרפוס של
אחאב והוצא כל ממונו לצדקה וזן את העניים והיה לוה בנשך
מיהורם וכו'.
We notice here an even verbal agreement between the
Jewish narrative and that of Ephraem.

V. 2 *Kings* v. 1 (I. 531):— ומן מלתא הדא נסבו אנשין
תחוירתא ואמר (ואמרו?) דהנא איתוהי הו גברא הו דקטליה
ביד נארא דנפק מן אידה תמימאית··· אלא הלין מן תחוירתא
שרירתא גליזין אנון. "Hence many derived the fable that

this [Naaman] was the man who had accidentally slain [Ahab] with an arrow." This noteworthy Agada I could find nowhere else.

VI. 2 *Kings* iv. 35 (I. 529, 530) :—אסברו אנשין מן כפרא
דהן מנינא ראזהו דאלפא שביעיא' דבה מתנחמין כלהון מיהא
ואמרו דזבנא דעלמא לה להנא מנינא תחם ברויה' שבועא גיר
תחום איתוהי מפרשנא דזבנא.

This view of the duration of the earth entirely agrees with the familiar Agada in T. B. *Sanhedrin,* 97a :—תנא דבי
אליהו ששת אלפים שנה הוי עלמא.

A similar tradition in Jerome is treated by Rahmer:— "*Die hebräischen Traditionen in den Werken des Hieronymos*" (Breslau, 1861), p. 22. A multitude of opinions on *Chiliasm* has also been collected from the Church Fathers and Talmudic doctors by Grünwald, *Verhältniss der Kirchenväter zur talmudischen und midraschischen Literatur* (in Königsberger's *Monatsblätter*, p. 102, also separately printed, Jungbunzlau, 1891).

S. Krauss.

DEMETRIOS J. CONSTANTELOS

JEWS AND JUDAISM IN THE EARLY
GREEK FATHERS (100 A.D. - 500 A.D.)

There are very few books which deal with the attitude of the Greek Fathers and Ecclesiastical writers toward Jews and Judaism. A few broad surveys that exist[1] are limited in scope and chronology. They are hardly adequate to vanquish old myths and stereotypes. Thus the cliché is perpetuated that the Greek Fathers were anti-Semitic, intolerant, and narrow-minded. May I state from the outset that, in my opinion, it is an error to accuse the Greek Fathers of being "anti-Semitic." Anti-Semitism in a modern context was foreign to the Greek Fathers.

We need a series of specialized studies, such as the recent *Origen and the Jews,*[2] before a synthesis on the Greek Fathers and Judaism is even attempted. To draw conclusions from inferences and general statements is to perpetuate misunderstandings. The problem with themes like the present is, indeed, how to interpret various sermonary pronouncements and rhetorical remarks made by different authors, for diverse occasions and for a variety of audiences in the course of many centuries.

"Jews and Judaism in the Early Greek Fathers" is a very large topic, and it cannot be treated exhaustively in the confines of a conference of this nature. Therefore, what I have to offer is only an overview. For our purpose I have selected Greek Fathers and ecclesiastical writers of different geographical areas and of diverse theological schools in the first five centuries of our era.

The attitude of the Greek Fathers toward Jews and Judaism should be examined in the context of the religious climate and the historical milieu in which they lived. The chronological period between the Apostolic Fathers and the Chalcedonian

A paper delivered at tha annual Conference of Christians and Jews in Philadelphia, Pa., May, 1977.

1.   Robert Wilde, *The Treatment of the Jews in the Greek Christian Writers of the First Three Centuries* (Washington, D.C., 1949). For a comprehensive summary of the attitude of the Greek Fathers toward Jews and Judaism see also A.C. McGiffert, *Dialogue between a Christian and a Jew* (New York, 1889), pp. 1-20.

2.   N.R.M. deLange, *Origen and the Jews* (Cambridge, 1976).

Fathers was a period of cosmogonic events. Political upheavals, social changes, intellectual reorientations, the quest for new moral and spiritual values, the crisis of the third century and breakup of the unity of the Mediterranean world, and the decline of the ancient and emergence of the medieval mind affected the psyche and the outlook of all. One crisis after another gave rise to eschatological expectations and the search for scapegoats. Religious antagonisms, conversions, polemical and apologetic controversies, intolerance and theological self-righteousness had replaced the religious syncretism and tolerance which prevailed for several centuries in the Hellenistic and Roman worlds. Jewish exclusiveness was inherited by Christianity, which had come to claim possession of absolute truth and of a special election. In the struggle between Christianity, Judaism, and the Greco-Roman pantheon, Judaism was humiliated, Greek and Roman paganism vanished and went underground to reemerge later in cultic forms, while Christianity emerged as the victor and the dominant religion of the Western world.

The Greek Fathers were the product of those transitional years, and they bear all the characteristics of the mind and the ethos of the times in which they functioned. It can be stated from the outset that only a few of the Greek Fathers wrote systematic diatribes against or apologies for the Jews as a people or against Judaism as a religion. Most Greek Fathers incidentally referred to Jews and Judaism. Furthermore, it should be emphasized that at no time were the Jews and Judaism singled out for either kinder or more ruthless treatment than was accorded to other religious minorities and creeds during the first five centuries of our era. Those of the Greek Fathers who dealt with non-Christian subjects and faiths wrote just as much against Jews and Judaism as they wrote against "Hellenes" and Hellenism, pagans, heretics, and schismatics alike. They condemned the "superstitions of the Jews" with as much zeal as they attacked "the gods and the wisdom of the Hellenes"; they opposed Judaism for the same reason that they objected to Greek, Roman, Persian, or any other religious faith.

To be sure, Jews and Judaism were condemned by a number of Greek Fathers but, as far as the Fathers were concerned, the opponents of Christianity were not only the Jews and Judaism but every non-Christian and non-Christian religion and creed. The Greek Fathers did not single out Judaism, but they made the whole non-Christian world their target. Their hostility, whether in the form of a mild antipathy or violent reaction, was directed toward all the non-Christian world. The Jewish nation, however, was condemned because it had rejected Jesus, who was perceived by the Jewish Christians as the Messiah. The Christian Community was born in the bosom of Judaism, and yet it was repudiated and persecuted by the Jews. When Christians and Jews separated and each community followed its own course, polemics were initiated by both sides.

Evidence confirms that we cannot speak of one uniform or monolithic position of the Greek Fathers toward Jews and Judaism. There were various and diverse attitudes and stands not only among the Greek Fathers collectively, but also among the Fathers of the same ecclesiastical climate, the same theological school, and the same geographical district. Thus there were differences among the Apostolic Fathers, the Apologists, the Alexandrians, the Antiochians, the Cappadocians, and so on. Notwithstanding the diversity, there are certain common denominators that underlie their treatment of Jews and Judaism.

Not all Jews were invariably criticised or condemned. After all many of them were Christians. Few Greek fathers held all Jews collectively responsible or guilty for the death of Jesus. When Jews were condemned, they were blamed because even though they had enjoyed the favor and the trust of God, they had betrayed the Almighty by persecuting his messengers, the prophets. There was both pity for and denunciation of those Jews who stubbornly refused to recognize, in the person of Jesus, the expected Messiah. Several Fathers criticised the Jews for arrogance and exclusiveness, for self-righteousness and superstition.

Concerning Judaism as a religion, the Greek Fathers viewed it as the most important vehicle of God's revelation to mankind before Christ. But for them, Judaism had fulfilled its propaedeutic mission, and it was expected to give way to Christianity. Certain fathers attacked Judaism for its rituals, sects, celebrations, and practices, such as the rite of circumcision, the Trumpets of the New Year, the Tabernacle, the Fasts, the charms, and amulets. But as a whole, Jews and Judaism fared

much better in the writings of the Greek Fathers than the pagan
Hellenes, the heretics, the Manichaeans, and other religious
minorities and creeds.

The Jews as a people and Judaism as a religion are either
ignored or seldom mentioned by the Apostolic Fathers. When
they are noted, they are usually discussed in connection with
the Judaizer Christians. While the Apostolic Fathers drew some
of their teachings from several Old Testament books, they did
not feel that they borrowed from the Jewish heritage for they
considered the events and the personalities of the Old Testament of universal significance and as a patrimony of their own
heritage.

Clement of Rome writes nothing negative about Judaism. In
fact, he finds in Old Testament personalities prototypes of the
virtuous life, peace, and harmony. Prophets are highly regarded
and are called *"Leiturgoi charitos"* or "servants of grace."[3] Even
though there was a suspicion, if not a conviction, that Jews
provoked in part the persecution of the Christians under
Domitian, Clement makes no use of the rumors. The only
repudiation of the Jews that we find in Clement is when he
compares them with the Christians. The latter have replaced the
Jews in the relationship between God and mankind, and Jews
can no longer make claims to exclusiveness and special relationship with God.[4]

Ignatios of Antioch has been one of the most influential of
the Apostolic Fathers. He refers to the Jews and Judaism in
general terms. His specific polemics were directed against the
Judaizer Christians. For example, he attacked their keeping of
the Sabbath instead of the Lord's Day,[5] their dependence on
the tradition and the archives of the ancients instead of the
kerygma about Christ.[6] Once a Jew becomes a Christian, he no
longer needs to observe Judaism. For Ignatios, Judaism and
Christianity were two different faiths, and Christianity was the
older of the two because Christ as God pre-existed the Patriarchs, Moses, and the Fathers of Judaism. He emphasized

3.   *First Epistle to the Corinthians* 4.7-18.

4.   Ibid., 29, 30; cf. Stanley S. Harakas, "The Relationship of Church and
Synagogue in the Apostolic Fathers," *St. Vladimir's Seminary Quarterly*. 11.3 (1967).
124-26. Wilde.

5.   *Magnesians* 9:1.

6.   Ignatios, *Philadelphians* 8:3.

that since Christianity antedated Judaism, it did not base its faith on Judaism but Judaism relied on Christianity.

Since Christianity is all encompassing and supersedes Judaism, Ignatios advised: "Should anyone expound Judaism, do not listen to him. It is preferable, surely, to listen to a circumcized man preaching Christianity than to an uncircumcized man preaching Judaism." The task of both, the uncircumcized and the circumcized, was to preach Christ.[7] Therefore it is absurd to talk of Jesus Christ and at the same time to practice Judaism, observing the rituals, keeping the Sabbath, honoring tradition.

Everyone who professed faith in God was in a state of grace and a Christian, even though he lived before the incarnation of Christ. Thus the Old Testament prophets, who lived in accordance with the ways of Christ, who announced His coming, who hoped in Him, who were persecuted for Him, "won the full approval of Him."[8] They were Christians before the coming of Christ.

Along with the prophets, Jesus, too, was persecuted and crucified, but Ignatios did not place the blame on any one person or people. The crucifixion was part of God's plan, and the purpose of Jesus' death was to draw to Himself saints from among all nations, Jews as well as Gentiles.[9] Ignatios viewed Judaism, especially the prophets, as God's instruments for the salvation of humankind, but mankind's expectations have found their fulfillment in Christ.[10] Ignatios' understanding of Judaism appears like a refrain in the writings of many Christian authors.

It can be said that the prototype for Ignatios and other Fathers, in their attitude towards Jews and Judaism, was Paul—the Hellenized Jew, citizen of the Roman Empire—who had stood above Hellenism, Judaism, and Rome. Like Paul, they attacked the literal interpretation of the law and saw in Christ the fulfillment of all prophecies and God's promises. Even though the *Ekklesia* and the *Synagoge* were rivals, the early *Ekklesia* was a reformed *Synagoge*. The Fathers were concerned less with condemnation of the Jews and more with the need to

7.   Ignatios, *Philadelphians* 6.

8.   Ignatios, *Magnesians* 8 and 10.

9.   Ignatios, *Smyrneans* 10.

10.   Ignatios, *Magnesians* 9:1-2.

transform Judaism in the light of Christianity.

The author of a tract on Judaism which has survived under the name of Barnabas is one of the harsher repudiators of Judaism. The unknown author extensively used the allegorical method and was greatly influenced by Philo the Jew. He is over-zealous in his Christian faith and seeks to demonstrate that the Jews misinterpreted the law because they interpreted it literally. Even though scholarship has not established the author's identity, his use of the allegorical method and Philo's influence indicate that he came from Alexandria and that he might have been a convert from Judaism. Let us note in passing that some of the harshest attacks on Jews and Judaism came from Jewish converts to Christianity.

Another Apostolic father, the anonymous author of the Epistle to Diognetos, is critical of both Jews and Judaism, but he is no more caustic toward Jews and Judaism than he is toward the Greeks and Greek religion. He acknowledges that the Jews are different in the sense that they believe in one God. But their sacrifices, their attachment to ritual, their superstitions, and their burnt offerings make them in no way better than those who show the same respect to deaf-mute images. Further-more the author ridicules the tedious Jewish attitude toward food, their superstitious attitudes toward the Sabbath, and their pride in circumcision, the feast of the new moon, and other practices. He writes:

> And what does it deserve but ridicule to be proud of the mutilation of the flesh [circumcision] as a proof of election, as if they were, for this reason, especially beloved by God? And their attention to the stars and moon, for the observance of months and days, and for their arbitrary distinctions between the changing seasons ordained by God, making some into feasts, and others into occasions of mourning—who would regard this as proof of piety, and not much more of foolishness.[11]

The anonymous author considered many Jewish practices silly and condemned the Jews for deceit, fussiness, and pride. To what degree that author was well-informed about Jewish practices in the second or the third century, we cannot discuss here. The fact is that here we have a panegyric on Christian

11. *The Epistle to Diognetos* 3, 4.

beliefs and character and an exposition of the inadequacies of both the Greek and Jewish religions. The Greeks were condemned for foolishness and the Jews for superstition and, in a way, for foolishness, too. Both nations are guilty of persecuting the Christians. "They are warred upon by the Jews as foreigners and are persecuted by the Greeks who . . . cannot state the cause of their enmity."[12]

The Jews were invariably condemned when they sided with the Roman authorities and the gentiles in the early persecutions of the Christians.[13] In some of those persecutions the Jews are described as more fanatic and "extremely zealous" in assisting in the work of the persecutors.

The author of the *Didache*—The Teaching of the Twelve Apostles—speaks of the break between the Christian *Ekklesia* and the Jewish *Synagoge* and indicates that a widening gulf separates them but he does not indulge in any anti-Jewish or anti-Judaism statements.[14]

The first systematic and the oldest apology for Christianity and repudiation of the Jews is "The Dialogue with Trypho" by Justin the Philosopher and Martyr. Justin's concern is to defend Christianity and explain it to both Jews and Hellenes. For Justin the Old Testament had a propaedutic purpose and the Mosaic law only a temporary jurisdiction. In discussing the Old Testament, Justin selects passages which indicate that Israel was rejected by God and the "Gentiles" were chosen in Israel's place. He writes that the truth is to be found with Moses and the prophets, but vestiges of the true knowledge of God can be found in the teachings and writings of the Greek philosophers and thinkers as well.[15]

While some early apocryphal writers, such as the author of the Gospel According to Peter, place the responsibility for the death of Jesus exclusively on the Jews, Justin placed the blame on the demons who blinded and instigated the Jews to inflict the sufferings on Jesus.

Among the early writers of Alexandria, Origen was the most

12. Ibid.

13. *Martyrdom of Polycarp* 12, 13.

14. *Didache* 8:3, 8:1; cf. Harakas, pp. 126-27.

15. For Justin's attitude toward the Mosaic law see the penetrating monograph of Theodore Stylianopoulos, *Justin Martyr and the Mosaic Law* (Scholars Press, 1975). For Justin's attitude toward the Jews see pp. 32-44.

prolific and the most tolerant of all. Modern scholarship on the subject confirms Origen's sympathies and debt to Judaism. Origen personally knew several Jewish teachers of his time. He makes use of Jewish methods in his exegesis of the Old Testament and gives a sympathetic view of the Jews and their relations with non-Jews. Modern scholarship reveals that there is a substantial influence of Jewish thought on Origen.[16] The Jews have a long tradition of Biblical exegesis, and Origen as well as other Biblical commentators borrowed from Jews in their interpretation of the Old Testament. But in certain areas, especially in their interpretation of prophecy, the Greek Fathers went far beyond Jewish exegesis.[17]

The attitude of several Church Fathers changed after Christianity became the state religion in 392 under Theodosios I. The most polemical of them came from cities or districts with large Jewish populations—Antioch, Caesarea in Palestine, and Alexandria. John Chrysostom, the fiery preacher of Antioch, Eusebios of Caesarea, and Cyril of Alexandria devoted special treatises and wrote extensively about Jews and Judaism. On the one hand they tried to protect their own flock from Jewish influences, and on the other they intended to make converts of the Jews.

St. John Chrysostom, as presbyter in Antioch, delivered many sermons in which he is critical of the Jews as a people. In fact, Chrysostom was more critical than most Greek Fathers from any geographical region. He criticized the Jews for pride, arrogance, malice, vainglory, hypocrisy, betrayal and ingratitude, covetousness, exclusiveness, and reliance on their descent. John's arguments are based not only on the fact that they did not receive Christ but also on the treatment that the Old Testament prophets received from them. He condemned their pride and arrogance which, in his eyes, had no justification. For example, Chrysostom exclaimed in the following words: "Why do you exalt yourself, O Jew? Why are you so arrogant? You, like all the world, are guilty, and, like others, are placed in need of being justified freely." He reminds the Jews of Antioch that "pride is the beginning of sin" and "every one who is proud in heart is an abomination to the Lord," citing the books of

16. N.M.R. deLange, pp. 1-2.
17. Ibid., pp. 133-35.

Ecclesiastes and the Proverbs (Eccles. 10:13; Prov. 16:5).[18]

For their haughtiness and pride, resulting from their belief that they were the chosen people of God, as well as for parading Abraham's name as evidence of their origin and of their virtue, the Jews were ridiculed by churchmen such as Chrysostom. These evil attributes were considered to be the source of God's displeasure and of the troubles that the Jews had with other nations.[19] To what degree the Jews of Chrysostom's times behaved arrogantly and how much of Chrysostom's condemnation rests on undisputed evidence are questions beyond the purpose of this paper. Nevertheless, Chrysostom relied on the words of Jesus, who himself condemned repeatedly the continual references and appeals of his compatriots to their ancestry and to Abraham in particular. Actually, Chrysostom was repeating a well established stereotype.

Even though Chrysostom did not attribute the guilt for the crucifixion of Jesus to all Jews, he described Jewish justice in the trial of Jesus before the chief priest Caiaphas as perverted.[20] He condemned the Jews at the trial who cried out to Pilate "His blood be on us, and on our children" (Mat. 27:25), but he did not accept it as a curse which affected the life of later generations. In the words of Chrysostom: "The lover of man, though the Jews acted with so much madness, both against themselves and against their children so far from confirming their sentence upon their children, confirmed it not even on them... and counts them worthy of good things beyond number."[21] Nevertheless, Chrysostom regarded the Jews present at the trial and the crucifixion as "authors of the spiteful acts done by the [Roman] soldiers... becoming accusers, and judges, and executioners."[22]

It should be noted that Chrysostom was not less critical of Hellenes or heretics. His criticism emanated from his desire to see all in the fold of the Christian *Ekklesia*, to see "the heathen and the Jews... come to the right faith."[23] There is very little

18. John Chrysostom, *Homilies on St. John*, No. 10.2.

19. John Chrysostom, *Homilies on the Gospel of St. Matthew*, No. 3.3.

20. Ibid., No. 84.2.

21. Ibid., No. 86.2.

22. Ibid., No. 87.1.

23. Ibid., No. 28.19-20.

evidence that Chrysostom's condemnation of the Jews was motivated by the crucifixion. For him, the rejection of Christ as the Messiah meant rejection of Moses and the Prophets.

Chrysostom's homilies against the Jews were intended primarily for his Christian flock and only incidentally for Jews. It should be noted that when Chrysostom delivered his famous homilies, the Jews of Antioch were still an influential power engaged even in proselytism.[24] Chrysotom tried to protect his flock from their influence, and in his pastoral zeal he was driven to hyperbole.

Chrysostom wrote, of course, a specific but incomplete treatise against the Jews. But this, too, was not intended exclusively for them. The Greek name of his essay is translated into English as "A Demonstration to Jews and Greeks That Christ Is God, From the Sayings Concerning Him Everywhere in the Prophets." In this essay Chrysostom writes that the Jews have been punished for their rejection of the Messiah and for their treatment of Christ.[25]

Another Antiochian, who wrote a special diatribe against the Jews, was Theodoretos, who became bishop of Cyrus. His treatise, however, is lost. It is only from surviving letters that we can infer what he had to say about the Jews. The main purpose of his *Contra Judaeos* was to show "that the prophets foretold Christ."[26]

Perhaps the most zealous polemicist among the Greek Fathers not only against Jews, Judaism, Hellenes, and Hellenism but against all heretics, schismatics, and opponents was Cyril of Alexandria. His intemperate polemic against paganism and Judaism, as well as other dissidents, is evident in many of his writings, especially in his Paschal Letters.[27] He was uncharitable not only to Jews, pagans, Novatians, and other non-Christian faiths and Christian heresies, but also to adversaries and theological antagonists. He was responsible for the Greek philosopher Hypatia's death as he was responsible for the expulsion of the Jewish inhabitants of Alexandria.[28]

24. Cf. Socrates, *Eccl. Hist.* 7.16, 17.

25. *Homilies*, P.G. 48:843-942.

26. Epistle 145.

27. P.G. 77:401-982.

28. Socrates, *Eccl. Hist.* 7.12, 13.

Some of the Fathers did not write directly against Jews and Judaism, and though they glow with enthusiasm for Christianity they do not indulge in any systematic polemics. For example, Eusebios of Caesarea is critical of Judaism, but he wrote against Judaism in order to answer accusations of the Jews that the Christians accepted Judaism's blessings promised for the Jews themselves without accepting the obligations of the law. But for Eusebios the Mosaic Law was given as a temporary economy, to serve as the guide for a transition between the Age of the Patriarchs and the Age of Christ.[29] Even these observations were not directed as a polemic against the Jews but the whole treatise of *Demonstratio Evangelica* was aimed at Porphyry's essay *Against the Christians.*

Certain Greek Fathers such as Athanasios[30] and Basil viewed Judaism as a Trojan Horse which tried to infiltrate Christianity and undermine its doctrines of the Trinity or the divinity of Christ through heresies that derived from it. To deny the divinity of Christ meant to deny the possibility of the divination of man through Christ. The God-made-man event meant the man-made-God result. Christian heresies such as Sabellianism and Monarchianism drew their arguments from Judaism. They stressed the Monarchy of God the Father and taught that Jesus is either a manifestation of the God of the Old Testament in the New Testament, or a power of the Old Testament God. But denial of the incarnation of God meant denial of the deification of man.

The early Fathers of the Eastern Roman Empire, thought of Greek origin or of Greek cultural and intellectual background, or simply Greek speaking persons, viewed Christianity as a faith and way of life above racial and cultural boundaries. As religious persons they were neither Greek nor Jewish. For them Greeks and Jews were united in the Messiah, who destroyed the enmity between the two. As the cosmopolitan Paul of Tarsus (a Hellenized Jew, citizen of Rome) wrote to the small Greek Christian Community of Ephesos: "Remember that at one time you Gentiles in the flesh . . . were . . . alienated from the Commonwealth of Israel . . . But now in Christ Jesus . . . you have been brought near to us in the blood of Christ . . . He has made us both one, and has broken down the dividing wall of

---

29. *Demonstratio Evangelica* 1 and 2.

30. Athanasios, *Against the Arians* 1.38.

hostility, ...that he might create in himself one new human being in place of the two, so making peace, and might reconcile us both to God in one body through the cross, thereby bringing the hostility to an end" (Eph. 2:11-16).

On the whole, the attitude of the Greek Fathers toward Jews and Judaism was determined by the New Testament writings. Christians represented the new breed, the reborn humanity, and it was on that basis that church Fathers condemned all those who stubbornly refused to see "the new humanity" and insisted on the old dividing wall between Greeks and Jews, Gentiles and Israelites.

To summarize: The Jews as a people were treated no differently from other people. Judaism as a religion introduced by Moses had only a temporary mission. The law of Moses was given as a propaedeutic instrument, while the law of Christ was perceived as the new and eternal covenant with universal jurisdiction. The old Israel of the Old Testament betrayed the trust of God, who removed his promises and replaced the old with the new Israel, the believers and followers of Christ.

According to the collective mind of the Greek Fathers,[31] Christian truth antedates Christ. The Old Testament prophets, as well as some Greek philosophers and thinkers who wrote about the Logos, were Christians before Christ. Thus Jews and Greeks were admonished to dispense with their old beliefs and practices and adopt the new dispensation. It was under the influence of this mind that the Greek Fathers expected both "gentiles" and "barbarians" to merge and become a new humanity, "a chosen race, a royal priesthood, a holy nation."[32]

The Persecutions: some Links between Judaism and the Early Church[1]

by W. H. C. FREND

University Lecturer in Divinity and Fellow of Gonville and Caius College, Cambridge

Each generation of historiographers has had its own interpretation of the persecutions. In their hour of triumph in the years following the Council of Nicaea, Christians in both halves of the Roman Empire looked back to these events as the heroic age of the Christian faith. The sufferings of the Church were linked to the sufferings of the children of Israel[2] and this time, too, anti-Christ and his abettors, the pagan emperors, their officials and the mobs had been worsted. Like the Egyptians they had perished miserably. But, as so often happens, victory dissolved the common bonds which united the victors. In the next centuries the relations between Church and State in the East and West were to follow different paths. In the East the 'martyrdom in intention'[3] of the monastic life tended to replace the martyrdom in deed in opposition to the emperor. In the West, the martyr tradition was to underline that same opposition. Tertullian, Hilary, Ambrose, Gregory VII, Boniface VIII embody a single trend of ideas extending over a thousand years.

If one seeks to trace back these ideas to their origins, one is at once thrown into the long drawn out debate on the relations between early Christianity and the Roman Empire. 'Coercitio' or 'institutum neroniarum', the protagonists of each have left their mark on three-quarters of a century of historical writing.[4] But the approach is narrow, and it is noticeable that even Grégoire[5] and his pupil Moreau,[6] in two of the latest assessments of the persecutions, have not sought to enlarge it significantly. It is, moreover, difficult to accept, because it appears to isolate one

---

[1] I would like to acknowledge the advice I have received from G. E. M. de Ste. Croix in preparing this article.

[2] Paulus Orosius, *Historia adversum Paganos*, C.S.E.L., v, vii. 27. Cf. *Liber Genealogus* (*Chronica Minora*, i. 196, ed. Mommsen). Seven persecutions before the coming of Antichrist—a Donatist view.

[3] The phrase is taken from the seventh-century novel, *Barlaam and Joasaph* (ed. Woodward and Mattingley, xii. §103). Monasticism arose 'from men's desire to become martyrs in will that they might not miss the glory of them that were made perfect by blood'.

[4] See the brilliant summary by A. N. Sherwin White, 'The Early Persecutions and Roman Law again', *J.T.S.*, N.S. iii (1952), 199–213.

[5] Henri Grégoire, 'Les Persécutions dans l'Empire romain', in *Mém. de l'Académie royale de Belgique*, Cl. des Lettres, xlvi, fasc. i, 1951.

[6] J. Moreau, *La Persécution du Christianisme dans l'Empire romain*, Mythes et Religions, Paris 1956.

141

particular aspect of the problem which a militant, apocalyptic and monotheistic religion presented to the Mediterranean world. The initiative was not always on the pagan side. Persecution had its counterpart in martyrdom, and the consideration of the one cannot be divorced from consideration of the other. Without the suffering and the death of the righteous at the hands of earthly rulers the Messianic Age would not dawn nor would the Second Coming take place. In addition, the emphasis on the legal and official aspects of the persecutions tends to ignore the background of long-standing and endemic religious hatred in the cities of the Hellenistic East, which the Christians inherited. As Grégoire points out, up to the time of Origen the Christian mission was essentially Greek, even in the Western provinces of the Empire.[1] If one understands the nature of these hatreds, one may be well on the way towards understanding the relations of the Church and the pagan world in the first two centuries. We will try to show how some of the elements of the crises in which the Church was embroiled during that period were present in the antagonism of Jew and Greek in the previous era. Moreover, part of the confusion over the legal status of Christians may possibly have its origins in the different standing enjoyed by Jews in Rome and in the Hellenistic East respectively. We will try to understand the history of the early Christian mission as a continuation of the great internal problem which confronted the Roman Empire, namely the containment of Judaism.

As Casey has recently stated, in a discussion on the origins of Gnosticism, 'however much philosophy may have softened the blow, conversion to Christianity involved submission to the Jewish way of conceiving the origins of the universe and much of the history of mankind.'[2] This appears to be true in the first two centuries, both as regards the outward organisation and outlook of the Christians,[3] and more important from our point of view, as regards the attitude of the provincials towards them. Though the writer of the Letter to Diognetus could claim justifiably that Christians had abandoned the fussiness and ritualism of Jewry,[4] many of those things which interested Christians most could hardly be understood apart from current Jewish usage. Let us take two examples out of many. For instance, it seems evident that as late as A.D. 170 the Christians in the province of Asia continued to observe the Jewish Passover, and that the recently published Homily on the Passion of Melito of Sardis is to be regarded as a Paschal Haggadah closely parallel to the type used by Jews to-day.[5]

[1] H. Grégoire, op. cit., 18.
[2] R. P. Casey, 'Gnosis, Gnosticism and the New Testament' in The Background of the New Testament and Eschatology, ed. W. H. Davies and D. Daube, 1956, 56.
[3] The literature on this subject is very extensive. Here one would direct attention to F. Gavin, The Jewish Antecedents of the Christian Sacraments, S.P.C.K., 1928; C. W. Dugmore, The Influence of the Synagogue upon the Divine Office, Oxford 1944; T. G. Jalland, The Origin and Evolution of the Christian Ministry, London 1948, iv, and the paper by Gerh. Loeschke, Jüdisches und Heidnisches im Christlichen Kult, Bonn 1906.
[4] Ep. ad Diognetum (ed. Kirsopp Lake), iv. 6.
[5] F. L. Cross in a paper read to the Cambridge Theological Society on 28 February 1957, and summarised in the Cambridge University Reporter lxxxvii. No. 45, 1957, p. 1468.

142

Nearly half a century later the dispute between Callistus and Tertullian on the ability of the Church to forgive deadly sins had an equally synagogal background. These sins, idolatry, apostasy and bloodshed are just those which in A.D. 132 Rabbi Akiba had defined as ones to be avoided, if necessary, by martyrdom.[1] That is, they were sins against God for which there could be no earthly forgiveness. The problem in A.D. 220 was whether the Christian Church should continue to maintain the Jewish standpoint or not, and the victory of Callistus was a significant step along the road of full emancipation from Judaism.

Though the authorities had made a clear distinction between Christians and Jews since A.D. 64, that did not prevent them from associating them both as adherents of a single monotheistic creed springing from the same root and potentially hostile to Greco-Roman society.[2] Thus in A.D. 202 Septimius Severus forbade proselytism to Judaism and Christianity alike.[3] Celsus, writing some twenty-five years earlier, assumed that Christians were primarily rebels against Judaism.[4] Galen follows the same line when he brackets 'the followers of Moses and the followers of Christ' as people on whom rational argument was a waste of time.[5] These indications suggest that an effort to consider the general problem of the persecutions within the framework of the relationship between Judaism and the Ancient World has at least the merit of being the way in which its inhabitants were wont to regard Christianity.

This accepted, the story of the persecutions should begin not with Nero but with the Maccabees. The great struggle between the Jews and the Seleucid kings foreshadows the characteristic outlook of the Jews and Christians, on the one hand, and the authorities and their supporters on the other. These outlooks persist to a remarkable degree down to the conversion of Constantine. For, whatever the incidental causes of the conflict,[6] such as the greed of Antiochus IV, his ill-advised interference in a purely internal Jewish quarrel, or his desire to punish specific acts of Jewish disloyalty, the issue came to be dominated by religion. Both the earlier and later Diaspora traditions, represented by II and IV Maccabees respectively, and the Palestinian tradition enshrined in I Maccabees make this quite clear. Antiochus's edict of 168/67 B.C. had as its object 'that they (the Jews) should forget the Law and change the ordinances' (I Macc., i. 49) or 'that they should leave the law of their fathers' (II Macc., vi. 1)

---

[1] L. Finkelstein, *Akiba: Scholar, Saint and Martyr*, New York 1936, 261. The question was a burning one, and Akiba's view was upheld by a majority vote only at the synod of Lydda in 135. *Talmud Babli*, Sanhedrin, ii. 74a (ed. Epstein, London 1935, 502).
[2] For a trace of this view, perhaps taken direct from Tacitus, see Sulpicius Severus, *Chronicon* (ed. Halm, C.S.E.L., i) ii. 30. 7.
[3] Spartian, *Vita Severi*, 17. 1.
[4] Celsus in Origen, *Contra Celsum* (ed. Koetschau, tr. H. Chadwick), ii. 1 and ii. 4.
[5] Galen, *De Differentiis Pulsuum* 3, cited from G. Waltzer, *Galen on Jews and Christians*, Oxford 1949, 37 ff. Cf. Origen, *Contra Celsum*, iv. 23.
[6] For emphasis on the political aspects of Antiochus's measures, see E. Bickermann, *Der Gott der Makkabäer*, Berlin 1937, and a corrective by J. Dancy, *1 Maccabees: a Commentary*, Oxford 1954.

143

or, in detail, 'that each individual of the nation should taste unclean food through tortures and abjure Judaism' (IV Macc., iv. 26). The penalty for disobedience was death. But in the eyes of the Jew the name of God was being blasphemed (II Macc., viii. 4) and he, like the Christian after him, knew that he must give his life for the sanctification of the Name.[1]

The object of the pagan rulers is portrayed as securing abjurations (ἐξόμνυσθαι τὸν 'Ιουδαισμόν).[2] This would be involved by the public (b'parhesia) transgression of the prohibition of idolatry coupled with the profanation of the divine name. The same means were employed by the Alexandrines against Jewesses in the great pogrom of A.D. 38.[3] The objective was, therefore, identical with that of the magistrates conducting trials of Christians. For a Hierocles in Bithynia during the Great Persecution[4] or for a Carthaginian magistrate in Tertullian's time the moment of triumph was when the Christian recanted.[5] The story of the Maccabees, too, shows that in certain circumstances the profession of Judaism could be a crime. In II Macc., xiv. 38–46 Razis is actually accused of Judaism and prefers to anticipate his fate by committing suicide. The case does not stand alone. In Wisdom, ii. 18–19, there is an interesting passage that can hardly refer to anything else but a trial on the charge of Judaism.[6] Though the identification of the accusing party is uncertain, the words 'Let us examine him with despitefulness and torture . . . let us condemn him with a shameful death' are susceptible of no other meaning. Clearly, in the Hellenistic East the Jewish 'nomen' could be the subject of persecution long before the Romans or Christianity appeared on the scene.

In opposition to this persecuting activity by the Hellenistic rulers one may trace the Jews' glorification of the martyr's lot, and the duty of destroying the symbols of pagan civilisation. This, as recent discoveries at Cyrene have shown, was taken quite literally. In A.D. 115 the great temple of Zeus there was destroyed by the Jewish rebels.[7] The story of the scribe Eleazer as told in II Macc., vi. 24–vii. 42 taught that no deviation from Torah was permitted and, secondly, that the reward for martyrdom was eternal rest with the patriarchs hereafter. The martyr represented Israel. Personally innocent, he expiated the sin of a guilty people. His death hastened the coming of God's mercy. Martyrdom was thus both the means of personal resurrection and an act of atonement on behalf of God's

---

[1] Note for instance, Pesaḥim, 53b (ed. Epstein, London 1935, 261), citing the example of the Three Holy Children. For Christian suffering for the Name, Hermas, Vis., iii. 1. 9 and Simil., ix. 28.
[2] IV Macc., iv. 26 (ed. Hadas, 167–168).
[3] Philo, In Flaccum (ed. Colson), xi. 96.
[4] Lactantius, Div. Inst. (ed. Brandt, C.S.E.L., xxvii. i), v. 11. 15.
[5] Tertullian, Apol., ii. 13.
[6] The expression κρίσιν εἰσενηνεγμένος 'Ιουδαισμοῦ, is strong, suggesting a legal charge, but what the χρόνοις τῆς ἀμιξίας were, which provided the pretext, is uncertain.
[7] Information from R. G. Goodchild, Director of Antiquities in the Kingdom of Libya. The inscription recording the event is being published by Miss J. M. Reynolds.

144

people as a whole. Both these ideas played their part in Christian martyrdom.

One need not be surprised, therefore, that martyrdom came to be regarded as a natural and integral part of the Jewish way of life. In the great crises of A.D. 40 and A.D. 66 Josephus describes in detail how thousands of Jews were prepared to die rather than perform an idolatrous act.[1] No friend of extremism himself, he wrote in c. A.D. 95, 'For it becomes natural to all Jews immediately and from their very birth to esteem those books (of the Law) and, if occasion be, willingly to die for them.'[2] Such conduct could be expected from the citizens of 'a theocracy'.[3] Such tendencies were powerfully reinforced by a development to which Fischel has recently drawn attention, namely, for the figure of the prophet to become merged with that of the martyr.[4] The killing of the prophets had become a commonplace in Judaism by the time the Synoptists wrote (Mt., xxiii. 35–37 and Lk., xiii. 34), and the story of the sawing asunder of Isaiah or the murder of Zechariah may be regarded as typical. These facts, coupled with an apocalyptic view of history involving the utter destruction of the Gentiles, complete the background of the tense and horrible situation which developed in the Hellenistic East in the last two centuries B.C.

Two cultures, religious and secular, confronted one another. One must remember, too, that the lines were not static. Jewish proselytism was proverbial (Mt., xxiii. 15), and successful proselytism was destructive alike of the institutions and family life of the classical world.[5] On the other hand, lapses and outright apostasies from Judaism were not infrequent, and these in their turn released fresh waves of hatred.[6] Our sources, pagan and Jewish alike, leave no doubt as to the intensity of ill-feeling which separated Jew and non-Jew in the Greek East throughout the whole period between the Maccabaean wars and Bar Kochba's revolt. There is no need to overstress the point. Alexandria, Antioch, Damascus, Caesarea, Halicarnassos, Miletus, Ephesus and Laodicea, to mention some examples only, were the scenes of pogroms and acts of repression.[7] Pagan rulers were described as plotting the utter destruction of Jewry in their dominions.[8] One incident out of very many deserves record. In c. A.D. 67 the Jews were massacred at Antioch because they were accused (falsely) of attempting

[1] Particularly, *Antiquities*, xviii. 8 and *Wars*, ii. 10, recording the incidents at Ptolemais and Tiberias in A.D. 40.
[2] Josephus, *Contra Apionem* (ed. Niese, tr. Whiston), i. 8. 42.
[3] Josephus's term: *Contra Apionem*, ii. 16. 165.
[4] H. A. Fischel, 'Prophet and Martyr', *Jewish Quarterly Review*, xxxvii (1946/7), 265 ff. and 363 ff.
[5] The view expressed by Tacitus, *Histories*, v. 5. 2. The Jewish convert 'exuere patriam, parentes, liberos, fratres vilia habere'. For the Christian's similar attitude, Tertullian, *Ad Nationes*, ii. 1 (C.S.E.L., xx. 94 lines 8–12) and *Passio Perpetuae* (ed. Knopf), 3.
[6] See, for instance, III Macc., vii. 10–23 (Hadas, 81).
[7] The situation is described in Philo, *In Flaccum*, iv. 18–xvii. 145 and Josephus, *Antiquities*, xiv. 10 ff., xvi. 2. 3, *Wars*, ii. 18. 1–2 and 7; 20. 2 and vii. 3. 3.
[8] The theme of Esther and III Maccabees.

145

to set fire to the city—an interesting parallel to the accusation against the Christians in Rome three years earlier. Furthermore, the test applied by the magistrates to identify Jews and proselytes was that of sacrifice.[1] The Jews, it was believed, had forfeited their special status and therefore must sacrifice 'ὥσπερ νόμος ἐστὶ τοῖς "Ελλησιν'. 'Sacrifice or die'. Here is the situation which was to be all too familiar in pagan-Christian relations. So also were the charges of 'atheism', 'haters of the human race', 'sacrilegious' and 'ritual murderers', hurled against the Jews[2]. It is not difficult to understand how this pattern of embittered relationships could be transferred to a body which popular opinion regarded as a criminal and dangerous off-shoot of Judaism. The same fears and prejudices which produced the pogroms of the period 170 B.C.–A.D. 135 contributed to the anti-Christian outbreaks in the same areas in the second and early third centuries A.D.

So much for the Hellenistic world. In Rome itself, by contrast, the Jews were in an exceptional position. First, they were only one of a large number of foreign cults which the crowds of immigrants from the east had brought with them from the second century B.C. onwards. Secondly, Jews and Romans begin their association as friends and allies against the Seleucids. Indeed, right through the second and first centuries B.C., Rome found the Jews a useful counterpoise in Asia Minor and later in Syria and Egypt against the perpetual grumbling hostility of the Greek autonomous cities. The protection of valuable Jewish privileges in these cities by Julius Caesar and Mark Antony was the result.[3] Hence, in Rome there was the tendency to regard Judaism as a national cult, albeit an unattractive one, and to apply to it the same regulations as governed other foreign cults.[4] From the outset, however, proselytism among Roman citizens was discouraged, if not actually forbidden. The expulsion of the Jews by the Praetor Peregrinus Cornelius Hispalus in 139 B.C. on the ground that they were 'tainting Roman manners with the worship of Jupiter Sabazius'[5], and the affairs of Fulvia in Tiberius's reign[6], and probably also of Pomponia Graecina in A.D. 57, are illustrations.[7] Such recorded instances were few and far between. Relations between Rome and the Jews were on a different and more cordial plane from those of Jews and Greeks in the Hellenistic East, and the fact was acknowledged in the speech which Josephus puts into the mouth of Titus in A.D. 70 (*Jewish War*, vi. 6. 2). No Greek city would have bestowed even-handed justice on Jews and Isis-worshippers alike as did Tiberius in A.D. 19.[8] Where action was taken against the Jews it was on grounds of acts violating the

[1] Josephus, *Wars*, vii. 3. 3.
[2] For the catalogue of accusations and reproaches showered on the Jews found in classical authors, J. Juster, *Les Juifs dans l'Empire romain*, Paris 1914, 45. n. 1.
[3] Josephus, *Antiquities*, xiv. 8. 3, and xiv. 10.
[4] On Rome's relations with the Jews, E. G. Hardy, *Christianity and the Roman Government*, 1925 ed., ii, and G. J. Foakes Jackson and Kirsopp Lake, *The Beginnings of Christianity*, i. 163 f.
[5] Valerius Maximus, i. 3. 2.
[7] Tacitus, *Annals*, xiii. 32.
[6] Josephus, *Antiquities*, xviii. 3. 5.
[8] Josephus, *Antiquities*, xviii. 3. 4.

146

pax deorum, or disturbing the peace,[1] complaints which could be levelled at other cults besides theirs.

In the first decades of the first century A.D. there is some evidence that, quite apart from the mad act of Caligula directed against the Jews in Palestine, the official friendship between Rome and the Jews was breaking down. In the first place, the rebellious tendencies of the Greeks in Asia Minor were lessening. The cult, first of Dea Roma, and then of Augustus, at last provided them with a focus of religious loyalty. Outside of Alexandria, where the *Acts of the Pagan Martyrs* show how the Roman administration continued to be regarded as anti-Hellenic and pro-Jewish until well into the second century A.D.,[2] the Greek became as loyal to the Imperial idea as any other citizen of Augustus's empire. Thus, Rome no longer needed the Jewish counterpoise. Moreover, the establishment of the Imperial cult for the first time linked the fortunes of Rome with those of Hellenism against the Jews. Then came the Alexandrine riots of A.D. 38 and 40. Claudius's solemn warning to the Jewish embassy of A.D. 41 is significant of what was to follow.[3] After confirming Jewish privileges as they stood in the reign of Augustus, he concluded, 'if they continued to introduce or invite Jews who sail down from Syria and Egypt, thus compelling me to conceive greater suspicion, I will by all means take vengeance upon them as fomenting a general plague on the whole world.'[4] The Jewish threat was now seen as world-wide. Would that of the Christians be regarded otherwise? The Christian Church could hardly have entered on the stage of history at a less favourable moment. Within twenty years the charge of moving sedition among all the Jews throughout the world was to be made against them (Acts, xxiv. 5). Rome's position in the East no longer depended on the loyalty of the Jews; it would hardly require concessions to the 'tertium genus'.

But had Rome the means to hand for dealing with a 'world conspiracy'? Much as modern historians may stress the relevance of measures designed to frustrate the effects of astrologers, magicians, Druids, and other violators of the '*pax deorum*',[5] it is questionable whether these provide the full answer. In the East these measures seem to have been combined with the sanctions long adopted in the Greek cities against 'atheism'. This term was not readily naturalised into Latin usage,[6] but as we shall see, was very relevant with regard to Christianity. It may well form the connecting link between the Roman and Hellenistic legal systems in

---

[1] Suetonius, *Claudius*, 25. 4.
[2] Ed. H. A. Musurillo, *The Acts of the Pagan Martyrs*, Oxford 1954. The *Acta Appiani* may relate to events as late as A.D. 190, while the *Acta Hermaisci* must be Trajanic or later. (Musurillo, 211 and 168).
[3] See H. I. Bell, *Jews and Christians in Egypt*, Oxford 1924, 25.   [4] Ibid.
[5] For the importance of these measures in understanding the attitude of the authorities towards the Christians, see H. Last, 'The Study of the "Persecutions"', *J.R.S.*, xxvii (1937) 80–92 and art. 'Christenverfolgung', *Reallexicon für Antike u. Christentum*, ii. :159 f. and 1208 f.
[6] It is not until Arnobius (*Adv. Gentes*, i. 29) writing at the end of the third century, that the term is used in Latin in the pagan-Christian controversy.

147

dealing with the early Church. In the mind of Dio Cassius writing in the 220s, magic and atheism were the twin dangers threatening the religious peace and therefore the prosperity of the Empire.[1] Misbelief was such an offence in the Hellenistic rather than the Roman world.[2] The Latin 'sacrilegium' implied more positive action—'deos destruere'.[3] Rome left unchanged so many of the characteristic institutions of the Hellenistic East. Like the *angareia*, was not 'atheism' and the public trial before the authorities on grounds of religion another of the legacies of Hellenism to Rome in the administration of the Empire?

How far then does the history of the early Church's relations with the pagan world in fact continue these same developments? Let us first take the meaning attached to martyrdom in the early Church. Here the *praeparatio evangelica* of Judaism seems obvious enough. Similarities of detail apart, such as those illustrated by Fischel in the Jewish and Christian *Acta Martyrum*,[4] the broad development from the one to the other seems undeniable. Complete obedience to God, where necessary in defiance of the authorities, expiatory sacrifice, self-abnegation on behalf of the People, and the reward of blessed immortality in anticipation of the approaching end of the world, are already firmly established ideas. Perhaps it is no accident that the term μαρτυρεῖν or διαμαρτυρεῖν applied to 'blood witness' first occurs in IV Maccabees.[5] The Jewish martyr bore witness to the Law, the Christian to the New Law. Those things which the Jew resisted to the death, such as idolatry, including the eating of 'impure' meats, and blood-shed, including duty in a pagan army, the Christian was to resist also. Yet martyrdom in Judaism was something of a *Hamlet* without the Prince. However much the Law might be regarded as 'pre-existent from Creation' and the 'breath of the Power of God',[6] the Jews' sufferings were in hope and anticipation only. The Law remained impersonal, and for deep, sensitive minds, such as St. Paul's, an 'occasion for sin' rather than for salvation (Rom., vii. 11). In the last resort the Jew died under the impulse of religious nationalism, as a member of a chosen race.[7] It was left to Christianity to extend this impulse to the individual, regardless of race, and eventually purge religion of the purely national element.

It needed the sacrifice and death of Jesus Christ to give the doctrine of martyrdom a permanent validity. The Christian accepted Jesus as Lord, and as 'the one faithful and true martyr',[8] whose death he should

---

[1] Dio Cassius (ed. Melber), lii. 36, 3 (in the mouth of Maecenas): μήτ' οὖν ἀθέῳ τινὶ μήτε γόητι συγχωρήσῃς εἶναι.

[2] See for instance Josephus, *Contra Apionem*, ii. 38. A. B. Drachmann, *Atheism in Pagan Antiquity*, Gyldendal, 1922.

[3] Cf. Apuleius, *Metamorphoses*, ix. 14, and art. Pfaff, *P.W.*, 'Sacrilegium'.

[4] H. A. Fischel, op. cit., 383 ff.

[5] IV Macc., xii. 16, but in the Alexandrine MS. only (Hadas 208), ἡ διαμαρτυρία occurs, however, at IV Macc., xvi. 16 with the implied meaning of 'bearing witness by death' on behalf of the law.

[6] Wisd., vii. 25 and ix. 9.

[7] See G. F. Moore, *Judaism*, ii. 312.

[8] Eusebius, *H.E.*, v. 2. 3, τῷ πιστῷ καὶ ἀληθινῷ μάρτυρι, citing Rev. i. 5 and iii. 14.

148

imitate. He believed that by bearing witness of his faith until death, he would also witness His glory.[1]

It has been urged with some justice[2] that the Passion narrative in St. Luke's Gospel is designed to portray the Ideal Martyr. 'St. Luke's portrait in the Passion story is that of the suffering but faithful servant of God, we may even say, the martyr.' His death atoned, however, not only for the sins of Israel, but those of all humanity (Heb., ix. 28). In St. Mark's account of the Passion, too, Christ prophesies a vision of God's power and glory (Mk., xiv. 62), such as may be found in the *Ascension of Isaiah* (v. 7) or in the account of Stephen's martyrdom in Acts (vii. 55). All three Synoptics recount signs and wonders which accompanied Christ's death, and throughout the New Testament suffering has the eschatological significance that it has in late Judaism. Wars, plagues, the persecution of the faithful on earth will precede the coming of the Messiah. The climax of evil was the immediate herald of the destruction of the heathen world by Christ. The sufferings of Christians would hasten the coming of the Messianic Age, and for that reason St. Paul rejoices in his sufferings (Col., i. 24) and hopes to participate in those of his Master (Phil., iii. 10). His message to the Thessalonians (II Thess., i) contains references to persecutions and sufferings which would precede the Parousia.[3] As Irenaeus stated (*Adv. Haer.*, v. 14.1), Christ's death was a recapitulation of (righteous) effusion of blood from the beginning— once again, the theme of human religious history is of righteous suffering and death. These ideas form one of the links between the Old Dispensation and the New.

Indeed, so long as the Second Coming was believed to be at hand, martyrdom and persecution at whomsoever's hands were bound to play a disproportionate part in the life of the Church. It is quite natural that at the end of the first century martyrdom had come to be accepted as the goal of a Christian life. Ignatius of Antioch begged the Roman Christians not to intercede on his behalf.[4] The martyrs of Lyons more than fifty years later defined a true disciple as one who 'follows the Lamb whithersoever He goeth',[5] i.e. to a martyr's death. But not only did martyrdom atone for sin, it had also become a touchstone of catholic orthodoxy. Ignatius uses it as an argument against his Jewish-Docetic opponents,[6] just as Tertullian does against the Gnostics in the next century.[7] In addition, it has become linked to a whole system of penitential discipline, particularly in the West. It was the supreme counsel of the Holy

[1] See K. Holl, 'Die Vorstellung vom Märtyrer und die Märtyrakte in der geschichtlichen Entwicklung', *Gesammelte Aufsätze*, ii. 71 ff.
[2] R. H. Lightfoot, *History and Interpretation in the Gospels*, 1934, 176. Also D. W. Riddle, *The Martyrs*, Chicago 1931, ch. viii with reference to St. Mark's Gospel.
[3] On this question, see G. Best, *One Body in Christ*, London 1955, 130–136.
[4] Ignatius, *Ad Romanos*, ii and iv. Cf. Irenaeus, *Adv. Haer.*, v. 28. 4.
[5] Eusebius, *H.E.*, v. 1. 10.
[6] Ignatius, *Ad Smyrn.*, iv. 2 and *Ad Trall.*, ix. 1.
[7] Tertullian, *Scorpiace*, passim. Cf. art. by the writer 'The Gnostic Sects and the Roman Empire', *J.E.H.*, v. 1 (1954) 25–37.

149

Spirit. Baptism by water merely prepared the way for suffering and the baptism of blood.[1] The intense belief prevalent in North Africa of the supreme value of martyrdom underlay the baptismal issue between Carthage and Rome, and it was to dominate the Donatist controversy.

For the individual, moreover, martyrdom brought immediate benefits, and here also we find that the Church has built on the well-laid foundations of late Judaism. Like the martyr-prophet of that age, the Christian martyr was credited with visions of divine glory,[2] converse with the Lord,[3] prophetic powers,[4] and immediate entry into Paradise where he would judge his enemies.[5] More than that, he and he alone held the 'claves Petri', the power to bind and loose on earth and hereafter.[6] He was already an angel.[7] Above all, Christ speaks and suffers through him, thus manifesting the type of victorious suffering which would precede the Last Days.[8] The persecutors were faced with the hopeless task of fighting against God.[9] Their methods were merely the means to Christian victory. There was every reason for the Christian to defy the authorities.

And so, one notices in the early Church that same aggressive side to martyrdom that one can see from time to time in Judaism. There was a strong element who agreed with the writer of Revelation rather than I Peter. It was difficult to dissociate Rome from idolatry, and the Christian duty of destroying idols could easily take on an anti-Roman bias. In Asia Minor and Africa at the turn of the third century there were plenty of zealous Christians who were prepared to provoke the authorities and rejoiced at the consequences.[10] But the precedent for voluntary martyrdom had already been established by the young men whom Josephus describes, as boasting of cutting down Herod's Golden Eagle over the gateway of the Temple with the express object of being executed, 'for they would enjoy greater happiness after they were dead'.[11] No Montanist or Donatist asked more.

The extraordinary fact is that, granted the state of exaltation among so many of the early Christians and the firm dogmatic basis for their outlook, so few were put to death. Origen, himself no despiser of the martyr's crown, writing just before the Decian persecution, claimed that

---

[1] *Passio Perpetuae*, iii. 3: 'Mihi Spiritus dictavit: Non aliud petendum ab aqua, nisi sufferentiam carnis'.

[2] Acts, vii. 55; *Acta Carpi* (ed. Knopf), 13. 3 and 39.

[3] *Passio Perpetuae*, 4: 'et ego quae me sciebam fabulari cum Domino'. *Mart. Polyc.*, (ed. Knopf), 1. 2 and 2. 2.

[4] *Mart. Polyc.* (ed. Knopf), 5.

[5] *Passio Perpetuae*, 17; Eusebius, *H.E.*, vi. 42. 5; *Mart. Polyc.*, 19. 2. Cf. Wisd., v. 1 and v. 5. For further references Holl, op. cit., 72–73.

[6] Eusebius, *H.E.*, v. 2. 5; cf. Tertullian, *De Pudicitia* (C.S.E.L., xx), 21.

[7] *Mart. Polyc.*, 2. 3.

[8] Eusebius, *H.E.*, v. 1. 23 (the deacon, Sanctus).

[9] *Acta Saturnini*, 6: 'Peccatis, infelices, adversus Deum facitis.' (P.L., viii. 707).

[10] *Acta Carpi*, 42; *Mart. Polyc.*, 4. Tertullian, *Ad Scapulam*, 5. Cf. *Apol.*, 50. 3 and *De Spect.*, 1.

[11] Josephus, *Wars*, i. 33. 3.

one could easily enumerate the number of martyrs to date.[1] The biggest recorded massacre, that of Lyons in 177, seems to have claimed only 48 victims.[2] In the same period, the numbers of Jewish dead by pogrom and persecution must have run into many thousands. Perhaps this is in itself an indication of the relative importance of the Jewish compared with the Christian problem in the Mediterranean world in the first two centuries.

Is it possible to say, before one leaves the Christian side of our problem, whether these parallels between late Judaism and Christianity were conscious or not? Thanks to the excellent work done by Perler[3] and Surkau[4] on IV Maccabees, it seems that the answer is in the affirmative, that is to say, that late Jewish literature provided the literary models as well as the ideas of some of the earliest Christian *Acta Martyrum*. That the Christians of the first generation were well acquainted with the *Assumption of Moses* and the *Ascension of Isaiah* is well known.[5] More recently, however, detailed studies of IV Maccabees have established what would appear to be the direct influence of this work on the letters of Ignatius, the martyrdom of Polycarp and the account of the martyrdoms at Lyons. The borrowings include style and vocabulary as well as general ideas, and even without following Perler into mazes of linguistic analysis, it is perfectly clear, for instance, that the description of Blandina at Lyons is modelled on the mother of the Maccabaean youths, and that bishop Pothinus finds his prototype in the scribe Eleazer. There seems to be little doubt that with IV Maccabees 'the historian is dealing with one of the roots of early Christian enthusiasm for martyrdom and martyr literature'.[6] The continuity between Jewish and early Christian ideas of martyrdom seems remarkably complete, and to deny the fact, as even Delehaye[7] and Campenhausen[8] have sought to do, merely makes unnecessary difficulties.

We can now go on to the second stage of our argument and investigate possible affinities in the treatment of Jews and Christians by the Imperial and local authorities in the Roman Empire. The Jews, we have seen,

---

[1] Origen, *Contra Celsum*, iii. 8. H. Grégoire, *Les Persécutions*, 12.

[2] H. Quentin, 'La liste des martyrs de Lyon de l'An 177', *Analecta Bollandiana*, xxxix (1921), 113–138.

[3] O. Perler, 'Das vierte Makkabäerbuch, Ignatius von Antiochen und die ältesten Märtyrerberichte', *Riv. di arch. crist.* xxv (1949), 47–72.

[4] H. Surkau, *Martyrien in jüdischer und frühchristlicher Zeit*, Göttingen 1938.

[5] R. H. Charles, *The Ascension of Isaiah*, London 1900, xliv and *Assumption of Moses*, London 1897, lxii.

[6] O. Perler, loc. cit., 64: 'Wir sind an einer Wurzel der altchristlichen Martyrerbegeisterung und Martyrerliteratur'.

[7] H. Delehaye, 'Martyr et Confesseur', *Analecta Bollandiana*, xxxix (1921), 36–64 at pp. 45–46: 'Et pour le dire en passant, nous ne reconnaissons nullement l'influence des idées juives, par l'intermédiaire du livre ii des Macchabées et de certaines légendes des prophètes, sur les Actes historiques des martyrs'.

[8] H. von Campenhausen, *Die Idee des Martyriums in der alten Kirche*, Göttingen 1936, 1: 'Die Idee des Martyriums und die Vorstellung des Märtyrers sind christlichen Ursprungs.'

151

were the victims of constant strife in the Greek cities but were comparatively free from molestation in Rome itself. How far can the same be said of the Christians? The evidence for the first two centuries preserved by Eusebius suggests that this may also have been the case. The Greek cities were obviously the main centres of anti-Christian agitation. By the end of the second century, however, this had extended to other great cities where there was a large Jewish community, such as Carthage.[1] Melito of Sardis is quoted as referring to Hadrian's instructions to the cities of Larissa, Thessalonica and Athens and 'to all the Greeks' that 'no new measures should be taken against us (Christians)'.[2] Eusebius prefaces the account of the persecution at Lyons, where the Christians also seem to be in the main Greek-speaking Asiatic immigrants[3], with the statement, 'In this time the persecution of us in some parts of the world was rekindled more violently by popular violence in the cities.'[4] In Rome after A.D. 64 we hear of isolated denunciations and individual trials, such as that of Justin in A.D. 163, but on the whole, the Christians there seem to have been left alone. Irenaeus's statement that in Rome the 'faithful from everywhere'[5] met, is confirmed by what is known of the careers of figures such as Marcion, Valentinus and Polycarp. And they met and disputed openly. The Church also accumulated property. If the persecution of A.D. 64 had really had the immediate and decisive importance that is claimed for it, one would expect Rome to have been one of the main centres of anti-Christian repression. This does not seem to have been the case. Eusebius clearly regarded Gnostic heresy as a worse danger to the Church in the second century than persecution.[6] Sporadic pogroms in the Hellenistic cities were the feature of the period and continued to be so up to the very eve of the Decian persecution.[7]

It might perhaps be suggested that the policy of the Roman authorities towards the Church was a patchwork of separate and scarcely coordinated ideas. First, in Rome itself there was concern for the maintenance of the *pax deorum*, and the consequent dread of the violation of the Roman gods by the practice of unholy rites and black magic. Secondly, there was a deep-felt loathing for converts to Judaism—the 'national apostates'[8]—and a tendency where possible to fasten the term borrowed from the Greeks of 'atheist' on to them.[9] Added to this, there was the

---

[1] P. Monceaux, 'Les colonies juives dans l'Afrique romaine', *Rev. des Etudes juives* (1902), 1 ff.

[2] Eusebius, *H.E.*, iv. 26. 10.   [3] See Grégoire, op. cit., 20.

[4] Eusebius, *H.E.*, v. 1. 1.   [5] Irenaeus, *Adv. Haer.*, iii. 3. 2.

[6] Eusebius, *H.E.*, iv. 7. 1.

[7] The last great anti-Christian outbreak was that which took place in Alexandria in A.D. 248. Eusebius, ibid., vi. 41. 1 ff.

[8] Mommsen's phrase, in his famous 'Der Religionsfrevel nach römischen Recht', *Historische Zeitschrift*, lxxv (1890), 389–429 at p. 407. See also, his letter in *Expositor* (1893), 1–7, under the title of 'Christianity in the Roman Empire'.

[9] A. Harnack, 'Der Vorwurf des Atheismus', *Texte u. Untersuchungen*, xii. 4 (1903), and Mommsen, art. cit., 393. For the unpopularity of proselytes, Tacitus, *Histories*, v. 5, Juvenal, *Sat.*, xiv. 96 ff., Origen, *Contra Celsum*, v. 41.

152

continuous, bitter hostility of the Jews towards the Christians, which ensured that there would lack neither accusers nor mobs to shout 'down with the atheists' at the appropriate moment.

The affair of A.D. 64 is quite clearly the application of the first of these principles to the problem of Christianity. Coupled with reproaches of 'hatred against the human race' applicable to Jews,[1] one can point to the parallel of the Bacchanal conspiracy. With Last[2] and Sherwin-White[3] we can see common ground between the Republican treatment of the Bacchanals, the Claudian treatment of the Druids and Magi and the Neronian persecution of the Christians. Tacitus's description of the searching out of the Christians in Rome involving an 'ingens multitudo' suggests almost word for word Livy's account of the famous days of 186 B.C.[4] Suetonius's language 'nova et malefica superstitio' indicates magic as the underlying fear of the authorities.[5] So far as one can tell, there was no sacrificial test. The victims are said simply to 'have confessed', and no attempt appears to have been made to secure recantations —no more so than with the Bacchanals. But this great round-up remained a unique event. It was designed as an act of reprisal against a conspiracy or a spectacular *alibi* to cover the tracks of Nero himself.[6] If there had been no other factors to influence the relations between Church and Empire, the Church might soon have gained the status of relative respectability obtained by the Druids and Bacchanals after similar acts of repression. But from the end of the first century onwards the centre of anti-Christian action switches to the Hellenistic world,[7] and there, there were plenty of factors which favoured religious strife. It did not need the precedent of the Neronian persecution[8] to stir up an anti-Christian pogrom.

The basic religious problem which Rome inherited from the Hellenistic governments was the containment of Judaism and its ramifications. These, if our thesis is correct, included Christianity and also the extension of Judaism to neighbouring peoples in Palestine, such as the Samaritans. Whatever villainies they might commit, whatever the results of their frustrated universalist ambitions, the Jews remained a 'people' (an ἔθνος) with a right to their own laws and customs established by antiquity.[9]

---

[1] Cf. Tacitus, *Histories*, v. 5. 2. The Jews were characterised as 'apud ipsos fides obstinata, misericordia in promptu, sed adversus omnes alios, hostile odium'.

[2] See H. Last, 'Christenverfolgung', 1208–1228, and 'The Study of the Persecutions', 88 ff.

[3] A. N. Sherwin-White, 'The Early Persecutions and Roman Law', 211.

[4] Tacitus, *Annales*, xv. 44: 'ingens multitudo'. Livy, xxxix. 13: 'multitudinem ingentem, alterum iam populum esse'.

[5] Suetonius, *Vita Neronis*, 16. Cf. also Pliny's views.

[6] Tacitus, though he did not believe that the Christians actually fired Rome, thought them guilty of something. They were 'sontes et novissima exempla meritos'. See, H. Fuchs's scholarly discussion of the problems arising from Tacitus, *Ann.*, xv. 44, in 'Tacitus über die Christen', *Vigiliae Christianae* (1950), 65–93. Also H. Last, art. cit., 1211.

[7] Cf. Rev., ii. 13 (martyrdom of Antipas).

[8] As suggested by A. N. Sherwin-White, art. cit., 209.

[9] Tacitus, *Histories*, v. 5: 'Hi ritus quoque modo inducti, antiquitate defenduntur.' Also, *Contra Celsum*, vol. 25.

The authorities were prepared to uphold these. But this policy did not apply to their converts and imitators,[1] and this was clearly understood by ordinary Greek provincials of the time. One of the first reactions of the people of Thessalonica to St. Paul's missions was that 'these men being Jews' were teaching practices which were illegal for Romans to observe (Acts xvi. 20–21). Forty years later, the cases of Flavius Clemens and Domitilla provided the classic examples of the charge of Atheism (ἀθεότης) being levelled at Roman citizens who 'had lapsed into Jewish customs'.[2] And not only citizens. There is an interesting passage in Origen, *Contra Celsum*, ii. 13 in which Origen, in a somewhat obtuse way, draws attention to the more favourable treatment accorded to Christians in contrast to unauthorised imitators of Judaism. The Samaritans, he points out, who accept Jewish practices 'are put to death on account of circumcision as Sicarii, on the ground that they are mutilating themselves contrary to the established laws and are doing what is permitted to the Jews alone'. Mere evidence of the fact was sufficient warrant for a death sentence. The Christians, however, were given a chance to recant even at the last moment by taking an oath and sacrificing. Small comfort perhaps, but it shows that punishment on religious grounds, where an extension of Judaism was concerned, had its place in third-century Roman practice in the Hellenistic East. Indeed, Roman policy, as illustrated by Antoninus Pius's rescript equating the circumcision of non-Jews with the criminal offence of castration,[3] and that of Septimius Severus[4] aimed against Christian and Jewish proselytism, seems to have been consistent throughout the second century. The background and justification lay in the great revolt of the Dispersion Jews in A.D. 115–117, and the continued disaffection of Jewry in general for a generation after the crushing of Bar-Kochba's rebellion in A.D. 135.[5] In these years 'the King of the Jews' upheld by Zealots and opposed to the authority of the Emperor was no myth.

One can go even further and point to the actual persecution of the Jews by the Romans in moments of crisis during the period A.D. 70–135. Thus, at the end of the desperate Jewish War, Josephus records how in the face of countless tortures the defenders of Masada preferred to be done to death rather than give even the mere appearance of confessing Caesar as lord.[6] The Midrash of the Ten Martyrs referring to the period after the

[1] On this subject, J. Juster, *Les Juifs dans l'Empire romain*, i. 232 ff. and G. La Piana, 'Foreign Groups in Rome during the first centuries of the Empire', *Harvard Theol. Review*, xx (1927), 183–403 at 387 ff.
[2] Dio Cassius, 67. 15; cf. E. T. Merrill, *Essays in early Church History*, 1924, vi.
[3] *Digest*, xlviii. 8. 11. 1 (Modestinus), and Paulus, *Sententiae*, v. 22. 3 for the specific prohibition on pain of exile for Roman citizens. Th. Mommsen, 'Der Religionsfrevel', 409.
[4] Spartian, *Vita Severi*, 17. 1.
[5] Ammianus Marcellinus (ed. Rolfe), xxii. 5. 5. Rabbis in the third century A.D. continued to boast that 'Jews are like wild beasts to the heathen and like doves before God'. Juster, op. cit., 220, n. 8; cf. O. Cullmann, *The State in the New Testament* (Eng. tr. 1957), ii.
[6] Josephus, *Wars*, vii. 10. 1.

154

end of the revolt of Bar-Kochba mentions that Rabbi Ishmael was urged to renounce his faith, but that he refused.[1] Akiba was martyred for teaching Torah when this had been declared illegal.[2] Nathan, the Babylonian Jewish sage, writing of the same period about conditions in Palestine, is reported as saying 'The expression in the Decalogue "Those who love me and and observe my commandments" applies to the people who live in Palestine and give their lives for the Law. "Why art thou being taken to execution?" Because I circumcised my son. "Why art thou being taken to crucifixion?" Because I read the Torah and ate the mazzot. "Why art thou being beaten with a hundred stripes?" Because I took the *lulab*" '.[3] This evidence, taken with Hadrian's other measures[4] against the Jews which precipitated the crisis of A.D. 132 suggests that Rome, when faced by the problems of militant Judaism, reacted in much the same way as had the Seleucid kings three centuries before. Indeed, the continuation in the East of the divine aspects of the Hellenistic monarchs by the Roman Emperors would make this almost inevitable. Religious persecution and trials were not a misfortune reserved for Christians alone.

These facts should put Rome's policy towards the Christians in its right perspective. The 'obstinacy' of the Christians and the fact that they were accused of criminal offences as well, made their case worse. The real complaint against them, however, was membership of an unrecognised Judaistic society engaged in spreading atheism[5] and social disruption.[6] The 'flagitia' alone would not have proved deadly unless linked to more fundamental charges, as the history of the Gnostics in this period shows.[7] More serious was that, while living as members of a community, they deliberately rejected the gods on whom the prosperity of that community rested. In addition, like the extreme Jewish sectaries recorded by Josephus[8], they refused to give even nominal recognition of Caesar as lord by swearing on his genius.

Though Pliny himself shared the views of his Roman upper-class

---

[1] H. A. Fischel, art. cit., 366.

[2] L. Finkelstein, *Akiba*, 272 ff.

[3] *Mechilta, Jethro Bahodesh*, vi (Winter u. Wünsche, 213). See L. Finkelstein, *Akiba*, 270.

[4] Including, of course, the building of a temple to Jupiter Capitolinus on the site of the Temple of Jerusalem, an act not far removed from Antiochus's 'abomination of desolation'.

[5] This is my interpretation of Origen, *Contra Celsum*, i. 1 and 2, 'societies which are public are allowed by the laws, but secret societies are illegal . . . The doctrine was originally barbarian, obviously meaning (Origen comments) Judaism with which Christianity is connected'. Lucian's description of Peregrinus in his Christian days as a προφήτης καὶ θιασάρχης καὶ ξυναγωγεὺς (*De Morte Peregrini*, 11) suggests a 'Judaistic *collegium*'.

[6] For instance, Origen, *Contra Celsum*, iii. 55 and Min. Felix, *Octavius* 8.

[7] See the present writer's 'The Gnostic Sects and the Roman Empire', 31 ff. For the attribution of *Flagitia* to Gnostics by orthodox Christians, Justin 1 *Apol.*, 26. 7 and Clement, *Stromata*, iii. 10. 1.

[8] Josephus, *Wars*, vii. 10. 1 and ii. 8. 10.

155

contemporaries, and like Suetonius regarded Christianity as a 'prava superstitio',[1] the imposition of a sacrificial test suggests that atheism also was implicit. As Mommsen pointed out, the Bithynian Christians were executed because they refused to sacrifice.[2] By c. 130, however, the charge of atheism seems to have become general. From Justin one learns that it was among the charges spread by the Jews in Asia Minor against the Christians.[3] It was the cry taken up by the people of Smyrna against Polycarp and his community.[4] It was the first of the three major accusations rebutted by Athenagoras.[5] It is reflected in Lucian's account of the charlatan Alexander of Abonuteichos forbidding access to his shrine in Bithynia to 'Christians' and 'atheists'.[6] It is clear from the forged decree of Antonius Pius to the Council of Asia that the population regarded Christians as atheists.[7] So did the people of Lyons.[8] In Africa the charge figures prominently in Tertullian's *Ad Nationes*.[9] Its existence ensured that pressure against the Church would not be relaxed. It was the atheistic 'nomen' rather than the 'flagitia' that mattered.[10]

But compared with the Jews, the Christians were, in general, peaceable and well-affected citizens. They did not behave like the Sicarii, even though the first reaction of the Roman authorities in Palestine was that they were members of this sect (Acts xxi. 38). Therefore, the authorities were prepared to temper the wind for them. Thus the instruction 'conquirendi non sunt'; thus the acquittals of Christians[11]; and, as Origen makes clear in the passage from *Contra Celsum* already cited, the chance of last-minute recantation. It was an illogical system. Tertullian's legal mind could drive a coach and four through it,[12] but it was the only system that could be evolved, having regard both to the religious history of the Hellenistic East and to the Christians' own impulse towards martyrdom. If there ever was a Neronian edict, there is no evidence that a Proconsul of Asia or Africa ever referred to it. While the magisterial right of *coercitio* may have been invoked, it would be more reassuring if specific evidence existed that it was.

In the last resort, the troubles of the early Church were due as much to the virulence of the Christian-Jewish controversy as to any other cause.[13] The literary warfare which has left its mark on the *Epistle of Barnabas*, and

[1] Pliny, *Ep.*, x. 96.
[2] Th. Mommsen, art. cit., 395.
[3] Justin, *Dialogue*, xvii. 1.
[4] Eusebius, *H.E.*, iv. 15. 19. See also ibid., v. 1. 9 (martyrdoms at Lyons in 177).
[5] Athenagoras, *Supplicatio*, 3.
[6] Lucian (ed. Harmon), *Alexander*, 25 and 38.
[7] See A. Harnack, 'Das Decret des Antoninus Pius', *Texte und Untersuchungen*, xiii. 4, 1895.
[8] Eusebius, *H.E.*, v. 1. 9.
[9] Tertullian, *Ad Nationes*, i. 1–3.
[10] Tertullian, *Apol.*, ii. 3: 'confessio nominis, non examinatio criminis'.
[11] See, in particular, Eusebius, *H.E.*, v. 18. 9, and Tertullian, *Ad Scapulam*, 3–5.
[12] Ibid., 1 ff.
[13] For a contrary view, M. Simon, *Verus Israel*, Paris 1948, 144 f. and J. Parkes, *The Conflict of the Church and the Synagogue*, London 1934, 125 ff.

156

the ideas of Marcion, became warfare indeed. There is strong circumstantial evidence that the Jews shifted the blame for the fire at Rome in A.D. 64 to the Christians, but the charge cannot be proved conclusively.[1] During the period, however, between A.D. 60 and A.D. 90, when Acts and the Gospels were being written, it is clear that Christians were concerned with Jewish rather than official hostility. In Acts the reasonable attitude of the Roman authorities is contrasted with the hatred of the Jews. In the Gospels the authorities are acquitted of condemning Jesus to death, though it would have been easy to have branded the Roman persecutors with that crime also. The conflict, however, at the end of the first century was less with the Roman Empire than with the 'synagogue of Satan'.

In the second and third centuries, Christian writers in both East and West make specific references to Jewish hostility towards the Church. Taken together, Justin, the account of Polycarp's martyrdom, Tertullian and Origen make convincing reading. Cursings,[2] and beatings in the synagogues,[3] the spreading of anti-Christian rumours,[4] active assistance at martyrdoms,[5] alliance with pagans in war against the Church, all this justified the charge that 'the synagogues of the Jews were the fountains of persecution'.[6] The parties were evenly matched, for the Christians, if they won the Hellenistic world, lost Palestine and with it all eastern Judaism. The bitter warfare carried on with such tenacity for so long must have been a powerful factor in maintaining popular hostility against the Church. The Greek cities where Diaspora Jew and Christian lived side by side were the natural centres of this strife.

Once the Christians had failed to make good their claim in the eyes of the majority of the Jews to be the New Israel, and at the same time had abandoned the outward signs of Judaism, their position was bound to be precarious. Their claim to the same privileges as Judaism, e.g. freedom from military service, from performance of sacrifices and public service, in exchange for prayer, could not be entertained.[7] The continued closeness, however, of their religion to that of orthodox Judaism would render them liable to the legal and popular penalties reserved for converts to Judaism. To these were added suspicion of black magic and cannibalism, charges calculated to rouse the anger of the city mob.[8] The result was, as the writer of the *Letter to Diognetus* lamented, 'They (Christians) are warred upon by the Jews as foreigners (ἀλλόφυλοι) and are persecuted by the Greeks, and those who hate them cannot state the cause of their enmity'

---

[1] See L. H. Canfield, 'The Early Persecution of the Christians', *Columbia University Studies in History*, lv (1913) 44 ff.

[2] Justin, *Dialogue*, xvi. 4.

[3] Eusebius, *H.E.*, v. 16. 12.

[4] Justin, *Dialogue*, xvii. 1; Origen, *Contra Celsum*, vi. 27 and *Comment. in Deuteron.* xxxi. 21.

[5] *Mart. Polycarpi*, 13 and 17.

[6] Tertullian, *Scorpiace*, 10 and *Adv. Nationes*, i. 14.

[7] For this claim, Origen, *Contra Celsum*, viii. 73.

[8] As they in fact did at Lyons in A.D. 177; Eusebius, *H.E.*, v. 1. 14.

157

(v. 17). The general interest of the Roman government of the 'containment of Judaism' led to the firmly-held but illogical legal position against which the Apologists stormed in vain.

Persecution for religion and martyrdom do not start with Christianity. The problem of a monotheistic religion, exclusive in its outlook towards surrounding society and yet universalist in its claims, confronted every ruler of Asia Minor and the Near East from the second century B.C. onwards. Culturally and politically Christianity was the more formidable successor of Judaism. Rome eventually tried to handle the problem on similar lines to her Hellenistic predecessors. The policy failed. Supported by the assurance of immortality and revenge which his doctrine of martyrdom gave him, the Christian like the Jew was proof against both pogrom and, later, official persecution.[1] Up to the end of the second century A.D. the Hellenistic world was the battleground. Then, gradually the emphasis shifts, and one finds that during the fourth century the more extreme aspects of the martyr's creed have entrenched themselves in the theology of the West. Petilian of Constantine[2] is the final representative of the philosophy of history asserted in IV Maccabees. How and why this took place is beyond the scope of this paper. But there can be no doubt of the great importance of this development. Conflict has been the mark of Church-State relations in the West down to the present day. By tracing the origins back into the pre-Christian past one may gain a clearer insight into the foundations of the Western standpoint.

---

[1] On the 'conditioning' of Christians for martyrdom, see Riddle, *The Martyrs*, iii.
[2] Augustine, *Contra Litteras Petiliani*, ii. 92. 202 (P.L., xliii. 322–323).

The Confutation of Judaism in the Epistle of Barnabas

IN discussing the general atittude of the Church Fathers towards the Jewish fast,[1] I had occasion to refer to the *Epistle of Barnabas* ch. III[2]. However, after a thorough examination of this work one realises that its unique radicalism is one which has almost[3] no counterpart in all patristic literature. Superficially, Barnabas' words on fasting are almost identical with those of Justin Martyr.[4] Both are sparing with their own words and let the Prophet (*Isa.* lviii) speak for them. Both even reach the same conclusion, that the rules of the fast (as well as all other Jewish rites) were not meant literally. But careful observation of their respective presentation of the verses reveals immediately a world of difference between them. Justin quotes the verses to prove from the Prophet that the "true" sense of fast is the ethical and not the ritual one. He adduces the Scriptures as evidence for his opinion the "new law" (i.e. abrogation of rites) had already existed in the mind of the Prophet.[5]

In contrast with this, Barnabas splits up the verses into two parts: "to them" (i.e. Jews, verses 4, 5) and "to us" (i.e. Christians, v. 6-10). By this device[6] he proves his radical thesis: the Jews misunderstood the law when applying it in its literal sense. Fasting was never intended to be a practical institution, and the verses were meant to bear a "spiritual" interpretation, which alone was originally intended to be the true exegesis of the Law. The purpose of his preaching is to prevent the Christians from being misled by Jewish law, by expounding

---

[1] *JJS.* ix (1958), p. 25 n. 59.

[2] As regards the authorship of this epistle cf. (F) X. FUNK, *Kirchengeschichtliche Abhandlungen u. Untersuchungen*, (1899) p. 80 ff.

[3] "Dieser 'Barnabas' vertritt einen Standpunkt, welcher in ganzen Geschichte der Verhandlungen über Christentum und Judentum niemals mehr von seiten eines kirchlichen Theologen geltend gemacht worden sein dürfte". O. BARDEN-HEWER, *Geschichte der altkirchenlichen Literatur* (Freiburg, 1913), I p. 104. With other extreme writers (e.g. n. 197 *infra*) we will deal elsewhere (cf. n. 37).

[4] *Dial. c. Try.*, ch. xv.

[5] Justin's last sentence in the chapter explains this: "Circumcise therefore the foreskin of thy heart, as the words of God in all these passages demand". cf. also *ibid.* c. vii.

[6] This system is often used by him (as e.g. on the sacrifices, early in ch. ii).

1

the scripture in the "innocent" way which was intended for Christians.[6a]

It is obvious that Barnabas' extremism is prompted by the fear of Judaising tendencies or even total conversion to Judaism. To appreciate this background the problem has to be further investigated in the following order:—(a) The significance of the polemics against fasting, and (b) comparison of these with the general tone of the Epistle as a whole; these may shed light on (c), the motivation of the conflict.

What is the nature of the fasting to which Barnabas refers? If the Day of Atonement[7] was meant, his remarks should have been connected with Chapter vii, where he allegorises in general the ritual of that day.[8] It is true that proselytes, and even semi-proselytes, adhered rigorously[9] to the observance of this fast, but Barnabas as a rule does not enumerate all the laws which such Judaisers might practice.[10] It is also unlikely that such strong arguments would be used against a fast that occurred but once a year; it is more likely that Barnabas is concerned with frequent and regular fasting.[11]

Since the closest parallel with our Epistle is the *Didache*,[12] and we

---

[6a] "So then, brethren, the long suffering one foresaw that the people whom He prepared in his Beloved should believe in guilelessness, and made all things plain to us beforehand that we should not be shipwrecked by conversion to their law". iii, 6.

[7] The same scriptural *periscope* is used for the *haftarah* on the Day of Atonement. On the other hand it served as matter for broad exhortation on public fasts. Tos. *Ta'an*. i, 8, (ZUCKERMANDEL, p. 215); J. *Ta'an*. ii, 1, 65b.

[8] There are even contradictions to be seen between the two chapters. In vii, 3, he says "Whosoever does not keep the fast should be put to death, and the Lord commanded this because He Himself was going to offer etc.". Here it speaks of literal fasts enjoined by Jesus.

[9] J. *Meg*. i, 27b. The discussion concerns whether Antoninus was a proselyte or merely "God-fearing", because he observed the day. The delicate problem of differentiating between proselytes and "God-fearers" cannot be dealt with here. Cf. I. LEVI, *Le prosèlytisme juif*, *REJ*, l, p. 1-9; li, 1-31; M. GUTTMANN, *Das Judentum u. seine Umwelt* (Berlin, 1927), p. 62f.; S. LIEBERMAN, *Greek in Jewish Palestine* (1942), p. 77.

[10] Josephus (*c. Apion*, x, 123) mentions the Sabbath, fasts (plural) kindling the lights (?) and the dietary laws. Juvenal (xiv, 95 f.) mentions only the Sabbath, prayers to God, and abstaining from pork. It seems that there was no unanimously fixed practice.

[11] It is most remarkable that Barnabas does not mention Passover; cf. n. 195, *infra*. Possibly the words "these things" (iii, 1) denote that he refers not to one fast only. Josephus (cf. n. 10) also speaks about fasts. If he had meant the Day of Atonement he would not have used the plural. (νηστεία, like the hebrew צום in the singular, was used as a technical term for the Day of Atonement. cf. *JSS*, ix, p. 19 n. 1).

[12] Cf. (F) X. FUNK, *Didache u. Barnasbabrief*, *Theologische Quartalschrift*, lxxvii (1905), p. 161f.

2

may compare the polemics against Jewish fasting expressed there:[13] 'Let not your fasts coincide with those of the hypocrites (i.e. Jews) for they fast on Mondays and Thursdays, but you fast on Wednesdays and Fridays'. We may safely assume that Barnabas' polemics are aimed against the same fasts, but while the *Didache* in general has a flexible attitude towards Jewish rites, that of Barnabas is more inflexible.

Before entering into the reasons for Barnabas' extremism, the character of the fasts on Mondays and Thursdays must be further explained.[14] These fast days—which had a controversial history in the Church[15]—were known as *Stationes*.[16] In the *Shepherd* of *Hermas*[17] they are referred to in a conversation as being customary fasts. This Latin term which in its translierated form penetrated into Greek has hitherto been explained as having been borrowed from Roman military language. This explanation is certainly true concerning its usage by the Fathers of the Church, and especially of Tertullian's usage.[18] But since military terms were employed in religious usage according to certain logical associations, we must look further into its origin. We have seen that these fasts originate in some Jewish practice; their name must therefore be deemed to have been borrowed from the Hebrew. The literal translation of *stationes* would be מעמדות.[19]

A *Baraitha*[20] mentions these fasts in connection with a special prayer which commemorates the significance of these special days in the *'Amidah:* '. . . Mondays and Thursdays and Public fasts and *Ma'amadoth'*. Regarding this the Talmud asks: 'Mondays and Thursdays, what is their significance?' And the question is answered: 'The Mondays and Thursdays of public fasts, and Ma'amadoth'. *Ma'amadoth* here cannot mean the fasts of the representatives who fasted from Monday to Thursday four days a week, but rather the popular

---

[13] viii, 1. For the *Didache*, the changing of the days of fasting is sufficient to divorce them from their Jewish origin; but Barnabas aims at their total eradication.

[14] On the Jewish origin and extent of these fasts, cf. G. ALLON, *Leyishshuva shel Baraitha 'aḥath, Tarbiz* iv (1933), pp. 285-291.

[15] Cf. *JJS*, ix, p. 28 n. 89.

[16] Tertullian, *De ieiunio* i, 10, and ch. x.

[17] *Sim.* v, i, 1-2.

[18] He (like many others) uses it also for Christian religious assemblies (e.g. *Ad Uxorem* ii, 4; *Adv. Psych.* i and x; *Orat.* 29 etc.), in the sense of *guard duties*.

[19] It was not the Latin origin of the term which caused its penetration into Greek, but rather the fact that when this term was translated from the Hebrew, *station* was already a well known term in the jargon of the Hellenistic world.

[20] *Shab.* 24a.

3

fasts observed voluntarily by individuals,[21] but limited like the public fasts, to these two days only.[22] But to the popular mind, prior to the crystallisation of the technical terms for fasting, all fasting on Mondays and Thursdays was connected with the *Ma'amadoth*,[23] and the early source had this association of ideas when *Ma'amadoth* were incorporated into the Tractate *Ta'anith*.[24]

The fact that these fasts were adopted by Christianity and practised (despite the controversy around them) for centuries, is a proof of the antiquity of this custom and indicates that it originates from a time earlier than Christianity itself. It would not be considered a Christian virtue, had it been a custom but newly invented by the Jews.[25]

There remains still one difficulty. Why should such Jewish fasts survive at all in Christianity after their general rejection of the Law?

[21] Tos. Ta'an ii, 4 is obviously corrupt and should read: יום שני ויום חמישי ציבור (היחיד וציבור בתענית) יחיד יושב בתענית the error is due to *homoioteleuton* of תענית. In the Vienna MS and *Editio Princeps* (cf. ZUCKERMANDEL p. 217) there is still a clue to the original reading in the addition of the unintelligible word הוחרו, which is a corruption of (צבור) היחיד ו. Megillath Ta'anith (xii,=B. *Ta'an.* 12a) elaborates the voluntary background of these fasts. There is a unique expression at the end of *Meg. Ta'an.*: ועוד גזרו רבותינו which could mean that it was compulsory. (cf. n. 24, *infra*). But all the sources show that it was not in fact a *halakhah* but rather custom (J. *Pes.* iv, 1, 30 c-d). Cf. ALLON, loc. cit. The late Allon did not interpret *Ma'amadoth* in this way, but took it to refer to the fasts of the representatives of the people in the Temple only. He believed (with Rashi *ad. loc.*) that Mondays and Thursdays are singled out in this prayer from the four-days-a-week fast of the *Ma'amadoth*. But there is no attempt made to explain why it is that these days only out of the four have this special prayer. ALLON thought that the compilers of the Babylonian Talmud did not know the reason for this special prayer (which was forgotten in Babylon) and consequently the *Baraitha* has become corrupted, as if the fasts of two days a week refer only to the Monday and Thursdays of Public fasts and *Ma'amadoth* (in the ordinary sense). But it is obvious that the Talmud gives the correct interpretation (cf. ALLON's difficulties there, n. 18), i.e. the fasts of Mondays and Thursdays all the year round are identical with *Ma'amadoth*. It goes without saying that all the proofs and sources adduced by ALLON in his article can easily be adapted to *Ma'amadoth* in the sense understood by us.

[22] Cf. *JJS*, ix, p. 28.

[23] The reason given by ALLON for the fasts of Monday and Thursday as "days of assembly" likewise fits our theory very well. We may go even further and suggest that it originates in the *Ma'amadoth*, and that יום כניסה originates from the phrase וישראל שבאותו משמר מתכנסין בעריהם (*Ta'an.* iv, 2).

[24] ii, 6-7; *Tos. Ta'an.* ii, 1-4. It has to be admitted that (as in Ch. iv) the connection is due to their being occasions for fasting. However, features of the public fast (as for example the נעילה prayer, cf. also *Ta'an*, ii, 5 etc.) show that it was based on the *Ma'amadoth*. The observance of the regulations concerning the "representatives" prevailed after the destruction of the Temple (*Tos. Ta'an.* ii, 3) and it is more than probable that the element of fasting was strengthened as a substitute for sacrifices. Possibly this is the explanation of the curious passage at the end of *Meg. Ta'an.* ועוד גזרו רבותינו. On the delicate problem of differentiation between *Ma'amadoth* and *Mishmaroth* cf. A. BÜCHLER, *Studies in Sin and Atonement*, p. 446.

[25] ALLON, loc. cit.

4

Even taking into consideration the fact that the Church realised the immense religious value of fasting, and did not wish to oppose these practices completely, why did it spare the *Ma'amadoth* (*stationes*) and not the Day of Atonement? There must have been some special historical circumstances which influenced this development.

In the custom of the disciples of John the Baptist[26] we may find a solution to our problem. The followers of John expected Jesus' disciples to fast, because this Pharisaic practice was one of the common principles which characterised both of the new movements.[27] From the answer of Jesus it is clear that this practice is connected with messianic expectations.[28] On the other hand we know that the common feature of both movements concerning messianism was the call: 'Repent ye, for the Kingdom of Heaven is at hand', preached first by John[29] and adopted by Jesus.[30] Since repentance is connected with fasting in the Hebrew Bible[31] and in the Apocrypha,[32] it is safe to assume that the same was the rule in the Judaism of the first century. The fasts which were expected of the disciples of Jesus could not be other than those of Monday and Thursday of the *Ma'amadoth*, which had gained additional significance through Messianic speculation. That is the secret of their survival in ancient Christianity despite the Christian abrogation of the Law; they were accepted as being the way of repentance, in order to hasten the advent of the Kingdom of Heaven.

There is very little mention of this messianic import in these fasts in talmudic literature. That, however, is small wonder, since these sources were edited and classified by the compilers when put into

---

[26] "Why do we and the Pharisees fast but thy disciples fast not?" (*Matth.* iii: 2, and parallels in the synoptics).

[27] Just as the Pharisees reproached Jesus on the matter of the washing of the hands (*Matth.* xv), the Sabbath (*ibid.* xii: 8), and divorce (*ibid.* xix: 3f.) and the Sadducees regarding the resurrection of the dead (*ibid.* xxii) because they were principles of importance to them, so John's followers expected Jesus to fast.

[28] "The bridegroom" is a symbol of the Messiah. This passage gave rise to much controversial exegesis. Cf. Tertullian, *c. Marcionem* iv, ii; *De ieiunio* 2; Origen, *Lev. Hom.*, x, 2. *Didascalia*, Ch. xxi, etc.

[29] *Matth.* iii: 2 and parallels.

[30] *ibid.* iv: 17.

[31] 1 *Sam.* vii: 6; *Jer.* xiv: 12, *Jonah* iii: 8; *Neh.* ix: 1.

[32] *Ps. Sol.* iii: 8-10; *Ecclesiasticus* xxv: 31 (=xxvi: 34); *Test. Reuben* i: 10; *Test. Simeon* iii: 4; *Gad* v: 6-8; *Joseph* iii: 4.

5

writing.[33] Repentance was the cardinal motive emphasised in the Jewish public fasts[34] though without any messianic tinge.[35] On the other hand we also find a strong emphasis on repentance as preparation for redemption.[36] It is thus quite logical to say, even in default of literary evidence, that since repentance is the main element in fasting, and repentance is the preparation for redemption, "the fast" was employed in Judaism also for messianic purposes.[37]

Support for this assertion can be found in a discussion of R. Eliezer (b. Hyrcanus) and R. Joshua (b. Ḥananya).[38] These two personalities represent conflicting contemporary opinion about pharisaic messianic speculations. R. Eliezer holds that 'if the children of Israel do not repent they will never be redeemed'. This is categorically denied by R. Joshua. The problem is whether the coming of the messianic era can be hastened by human works (R. Eliezer) or whether it depends entirely on Divine grace (R. Joshua).[38a]

These two motives, which had co-existed in the apocalyptic speculations of old, became rival theories when opinions started to become

---

[33] This was already noted by JOEL (Blicke in d. Religionsgeschichte, II, p. 99-131). Silence about the period of Bar-Kokhba, and restrained expressions in general testify to this. Even so careful a scholar as G. F. Moore writes: (Judaism II, p. 346): "There is a notweorthy reticence, an evident disposition not to be wise beyond what is written, a sobriety in striking contrast to the enthusiastic constructions of the apocalypses".

[34] Ta'an. ii: 1, Baraitha, B. Ta'an. 16a.

[35] Most probably because of the reasons mentioned (n. 33 supra) and because of the practical motivation e.g. rain, persecution, etc.

[36] "Great is repentance, for it brings near redemption as it is said . . . (Is. lix: 20)" Yom. 86b; Yalq. Shim. ii, 358; ibid. 865 (on Ps. cvii), and, with variations, Deut. R. ii, 14. In Yoma the saying is ascribed to R. Jonathan but it should be R. Jose Ha-Gelili, cf. BACHER, Agada d. Tannaiten I, p. 369, n. 3.

[37] It is quite possible that the fasts of R. Ṣadoq (Giṭ 56a; Lam. R. i, 31) and R. Eliezer Ha-Moda'i (J. Ta'an. iv, 8, 68d; Lam. R. ii, 4). were of this character. A further elaboration of these historical phenomena will be attempted in my paper "Religious Polemics as the Background of Historical Events of the early Second Century" (read at the Institute of Jewish Studies, 16th March, 1960).

[38] J. Ta'an. i, 1, 63d; B. San. 97b-98a.

[38a] It is tenous to explain the background of this controversy as it has been explained by some Christian theologians—that the question is whether the time fixed by God for the redemption belongs to the past or to the future. (Cf. STRACK-BILLERBECK, Kommentar zum N.T. etc. I, p. 163). It is not logical that R. Joshua should deny so emphatically the role of repentance unless for some serious polemical reasons. On the other hand, had R. Eliezer thought that redemption was overdue in time but had been postponed because of sin, that would imply a very harsh judgment of the virtues of his generation. The opposite is evident from the sources (cf. Meg. 25b.).

6

systematised into fixed theological dogmas.[39] R. Eliezer, who is known for his extremism,[40] gave in completely to the Apocalyptic trend[41] which demanded repentance and fasting.[42] The moderate leaders, being more realistic, opposed this extremism and preached moderation. Their aim was the normalisation of life (including the religious life) after the great catastrophe. The extreme messianic tension prompted by exhortations to repent and fasts became too dangerous, and, as in similar cases, there were always some moderate scholars who tended to water them down.[43] R. Joshua belonged to this school of thought[44] and his opposition to R. Eliezer was based on this motive. By argument he silenced his great opponent, in order to slacken the highly active messianic tension that was in his opinion disturbing the normalisation of life which was a necessary condition of the perpetuation of national survival after the catastrophe. R. Joshua would be the last to discourage people from repentance or fasting had it not been for this danger. No wonder that when, after the failure of the Bar Kochba revolt, this moderate tendency became the dominant one, it was formulated in the words of the 'Amora'im in terms of divine vows enforced on Israel to the effect that they should not revolt against the domination of the nations and not "hasten the

---

[39] For a similar development in Christianity, cf. n. 65f. However, one motive did not completely exclude the other. Emphasis was but put on one motive, keeping the other in the background.

[40] Called *Shammuthi* as e.g. J. *Shevi'ith* ix, 9 (39a).

[41] At this period, when there were still many common features between Jewish and Christian Messianic thinking (cf. *infra*), the Roman authorities could easily make the mistake of thinking him a Christian because of his extreme messianic bias (cf. b. *'Avoda Z.* 16b).

[42] His well-known saying on the subject of permanent repentance, *'Avoth* ii, 10 (*Shab.* 153a; *Eccl. R.* x; *'Avoth d. R. Nathan*, version a, xv version b xxix ed. Schechter p. 62) shows his preoccupation with this problem. On his proclamation of the thirteen public fasts, cf. *Ta'an.* 25b. It may be that the conversation with the student about repentance, and the eschatological preaching in *Tana debe Eliyahu Zuta* (xxiii) have also some historical background. (but cf. *'Avoth d. R. Nathan, loc. cit.*).

[43] Even when messianic agitation reached its peak and conditions supported it, as in the times of Bar-Kokhba, there were some who opposed. cf. J. *Ta'an.* iv, 8, 68d.

[44] *Tos. Sot.* xv, 11 (ed. Zuckermandel p. 322) (=*B. Bath.* 60b); *Gen. Rab.* lxiv, 10 (ed. Theodor-Albeck p. 710). Maybe the congruence of some features with the Christian messianic movement (cf. n. 47) also prompted his opposition. R. Joshua is well-known (*Ḥag.* 5b) as the great defender of Judaism against Christian and heretical dangers. An occasional expression here and there (of R. Eliezer or R. Joshua) should not disturb our reliance on the main body of sources. It is a well-known fact that even in matters of *halakhah* their opinions are quite frequently interchanged. Cf. J. N. Epstein, *Mavo' Le-nusaḥ Ha-Mishnah* i, p. 6.

7

end".[45] Nevertheless, some echoes of the previous situation lingered on in these writings.[46]

One may seem justified in asking how it is possible to compare the messianic movement in Christianity to that of Judaism; but the truth is that at the turn of the first century they had still much in common.[47] The commonly held opinion, which is based on messianic descriptions of both religions after their final crystallisation into fixed dogmas, is most distorting. Most features such as the "transformation of ideals from national deliverance to the salvation of the individual soul from sin", or, as others put it, from nationalism to universalism, were barely noticeable at this period.[48] The salvation of the N.T. was also couched in terms of Jewish nationalism,[49] to the extent of even using the same eschatological terms.[50] Not only was the restoration of the Kingdom of Israel[51] expected, but even the ingathering of the exiles.[52] Furthermore, the affinity between the *Revelations* of John and the Jewish (Sectarian?) Apocalyptics proves also[53] how close was the

[45] שלא ידחקו על הקץ There are different versions of the number of vows. *Cant. R.* (on ii: 2) has four, and the Talmud (*Kethub.* 111a) six. It is clear from both sources that "hastening the end" does not refer to political or military activities, but rather to religious ones such as prayer, repentance fasting, etc. Rashi (*ad. loc.*) grasped this. Otherwise "hastening the end" would be identical with the previous vows.

[46] Later we find fasting as a substitute for offering (*Ber.* 17a; *Shoḥer Ṭov*, ed. BUBER 105b on *Ps.* xxv: 3). Later still, תשובה was identified with fasting in the prayers for New Year and the Day of Atonement. Regarding *Ma'amadoth* (emptied of their literal content) and their significance, cf. *Ta'an.* 27a; *Meg.* 31b.

[47] Regarding fasting, for example, we know that Jewish-Christians participated in the public fasts. *Kerithoth* 6b (cf. *JJS* ix, p. 25 n. 57), cf. also n. 41 *supra*. (R. Eliezer suspected of being a Christian).

[48] This subject will be dealt with broadly elsewhere (cf. n. 37).

[49] *Matth.* i: 21; *Acts* iii: 21, etc.

[50] The "world to come" for the Messianic *Aeon* comes from Jewish usage (*Matth.* xii: 32, *Eph.* i: 21). In rabbinic writing also it was only later that the terms were crystallised (cf. *San.* 91b=*Ber.* 34b). Even the Palestinian Talmud (in the controversy of R. Eliezer and R. Joshua, *Ta'an.* i, 1, 63d) speaks first of the resurrection of the dead and immediately afterwards of redemption (=Messiah), which indicates that there was as yet no clear cut differentiation. The usage of "Son of David" as the Messiah shows the same background. *Matth.* ix: 27; *ibid.* xv: 22; *ibid.* xx: 30-31 and parallel; *Rev.* v: 5; *ibid.* xxii: 16, etc. Even the genealogies of *Matth.* and *Luke* in one way or another trace Jesus back to David. On the other hand cf. Jesus' comment on *Ps.* cxi: 1 (*Mk.* xii: 35=*Matth.* xxii: 41f.).

[51] *Acts* i: 6.

[52] *Matth.* xvii: 36f. Cf. also *Apocalypse of Abraham* xxxi (ed. Box p. 84, and the editor's note 7, *ibid.*). *Didache* ix, 4; *ibid.* x, 5. On this cf. G. ALLON, *The Halakhah in Didache*, (in Hebrew) *Tarbiz* xi, (1939) p. 142. On the Christian prayers and expressions against the Roman Empire cf. G. KLEIN, *Der älterste christliche Katechismus und die Jüdische propaganda Literatur* (Berlin, 1909), p. 222. While we would today reject the thesis of this author, there are still numerous interesting points in his book that are worth further investigation.

[53] Cf. G. F. MOORE, *Judaism*, ii, p. 339 f.

8

eschatological speculation in both religions.[54] Even motives, the existence of which within Jewish messianism had been emphatically denied,[55] like the suffering of the Messiah and similar "Christian" inventions,[56] are in point of fact traceable to Jewish sources.[57]

As in the development of Judaism, the problem as to whether salvation depends on grace only or rather on repentance (works) existed in ancient Christianity; both views existed at its beginnings. With the expansion of Christianity among the Gentiles both trends, taken in their extreme forms, became more and more dangerous. The preaching of grace (or faith) as against and opposing works,[58] could easily lead to libertinism among the newly converted Gentiles.[59] The call for repentance (demanding works), on the other hand, could easily cause misunderstanding as it looked too much like the re-adoption of Jewish practices.[60] This danger was much greater if we

[54] There are certain "twists" in *Revelations*, as e.g. concerning the "New Jerusalem" xxi: 2, 10. cf. *Enoch* xc: 28, 29, *II Esdr.* vii: 26; xiii: 36; *Apoc. Bar.* xxxii: 2.

[55] In many circles these nineteenth century ideas are still the dominant ones. They depend on V. N. STANTON who writes (*The Jewish and Christian Messiah*, London, 1886, p. 124) on the preaching of the suffering Messiah to the Jews: '. . . repugnance to such an idea is the greatest difficulty they had encountered in preaching to their countrymen". Cf. also his treatment on the transformation of messianism by the Church, p. 149 f. and his article in HASTINGS *Dictionary of the Bible, s.v. Messiah.*

[56] Cf. J. KLAUSNER, *The Messianic Idea in Israel*, N.Y. 1955, p. 440f. followed by many authors.

[57] One must admit that Justin's frequently mentioned reference (*Dial, c. Tryph.* chaps. lxviii, lxxxiv, xc) to the suffering Messiah without the eliciting of comment or objection on the part of Trypho, is not a strong proof (cf. STANTON, *op. cit.* p. 123). But on the other hand, had the idea been repugnant to Jewish thought, Justin would not have been able to pass over it in silence. If we add to this the few similar expressions from Jewish sources, this becomes even more evident: *Yalq. Shim.* II 620 (on *Ps.* xi) hints, in the "son of King", at the Messiah. That this is not "late Christian influence" we can see from the *Mekhilta* (*Shir.* vii, 4a) about Gog and Magog. Cf. also *Yalq. Shim.* II, 476, (on *Is.* liii, 5) and *Ruth R.* v, 6. (Parallel in *Yalq.*). Of interest in the last passage is the "vinegar" as the symbol of his sufferings. Cf. *Luke* xxiii: 36; *John* xix: 29; *Barnabas* vii, 4f. There are other expressions as well which "do not suit" Jewish Messianism, such as that of R. 'Aqiba (*Hag.* 14a. cf. R. Jose Ha-Gelili, opposing him). Even as late as R. Joshua b. Levi such expressions were not yet completely censured. (*San.* 98a, cf. *Matth.* xxiv: 30).

[58] *Rom.* iii: 28; *Gal.* ii: 16; *ibid.* iii: 11, etc.

[59] The denunciations of abortion, infanticide, sodomy, etc. in the "Two Ways" (*Didache*, ch. 11f.; *Barnabas*, ch. xixf.) are most probably taken from the actual life of those who have fallen back to their previous heathen ethics. Possibly this is the background of some of the denunciations in the Apostolic Epistles (*I Cor.* v; *Thess.* iv: 1-8; *James* iv). The problem is explicitly brought forward by 1 *Clement*, xxxiii, 1f.

[60] From the *Epistle to the Galatians* we can see how Gentiles, recently converted to Christianity, turn Judaisers, and it is against them that Paul (the Jew) polemises. Cf. T. F. TORRANCE, *The Doctrine of Grace in the Apostolic Fathers* (Edinburgh, 1948) and his remarks on the difficulty experienced by the first gentile Christians in understanding the teachings of Grace (pp. 135-141).

9

THE JOURNAL OF JEWISH STUDIES

take into consideration that there was a considerable proselytising tendency at this period.[61] So far this movement and its fostering background has not been satisfactorily explained, particularly if we bear in mind the disasters which followed the destruction of the Temple.[62] Only by inferring an analogy from Christianity, and presuming that there then existed a Jewish messianic movement the activities of which caused (directly or indirectly) this proselytising movement, can we satisfactorily motivate this phenomenon. It is more than probable that this proselytising tendency was not sanctioned by the religious leadership of the nation, but that, like the whole messianic urge, it was a popular one, using mainly personal contact and influence by the masses on the gentile or even gentile-Christian surroundings, and relying on social, political, and other "signs" to prove the nearness of the Messiah.[63] Thus preaching that demanded repentance within Christianity, accompanied by frequent fasts (like the Jewish ones), tended to increase misconception among Christians and supported the Judaising tendencies among the newly converted Gentile-Christians.

Keeping this background in mind, we can understand why Barnabas concludes his polemics against these fasts with the following words: 'that we should not be shipwrecked by conversion to their law'.[64] This language denotes that there was a close conection between fasting (as a rite of repentance and "hastening the end") and conversion.

Contrary to all expectation, Barnabas does not exploit the Doctrine of Grace (or faith, or love) as an antidote to "works".[65] Instead, he finds his own way to counteract Jewish influence with weapons borrowed from the Jews themselves. He employs "Knowledge" which

[61] GRAETZ, *Die jüdischen Proselyten im Römerreiche unter den Kaisern Domitian, Nerva, Trajan und Hadrian, Bericht des Jüd-theol. Seminars,* (Breslau) 1884. Cf. also n. 139 *infra.*

[62] The hypothesis about Judaism turning from narrow nationalism to universalism after the destruction of the Temple is based upon imagination. There is a better explanation, viz. that the courageous stand of the Jews caused the proselyte movement. But the Christians were also not short of martyrs, and they were active missionaries. If, therefore, there were some Jewish proselytes (or Judaisers) from amongst the Christians, this can be explained by a similar Jewish activity only.

[63] This problem is widely dealt with elsewhere (cf. n. 37).

[64] iii, 6. This is according to the Greek text, but the Latin translation has a similar connotation.

[65] The Pauline Epistles are full of the contrast of law and grace. This doctrine is well known as the "orthodox" opinion; cf. e.g. Ignatius *Ep. to the Magnesians* viii, 1-2; x, 1-3; *Ep. to the Philadelphians,* vi, 2 etc. Barnabas does not deny grace, but he fails to emphasise it as against the law.

10

allegorises the Law, and at the same time he firmly adheres to the Scriptures as the basis for christological and ethical teachings. By this device his *gnosis* escaped the dangers of extreme antinomy in the ethical field, while at the same time so expounding the Scriptures as to support the claim of the abrogation of Judaism.

*   *   *

Our next task will be to go through the *Epistle* and to endeavour to discover by comparison whether our hypothesis is tenable. All previous solutions have contained some weak points.[66] Once these difficulties are solved in a homogeneous system they may also reflect the historical need which motivated this *Epistle*.[67] Since we dare not depend on arbitrarily selected passages, the bulk of the work must be thoroughly examined.

I. 1-4. The preface of the author is followed by his expression of love towards his readers and his rejoicing in them because of their adherence to the teachings of Christianity. This passage shows clearly the group at which it was aimed.[68] The tone of the introduction and similar personal tones elsewhere[69] do not prove that there is no polemical intention in the *Epistle*.[70] It is true that in comparison with the Pauline Epistles it is not so outspoken, but there are many examples of a disguised polemical approach.[71]

1. 5-8. He therefore comes to perfect their knowledge[72] and teaches

[66] We cannot enter here into all the different theories, which vary from one extreme to the other. All these systems and the literature are excellently summed up by H. WINDISCH (*Der Barnabasbrief*, 1920). We shall frequently refer to this work.

[67] Our inquiry here is strictly limited to the historical aspect, while other important problems which deserve investigation (e.g. textual problems) are left for scholars more competent in these fields. Even comparison with rabbinic sources must be limited to those relevant to our subject matter. On such comparisons much has been written. For the *Halakhah* cf. G. ALLON's brilliant article, *Tarbiz* xi (1939), pp. 23-38. For *'Aggada*, A. MARMORSTEIN, *L'épitre de Barnabé et la polémique juive*, *REJ* LX (1910), pp. 213-220. While the sectarian theories in this article are now antiquated, the rabbinic material gathered is still helpful.

[68] After almost a century we can still accept (with modifications) HILGENFELD's view in his introduction to his edition (Leipzig, 1866) that it was written (about) the end of the first century by a Gentile Christian of the Alexandrian School to win back Gentiles Christians from Judaism or to protect them from it. Unfortunately, H. does not explain what caused this danger.

[69] Cf. iv, 9; vi, 5 etc.

[70] Cf. J. WEIS, *Der Barnabasbrief kritisch untersucht* (Berlin, 1888) p. 87f. This work is an example of critical exaggeration; whatever does not suit the author's thesis he extracts from the "Grundlage", and brands as interpolation. Nevertheless, it has influenced other scholars.

[71] Cf. 2 *John* i: 4; 3 *John* i: 4f.

[72] WINDISCH is right in asserting (*op. cit.*, p. 307-8) that γνῶσις occupies the main position in his teaching. This should not be confused with Gnosticism, with which *Barnabas* has little in common.

11

the three (main) ordinances of the Lord. This verse (6) about principles is not an interpolation,[73] but an introduction to all his preachings later with regard to "the present circumstances". Obscure as this verse may be, it was meant to teach the three doctrines on which Christianity rests.[74] Understanding of these principles as ordained by the Divine Will will give the real "Knowledge" of past and present.[75]

II. 1-3. Elaboration of the above-mentioned "present circumstances" which prompted the *Epistle*. Because of the "evil days" in which "The Evil",[76] dominates there is a particular need of diligent understanding and observation of the law.[77] In such circumstances when the "worker of evil" gains power, the demand for patience and long suffering is natural,[78] to counteract misleading eschatological (and missionary?) preaching. Those ideas only which are purely Divine (in his sense, i.e. spiritual=allegorical) are considered real "Knowledge". The greatest part of the book (up to ch. 17) demonstrates this idea from the Scriptures.

II. 4-9. His first example to prove the "real" will of God from Scripture[79] is his polemics againt sacrifices. Using the same system as

[73] WINDISCH, p. 408.

[74] The Latin translation has preserved, most probably, the first principle only, while the Greek is hopelessly corrupt. It would be presumptuous on the part of the present writer to try to reconstruct the Greek text after the vain attempts of eminent Greek scholars. However, we may compare this to other teachings of main principles. It is certain that Barnabas did not have in mind *Matth.* xxii: 40, since two principles only are mentioned there. The number *three* recalls the Jewish sayings ('Avoth i, 2 and *ibid.* 18). Simon the Just's famous maxim could easily serve Barnabas as a basis for his own principles if it is twisted around according to his needs, thus:
  1. *Torah* is equated by Barnabas with *gnosis*, which is "hope of life".
  2. עבודה or sacrifices is equal to Righteousness (cf. Ch. ii).
  3. Since righteousness has already been accommodated he turns the third principle, גמילות חסדים into "Love, Joy and Gladness". Cf. also *Menahoth* 110a, where 1 and 2 are identified.

[75] Verse 7. Barnabas does not pretend to be the master of the future course of events. The expression "the first fruits of the future" is explained by him: "and when we see these things coming to pass one by one", i.e. that the future is only hinted at and it is assumed that only by the development of events is it revealed. cf. nn. 181-186.

[76] i.e. Antichrist (cf. 1 *John* ii: 18f.). Barnabas does not say this explicitly but the sense is clear as in *Didache* ch. xvi, *supra*. ch. iv. It is commonly agreed that there was some special danger at this time (WINDISCH p. 322). It is certain that the Jewish Messiah—or Messianism, which was very influential at this period—was meant.

[77] According to his "gnosis" which opposes the Jewish literal practice of the rituals.

[78] The punctuation of this verse (3) is difficult, but if connected with the previous one (v. 2, which is not an interpolation, cf. WINDISCH p. 408f.) it gives perfect sense. This is a general introduction to his scriptural exegesis.

[79] Barnabas' quotations are from the Hebrew Bible and Apocrypha. On his system of scriptural exegesis, cf. WINDISCH pp. 313-316.

12

in the case of fasting, he quotes verses[80] to show that the Prophets were already opposed to "their" (=Jewish) practice and that there are indications (through *gnosis*) for "us" (=Christians) as to the nature of the "real" sacrifice.[81]

II. 10. We have here a warning for a careful inquiry concerning salvation (=Knowledge) in order that the "evil one" should not gain a victory by deceit. Such a conclusion on the subject of sacrifices is unaccountable at this period, unless the discussion of the problem of sacrifices was opportune.[82] Only a few decades later we hear Justin's triumphant exclamation:[83] Jerusalem alone was chosen because it was forecast that it would be destroyed, and consequently "all sacrifices will cease". Hence Justin uses the offerings as an excuse against the form of Jewish worship in general. Why, then, should Barnabas, who is more extreme and outspoken, be afraid lest "we" are going astray like "them"?

We are far from suggesting that there was an actual Jewish sacrificial cult at this period.[84] What, however, we certainly can gather from this chapter is, that the Jewish messianic movement used the prospect of sacrifices and the early rebuilding of the Temple as a main item in their propaganda to win over converts. Nevertheless, it has to be admitted that such propaganda could have had only a very slight factual basis. The expression, "the Evil One may achieve a

[80] *Is.* i: 11-14 then a combination of *Jer.* vii: 22; *Zech.* viii: 7.

[81] *Ps.* li: 19 and other verses not found in the Bible. With regard to certain virtues, we find also in rabbinic writings that they are of equal value to sacrifices (*Soṭ.* 5b; *San.* 53b; *Lev. R.* vii, 2; *Yalq. Shim.* II 766 etc.), but only so because the Temple does not exist and they can act as a substitute. On verse 6 (which differs in the reading in the Latin translation) there are widely diverging opinions. There is no need to interpret it as if the Old Law was abolished by the New, since no such idea occurs elsewhere in the *Epistle*. The meaning is: He abolished these things (through the Prophets) in order that the new one which has not been misinterpreted by men (as if implying actual sacrifices) should be established. Barnabas holds that the literal meaning was never intended by God, but was invented by men.

[82] This was already noted by JOEL, *op. cit.*, I, p. 32. Cf. also M. GÜDEMAN, *Religionsgeschichtliche Studien* (Leipzig, 1876) p. 114f.

[83] *Dial. c. Try.* xl. One is forced to the conclusion that the historical climate had changed in the meanwhile.

[84] There was a lengthy controversy on this subject more than a century ago in the pages of the *Lietraturblatt des Orient* x (Leipzig, 1849) between FRIEDENTHAL (p. 328f.) and FRIEDMANN (p. 401f.). Nevertheless, the view that the sacrificial cult continued between the years 70 and 135 did not die out despite the fact that great scholars including GRAETZ and J. DERENBOURG, (*Essai sur l'histoire et la géographie de la Palestina*, Paris 1867, 1, 480f.) opposed it. Cf. also M. GUTTMANN, *Palestine in Midrash and Talmud, Festschrift zum 75 jährigen jüd. theol. Seminars* (Breslau, 1929) Vol. I, p. 99f.

13

deceitful entry"[85] suggests that every little hope was greatly inflated by legendary eschatological exaggerations.

From Ch. IV onwards[86] many chapters are devoted to a central problem in the Jewish-Christian controversy, namely that of the "covenant". In the N.T. we already find that gentile Christians are partakers of the covenant, whether as converts[87] or as a continuation of the role of Israel.[88] Barnabas, however, considers such sitting on the fence as sin (iv, 6). The Jews have no part in the covenant, which belongs exclusively to the Christians. This extremism is certainly a result of polemics which have left their deep imprint in rabbinic literature as well.[89] Since the covenant, or "Merit of the Fathers", was a part of the hope of Jewish redemption,[90] it is not to be wondered at that it was radically denied by Barnabas. This theme is widely discussed in chapters IV, V, VI,[91] XIII and XIV.

IV. 1-2. The present situation demands[92] that we must avoid error[93] and not be overcome by it[94] and become like "them".

IV. 3-5. "The final stumbling block"[95] i.e. false Messianism is a part of the Divine plan. Because of the Divine will they (the advocators of it) seem successful. From here it is evident that this danger

[85] παρείσδυσις Cf. also vi, 9. The phenomenon of the exaggerating of miracles and signs at a period of messianic tension is well known. Cf. G. SCHOLEM, *Shabbethai Ṣevi*, (Tel-Aviv, 1957) I, p. 209f., 265f. For the spreading of exaggerated rumours among Christians cf. *ibid.* p. 272f., II p. 394f., p. 460f.

[86] Ch. III was dealt with in the introduction.

[87] 1 *Peter* ii: 9, 10.

[88] *Eph.* ii: 11f.

[89] The controversies of the Rabbis and the Christians are very often motivated by such arguments, the Christians maintaining that God had forsaken Israel, while the Rabbis defend the continuation of His benevolence towards Israel. (ברית). *Ḥag.* 5b; '*Eruvin* 101a; *Ber.* 10a; *Yom.* 56b-57a. With the view of Berurya (*Ber.* 10a) cf. 1 *Clement* ii, 1-4; Justin Martyr, 1 *Apol.*, liii, Cf. also MARMORSTEIN, *op. cit.*

[90] J. *Ta'an.* i, 1, 64a; *Yalq. Shim.* I, 827; *ibid.* II, 865 (on *Ps.* cvi); *Deut. R.* ii, 14. The verses referring to the covenant (*Deut.* vi: 31; *Ps.* cvi: 45, etc.) were explained as זכות אבות.

[91] The interruption of this theme in ch. VII-XII is due to associative thinking, which continues with the "spiritual" and typological examples given in ch. VI.

[92] As in II, 1 and 10.

[93] i.e. Judaism, cf. ch. II and III.

[94] Cf. III, 6.

[95] τέλειον σκάνδαλον (cf. n. 76 *supra*) WEIL already saw the affinity of this with *Didache* ch. xvi (cf. E. HENNECKE, *Handbuch z.d. neutestamentliche Apocryphen*, 1923, p. 222) where it speaks of the appearance of "the deceiver of the World as a Son of God". It is possible that the expression ὡς πρέπει υἱοῖς θεοῦ does not refer to the Christians, but to the deceiver (πρέπει introduced by ὡς in the sense of being similar, appears as, or pretends); the sense of the sentence would then be: unless we resist at this present evil time, offenders which are to come pretending to be Sons of God, that the Black one ... The great difference between the Greek and the Latin translation of these sentences calls for elucidation.

14

was connected with the Roman Emperors, who directly or indirectly supported Jewish hopes.[96]

IV. 6-8. Personal exhortation[97] to understand the situation, and not to be waverers concerning the Christian exclusive ownership of the covenant.

IV. 9. He writes of that only which is necessary to understand the "present" situation, "for the whole time of your life and faith will profit us nothing"[98] unless the present evil is resisted.

IV. 10-12. This should be done by fleeing from the vanity[99] and evil of the Jews, who seek to be justified (by their separation and) their covenant and laws.[100] Instead, Christians assemble[101] to discuss and practise the spiritual way.

IV. 13-14. Warning not to rest as though they have been "called";[102] Barnabas adduces the misfortunes of Israel as an example to demonstrate his thesis.[103]

V. This chapter is an elaboration of what has been said before: that the Jewish covenant was broken, in order to make way for a new one (IV, 8).

V. 1. That is the reason of the coming of Jesus in the "flesh" and his "Passion".

V. 2. At the same time as this brought about the salvation of Christians, it also sealed the destiny of Israel.[103a]

V. 3-4. He therefore thanks God for "making known the past" (=fate of Israel) and giving wisdom for the present (to withstand the evil of the time) and some[104] for the future. Israel deserved its fate, since they had the knowledge but nevertheless they went astray.

---

[96] On the 10 Emperors, their period etc. and literature, cf. WINDISCH p. 319-20.

[97] The expression "loving you above my life", like others in this chapter, appears also in the *Didache* (ii, 7). This clause indicates that he regards his readers as being of the highest class of Christians. They do not belong to the category of those whom one "should reprove", or those whom one "should pray for". This expression thus comes to soften the exhortations, since they are addressed to those whom he is commanded to "love more than his own life". This is also the meaning of the conclusion of the passage (9a).

[98] *Didache* xvi, 2.

[99] i.e. boasting of their covenant and Law.

[100] One of the reasons that Barnabas does not stress justification by grace is because among the Jews also there were those who relied on the covenant and the "Merit of the fathers". He preaches rather the keeping of the commandments (but in his "spiritual" way), and stresses very much reward and punishment (v.12).

[101] Cf. nn. 97, 98. These similarities to the *Didache* deserve further study.

[102] Again a hint against dependence on the covenant.

[103] Cf. *Matth.* xxii: 14. Again a twist against the Jewish concept of "Election".

[103a] The prophecy on which Barnabas builds his hermeneutics (*Is.* liii) has a "practical reference to Israel" explained in this way (v. 4).

[104] Cf. n. 75.

B

15

V. 5-7 (and 10). The passion which the Prophets foretold, was "in order to fulfil the promise made to the Fathers",[105] raise the dead, and save the believers.

V. 8-9. "He taught and loved Israel",[106] but "he came not to call the righteous[107] but the sinners".

V. 10-14. The other reasons for the "coming in the flesh".[108]

VI. Further proofs from the Prophets on the same lines (a new covenant and the suffering of Jesus).

VI. 1-2a. Direct continuation of the end of the previous chapter.[109]

VI. 2b-4. Typological explanation on "stone" with an obvious hint against the Jews who believe in the literal sense of the scripture.[110]

VI. 5-7. Further and more explicit scriptural proofs of the Jewish error concerning Jesus.[111]

VI. 8-19. Scriptural evidence[112] concerning the Christian[113] inheritance of the covenant (=the promises to the Patriarchs), is the promise of inheriting the land flowing with milk and honey (v. 8). But "Knowledge" says it is not meant literally, but the Earth is Jesus (v. 9) and flowing milk etc. is a symbol of "the new creation" through Jesus (10-17). Rule over the fish, which does not exist at present, was

[105] But for the "new people". This is aimed against the Jewish concept of זכות אבות and covenant, which belongs now to the new people (Christians).

[106] That is, the reference to Israel in the Scriptures (v. 2).

[107] Righteous in the sense of literal observants of the law. Such was also his hint above "as if you were already righteous (IV, 10)". Otherwise it is very difficult to comprehend why he calls the Apostles "sinners above all sin". Cf. also VIII, 2f.

[108] Cf. v. 2 *supra*. Obviously "that he might complete the total of the sins" of the Jews (v. 10) contradicts v. 8. On the parable of the sun cf. *Ḥul.* 60a, and GÜDEMANN (*op. cit.* p. 116). While GÜDEMANN's theories are far fetched, he is right in pointing out the uniqueness of Barnabas' use of this parable of the sun for the incarnation in the flesh.

[109] Continuation of the exposition of scripture (*Is.* l) on the faults of Israel.

[110] The sarcastic remark: "Is then our hope on a stone?" (v. 3) refers to the Jewish messianic hope in which the building of the Temple (or the altar) occupied such a great part. Cf. XVI, 1, "putting their hopes on the building, and not on God, etc."

[111] Possibly the personal note "I write to you more simply that you may understand" implies an additional hint: In expounding (*Is.* xxviii: 16), the word "stone" in its typological meaning and then continuing with the error of the Jews, one could easily connect the two concepts and make them identical (as in *Rom.* ix: 33; 1 *Pet.* ii: 6). But Barnabas does not like this interpretation since his "stumbling stone" is the Jewish Messiah (cf. n. 95).

[112] The connection is quite natural, and vv. 8-19 are not, as WINDISCH thought (p. 409), a different unit. After bringing evidence from the Prophets of the Jewish failure, he goes on to prove the Christian succession from the same sources.

[113] It is evident that there is a mistake here and instead of "Moses says to *them*" it should be, "to us". The whole passage refers to Christians and not to Jews. Moreover, v. 13, "*Again I will show you how he speaks to us*", indicates that the former must have been also to "us". Finally, the whole passage is made to prove that "We then are they whom he brought into the good land" (v. 16). Cf. also XI, 9.

16

promised "When we ourselves also have been made perfect as heirs of the Covenant of the Lord".

The least that one could say about this last ambiguous piece of hermeneutics is that it sounds very forced.[114] It is obvious that here is a desperate attempt to play down by all means the Jewish hopes of re-inheriting Palestine, which was the cardinal aim of their messianic movement. This attempt to eliminate by allegorisation the significance of "the land flowing with milk and honey"[115] shows that it was a polemical background which prompted this exegesis. The exaggerated fables about the wealth of the products of the Holy Land in the messianic era are numerous. From the Apocrypha[116] and the Talmud[117] we learn that it occupied a great place in Jewish apocalyptic speculation and it had an influence an Christianity as well.[118] Barnabas' aim here is to eliminate this dangerous motive, which was stressed by Jewish messianic propaganda, through his usual, arbitrary, "spiritual" exegesis. It is no wonder that such allegorical explaining away appears greatly forced.

This heated argument caused him also to depart from his main subject (the covenant) and to indulge in similar extravagant allegorisations on other precepts of the Jews. It is only in ch. XIII that he resumes his main subject.

VII. The Temple rites of the Day of Atonement (scape-goat and other offerings) are explained as Types of Jesus.

VIII. The red heifer is explained in a similar way. He concludes this allegorising of the sacrifices (which is one of the aims of his polemics)[119] with an apt reference to the "evil and polluted days"[120] and an instructive remark to the effect that this spiritual knowledge is "plain to us (=Christians) but obscure to them (=Jews), because they did not hear the voice of the Lord" (7). In the next chapter this remark is elaborated: the reason why the Jews failed to hear is because their ears and hearts were not circumcised.

IX. Circumcision, which in this chapter is made to refer in a meta-

---

[114] In addition to the ambiguity of the allegorizations, there is no consistency in the system, e.g. the rule over the fish is not allegorised but taken literally.

[115] He does not allegorise many other expressions as e.g. land of Canaan etc. which would be easier than this one.

[116] Syriac *Baruch* xxix: 5f.

[117] J. *Ber.* vi, 1, 10a; J. *Sheq.* vi, 2, 50b; B. *Shab.* 30b; *Meg.* 17b; *Keth.* 111b; *Bab. Bath.* 75a, etc.

[118] Irenaeus (*Haer.* V 33) quotes from Papias similar exaggerations of features of the messianic age.

[119] Cf. ch. II, and notes there.

[120] Cf. nn. 76 and 95.

17

phorical sense to the ears and the heart, is a well-known theme.[121] But even in this Barnabas is almost unique[122] in his extremism. He considers the literal circumcision of the flesh as an error "because an evil angel was misleading them" (v. 5). Another sarcastic remark follows (v. 6), in which he ridicules the belief that circumcision serves as a seal of the covenant.[123] If this were so "all priests of the idol" are within their covenant. Both the covenant and circumcision are the targets of his polemics here. One can hardly escape the thought that he has a practical danger to counteract, namely, a movement which claimed proselytes by literal circumcision. All the weapons of mystical allegory are arrayed against this strict adherence to literal sense which, according to Barnabas' convictions, is wrong. Hence the boasting of Barnabas (v. 9) about his hermeneutics on number 318 as if it represents letters[124] (v. 7-8); he is sincere in believing that this "knowledge" is a "gift" implanted by God.[125]

X. In a similar way to circumcision the dietary laws are here allegorised. Once more his unique extremism[126] is apparent when he asserts that the Jews erred in taking the dietary laws literally, which was never intended, because of "the lust of their flesh".[127]

XI-XII. Continuing his exposition in the spirit of his "knowledge", Barnabas proves that Baptism (XI, 1-11), the Cross (XI, 8-11, XII, 1-7), and Jesus (XII, 8-11) were mystically implied in the Scriptures. Here too the polemical tone is not absent. The Jews, by denying baptism, are excluded from the remission of sins (XI, 1f.) and will share the fate of all the wicked (*ibid.* 7, 8). The Sign of the Cross, hinted at in the outstretched hands of Moses, is also brought in to show that Jews cannot be saved, because of their disbelief (XII, 3). The brazen serpent had a similar significance (*ibid.* 6-7).[128]

---

[121] Cf. *Rom.* ii: 27f. The first few verses of Barnabas (1-3) still follow this "traditional" line.

[122] Another exception is the *Epistle* to Diognetus (iv, 1, 4) with which I deal elsewhere (cf. n. 37).

[123] If one realises the gradual system of Barnabas, (verses 1-3 in the Gospel sense, v 4-5 error, 6-9 no covenant), the chapter is seen to be homogeneous (ci. WINDISCH, *in loc.*).

[124] For Jewish *Gemaṭria* on this number (אליעזר=318) cf. *Ned.* 32a; *Gen. R.* xliii, 2 and parallels.

[125] He is interested in showing "gnosis". Therefore he does not use *Gen.* xvii: 4, 5 as he does later in xiii, 7. In this context it would be too literal.

[126] Cf. n. 122.

[127] Such general polemical outbursts should not be taken very seriously. If there were any special carnal corruption in the movement he polemisizes against, he would not fail to elaborate on it, and hold it up against them. It seems that "lust of the flesh" means uncircumcised ears and heart. (cf. also *Col.* ii: 23).

[128] For Jewish polemics against these cases cf. *Rosh Hash.* iii, 5.

18

To all of these he adds a polemical note against the Jewish concept of the Messiah as the "son of David" (*ibid.* 10-11). Here again a motive well-known from the Gospels[129] is used by Barnabas in his supererogatory way. While the Gospels admit the Davidic descent of Jesus, Barnabas considers it as "the error of sinners".[130]

XIII-XIV. The conclusion of his main theme is thus that "this people" (the Christians) and not "the former people" (Jews) are the legitimate heirs of the covenant. The Patriarchs demonstrated that the birthright of the firstborn may be transferred to the younger brother. The example of Isaac, Rebecca and their two sons (XIII, 2-3) is allegorised[131] in contrast with the literal meaning. Ephraim and Menasseh (*ibid.* 4-6) typify the Church and the Synagogue.[132] Finally, the proof from Abraham (v. 7) is not (contrary to expectation) from the story of his two sons,[133] but according to the "knowledge" which, in its perfect form,[134] teaches fatherhood to the uncircumcised.[135] This last example of Abraham's relationship to the Gentiles shows their inheritance of the covenant.[136]

Despite the allegorical explanations, one cannot altogether explain away the literal meaning of the actual promises of God which all refer to real descendants. This is made to appear due the fault of the Jews, (XIV, 1 and 4a) "who were not worthy to receive it". Barnabas repeats the story of the breaking the tablets of the covenant by Moses

---

[129] *Matth.* xxii: 41-6; *Mark* xii: 35-7; *Luke* xx: 41-4 for the Davidic descent of Jesus, cf. n. 50.

[130] It is characteristic that the interrogative of the Gospels ("how is he his son?") was changed by Barnabas into an absolute negative (καὶ υἱὸν οὐ λέγει).

[131] He does not say explicitly what each symbolises. But from VII, 3 one can infer that Isaac=Jesus. Of the two sons, Jacob=the Church, Esau=Israel (!). This paradox can be explained by Barnabas' unbridled malice in polemical derogation of the Jews and the desire to present the Church as "spiritual Israel".

[132] Here, however, there is no allegorisation of all the characters. Barnabas allegorises only when it suits his polemics.

[133] After Jacob and Esau the example of Isaac and Ishmael would not add anything, and it moreover lacks polemical sting.

[134] What was not spiritual enough to prove that Abraham was uncircumcised (IX, 7-8, because there in this sense it is almost literal) fits in here very well. Talking about the preference of the younger brother to the older, it proves (according to his *gnosis*) that the younger brother who inherits the covenant is the uncircumcised one.

[135] In *Rom.* iv: 12, ἀκροβυστία is justified as merely being equal to circumcision (with belief). Barnabas is more radical—for him circumcision is an error (IX, 5).

[136] Throughout his examples it is evident (even though not stated explicitly) that his polemical aim is to exalt the Church as the spiritual Israel. This becomes even clearer by comparison with Justin (*Dial. c. Try.* xi) . . . "for the true spiritual Israel and descendants of Judah, Jacob, Isaac and Abraham (who in uncircumcision was approved of and blessed by God on account of his faith, and called the father of many nations) are *we*, etc.

19

(XIV, 2-4=IV 7-8) to strengthen this argument, and to prove the temporary nature of the Jewish covenant in contrast with the Christian one, which is eternal. He goes a step further in trying to show that the covenant was never intended to refer to the Jews, by quoting a series of scriptures on "light for the Gentiles" (XIV, 1-9). With these terms and proofs he comes to convince his fellow gentile-Christians that they were meant to be the only "holy people" (*ibid.* 6).[137]

XV. The Sabbath, one of the cardinal tenets of Judaism, is also connected with his main topic since Scripture called it a "perpetual covenant".[138] That reason alone would suffice for our author to attempt to mullify its literal meaning. This could easily be done in accordance with the line taken by Jesus. Barnabas, however, ignoring this aspect completely, employs various other systems. His manifold efforts hint that he is aiming at counterbalancing Jewish propaganda.[139] One of his arguments (v. 3-5) originates in apocalyptic

---

[137] Cf. the previous note.

[138] *Exod.* xxxi: 16.

[139] On *Exod.* xxxi: 13, the *Mekhilta* comments (ed. FRIEDMAN, 103b. and again 104b): ולא ביני ובין אומות העולם and later (ed. FRIEDMAN 104b): מגיד שאין לעולם מישראל במלה שבת ה. From such expressions, however, there is no proof that Jews could not propagandise Sabbath observance to Gentiles. All the extreme expressions about Gentiles observing the Sabbath (*San.* 58b; *Deut. R.* i, 18 etc.) originate from the third century, from the circle of R. Yoḥanan and Resh Laqish (and their disciples). Even in the Talmud (*San.* 59a) there is a contrast between R. Yoḥanan's opinion and R. Me'irs universalistic approach. There is an interesting tradition to illustrate the development and the change in attitude: R. Yoḥanan brings forward a tradition in the name of R. Simeon b. Yoḥai: "If the children of Israel would observe two Sabbath days properly according the law, they would be immediately redeemed, as it says (*Is.* lvi: 5) (שבתותי in the plural, therefore the minimum is two) . . . and it is written after it: (*ibid.* 7) והביאותים etc." The strange thing about this Midrash is that verse 7 which is quoted does not refer to Jews but to the "sons of the strangers" (Cf. J. *Ta'an.* i, 1, 64a, where a disciple of R. Yoḥanan uses completely different verses, most probably because of this difficulty). It is obvious that something is missing in this Midrash between the two scriptural quotations, and it looks as if R. Yoḥanan shortened it according to his own taste leaving out a passage which he opposed. But we have another Midrash from R. Yoḥanan (most probably originating from R. Simeon b. Yoḥai) which runs as follows: "Every one (not only Israel) who keeps the Sabbath properly, even if he is an idol-worshipper like the generation of Enoch, his sins are forgiven etc.". From there we may conclude that R. Yoḥanan had a tradition (otherwise he would not state something opposed to his own views) that if Idol-worshippers (=Gentiles) would keep one Sabbath their sins would be forgiven (=Redemption ?). According the the last Midrash we may quite safely reconstruct the corrupt (or censured) Midrash and add between the two scripture quotations: "And for the Nations of the World even one Sabbath suffices, as it says "Sabbath" . . . (*Is.* lvi: 2 or 6 is in the singular, therefore one suffices). Now if in the time of R. Simeon b. Yoḥai and R. Me'ir it was still possible to advocate the keeping of precepts by Gentiles, in the period, before Bar Kokhba it seem even more likely.

20

circles,[140] namely, that the six days of creation are not meant literally but as an allegory of the six millenia of this world leaving the seventh for the redemption. Consequently, the Sabbath is not the seventh day of the week, but redemption at the seventh millenium, the final and only Sabbath.[141] Another sharper argument (v. 1, 2, 6-7) denies the possibility of Sabbath observance at the present as it was commanded (with purity), because of sins. If the Jews' claim that they observe the Sabbath properly were true, then "we (=Christians) are astray in all things".[142] The thrid argument (v. 8) shows from Scripture that the present Sabbath is not acceptable to God.[143]

XVI. With the allegorisation of the Temple Barnabas concludes the polemical section of his work. On this most controversial chapter much ink has been spilled, and the opinions of scholars diverge widely.[144] With reference to our main problem,[145] it is safe to assume that at least the hope of the rebuilding of the Temple was a probability which had some reasonable chances of materialisation in this historical milieu.[146] For the Jews, it was not only actually looked forward to but even exploited (when social or political conditions were favourable) as a propaganda device. Barnabas' heated arguments are aimed at nullifying this hope and the danger which it contained for Christianity. He ridicules the Jews who hope for a building and not for God (v. 1) and compares their Temple cult to that of the heathens

[140] *Rev.* ch. xx etc., cf. also 2 *Pet.* iii: 8. There is however a great difference; Barnabas' chiliasm definitely puts off the final redemption to the end of the sixth (or seventh) millenium. For Jewish millenarianism cf. *San.* 97a; *Rosh Hash.* 31a.
[141] This argument is aimed also against messianic vacillations in general based on the belief of a very early coming of this age. He does not mention this part of the polemic explicitly, because the Christians of this period still believed that the "second coming" would be in their own days.
[142] This passage shows more clearly than any former one that he is writing his *Epistle* for convinced Christians whose belief in Jesus is so strong, that he can use it as an argument against the Law. For similar argumentation cf. *Rom.* iv: 14; Ignatius, *Ep. to the Magnesians* viii, 1.
[143] It therefore supports the former arguments: the Sabbath of the Jews is proclaimed as wrong by God. Only the final Sabbath when "we" will become pure, is acceptable.
[144] On the basis of this chapter, WEIL (*op. cit.*) and A. SCHLATTER (*Die Tage Hadrians u. Trajan* (Gütersloh 1897), p. 61f.), and many Jewish scholars who share their opinion, believe in an actual rebuilding of the Temple at this period. The opposite view has been taken by most Christian scholars since HARNACK, but they vary greatly in their opinions. Cf. e.g. J. D. BURGER, *L'Enigme de Barnabas*, *Museum Helveticum*, III (1946), p. 189.
[145] An excellent analysis of this chapter and its historical background was given recently by G. ALLON, *Toledoth Ha-yehudim* etc. (Tel Aviv, 1954), vol. I, p. 279-282.
[146] We cannot enter here into the problem of the historical background cf. n. 37).

21

(v. 2).[147] The Temple should be spiritualised (v. 6-8) so as to mean the human heart.[148] How is such a Temple built?[149] By God's words (faith, promise, ordinances, prophecy) which dwell inwardly in the heart, and lead towards the establishment of the incorruptible Temple[150] (v. 9). The Divine message, amazing and unexpected as it may sound, rather than the personality of the man who preaches it, is the "spiritual Temple *being* built", (v. 10).

XVII. In summing up the first part of his *Epistle* some finishing strokes are added by the author, explaining why he does not elaborate the future[151] of Christianity. It was to be expected that the master of "Knowledge" would indulge more in eschatology; our author's over-cautious reluctance to commit himself as regards the future is symptomatic. The aim of the *Epistle* is to counteract a tendency based on a form of propaganda for the future in which imagination runs wild, and it preaches the restraint of such "authority" of the soul.[152] Therefore Barnabas is content with "knowledge" applicable to the present (to save his audience from the dangers of Jewish preaching), and he refrains from entering into details about the future, which they would not understand because they "are hidden in parables".

XVIII-XX. In addition to the "spiritual" part there is subjoined a practical part called by our author "another knowledge and doctrine",[153] that of the "Two Ways". This part serves to counterbalance the "spiritual" part which, by opposing in such an extreme manner the literal observance of the law, might have led to misunderstanding. Our author, while concentrating on opposing any Judaistic influence realised the danger of antinomianism which might result from such preaching. The "Two Ways" represent for him the law which, although emptied of its literal content, was allegorised into ethical

[147] The polemical exaggeration is obvious. Such distortions of the truth are quite common in polemical literature. Cf. the *Epistle to Diognetus* iii, 3.

[148] This has already been mentioned by him (IV, 11 and VI, 15). The only difference here is that it contains an additional polemical motive, postponing the building of the Temple till the end of the "week" (cf. n. 144). This is a further scriptural proof that the hope for a Temple in the present *aeon* is vain.

[149] He tries to reconcile the apparent contradiction between the "future" Temple (cf. former note) and the permanent demand to turn the heart into a Temple.

[150] An obvious allusion to the Jewish Temple which had already twice been destroyed and, if rebuilt, would still be liable to fall.

[151] HEFELE's reading is here preferred to that of Cod. Sin. Internal evidence (not textual criticism) forces us to accept this reading. Otherwise the purpose of the *Epistle* becomes meaningless, since it is motivated by the "present evil times". Cf. II, 1 and 10; IV, 1f and 9; XVI, 4; XVIII, 2 (in Cod. Sin.).

[152] IV, 2.

[153] ἑτέραν γνῶσιν καί διδαχὴν (Cf. *Didache*, ch. i-iii).

22

precepts[154] and christologies, thus avoiding the relapse into heathen libertinism.[155]

XXI. The final exhortation is blended with personal emotional encouragements (v. 7 and 9) and prayers for the guidance of God (v. 5). As a summary of his work, almost all its features are hinted at (4-5) in the conclusion. He stresses that the main purpose of his writing is focused on preparation (according to "knowledge") for the *real* salvation (v. 1-3, 6, 8).

* * *

We now have to review all the possible solutions, in order to reach a final decision on our problem. Exposition of the *Epistle* has helped us to realise that it *is* possible to treat it as a homogeneous work despite its discrepancies, once we have a logical explanation for them. It is certain that the main purpose of the *Epistle* is the "divorcing the Church from association with the Jewish nation and religion".[156] But this explanation does not answer any of the main problems. Windisch, therefore, rightly states that Barnabas proves that separation is an accomplished fact rather than that he had actively participated in its being brought about. He gives a different solution to the problem,[157] and regards the polemical features in the *Epistle* as an inheritance which came to Barnabas through his sources. He used christological testimonial literature (*Testimonien-lehre*, consisting of the collection of texts arranged according to topics, with introductions and notes, aimed at proving the truth of the Church against the Jews when such points were raised), which by its very nature was anti-Jewish. This theory is based on the general tone of the *Epistle*, which (according to Windisch) gives the impression that "Judaism has been annihilated, we have been victorious, there is no danger to the Church from them". All the actual dangers (evil days, Temple building, etc.) are not sufficiently stressed for them to be taken seriously. The *Epistle* was not meant for any other purpose than to prompt and encourage the spirit of his readers.[158] The difficulty as to why Barnabas' extremism in the confutation of the Jews exceeds even that of the N.T. and all the other Church Fathers has also been dealt with by Windisch[159]; Barnabas' radicalism is a pro-

---

[154] Cf. ch. II, III, IX, X, XV and XVI.
[155] Cf. n. 59.
[156] K. WEIZSÄCKER, *Zur Kritik d. Barnabasbrief,* etc. (1863) p. 2.
[157] pp. 322-323; 410.
[158] . . . "der Verfasser einige Testimonien in eschatalogische Mahnungen zusammengestelt hat zur Erbauung seiner Leser".
[159] p. 395.

23

duct of his "spiritual" law exegesis. He adopted his exegetical system from the (Alexandrian) Jews, but he uses it against them. Barnabas is similar to, but more consistent than, his predecessors (Philo and Aristeas), and his allegories exclude the literal meaning.

Windisch's brilliant but, unfortunately, over cautious analysis suffers from several weak points:

1. Why should Barnabas' scriptural interpretation oppose the teachings of the N.T. and of the Church? There must be a more profound reason than exegetical consistency for Barnabas' usurpation of the "authority" to do it. He himself repeats, in the teaching regarding the "Two Ways", a warning against Schism.[160]

2. Except in a very few chapters, there is very little evidence in sequence, connection or exposition to suggest that they are based on "Testimonial literature".[160a]

Furthermore it has been proved by Allon[161] that Barnabas used a Jewish written tradition current among the Jews in Alexandria which was attached to the whole scripture. It was a kind of Midrash written in Greek, interlocated into the scripture[162] and considered as an entity with it. Similar phenomena of Midrash interwoven into scripture and fused into one unit, we find also in other books of the period.[163] Allon suggests that the source which Barnabas used was probably similar to the Targum of Pseudo-Johnathan, but composed in Greek; for in that paraphrase we also have *Halakhah* and *'Aggada* grafted into the verses of Scripture.

Once the foundation of Windisch's thesis is refuted the whole system becomes shaky. Allon, like many other scholars, follows in many points the cautious approach of Windisch,[164] but about the problem of Barnabas' Jewish polemic he has a different explanation[165]: the *Epistle* was written at a time of *local* persecutions against the Christians. Many Christians returned (?) to Judaism in order to escape persecutions, but they did not give up their faith. This situation of

---

[160] XIX, 12.
[160a] Possibly regarding chapters XI-XII WINDISCH is right, and they are based on such *Testimoniallehre*. As has been clearly demonstrated in our analysis of the chapters, many of WINDISCH's assumptions regarding interpolation, contradiction etc. are superfluous.
[161] *Tarbiz* xi (1939), p. 23-238.
[162] Cf. VII 3-7; VIII 1-4; X 7; XV 1.
[163] e.g. *Jubilees, liber Antiquitatum biblicarum*, etc.
[164] He disagrees with WEIL, GRAETZ, JOEL, etc. on the interpretation of ch. XVI (concerning the Imperial order to rebuild the Temple) and accepts wholeheartedly the view that this matter is not really stressed in the *Epistle*.
[165] *Toledoth Ha-yehudim*, etc. (Tel-Aviv 1954), vol. I, p. 282.

24

Christians observing the Jewish law prompted his warning against the danger of "becoming a convert to their law". The passage concerning the building of the Temple is introduced into his treatise only as an afterthought. Perhaps some rumours (substantiated or otherwise) reached him when writing the *Epistle*, and he added in a hurry some doubtful remarks in order to console and encourage his readers.

In examining this solution critically, we cannot help pointing out certain difficulties.

1. Were it true that the *Epistle* was written because of persecutions this fact would have been mentioned if not stressed. If, because the question of the Temple is not completely stressed, we reject the theory that the author was instigated to write his *Epistle* by any actual attempt at rebuilding it, we ought not to jump from the frying pan into the fire by inventing a background which is not even hinted at. Moreover, we often find in the writings of this period exhortations to accept martyrdom, to follow the example of the martyr and other similar features characteristic of a period of persecution. These make a very good background for preaching and influence, and Barnabas, who used all artificial devices for this end, would not shy away from using such a natural method if only it were opportune. Furthermore there are some passages where martyrology would be expected even under normal conditions because of the subject matter,[165a] and how could this escape his attention unless his mind was preoccupied by a danger which threatened his readers to the uttermost degree?

2. The chapter about the Temple does not differ from the other parts of the book, and it is hard to see why it should be regarded as a strange or an interpolated element. A great part of the *Epistle* deals with sacrifices, the Temple, etc. but there is not even a hint that these are matters belonging to the past. The destruction of the Temple is mentioned, but not exploited as an argument against the Jews, as was done later by Justin.[166] The whole temple cult is discussed and attacked as a matter of fact, which means that despite the temporary discontinuation of this cult due to the destruction, some historical circumstances forced even a cynical and hostile observer to admit the belief in its restoration (at least temporarily). Even the claim that it is not sufficiently emphasised is but only part of the truth. If we consider

---

[165a] In II, 1, speaking on the "present evil days" at least some encouragement would be expected. Although he speaks of the sufferings of Christ and the Christians and of achieving everything by pain, there is never a hint of martyrology. Similarly VIII, 6.

[166] 1 *Apol.* xlvii; *Dial. c. Try.* xcii, *ibid.* cxvi.

25

that the polemics are aimed against the messianic movement—as we noted in our analysis of the chapters—we get a different picture. The *Epistle* begins its polemics with sacrifices (ch. II) and concludes with the Temple (ch. XVI). Similarly it does not miss any opportunity to hit out against Jewish "hopes".[167] The fact that he uses an implicit rather than an explicit style does not detract from the powerful nature of the evidence.[168]

3. The "evil days" cannot be explained as persecution and dangers of a similar physical kind, but as fear of conversion and of spiritual conquest deceitfully achieved by the "prince of the time".[169] Similarly the emperor connected with this "evil time" does not appear as a persecutor, nor even as the "stumbling block". Even if we do not agree with Weil on the theory of the reconstruction of the Temple being by order of the emperor, what the passage does at least indicate is that the Roman authorities supported (perhaps sub-consciously?), or were connected with the course of the "evil time".

4. If we were to suppose that the *Epistle* was meant for Christians, who for the sake of an easy way out reverted to Judaism, the exhortations would have been different. For what reason do such Christians, forced into Judaism by circumstances, need the chapters on Baptism and the Cross?[170] Such chapters are needed only if we assume that there existed a danger to the very principles of Christianity either from a declared total war against its dogmas, or at least from propaganda (based on the expectations raised by promised events) which would make Christian beliefs void.

5. The same applies to the chapter on the "Two Ways". Were the Judaising tendencies to which he addresses himself caused by pressure only, there would not be any need for the commandments[171] being given such emphasis. Such exhortation would in no way counter-balance the strict Jewish adherence to the precepts. If it had been the case that Barnabas' audience consisted of Christians who accepted the Jewish Law under duress, the preaching of "Grace", brought by

---

[167] e.g. in VI, 3 the sarcastic remark: "is our hope on a stone?" is an allusion against the Temple and altar built of stone. The same applies to the allegorisation of the "land flowing with milk and honey" (v. 13), which denies its reference to the Holy Land, etc.

[168] For his system of hinting instead of using explicit language cf. n. 179 and text, *infra*.

[169] Cf. e.g. II 10.

[170] Ch. XI-XII. cf. nn. 142 and 160a.

[171] IV, 11-12; VI, 19; XVI, 9; XX, 1, 6-7, 8.

26

Christ, ought to have been used for the confutation of the law. However, this element is very little stressed in the *Epistle*.[172]

6. Barnabas' frenzied and sophisticated methods of proving the most extreme anti-Jewish arguments indicate that he did not aim at an audience that was merely sitting on the fence. On the contrary, it is a war of life and death in which he tries to uproot all Jewish existence. Even Justin, one of the fiercest of apologists, is more tolerant.[173] Only an extraordinary historical background[174] could produce such violent outbursts.

Scholars who have advocated the view that there did take place an actual rebuilding of the Temple with Roman backing, and that it was this which provoked Barnabas to write his *Epistle*, were close to the truth in certain points. It is evident from the *Epistle* that the Jews' religion and way of life had a profound effect even on Christians, and that their victorious mood, or prosperity, or propaganda (or all three together) endangered the beliefs of Christians. Unless we accuse Barnabas of slander (or tilting at windmills), this is no way to write about the Jews had they been totally defeated and the victims of persecution.[175]

A cautious approach in this field is overwhelmingly justifiable. Nevertheless, the evidence speaks for itself. Even such a painstaking scholar as the late G. Allon,[176] while speaking on the significance of Barnabas' chapter on the Temple, had to yield to the implications of historical evidence. The following is his presentation: The author wants to minimise the significance of the Temple in the past, and of all hopes for the future. This is done on behalf of his fellow Christians, in order to prevent them from accepting Judaism. Had there not in reality been any hope for the reconstruction of the Temple, the author would not shy away from inferring from the available facts, *viz.* that all hopes for Israel are vain and void, a decisive proof of the victory of Christianity and the worthlessness of Judaism. And the prophecy about the future depending on Scripture, to the effect that the "The city, Israel, and the Temple will be delivered up . . . ", proves it even

[172] This has already been stressed by J. WEISS (op. ct. p. 94) and many others after him.
[173] For example, on the problem of a Christian observing the Law he comments: "Such a one will be saved if he does not strive in any way to persuade others. I mean those Gentiles who have been circumcised from error by Christ, to observe the same thing as himself, telling them that they will not be saved unless they do so". (*Dial. c. Try.* xlvii).
[174] Cf. n. 61.
[175] Cf. SCHLATTER (*op. cit.*) p. 66.
[176] *Toledoth*, etc., vol. I p. 281.

27

more. It seems, therefore, that Barnabas himself is perplexed by the situation and endeavours to console himself and his readers with prophecies of the future; and in this way to show that the prosperity of the Jews is temporary only.

Because the question of the Temple is not sufficiently stressed in the *Epistle* as a whole it has not been taken sufficiently into account by careful scholars. This would not seem to add weight to our theory concerning the Jewish messianic movement as the cause of the writing of the *Epistle*. However, our analysis of the book had greatly minimised this lack. But the best proof of all for our thesis is the fact that it is a characteristic of Barnabas not to speak explicitly on the important issues but to hint at them, relying on their familiarity to his readers. We have now to consider how far this method is evident in the most important and central issues in the *Epistle*.

1. With regard to "Evil days" and "the worker of evil" against which all his exhortation is aimed,[177] the character, identity, function etc. of these evils are never revealed. We have to guess what is meant by inference from elsewhere.[178] He purposely avoids mentioning the crucial points. When warning about this "final stumbling block"[179] and in his apocalyptic speculations on the emperors (indicating at least their connection with it) he limits himself to hints. "*You ought then to understand*"[180] is his motto, because the identity of his target is never in doubt.

2. It was long ago noted by Windisch[181] that there is a discrepancy between the author's deep and intensive eschatological urge and aim,[182] and his preaching on the other hand of "patience"[183] and Chiliasm.[184] But all this is due to the mystical style in which he wraps up his cardinal points. He has two separate events distinctly in his mind: (*a*) The present "evil days" which are a part of the Divine plan to hasten the redemption (by trial of the real believers); (*b*) The final and second coming of the Messiah which is to signify a new world.[185] Because of the confusion in these matters among Christians (which

---

[177] II, 1, 10.
[178] Cf. e.g. 1 *John* ii: 18 (=iv: 3); 2 *John* i: 7.
[179] VI, 2. Cf. *ibid.*, 1, "things which *now* are".
[180] *ibid.*, 6.
[181] *op. cit.* p. 365.
[182] XXI, 3, "the day is at hand".
[183] II, 2, XXI, 5.
[184] XV, 4-5.
[185] The same contradiction as between בעתה and אחישנה (*Is.* lx: 22) is manifested in the Talmud, as we have seen in the case of R. Eliezer and R. Joshua; and it went on developing into ammoraic times.

28

could easily be exploited by their opponents), he is content with hints only.[186] A striking similarity to this attitude can be found in the *Gospel of St. John*,[187] which has many affinities with our *Epistle*.

3. Scholars have paid very little attention to Barnabas' exclusive usage of the words "they" and "we" instead of Jews (including Jewish-Christians) and Gentiles.[188] The main issue that concerns Barnabas—the Jews and Judaism—is not mentioned explicitly.[189] Israel, which is mentioned, refers to the scriptural Israel, mainly in connection with quotations.[190] Gentiles in the *Epistle* are identical with heathen.[191] Only in connection with texts where there is reference to their origin, to prove that salvation was intended for other than Jews, do Gentiles appear again.[192] The inference is simple: *We* are now the real Israel. Since the covenant belongs to Christians, the latter are not Gentiles any more.[193] Again an analogy may be drawn from *John*.[194] The same applies to the curious omission of the Pascal offer-

---

[186] Cf. notes on ch. XVII.

[187] *John* xvi: 12. On the theological background of the Fourth Gospel there are divided opinions. It needed a mystic, W. R. Inge, to express the most striking one: "It marks the final severance between Christianity and Messianism". (The Theology of the fourth Gospel in *Cambridge Biblical Essays*, ed. H. B. SWETE, London, 1909, p. 255). Later he writes: "In spite of the respectful treatment of Messianism it was really Jewish-Christianity which was thrown overboard . . ." (p. 257).

[188] Most outstandingly in Chapters II and III, where he divides the Scriptures to make them refer partly to "them" and partly to "us".

[189] The Latin translation is not reliable in this respect. If often translates "Israel" as *populo Judeorum* (e.g. IV, 14 etc.).

[190] IV, 14. The "signs and wonders wrought in Israel" are those mentioned in Scripture; V, 2, 8. Also in connection with the sufferings of Jesus, which were predicted by the Prophet. Similarly VI, 7; VIII, 1 and XI, 1; In XVI, 5 it is also connected with what the "Scripture says".

[191] XVI, 2.

[192] As in the case of Abraham, who is called πατέρα ἐθνῶν (XIII, 7) or φῶς ἐθνῶν (XIV, 7, 8), all from Scripture.

[193] These sentiments are stressed explicitly by Justin: "but when he says that they as Gentiles rejoice with His people, He calls them Gentiles to reproach you. For even as you provoked Him to anger by your idolatry, so also He has deemed those who were idolaters worthy of knowing His will, and of inheriting his inheritance". (*Dial. c. Try.* cxxx). Or, "Since then God blessed this people, and calls them Israel, and declares them to be his inheritance" (*ibid.* cxxiii), cf. also *ibid.* cxxv.

[194] Jews mentioned in *John* are meant in rather a derogatory sense. Whenever the author means to praise them, the term Israel is used (*John* iii: 10; xii: 14). The classical example, the text *Israelite indeed in whom is no guile* (*ibid.* i: 47), may have served as an example to consider as Israel those only "in whom there is no guile" (according to Christian thinking, the Jews were branded as hypocrites). The word *Gentiles* appears once only (3 *John* i: 7) referring to heathens.

29

ing, because it is difficult to explain away the censure it contained of the Gentiles.[195]

4. The nature of Barnabas gnosis was excellently presented by Windisch.[195a] However, this main concept of Barnabas' mysticism has an even deeper meaning. It is a commonplace that this "knowledge" is a Divine gift (I, 7; VI, 10; IX, 9) equal in character to the knowledge of the Prophets (IX, 8; X, 1 and 10). Nevertheless, Barnabas does not mention the Prophets of his own time even once, despite the fact that they were still plentiful even in later periods.[196] It is only once that he partly gives the game away, by asserting that God is "prophesying in us".[197] It is certain that in this instance he is not referring to the prophecies of the past because immediately afterwards comes the exhortation not to look upon the personality of the preacher but on his Divine message. Furthermore if "knowledge" is equal to prophecy Barnabas, as the master of "knowledge", must have considered himself a contemporary prophet. But because of his mystical system he does not reveal this openly. When introducing the "Two Ways"[198] he calls it "another knowledge and teaching". But following immediately on this, when enumerating the points of this knowledge, he says "Two Ways of teaching and authority". Analogy shows that to our author "knowledge" is equal to "authority".[199] This is the same authority (or power)[200] which was given to the twelve Apostles to

---

[195] On the paschal lamb in *John* there are divided opinions. But the plain explanation is that it was purposely omitted. STRACK-BILLERBECK's (*Kommentar etc.* II, p. 838f.) efforts to reconcile the "last supper" of *John* with this event in the other Gospels (as referring to the "Paschal offering") is most ambiguous. The "passover of the Jews", mentioned many times, is not complementary and cannot serve as a "Type" for the Messiah. There is no proof that *John* xix: 36 is a paraphrase of *Num.* ix: 12. It may as well be one of *Ps.* xxxiv: 21 (cf. STRACK-BILLERBECK, II, p. 583). The "Lamb", which is a beloved symbol, is likewise not the Paschal lamb, but rather this of *Is.* liii: 7 (which was one of the main Christological chapters, cf. Justin, *Dial c. Try.* cxi). At the beginning this attack on Gentiles caused confusion (exploited most probably by Jewish-Christians), and it was therefore avoided. Such development may still be traced in the case of "Give not that which is holy unto the dogs" (*Matth.* vii: 6, cf. *ibid.* xv: 24, 26) which was explained away by the *Didache* (xi, 5) forbidding any unbaptised person to partake of the Eucharist. Possibly that is how they later explained also וכל ערל לא יאכל בו (*Ex.* xii: 48).

[195a] *op. cit.*, pp. 308-9.

[196] Cf. H. WEINEL, *Propheten*, etc. in HEINNECKE's *Neutestamentliche Apocryphen*,[2] p. 290 ff.

[197] *ibid.* xvi, 9. He says this of himself, cf. n. 206.

[198] XVIII, 1.

[199] γνῶσις = ἐξουσία.

[200] But "power" only in this sense. For power in the ordinary sense he uses δύναμις (cf. e.g. XV, 6).

30

preach the Gospel,[201] and the very same which in the Gospels is opposed to the *teaching* of the Scribes.[202] From the *Didache* we have learnt what was the difference in the Church between teacher and prophet. The teacher cannot deviate in any detail of his teachings from the doctrines of the Church.[203] The prophet on the other hand has much more freedom (he speaks with *authority*, or "in the spirit"). He is not to be challenged on what he "speaks in the spirit".[204] Only "from his behaviour, then, the false prophet and the true prophet shall be known".[205]

We can now understand a little better why Barnabas stresses that he writes "not as a teacher"[206] but as one of them. His doctrines were not exactly those of the teaching of the Church, but he writes as one of them but "in the spirit" or with authority.

In this case it is easy to guess why he does not mention prophecy explicitly. It was an "evil time", when the "worker of evil has authority",[207] and there is a danger that this "wicked ruler" may gain power over us[208]; he therefore preaches for the limitation of this spiritual "power", not to associate with the wicked "lest we be made like them".[209] If we think of Jewish "prophets" who acted in the service of the messianic movement (as may be seen in the apocalyptic literature, and in some chapters of the *Sibylline Oracles* which belong to this period) the above passages become self-explanatory.

This gives us a clue to the reason that Barnabas avoids mentioning all the main issues explicitly. The Jewish polemical activities which endangered the beliefs of some Christians were not clearly crystallised at this time, and Barnabas did not want to commit himself in those days of confusion; but he was also unwilling to wait until the matter was completely cleared up, since it was rumour which more than anything else was injurious to the faith. He therefore used this ambiguous method of expressing himself in order to exhort his fellow Christians,

---

[201] VIII, 3. cf. 2 *Cor.* x: 8. Possibly this is the reason that the *Epistle* was ascribed to Barnabas?

[202] *Matth.* vii: 29; *Mark* i: 22, ;*Luke* iv: 32. (cf. STRACK-BILLERBECK, *Kommentar, etc.* I p. 470).

[203] *Didache* xi, 1.

[204] *Ibid.*, 7.

[205] *Ibid,.* 8.

[206] I, 8; IV, 9. This explains the odd construction. (He would like to elaborate but is in a hurry because of his devotion, as it becomes—not a teacher—but one who loves, to leave out nothing of that (prophecy) which we have).

[207] II, 1.

[208] VI, 13.

[209] *Ibid.*, 2.

c

31

who knew exactly what he was driving at. While declining the honour of being a teacher (most probably because of his extremism), he maintained his claim of prophecy but in a veiled way—because prophets were numerous just then; but he nevertheless wanted to imply that it was only such "authority" which can teach the kind of "knowledge" that is valid.

If we realise that this lack of explicit stressing of the most important points is a system deliberately chosen by Barnabas, the main difficulty is solved. For the rest of the explanation we can depend on our analysis of the chapters of the *Epistle*, which demonstrated not only that there is no single instance which contradicts our hypothesis but also solves most of the difficulties.

We may now formulate the answer to our main problem: the *Epistle* was written as an answer to the Jewish messianic movement which prophesied the early reconstruction of the Temple, the ingathering of the exiles, the coming of the Messiah, political freedom, etc. These aspirations were given a fillip by certain political and social events, which could be explained as favouring Jewish hopes, and they were consequently used as a proof that such hopes were going to be fulfilled. The Roman Empire was considered as being in favour (consciously or otherwise) of these hopes. By its preaching, prophecies and supposed success, the movement drew converts and sympathisers to Judaism and the Law, including some from the rank and file of Christianity. The similarities between the two religions at this period increased the danger, to check which the author wrote his extremist *Epistle* to prove: (i) that there was never a Jewish covenant and that, consequently, (ii) all Jewish hopes were based on a misunderstanding.

Leeds   S. LOWY

ADDITIONAL NOTES

I Concerning the tendency in the Talmud towards minimising the messianic movements (cf. n. 33) one has to add an additional factor. There existed an overwhelming denial of the continuation of the apocalyptic tradition in rabbinic Judaism, based on the controversial and polemical bias of Jewish and Christian scholars respectively. Cf. G. G. SCHOLEM, *Zum Verständnis der messianischen Idee in Judentum*, Eranos Jahrbuch xxviii (1960), pp. 203f.

II The continuation of the sacrificial cult after 70 C.E. (cf. n. 84) has again been advocated recently. Cf. K. W. CLARK, *Worship in the Jerusalem Temple After A.D.*70, New Testament Studies VI (1960) p. 269f. Most of the sources on which this article is built have been previously considered. The only new "evidence", the New Samaritan Chronicle published by E. N. ADLER and M. SELIGSOHN, (*REJ* xlv, 1902, p. 80f.), is historically most unreliable. Furthermore, the story seems to be a Samaritan version of the Jewish legend regarding the subsitution of the two sacrificial lambs by pigs during the siege of Jerusalem in 63 B.C.E. (according to T. B. *Soṭah* 49b and parallels) and in the war of 70 C.E. (according T. J. *Ber.* i, 4, 7b and parallels).

32

III To the diversity of opinions on the background of the Fourth Gospel (cf. n. 187) a new theory has been added recently by J. A. T. ROBINSON (*The Destination and Purpose of St. John's Gospel*, New Testament Studies VI, 1960, p. 117f.). The Author claims that this Gospel was meant for Hellenistic Jews, and was written by their brethren from Judea (who came to the Diaspora as refugees) in order that they might not err like the Jews who denied Jesus. But the Author does not educe any historical evidence for these theories. Furthermore, the "other sheep" (x: 16) cannot refer to Jews, as is evident from xi: 52. The universal character of the preaching is quite clear (xii: 31, cf. STRACK-BILLERBECK, *Kommentar, etc.* vol. ii, p. 548), its purpose being to "save the world" (xii: 47).

33

ORIGEN AND THE EARLY JEWISH-CHRISTIAN DEBATE

By A. J. PHILIPPOU

The early rejection of God's revelation in Jesus Christ by the Jewish people has, inevitably, much troubled the Christian mind, and it is natural that an immense literature has been accumulated on the subject.[1] Yet at the death of St. Paul, Christianity was still part of the Hebraic religion and was regarded by most as a Jewish sect. The earliest Christians were not aware of any discontinuity between the new and the old covenant.[2] In point of fact, primitive Christianity had a geographical centre and this was Jerusalem. By the middle of the second century Christianity is seen more and more as a separate religion busily engaged in apologetics to the Greek and Roman world, rather anxious to establish its roots in antiquity. So long as the rejection of Christianity by the Jewish people remained in doubt it was only natural that the main effort of the early apologists should be to explain and justify it to their Hebrew brethren while at the same time advocate the view that Christianity was firmly rooted in the Hebraic tradition.

This becomes apparent in Justin's celebrated essay *Dialogos pros Tryphona* in which three main ideas are developed: viz. the transitoriness of the Old Covenant and its precepts, the identity of the Logos with the God who appears in the Old Testament, and the new vocation of the Gentiles to take the place of Israel.

A few years later the whole Christian literature relating to this theme loses its irenic spirit and becomes a polemic against the Jews. Tertullian opened the way with his *Adversus Judaeos* while Hippolytus of Rome soon followed with his essay on *Demonstratio Contra Judaeos*. From here on an open polemic or a missionary activity is adopted by the Christian Church as regards the Jewish people.

---

[1] It is only recently that historical theology began to cut across the confessional differences and to treat the relationship of Church and Synagogue from an unbiased perspective.

[2] Ensebius notes that the community of Jerusalem was entirely made up of faithful Hebrews, HE, IV, 5, 2.

Now to decide on the date at which the separation of the Church from the Synagogue took place is no easy task for the historian, for there are so many factors to be considered. When the armies of Titus advanced on Jerusalem, the Judeo-Christians retired to Pella, while at the same time, the rabbinical leaders retired to Jabne. To the fall of the city and the loss of the temple the two different religious groups reacted differently. For the rabbinical leaders, it meant a punishment for the sins of the people. But the Judeo-Christians saw in this God's condemnation of the Jewish people for their refusal to accept Jesus Christ and the final departure of God's grace from Israel.

It is safe to presume that shortly thereafter all the synagogues of the diaspora had been informed by the Jewish religious leaders of Palestine of a new malediction and warned not to have any dealings with the Christians. Of the actual wording of the original malediction we cannot be certain. It was an insertion into the daily Blessings recited in the Synagogue as a declaration about heretics worded by the rabbis of Jabne in such a manner that the Judeo-Christians should not pronounce it.[3] In other words, this act shows clearly that the Judeo-Christians still frequented the services in Synagogues.

The frequent references in patristic literature show that the matter touched the diaspora even more closely than Palestine itself. If we examine closely Justin, Ensebius and Jerome, we can make a fair construction of a letter sent to the diaspora by Palestine. It held a formal denial of the truth of the Christian account of the teaching and resurrection of Jesus. Furthermore, Christianity was interpreted as a denial of the God of Israel and of the Torah. It was a dignified but firm denunciation of the Christian accompanied by an order to have no fellowship with them, and a copy of the new malediction to be included in the service of the Synagogue.

When the Jew had lost everything, Jerusalem and the Temple, Christians like Tertullian and Hippolytus tried to disinherit the Jew from his own sacred writings at a time when these provided his only comfort. For all the Law and the Prophets led on to Christ the Messiah. Rejecting Him, the Jew was no longer part of the Covenant community of grace in which God has the initia-

---

[3] Jerome, in *IS.* V, 18, P.L. XXIV, 87.

tive, in which God remains the faithful and loving partner despite man's obedience at disobedience.

In the *Contra Celsum*, the reader cannot fail to be impressed with the theological sensitivity and the irenic spirit with which Origen approaches the Jews. The *Contra Celsum* is at once too long a work, and too well known by numerous excellent exegetical essays, to require or permit a detail introduction.[4] We must be content to presume the reader's acquaintance with this classic of early Christian apologetic, which Ensebius regarded as the final answer to the heresies of all centuries to come. The aim of Celsus was to show how shallow the Christian religion was. He had studied his subject well and had relied heavily on a host of pagan arguments to attack both Judaism and Christianity and it is interesting to note that Origen does not hesitate to resort to the stock-in-track of the corresponding Jewish apologetic. Furthermore, as against Celsus using Jewish anti-Christian polemic, Origen far from attacking the Jews, refutes the argument of his learned opponent by denying that a Jew would have used such language against the Christians.

It was the duty of scholars to warn the upper classes against the insidious advance Christianity makes in the world and this is what motivates Celsus to write *The True Doctrine*, ἀληθὴς λόγος, as he entitles his work.[5] Origen is called to refute it, and his method of quoting Celsus almost sentence by sentence, has ensured that a substantial part of *The True Doctrine* is preserved in its original usage.[6] To put the matter quite simply, Celsus' discourse may be divided into three distinct categories: First, an array of the traditional pagan arguments against the Jews adopted by him as ammunition against the Church; second, Jewish arguments against Christianity; and lastly, pagan charges levelled at Christianity but inapplicable to Judaism. Of these only the first

---

[4] See the excellent introduction of Henry Chadwick, *Origen: Contra Celsum* (Cambridge University Press, 1953), pp. ix-xxxii.

[5] The title as has been pointed out has a strongly Platonic flavor: cf. R. Bader, *Der Alethes Logos des Kelsos*, Tübinger Beiträge zur Altertumswissenschaft, Heft 33 (Stuttgart-Berlin, 1940), pp. 2-3; cf. A. Wifstrand, *Die wahre Lehre des Kelsos*, Bulletin de la Société royale des lettres de Lund (1938-1939), II. p. 399; H. Chadwick, *op. cit.*, p. xxi.

[6] Many attempts have been made to reconstruct Celsus' text, but the most competent work is that of Robert Bader, *op. cit.*

two interest us here and we shall look at them briefly.

Celsus opens his polemic by referring to the barbarian origins of Christianity (I. 2). Whereas many of the older non-Greek nations have had some insight into the Common truth (I. 14), the Jews have no original or true ideas (I. 4, V. 41). Moses' philosophy was derivative and by definition false, and his people were misled by him into accepting it (I. 21, 23, 26 ff.; cf. V. 41).[7]

To be a new nation was to be historically insignificant and culturally unoriginal, and to challenge this a negation was a top priority for any nation in antiquity, as Vergil's epic of the ancient history of Rome demonstrates.

Again monotheism comes to the Jews as Moses' outstanding deception, who persuaded his ignorant followers to abandon the worship of their many gods and believe in the one God (I. 23, V. 41).[8] The Jews were believed to have cut themselves off from common and decent intercourse with their fellowmen, having nourished a hatred for the rest of the human race and encouraging "secret associations." The argument is to be found in the anti-Jewish polemic of the Egyptians, Manetho, Lysimachus, Chaeremon and Apion quoted by Josephus in his *Contra Apionem* (I. 219, 24 to II. 32, 3).

But perhaps the most important indictment is that God was not on the side of the Jews (VIII. 69). Celsus, like Cicero (*pro Flacco* 28 (69) points to the fact that they were expelled from their homeland with impurity and far from having divine protection a number of disasters had fallen upon them. The old charge that the Jews were originally rebels (III. 5) was given a new twist by Celsus who turns to accuse the Christians of rebelling in the same manner against the Jews (III. 5; V. 33).

By using the person of a Jew, Celsus puts forward some of the fables about Jesus already current which were later woven to form the "Sepher Toldoth Jeshu." According to these Jesus was not God (I. 69 ff.) nor the Son of God (I. 39, 41; II. 30) but

---

[7] This claim goes back to the Egyptian anti-Jewish writers quoted by Josephus in his *Contra Apionem*, which makes its starting-point the proof of the antiquity of the Jews.

[8] Compare Manetho *apud Jos. c. Ap.* I, 239 (26); Apollonius Molon, *ibid.* and *ap. Diod. fic.* 34.1 (Photius p. 524); Apion, *Jos. c. Ap.* II 65 ff (6).

a mere man (II. 79) and wicked sorcerer hated by God (I. 79) who was rightly punished (II. 44). Due to poor leadership he lost the support of his followers (II. 12) who even betrayed him (II. 11). It was after his death that stories were invented of his divinity (I. 41, II. 47), the power of prophecy was attributed to him (II. 13, 15, 44) and multitudes were won over to his name (II. 46).

Origen examines in detail Celsus' arguments, replying at length to each. With Josephus, whose works he quotes by name, he begins by saying that the Jews are among the most ancient and most cultivated peoples, and rebukes Celsus for not knowing that Moses antedates Homer and Hesiod (IV. 11 ff.; 21, 36; VI. 43, 47; VII. 30 ff.). He then goes so far as to maintain that the Mosaic laws provide a blueprint for the perfect *polis* (V. 43) and, when properly read, what he has to say about God is far more profound than what the Greek poets and philosophers had to say about Him (I. 17). Moses is less esoteric and what he presents has more universal significance and is more immediate in its appeal. With Justin and Tatian as well as with Philo and Josephus he argues that Greek philosophy was, partly if not wholly, derived from Hebraic sources.

Thus Origen replies to Celsus' allegations by insisting on the antiquity of the Jewish people, on the validity of Moses' teaching and on the peculiar case which, despite appearance, God has for his chosen people. Having endowed the Church with antiquity and respectability as the offspring of Judaism, Origen turns to expound the religious ideas of the Hebrews.

By pointing to the futility of the pagan pantheon, he draws a contrast between the superiority of the Jewish monotheism (I. 23; VIII. 3 ff.) as against the indignity of worshipping man-made idols (Pagan gods: I. 23; IV. 48; Images: I. 5; III. 40; VII. 64 ff.). Far from accepting the charge that God was angry with the Jews, he points to His care and love for His people and for their ancient and sacred society (VI. 80). As a Christian he must at the same time insist that God's special care has now passed from the Jews to the Gentiles, but he is convinced that this will come to an end at a future date when "all Israel will be saved."

In putting his argument against Jesus into the mouth of a

Jew,[9] Celsus had taken a bold and original step, which enabled him to exploit the well-developed Jewish polemic against the Church. This is perhaps the most interesting part of the debate, since it provides an invaluable insight into the Jewish-Christian dialogue of the time.

The real purpose of this essay, so far as it has any purpose beyond the rejection of Celsus' argument, is to consider not the legends Celsus puts forward, but what the Christian Church teaches on the matter. Addressing an educated Greek audience, Origen clearly points out with some detail that the discourse which Celsus presents is implausible and unworthy of serious consideration. He is not at all impressed by the figure of Celsus' Jew whom he proves to be false in his account of Jewish beliefs (II. 31, 57, 28, 77; IV. 2; V. 6, 8 ff.). He then takes advantage of this rhetorical scheme to introduce "genuine" Jewish arguments which Celsus has failed to quote, but which he himself is aware of and having quoted them he then successfully refutes. We have to remember that Origen often alludes explicitly to Jewish traditions. The passages in which he does so were first collected by Harnack and recently by M. Bardy.[10] Furthermore Origen had spent time in Palestine[11] where, as he tells us, he had carried on both a dialogue and a debate with Jews while his tremendous scholarship and knowledge of the Old Testament gives him an undisputed superiority over his pagan opponent.

The appeal of miracles obviously holds a fascination for the primitive mind and he ridicules Celsus for putting his criticism of the New Testament miracles into the mouth of a Jew. Jews have no reason for doubting these miracles: they must believe that these miracles are possible since they also occur in the Hebrew Bible. Again, they cannot be challenged by them as historically unauthenticated, since they are more recent and are better sup-

---

[9] Celsus represents this Jew, first, as disputing with Jesus and often refuting Him (I. 28-71) and then arguing with Jewish Christians (II).

[10] A. von Harnack, *Der Kirchengeschichtliche Ertrag der exegetischen Arbeiten des Origenes;* M. Bardy, "Les traditions juives dans l'oeuvre d'Origène," *Rev. Bibl.* (1925), pp. 194 ff.

[11] The *Contra Celsum* was composed in 248, as Prof. H. Chadwick shows in the introduction to his translation of this work. At this time Origen had been permanently resident in Caesarea for seventeen years.

ported by independent testimony than those in the Old Testament (I. 43 ff.).

Now if a Jew doubts the authenticity of the miracles in the New Testament, how can he explain the fact that prophecies contained in the Old Testament not only foretell that there will be signs and wonders when the Messiah comes, but even describe in considerable detail the chief events in Jesus' life? Here Origen brings into play the argument of prophecy on which he relied in his dialogue with Jewish sages (I. 55, 56).[12]

The miracles of Jesus are next compared with those of Moses. If Moses welded the Israelites into one people with God's help even through miracles, Jesus welds the whole of mankind into his people. Moses gave the Israelites the "literal" Torah while Jesus' message is the "spiritual" Gospel addressed to all the world (II. 52; I. 43; IV. 4; cf. De Principiis IV. 1, 1). In substance, it is in this universal appeal that Jesus was superior to Moses. Also he is recognized by the prophets who speak of him as the Messiah and the Saviour of mankind.

While Judaism is essentially a national religion, Christianity is one that is universal, not superior to that of the Jews only, but overcoming the religions of the Pagan world (IV. 22, 32). This makes the Christian Church grow amazingly rapidly in the world, while Jewish faith is limited in its appeal, being addressed only to the Jewish people. By using the argument from history in discussing the triumph of the Church over the Synagogue, Origen maintains that God's rejection of the Jewish people is in itself a manifestation of this defeat which in history is marked by the expulsion from Jerusalem and the subsequent humiliation and persecution that falls upon the Jews. It was generally admitted in the ancient church that the destruction of the Temple, the sack of Jerusalem and the dispersal of the Jewish people was a living proof of the triumph of the Church over the Synagogue. This attitude to the historical events of the end of the Jewish Commonwealth is not dissimilar to that of the Pharisaic Rabbis; Origen contrasts it to the rapid spread of Christianity throughout the Oecumene.

---

[12] The use of Christian biblical prophecies by Christian apologists is amply illustrated by Justin's Dialogue and Ps. — Cyprian's Testimonia adversus Judaeos.

We must now close this section by going beyond the *Contra Celsum,* directed self-consciously to a pagan audience, and examine his theme of the Church as the true successor of the Israel of God.

Central to Origen's general approach is the spiritual interpretation of the Bible. The Christians must go beyond the Jewish attitude to religious law with its literalism and mythology if they are to understand its full message and significance. The very text of the Bible is comparable to the Incarnate Christ: The Jews just as they failed to see through the body of Jesus to the spiritual being beyond, likewise see only the "carnal" letter of the Law and failed to grasp its true spirit. The Jews have been vouchsafed a "shadowy image of the truth" (in Lev. hom. 12:1) and so should have been the first to believe, but instead they rejected the reality and clung firmly to the shadow (in Isa. Nom. VI. 6).

Origen thus identifies the Jews' rejection of Jesus with their literalistic approach to the Law which he himself completely rejects as we read in the fourth book of *De Principiis.* By using the allegorical interpretation of Scripture, a technique derived ultimately from the commentators on Homer and from Philo, he sets out to demonstrate that the Old Testament is now a Christian document and that the New Testament is a continuation of the Old.[13]

The most characteristic feature of Origen's theology, for most of his readers at any rate, is his doctrine that there are three separate progressive revelations of God: the Natural Law, the Law of Moses, and the Gospel. The fourth is still to come and this is the Eternal Gospel. We now come to examine briefly the Mosaic legislation which is the main point of difference between the Church and Synagogue in the early Church. Both Justin and Cyprian held that the Mosaic legislation was never intended to be a permanent institution but was given to the Israelites until such a time as a more comprehensive and universal law could be given.

> A law which is given in contrast to another cancels the previous one, and similarly a later covenant renders the former one void. Christ has been given to us as an everlasting and final law, and this covenant is reliable, after which there is no other law, no ordinance and no commandment.[14]

---

[13] As A. Harnack points out, Origen found a great exegetical tradition

As against this interpretation Origen stressed rather the allegorical approach to the Law.[15] Not that he denied that their literal observance ever had any validity; he held that old laws were a type or shadow of the truth, the meaning of which would become fully apparent only later, when the whole truth had been revealed. In his words, "Those ceremonies were a type, while' the ultimate reality was that which the Holy Spirit was to teach them." The Law had once served a saving purpose but had now been superseded. By using an image he took from Melito,[16] he compares the Law to the model a sculptor makes for a statue. The model serves to determine the shape of the statue, but once the statue is completed it no longer has any pressing relevance. The following passage quoted at some length underlines what is going to become the formal Christian position on this burning issue:

> We who belong to the Church accept Moses, and with valid reason. We study his works because we believe that he was a prophet and that God revealed Himself to him. We believe that he came to describe the mysteries to come, but using symbols, figures and allegories, whereas before we ourselves began to teach men about the mysteries, they had already taken place, at the time appointed for them. It does not matter whether you are a Jew or one of us; you cannot maintain that Moses was a prophet at all unless you see him in this light. How can you prove that he was a prophet if you say that his works are rather ordinary, that they imply no

which he was at pains to master: *Der Kirchengeschichtliche Ertrag,* I., p. 22; cf. J. Daniélou, *Origen* (London, 1955), pp. 139 ff. On Origen's influence on later commentaries see H. de Lubac, *Exégèse médiévale,* I. i (Paris, 1959), pp. 198 ff.

[14] Justin, *Dial.* 18; cf. Cypr. *Test.* I: 8-17. Both quote Jer. 38 (31). 31 ff.

[15] The allegorical interpretation of the Law was by no means new; it is to be found in the *Letter of Aristobulus* (Ps. Arist. 128 ff.) in the *Epistle of Barnabas* and above all else in Philo: cf. J. Pepin, *Mythe et Allégorie* (Paris, 1958), and for more information on the history of allegory see J. Tate, "The Beginnings of Greek Allegory," *Classical Review,* XLI, pp. 214 ff.; W. B. Stanford, *The Ulysses Theme,* pp. 36 ff., 125-7. The practice of allegorizing a classical text had begun at least three centuries before Philo.

[16] *Homily on the Passion,* ed. Campbell Bonner, pp. 29-30.

knowledge of the future and have no mystery hidden in them? The Law, then, and everything in the Law, being inspired, as the Apostle says, until the time of amendment, is like those people whose job is to make statues and cast them in metal. Before they start on the statue itself, the one they are going to cast in bronze, silver, or gold, they first prepare a clay model to show what they aim to create. The model is a necessity, but until the real statue is completed. The model is made for the sake of the statue, and when the statue is ready the sculptor has no further use for the model. So it is with the Law and the Prophets. The things written in the Law and the Prophets were meant as types or figures of things to come. But now the Artist Himself has come, the Author of everything, and He has cast the Law aside, because it only contained the shadow of the good things to come (Heb. X. 1), whereas He brought the things themselves.[17]

This, however, is just the point at which the difficulty arises. There was a fundamental difference between the Christian and the Rabbinic attitude to the Law; the Rabbis were concerned to make the laws practicable and relevant to the times in which they lived, while Christians like Origen had no patience at all for the Mosaic Law as Law, and uncompromisingly rejected the halachic refinements of the Rabbis. Under the circumstances the grand for the debate cannot have been very fruitful. Origen moves from the focus-points of the debate, viz. circumcision, the Sabbath and the dietary laws to the coming of a new age, the revelation of a new meaning for the Scriptures and the obsolescence of all the traditional observances.

As a whole Origen unlike Justin does not give us in his writings an account of his discussion with the Jews. But we have certain snatches of these and his aim is clearly twofold. On the one hand to show that the election of the Gentiles as taught by the Church was prophesied in the Hebrew Bible, while on the other to confirm this interpretation of the biblical passages in question by reference to the history of the Jews and the Christian Church since the advent of Christ. Of these two arguments it was the second to which he attached greater importance and which be-

---

[17] *Hom. Lev,.* X. 1; cf. *Comm. Matt.,* XI, 11; XIV. 19 and XII. 4.

came the focal point of the Jewish replies.[18]

At the beginning of the *De Principiis*, where he is expounding on the traditional teaching of the Church before he comes to elaborate his own personal views, Origen writes the following:

> We believe that the Scriptures were written by the Spirit of God and that in addition to their literal meaning they have another, which the majority of the people are unaware of. The things written in the Scriptures are signs of certain mysteries and images of the things of God. The teaching of the whole Church is the same, viz., that the whole of the Law is spiritual but that what it truly means in the spiritual sense is not known to all: only to those who have received such grace from the Holy Spirit as enables them to speak with wisdom and knowledege (1 Cor. XII. 8) know what it is.[19]

Thus the inheritance of the Israel of God is now passed on to the Church, the New Israel. The transition from the old economy to the new and the unity of the two Testaments had a dramatic side to it. In so far as Christ had identified himself with old Jewish orders of things, He had to die and to rise again before He could set up the new Temple, His risen body, the Church.

Origen will not admit that the Law is in any sense the cause of sin. On the contrary, before Christ it was the Law that struck the first blow against sin.[20] He understands a progressive movement beginning with the Law, supplemented by the Prophets and completed in Christ.[21] For him, the faith of Law and Gospel are one but the Law is inferior, because to the Jews God was obeyed through fear. The thoughts of Origen rise above the level of the majority of apologists, whose primary conception is the purely intellectual argument of the congruity of the messianship of

---

[18] *C. Celsum* II: 78; V.

[19] *De Princ.*, I, preface, 8 (Koetschau, p. 14, 6-13). On Origen's principles of Biblical exegesis see the following: H. de Lubac, *Histoire et Esprit* (Paris, 1950); *Exégès médiévale* I. 1 (Paris, 1959); R. P. C. Hanson, *Allegory and Event* (London, 1959); R. M. Grant, *The Letter and the Spirit* (London, 1957); J. Daniélou, *Sacramentum Futuri* (Paris, 1949).

[20] *In Rom.* V. 1, 'Per legem enim purificatio peccatorum coepit aperiri et ex parte aliqua tyrannidi eius obsisti per hostias, per expiatones varias, per sacrificia varia, per praecepta.'

[21] *In Rom.* III. 2; cf. *In Jesu Nave*, Hom. XVII. 2.

Jesus with Old Testament prophecy, to the new reality of grace which now embraces history. As he puts it:

> Those who observed the Law which foreshadowed the true Law possessed a shadow of divine things, a likeness of the things of God. In the same way, those who shared out the land that Juda inherited were imitating and foreshadowing the distribution that will ultimately be made in heaven. Thus the reality was in heaven, the shadow and image of the reality on earth. As long as the shadow was on earth, there was an earthly Jerusalem, a temple, an altar, a visible liturgy, priests and high priests, towns and villages too in Juda, and everything else that you found described in the book. But at the coming of our Lord Jesus Christ, when the truth descended from heaven and was born on earth, and justice looked down from heaven (Ps. LXXXIV. 12), shadows and images came to an end. Jerusalem was destroyed and so was the temple; the altar disappeared. Henceforth neither Mount Garizim nor Jerusalem was the place where God was to be worshipped: His true worshippers were to worship Him in spirit and in truth (John IV. 23). Thus, in the presence of the truth, the type and the shadow came to an end, and when the temple was built in the Virgin's womb by the Holy Spirit and the power of the Most High (Luke I. 35), the stone-built temple was destroyed. If then, Jews go to Jerusalem and find the earthly city in ruins, they should not weep as they do, because they are mere children when it comes to understanding these things. They ought not to lament. Instead of the earthly city, they should seek the heavenly one. They have only to look up and they will find the heavenly Jerusalem, which is the mother of us all (Gal. IV. 26). Thus by God's goodness their earthly inheritance has been taken from them to make them seek their inheritance in heaven.[22]

And so we come to the very heart of Origen's teaching on the Israel of God. The life and ordeal of Israel may be remedied, according to our author only if the Synagogue accepts the teachings of the Church.

In judging the teaching of Origen on this problem as a whole

---

[22] *Hom. Jos.*, XVII, 1 (Baehrens, pp. 401-2).

it is important to remember two things. On the one hand many of his ideas are not his personal invention for they reflect the general view of early Christianity and its sanguine belief that the Church in the light of God's revelation in Jesus Christ had now become the New (True) Israel of God. On the other hand true to the tradition of Clement and Philo, Origen allowed philosophical theology to bypass the mould of biblical Revelation and history. This means that the generation of theologians influenced by Origen, especially those of the fourth century, inherited his theological detachment from the historical covenant placing more and more emphasis on Hellenic patterns of thought. Thus, with Prof. Torrance we have to agree when he writes, "it is surely clear that it belongs to the Christian Church as one of its greatest tasks to wrestle with Israel in the prayer for understanding and reconciliation. Only through the Church that enters into the fellowship of Israel's sufferings can Israel find its way through the *Eli, Eli, lama sabachthani?* into resurrection and new creation. So long as Israel persists in unbelief the Church itself is denied its fulness both in regard to Revelation and in regard to Reconciliation."[23] The debate between the Church and Synagogue is not over, it is not an easy debate, yet it is essential that it be continued both for the Christian and the Jew.[24]

---

[23] T. F. Torrance, *Conflict and Agreement in the Church*, vol. I (London, 1959), pp. 302-3.

[24] We can expect much from the recent research of my some-time pupil, N. R. M. de Lange, who is now writing his doctoral dissertation on Origen and the dialogue between the Church and Synagogue under Henry Chadwick at Oxford. To both Mr. de Lange and his reader Dr. Chadwick I am indebted for many illuminating observations on Origen, and to the former even for some specific details.

BOSTON UNIVERSITY
SCHOOL OF THEOLOGY

Jews and Christians at Edessa*

HAN J. W. DRIJVERS

INSTITUUT VOOR SEMITISTIEK, UNIVERSITY OF GRONINGEN

Various and manifold reasons make an inquiry into the relations of Jews and Christians at Edessa a subject of more importance than the thousand and first variant of the general theme Judaism and Christianity during the first centuries C.E. of which the conclusions are predictable.[1] The specific local circumstances in which Christianity manifested itself in various forms in this city, which was to become the cradle of early Syriac-speaking Christendom, the supposedly paramount rôle that the large Jewish community of Edessa played in this whole process of introduction and further development of its messianic offspring that was to become its most threatening rival religion, all this asks for a more thorough investigation of social relations between the different groups in this North-Mesopotamian city.[2] Although we do not possess historical sources that would enable us to write the history of Jews and Christians at Edessa like E. Le Roy Ladurie did for Cathars and Catholics at Montaillou, the extant sources allow of more precise conclusions than a general labelling as Jewish Christianity which suggests intense relations between Jews and Christians without any

---

*Abbreviations

ANRW	Aufstieg und Niedergang der römischen Welt
BSOAS	Bulletin of the School of Oriental and African Studies
CSCO	Corpus scriptorum christianorum orientalium
EJ	Encyclopaedia Judaica
EPRO	Études préliminaires aux religions orientales dans l'empire romain
JJS	Journal of Jewish Studies
OrChr	Oriens Christianus
OrChrAn	Orientalia Christiana Analecta
VigChr	Vigiliae Christianae
ZThK	Zeitschrift für Theologie und Kirche

[1] Cf. int. al. L. Goppelt, *Christentum und Judentum im ersten und zweiten Jahrhundert. Ein Aufriss der Urgeschichte der Kirche*, Gütersloh 1954; M. Simon, *Verus Israel. Étude sur les relations entre chrétiens et juifs dans l'empire romain (135-425)*, Paris 1964; K.-H. Rengstorf/S. von Kortzfleisch, *Kirche und Synagoge. Handbuch zur Geschichte von Christen und Juden. Darstellung mit Quellen*, 2 Vols. Stuttgart 1968-1970; K. Hoheisel, *Das antike Judentum in christlicher Sicht, Ein Beitrag zur neueren Forschungsgeschichte*, Studies in Oriental Religions 2, Wiesbaden 1978.

[2] Cf. Simon, *Verus Israel*, 154; J. B. Segal, *Edessa "the Blessed City"*, Oxford 1970, 41-43; 60ff; 63ff.; idem, "When did Christianity come to Edessa?", B. C. Bloomfield (ed.), *Middle East Studies and Libraries. A Felicitation Volume for Professor J. D. Pearson*, London 1980, 179-191; Drijvers, *East of Antioch. Studies in Early Syriac Christianity*, London 1984, esp. I and VI.

indication what these relations were like.[3] Moreover, the bulk of the Edessene population was pagan, and remained pagan for a much longer period than has usually been assumed.[4] Pagans, Jews and Christians did not live in splendid isolation in an antique town in which a good deal of life was lived in public, and privacy was an almost unknown concept. Ideological conflicts and struggles like those between Christians, Jews and pagans found their origin in daily experiences of different religious, and consequently social, behaviour because religion in the ancient world was mainly a matter of public conduct according to traditional standards.[5] The religious debate, therefore, often centres around proper behaviour and the rules that should be followed. In contrast to Judaism and paganism, Christianity was a newcomer on the religious scene with revolutionary ideas and deviant behaviour, but the whole social context set bounds to such deviations. For significantly different conduct the only milieu was the solitude of the desert. In other words, Jews, pagans and Christians behaved differently, but had a lot in common, just because they all lived densely packed on a small area within the city walls. We will restrict ourselves to the relations between Jews and Christians, keeping in mind that both lived in a largely pagan city, at least in the early Christian period.

Edessa must have had an important Jewish community and several synagogues, one of them in the centre of the city near the intersection of the two principal streets. This synagogue was converted into a church dedicated to St. Stephen at the beginning of the fifth century when Rabbula was bishop of Edessa.[6] Some members of the Jewish congregation were merchants in silk, since Edessa was a main station on the silk road to China.[7] They must, therefore, have been men of a certain wealth and

[3]   Cf. *int. al.* R. Murray, *Symbols of Church and Kingdom. A Study in Early Syriac Tradition,* Cambridge 1975, 279ff.; A. F. J. Klijn, "The Influence of Jewish Theology on the Odes of Solomon and the Acts of Thomas", *Aspects du Judéo-Christianisme,* Paris 1965, 167-179; G. Quispel, "L'évangile selon Thomas et les origines de l'ascèse chrétienne", *Aspects du Judéo-Christianisme,* 35-52 and many other papers.

[4]   Drijvers, Cults and Beliefs at Edessa", EPRO 82, Leiden 1980; *idem,* "The Persistence of Pagan Cults and Practices in Christian Syria, East of Byzantium": *Syria and Armenia in the Formative Period,* ed. N. Garsoïan – Th. Mathews – R. Thomson, Washington-Dumbarton Oaks 1982, 35-43 (repr. in East of Antioch).

[5]   R. MacMullen, *Paganism in the Roman Empire,* New Haven-London 1981, *passim;* it seems highly questionable that D. Rokeah, *Jews, Pagans and Christians in Conflict,* Studia Post-Biblica 33, Leiden 1982, is right when he states that the Jews did not have part in this ideological conflict and that there actually did not exist a Christian-Jewish polemic.

[6]   Chronicon Edessenum, li, ed. I. Guidi, *Chronica Minora* I, CSCO 1, Louvain 1903; cf. J. B. Segal, "The Jews of North Mesopotamia before the Rise of Islam", *Sepher Segal,* Jerusalem 1965, 40; idem, Edessa, 41f; G. G. Blum, *Rabbula von Edessa. Der Christ, der Bischof, der Theologe,* CSCO, Subs. 34, Louvain 1969, 105f.

[7]   *Doctrina Addai,* ed. and transl. by G. Howard, Scholars Press 1981, 34 (Syriac text); cf. Segal, "The Jews of North Mesopotamia", 45f.; Drijvers, "Hatra, Palmyra und Edessa. Die Städte der syrisch-mesopotamischen Wüste in politischer, kulturgeschichtlicher und religionsgeschichtlicher Beleuchtung", ANRW II, 8, Berlin-N.Y. 1977, 864.

position in society. Some of them were buried in one of the ancient cemeteries of Edessa, Kirk Mağara, the Forty Caves, where three Hebrew and one Greek inscription commemorate their burials among their pagan fellow-citizens.[8] The inscriptions are all of different dates between the first and fourth century C.E., and contain proper names such as Joseph, Samuel, Seleucus and Izates. This might be considered an indication of a certain hellenistic element in local Judaism and of assimilation of Jews to their pagan fellow-citizens. Four Jewish tomb inscriptions, however, in comparison with at least fifty pagan examples from the same period, give a rough idea of the Jewish component of the whole population. If about ten percent belonged to the élite who could afford a wealthy burial-place, a substantial number among the Jews must have belonged to the rank and file Edessenes.[9] At the other end of the social scale, the local dynasty of Edessa might be related to the royal house of Adiabene which converted to Judaism. King Abgar VII bar Izates (109-116 C.E.) was probably a descendant of the royal Izates family of Adiabene with which Edessa also had political ties.[10] In addition, Edessa's significance in Jewish eyes appears in the Targumic tradition that the city, identified with biblical Erekh, was founded by Nimrod.[11] But the main argument for the importance and distinction of Edessa's Jewish inhabitants is provided by the supposedly rapid growth of Christianity and the rôle attributed to the Jews in that process.[12] Hence local Christianity is labelled Jewish-Christianity, since its first missionaries and adherents were Jews, who gave Edessene Christendom its typical semitic flavour and *couleur locale* untouched by hellenism.[13] Their contribution to Christian origins at Edessa is deduced from their rôle in the *Doctrina Addai,* the official foundation legend of the Edessene church. And that is the main reason why all other early Christian writings that are related to Edessa are considered Jewish-Christian products too.[14]

[8]   H. Pognon, *Inscriptions sémitiques de la Syrie, de la Mésopotamie et de la région de Mossoul,* Paris 1907, 78ff.; J. B. Frey, *Corpus inscriptionum judaicarum* II, 340ff.; Segal, "The Jews of North Mesopotamia", 40f.; *idem, Edessa,* 42.

[9]   For ancient tomb inscriptions see Drijvers *Old-Syriac (Edessean) Inscriptions,* Leiden 1972.; *idem,* "Some New Syriac Inscriptions and Archaeological Finds from Edessa and Sumatar Harabesi", BSOAS 36, 1973, 1-14; *idem,* "A Tomb for the Life of a King. A recently discovered Edessene Mosaic with a Portrait of King Abgar the Great", Le Muséon 95, 1982, 167-189.

[10]   Rubens Duval, *Histoire d'Édesse, politique, religieuse et littéraire,* Paris, 1892 (repr. Amsterdam 1975), 52; Drijvers, "Hatra, Palmyra und Edessa", 872ff.

[11]   Rubens Duval, *Histoire d'Édesse,* 104; EJ s.v. "Edessa", Vol. 6, 366f. cf. Targum Palest. on Gen. 10,10.

[12]   Segal, "The Jews of North Mesopotamia", 41ff.; Rubens Duval, *Histoire d'Édesse,* 107ff.

[13]   e.g. R. Murray, *Symbols of Church and Kingdom,* 4ff.; W. Cramer, *Der Geist Gottes und des Menschen in frühsyrischer Theologie,* Münster 1979, 7ff.; cf. Drijvers, *East of Antioch,* I, 2ff. where relevant literature is listed.

[14]   Drijvers, "Edessa und das jüdische Christentum", VigChr 24, 1970, 4-33 (repr. in East of Antioch).

What then does the *Doctrina Addai* tell us about contacts between Jews and Christians and the way in which the Christians saw their Jewish fellow-citizens? The nucleus of the *Doctrina Addai*, i.e,. the story of king Abgar's embassy to the Roman governor which passed through Jerusalem and reported to the king about Jesus' appearance, the subsequent correspondence between Abgar and Jesus, and Addai's coming to Edessa, healing of Abgar and public preaching, dates back to the end of the third century C.E. and originates in a Christian minority group which produced this propaganda story in order to vindicate its religious claims against its rival fellow-Christians and Edessene Jews and pagans.[15] This writing, therefore, does not describe historical events but mirrors a particular historical situation in which this minority group addresses itself to religious opponents, tries to refute them, and above all to win them over. The most threatening rivals were the Manichees from whom these Christians borrowed the apostle Addai, one of the best known early Manichaean missionaries in the Syrian area, and transformed him into Addai, apostle and eye-witness of Jesus' miracles and crucifixion.[16]

In the course of time, this "original" *Doctrina Addai* was extended with various additions, all with a propagandistic aim, till it reached its final form in the beginning of the fifth century.[17] One of the main additions relates how the empress "Protonice", the wife of Claudius Caesar, came to Jerusalem as a pilgrim, visited Christ's tomb and discovered the True Cross. Protonice gave it to James, the leader of the Christian community at Jerusalem, and ordered that a large building be built over Golgotha and Christ's tomb. This story alludes to the Constantinian buildings over Golgotha and the Holy Grave, and clearly reflects the account of how Helena, the mother of Constantine, found the True Cross when she made a pilgrimage to Jerusalem.[18] This legend attributing the discovery of the Holy Cross to Helena emerges at the end of the fourth century and is most likely a Christian reaction to Julian's plan to rebuild the Temple at Jerusalem in 363 C.E., which evoked such a shock in the Christian Church that it claimed Jerusalem as a Christian place par excellence where the True Cross was found, notwithstanding severe Jewish opposition.[19] The whole story has a

---

[15] *The Teaching of Addai,* ed. and transl. by G. Howard, Scholars Press 1981; cf. Drijvers, "Facts and Problems in Early Syriac-Speaking Christianity", The Second Century 2, 1982, 157-175; *idem,* "Addai und Mani, Christentum und Manichäismus im dritten Jahrhundert in Syrien", OrChrAn 221, Roma 1983, 171-185.

[16] Drijvers, "Addai und Mani".

[17] According to T. D. Barnes, "The Date of the *Teaching of Addai*", paper given at the Patristic Conference Oxford 1983, the Doctrina Addai got its final form well after 410 which seems convincing; cf. A. Desreumaux, 'La Doctrine d'Addaï. Essai de classement des témoins syriaques et grecs', Augustinianum 23, 1983, 181-186.

[18] *The Teaching of Addai,* ed. Howard, 21-33; cf. C. Coüasnon, *The Church of the Holy Sepulchre in Jerusalem,* London 1974.

[19] Cf. Cl. Aziza, Julien et le Judaïsme, L'empereur Julien. De l'histoire à la légende (331-1715), Études rass, par. R. Braun-J. Richer, Paris 1978, 141-158; S. P. Brock, "A letter attributed to Cyril of Jerusalem on the rebuilding of the Temple", BSOAS 40, 1977, 267-286, where the relevant Syriac texts are listed.

strong anti-Jewish tendency and emphasizes that when Protonice wished to see Golgotha where the Messiah was crucified, the wood of his cross on which he was hung by the Jews, and the grave where he was laid, the Jews control these three and "do not permit us to go and pray there before Golgotha and the grave. They are not even willing to give us the wood of his cross. And not only this, but they persecute us, in order to prevent us preaching or claiming in the name of the Messiah. Often also they confine us in prison".[20]

The literary history of the *Doctrina Addai,* therefore, reflects in this way the attitude towards the Jews over a period of more than two hundred years and enables us to detect changes in it. Other sources used in addition may reinforce and differentiate the results.

The oldest stratum of *Doctrina Addai,* at least in the Syriac version, shows two at first sight contrasting views of Judaism. When Abgar's embassy came to Jerusalem, "they saw the Jews standing in groups and plotting what they might do to him, for they were distressed at seeing that some of the multitude of the people believed in him". The royal envoys apparently reported accurately to Abgar, because in his letter to Jesus he wrote: "Furthermore I have heard that the Jews murmur against, persecute, and are seeking to crucify you in an effort to destroy you". Jesus received Abgar's letter in the house of the chief priest of the Jews, obviously during his trial before the high priest (John. 18, 15ff). His answer to Hanan the archivist also contains a clear anti-Jewish tenor: "Blessed are you who though not having seen me have believed in me. For it is written concerning me that those who see me will not believe in me, but those who do not see me will believe in me" (cf. John 20,29).[21] The Jews, who were eye-witnesses of Jesus' activities, are labelled as unbelievers in this phrase, in clear contrast to its original meaning. When later Judas Thomas sent Addai to Edessa, "he dwelt in the house of Tobia, the son of Tobia the Jew, who was from Palestine". That Tobia son of Tobia was a Jew from Palestine is only reported in the Syriac version of the *Doctrina Addai,* and is missing from the Greek text of Eusebius, h.e. I, xiii, 11. The usual interpretation of this remarkable detail is that Edessene Christianity owed its origin and early spread to converts from Judaism, of which Tobia bar Tobia was one. Many scholars consequently stressed the Jewish-Christian character of that branch of Christianity and its close ties with traditions current in the Jerusalem community.[22] This interpretation seems doubtful, taking into

---

[20]   *The Teaching of Addai,* ed. Howard, 23.

[21]   *The Teaching of Addai,* ed. Howard, 9; on this passage see Drijvers, "Addai und Mani", 179ff.

[22]   E.g. J. C. L. Gibson, "From Qumran to Edessa or the Aramaic Speaking Church before and after 70 A.D.", The Annual of Leeds Oriental Society V, 1963-65, 24-39; G. Quispel, "The Discussion of Judaic Christianity", VigChr 22, 1968, 81-93; L. W. Barnard, "The Origins and Emergence of the Church in Edessa during the First Two Centuries A.D.", VigChr 22, 1968, 161-175; Neusner, *A History of the Jews in Babylonia I. The Parthian Period,* Leiden 1965, 166ff.

consideration the whole tenor of the *Doctrina Addai*. Tobia bar Tobia on the one hand serves to construct the link with Christian origins like Addai himself; on the other hand, he is part of the propaganda to convert the Jews together with other non-Christians. That becomes clear from the other passages in which the Jews are mentioned and where the same ambivalence can be detected. When Tobia brought Addai to Abgar's court the king welcomed the apostle and told him, "I have so believed in him that against those Jews who crucified him I wish that I might lead an army myself and might go and destroy them. But because that kingdom belongs to the Romans I have respect for the covenant of peace which was established by me as by my forefathers with our Lord Caesar Tiberius". The same motif occurs later again in the *Doctrina Addai*, when it is reported that Abgar wrote a letter to Tiberius Caesar informing him of the crucifixion performed by the Jews. Tiberius Caesar confirmed the receipt of the letter "concerning that which the Jews did with respect to the Cross". From the rest of the answer, in which we are told that Tiberius is engaged in a war with the Spaniards, who have rebelled against him, it becomes clear that this whole passage must be dated to the beginning of the fifth century after Constantius' operations against the Visigoths in Spain between 414 and 416, a date in perfect concordance with the important rôle attributed to the Cross.[23]

Nonetheless, the Jews formed part of the whole population which assembled to hear Addai's preaching, summoned by royal order. After princes and nobles of the king, came "the officers and all of the workmen and craftsmen, both Jews and Gentiles, who were in the city, the foreigners of the regions of Soba and Harran and the rest of the inhabitants of the whole region of Mesopotamia. They all stood in order to listen to the teaching of Addai, of whom they had heard that he was a disciple of Jesus, who had been crucified.[24] Here again the Jews were the object of religious propaganda and according to our treatise some of them at least converted to Christianity. Addai addresses himself directly to the Jews, after quoting the well-known text from the Gospel, "Behold, your house is left desolate" (Matthew 23:38):[25] "For behold unless those who crucified him had known that he was the Son of God, they would not have proclaimed the desolation of their city, nor would they have laid sorrow upon themselves. Even if they had wished to turn away from acknowledging this, the frightful horrors which happened at that time would not have permitted them. For behold some of the sons of those who performed the crucifixion have today become

---

[23] *The Teaching of Addai*, ed. Howard, 21; 77-79; the same motive occurs in *The History of the Blessed Virgin Mary and the History of the Likeness of Christ*, ed. E. A. Wallis Budge, London 1899, 97f. (Syriac text), 100ff. (English transl.).

[24] *The Teaching of Addai*, ed. Howard, 37.

[25] *The Teaching of Addai*, ed. Howard, 55; Luke 13;35; this text is considered the main proof of the rejection of the Jews and occurs from Justin, *Dial.* 16,12 on with all church fathers.

preachers and evangelists with the Apostles, my companions, throughout the Land of Palestine, among the Samaritans, and in all the land of the Philistines".[26] And Jesus is explicitly proclaimed "the God of the Jews who crucified him" in Addai's sermon.[27]

The Apostle's preaching met with great success. When the pagan high priests of the city had destroyed the altars on which they sacrificed to Nebo and Bel, and were baptized,[28] "Even the Jews who were learned in the Law and the Prophets, who traded in silk, submitted and became followers and confessed that the Messiah is the Son of the living God".[29] The anonymous author of the *Doctrina Addai* considered it, however, necessary to emphasize that "neither King Abgar nor the Apostle Addai forced anyone by constraint to believe in the Messiah, because without human compulsion, the compulsion of signs compelled many to believe in him". This remarkable sentence may be a later addition dating back to the beginning of the fifth century, when under Rabbula, the tyrant bishop of Edessa, religious coercion was not unusual and many Jews were forced to be baptized.[30] If this text, however, does belong to the oldest stratum of the *Doctrina*, it is certainly meant to stress the self-evident strength of the Gospel that is accepted of one's own free will.

The same opponents, Jews and pagans, occur in Addai's farewell sermon, which has all the characteristics of early third-century Syriac theology.[30a] Addai quite earnestly warns his flock, "Do not be a stumbling block to the blind, but make the path and road smooth in a rough place, between the crucifying Jews and the erring pagans. With these two parties alone you have a warfare that you might demonstrate the truth of the faith which you hold! Those fighters for the truth are, however, not very militant or warlike. When you are silent, your modest and honourable appearance joins the battle for you with those who hate truth and love falsehood".[31] Such words are typical of a minority group without real power to convert people of different beliefs. The Jews by contrast do not shrink from religious dispute with the Christians, who are reminded by Addai of the christological interpretation of the prophets: "Beware, therefore, of the crucifiers and do not be friends with them, lest you be responsible with those whose hands are full of the blood of the Messiah. Know and bear

[26]   *The Teaching of Addai*, ed. Howard, 55-57.
[27]   *The Teaching of Addai*, ed. Howard, 59.
[28]   *The Teaching of Addai*, ed. Howard, 69; cf. Drijvers, "Cults and Beliefs at Edessa", 34f.
[29]   *The Teaching of Addai*, ed. Howard, 69.
[30]   *The Teaching of Addai*, ed. Howard, 69-71; cf. J. J. Overbeck, *S. Ephraemi Syri, Rabulae Episcopi Edesseni, Balaei aliorumque opera selecta*, Oxford 1865, 194-95; Blum, *Rabbula von Edessa*, 104ff.; for the problem of religious coërcion, cf. P. Brown, *Religion and Society in the Age of Saint Augustine*, London 1972, 301-331.
[30a] Cf. *East of Antioch*, London 1984, I, 1-27; V, 187-217; and my forthcoming study "Early Forms of Antiochene Christology", *Mélanges van Roey*, Louvain 1985.
[31]   *The Teaching of Addai*, ed. Howard, 85-87.

witness that everything which we say and teach in regard to the Messiah is written in the books of the Prophets and is laid up with them, . . . They do not know that when they rise up against us, they rise up against the words of the Prophets. Just as they persecuted the Prophets during their lives, so also now after their deaths they persecute the truth which is written in the Prophets".[32]

Three days (!) after this impressive sermon, Addai died, and "all the city was in great lamentation and bitter sorrow over him. Nor were the Christians alone in grieving over him, but Jews and pagans who were in the city grieved as well".[33] This motif of the Jews mourning for the death of a Christian also occurs in the story of the martyrdom of Habbib the Deacon[34] and even in the Vita of Rabbula.[35] Although it might therefore be a traditional element, it fits perfectly into the whole pattern of the *Doctrina Addai* and its view of the relations between Christians and Jews. What picture of those relations emerges from the official foundation of Edessene Christianity and its propagandistic tenor as intended for both an inner and an outer public?

The *Doctrina Addai* proclaims the true belief and the *prestige de l'origine* of a small group of Christians which tried to win over Manichees, Jews and pagans to its religious views. It tried to convert Manichees by introducing the Christian preacher Addai at the court of king Abgar, just as Mani stayed and preached at other royal courts, and it tells how Jews and Gentiles did indeed convert. The *Doctrina Addai* is thus not characterized by a tone of hostility towards its opponents. It stresses that it was the Jews who crucified Jesus, but they did so through lack of real knowledge and insight. Otherwise they would have known that Jesus was their God. Even king Abgar did not undertake a military campaign against the Jews, but simply offered a safe refuge to Jesus. The main tenor of this propaganda tract is that Jews and pagans alike embraced Christian belief completely of their own free will without any coercion.

The propaganda against the Manichaean community had little if any success. The Manichees were a group of substantial importance at Edessa and the main opponents of Ephrem Syrus in the second half of the fourth century, roughly one century after the coming into existence of the *Doctrina*.[36] At that time a considerable part of the population was still

---

[32]   *The Teaching of Addai*, ed. Howard, 87; cf. Simon, *Verus Israel*, 205ff.

[33]   *The Teaching of Addai*, ed. Howard, 97-99.

[34]   F. C. Burkitt, *Euphemia and the Goth. A legendary Tale from Edessa, with the Acts of Martyrdom of the Confessors of Edessa*, London-Oxford 1913, 126.

[35]   J. J. Overbeck, *S. Ephraemi Syri, Rabulae Episcopi Edesseni*, 207, 5-9.

[36]   E. Beck, *Des Heiligen Ephraem des Syrers Hymnen contra Haereses*, CSCO, 169-170 and C. W. Mitchell, *S. Ephraim's Prose Refutations of Mani, Marcion, and Bardaisan*, 2 Vols, London 1912-21 are the main sources from Manichaeism at Edessa in Ephrem's time; it is noteworthy that the Syriac translation of Titus of Bostra, Contra Manichaeos, is to be found in the oldest preserved Syriac MS. that was written in 411 C.E. at Edessa. A separate study of Manichaeism at Edessa in relation with local Christian traditions is an urgent task.

pagan, or clung to Bardaisan's doctrine or to Marcionitism.[37] It is consequently very unlikely that local Judaism during the second or third century was the main source for the members of the Christian community. On the contrary, Judaism seems to have had a certain attraction for the Christians, who are warned not to be friends with them.

Second and third century Christianity at Edessa was dominated by Marcionites, Bardaisanites and adherents of an encratite form of Christian belief of which Tatian was an exponent.[38] Marcionites and Bardaisanites, like later Manichees, were in all likelihood of mainly gentile origin and background, whereas the typical encratite Christian writings show no sign of Jewish influence. It is, therefore, not without good reason that the author of the *Doctrina Addai* in particular tried to win over the Jews, his group being especially attracted to Jewish religious behaviour since it was so close to it! But even in the *Doctrina Addai* there are no traces of effect by Jews, only the early primitive beginnings of the religious debate. Our first tentative conclusion, therefore, is that until the end of the third century C.E. the larger part of Edessene Christianity shows no substantial influence on the part of, or close contacts with, the Jewish section of the population with the exception of that small group which was to become Edessa's orthodox church in later times and was probably called after Palut. They were obliged to enter into discussion with the Jews because they retained the Jewish Bible as part of the whole revelation. But most of Edessa's Christianity is clearly of pagan origin and consists in vast majority of semi-gnostic, gnostic and encratite groups which show no great interest in the religion of their Jewish fellow-citizens, or clear traces of Jewish impact. In particular, the Marcionites kept Jews at a distance since it was essentially an emancipation movement to free the Gospel from the Law.[39] Hence it is not surprising that the most "pagan" Christian group, that of the Bardaisanites, was closest to Jewish hellenistic circles with a strong philosophical element.[40] For the author of the *Doctrina Addai,* and for the group he represents, Jews and pagans belong together as they actually may have done at Edessa. They represent traditional value and belief systems, well rooted in the Greco-Roman and Oriental world, whereas the Christians were revolutionary newcomers.[41] That situation forms the background

---

[37]   Cf. Drijvers, "The Persistence of Pagan Cults and Practices in Christian Syria"; B. Aland, "Marcion. Versuch einer neuen Interpretation", ZThK 70, 1973, 420-447 is mainly based on Ephrem's polemic with the Marcionites, which, however, needs a fresh investigation after the appearance of R. J. Hoffmann, *Marcion: On the Restitution of Christianity. An Essay on the Development of Radical Paulinist Theology in the Second Century,* Scholars Press 1984.

[38]   Cf. Drijvers, *East of Antioch,* I, 1-27, where Tatian's rôle in Early Syriac Christianity is discussed.

[39]   Harnack, *Marcion,* 30ff.; but see now Hoffmann, *Marcion,* 155ff.

[40]   Cf. Drijvers, "Bardaiṣan of Edessa and the Hermetica. The Aramaic Philosopher and the Philosophy of his Time", *East of Antioch* XI, 190-210.

[41]   Cf. R. L. Wilken, *The Christians as the Romans saw them,* New Haven-London 1984.

against which a nascent Christian orthodoxy at the same time combats its heretical opponents, in particular the Manichaeans, and tries to win Jews and pagans alike to the Gospel. That same situation provides us with an explanation of the ambivalent attitude towards Jews. On one hand, they are pictured as the link with Christian origins, i.e., Jerusalem, and as the first converts with real insight into the message of Law and Prophets. On the other hand, they crucified their God. It seems very likely that association with, and influence by, the Jewish population of Edessa increased together with the growing status of these Christians who were to become Edessa's orthodox during the fourth century. During that period the Jewish impact on, and tensions with, at least that part of the Christians strengthened.

The works of Ephrem Syrus (d. 373) throw light onto the religious developments during that part of the fourth century in which he was the main spokesman of Edessene orthodoxy, and in that rôle provides us with interesting information on other religious groups as well. Ephrem Syrus spent most of his life at Nisibis, which had a large and important Jewish community and was the main Jewish centre in Northern Mesopotamia.[42] After the sudden death of Julian the Apostate in 363 C.E., Nisibis was ceded by Jovian to the Persians and the Christian élite left the town to find a refuge in the Roman West.[43] Ephrem ended up at Edessa, where he spent the last ten years of his life. Throughout his many works are to be found polemics with the Jews referring to the situation at Nisibis and at Edessa, according to the place where they were written, although circumstances in both cities were not fundamentally different.[44] Ephrem Syrus was the champion of Edessene orthodoxy and his whole oeuvre aims at purifying his flock from heretical views and customs. Within this overall context, polemics with the Jews, and his sometimes nasty and offensive remarks about them, find their place.

Ephrem Syrus does not address himself to the Jews as a separate community in the city but deals with members of the Christian church who were attracted to Jewish customs and frequented the synagogue. From that viewpoint, Jews were on a par with Arians, Marcionites, Bardaisanites, Manichaeans, and even pagans insofar as Christians still clung to pagan practice. That is the reason why Ephrem also comments on Jews and pagans in the *Hymns contra Haereses* that are mainly directed against Marcionites,

---

[42] Segal, "The Jews of North Mesopotamia", 38f.; J. Neusner, *A History of the Jews in Babylonia* I, 121ff.

[43] G. W. Bowersock, *Julian the Apostate*, Cambridge, Mass. 1978, 106-119; cf. Ephraem Syrus, *Hymns contra Julianum*, ed. E. Beck, CSCO 174-75.

[44] Segal, "The Jews of North Mesopotamia", 38-43; S. Kazan, "Isaac of Antioch's Homily against the Jews", OrChr 46, 1962, 95-98; 47, 1963, 89-92; a survey of the relevant texts is given by T. Kronholm, *Motifs from Genesis 1-11 in the genuine Hymns of Ephrem the Syrian with particular reference to the influence of Jewish exegetical tradition*, Lund 1978, 30f.

Bardaisanites and Manichaeans.[45] A good example is *Contra Haereses* LVI, 8, where Ephrem praises the church that is free from the dirt and dregs of the Marcionites, of the Manichaeans and of the Bardaisanites and "of the stink of the stinking Jews".[46] It is noteworthy that polemics with the Jews are almost totally absent from Ephrem's Prose Refutations, which were certainly written at Edessa and directed against Marcionites, Bardaisanites and Manichaeans. Like these, Judaism was attractive for Ephrem's flock, because "he who prays with the Jews prays with Barabbas, the robber".[47]

The comparison with Barabbas, the robber, has solid grounds. Jewish religious customs such as the keeping of the Sabbath, the laws of purity, circumcision and the great festivals, charmed and fascinated many Christians, and so in Ephrem's view the Christian community was "robbed". When Ephrem attacks the Arians in his *Sermones de Fide,* he treats within that context of Jewish practices common among Christians, in particular circumcision, Sabbath observance and the great feasts, to which a substantial part of the third Sermo is devoted.[48] It is not a public assault on Judaism as such, but in first instance intended for internal Christian use. Ephrem is obsessed by deviating views and practice within the church, and not by hatred of the Jews. The situation in Edessa in his time can be compared to religious relations at Antioch under John Chrysostom, who attacked Jewish practice in the Church with all his rhetorical skill.[49] Polemic with the Jews was a set element of Christian self-definition.[50]

Such a self-definition became of paramount importance following the failure after a few weeks of Julian the Apostate's plan to rebuild the Temple at Jerusalem.[51] The Christian character of the Empire in the fourth century was not self-evident at the time, especially not after Julian's short reign, and more particularly not in Northern Mesopotamia, where Nisibis was ceded to the Persians and Edessa's Christian community was for the greater part still heretic and semi-pagan. Julian's plans were more threatening to the

---

[45]   E. Beck, *Des Heiligen Ephraem des Syrers Hymnen contra Haereses,* CSCO 169-170, Louvain 1957; a systematic study of Ephrem's polemical works is a desideratum; on pagans in the Hymns contra Haereses see Drijvers, "The Persistence of Pagan Cults and Practices".

[46]   Cf. E. Beck, *Des Heiligen Ephraem des Syrers Carmina Nisibina* II, CSCO 240-241, Louvain 1963, LXVII, 14-17 and P. Hayman, "The Image of the Jew in the Syriac Anti-Jewish Polemical Literature".

[47]   Ephrem Syrus, *Prose Refutations,* ed. Mitchell, I, p. cxix.

[48]   E. Beck, *Des Heiligen Ephraem des Syrers Sermones de Fide,* CSCO 212-213, Louvain 1961, Sermo III, 167-419; cf. E. Beck, "Ephraems Reden über den Glauben", Studia Anselmiana XXXIII, Rome 1953, 118-120; S. Kazan, *Isaac of Antioch's Homily against the Jews,* 96-98.

[49]   R. L. Wilken, *John Chrysostom and the Jews. Rhetoric and Reality in the late 4th Century,* Berkeley-London 1983; W. A. Meeks-R. L. Wilken, *Jews and Christians in Antioch in the First Four Centuries of the Common Era,* Scholars Press 1978, 25-36.

[50]   Cf. L. C. Ruggini, "Pagani, Ebrei e Cristiani: Odio sociologico e odio teologico nel mondo antico", *Gli Ebrei nell'Alto Medioevo,* Settimane XXVI, Spoleto 1980, 15-101.

[51]   Cf. G. Bowersock, *Julian the Apostate,* Appendix 1: The Chronology of the Attempt to Rebuild the Jewish Temple, 120-122.

Christians than promising for the Jews, and that is why the attribution of the crucifixion to the Jews plays such a paramount rôle in Ephrem's polemics. The Jews thereby caused the desolation of their Temple and City, and made way for the Christians, *verus Israel*. The issue of the crucifixion and the Holy Cross was essential to Christian self-confidence, which was seriously shaken during Julian's reign and long thereafter.[52] There lies the explanation of at least part of the additions to the *Doctrina Addai* dating back to the beginning of the fifth century.

Our second conclusion, therefore, is that the statement that in Northern Mesopotamia "the local Christian population and Jewish communities hated one another"[53] is only half of the truth, and thus a distortion of the historical and social situation. They were, on the contrary, in close touch in many cases on the initiative of the Christians. They were friends with the Jews (cf. the *Doctrina Addai*), visited the synagogue, prayed with the Jews and observed Jewish religious practice. Some of them may have been Jewish converts. This may have caused feelings of animosity with church leaders like Ephrem, but that is something rather different from hatred between the two communities as a social phenomenon.

Two other areas in which Jews and Christians had much in common corroborate this thesis. The first is what is usually, but wrongly, called magic. The rabbis were well-known soothsayers, magicians and healers, who were held in high esteem by the Christians also, who often used their services or consulted them. A famous homily by Isaac of Antioch falsely attributed to Ephrem Syrus testifies to such practices.[54] But when Ephrem polemizes with the Jews in his III Sermo de Fide, he frequently uses metaphors borrowed from medical practice. The Jews do not provide the right healing or effective medicine, which may be considered an allusion to current customs of consulting Jewish experts in case of illness.[55] Healing was a matter of keen competition much as it is nowadays! Rabbis, Christian saints and hermits, Manichaean electi and pagan philosophers, all offered healing, mental and physical health, and the best protection against all kinds of perils. In the fluid society of the fourth century in Northern Mesopotamia where new groups, in particular the Christians, tried to attain to some sort of cohesion, with all sorts of consequences for other parts of society, accusations of magic and witchcraft and the public display of the effectiveness of various practices and miracles belonged together as the two sides of a coin.[56] This is the paramount reason why Ephrem warned against

[52]   Simon, *Verus Israel*, 139-144;

[53]   J. Neusner, *A History of the Jews in Babylonia* IV, 34.

[54]   Th. J. Lamy, *Sancti Ephraem Syri Hymni et Sermones* II, Mechelen 1886, 393-426; cf. Simon, *Verus Israel*, 416ff.

[55]   *Sermo de Fide* 197-213; 225; 291-295.

[56]   Cf. E. Peterson, "Die geheimen Praktiken eines syrischen Bischofs", *Frühkirche, Judentum und Gnosis*, Rom-Freiburg-Wien 1959, 333-345; a systematic enquiry into magic, allusions to medical practices and the like in Ephrem's works would yield interesting results.

the magic arts of the rabbis. But it is the best proof of how little cohesion
the Christian community had in comparison with their Jewish neighbours!

The second area of some interest is theology and scriptural exegesis. It
has often been stated that biblical and homiletical literature in Syriac owes a
lot to Jewish writings and exegetical techniques.[57] "Our authors appear
simply as Christian midrashists", says Robert Murray; but when he
continues, "There is no need to suppose, just as there is no likelihood, that
they had any contact with Jewish rabbis", he seems to be wrong.[58] Ephrem
Syrus' works like those of Aphrahat and Origen in the third century reflect
Jewish learning and actual discussions on theological matters with Jewish
rabbis and scribes.[59] It is often difficult to strip Ephrem's exuberant poetry
of all the rhetoric of abuse and nasty invective in order to detect the real
issues at stake in the profound theological debate. A good example is found
in *Contra Haereses* 3,10-12:

> The Jew also did not investigate the hidden things,
> Although in his scriptures hindrances certainly lay hidden for him.
> Questioning with passion blinded him through its obfuscation.
> He confesses the Holy Spirit without further dispute
> but when he is questioned, he denies, and when he is completely defeated, he
> blasphemes.
>
> Their crown is death, and their armour despair.
> When he denied the Son, the buried came out of their graves,
> they confuted him there, and here when he denies the Spirit, that it is non-
> existing.
>
> then the Scriptures will charge him,
> that the Spirit is the breath of the mouth of the Lord (Ps. 33,6)
> And his Spirit is with Him, and if there was a time
> When He was without the Spirit, let them demonstrate that without dispute.
> And instead of what is proper, that He created through the Son,
> They tried to prove that when He created, someone created with Him
>
> She who created with Him the heaven and the creatures.
> They are mad and deny the Son and reject him
> But the other Maker, who helped him, of Her they are proud.
> Because they abjured and rejected the Truth, they have found shame.[60]

[57] R. Murray, *Symbols of Church and Kingdom*, 281ff.; N. Séd, "Les hymnes sur le
Paradis de saint Ephrem et les traditions juives", Le Muséon 81, 1968, 455-502; T. Kronholm,
Motifs from Genesis 1-11 in the genuine Hymns of Ephrem the Syrian, Lund 1978, 215ff.

[58] Murray, *Symbols of Church and Kingdom*, 281.

[59] J. Neusner, *Aphrahat and Judaism. The Christian-Jewish Argument in Fourth-Century
Iran*, Leiden 1971, 150ff.; N. R. M. de Lange, *Origen and the Jews. Studies in Jewish-
Christian Relations in Third-Century Palestine*, Cambridge 1976.

[60] E. Beck, *Des Heiligen Ephraem des Syrers Hymnen contra Haereses*, CSCO 169-170,
Louvain 1957, 14.; cf. CH XXI,11; XXV,5; L,4; HdF XLIV, 4f.

This remarkable mixture of theological reasoning and rhetorical abuse unmistakably mirrors actual debates on the nature of the Spirit and her relationship with Father and Son in the process of creation. The Jewish interlocutor undoubtedly emphasized the rôle of God's wisdom in the creation instead of God's eternal creative Logos as His Son, which may have aroused further discussions.

Ephrem's indebtedness to Jewish exegetical methods was often discussed, and substantial elements from Jewish Haggada and Targumic traditions are undeniably present in his hymns and commentaries.[61] It is in particular noteworthy that the influence of Jewish Haggada is not literary; Ephrem and the Haggada share common traditions but often develop them in opposite directions. This may be an indication of personal contact between Ephrem and the Rabbis. In particular, traditions found in apocryphal and pseudepigraphical works of the Second Temple Period, e.g., works relating to Adam, have many features in common with Ephrem's exegesis; they were translated into Syriac in an early period, and played a paramount rôle in later exegetical traditions stemming from Ephrem's school that are found, e.g., in the well-known Cave of Treasures.[62] Especially this last work, a re-telling of the biblical story like the Book of Jubilees, is a good example of how Jewish traditions and polemics with the Jews go together in the same work; Adam, Seth and the Patriarchs have knowledge of Christ, his Crucifixion, the Church and the Sacraments, and were Christians *avant la lettre,* namely, before the Jewish nation came into existence through Moses' activities and law-giving.[63] As the existence of the Jews and their ritual observances was, in Ephrem's view, an intermediary state preparing the coming of Christ, after his appearance they had lost their right to exist as a nation according to the prophecies of Daniel and Jesus' words.[64]

The simple existence of Jews and their synagogue, where even Christians attended the feasts and went to pray, was a real threat to Edessa's nascent orthodoxy, because it could neither exist without the Jews nor together with the Jews. The real debate of the early Church was with the Jews and not with the Gentiles, and of that debate Ephrem Syrus is a first-class witness.[65]

[61]   Cf. n. 57 and S. Hidal, *Interpretatio Syriaca. Die Kommentare des Heiligen Ephräm des Syrers zu Genesis und Exodus mit besonderer Berücksichtigung ihrer Auslegungs-geschichtlichen Stellung,* Lund 1974, 101ff.; S. Brock, "Jewish Traditions in Syriac Sources", JJS 30, 1979, 212-232.

[62]   C. Bezold, *Die Schatzhöhle "Me'ārath Gazzē",* Leipzig 1883-1888; Brock, Jewish Traditions in Syriac Sources, 227ff.; M. E. Stone, *Armenian Apocrypha relating to the Patriarchs and Prophets,* Jerusalem 1982, 41f.; S. E. Robinson, *The Testament of Adam, An Examination of the Syriac and Greek Traditions,* Scholars Press 1982, 156ff.

[63]   C. Bezold, *Die Schatzhöhle,* 5,7,9,35; cf. E. A. Wallis Budge, *The Book of the Cave of Treasures,* London 1927, 33ff.

[64]   Simon, *Verus Israel,* 178ff.; 205ff.; C. Bezold, *Die Schatzhöhle,* 56f.

[65]   Contra D. Rokeah, *Jews, Pagans and Christians in Conflict,* Jerusalem-Leiden 1982, see his conclusions, 209ff.; cf. J. Gager, "The Dialogue of Paganism with Judaism: Bar Cochba to Julian, HUCA 44, 1973, 89-118.

This is why Julian's plans to rebuild the Temple were so threatening to the Church; they would have deprived the Church of its legitimation.[66]

After Ephrem's time, the situation did not fundamentally change. The Vita of Rabbula, bishop of Edessa from 412 till 436 C.E., shows the same ambiguity towards the Jews. They were continually exhorted, many thousands were baptized, and they suffered deep grief when Rabbula died, as the hagiographer tells us. But the *Chronicon Edessenum* reports that Rabbula transformed the synagogue into a church dedicated to St. Stephen.[67] It is highly unlikely that thousands of Jews were converted and baptized, but the Vita makes clear how important the conversion of the Jews was in Christian eyes and, therefore, how threatening the existence of the Jews at Edessa was. The expropriation of their synagogue was certainly a means to put an end to that danger, because it deprived the Jews of their social and religious centre that was so acceptable to many Christians!

The Jews at Edessa made their Christian fellow-citizens feel uncertain and often unsafe, whereas they themselves were self-confident as adherents of an old and traditional religion. As such they served as a real magnet to many Christians and gave rise to very ambivalent feelings, especially among church leaders and theologians, who warned their co-religionists against the Jewish danger with all the exuberance of traditional rhetoric. But side by side with such verbal violence went a continuous debate in which Christian theologians took the initiative. And last but not least there were the ordinary people who went to the synagogue – Jews, many Christians and even some pagans. They at least saw the Jews as a source of help against the dangers in their lives.

[66] A late source *The Chronography of Bar Hebraeus*, ed. E. A. Wallis Budge, 2 Vols, London 1932, Vol. I, 62 even mentions about Julian the Apostate: "And he offered sacrifices to idols and paid honour to the Jews. And when the Christians who were in Edessa heard (this), they became filled with envy and wrath, and slew the Jews who were their neighbours".

[67] *Chronicon Edessenum*, ed. I. Guidi, *Chronica Minora* I, CSCO 1-2, Louvain 1907, LI: Anno 723, fuit Rabbulas episcopus Edessae. Hic aedificavit aedem Mar Stephani quae antea domus sabbati, synagoga Iudaeorum fuerat; aedificavit autem iussu imperatoris.

THE JEWISH-CHRISTIAN ARGUMENT IN FOURTH-CENTURY IRAN: APHRAHAT ON CIRCUMCISION, THE SABBATH, AND THE DIETARY LAWS

by

JACOB NEUSNER

PRECIS

Aphrahat was a remarkable fourth century Iranian Christian monk. He was remarkable because he was fair and objective in debate with Jews in the Mesopotamian area where he lived. Free from any anti-semitism, he argued almost entirely on the basis of historical facts as he understood them. Concerning circumcision Aphrahat contends that it never had any salvific value except where combined with faith, and Israel was unfaithful as the prophets themselves contended. But without faith what is the use of circumcision? Actually it was only one among many signs of the covenant and has only a "this-worldly" importance. It is also interesting to note that other people practiced circumcision. Turning to the Sabbath, Aphrahat likewise claims its observance never led to salvation. The Sabbath is simply a day of rest and even cattle rest then, whereas other animals ignore it with impunity. Obviously there is nothing spiritually essential in its keeping. Furthermore Adam, Enoch and Noah didn't observe the day, yet they were saved. Joshua made war on the Sabbath and others sometimes ignored it of necessity. Similarly Aphrahat follows the New Testament in thinking dietary laws pertain only to externals. It is interesting that he thinks these laws were instituted only after the Hebrews' contact with the Egyptians who worshipped animals. For all "practical" commandments Jesus substituted the law of love.

I. INTRODUCTION

The first great father of the Iranian church, Aphrahat, a monk of the rank of bishop at Mar Mattai, north of Nineveh, near the present-day Iraqi town of Mosul, wrote, in elegant, classic Syriac, twenty-three demonstrations. The first ten, composed in 336-7, present a systematic account of Christianity, addressed to his fellow-monks. The next thirteen, written in 344-5, deal with various pressing issues facing the Iranian church, which was severely persecuted because of its resistance to the war-taxes Shapur II levied to pay for his war with Christian Rome. Among these demonstrations, XI, XII, XIII, XV, XVI, XVII, XVIII, XIX, and XXI, as well as parts of XXIII, deal with the Jewish critique of Christianity. Since the Iranian church

Professor Jacob Neusner (Jewish) teaches in the Department of Religion at Brown University, Providence, Rhode Island. He is author of *History and Torah: Essays on Jewish Learnings, A History of the Jews in Babylonia, I. The Parthian Period*, and II, *The Early Sasanian Period*, and other books.

282

included large numbers of converted Jews—in the first instance having been established in some measure by Jews[1]—the Jewish-Christian argument represented a primary concern for Aphrahat. He himself was a convert, born of probably Iranian parents, but obviously he had mastered both Scripture and Christian doctrine. The Jewish critique was re-enforced by the peace and prosperity enjoyed by Jewry in a time of Christian suffering.[2] The relationship between the two communities was vigorous, intimate, and competitive.

What is striking is the utter absence of anti-Semitism from Aphrahat's thought. While much provoked, he exhibits scarcely a trace of the pervasive hatred of "the Jews" characteristic of the Greek-speaking churches of the Roman orient, indeed of his contemporary John Chrysostom. On the contrary, Aphrahat conducts the debate through penetrating criticism, never vilification. Though hard-pressed, he throughout maintains an attitude of respect. He must be regarded as the example of the shape Christianity might have taken had it been formed in the Semitic-Iranian Orient, a region quite free of the legacy of Greco-Roman anti-Semitism. In the Iranian empire, the Jewish-Christian argument was carried on heatedly, but entirely within reasonable limits, along exegetical-historical lines, through generally rational and pointed discussion.[3]

Aphrahat's mode of argument is of special interest. He presents a case based almost wholly on historical facts derived from sources universally acknowledged as accurate by all parties to the argument. He does not rely on interpretation based upon convictions held by Christians but not by Jews, although he does hold with Christian affirmations. He copiously cites the Hebrew Scriptures, but rarely the New Testament, and then chiefly when addressing himself to his Christian reader. His exegeses of Scriptures are reasonable and rational, for the most part *not* based on a tradition held by the church and not by the synagogue, but rather on the plain-sense of Scripture as he thinks everyone understands it. It is frequently alleged that his

---

[1] On Christianity in the Sasanian Empire an its relationships to Judaism, the following works by this writer contain bibliographies and summaries of the Talmudic and related evidence: *A History of the Jews in Babylonia, I. The Parthian Period* (Leiden, 1965), pp. 166-9; II. *The Early Sasanian Period* (Leiden, 1966), pp. 19-26, 72-91; III. *From Shapur I to Shapur II* (Leiden, 1968), pp. 9-16, 24-29, 354-358; IV. *The Age of Shapur II* (Leiden, 1969), pp. 20-26, 56-61; V. *Later Sasanian Times* (Leiden, 1969), pp. 6-8, 19-29, 43-4, 92-5, 119-122.

[2] Vol. IV, pp. 20-27, 35-56.

[3] See especially A. Vööbus, "Aphrahat," *Jahrbuch für Antike und Christentum* 3 (1960), pp. 153-4 for an excellent summary.

283

arguments are exegetical, but this seems to me far from the case. The arguments are, as I said, *historical*; exegesis of Scriptures plays a small part. What dominates is, rather, *citation* of Scriptures as one would cite a historical document—for facts available to anyone, not for interpretations acceptable only to the believer. The Jewish-Christian argument in Aphrahat's formulations is an argument about the facts of history, not about theological doctrines, and the assumption is that the Christian side wins because it is right about what has happened. Doctrine, faith, revelation, play no considerable role in such an argument.[4]

II. CIRCUMCISION

Aphrahat's arguments on circumcision stand nearer to the Occidental church tradition than those pertaining to the Sabbath and the dietary laws. The reason is that all parts of the church read the same Scriptures, particularly Hebrews and Paul, and one should not be surprised to see a consistency of argument. All Christian writers on Judaism tend to spiritualize the commandments, the people of Israel, and various concrete religious symbols, practices, and categories of Judaism. While the Alexandrians are given credit for such spiritualized exegeses, in fact the New Testament shows the way. But Aphrahat adds a completely original argument, which in no form occurs elsewhere in any antecedent Church father. It concerns the origin and purpose of circumcision, its purely this-worldly value. Aphrahat never articulately admits that the practical commandments ever served to bring salvation for any man—a position far more extreme than anything in Paul or in most of his precedessors.

As in all of the anti-Judaic demonstrations, Aphrahat draws upon a considerable repertoire of prophetic passages to prove that ancient

---

4 Earlier studies: W. Wright, *The Homilies of Aphraates, the Persian Sage. Edited from Syriac manuscripts of the Vth and VIth centuries in the British Museum, with an English translation. Vol. I: The Syriac Text* (London, 1869, no further volumes) was the first edition of the text. I followed the text of *Aphraatis Sapientis Persae, Demonstrationes*, ed. Ioannes Parisot, *Patrologia Syriaca I*, i (Paris, 1894) and I, ii (Paris, 1907), and afterward compared my translation from the Syriac with the text of Wright. Among translations I consulted Parisot and Georg Bert, *Aphrahat's des persischen Weisen Homilien, aus dem syrischen übersetzt und erläutert* (Leipzig, 1888). Demonstrations I, V, VI, VIII, X, XVII, XXI, and XXII were translated into English by John Gwynn, *Selections . . . from the Demonstrations of Aphrahat the Persian Sage*, in Philip Schaff and Henry Wace, eds., *A Select Library of Nicene and Post-Nicene Fathers*, second series, XIII, Part ii, *Gregory the Great, Ephraim Syrus, Aphrahat* (repr., Grand Rapids, 1956), pp. 345-412. Numbers in square brackets refer to the page in Parisot's text. All three demonstrations under discussion here appear in vol. I. Numbers in parentheses refer to pages in Wright's text.

Israel was rebellious, therefore was rejected. For Demonstration XI, *On Circumcision,* the following is representative:

Moses their leader testified concerning them, saying to them, "You have been rebellious from the day that I knew you" (Deut. 9: 24). Furthermore, he reiterated in the hymn of testimony, "Your vine [is] from the vine of Sodom and from the planting of Gomorrah. Your grapes are bitter grapes, and your clusters are bitter for you" (Deut. 32:32). He hinted [469] in that [same] hymn of testimony about the people which is (203) from the peoples [=the Church of Christ] when he said to them, "I shall provoke you with a people which is no people, and with a foolish people I shall anger you" (Deut. 32:21). And through Isaiah, the Holy One testified, saying, "I have planted a vineyard and have worked it. But instead of grapes, it brought forth wild grapes" (Is. 5:2). Again Jeremiah the prophet also said concerning the congregation of the people, "I have planted you as a shoot which was entirely a true seed, but you have changed and rebelled against me as an alien vine" (Jer. 2:21). Ezekiel testified about the vine: "Fire has consumed the twig, its middle is dried up, and it is not again useful for anything" (Ez. 15:4). "The shoot was planted, a true seed" [refers to] their original fathers. But the children have turned to the unclean deeds of the Amorites.

When [any] of all the peoples do righteousness, they are called children and heirs of Abraham their father. But when the children of Abraham do an unclean deed of the alien peoples, then they become Sodomites and the people of Gomorrah, as Isaiah testified concerning them, "Hear the word of the Lord, rulers of Sodom and people of Gomorrah" (Is. 1:10).

Here Aphrahat turns to a long digression, in which he proves that Isaiah's reference was intended to characterize the Israelites of his day as Sodom. This further demonstrates the spiritual character of prophecy: A Sodomite is one who does the deeds of the Sodomites, not one born there. And likewise, a true Israelite is one who does God's will, not merely one born of Israel after the flesh.

Aphrahat now turns to the classic argument about circumcision and faith:

XI-2. Any who considers [matters] closely know this: Circumcision without faith has no use nor profits anything, for faith precedes circumcision, and circumcision was given as a sign and a covenant to Abraham, as God said to him, "This is my covenant which you will keep, that you will circumcise every male" (Gen. 17:10). So long as it [circumcision] pleased its Giver, it was observed with the commandments of

285

369

the law, profited and gave life. But when the law was not observed, circumcision was of no value. Jeroboam [473] the son of Nabat of the children of Joseph of the tribe of Ephraim was circumcised as the Holy One commanded Abraham and [as] Moses instructed in the law. All the kings of Israel who walked in the law of Jeroboam were circumcised and [thereby] distinguished. But a good memory was not preserved concerning them, because of their sins. What [then] did Jeroboam profit in his circumcision—he and all the kings of Israel who walked in his path? Or what use and value [from circumcision] did Manasseh the son of Hezekiah have, on account of whose sins, that were many, God was not able again to forgive Jerusalem?

Thus circumcision without faith is of no salvific consequence. But circumcision with faith is foolish, for faith obviates the need for circumcision. Indeed, baptism is the circumcision of the new age.

Aphrahat then asks, How is it possible that circumcision, once the sign of the covenant, no longer avails? He shows, first, that circumcision was not *the* sign, but one among many.

> XI-3. With all generations and tribes God made his covenants, in each generation as it pleased him, and they [the covenants] were kept in their times but [then] changed. He commanded Adam that he should not eat from the tree of the knowledge of good and evil, but because he [Adam] did not keep the commandment (205) and the covenant, he was condemned. As to Enoch who was pleasing before God, it was not because the commandment concerning the tree was kept by him that he was translated alive, but because he believed, and the [act of] pleasing does not seem [to have been] the commandment not to eat from the tree. [God] saved Noah, who preserved his innocence and righteousness, from the wrath of the flood, and made a covenant with him and with his descendants after him, that they should be fruitful and multiply, and [he made] the covenant of the bow in the clouds between God, earth and all flesh. With not one of [476] these covenants was circumcision given.
>
> Thus those who believed even while not circumcised live, but those who circumcised but did not believe—their circumcision availed them not at all. Abel, Enoch, Noah, Shem, and Japheth were not in the circumcision, [yet] were pleasing before God, for each one of them kept their covenants in their time and believed that one is he who gave his covenant in each generation as he willed. Melchizedek was the priest of God most high. He blessed Abraham when he [Abraham] was not

286

circumcised, and this matter is known, that the lesser will be blessed by him who is greater than he.

Here, following the New Testament, Aphrahat seems to be prepared to admit circumcision once did serve a salvific end. However, the whole thrust of his arguments on the practical commandments is to prove otherwise. Circumcision was important, but only for a modest, this-worldly purpose:

He commanded him to circumcise the flesh of his foreskin as a sign and a signification of the covenant, so that when his seed would multiply, they might be distinguished from all the nations among whom they would go, so that they might not be mingled with their [the pagans'] unclean deeds. So Abraham circumcised the flesh of his foreskin at the age of ninety-nine years, and he circumcised Ishmael, his son, at the age of thirteen years; and those who were born of his house and purchased of his money did Abraham circumcise on that day, just as God had spoken with him. After he was circumcised, Isaac was conceived, born, and circumcised on the eighth day. Circumcision was observed by the seed of Abraham, [480] by Isaac and Ishmael, by Jacob and his son, and by Esau and his sons, one hundred ninety years, until Jacob entered Egypt.

In Egypt the children of Jacob kept it [circumcision] two hundred twenty-five years, until they went forth to the wilderness. Also when Lot saw that Abraham his uncle circumcised, he too circumcised his son, after he had separated from him [Abraham], so they retained circumcision as a custom without faith.

XI-6. This should stand firm for you, my beloved, that circumcision is a sign so as to separate [the Jews] from the unclean peoples. Note that when he brought them forth from Egypt, and they walked in the wilderness for forty years, they did not circumcise, for the people was one [alone] and not mixed among other peoples. There he did not mark them because they pastured by themselves. And that he marked out (208) the seed of Abraham—it was not because all the peoples were not his that he separated the seed of Abraham as his own flock; but all the people who do evil deeds of idolatry he abandoned because of their deeds.

And as to his marking them as his people, it was not to inform himself that [484] they are the seed of Abraham, for before he marked them, he knew them. But [it was] that they themselves might know one another, so that they might not be traduced through lies. For it might come to pass, if they were not [clearly] marked, that when some of them might be found worshipping idols, or committing fornication, or adultery, or

287

stealing, or doing anything which was outside of the law, then some of them who were found in these things might deny and lie, [saying] We are not the children of Abraham, so that they might not be killed or receive capital punishment. But the decree of death, which is written in the law, is upon those who do these things. So whoever is found transgressing the law and does any of these odious deeds no longer is able to take refuge through lying, [saying] I am not of the seed and a child of Abraham. For if he is found to deny, they find it out through his circumcision and inflict capital punishment as is right according to his transgression.

Now if circumcision were not given for *this* reason, it should have been required even in the wilderness that they circumcise. But because they were set apart from the peoples and pasturing by themselves in the wilderness, they were not marked. But when they crossed the Jordan, the Lord commanded Joshua the son of Nun, saying [485] to him, "Once again circumcise the children of Israel a second time" (Jos. 5:2). And why did he say to Joshua (209) that he should circumcise them a second time? Because they were [already] circumcised in their hearts, as he said through the prophet, "Circumcise the foreskin of your heart and do not again stiffen your neck" (Deut. 10:16). Joshua again circumcised them, and a second time marked them in their flesh. But how do you understand the saying that Joshua circumcised the people a second time? They were *not* [yet] circumcised in their flesh, for after Joshua circumcised them, Scripture testifies, "Joshua circumcised all those who were born in the wilderness, for no child that was born in the wilderness was circumcised" (Jos. 5:5,6).

Aphrahat here proves that other peoples of antiquity practiced circumcision as did Israel. He shows that the Egyptians, Edomites, Moabites, Ammonites, and others did so (Jer. 9:25-6), and he says they were circumcised in uncircumcision, and just so where the Israelites: "Whoever does not circumcise the foreskin of his heart, then also the circumcision of his flesh is of no value to him."

Proof that the Egyptians practiced circumcision is derived from the Moses-story:

And furthermore, my beloved, there are men who say that when the daughter of Pharaoh found Moses, she realized from the covenant which was in his flesh that he was of the children of Israel. But the meaning of the Scripture is not as it appears to be. For the covenant of the circumcision of Moses was in no way different from the circumcision of the children of Egypt. Whoever does not know that the Egyptians were circumcised,

288

let him learn from Jeremiah. For when the daughter of Pharaoh [489] found Moses and saw that he was floating in the river, she [thereby] knew that he was of the children of the Hebrews, because it was not commanded for Egyptians to be thrown into the river as Pharaoh had commanded concerning the children of Israel, saying, "Every male child who is born will be cast into the river" (Ex. 1:22). She knew that on account of fear of the commandment [of Pharaoh] this thing had been done. When she saw that he had been placed in an ark of wood, she knew that they had hidden him and made the ark and threw it in the river, so that his [Pharaoh's] men would not find [him].[7] Now if by means of circumcision the children of Israel had been distinguished, while the Egyptians were not circumcised, Moses could not have been brought up in the house of Pharaoh, because in his childhood at any time the covenant of his flesh would have been found out. If the daughter of Pharaoh had transgressed the law and commandment of her father, then in the whole of Egypt (211) the commandment and law of Pharaoh would no longer have been carried out.

Aphrahat returns to the theme of the changing of the covenants and the signs of the covenants:

XI-11. In all things the law and the covenant have been changed. From of old God changed the covenant of Adam, and he gave another to Noah. Then again he gave it also to Abraham. He changed the one of Abraham and gave another to Moses. Then when that of Moses was not kept, he gave another in the final generation [= that of Jesus], a covenant which will not be changed.

Adam's was the covenant not to eat from the tree; Noah's was the bow in the clouds; Abraham's was at first his chosing him because of his faith, and then was [the covenant of] circumcision, a sealing and a sign [500] for his descendants. Of Moses [the sign of the covenant was] a lamb which was slaughtered in behalf of the people. None of all of these covenants is like the next.

He concludes the demonstration with a typology of Joshua b. Nun and Joshua=Jesus our redeemer, a favorite rhetorical flourish in Aphrahat's writings:

XI-12. Joshua the son of Nun circumcised the people a second time with knives of stone when he and his people crossed the Jordan; Joshua [Jesus], our redeemer a second time circumcised the peoples who believed in him with the circumcision of the heart, and they were baptized and circumcised with the

289

knife which is his word that is sharper than the two-edged sword (Heb. 4:12). Joshua the son of Nun led the people across to the Land of Promise; and Joshua our redeemer promised the land of the living to whoever passed through the true Jordan and believed, and circumcised the foreskin of his heart. Joshua the son of Nun raised up stones as a testimony in Israel; and Joshua our redeemer called Simon the true stone and set him up as a faithful testimony among the peoples. Joshua the son of Nun made a paschal sacrifice in the camp at Jericho in the cursed land [504] and the people ate from the bread of the land; and Joshua our redeemer made a paschal sacrifice with his disciples in Jerusalem, the city which he cursed (216) [saying] "There should not remain in it stone on stone" (Matthew 24:2), and there he gave the mystery in the bread of life. Joshua the son of Nun condemned the avaricious Achan who stole and hid, and Joshua our redeemer condemned the avaricious Judah who stole and hid money from the purse which he was holding. Joshua the son of Nun wiped out unclean peoples; and Joshua our redeemer threw down Satan and his host. Joshua the son of Nun held up the sun in the sky; and Joshua our redeemer brought on sunset at noon when they crucified him. Joshua the son of Nun was redeemer of the people. Jesus was called redeemer of the peoples. And blessed are those whose hearts are circumcised from the foreskin and who are born through water, the second circumcision, for they are inheritors with Abraham, the first believer and the father of all peoples, whose faith was reckoned for him as righteousness.

Acknowledgments

Kraft, R.A. "In Search of 'Jewish Christianity' and Its 'Theology': Problems of Definition and Methodology." *Recherches de science religieuse* 60 (1972): 81–92. Courtesy of Yale University Seeley G. Mudd Library.

Simon, Marcel. "Problèmes du Judéo-Christianisme." In *Aspects du Judéo-Christianisme* (Paris: Presses Universitaires de France, 1965): 1–17. Reprinted with the permission of Presses Universitaires de France. "Travaux du Centre d'Études Supérieures Spécialisées d'Histoire des Religions de Strasbourg, 'Aspects du Judéo-Christianismé.'" Courtesy of Presses Universitaires de France.

Strecker, Georg. "On the Problem of Jewish Christianity." In Robert A. Kraft and Gerhard Krodel, eds., *Orthodoxy and Heresy in Earliest Christianity* (Philadelphia: Fortress Press, 1971): 241–85. Reprinted with the permission of SCM Press, Ltd. 1971. Copyright Fortress Press, 1971. Courtesy of Yale University Cross Campus Library.

Murray, Robert. "'Disaffected Judaism' and Early Christianity: Some Predisposing Factors." In Jacob Neusner and Ernest S. Frerichs, eds., *"To See Ourselves As Others See Us": Christians, Jews, "Others" in Late Antiquity* (Chico, CA: Scholars Press, 1985): 263–81. Reprinted with the permission of Scholars Press. Courtesy of Yale University Cross Campus Library.

Klijn, A.F.J. "The Study of Jewish Christianity." *New Testament Studies* 20 (1974): 419–31. Reprinted with the permission of Cambridge University Press. Courtesy of Yale University Seeley G. Mudd Library.

Munck, J. "Jewish Christianity in Post-Apostolic Times." *New Testament Studies* 6 (1960): 103–16. Reprinted with the permission of Cambridge University Press. Courtesy of Yale University Seeley G. Mudd Library.

Schoeps, H.J. "Ebionite Christianity." *Journal of Theological Studies* n.s. 4 (1953): 219–24. Reprinted with the permission of Oxford University Press. Courtesy of Yale University Seeley G. Mudd Library.

Moxnes, Halvor. "God and His Angel in the Shepherd of Hermas." *Studia Theologica* 28 (1974): 49–56. Reprinted with the permission of *Studia Theologica*. Courtesy of Yale University Divinity Library.

Rordorf, W. "Un chapitre d'éthique judéo-chrétienne: les deux voies." *Recherches de science religieuse* 60 (1972): 109–28. Courtesy of Yale University Seeley G. Mudd Library.

Gavin, F. "Rabbinic Parallels in Early Church Orders." *Hebrew Union College Annual* 6 (1929): 55–67. Courtesy of Yale University Divinity Library.

Rankin, O.S. "The Extent of the Influence of the Synagogue Service upon Christian Worship." *Journal of Jewish Studies* 1 (1948): 27–32. Reprinted with the permission of the Oxford Center for Postgraduate Hebrew Studies, Oriental Institute. Courtesy of Yale University Sterling Memorial Library.

Gutmann, Joseph. "Early Synagogue and Jewish Catacomb Art and its Relation to Christian Art." In Hildegard Temporini and Wolfgang Haase, eds., *Aufstieg und Niedergang der Römischen Welt* (Berlin: Walter de Gruyter & Co., 1984): 1313–42. Reprinted with the permission of Walter de Gruyter Inc. Courtesy of Yale University Sterling Memorial Library.

Krauss, S. "The Jews in the Works of the Church Fathers." *Jewish Quarterly Review* 5 (1893):122–57; 6 (1894): 82–99. Courtesy of Yale University Sterling Memorial Library.

Constantelos, Demetrios J. "Jews and Judaism in the Early Greek Fathers (100 A.D.–500 A.D.)." *Greek Orthodox Theological Review* 23 (1978): 145–56. Courtesy of Yale University Divinity Library.

Frend, W.H.C. "The Persecutions: Some Links between Judaism and the Early Church." *Journal of Ecclesiastical History* 9 (1958): 141–58. Reprinted with the permission of Cambridge University Press. Courtesy of Yale University Seeley G. Mudd Library.

Lowy, S. "The Confutation of Judaism in the Epistle of Barnabas." *Journal of Jewish Studies* 11 (1960): 1–33. Reprinted with the permission of the Oxford Centre for Postgraduate Hebrew Studies, Oriental Institute. Courtesy of Yale University Sterling Memorial Library.

Philippou, A.J. "Origen and the Early Jewish-Christian Debate." *Greek Orthodox Theological Review* 15 (1970): 140–52. Courtesy of Yale University Divinity Library.

Drijvers, Han J.W. "Jews and Christians at Edessa." *Journal of Jewish Studies* 36 (1985): 88–102. Reprinted with the permission of the Oxford Centre for Postgraduate Hebrew Studies, Oriental Institute. Courtesy of Yale University Sterling Memorial Library.

Neusner, Jacob. "The Jewish-Christian Argument in Fourth-Century Iran: Aphrahat on Circumcision, the Sabbath, and the Dietary Laws." *Journal of Ecumenical Studies* 7 (1970): 282–90. Reprinted with the permission of the *Journal of Ecumenical Studies*. Courtesy of the *Journal of Ecumenical Studies*.